THE
g
FACTOR

D0087109

THE
g
FACTOR
The Science of Mental Ability

Arthur R. Jensen

Human Evolution, Behavior, and Intelligence
Seymour W. Itzkoff, Series Editor

PRAEGER

Westport, Connecticut
London

WILMETTE PUBLIC LIBRARY

Library of Congress Cataloging-in-Publication Data

Jensen, Arthur Robert.
    The g factor : the science of mental ability / Arthur R. Jensen.
       p. cm.—(Human evolution, behavior, and intelligence, ISSN
  1063–2158)
    Includes bibliographical references and index.
    ISBN 0–275–96103–6 (alk. paper)
    1. General factor (Psychology) 2. Intellect. 3. Nature and
  nurture. I. Title. II. Series.
  BF433.G45J46   1998
  153.9—dc21   97–22815

British Library Cataloguing in Publication Data is available.

Copyright © 1998 by Arthur R. Jensen

All rights reserved. No portion of this book may be
reproduced, by any process or technique, without the
express written consent of the publisher.

Library of Congress Catalog Card Number: 97–22815
ISBN: 0–275–96103–6
ISSN: 1063–2158

First published in 1998

Praeger Publishers, 88 Post Road West, Westport, CT 06881
An imprint of Greenwood Publishing Group, Inc.

Printed in the United States of America

♾️

The paper used in this book complies with the
Permanent Paper Standard issued by the National
Information Standards Organization (Z39.48–1984).

10 9 8 7 6 5 4 3 2 1

Every reasonable effort has been made to trace the owners of copyright materials in this book, but
in some instances this has proven impossible. The author and publisher will be glad to receive
information leading to more complete acknowledgments in subsequent printings of the book and in
the meantime extend their apologies for any omissions.

Quote from Charles Murray on the jacket reprinted with permission of *National Review*, 215
Lexington Avenue, New York, NY 10016.

153.9
JE

Dedicated to the memory of
CHARLES EDWARD SPEARMAN
the discoverer of g

Contents

Preface

This book about the g factor has its origin in the aftermath of an almost book-length article (my 77th publication) that I wrote almost thirty years ago, titled "How Much Can We Boost IQ and Scholastic Achievement?" and published in the *Harvard Educational Review* in 1969. It had five main themes: (1) the malleability of IQ (or the latent trait it measures) by special psychological and educational interventions in the course of children's mental development; (2) the heritability of IQ; (3) social class and race differences in IQ; (4) the question of cultural bias in mental tests; (5) the need for universal education to tap types of learning ability that are relatively unrelated to IQ in order to achieve the benefits of education for all children throughout the wide range of abilities in the population. It made four main empirically based claims: (1) individual differences in IQ are largely a result of genetic differences but environment also plays a part; (2) the experimental attempts to raise the IQs of children at risk for low IQ and poor scholastic performance by various psychological and educational manipulations had yielded little, if any, lasting gains in IQ or scholastic achievement; (3) since most of the exclusively cultural-environment explanations for racial differences in these important variables were inconsistent and inadequate, genetic as well as environmental factors should be considered; (4) certain abilities, particularly rote-learning and memory, had little relation to IQ, which suggested that these non-IQ abilities could to some extent compensate for low IQ to improve the benefits of schooling for many children at risk for failure under traditional classroom instruction.

According to the Institute for Scientific Information (ISI), which publishes the *Science Citation Index* (SCI) and the *Social Science Citation Index* (SSCI), this 1969 article soon became what the ISI terms a "citation classic"—an article (or book) with an unusually high frequency of citations in the scientific and professional journals. The onslaught of critiques and commentaries on the article, in both the popular media and the professional literature, made it clear that there was sufficient misunderstanding and misinformation, as well as reasonable criticism and argument, concerning some of the article's main topics to warrant a more thorough explication of the issues and the empirical evidence than was possible in the 124-page journal article. Moreover, certain questions raised in my article could not be answered adequately without doing further research based on adequate data—inquiries that had not been undertaken by anyone at that time.

Hence some of the issues raised by my 1969 article in the *Harvard Educational Review* determined my research and publication agenda during the subsequent years—empirical studies, methodological papers, and reviews, which, over a period of nearly thirty years, averaged over ten publications a year in journals and book chapters. The main themes in much of this work, I decided, should be consolidated into separate books, each dealing with one of the key topics of my 1969 article.

The first book in this series was *Educability and Group Differences* (1973), which dealt almost entirely with social class and racial differences in IQ and other psychometric abilities and their important role in accounting for individual and group differences in scholastic achievement. Probably the book's most controversial conclusion was that all of the most popular and purely environmental theories of the causes of the well-established average black-white differences in IQ and scholastic achievement were either contradicted by the factual evidence or were inadequate as a scientific explanation, and that the total body of evidence at that time was better explained by the hypothesis that the racial differences involved both genetic and environmental factors and in about the same proportions as they determined individual differences within either racial group. ISI, in its journal *Current Contents* (1987), announced that this book had also become a "citation classic."

The second book in the series was *Bias in Mental Testing* (1980), in which I examined as comprehensively as was possible at that time the then controversial question of whether the psychometric tests of mental ability that were widely used in schools, colleges, industry, and the armed services yielded biased scores for those racial and cultural minority groups in the United States that, on average, score below the mean of the rest of the population. My conclusion from this research was that the currently most widely used standardized tests of mental ability yield unbiased measures for all native-born English speaking segments of contemporary American society, regardless of their sex, race, or social class background, and that the observed mean differences between various groups are not an artifact of the tests themselves, but are attributable to factors that are causally independent of the tests. In brief, the tests do not create the observed group differences, they simply register them. This conclusion has since been accepted and affirmed by the majority of experts in the field of psychometrics. This book, too, was later written up as a "citation classic" in the ISI's *Current Contents* (1987).

The following year I wrote a smaller, popular book, *Straight Talk about Men-*

tal Tests (1981), to explain the gist of the two previous books to readers without a background in psychometrics and behavioral genetics. (Those about to delve into the present volume may find this little book a helpful introduction.)

Having addressed those points, I realized that the critical issue was the existence and nature of the *g* factor itself. Although it was mentioned in my 1969 article, *g* was largely taken for granted, as if there had long ceased to exist any serious controversy about the sovereignty of *g* in the study of human mental abilities. Yet some people, mostly from outside the field, viewed *g* not as a phenomenon of nature, but as merely an artifact created by subjecting a particular set of mental tests to the arcane mathematical machinations of factor analysis. And I discovered that more than a few psychologists had misconceived notions or prejudices about *g*. It became clear to me that the real basis of my 1969 article was *g* itself and that it deserved a book-length exposition in its own right, even more than the other topics that, at the time, I thought were most interesting and in need of investigation.

So this—*The g Factor*—became the third volume in the series of books growing out of my 1969 article. Charles Spearman's great work, *The Abilities of Man* (1927), in which he summarized the results of his pioneer studies of *g*, was then the best exposition of the subject, and it is still well worth reading. But Spearman's book, of course, does not take account of the important research involving *g* that has accumulated during the seventy years since its publication. Also, not all of the issues related to *g* that are the focal point of psychometrics and differential psychology today are the same as the problems faced by Spearman in his day.

Therefore, since the publication of my last major book, in 1980, I have devoted my research to the empirical study of *g*. As this line of study was actually begun by Sir Francis Galton more than 100 years ago, I decided to take up where he left off in his attempt, which appeared unsuccessful at the time, to relate measurements of reaction time to other criteria of general mental ability. The initial success of this work in my chronometric laboratory encouraged me to institute a long-term research program using modern electronic techniques for precisely measuring an individual's reaction time (RT) in performing extremely simple elementary cognitive tasks (ECTs, as they are now called), and determining how these RT measures are related to performance on complex tests of mental ability, such as those used for measuring IQ. This Galtonian paradigm has proved a successful tool for probing the essential nature of psychometric *g* at the behavioral level, and it has pointed up fruitful hypotheses for further investigations of *g* at a physiological level, the new frontier of research on mental ability. All of my own empirical and methodological studies related to *g*, as well as virtually all of the research by the great many other investigators cited in the present book, have been published in the peer-reviewed scientific literature. I hope that my synthesis and theoretical interpretation of this massive body of research have done it justice. In any case, it had to be done.

My research has led me to regard the *g* factor in a much broader perspective than I had envisaged at the outset. I have come to view g as one of the most central phenomena in all of behavioral science, with broad explanatory powers at least as important for understanding human affairs as E. L. Thorndike's Law of Effect (or Skinner's reinforcement principle). Moreover, it became apparent that the g construct extends well beyond its psychometric origin and definition. The g factor is actually a biologically based variable, which, like other biological functions in the human species, is necessarily a product of the evolutionary process. The human condition in all of its aspects cannot be adequately described or understood in a scientific sense without taking into account the powerful explanatory role of the g factor. Students in all branches of the behavioral and social sciences, as well as students of human biology and evolution, need to grasp the essential psychometric meaning of g, its basis in genetics and brain physiology, and its broad social significance.

A NOTE TO THE READER

Although much of the material in this book is admittedly, though unavoidably, at a fairly difficult conceptual level, I have tried to present it in such a way that it can be understood not only by specialized readers with a background in psychology, psychometrics, statistics, or behavioral genetics, but by any interested persons of whatever educational background whose reading comprehension is up to the level of what I presume is typical of college graduates. I had thought of providing a glossary of the more specialized terms, but discovered that nearly all of the entries I would have included are given quite adequate definitions in the *Random House Unabridged Dictionary* (Second Edition, 1993).

Each chapter is preceded by a brief summary of its content, as an ''advance organizer'' for the reader. Notes at the end of each chapter are keyed by numerical superscripts in the text; they are of two kinds: (1) definitions or explanations of technical terms or statistical concepts, or a more detailed explanation or analysis of some point in the text, that appear as end-notes to avoid interrupting the main text (indicated in the text by superscript numbers); and (2) literature *citations* accompanied by little or no commentary (indicated in the text by *bracketed* superscript numbers). Germane but more specialized topics are explicated in the appendices. The references (all of them cited at some point in the text) provide a comprehensive bibliography of the scientific literature on human mental ability.

Acknowledgments

Mere thanks to all of those who have helped me in a variety of ways that eventually led to my writing this book, and indeed provided the conditions that made it possible, seems hardly enough. Many persons are owed my gratitude—my graduate research assistants and postdoctoral fellows at Berkeley who helped me in conducting many of the studies cited herein, my distinguished colleagues and friends who generously offered their expertise in specialized areas by reading portions of the manuscript with a critical eye and providing advice for improving it, and those experts in fields relevant to certain topics in this book who were always willing to engage in helpful and encouraging discussions about my inquiries, often providing reprints and references. Especially deserving of credit for supporting much of the empirical research I have done on the g factor and its educational, social, and biological correlates, at a time when few foundations or granting agencies would consider supporting research aimed at exploring the nature and implications of g in areas considered politically sensitive, are The Pioneer Fund and its admirably intrepid president, Harry F. Weyher, whose mission has been to lend support to pioneering efforts in scientific research areas that in academe are often considered unpopular or even taboo, at least initially. Similarly, I am grateful to the publishers of this book, particularly Dr. James Sabin, Director, Academic Research and Development, and Professor Seymour Itzkoff, the series editor, for supporting this book on a topic that other firms may have thought unwise or unprofitable to consider publishing.

Finally, and above all, I must acknowledge how very indebted I am to my remarkable wife, Barbara, who has not only been of direct assistance in my work, but whose superior capability, ingenuity, and efficiency in managing all of the practical and financial responsibilities of daily life have completely freed me from every chore and care that is not directly germane to my research work.

For granting permission to reprint the figures or graphs in this book (indicated in parentheses), I am grateful to the following publishers: Ablex Publishing

Corporation (4.1, 4.2, 4.3, 4.4, 5.3, 6.3, 8.4, 8.5, 10.2, 11.8, 14.4), American Psychological Association (7.2a, 7.2b), Boxwood Press (figure in Appendix C), Cambridge University Press (7.1), Elsevier Science Ltd. (8.6, 11.4, 11.9, 12.11), Erlbaum Associates Inc. (12.13), The Free Press (5.2, 9.1, 10.3, 11.2, 11.3), Methuen, Grune & Stratton (12.12), Kluwer Academic Publishers (8.7), Plenum Publishing Corporation (9.2), Princeton University Press (12.1, 12.2, 12.3), SAGE Publications Inc. (14.1), and John Wiley & Sons (5.1).

Chapter 1

A Little History

In the 2,000-year prehistory of psychology, which was dominated by Platonic philosophy and Christian theology, the cognitive aspect of mind was identified with the soul, and conceived of as a perfect, immaterial, universal attribute of humans. This vastly delayed the study of mental ability, or intelligence, as an attribute discernible in people's idiosyncratic behavior and therefore as manifesting individual differences.

The formal recognition of individual differences in mental ability as a subject for study in its own right arose as an outgrowth of the idea of evolution in the mid-nineteenth century. For the first time in history, animals' behavioral capacities and humans' mental ability were recognized as a product of the evolutionary process, just as the physical systems of organisms. Darwin's theory of natural selection as the mechanism of evolution implied that organisms' behavioral capacities, along with their anatomy and physiology, evolved as adaptations to particular environments. In Darwin's theory, hereditary variation is a necessary condition for the working of natural selection. From this insight, Herbert Spencer, the early philosopher of evolution, interpreted individual differences in intelligence as intrinsic to the human condition. He further introduced the notion that human intelligence evolved as a *unitary* attribute.

Individual differences in mental qualities, however, did not become a subject for empirical study in its own right until the latter half of the nineteenth century, with the pioneer efforts of Sir Francis Galton, who is generally regarded as the father of differential psychology (the study of individual and group differences in human traits, which includes behavioral genetics). Galton introduced the idea of objective measurement of human capacities, devised tests to measure simple sensory and motor functions, and invented many of the statistical concepts and methods still used in the study of individual differences. He was the first to apply empirical methods to studying the inheritance of mental ability. Galton's conclusions, or beliefs, are consistent with his empirical findings but are not at all adequately supported by them. They may be briefly summarized as follows:

Human mental ability has both *general* and *specific* components; the general component is the larger source of individual differences; it is predominantly a product of biological evolution, and is more strongly hereditary than are specific abilities, or special talents. Mental ability, which ranges widely in every large population, is normally distributed, and various human races differ, on average, in mental ability. General ability is best measured by a variety of fairly simple tests of sensory discrimination and reaction time.

Thus, Spencer and Galton, in putting forth their ideas, which harmonized with the Darwinian revolution in biology, set the stage, by the end of the nineteenth century, for nearly all the basic ideas and questions that have dominated research and theoretical controversy in twentieth century differential psychology.

History helps us understand the present. In science, past events set the stage for the substantive questions and arguments that face contemporary researchers. Current methods of investigation and standards of evidence are based on the philosophy of science, a viewpoint so deeply embedded in modern Western thought that it is unquestioned by working scientists. It has two outstanding virtues: Its rules of empirical observation, controlled experimentation, and hypothesis testing produce eventual agreement on statements about natural phenomena, and the knowledge so produced often has consequences that affect other disciplines and life in general.

It is worthwhile, therefore, to sketch the origins of the study of human mental ability.[1] The "prehistory" of this topic extends from ancient times to approximately the beginning of the twentieth century. Since then, at least, no major issue has arisen that lacks historical precedent. As in other branches of science, the main lines of contemporary thought in the study of mental ability can be traced back to a few principal themes.

THE LATE ARRIVAL OF THE CONCEPT OF INTELLIGENCE IN PSYCHOLOGY

Almost a hundred years ago, the German psychologist Hermann Ebbinghaus (1850–1909) remarked that psychology has a long past, but only a short history. This is still true, particularly for the branch known as *differential psychology*, the study of individual differences in behavior. Surprising as it may seem, ability, intelligence, and individual differences were not mentioned in most of the early textbooks of psychology (written during the last half of the nineteenth century). One of the most important and comprehensive textbooks, William James's *Principles of Psychology* (1890), mentions "intelligence" only once—as a synonym for "intellect" and "reason," and that only in the context of defining the properties of the mind. Totally absent is any notion of mental ability or individual differences. The same is true of James's *Talks to Teachers* (1899), the first influential textbook of educational psychology in America.[2] Another well-known textbook, James Mark Baldwin's *Handbook of Psychology* (1890), briefly mentions "intellect," but completely ignores individual differences. Baldwin's encyclopedic *Dictionary of Philosophy and Psychology* (1901) has no separate entry for "intelligence," which is merely listed in a generic sense as a synonym under "intellect."

It may seem puzzling that such intentionally comprehensive textbooks and dictionaries of psychology, even as late as 1900, are devoid of such a conspicuous and often controversial psychological topic as individual differences in mental ability. Why was this phenomenon, so universal to human experience, absent from academic psychological discourse for so long, in stark contrast to the prominence of the "IQ controversy" in contemporary psychology and social science?

The reason was clearly not a lack of awareness in the past. Individual differences in mental ability and other personality traits have been portrayed in literature (often in detail) since ancient times. Fictional characters were described as clever, bright, keen-witted; or dull, addled, and stupid. Geniuses and the feebleminded have figured in novels and plays for centuries. Historians and biographers recognized exceptional abilities or their absence. Nor was the subject ever shunned because of an egalitarian taboo against openly recognizing human differences in abilities. Thinkers of the past were hardly egalitarians. Rather they accepted a highly stratified society as a matter of course. To most, it was simply part of the natural order that individuals were born and remained in rigid classes, as aristocrats, artisans, peasants, serfs, and slaves. Every civilization has had at least a two-tiered society, but more typically a three-tiered one. Plato, in *The Republic* (circa 400 B.C.), classified individuals as gold, silver, and bronze, according to the rarity of their valued qualities, and suggested that in the ideal society—in his view, a pure meritocracy—they should be selected for different occupations according to these qualities.

PREHISTORY OF PSYCHOLOGY

Why, then, was the subject of individual differences in mental ability per se absent from systematic thought before the latter part of the nineteenth century? Two main factors seem to be responsible. One was the pervasive influence of Plato on the concept of the *mind* in philosophical and theological thought. The other was that the discipline of psychology itself grew out of the philosophic tradition.

Plato (427–347 B.C.). Since Plato's time, the doctrine of dualism—the separation of mind and body, each as a distinct entity—has been deeply entrenched in Christian theology and Western philosophy. This dogma influenced the development of psychology. In Platonism, *mind* and *soul* are almost synonymous. The soul, with universal and eternal properties, was a central theme. The perfect and immaterial soul was the essence of being human, the defining attribute that unequivocally separated humankind from all other creatures. The idea of soul, or divine mind, as a perfect and universal quality of humans, therefore, was incompatible with the notion of individual differences in this attribute. The soul transcends all that is mundane, including individual differences in behavior. Reason, thought, and intellect, as the essence of mind (or soul) were regarded as universal qualities, distinct from behavioral idiosyncracies. Plato also distinguished two lower aspects of the human psyche, *emotion* and *will*. There is a famous metaphor in Plato's *Phaedra* depicting intellect as the charioteer who holds the reins, with emotion and will as the horses that draw the chariot. This triarchic model of the human psyche, comprising intellect, emotion, and will, is perhaps the most easily recognizable aspect of philosophy's legacy to psychology.

Aristotle (384–323 B.C.). Plato's illustrious student Aristotle came closer to a naturalistic or scientific conception of psychology than did his mentor. He wrote about psychological functions, such as sensation, reaction, desire, recognition memory and recall memory, knowing, and thinking. These all resemble modern distinctions. More significantly, Aristotle rejected Plato's dualistic partition of mind and body. Instead, he claimed that the mind's higher functions—acquiring knowledge, thinking, and reasoning—depended on sensation and memory, although because these functions are also possessed by animals, he assigned them a lower status than thought and reason. He also held that intentional behavior is causally connected to the mental state that immediately precedes it. His description of *thought* as "deliberation preceding action" anticipated the Watsonian behaviorism of the 1920s. Although this approach implies that consistent individual differences in *behavior* (judged as clever or stupid) have an underlying *mental* counterpart, Aristotle did not develop this point or discuss individual differences in mentality.

Aristotle was also responsible for the word *intelligence*, although indirectly. He had reduced Plato's triarchic division of the psyche to only two main functions, termed *dianoetic* (cognitive functions) and *orectic* (emotion, will, and moral sense). The Roman orator and statesman Cicero (106–43 B.C.), in translating Aristotle's Greek, coined the equivalent of "dianoetic" in Latin as *intelligentia*—Anglicized as *intelligence*. Thus originated this now commonplace term, which later became perhaps the most controversial subject in all of psychology.

Social Factors in Past History. Another historical factor that probably accounts for the scarcity of references to individual differences in the philosophic literature of ancient and medieval times was the social system itself. Consisting of aristocracies and serfdoms, it allowed narrow scope for the salience of individual differences in mental ability. The coming of industrialization, with the proliferation of specialized occupations and the availability of formal schooling for a large part of the population, made individual differences in ability more clearly visible. In preindustrial eras, an individual's social status at birth severely restricted his chances for education and choice of occupation. Formal schooling, which tends to highlight differences in mental ability, was the privilege of a small elite. Thus the great inequality of opportunity in education and occupational choice obscured the perception of individual, inborn differences in mental ability.

The earliest explicit statement regarding individual differences that I have been able to find in the philosophic literature is attributed to the Roman orator Quintilian (A.D. 35–95). His advice to teachers would not look out of place in a present-day textbook of educational psychology: "It is generally, and not without reason, regarded as an excellent quality in a master to observe accurately differences in ability in those whom he has undertaken to instruct, and to ascertain in what direction the nature of each particularly inclines him; for there is in talent an incredible variety, and the forms of mind are not less varied than those of bodies" (quoted in Stoddard, 1943, p. 79). But Quintilian evidently had no impact on psychology. His name was not even indexed in Wiley's four-volume *Encyclopedia of Psychology* (1984).

Locke and British Empiricism. The English philosopher John Locke (1632–1704) made a lasting mark on our topic. He was probably the first formal "environmentalist." In his famous *Essay Concerning Human Understanding* (1690), he expounded that the human mind, at birth, is a *tabula rasa*, or blank tablet. Through the special senses—vision, hearing, touch, taste, and smell—the mind accumulates impressions from the environment. All knowledge, Locke argued, comes from only two sources, *sensation* and *reflection* (or the "association of ideas"). Experience, he said, is the sole basis of mind. Thus he opposed *nativism*, the notion that the mind comes equipped with certain built-in propensities, instincts, ideas, or qualities. He advocated *empiricism*, the belief that the properties of mind are wholly attributable to individual experience. Locke's *tabula rasa* theory implied to followers that differences in intelligence resulted from differences in people's life experience. The philosophic argument between the rival doctrines of nativism and empiricism moved into psychology, where it had profound ramifications, most notably the so-called nature-nurture controversy over the relative importance of heredity and environment as causes of variation in psychological traits.

THE DARWINIAN REVOLUTION

Full recognition of individual differences in psychological traits, however, had to wait for the revolution in biological thought ushered in by Darwin's theory of evolution through natural selection. The British philosopher Herbert Spencer

(1820–1903) was ready and waiting to make the connection. He had originally promoted his own pre-Darwinian theory of evolution along Lamarckian lines, which held that characteristics acquired through experience could be passed from parents to offspring through biological heredity. According to this theory, particular learned behavior, if habitual, could be passed on to later generations as an inborn instinct. The publication of *The Origin of Species* (1858), however, converted Spencer to Darwin's theory of natural selection as the mechanism of biological evolution, and he became the leading philosopher of Darwinism. But even before he had read Darwin, he wrote a textbook, *The Principles of Psychology* (1855), which had an evolutionary orientation. It has the important distinction of being the first psychology textbook to use the word *intelligence* and to pay specific attention to the fact of *individual differences* in intelligence.

Spencer considered intelligence a *unitary* biological characteristic that evolved through the differential adaptation of organisms to their environment over time. Behavior itself evolved biologically in conjunction with physical systems. This was a clear break from the dualism handed down since Plato. The mind— intelligence in particular—was for the first time viewed in the same way as anatomical and physiological systems, that is, as an organically evolved adaptive mechanism used in the competition for survival in a particular environment. This was a large step, for which Spencer is seldom given enough credit. His notion of intelligence as a *unitary* trait, instead of as a number of separate faculties, also marks the beginning of another long-lived controversy. Still a lively issue in psychology, it is taken up in a later chapter.

Darwin's theory of evolution emphasized hereditary variation as the raw material on which natural selection operates. From this new perspective, Spencer realized the biological significance of individual differences, because *Homo sapiens* would not have evolved without the existence of individual variation. Therefore, Spencer saw individual variation in hereditary traits as intrinsic to the human condition. In his philosophizing about society, he used the catchy phrase "survival of the fittest," and produced a primitive precursor of sociobiology known as Social Darwinism. Both the term and the concept eventually were strongly reproached. Anthropologists and sociologists, in particular, decried its antiegalitarian overtones and reviled the whole idea as misconstrued Darwinian theory. However, Spencer's view of intelligence as a biologically adaptive function for achieving, in his words, "the adjustment of internal to external relations" was a precursor of later efforts to investigate the continuity of brain and intelligence in animals and humans from an evolutionary perspective. This has become a major frontier of research in biological psychology.

GALTON AND THE COMING OF EMPIRICAL PSYCHOLOGY

All the early influences on differential psychology mentioned so far came from philosophers. None was an empirical scientist. Darwin was, of course, but Darwinian ideas were introduced into psychology by Herbert Spencer, a professional philosopher. The empirical study of mental ability and individual differences could not begin until someone took up the methods of empirical science, that is, asking definite questions of nature and discovering the answers through analysis of data based on systematic observation, objective measurement, and experimentation. The first person to do this was the Victorian eccentric, polymath, and genius Sir Francis Galton (1822–1911).[3] Galton was Charles Darwin's younger half-cousin—half-cousin because they had only one grandparent in common, Erasmus Darwin, a noted physician, physiologist, naturalist, and poet. Born into a prominent and wealthy family, Galton was a child prodigy, who could read and write before the age of four. He intensely disliked school, however, and his parents transferred him from one private boarding school to another, each as boring and frustrating to him as the others, and he begged his parents to let him quit. In his *Memories of My Life* (1908), written when he was 86, he still complained of his unsatisfying school experience. At age fifteen, he was sent away to college, which offered more challenge. To satisfy his parents' ambition that he follow in his eminent grandfather's footsteps and become a physician, he entered medical school. There he soon discovered that the basic sciences—physics, chemistry, biology, and physiology—were far more to his liking than medical practice. So he left medical school for Cambridge University, there to major in mathematics in preparation for a career in science.

Soon after Galton graduated, at age twenty-one, his father died, and Galton received a large inheritance that made him independently wealthy for the rest of his very long life. It allowed him to pursue his extremely varied interests freely in all things scientific. His enthusiastic and catholic curiosity about natural phenomena drove him to became perhaps the greatest scientific dilettante of all time. Because he was also a genius, he made original contributions to many fields, some of them important enough to be accorded chapters in books on the history of several fields: criminology, eugenics, genetics, meteorology, psychology, and statistics. He first gained fame in geography, as an explorer, expertly describing, surveying, and mapping previously unexplored parts of Africa. For this activity, his name is engraved on the granite facade of the Royal Geographical Society's building in London, along with the names of the most famous explorers in British history. (His fascinating book *The Art of Travel* [1855] was a long-time best seller and went through nine editions.) He also made contributions to meteorology, inventing isobar mapping, being the first to write a daily newspaper weather report, and formulating a widely accepted theory of the anticyclone. He made other original contributions to photography, fingerprint classification, genetics, statistics, anthropology, and psychometrics. His prolific achievements and publications brought worldwide recognition and many honors, including knighthood, Fellow of the Royal Society, and several gold medals awarded by scientific societies in England and Europe. As a famous man in his own lifetime, Galton also had what Hollywood calls "star quality."

Biographies of Galton also reveal his charming eccentricities. His profuse intellectual energy spilled over into lesser achievements or activities that often seem trivial. He was almost obsessed with counting and measuring things (his motto: "When you can, count!"), and he devised mechanical counters and other devices to help in counting and tabulating. He loved data. On his first visit to a city, for example, he would walk around with a small, hand-held mechanical counter and tally the number of people passing by, tabulating their character-istics—tall, medium, short; blond, brunette, redhead—separately for males and females, the latter also rated for attractiveness. To be able to manage all these data while walking about, he had his tailor make a special vest with many little pockets, each one for a particular tabulated characteristic. He could temporarily store the data from his counters by putting into designated pockets the appro-priate number of dried peas. Back in his hotel room, he counted the peas in each pocket and entered the numerical results in his notebook for later statistical calculations.

He devised an objective measure of the degree to which a lecturer bored the audience, and tried it out at meetings of the Royal Society. It consisted of counting the involuntary noises—coughs, feet shuffling, and the like—that is-sued from the audience, and, with a specially rigged protractor, he measured the angle that listeners' heads were tilted from a vertical position during the lecture. A score derived from the data obtained with this procedure showed that even the most eloquently written lecture, if read verbatim, was more boring than an extempore lecture, however rambling and inelegant.

He also invented a special whistle (now called a Galton whistle), which is familiar to many dog owners. Its high-frequency pitch is beyond humans' au-dible range and can be heard only by dogs and certain other animals. Galton made a series of these whistles, ranging widely in pitch, and used them to find the upper limits of pitch that could be heard by humans of different ages. To compare the results on humans with the auditory capacities of many species in the London Zoo, he would attach the whistles to the end of a tube that could be extended like a telescope, so it could reach into a cage and direct the sound right at the animal's ear. While quickly squeezing a rubber bulb attached to one end of the long tube to force a standard puff of air through the whistle attached to the other end, he would note whether or not the animal reacted to a particular pitch.

In another amusing project, he used the mathematics of solid geometry to figure out the optimal way to cut a cake of any particular shape and dimensions into any given number of pieces to preserve the freshness of each piece. He published his clever solution in a mathematics journal. There are many other quaint anecdotes about Galton's amazing scientific curiosity and originality, but the several already mentioned should suffice to round out the picture of his extraordinary personality.

Although he died (at age ninety) as long ago as 1911, his legacy remains remarkably vivid. It comprises not only his many pioneering ideas and statistical inventions, still in use, but also the important endowments, permitted by his personal wealth, for advancing the kinds of research he thought would be of greatest benefit to human welfare. He founded the Department of Eugenics (now Genetics) at the University of London and endowed its Chair, which has been occupied by such luminaries as Karl Pearson, Sir Ronald Fisher, and Lionel Penrose; he furnished a psychological laboratory in University College, London; he founded two prestigious journals that are still active, *Biometrika* and *The Annals of Human Genetics*; and he founded (in 1904) the Eugenics Society (recently renamed The Galton Institute), which maintains an extensive library, publishes journals and books, and sponsors many symposia, all related to the field now known as social biology.

THE TWO DISCIPLINES OF SCIENTIFIC PSYCHOLOGY

Galton's position in the history of behavioral science is stellar. He is acknowledged as one of the two founding fathers of empirical psychology, along with Wilhelm Wundt (1832–1920), who established the first laboratory of experimental psychology in 1879 in Leipzig. As Wundt is recognized as the father of *experimental* psychology, Galton can certainly be called the father of *differential* psychology, including psychometrics and behavioral genetics. Each is now a major branch of modern behavioral science. The leading historian of experimental psychology, Edwin G. Boring (1950), drew the following interesting contrast between the scientific personalities of Galton and Wundt:

> Wundt was erudite where Galton was original; Wundt overcame massive obstacles by the weight of his attack; Galton dispatched a difficulty by a thrust of insight. Wundt was forever armored by his system; Galton had no system. Wundt was methodical; Galton was versatile. Wundt's science was interpenetrated by his philosophy; Galton's science was discursive and unstructured. Wundt was interminably arguing; Galton was forever observing. Wundt had a school, a formal self-conscious school; Galton had friends, influence and effects only. Thus, Wundt was personally intolerant and controversial, whereas Galton was tolerant and ready to be convicted of error. (pp. 461–62)

Wundt and Galton were the progenitors of the two main branches of scientific psychology—experimental (Wundt) and differential (Galton). These two disciplines have advanced along separate tracks throughout the history of psychology. Their methodological and even philosophical differences run deep, although both branches embrace the scientific tradition of objective testing of hypotheses.

Experimental psychology searches for general laws of behavior. Therefore, it treats individual differences as unwanted variance, termed "error variance," which must be minimized or averaged out to permit the discovery of universal regularities in the relation between stimulus and response. The method of experimental psychology consists of controlling variables (or treatment conditions) and randomizing the assignment of subjects to the different treatments. The experimental conditions are intentionally manipulated to discover their *average* effects, unconfounded by individual differences. In general, the stimulus presented to the subject is varied by the experimenter, while the subject's responses are recorded or measured. But the data of primary interest to the experimental psychologist consist of the *averaged* performance of the many subjects randomly assigned to each condition.

Differential psychology, on the other hand, seeks to classify, measure, and then explain the variety and nature of both individual and group differences in behavioral traits as phenomena worthy of investigation in their own right. It uses statistical analysis, such as correlation, multiple regression, and factor analysis, applied to data obtained under natural conditions, rather than the controlled conditions of the laboratory. Obviously, when human characteristics are of interest, individual differences and many other aspects of behavior cannot feasibly or ethically be controlled or manipulated by the investigator. Therefore, scientists must study human variation as it occurs under natural conditions. During the latter half of this century, however, a rapprochement has begun between the two disciplines. Both experimental and correlational methods are being used in the study of cognition.

Galton's Methodological Contributions. Galton made enduring contributions to the methodology of differential psychology. He was the first to devise a precise quantitative index of the degree of relationship, or *co-relation* (as he called it) between any two metric variables obtained from the same individuals (or relatives) in a given population. Examples are individuals' height and weight or the resemblance between parents and children, or between siblings, in a given trait.

In 1896, Karl Pearson (1857–1936), a noted mathematician, who became a Galton disciple and has been rightly called the "father of statistics," revamped Galton's formulation of co-relation, to make it mathematically more elegant and enhance its general applicability. Pearson's formula yields what now is called "the Pearson product-moment coefficient of correlation." In the technical literature, however, the word *correlation*, without a modifier, always signifies Pearson's coefficient.[4] (The many other types of correlation coefficient are always specified, e.g., *intraclass* correlation, *rank-order* correlation, *tetrachoric* correlation, *biserial* correlation, *point-biserial* correlation, *partial* correlation, *semipartial* correlation, *multiple* correlation, *canonical* correlation, correlation *ratio, phi* coefficient, *contingency* coefficient, *tau* coefficient, *concordance* coefficient, and *congruence* coefficient. Each has its specialized use, depending on the type of data.) Pearson's correlation is the most generally used. Universally symbolized by a lower-case italic *r* (derived from Galton's term *regression*), it is a ubiquitous tool in the biological and behavioral sciences. In differential psychology, it is absolutely essential.

Galton invented many other statistical and psychometric concepts and methods familiar to all present-day researchers, including the bivariate scatter diagram, regression (related to correlation), multiple regression and multiple correlation (by which two or more different variables are used to predict another variable), the conversion of measurements or ranks to percentiles, standardized or scale-free measurements or scores, various types of rating scales, the use of the now familiar normal or bell-shaped curve (originally formulated by the great mathematician Karl Friedrich Gauss [1777–1855]) as a basis for quantifying psychological traits on an equal-interval scale, and using either the median or the geometric mean (instead of the arithmetic mean) as the indicator of central tendency of measurements that have a markedly skewed frequency distribution.

In his *Inquiries into Human Faculty and Its Development* (1883), Galton described an odd assortment of clever tests and techniques, devised mostly by himself, for measuring basic human capacities, particularly keenness of sensory discrimination in the different modalities, imagery, and reaction times to auditory and visual stimuli. Although Galton's use of gadgetry has been disparaged as "brass instrument psychology," it was a seminal innovation—the *objective measurement* of human capacities. Compared with modern technology, of course, Galton's methods were fairly crude, sometimes even inadequate for their purpose. His intense interest in human variation and his passion for quantitative data, however, led him to apply his "brass instrument" techniques to almost every physical and mental characteristic that could be counted, ranked, or measured.

Galton obtained many types of data on more than 9,000 persons who, from 1884 to 1890, went through his Anthropometric Laboratory in London's South Kensington Science Museum. Each had to pay threepence to serve as subjects for these tests and measurements. Unfortunately, Galton lacked the powerful tools of statistical inference that were later developed by Karl Pearson (1857–1936) and Sir Ronald A. Fisher (1890–1962), and therefore he could only draw much weaker conclusions than the quality of his massive data really warranted. He was dismayed that the measurements of sensory discrimination and speed of reaction appeared to show so little relationship to a person's level of general mental ability (as indicated by educational and occupational attainments). It soon became a widely accepted and long-lasting conclusion that the simple functions assessed by Galton are unrelated to individual differences in the higher mental processes, or intelligence. Galton's "brass instrument" approach to the study of human abilities, therefore, was abandoned for nearly a century.

Recently, Galton's original data have been analyzed by modern methods of statistical inference.[5] It turned out that his original hypotheses were largely correct after all. R. A. Fisher's method known as *analysis of variance* revealed highly significant differences between groups differing in educational and occupational level on Galton's discrimination and reaction-time tests. Galton's scientific intuitions were remarkably good, but the psychometric and statistical methods then available were not always up to the task of validating them.

Galton Introduces Genetics into Psychology. Galton's most famous work, *Hereditary Genius* (1869), was the forerunner of behavior genetics, nearly a century before either the term or the field of behavior genetics came into being. Galton was especially interested in the inheritance of mental ability. Because there was then no objective scale for measuring mental ability, he devised another criterion of high-level ability: *eminence*, based on illustrious achievements that would justify published biographies, encyclopedia articles, and the like. By this criterion, he selected many of the most famous intellects of the nineteenth century, whom he classed as "illustrious," and he obtained information about their ancestors, descendants, and other relatives. His extensive biographical and genealogical research revealed that the relatives of his illustrious probands were much more likely to attain eminence than would a random sample of the population with comparable social background. More telling, he noticed that the probability of eminence in a relative of an illustrious person decreased in a regular stepwise fashion as the degree of kinship was more remote. Galton noticed that the same pattern was also true for physical stature and athletic performance.

Galton made other observations that gave some indication of the power of family background in producing eminence. In an earlier period of history, it was customary for popes to adopt orphan boys and rear them like sons, with all the advantages of culture and education that papal privilege could command. Galton noted that far fewer of these adopted boys ever attained eminence than did the natural sons of fathers whose eminence was comparable to a pope's. From such circumstantial evidence, Galton concluded that mental ability is inherited in much the same manner, and to about the same degree, as physical traits.

Galton further concluded that what was inherited was essentially a *general* ability, because eminent relatives in the same family line were often famous in quite different fields, such as literature, mathematics, and music. He supposed that this hereditary general ability could be channeled by circumstance or interest into different kinds of intellectual endeavor. He also recognized *special* abilities, or talent, in fields like art and music, but considered them less important than general ability in explaining outstanding accomplishment, because a high level of general ability characterized all of his illustrious persons. (Galton noted that they were also characterized by the unusual zeal and persistence they brought to their endeavors.) He argued, for example, that the inborn musical gift of a Beethoven could not have been expressed in works of genius were it not accompanied by superior general ability. In *Hereditary Genius*, he summarized his concept of general ability in his typically quaint style: "Numerous instances recorded in this book show in how small a degree eminence can be considered as due to purely special powers. People lay too much stress on apparent specialities, thinking that because a man is devoted to some particular pursuit he would not have succeeded in anything else. They might as well say that, because a youth has fallen in love with a brunette, he could not possibly have fallen in love with a blonde. As likely as not the affair was mainly or wholly due to a general amorousness" (p. 64).

Galton's Anecdotal Report on Twins. The use of twins to study the inheritance of behavioral traits was another of Galton's important "firsts." He noted that there were two types of twins, judging from their degree of resemblance. "Identical" twins come from one egg (hence they are now called monozygotic, or MZ, twins), which divides in two shortly after fertilization. Their genetic makeup is identical; thus their genetic correlation is unity ($r = 1$). And they are very alike in appearance. "Fraternal" twins (now called dizygotic, or DZ) come from two different fertilized eggs and have the same genetic relationship as ordinary siblings, with a genetic correlation of about one-half (on average). That is, DZ twins are, on average, about one-half as similar, genetically, as MZ twins. DZ twins are no more alike in appearance than ordinary siblings when they are compared at the same age.

Galton was interested in twins' similarities and differences, especially in MZ twins, as any difference would reflect only the influence of environment or nongenetic factors. He located some eighty pairs of twins whose close physical resemblance suggested they were MZ, and he collected anecdotal data on their behavioral characteristics from their relatives and friends and from the twins themselves. He concluded that since the twins were so strikingly similar in their traits, compared to ordinary siblings, heredity was the predominant cause of differences in individuals' psychological characteristics.

Because Galton obtained no actual measurements, systematic observations, or quantitative data, his conclusions are of course liable to the well-known shortcomings of all anecdotal reports. Later research, however, based on the more precise methods of modern psychometrics and biometrical genetics, has largely substantiated Galton's surmise about the relative importance of heredity and environment for individual differences in general mental ability. But Galton's research on heredity is cited nowadays only for its historical interest as the prototype of the essential questions and methods that gave rise to modern behavioral genetics. It is a fact that most of the questions of present interest to researchers in behavioral genetics and differential psychology were originally thought of by Galton. His own answers to many of the questions, admittedly based on inadequate evidence, have proved to be remarkably close to the conclusions of present-day researchers. In the history of science, of course, the persons remembered as great pioneers are those who asked the fundamental questions, thought of novel ways to find the answers, and, in retrospect, had many correct and fruitful ideas. By these criteria, Galton unquestionably qualifies.

Galton's Concept of Mental Ability. Galton seldom used the word *intelligence* and never offered a formal definition. From everything he wrote about ability, however, we can well imagine that, if he had felt a definition necessary, he would have said something like *innate, general, cognitive* ability. The term *cognitive* clearly distinguishes it from the two other attributes of Plato's triarchic conception of the mind, the affective and conative. Galton's favored term, *mental ability*, comprises both *general* ability and a number of *special* abilities—he mentioned linguistic, mathematical, musical, artistic, and memorial. General ability denotes a power of mind that affects (to some degree) the quality of virtually everything a person does that requires more than simple sensory acuity or sheer physical strength, endurance, dexterity, or coordination.

Analogizing from the normal, bell-shaped distribution of large-sample data on physical features, such as stature, Galton assumed that the frequency distribution of ability in the population would approximate the normal curve. He divided the normal curve's baseline into sixteen equal intervals (a purely arbitrary, but convenient, number) to create a scale for quantifying individual and group differences in general ability. But Galton's scale is no longer used. Ever since Karl Pearson, in 1893, invented the *standard deviation*, the baseline of the normal distribution has been interval-scaled in units of the standard deviation, symbolized by σ (the lower-case Greek letter sigma). Simple calculation shows that each interval of Galton's scale is equal to 0.696σ, which is equivalent to 10.44 IQ points, when the σ of IQ is 15 IQ points. Hence Galton's scale of mental ability, in terms of IQ, ranges from about 16 to 184.

Galton was unsuccessful, however, in actually *measuring* individual differences in intelligence. We can easily see with hindsight that his particular battery of simple tests was unsuited for assessing the higher mental processes that people think of as "intelligence." Where did Galton go wrong? Like Herbert Spencer, he was immensely impressed by Darwin's theory of natural selection as the mechanism of evolution. And hereditary individual variation is the raw material on which natural selection works by, in Darwinian terms, "selection of the fittest in the struggle for survival." Also, Galton was influenced by Locke's teaching that the mind's content is originally gained through the avenue of the five senses, which provide all the raw material for the association of impressions to form ideas, knowledge, and intelligence. From Darwin's and Locke's theories, Galton theorized that, in his words, "the more perceptive the senses are of differences, the larger is the field upon which our judgement and intelligence can act" (*Human Faculty*, 1883, p. 19). Among many other factors that conferred advantages in the competition for survival, individual variation in keenness of sensory discrimination, as well as quickness of reaction to external stimuli, would have been positively selected in the evolution of human intelligence.

It seemed to Galton a reasonable hypothesis, therefore, that tests of fine sensory *discrimination* (not just simple acuity) and of reaction time to visual and auditory stimuli would provide objective measures of individual differences in the elemental components of mental ability, unaffected by education, occupation, or social status. The previously described battery of tests Galton devised for this purpose, it turned out, yielded measurements that correlated so poorly with commonsense criteria of intellectual distinction (such as election to the Royal Society) as to be unconvincing as a measure of intelligence, much less having any practical value. Statistical techniques were not then available to prove the theoretical significance, if any, of the slight relationship that existed between the laboratory measures and independent estimates of ability. Galton had tested thousands of subjects, and all of his data were carefully preserved. When recently they were analyzed by modern statistical methods, highly significant (that is, nonchance) differences were found between the *average* scores obtained by various groups of people aggregated by age, education, and occupation.[5] This finding lent considerable theoretical interest to Galton's tests, although they would have no practical validity for individual assessment.

Binet and the First Practical Test of Intelligence. At the behest of the Paris school system, Alfred Binet in 1905 invented the first valid and practically useful test of intelligence. Influenced by Galton and aware of his disappointing results, Binet (1857–1911) borrowed a few of Galton's more promising tests (for example, memory span for digits and the discrimination of weights) but also devised new tests of much greater mental complexity so as to engage the higher mental processes—reasoning, judgment, planning, verbal comprehension, and acquisition of knowledge. Test scores scaled in units of *mental age* derived from Binet's battery proved to have practical value in identifying mentally retarded children and in assessing children's readiness for schoolwork. The story of Binet's practical ingenuity, clinical wisdom, and the lasting influence of his test is deservedly well known to students of mental measurement.[7] The reason that Binet's test worked so well, however, remained unexplained by Binet, except in intuitive and commonsense terms. A truly theory-based explanation had to wait for the British psychologist Charles Spearman (1863–1945), whose momentous contributions are reviewed in the next chapter.

Galton on Race Differences in Ability. The discussion of Galton's work in differential psychology would be incomplete without mentioning one other topic that interested him—race differences in mental ability. The title itself of his chapter on this subject in *Hereditary Genius* would be extremely unacceptable today: "The Comparative Worth of Different Races." But Galton's style of writing about race was common among nineteenth-century intellectuals, without the slightest implication that they were mean-spirited, unkindly, or at all unfriendly toward people of another race. A style like Galton's is seen in statements about race made by even such democratic and humanitarian heroes as Jefferson and Lincoln.

Galton had no tests for obtaining direct measurements of cognitive ability. Yet he tried to estimate the mean levels of mental capacity possessed by different racial and national groups on his interval scale of the normal curve. His estimates—many would say guesses—were based on his observations of people of different races encountered on his extensive travels in Europe and Africa, on anecdotal reports of other travelers, on the number and quality of the inventions and intellectual accomplishments of different racial groups, and on the percentage of eminent men in each group, culled from biographical sources. He ventured that the level of ability among the ancient Athenian Greeks averaged "two grades" higher than that of the average Englishmen of his own day. (Two grades on Galton's scale is equivalent to 20.9 IQ points.) Obviously, there is no possibility of ever determining if Galton's estimate was anywhere near correct. He also estimated that African Negroes averaged "at least two grades" (i.e., 1.39σ, or 20.9 IQ points) below the English average. This estimate appears remarkably close to the results for phenotypic ability assessed by culture-reduced IQ tests. Studies in sub-Saharan Africa indicate an average difference (on culture-reduced nonverbal tests of reasoning) equivalent to 1.43σ, or 21.5 IQ points between blacks and whites.[8] U.S. data from the Armed Forces Qualification Test (AFQT), obtained in 1980 on large representative samples of black and white youths, show an average difference of 1.36σ (equivalent to 20.4 IQ points)—not far from Galton's estimate (1.39σ, or 20.9 IQ points).[9] But intuition and informed guesses, though valuable in generating hypotheses, are never acceptable as evidence in scientific research. Present-day scientists, therefore, properly dismiss Galton's opinions on race. Except as hypotheses, their interest is now purely biographical and historical.

NOTES

1. A considerably more detailed history of the differential psychology of mental abilities, extending from ancient times to the present, can be found in Jensen (1987a).

2. For comprehensive articles on the histories of topics discussed in the present chapter—educational psychology, educational and psychological measurement, statistical methodology—I recommend the book edited by Glover and Ronning (1987).

3. The literature on Galton is extensive. The most accessible biography is by Forrest (1974). Fancher (1985a) gives a shorter and highly readable account. A still briefer account of Galton's life and contributions to psychology is given in Jensen (1994a), which also lists the principal biographical references to Galton. His own memoir (Galton, 1908) is good reading, but does not particularly detail his contributions to psychology, a subject reviewed most thoroughly by Cyril Burt (1962). Galton's activities in each of the branches of science to which he made original contributions are detailed in a collection of essays, each by one of fourteen experts in the relevant fields; the book also includes a complete bibliography of Galton's published works, edited by Keynes (1993). Fancher (1983a, 1983b, 1983c, 1984) has provided fascinating and probing essays about quite specific but less well-known aspects of Galton's life and contributions to psychology. Lewis M. Terman (1877–1956), who is responsible for the Stanford-Binet IQ test, tried to estimate Galton's IQ in childhood from a few of his remarkably precocious achievements even long before he went to school. These are detailed in Terman's (1917) article, in which he concluded that Galton's childhood IQ was "not far from 200" (p. 212). One of Galton's biographers, Forrest (1974), however, has noted, "Terman was misled by Francis' letter to [his sister] Adèle which begins, 'I am four years old.' The date shows that it was only one day short of his fifth birthday. The calculations should therefore by emended to give an I.Q. of about 160" (p. 7). (*Note:* Terman estimated IQ as $100 \times$ estimated Mental Age (MA)/Chronological Age (CA); he estimated Galton's MA as 8 years based on his purported capabilities at CA 5 years, so $100 \times 8/5 = 160$.)

4. Pearson's correlation coefficient, *r*, is explained in virtually every introductory textbook of statistics. The basic formula is

$$r = \Sigma(X_i - \overline{X})\,(Y_i - \overline{Y})\,/N\sigma_x\sigma_y,$$

where Σ means "the sum of"; X_i and Y_i are paired individual measurements of variables X and Y; $\overline{X}$ and $\overline{Y}$ are the means of variables X and Y in the sample; σ_x and σ_y are the sample standard deviations of variables X and Y; and N is the number of *paired* measurements. (If the σ_x and σ_y are removed from the above formula, it becomes the formula for what is called the *covariance* of the variables X and Y.) The standard deviation of any variable (say, X), using the above symbols, is

$$\sigma = \sqrt{[\Sigma(X_i - X)^2/N]}.$$

What is known as the *variance* is simply σ^2.

5. This analysis of Galton's original data was conducted by a group of behavior geneticists (Johnson et al., 1985).

6. Ibid.

7. An excellent historical account of the development of Binet's test and of all the major tests of intelligence that followed Binet, up to the present, is found in Thorndike & Lohman (1990).

8. Estimate based on the weighted average IQ of eleven samples of African children and adults (total $N = 10{,}073$) taken from Tables 3 and 4 in Lynn (1991a).

9. Based on data from the 1980 National Longitudinal Study of Youth (NLSY), comprising 6,502 whites and 3,022 blacks, reported in Herrnstein & Murray (1994). The black-white difference of 1.36σ in this estimate is larger than the difference of about 1σ typically reported for IQ, mainly because the white sample in this study, unlike many other studies, is entirely of European ancestry and does not include Amerindians, Mexican-Americans, Asians, and Pacific Islanders.

Chapter 2

The Discovery of *g*

Spearman invented[1] a method, *factor analysis*, that permitted a rigorous statistical test of Spencer's and Galton's hypothesis that a general mental ability enters into every kind of activity requiring mental effort. A well-established empirical finding—positive correlations among measures of various mental abilities—is putative evidence of a common factor in all of the measured abilities. The method of factor analysis makes it possible to determine the degree to which each of the variables is correlated (or loaded) with the factor that is common to all the variables in the analysis. Spearman gave the label *g* to this common factor, which is manifested in individual differences on all mental tests, however diverse.

Spearman's two-factor theory held that every mental test, however diverse in the contents or skills called for, measures only two factors: *g* and *s*, a factor specific to each test. But later research based on larger numbers of tests than were available in Spearman's early studies showed that *g* alone could not account for all of the correlations between tests. So Spearman had to acknowledge that there are other factors besides *g*, called *group factors*, that different groups of tests, each with similar task demands (such as being either verbal, spatial, numerical, or mechanical), have in common.

By comparing tests with high and low *g* factor loadings, Spearman concluded that *g* is most strongly reflected in tests that call for the "eduction of relations and correlates," for example, reasoning to solve novel problems, as contrasted with recalling previously acquired knowledge or using already well-learned skills.

Spearman thought of *g* metaphorically as "mental energy" that could be applied to any and every kind of mental task, and likened group factors and specificity to specialized "engines" for the performance of certain types of tasks. Individual differences in potential performance on any mental task, according to Spearman, result from two sources: differences in the amount of mental "energy" that can be delivered to the specific "engine" that mediates performance of the task, and differences in the efficiency of energy utilization by the "engine." The efficiency of the various "engines" differs independently within the same person.

Although Spearman remained agnostic concerning the biochemical and physiological basis of this energy, it was his fervent hope that scientists would eventually discover a physical basis for *g*.

As was indicated in the previous chapter, the belief that mental ability is a general, unitary trait was introduced into psychology by Spencer and Galton. But their work was largely speculative with little, if any, empirical support. The idea of general ability had in fact existed in literature since ancient times. Samuel Johnson (1709–1784) expressed it tersely when he heard a noted historian proclaim that it was by virtue of their very different gifts that Caesar became a great commander, Shakespeare a great poet, and Newton a great scientist. Dr. Johnson replied, "No, it is only that one man has more mind than another; he may direct it differently, or prefer this study to that. Sir, the man who has vigor may walk to the North as well as to the South, to the East as well as to the West."[2]

The far more common academic belief, however, was that the mind is a multiplicity of separate and distinct functions, called *faculties*. This was the prevailing view in psychology at the end of the nineteenth century. *Faculty psychology*, as it was called, postulated the existence of a distinct faculty for each and every mental activity a psychologist could think of: perception, conception, judgment, reason, recollection, memory, imagination, intuition, wisdom, discernment, discrimination, aesthetic sensitivity—to name a few. Thinking they could identify an individual's strong and weak faculties, phrenologists examined people's skulls for bumps, depressions, and other irregularities that would indicate the relative development of parts of the brain that supposedly controlled these various, distinct mental faculties.

Did each name in the entire lexicon of human faculties really represent a different mental process? Or did the faculty psychologists simply take verbs and adjectives that describe various mental activities, convert them into nouns, and then reify them as distinct faculties? Was there a theoretical limit to the possible number of faculties beyond simply the total number of words in the unabridged dictionary that refer to mental activity? Such questions (not unlike the debates in medieval scholasticism over how many angels could dance on the head of a pin) were acknowledged and debated. But no one developed a means to answer them in a scientific manner (that is, objectively, empirically, and experimentally).

Such was the general state of affairs in psychology at the turn of the century. Galton had already provided the two necessary tools—*mental tests* and *correlation*—to answer the problems raised by faculty psychology. But Galton never used them expressly for that purpose. His rejection of faculty psychology in explaining individual differences and his belief in a general mental ability were, like Dr. Johnson's, based mainly on general impressions rather than explicit analysis of empirical data.

The actual employment of Galton's tools to tackle the questions about individual differences in mental ability remained for another Britisher, Charles Edward Spearman (1863–1945). He became Britain's most distinguished psychologist and one of the "greats" in the history of psychology. He invented an even more powerful quantitative method, *factor analysis*, and used it to discover a psychological phenomenon, *g*. For this reason, Spearman is more frequently cited in the present-day literature of empirical psychology than any other psychologist of his period.

It is often hard to pin down the exact origin of an important discovery, because usually most of the prerequisite concepts were already known but were not fully and systematically articulated. In Spearman's case, it is hard to tell from the literature exactly which came first, his invention of factor analysis or his discovery of *g*. Part and parcel of one another, they probably occurred simultaneously. I am reminded of a revealing passage in science writer Horace Judson's interview with the Nobel laureate Francis Crick (codiscoverer of the molecular structure of DNA):

> Discovery, examined closely, I said to Crick, seemed curiously difficult to pin to a moment or to an insight or even to a single person. "No, I don't think that's curious," Crick said. "I think that's the nature of discoveries, many times that the reason they're difficult to make is that you've got to take a series of steps, three or four steps, which if you don't make them you won't get there, and if you go wrong in any one of them you won't get there. It isn't a matter of one jump— that would be easy. You've got to make several successive jumps. And usually the pennies drop one after another until eventually it all *clicks*. Otherwise it would be too easy![3]

Spearman's discovery of *g* is probably another instance of the creative act as described by Crick. The discovery and the method needed to establish its validity came about by a series of successive steps.

The definition of *g* will be postponed momentarily, because a proper definition is impossible outside of the context in which Spearman formulated it. A purely verbal definition of *g*, such as "general intelligence," does not adequately convey the precision of Spearman's concept. He was extremely concerned with this, and with good reason, as *g*, like many other scientific constructs, cannot be expressed in common parlance. Therefore, it is essential for understanding the meaning of *g* as a scientific concept to have a clear idea of the methodology by which Spearman arrived at it. But first, a brief sketch of Spearman's life.[4]

In college, Spearman had a liking for mathematics, but after considering the prospects of earning a living as a mathematician, he decided to major in engineering. His greatest interest, however, was philosophy, which he read widely and assiduously.

While a graduate engineer, he became especially attracted, strangely enough, to the philosophies of India, and wanted to go there to study. He enlisted in the British army's Royal Corps of Engineers, hoping to be sent to one of its stations in India. He assumed that life as a military engineer would allow him substantial time to study philosophy.

Instead of being sent to India, however, he was stationed in Burma. His engineering activities there won him a medal for distinguished service, and he was soon advanced to the rank of major. Meanwhile, his initial interest in philosophy led him to psychology. He was enthralled by the opportunity this new field seemed to present for development as a natural science. He had come to believe that philosophy should adopt the methods of the natural sciences, and he considered the subject matter of psychology, such as it was at the end of the nineteenth century, to be the proper vehicle for achieving this aim.

Finally deciding at age thirty-four to make psychology his career, he resigned his commission in the army and headed for what was then the leading center for research in experimental psychology, Wilhelm Wundt's laboratory in the University of Leipzig. In Spearman's brief autobiography,[5] he regretted the years he wasted as an army officer before discovering his true vocation in psychology. His several years' sojourn in the army, he later remarked, resulted from the youthful illusion that life is long. Seven years passed before he completed his doctoral study under Wundt, because in the midst of it, alas, he was recalled to military duty during the Boer War.

While still a graduate student, however, he showed his unusual analytic ability by writing what is perhaps the single most important paper in the history of differential psychology and psychometrics: " 'General Intelligence' Objectively Determined and Measured.'' Published in 1904 in the *American Journal of Psychology*, it introduced Spearman's famous *two-factor theory*. This strikingly non-Wundtian paper was not Spearman's Ph.D. dissertation, which dealt with optical illusions in spatial perception, a subject strictly in line with Wundt's interest at that time.

Finally, with a Ph.D. in hand, Spearman returned to England to take the estimable position of Reader in Psychology at the University of London. Only four years later, he was promoted to a distinguished chair—Grote Professor of Mind and Logic—and for twenty-two years thereafter he headed the Psychology Department at the University of London. During his distinguished career, he received many honors in England and abroad, including election as a fellow of the Royal Society and (in the United States) the National Academy of Sciences. At age eighty-two, suffering from poor health and the frailties of old age, Spearman ended his life by jumping out of an upper-story window of the London University Hospital.

CORRECTION FOR ATTENUATION

While studying under Wundt, Spearman also read Galton and later claimed that these pioneers of scientific psychology were the two greatest influences in his life. He found Galton's writings especially stimulating. Spearman was most intrigued by Galton's idea that individual differences in simple mental processes, such as discrimination, are the basis of individual differences in the more complex function intelligence. He was aware of Galton's apparent failure to find much relationship between performance on simple tasks and the ordinary criteria of intelligence. He also knew of the failure to find such correlations in subsequent studies inspired by Galton. The idea of general ability was further shaken by the observation that the simple Galtonian tasks of discrimination, reaction time, and the like showed small correlation even among themselves, to say nothing of their near-zero correlations with "real-life" indicators of intelligence. Yet there were a few studies that did show more impressive correlations. Spearman puzzled over this inconsistency. The theoretical issue at stake seemed too important to him to dismiss Galton's hypothesis without further empirical investigation of his own.

Spearman noted that the Galtonian measures had poor *reliability*; that is, the same subject obtained different scores when the test was repeated. Besides measuring what they were intended to measure and appeared to measure, therefore, the Galtonian tests also contained a lot of *measurement error*. Spearman drew the analogy of firing a gun repeatedly while aiming at a mark on a target. The bullets scatter randomly around the mark, more of them hitting nearer the mark than farther away from it, and the more shots that are fired, the greater is the number of bullets that hit the mark. The scatter of bullets around the mark is analogous to measurement error. It is a part of every kind of measurement, to a greater or lesser degree, depending on the nature of the measuring instrument, the thing being measured, and how hard the experimenter works to reduce measurement error.

Neither Galton nor anyone else working on the measurement of mental abilities had taken into account the reliability of their measurements. Measurement error necessarily diminishes (the technical term is *attenuates*) the correlation coefficient. The larger the error (that is, the lower the *reliability*) in either one or both of the correlated variables, the lower will be the possible obtained correlation between them, because the measurement errors are by definition random and therefore uncorrelated. Even two variables that theoretically are perfectly correlated, such as the diameter and the circumference of circles, will not show a perfect correlation (i.e., $r = +1.00$) unless both variables are measured with perfect accuracy. Yet *perfect* accuracy of measurement is a pure abstraction never attained by any actual measurement. Actual measurements of any kind always have some "margin of error."

Spearman's formalization of this idea with respect to test scores is the basic postulate of what is now called *classic test theory*. It states that *any* and *every* actual (also termed *obtained*) score (or measurement), call it X, is composed of two elements—a *true score, t*, and a *random error* of measurement, *e*. (Neither *t* nor *e* can be directly observed.) Thus $X = t + e$. Because *e* can have either a positive or a negative sign and because it is random, its value tends toward zero as we average more and more of the measurements of X. Theoretically, the average of an infinite number of Xs contains zero error; it will consist purely of *t*. The way, then, to reduce measurement error is to average a number of repeated measurements of the thing being measured, and to include in the average as many repeated measurements as necessary to achieve the desired degree of accuracy, or, as it is termed, *reliability*, of the composite measure. The *t* (which is systematic) is repeatedly averaged in, while the *e* (which is random) is increasingly averaged out.

This postulate has an important corollary concerning the *variance* (σ_x^2) of a number of different values of X. The variance consists of the true score variance (σ_t^2) plus the error variance (σ_e^2), or $\sigma_x^2 = \sigma_t^2 + \sigma_e^2$. Only σ_t^2 represents the reliable component of individual differences in the measurements of X. This leads to the definition of the *reliability coefficient* (r_{xx}) as $r_{xx} = \sigma_t^2/\sigma_x^2$. Although the theoretical σ_t^2 cannot be determined directly, we can determine r_{xx} simply by obtaining two separate measures of the same variable, X, for every subject and then calculate the correlation between the two sets of measurements. This is r_{xx}, the reliability of the measurements of X.[6] As r_{xx} is the proportion of true score variance in test scores, $1 - r_{xx}$ yields the proportion of error variance.

These considerations led Spearman to invent a method to rid a correlation coefficient of the weakening effect of measurement error. It is known as the *correction for attenuation*. If the correlation between the obtained measures of the variables X and Y is r_{xy}, the correlation $(r_{x'y'})$ between the error-free true scores (termed X' and Y') is the raw correlation between X and Y divided by the geometric mean of the reliability coefficients of X and Y, that is, $r_{x'y'} = r_{xy}/(r_{xx}r_{yy})^{1/2}$. The correlation $r_{x'y'}$ thus is said to be *corrected for attenuation*, or *disattenuated*.

Realizing that the true correlations in earlier studies of Galton's hypothesis of the generality of mental ability had been seriously underestimated because of the low reliability of most of the measurements, Spearman applied his correction for attenuation to the correlations obtained in the earlier studies. Galton's measurements of reaction time, for example, had a reliability of only .18! The theoretically highest correlation that any variable can have with any other variable is the geometric mean of their reliability coefficients (i.e., the square root of the product of the two reliabilities). Obviously, it would be impossible to find substantial correlations between such unreliable measures. For example, Galton's measure of reaction time (RT), with a reliability of only .18 could not possibly correlate higher than $\sqrt{.18} = .42$ with any other variable, and if the true correlation between simple RT and g was, say, .15, the obtained correlation (if the reliability of RT was .18) would be only $.15 \times \sqrt{.18} \approx .06$. Measurements can be made more reliable, however, by aggregating repeated measurements.

Table 2.1
Spearman's Correlation Matrix[a] and *g* Loadings

Variable	C	F	E	Ma	P	Mu	*g*
Classics		.83	.78	.70	.66	.63	*.958*
French	.83		.67	.67	.65	.57	*.882*
English	.78	.67		.64	.54	.51	*.803*
Math	.70	.67	.64		.45	.51	*.750*
Pitch	.66	.65	.54	.45		.40	*.673*
Music	.63	.57	.51	.51	.40		*.646*
Mean *r*	*.720*	*.678*	*.628*	*.594*	*.540*	*.524*	

[a]Only the correlations given here appear in Spearman's original matrix; the *g* loadings and the mean *r*s (both in italics) have been included here only for didactic purposes.

Spearman obtained such aggregated data in a small and seemingly unimpressive experiment based on twenty-two high school boys. These data admittedly are not compelling from the standpoint of any substantive conclusions that can be drawn from them. It is only the novel procedure that Spearman applied to these meager data and the important insights he gained as a result that proved to be of such far-reaching methodological and theoretical consequence. It is also worth looking at his employment of a prototype of factor analysis, not only for its historical interest, but as a way of explaining the basic concepts underlying this complex mathematical procedure.

THE FIRST FACTOR ANALYSIS

Spearman obtained students' ranks based on their teachers' ratings in five school subjects (Classics, French, English, Math, and Music). Most important, as suggested by Galton's hypothesis, Spearman measured the pupils' ability in pitch discrimination, the crucial variable in his little study. The raw correlations between these six variables were reported by Spearman as shown in the correlation matrix in Table 2.1.[7]

A *matrix* is just an array of numbers arranged in columns and rows. A *correlation matrix* is such an array that shows the correlation of each variable with every other variable. In Table 2.1, for example, the correlation between rank in Classics and rank in French is .83. The correlation coefficient is a continuous variable, ranging from a perfect negative correlation ($r = -1.00$) to zero correlation ($r = 0$) to a perfect positive correlation ($r = +1.00$). (When no sign is shown, a positive correlation coefficient is understood. Negative signs are always shown.) When all correlations in the matrix are positive, it is called a *positive manifold*.[8]

Spearman was especially intrigued to find that pitch discrimination, although seemingly very different from the scholastic variables, was nevertheless correlated with each of the other variables, and was even more highly correlated with rank in classics, French, and English than with rank in music. Galton's belief that fineness of sensory discrimination is related to intelligence was perhaps correct after all!

Now let's go step-by-step through Spearman's analysis of the correlations in Table 2.1:

First, it should be noted that the six variables (Classics, French, etc.) in Table 2.1 can be listed in any arbitrary order. (The correlations themselves would, of course, remain unchanged.) But Spearman's insight led him to arrange the variables exactly as shown in Table 2.1. He did this to see if the matrix would show what he termed a *hierarchical* order. He reasoned that if only one common factor (i.e., a source of variance) were responsible for all of the correlations among a number of measurements, the matrix of correlations would show a hierarchical order. That is, the correlation coefficients would decrease in size the farther away (in any direction) they are from the upper left corner of the matrix. The easiest way to determine if the correlations form a hierarchy is to put the variables in the order of their average correlation with each of the other variables. (See the row labeled *Mean r* in Table 2.1). With the variables so ordered, one can see that the matrix of correlations here is extremely hierarchical. The slight deviations from a perfect hierarchy are probably due to random error.[9]

Second, it is a mathematical necessity that if there is only one factor that is common to all of the variables and no two (or more) variables have any other factor(s) in common, then any two columns of correlations will have a constant proportionality. This is a more stringent criterion of a single-factor matrix than merely a hierarchical order of the correlations. For example, examine the corresponding entries in columns C and F: $.78/.67 = 1.16$, $.70/.67 = 1.04$, $.66/.65 = 1.02$, $.63/.57 = 1.11$. Or the corresponding entries in columns E and P: $.78/.66 = 1.18$, $.67/.65 = 1.03$, $.64/.45 = 1.42$, $.51/.40 = 1.27$. Although all of the proportions are slightly greater than 1.00 and they obviously vary, we cannot be certain that the correlations in this matrix can be adequately explained in terms of only one factor.

Third, Spearman proposed a closely related means to test whether a matrix has only one factor (or, in the terminology of matrix algebra, it has *unit rank*; i.e., rank = 1). This is the most rigorous criterion of a single factor matrix and has the advantage that it can be subjected to a test of statistical significance. This tells whether the obtained correlations depart from theoretical expectation more than chance, or random error, would allow. Spearman called it the method of *vanishing tetrad differences.* A *tetrad* consists of any set of four correlations (arranged just as they are located in a hierarchically ordered matrix) between which two equal-length crossing diagonals can be drawn. For example, here are just four of the tetrads to be found in Table 2.1. (See if you can find them in the matrix):

(a)	(b)	(c)	(d)
.78 .67	.67 .64	.83 .66	.79 .63
.70 .67	.57 .51	.57 .40	.45 .40

The number of possible *distinct* tetrads in a matrix rapidly increases as the number of variables increases.[10] The total number of distinct tetrads that can be obtained from Table 2.1, with only six variables, is forty-five. Spearman's *tetrad equation* is illustrated by putting each of the four tetrads above into the following form:

a) $(.78 \times .67) - (.70 \times .67) = .054$

b) $(.67 \times .51) - (.57 \times .64) = -.024$

c) $(.83 \times .40) - (.57 \times .66) = -.044$

d) $(.70 \times .40) - (.45 \times .63) = -.003$

Each of the above equations is a *tetrad difference*. In a matrix that contains only one factor, all of the tetrad differences in the matrix should approach zero, hence Spearman's "vanishing tetrad differences" proof that only one factor exists in the correlation matrix. The tetrad differences shown above all depart slightly from zero; they average $-.017$. But these departures from zero are so small they could be just chance variation. Spearman would obtain all of the possible tetrad differences in the matrix and plot their distribution. If there was only one factor in the matrix, the average of all the tetrad differences would be very close to zero. One of Spearman's doctoral students, Karl J. Holzinger, helped him figure out the formula for the probable error of a tetrad difference. This statistic makes it possible to determine if departures from zero are greater than would be expected by chance for a correlation matrix based on any given sample size. If the tetrad differences are no greater than would be expected by chance, it proves mathematically that the correlations reflect only one factor. Another way of saying this is that all of the variables share only one common source of variance. The fact that the correlations between variables differ from one another implies that the variables have this common factor to varying degrees. In technical jargon, the variables have different *loadings* on the common factor. (The term *factor saturation*, which has gone out of fashion, has exactly the same meaning as *factor loading*.)

Because the matrix in Table 2.1 meets the vanishing tetrad proof (within the limits of probable error for the small sample of only twenty-two subjects), we can justifiably say that it can be explained in terms of only one common factor.

Spearman then faced two big questions: What *is* this common factor? And how loaded with this factor is each of the six variables shown in Table 2.1? The first question is a real stopper, and any attempt to give an answer that goes much beyond mere verbalization must be postponed. The second question is much easier to answer, and Spearman invented a method for doing so. It can be best illustrated if we begin with the simplest possible example, the correlation between only two variables. The variance (σ^2) of any set of measurements of any variable, when the measurements are expressed in standardized form,[11] is always unity (or 1). We can represent the variance of a variable graphically as the area of a rectangle, and the correlation between two variables as the over-lapping (or intersection) of the areas of two squares. The proportion of the area in each square that overlaps the other square represents the correlation between the variables and is equal to the correlation coefficient.[12] Consider the following diagram, which depicts a correlation of .25 (that is, $r_{XY} = .25$). The shaded area (C) represents the variance that variables X and Y have in common.

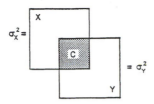

It is a kind of simplest possible common factor. The _factor loading_ of each variable on the common factor is the correlation between one variable, say X, and the factor it has in common with Y (i.e., the shaded area C). This correlation is equal to the square root of the shaded area ($\sqrt{r_{XY}}$). In this example it is $\sqrt{.25}$ = .50. When there is only one common factor, multiplying one test's factor loading by another test's factor loading yields the observed correlation between the two tests.

Now, say we want to determine the correlation that each of three correlated variables, X, Y, and Z, has with the one factor they all have in common, which we can call C. Technically, we want to determine each variable's loading on the common factor. The factor loading of variable X, for example, is r_{XC}, or the correlation of X with C (the factor that is common to variables X, Y, and Z). Spearman's formula for calculating the factor loadings of each variable:

$$r_{XC} = [(r_{XY} \cdot r_{XZ})/r_{YZ}]^{1/2}, \; r_{YC} = [(r_{XY} \cdot r_{YZ})/r_{XZ}]^{1/2}, \; r_{ZC} = [(r_{XZ} \cdot r_{YZ})/r_{XY}]^{1/2}.$$

For example, say our three variables have the following correlations: r_{XY} = .63, r_{XZ} = .45, and r_{YZ} = .35. Inserting these correlations into the formula gives r_{XC} = .9, r_{YC} = .7, and r_{ZC} = .5. These are called the factor loadings of variables X, Y, and Z. To reproduce the original correlations between any two variables, simply multiply their common factor loadings; for example, $r_{XY} = r_{XC} \cdot r_{YC}$ = .9 × .7 = .63; r_{XZ} = .9 × .5 = .45; and r_{YZ} = .7 × .5 = .35. The fact that all of the correlations can be perfectly reproduced from the variables' loadings on this one factor is taken as proof that the all of the variables have only this one factor in common and that we have correctly determined each variable's factor loading (that is, the correlation of each variable with the common factor).

The formula does not work on every set of correlations, however. For example, apply it to the following correlations: $r_{xy} = .90$, $r_{xz} = .80$, and $r_{yz} = .50$. The loadings of each variable on the common factor, according to the formula, are: $r_{xc} = 1.20$, $r_{yc} = .75$, and $r_{zc} = .67$. But $r_{xc} = 1.20$ is impossible, because no correlation coefficients can be larger than 1.00. This implies that there is more than one common factor in this set of three variables. Since X and Y are very highly correlated, they have another factor in common in addition to the factor that they share with Z.

All three variables must have one factor in common, or they would not all be positively correlated with each other. But X and Y are also loaded on a second factor that is not common to Z. A factor shared by three or more but not all variables in a matrix is called a _group factor_. It was not until some years after Spearman invented factor analysis that he acknowledged the existence of group factors. Earlier he had argued, using our example above, that X and Y overlap so much that they represent the same variable. Therefore, only one of them, or a combined measure of both, should be entered into a correlation matrix subjected to factor analysis. This would preserve the hierarchical structure of the matrix, which then would yield only one common factor.

It is evident that Spearman's method would work properly only if the variables are all sufficiently different from each other to rule out the emergence of group factors. His method for determining the variables' factor loadings, in fact, is capable of extracting only a single common factor from a correlation matrix; if the matrix contains more than one common factor, the method cannot correctly determine the loadings of the additional factors.[13] But Spearman's most remarkable empirical discovery was that quite different kinds of tests, so long as they all measured some kind of mental ability, all shared at least one common factor.

Spearman generalized the above formula for extracting the variables' loadings on the one common factor so that it could be applied to a correlation matrix having any number of variables.[14] With a large number of variables, however, the formula becomes quite complex and the sheer labor of calculating the factor loadings is enormous. As Spearman did all his calculations either by hand or with a mechanical calculating machine, it is little wonder that he occasionally made slight, but essentially trivial, errors in some of his calculations.[15]

When the correlation matrix is made up entirely of variables that represent a variety of what would be characterized as "mental abilities," Spearman referred to the one factor that all of the variables have in common as the _general factor_, which he designated by the symbol _g_ (always printed as a lower-case italic, as shown here).[16]

Returning to Table 2.1, the rightmost column shows the _g_ loadings of the six variables in this matrix. Note that they are in the same rank order of magnitude as the average correlation of each variable with all the others (_Mean r_ in bottom

Table 2.2
Correlations Reconstituted from the *g* Loadings

	C	F	E	Ma	P	Mu	*g*
Classics		.85	.77	.72	.65	.62	*.958*
French	.85		.71	.66	.59	.57	*.882*
English	.77	.71		.60	.54	.52	*.803*
Math	.72	.66	.60		.51	.49	*.750*
Pitch	.65	.59	.54	.51		.43	*.673*
Music	.62	.57	.52	.48	.43		*.646*
Mean *r*	*.719*	*.676*	*.628*	*.594*	*.544*	*.526*	

row). This tells us that the average of a variables' correlations with the other variables is a rough indicator of the relative size (but not the absolute size) of the *g* loading for that variable. (In this example, the correlation between the *Mean r* values and the *g* values is .999.) Spearman was particularly concerned to find that the *g* loading of pitch discrimination was as high as .673, and would be even higher if corrected for attenuation. This suggested to him that the *g* factor reflected something more basic than scholastic attainments, and that Galton was essentially on the right track in his belief that simple tasks involving discrimination or quickness of mental reaction reflect a general aspect of mental ability that enters into scholastic performance or other mentally demanding activities.

A test of how well the single *g* factor accounts for all of the correlations in Table 2.1 is to reconstitute the correlations by multiplying the *g* loading of each variable with that of every other variable. Take Classics and French, for example: the reconstituted correlation is .958 × .882 = .85. The obtained correlation is .83. All of the reconstituted correlations obtained in this manner are shown in Table 2.2. They closely resemble the obtained correlations in Table 2.1. The *g* loadings are identical, of course, because they are the values used to generate the correlations in Table 2.2. We can check this by subtracting the reconstituted correlations (Table 2.2) from the obtained correlations (Table 2.1). This yields what is termed the *residual matrix*, that is, whatever is left after all of the variance attributable to the *g* factor has been removed. The residual matrix is shown in Table 2.3. We see that no significant correlations remain. The average of the residual correlations is a mere −.001. The minuscule scraps of correlations that remain in the residual matrix reflect nothing but random error variance. No additional factor(s) can possibly be extracted.

If, however, the residual matrix had contained a few substantial correlations, we would know that the original matrix contains one or more common factors in addition to *g*. Termed *group factors*, they are loaded only in some subset of

Table 2.3
Residual Correlation Matrix after *g* Is Removed

Variable	C	F	E	Ma	P	Mu
Classics		-.01	.01	-.02	.01	.01
French	-.01		-.04	.01	.06	.00
English	.01	-.04		.04	.00	-.01
Math	-.02	.01	.04		-.05	.03
Pitch	.01	.06	.00	-.05		-.03
Music	.01	.00	-.01	.03	-.03	
Mean *r*	*.001*	*.002*	*.000*	*.000*	*-.004*	*-.002*

variables. For example, if Spearman had included three tests of pitch discrimination (say, using different musical instruments, or pitches in different ranges of the scale), then surely pitch discrimination would emerge as a group factor. Each test of pitch discrimination would be loaded on *g*, as before, but would also be loaded on a group factor, let's call it "pitch discrimination." In his early factor analytic studies, however, Spearman never allowed this to happen. He took pains to ensure that no two (or more) variables in the matrix were so alike as to violate the rule of vanishing tetrad differences and thereby risk the emergence of more than one common factor in the matrix.

SPEARMAN'S TWO-FACTOR THEORY

The *g* factor of the correlation matrix in Table 2.1 accounts for 62.9 percent of the total variance in the six variables. This is calculated simply by adding up the squared values of each variable's *g* loading, obtaining their average, and multiplying by 100.[17] But if *g*, in this case, accounts for 62.9 percent of the total variance, what accounts for the remaining 37.1 percent? Because *g* is the only common factor in this matrix, the remaining 37.1 percent of the total variance must be attributed to sources that are *unique* to each of the variables, and indeed the technical term for this unique source of variance in each variable is the variable's *uniqueness*, symbolized as *u*. Its variance is u^2. The unique variance is composed of two parts: error variance (e^2, due to random errors of measurement) and variance due to a true-score component that is *specific* to each variable in the matrix. The latter is technically termed the variable's *specificity*, symbolized as *s*. Its variance is s^2. The *s* is not a common factor, but a *specific factor*, and there are as many specific factors as there are variables. Since the standardized variable's total variance is one, and the variable's error variance, e^2, is equal to one minus the variable's reliability, or $1 - r_{xx}$, the variable's *specific variance*, s^2, is equal to $1 - g^2 - e^2$. The square root of this value, then, yields the variable's *specificity*, or *s*.

Spearman's famous *two-factor theory* states that individual differences in the true-scores (i.e., error-free scores) on any measurement of any mental ability are attributable to only two factors: a general factor, *g*, that is common to all mental ability measurements, and some factor, *s*, that is specific to each and every measurement.[18] Also, *g* and *s* are uncorrelated ($r_{gs} = 0$), and the various *s*'s are uncorrelated with each other.

Spearman's two-factor formulation has an important corollary: Because every mental test, no matter how distinctive, contains some *g* and each mental test contains a different *s*, and because *g* and *s* (and also *e*) are uncorrelated with each other, then a composite score based on a number of distinct tests will have relatively more *g* and less *s* than any of the individual scores that went into the composite. The more we increase the number of distinct tests in the composite, the more the *g* components cumulate in the composite score and the more the uncorrelated *s* components cancel each other (their average tending toward zero). Theoretically, then, the composite score from an infinite number of diverse mental tests would be a perfect measure of *g*.

THE DEMISE OF THE TWO-FACTOR THEORY

After the publication of Spearman's important 1904 paper and the invention of Binet's test in 1905, other psychologists began constructing and trying out a variety of mental tests. More adequate psychometric instruments for testing the two-factor theory appeared than were initially available to Spearman. The leader in this effort was the British psychologist Sir Cyril Burt (1883–1971). In 1931 Burt succeeded Spearman as head of the Psychology Department at the University of London.

As early as 1909, Burt's mental test data led him to doubt that the two-factor theory was adequate to explain fully the correlations among tests. It appeared there were common factors besides *g*. Between the extremes of complete generality and complete specificity there were factors (later termed *group factors*) that some, but not all, of the tests shared in common. Spearman maintained that his "vanishing tetrad differences" criterion of a single common factor, or *g*, was broken only by making the mistake of putting two or more tests into the matrix that were really more or less equivalent measures of one and the same ability. But Burt argued that there were sufficient differences among the subsets of tests that form group factors (in addition to *g*) to warrant their being regarded as more than just equivalent forms of the same test.[19] For example, in a correlation matrix of the following tests—adding mixed fractions, multiplying decimal numbers, long division, vocabulary, verbal analogies, and English grammar—Burt noted that even though all of the tests were substantially correlated with each other and therefore all were *g*-loaded to varying degrees, the correlations among the three arithmetic tests were larger than their correlations with any of the verbal tests; and the correlations among the three verbal tests were larger than their correlations with the arithmetic tests. Therefore, it appeared that each of the two clusters of tests—arithmetic and verbal—represents its own factor in addition to the *g* factor common to all six tests.

By 1911, Burt had collected data on so many different tests and showed that this kind of correlational clustering of certain groups of tests was the rule rather than the exception that Spearman's two-factor theory had to be abandoned. Other psychologists agreed with Burt's position that it was more reasonable to accept the existence of *group factors*, along with *g* and *s*. Spearman himself finally admitted the existence of group factors, but he did so reluctantly, because their presence not only destroyed the pleasing simplicity of his two-factor theory, but also greatly complicated the methodology of factor analysis. He regarded the admission of multiple factors as opening a Pandora's box, and in his great work *The Abilities of Man* (1927), he wrote a technically correct but surprisingly grudging chapter titled "Special Abilities and Group Factors":

> We have now arrived at the "group factors" which have played such a baffling part in controversial writings. They make their appearance here, there, everywhere, nowhere; the very Puck of psychology. On all sides contentiously advocated, hardly one of them has received so much as a description, far less any serious investigation. And yet they are of immense importance, not only theoretically, but also practically. . . . For a test only measures any ability other than *g* by having correlation with it other than that due to *g*. Such super-added correlation will, of course, be caused by any overlap of the specific factors; or in other words, by any "group factor." (pp. 222–223)

One could argue, of course, that Spearman's phrase "overlap of specific factors" is a contradiction in terms, because *specificity* is defined as that part of a test's variance that is not shared by any other test included in the factor analysis. But history finally tells the tale, which is that Spearman's simple two-factor theory was short-lived and was soon supplanted by a *multiple factor* theory of abilities. However, the theory of *g* as the common factor reflected by all mental tests remained fully intact.

SPEARMAN'S THEOREM OF THE "INDIFFERENCE OF THE INDICATOR"

This "theorem" has both theoretical and practical importance and remains very much alive in modern psychometrics.[20] Spearman complained that Binet's test was composed of a hodgepodge of various tasks, selected without any real theoretical rationale and justified simply by the fact that the test "worked." That is, the composite score based on all these varied tasks correlated quite well with children's future level of scholastic achievement and with teachers' subjective judgments of children's brightness or dullness, even though the diverse tasks were not specifically scholastic. Binet expressly avoided including items of the kind children were likely to have learned in school. To this day, he and many of his followers explain that the test works because the test items represent a fair sample of the particular skills and the bits of knowledge most children normally have had the opportunity to acquire by a given age. The composite score on the test thus reflects a simple average of the subject's performances on all of these diverse items that call on many separate cognitive skills and bits of knowledge. This averaging of the scores on many disparate items could be called a measure of "intelligence in general." This interpretation of a composite score based on many diverse items, it was argued, is preferable to interpreting the score as a measure of "general intelligence," with its implication that the test measures something broader and more general than just the arbitrary hodgepodge sample of particular skills and items of knowledge that compose the test. Spearman strongly disagreed with this idea of "intelligence in general." He dubbed it the "anarchic" theory of mental abilities. In his words:

> As for the prevalent procedure of throwing a miscellaneous collection of tests indiscriminately into a single pool this—whether or not justifiable by the theory which gave birth to it—certainly cannot be justified simply by claiming that the results give a "general level," an "average," or even a "sample." No genuine averaging, or sampling, of anybody's abilities is made, can be made, or even has really been attempted. When Binet borrowed the idea of such promiscuous pooling, he carried it into execution with a brilliancy that perhaps no other living man could have matched. But on the theoretical side, he tried to get away too cheaply. And this is the main cause of all the present trouble. (1927, pp. 70–71)

Spearman argued that a collection of items as found in Binet's test "works" only because *g* enters into any and every mental task. Therefore, according to Spearman's theory, each one of the items in Binet's hodgepodge measures both *g* and *s*. And thus the composite score contains the accumulated *g* and the averaged-out *s*'s. In Spearman's words:

> This means that, for the purpose of indicating the amount of *g* possessed by a person, any test will do just as well as any other, provided only that its correlation with *g* is equally high. With this proviso, the most ridiculous "stunts" will measure the self-same *g* as will the highest exploits of logic or flights of imagination. . . . And here, it should be noticed, we come at last upon the secret of why all the current tests of "general intelligence" show high correlations with one another, as also with *g* itself. The reason lies, not in the theories inspiring these tests (which theories have been most confused), nor in any uniformity of construction (for this has often been wildly heterogeneous), but wholly and solely in the above shown "indifference of the indicator." Indeed, were it worth while, tests could be constructed which had the most grotesque appearance, and yet after all would correlate quite well with all the others. (1927, pp. 197–198)

Spearman was quite right in this. If the many heterogeneous tasks that compose a test like Binet's were not all correlated with each other, the variance (or individual differences) of the total scores would be reduced to only 5 to 10 percent of what it actually is.[21] On the Stanford-Binet IQ test, for example, persons picked at random from the population differ from one another by eighteen IQ points, on average. If all of the many diverse items composing the whole test were not correlated with each other, the average difference between persons would be only about five IQ points. In other words, by far most of the difference in IQ between persons is not traceable to the specific skills or knowledge called for by the various items, but is due to the fact that all the items are correlated with each other.

Each item in a test contributes to the true-score only to the extent that the item is correlated with other items in the test. The item intercorrelations are the essential basis of common factors. Remove the correlations and you remove all of the test's true-score variance and all of the common factors. It is axiomatic in measurement theory that the true-score of any mental ability test composed of heterogeneous items consists only of common factors (typically _g_ and certain group factors in the mental abilities domain). Item _specificity_ is lumped together with random measurement error as the test's unreliability. Unreliability is the complement of the test's internal consistency reliability. Internal consistency, in turn, is directly related to the average correlation among the test items.[22] In the best modern tests, the true-score variance is about 90 to 95 percent of the total variance. The remaining 5 to 10 percent is error (random error plus item specificity).

SPEARMAN'S NOEGENETIC LAWS

Although Spearman had proved the statistical existence of _g_, he admitted that he did not know what _g_ is. What, one can ask, is _g_ beyond the mathematical operations of factor analysis that reveal its presence in a collection of mental tests? Spearman described this problem as follows:

> But notice must be taken that this general factor _g_, like all measurements anywhere, is primarily not any concrete thing but only a value or magnitude. Further, that which this magnitude measures has not been defined by declaring what it is like, but only by pointing out where it can be found. It consists in just that constituent—whatever it may be—which is common to all the abilities interconnected by the tetrad equation. This way of indicating what _g_ means is just as definite as when one indicates a card by staking on the back of it without looking at its face. ... Such a defining of _g_ by site rather than by nature is just what is meant originally when its determination was said to be only "objective." Eventually, we may or may not find reason to conclude that _g_ measures something that can appropriately by called "intelligence." Such a conclusion, however, would still never be the definition of _g_, but only a "statement about" it. (1927, pp. 75–76)

Spearman tried to describe the essential characteristics of the tests in which _g_ is most highly loaded by comparing strongly _g_-loaded tests with weakly _g_-loaded tests based on factor analyses of some 100 or so distinct tests given to school children.[23] Here are some of his examples of tests found to have high or low _g_ loadings (in parentheses):

High *g* Loading	Low *g* Loading
Matrix relations (.94)	Maze speed (.04)
Generalizations (.89)	Crossing out numbers (.12)
Series completion (.87)	Counting groups of dots (.14)
Verbal analogies (.83)	Simple addition (.23)
Likeness relations (.77)	Tapping speed (.24)
Problem arithmetic (.77)	Dotting speed (.27)
Paragraph comprehension (.73)	Paired-associates memory (.27)
Perceptual analogies (.70)	Recognition memory (.31)

It would be more informative, of course, if we knew more than just the names of these tests and could examine their various contents and task demands, as Spearman did in comparing the ways in which they were either similar or different. From these comparisons, he discerned that the relative magnitude of a test's *g* loadings was a function of the degree to which the test manifests two of his *noegenetic* "laws," in combination with having the quality of "abstractness."

In Spearman's terminology, *noegenesis* means the production of new knowledge, or mental content, from sensory or cognitive experience. Spearman pronounced three "laws" of noegenesis, which he regarded as self-evident and fundamental to cognition.

The *first noegenetic law* is the **apprehension of experience**. It states: "Any lived experience tends to evoke immediately a knowing of its characters and experiencer." The term "immediately" has no temporal connotation in the context of noegenesis; it means only that the knowledge is direct and not mediated by inference. The "apprehension of experience," in other words, is the awareness of oneself directly perceiving the attributes of whatever holds the present focus of attention.

The *second noegenetic law* is the **eduction of relations**. It states: "The mentally presenting of any two or more characters (simple or complex) tends to evoke immediately a knowing of relation between them." The "two or more characters" between which some relationship can be educed Spearman called *fundaments*. A test involving the "eduction of relations" is not deemed appropriate for a given person unless the person is fully capable of perceiving the fundaments between which the relation is to be educed and is already familiar with them; also, whatever response is appropriate for indicating the relation must already exist in the person's repertoire. Example: *Branch-Trunk → Tree*.

The *third noegenetic law* is the **eduction of correlates**. It states: "The presenting of any character together with any relation tends to evoke immediately a knowing of the correlative characters." Example: *High-Opposite → Low*.

Spearman concluded that the tests that best reflect *g* are those that most involve the "eduction of relations and correlates." These are the tests that require inductive and deductive reasoning, grasping relationships, inferring rules, generalizing, seeing the similarity in things that differ (e.g., *reward-punishment*) or the difference between things that are similar (*love-affection*), problem solving, decontextualizing a problem (that is, distinguishing between its general, or essential, features and its specific, or nonessential, features). These all manifest the second and third "laws" of noegenesis—the eduction of relations and of correlates. They are contrasted with tests that call mainly upon speed of execution of simple tasks, performance of repetitious acts, simple cued recall of prior learned responses, execution of a practiced sequence or chain of responses, and direct imitation of another person's specific action without conscious transformation.

It would be a serious mistake, however, to suppose that *g* is a dichotomous variable that some tests reflect and other tests do not. Inspection of a great many factor analyses of the widest variety of mental tests imaginable reveals without exception that tests' *g* loadings are a perfectly continuous variable, ranging from slightly greater than zero to slightly less than unity. The *g* loadings are always positive, provided all of the tests are scored so that higher scores (i.e., larger numerical values) represent better performance (e.g., the number of items gotten correct rather than number of errors; speed of response rather than the time taken for response; the reciprocal of number of trials rather than the number of trials to learn something to a given criterion of mastery). Every kind of mental test and every mentally demanding activity, as required in school and in most occupations, is to some degree loaded with *g*. If one wants to assess a person's level of *g*, it is more efficient, of course, to select highly *g*-loaded tests, provided they are otherwise appropriate for the person in terms of having familiar fundaments. Obviously, a highly *g*-loaded test given in the Tamil language would be wholly inappropriate for a typical American, although it may provide a valid assessment of *g* for a native of Madras, India. A highly *g*-loaded nonverbal test, one based on figural relations for example, could be equally appropriate for both the American and the Madrasi, assuming, of course, that its fundaments are familiar to both.

To incorporate his noegenetic laws in a mental test as ideally as seemed possible, Spearman invented a type of test that was entirely nonverbal, that was composed of fundaments (various geometric shapes) that are universally familiar to virtually all persons beyond three years of age in every culture, and in which every item calls for the eduction of relations and correlates. It also had the quality of "abstractness" in the sense that the fundaments (straight and curved lines, triangles, circles, squares, and the like) do not represent any real or tangible objects, like animals, plants, furniture, or vehicles. He called this type of spatial relations test "matrix relations," because each item consisted of eight panels of fundaments and a blank panel, all arranged in the form of a 3 × 3 matrix, from the examination of which one could figure out the rule that would determine the particular characteristics of the figure that should fit into the blank space in order to complete the logical pattern of the whole matrix. The one correct figure could be chosen from a set of six (or eight) alternatives presented

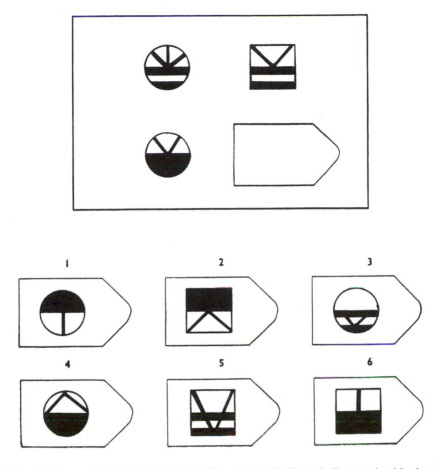

Figure 2.1 A matrix relations item similar to those in Raven's Progressive Matrices test.

below the matrix. (The incorrect alternatives in a multiple-choice test are called *distractors*.)

Spearman's test was further developed by one of his students, John Raven, and the eminent geneticist Lionel Penrose. The test is now known as Raven's Progressive Matrices—"progressive" because, as a person proceeds through the test, the items systematically increase in difficulty, based on the number of fundaments that simultaneously enter into the relations and correlates that must be educed to attain the correct solution. The test comes in three forms according to the level of complexity and difficulty: the Colored Progressive Matrices (for children); the Standard Progressive Matrices (for adolescents and adults); and the Advanced Progressive Matrices, for adults who score well above the average on the Standard form. Figure 2.1 shows a typical item of moderate difficulty.

When the Progressive Matrices test is factor analyzed along with a variety of other tests, it is typically among the two or three tests having the highest *g* loadings, usually around .80. Probably its most distinctive feature is its very low loadings on any factor other than *g*. Raven's Progressive Matrices is often used as a "marker" test for Spearman's *g*. That is, it is entered into a factor analysis with other tests of unknown factor composition, and if the Matrices has a high loading on the general factor of the matrix of unknown tests, its *g* loading serves as a standard by which the *g* loadings of the other tests in the battery can be evaluated. I have yet to see a factor analysis of any diverse collection of tests that includes Raven's Matrices in which the Raven's largest loading was found on any factor other than *g*.

SPEARMAN'S QUANTITATIVE PRINCIPLES OF COGNITION

In addition to the qualitative principles of noegenesis, Spearman introduced five quantitative principles that determine individual differences in any performance that involves noegenesis.

Mental Energy. The first and best known of these quantitative principles is *mental energy*, the hypothetical basis of *g*, which, according to Spearman, "enters into the measurements of ability of all kinds, and which is throughout constant for any individual, although varying greatly for different individuals" (1927, p. 411). Spearman's notion of mental energy as a characteristic in which people differ seems to be purely metaphorical. He suggested no mechanism that would link it to energy as defined in physics and measured in ergs. He also used the terms "power," "force," and "neural energy," as the hypothetical basis of *g*, but without specifying the physiological or metabolic mechanisms that presumably produce this "energy." He forever remained theoretically agnostic and noncommittal about the physical basis of this hypothesized energy, although he suggested such possibilities as the electrochemical potential in neurons, the richness of the branching of capillaries that supply blood to brain cells, and the energy released by catabolism of the brain's nutrients.

In Spearman's day, far too little was known about brain chemistry and physiology to afford a basis for much more than metaphorical explanations, and he was even willing, though reluctant, to settle for postulating a purely psychic form of energy, analogous to physical energy in its capability of being transferred from one system to another, in this case from any particular mental operation (or "engine") to another, like an electrical generator that powers a number of engines that perform different functions. He likened *g* to the power generator and *s* to the different engines, each of which is powered by *g* but also has its own level of efficiency independent of *g*. Spearman fully recognized the metaphorical nature of this speculation. But he hoped that eventually a true physical source of energy would be discovered to substantiate his metaphor, in his words, "whereby physiology will achieve the greatest of all its triumphs." In *The Abilities of Man*, he wrote: "And even should the worst arrive and the required physiological explanation remain to the end undiscoverable, the mental facts will none the less remain facts still. If they are such as to be best explained by the concept of an underlying energy, then this concept will have to undergo that which after all is only what has long been demanded by many of the best psychologists—it will have to be regarded as purely mental. Both by history and otherwise, the concept of energy belongs at least as much to the science of mind as to that of matter'' (1927, p. 408).

The measurement of g in individuals has been the most problematic aspect of Spearman's contribution and was nearly the sole subject of the first critical review of Spearman's most important book, *The Abilities of Man*.[24] The problem is the indeterminacy of factor scores. They cannot be determined exactly but can only be estimated from the data. In practice, this is usually accomplished by using the most highly g-loaded tests, although even scores on highly g-loaded tests are always contaminated to some degree by one or more other factors, including specificity, in addition to their g. However, these extraneous non-g factors can be reduced considerably by obtaining a "weighted average" of the individual's standardized scores on a number of highly g-loaded tests, in which the individual's standard scores (z) on the various tests are each weighted (i.e., multiplied) by their g-loadings and the resulting products ($g \times z$) are summed (Σgz). This sum is called a *g factor score*.[25] (It is usually transformed to a standard score, to make it easily interpretable in relation to a particular group or a representative sample of some population.)

Spearman's four other quantitative principles have faded with time or have been supplanted by other terminology and conceptual formulations, so they are mentioned only briefly here, and defined in Spearman's own words.[26]

Retentivity. "The occurrence of any cognitive event produces a tendency for it to occur afterwards." This is the basis of conditioning, learning, and memory in its several empirically distinguishable forms.

Fatigue. "The occurrence of any cognitive event produces a tendency opposed to its occurring afterwards." This is akin to Pavlov's hypothetical construct of "inhibition" and is even more closely akin to Clark Hull's postulate of "reactive inhibition."

Conative control. "The intensity of cognition can be controlled by conation." By "conation" Spearman means drive, motivation, will.

Primordial potencies. "Every manifestation of the preceding four quantitative principles is superposed upon, as its ultimate bases, certain primordial but variable individual potencies." This is a recognition of innate individual differences in predisposition to mental development and the evolutionary origins of mental organization.

NOTES

1. There is some dispute over priority in the invention of factor analysis, a subject covered comprehensively by Blinkhorn (1995). Spearman unquestionably invented a simple form of factor analysis. It is limited by being applicable only to a correlation matrix

of unit rank, that is, a matrix that has only one common factor. And he invented a method (tetrad differences) for determining whether a matrix is of unit rank and therefore suitable for the application of his method of factor analysis, which in the case of unit rank consists of obtaining the variables' loadings on the common factor, or *g*. And there is no question that Spearman was the first to apply factor analysis to mental test scores or psychological data of any kind. On all these counts, priority certainly belongs to Spearman. (See Lovie & Lovie, 1993.) The dispute arises, however, because, prior to Spearman (1904), Karl Pearson (1901) published an abstruse and purely mathematical paper that contains essentially the invention of what is now known as principal components analysis. It was further developed and made accessible to psychologists in a classic paper by the statistician H. Hotelling (1933). Principal components analysis permits the decomposition of a correlation matrix into as many perfectly uncorrelated axes, or components, as the number of variables, and it has been used extensively not only in psychology, but in many other fields, including economics, medicine, physics, political science, sociology, biology, paleontology, and archaeology. Because present-day methods of factor analysis are like principal components analysis in allowing the extraction of a number of uncorrelated factors, and because the whole procedure of modern factor analysis more closely resembles principal components analysis than Spearman's simple form of factor analysis, Pearson has some claim to the invention of factor analysis. Spearman's method may be regarded as a limited case implicit in the class of multivariate methods derived from Pearson's work. Also, a few years after Spearman's 1904 paper that introduced his method of factor analysis, Sir Cyril Burt invented a method of multiple factor analysis called simple summation. It is similar to Pearson's principal components, but is simpler to compute. Burt can be credited with being the first to apply a proper method of multiple factor analysis to psychological data. As his method allowed the extraction of more than a single factor from a matrix, it was clearly an advance over Spearman's method. Some years later, Louis L. Thurstone (1931) reinvented Burt's method, giving it the name *centroid* method; it is mathematically identical to Burt's method, although Thurstone (1947) introduced some new features in the way it is used in psychological research (e.g., rotation of factors, the simple structure principle, and oblique factors). The centroid method, which was widely used in the days of mechanical and electrical calculating machines, disappeared with the advent of high-speed electronic computers, which made it feasible to use the computationally more complex and more exact methods of modern factor analysis (see Harman, 1976).

Commemorating the fiftieth anniversary of Spearman's death, the *British Journal of Mathematical and Statistical Psychology* (1995, *48*, 211–253) published excellent in-depth articles on Spearman's role in the origin of factor analysis (D. J. Bartholomew), Spearman's contributions to test theory (P. Levy), the formulation of rank correlation (A. D. Lovie), and the resolution of the Spearman-Wilson debate over factor score indeterminacy (P. Lovie) (see p. 39 and Note 24).

2. Quoted in Burt (1972, p. 412).

3. Judson (1979, pp. 179–180).

4. Unfortunately, there is no book-length biography of Spearman. Fancher (1985a, pp. 84–98) gives a highly readable biographical sketch, but beware of the technical error in the last paragraph on page 88: a test's reliability is not the correlation between true scores and obtained scores, but is the square of this correlation. Jensen (1994b) gives a concise biography emphasizing Spearman's contributions to psychology and statistics, and also gives references to nearly all of the available biographical sources. A good

account of Spearman's two most important works is J. B. Carroll's (1991a) retrospective review of _The Nature of "Intelligence" and the Principles of Cognition_ and _The Abilities of Man: Their Nature and Measurement._ Sir Godfrey Thomson's (1947) obituary of Spearman is an excellent summary of Spearman's contributions to factor analysis and the theory of intelligence. It also contains the best of the several different photographs of Spearman that I have seen.

5. Spearman, 1930. More information about Spearman's life is contained in his autobiography than in probably any other single source, although it has comparatively little systematic explication of his work.

6. Reliability can also be expressed as the squared correlation between true scores and obtained scores, i.e., r_{tx}^2. The symbol r_{xx}, it should be noted, does not mean the correlation of test scores with themselves (which would equal 1), but the correlation between scores obtained from two separate administrations of the same test or from two different but equivalent forms of the test, such as two vocabulary tests each composed of words drawn from the same pool and both having the same level of difficulty. Reliability may also be determined by the so-called "split-half" method, in which the odd- and even-numbered items in a test are scored separately and a correlation (r_{OE}) is obtained between the odd and even scores. Because each of the correlated parts is only half as long as the whole test, the reliability coefficient (r_{FF}) of the scores based on the full-length test (i.e., odd + even items) is calculated by the Spearman-Brown formula: $r_{FF} = 2r_{OE}/(1 + r_{OE})$. This is just a special case of the generalized _Spearman-Brown prophecy formula_, which states the relationship between a test's length and its reliability. If we have determined the reliability (r_{LL}) of a test of a given length (i.e., number of items or number of trials), the reliability ($r_{L'L'}$) of a test n times as long (provided it is composed of similar items) will be

$$r_{L'L'} = nr_{LL}/[1 + (n - 1)r_{LL}].$$

7. The measures of five of these variables consisted of the boys' rank order in ability in each subject as judged by their teachers. Standardized achievement tests did not then exist. Spearman invented a method now known as Spearman's _rank-order correlation_ (also called _rank-difference correlation_), symbolized r_s. It is now universally used for correlating ranked variables and is described in most statistics textbooks. Rank correlation is a nonparametric statistic, in contrast to the Pearson r (which is parametric), because the sampling error of any obtained r_s based on n ranks involves no assumptions about the nature of the population distribution of the correlated variables. The probability of a particular r_s based on n ranks is simply the proportion a/b, where a is the number of all the possible permutations of n ranks that yield absolute values of r_s equal to or greater than the designated r_s, and b is the total number of possible permutations of n ranks. Pearson's r and Spearman's r_s calculated on the same ranked variables are numerically identical. However, the standard error of Pearson's r applied to actual measurements (rather than ranks) is slightly smaller than the standard error of Spearman's r_s applied to the ranks of the measurements. If there is evidence that the population distribution of one or both of the correlated measurements departs markedly from normal, the calculated standard error of the Pearson r becomes highly questionable. The standard error of Spearman's r_s for ranks is unaffected by the population distribution of the measurements underlying the ranked variables.

8. This usage of the term _positive manifold_ is a commonly accepted corruption of the more specialized original meaning of the term intended by its originator, Louis L.

Thurstone (1947, pp. 341–343). His specialized meaning refers to the condition in which every variable in the matrix has positive loadings on every factor. Because rotation of the factor axes extracted from a matrix of all positive correlations can yield a factor matrix of positive manifold, in Thurstone's sense, a correlation matrix of all positive correlations has also come to be loosely called a positive manifold, although that usage departs from its original Thurstonian meaning. (Thurstone's ideas on factor analysis are discussed in Chapter 4.)

9. Mathematical proofs of this and the following propositions are given in the Appendix of Spearman's *The Abilities of Man* (1927).

10. The possible number of distinct tetrads in a complete correlation matrix of n variables is $3n!/4!(n - 4)!$. (Note that $0! = 1$.)

11. A standardized score (or a standardized measurement of any kind), technically called a z score, simply expresses the score in terms of its deviation (in standard deviation units) from the mean of the sample or group of scores of which it is a member. That is, $z = (X - \overline{X})/\sigma$, where X is the raw score, $\overline{X}$ is the group mean, and σ is the standard deviation of the raw scores in the group. Consequently, in any distribution of z scores the mean $= 0$, the standard deviation $= 1$, and the variance $= 1$.

12. The meanings of correlations and the basic ideas of factor analysis are explained much more fully in Jensen, 1980a, Chapter 6.

13. There has been considerable misunderstanding on this point, and earlier factor analyses were often performed (not by Spearman but by others) on matrices with more than one factor. The factor common to all of the variables was extracted first, using Spearman's method, and then the same method was applied to the matrix of residual correlations. Thurstone (1947, pp. 279–281) has proved mathematically that this gives an incorrect result. Spearman himself insisted on demonstrating that all of the tetrad differences in the matrix must "vanish," thereby proving it has only one common factor, before determining each variable's loading on the common factor. To achieve this, he either eliminated or averaged overlapping variables that violated the "vanishing tetrads" criterion. Thurstone (1947, Chapter XII) gives a superb discussion of this limitation of Spearman's method. As with most prototypes, the limitations of Spearman's original method have made it now obsolete.

14. The generalized formula for the factor loadings is given in Spearman, 1927, Appendix, p. xvi, formula 20. This formula has scarcely been used for more than half a century, and is now only of historic and didactic interest. Mathematically more sophisticated methods for extracting multiple factors coupled with the use of high-speed computers have made modern factor analysis into something much more powerful than what Spearman had to work with.

15. At least some of Spearman's calculation errors have been detailed by Fancher (1985b). They are actually quite unimportant with respect to Spearman's overall method, theory, or general conclusions. It was possible to check his calculations because in his 1904 article he presented the raw data of his study.

16. The symbol g should never be used to stand for the largest common factor in a matrix that does not represent mental abilities. It is not used as the symbol for the general factor in strictly physical variables, personality variables, and so forth. To make this explicit, writers often refer to "Spearman's g" or "psychometric g." I prefer to reserve the qualified term "Spearman's g" for the g in Spearman's two-factor theory, that is, the matrix in which there is one, and *only* one, common factor. The broader term "psychometric g" refers to the general factor in a matrix of mental ability tests of any kind,

determined by any appropriate method of factor analysis, regardless of the number of other factors (i.e., group factors) in the matrix. The use of _g_ without a modifier usually refers to the common factor that accounts for the largest proportion of the total variance, as compared with any other factors in the matrix; but it also may refer to the _highest order_ factor (_g_ typically emerges at the second or third order) in a _hierarchical factor analysis_, regardless of whether or not it accounts for the largest proportion of variance. However, in the literature a hierarchical _g_ is usually designated as such. (Hierarchical factor analysis is described in Chapter 3.)

17. A variable's factor loading is simply the correlation, r_{Xg}, between the variable (X) and the factor (_g_). Also, the proportion of variance in one variable that can be accounted for by its correlation with another variable is the square of the correlation. Therefore, the sum of the squared factor loadings is the actual amount of variance accounted for by the factor. As each variable has a variance of one, the total variance in the matrix is equal to the number of variables. Thus the sum of the squared factor loadings divided by the number of variables is the proportion of the variance in all of the variables that is accounted for by their common factor, in this case _g_. This proportion, multiplied by 100, is customarily called the "percent of total variance explained" by the factor. In the example of Table 2.1, this is $3.77/6 = .629 \times 100 = 62.9$ percent.

18. A leading expert in factor analysis, the late H. F. Kaiser, has urged that I not call _s_ a factor, because, technically speaking, the term _factor_ should refer to a source of variance that is common to at least three or more variables. Hence, _s_ should simply be called _specificity_, not "specific factor." I will observe this rule in all the chapters following this one, in which it seems more appropriate to use Spearman's own terminology.

19. The key references here are to Burt (1909, 1911). Burt's (1949a) impressively erudite but quite technical treatment of the whole history of Spearman's two-factor theory traces its origins, its demise, and its replacement by what Burt refers to as the theory and methods of the "Galton-Pearson school," which recognized multiple factors as well as general ability, and of which Burt undoubtedly regarded himself as the chief exponent. Although Burt was exceptionally brilliant and amazingly erudite, he was not the creative genius that Spearman was, and his contributions were never as original or as fertile, scientifically, as Spearman's. But Burt's (1949b, 1955) views on the structure of mental abilities accorded more closely with recent formulations than did Spearman's, which should not be too surprising, since Burt's active career extended twenty-five years closer to the present day than did Spearman's.

20. I have written an article on the implications of Spearman's theorem of "indifference of the indicator" for some of the current issues in mental testing (Jensen, 1992a).

21. This all follows from a fundamental formulation in mathematical statistics, which states that the variance (σ^2) of the sum (Σ) of a number of different variables (i, j, . . . etc.) is equal to the sum of the variables' variances $[\Sigma(\sigma_i^2 + \sigma_j^2 + \ldots \text{etc.})]$ plus twice the sum of the covariances between all of the items $[2\Sigma(r_{ij}\,\sigma_i\sigma_j)]$. The translation of this statement into mathematical symbols is: $\sigma^2 = \Sigma(\sigma_i^2 + 2\Sigma r_{ij}\sigma_i\sigma_j)$. In psychometrics, where the variables are items that compose a test or various subtests within a test, the true-score variance consists only of the second term in the above equation, which is purely item covariances; the item variances (the first term in the above equation) constitute the error variance. The variance of the total scores on the test is the sum of these two terms, and the test's internal consistency reliability (assuming a large number of items) is defined as the fraction $(2\Sigma r\sigma_i\sigma_j)/\sigma^2$. An important point to notice about the above equation is that as the number of variables (e.g., test items) increases linearly, the

number of all their covariances increases exponentially. For *n* variables, the number of covariances is $n(n - 1)/2$. Therefore, the ratio of twice the sum of the item covariances to the sum of the item variances rapidly increases as the number of items in the test increases. Even though the item covariances are usually very small, their summation greatly exceeds the sum of the item covariances in a test containing thirty or more items. In most current standard tests of mental ability this ratio of $2\sum r_{ij}\sigma_i\sigma_j$ to $\sum\sigma_i^2$ is typically between 10 to 1 and 20 to 1.

22. A rearrangement of the terms in the well-known Spearman-Brown formula shows the relation between the average item intercorrelation (r_{ij}) and the internal consistency reliability coefficient r_{tt} of a test composed of *n* number of items:

$$r_{ij} = r_{tt}/[n + (1 - n)r_{tt}]$$

23. The final fruits of this effort are described in a posthumous book (Spearman & Jones, 1950), which, in 191 pages, succinctly summarizes Spearman's final position on factor analysis and mental abilities, including *g*, the then few established group factors, noegenesis, and certain quantitative aspects of cognition.

24. The Harvard mathematical statistician Edwin B. Wilson (1928) devoted nearly his whole lengthy review of Spearman's book in *Science* to a highly mathematical critique of just the brief mathematical appendix, focusing almost entirely on the problem of *g*-factor scores. He does not, however, dispute Spearman's important discovery of *g* as an empirical fact. He wrote, "Science advances not so much by the completeness or elegance of its mathematics as by the significance of its facts" (p. 244).

25. In a common factor analysis (principal factor analysis, also called principal axes analysis), factor scores, including *g*-factor scores, may be slightly correlated with one another, even when the factors themselves are perfectly orthogonal (i.e., uncorrelated with one another). The reason is that in a common factor analysis the obtained factor scores are only estimates of the true factor scores, the exact values of which cannot be determined. If it is important to assure perfectly uncorrelated factor scores, they may be obtained from a principal components analysis. (See Jensen & Weng [1994] for a simple explication of the difference between common factor analysis and principal components analysis, including references to the more technical literature on this subject.)

26. From Spearman (1923). This work is the first comprehensive statement of his theory, not just of abilities, but of the general psychology of mental activity. Thus it may be considered a major pioneering contribution to the field now known as cognitive psychology.

Chapter 3

The Trouble with "Intelligence"

The word "intelligence" as an intraspecies concept has proved to be either undefinable or arbitrarily defined without a scientifically acceptable degree of consensus. The suggested remedy for this unsatisfactory condition is to dispense with the term "intelligence" altogether when referring to intraspecies individual differences in the scientific context and focus on specific mental abilities, which can be objectively defined and measured. The number of mental abilities, so defined, is unlimited, but the major sources of variance (i.e., individual differences) among myriad abilities are relatively few, because abilities are not independent but have sources of variance in common.

The empirical fact that all mental abilities are positively correlated calls for an analytic taxonomy of mental abilities based on some form of correlation analysis. Factor analysis has proven to be the most suitable tool for this purpose. By means of factor analysis it is possible to describe the total variance of various abilities in terms of a smaller number of independent dimensions (i.e., factors), or components of variance, that differ in their degree of generality. "Generality" refers to the number of abilities that are correlated with a particular factor. The common factors in the abilities domain can be represented hierarchically in terms of their generality, with a large number of the least general factors (called first-order or primary factors) at the base of the hierarchy and the single, most general, factor at the apex.

Ability measurements can be represented geometrically and mathematically as vectors in space, with a common origin and with the angles between them related to their intercorrelations. Factors are the "reference axes" in this space and the number of orthogonal axes, or independent dimensions, needed to represent the ability measurements defines the number of factors. The dimensions found in the factor analysis of the correlations among a large variety of mental ability measurements can be arranged hierarchically according to their generality. This hierarchical structure typically has three tiers, or strata: a large number of narrow (i.e., least general) first-order factors, a relatively small number (six to eight) of broad (i.e., more general) second-order factors, and, at the apex, a single third-order factor, conventionally symbolized as _g_. The _g_ factor is the most general of all and is common to all mental abilities.

No other term in psychology has proved harder to define than "intelligence." Not that psychologists haven't tried. Though they have been attempting to define "intelligence" for at least a century, even the experts in this field still cannot agree on a definition. In fact, there are nearly as many different definitions of "intelligence" as there are experts.

The solution to this problem is to make a clear distinction between intelligence as an _interspecies_ phenomenon, on the one hand, and individual differences in mental abilities as an _intraspecies_ phenomenon, on the other. The term _intelligence_, then, would apply only to the whole class of processes or operating principles of the nervous system that make possible the behavioral functions that mediate an organism's adaptation to its environment, such as stimulus apprehension, perception, attention, discrimination, stimulus generalization, learning, learning-set acquisition, remembering, thinking (e.g., seeing relationships), and problem solving. These functions are subsumed in the term _intelligence_. In this sense, some of these aspects of intelligence are a property of virtually every organism in the animal kingdom. Intelligence, by this interspecies definition, therefore, is a broadly generic term. Hence, while it is meaningful, in this sense, to speak of _inter_species differences in intelligence, it is confusing to speak of _intra_species differences, at least for all biologically normal members of a species, that is, those without exogenously or endogenously caused defects of the central nervous system. All biologically normal members of a given species possess the same intelligence, that is, the same neural structures and processes that make whatever constitutes intelligent behavior possible for members of that species. From an evolutionary standpoint, it is most improbable that, by this definition, there are intraspecies differences, whether individual differences or group differences, in intelligence. This definition is absolutely moot regarding normal intraspecies variation. The definitional troubles begin when we talk about _intra_species differences among human beings, particularly individual differences and racial and ethnic group differences. Here we must come to grips with achieving scientific precision in our terminology. This can be accomplished most effectively by confining the term "intelligence" to its broadly generic interspecies definition and discarding its use entirely in discussing individual differences among _Homo sapiens_. I shall follow this rule throughout this book.

Some psychologists regard "intelligence" as the sum total of all mental abilities. This is a wholly open-ended concept, because obviously no one will ever be able to enumerate *all* mental abilities. Others define "intelligence" as the entire repertoire of a person's knowledge and skills available at any one time that are deemed "intellectual" by a consensus of psychologists—the very consensus that is so lacking! Still others identify "intelligence" as Spearman's g, but others then complain that this leaves out all the variance attributable to the many kinds of abilities other than g.

Contextualists and cultural relativists recognize the widest variety of knowledge and skills, but claim that what "intelligence" means in any particular culture is merely a limited selection from the entire human cognitive domain. In each culture it comprises those abilities considered important by that culture. In their view, "intelligence" is purely a cultural artifact. Some psychologists define "intelligence" so broadly as to include personality traits, motives, values, interests, attitudes (and even physical attributes) that may be correlated with whatever "real life" achievements are valued in a particular culture.

From a scientific standpoint, such failure to obtain a precise definition is hardly desirable. How can scientists make a consistent and concerted effort to research a phenomenon if they can't even agree on what that phenomenon is in the first place?

In hopes of finding a consensus definition of "intelligence," the editors of the *Journal of Educational Psychology*, in 1921, convened a symposium of fourteen American psychologists with distinguished reputations in this field.[1] They included such luminaries as Lewis M. Terman, Edward L. Thorndike, and Louis L. Thurstone. The symposium produced fourteen different definitions of "intelligence," each one scarcely resembling any of the others. Most of the definitions were mere verbalisms without empirical referents—"the power of good responses from the point of view of truth or fact" (Thorndike), "the power to think abstractly" (Terman), "that which can be judged by the incompleteness of the alternatives in the trial and error life of the individual" (Thurstone). One of the symposiasts stated that "so-called general intelligence tests are not general intelligence tests at all but tests of the special intelligence upon which the school puts a premium." There was a striking diversity even about which observable phenomena are the product of "intelligence" and which behavioral or mental attributes the term should encompass. The many definitions consisted only of supposed examples of "intelligence," not true definitions. The one point of implicit agreement was that "intelligence" was generally identified with "higher mental processes," not with elemental processes such as sensation and perception.

On reading this symposium, Spearman (who was not a participant) responded with evident exasperation: "Chaos itself can go no farther! The disagreement between different testers—indeed, even the doctrine and the practice of the selfsame tester—has reached its apogee. If they still tolerate each other's proceedings, this is only rendered possible by the ostrich-like policy of not looking facts in the face. In truth, 'intelligence' has become a mere vocal sound, a word with so many meanings that finally it has none'' (1927, p. 14). Spearman thereafter abandoned the use of the "mere vocal sound" *intelligence*, or else put it in quotation marks, as if to remind his readers that this "vocal sound" had no scientifically acceptable meaning in the context of human individual differences.

Sixty-five years later, in 1986, two leaders in the intelligence field, Robert Sternberg and Douglas Detterman, published another symposium, entitled "What Is Intelligence?"[2] This time, twenty-five well-recognized psychologists noted for their research on mental abilities and psychometrics were asked to state their definitions of "intelligence," how they thought it can best be measured, and their ideas for future research on "intelligence." The results were interesting but also dismaying. After sixty-five years, there was still no solid agreement among experts on how "intelligence" should be defined.

The editors then examined the degree of consensus between the 1921 statements and those of 1986 and tried to determine whether there was greater or lesser consensus among the experts within each period. They concluded that "substantial disagreement on a single definition still abounds" (p. 164). But they also note that there has been a shift of emphasis away from the strictly psychometric aspects of intelligence and its importance in education, emphasizing rather the concept of intelligence as information processing and as a scientific construct of interest in its own right. My impression is that the points of agreement among the contributors in 1986 concern the less critical attributes of the problem than do the points of disagreement. The overall picture remains almost as chaotic as it was in 1921, and Spearman would have reacted in much the same way to the 1986 symposium as he did to the earlier one. And he would be quite right again.

My study of these two symposia and of many other equally serious attempts to define "intelligence" in purely verbal terms has convinced me that psychologists are incapable of reaching a consensus on its definition. It has proved to be a hopeless quest. Therefore, the term "intelligence" should be discarded altogether in scientific psychology, just as it discarded "animal magnetism" as the science of chemistry discarded "phlogiston." "Intelligence" will continue, of course, in popular parlance and in literary usage, where it may serve a purpose only because it can mean anything the user intends, and where a precise and operational definition is not important.

Largely because of its popular and literary usage, the word "intelligence" has come to mean too many different things to many people (including psychologists). It has also become so fraught with value judgments, emotions, and prejudices as to render it useless in scientific discussion.[3] I have no quarrel with the typical dictionary definition of "intelligence," except that it does not adequately describe what I am actually writing about in this book. Indeed the attempt to provide a purely lexical definition is a hindrance to understanding the phenomena examined here.

I am certainly not proposing to offer still another definition of "intelligence," or another term to take its place, or suggesting that any existing definition can be made more acceptable if we modify it with adjectives, such as "academic intelligence" and "practical intelligence," or by making it plural, such as the currently popular "multiple intelligences." These "solutions" can only worsen the problem. As an intraspecies concept it is best simply to get rid of the term "intelligence" altogether in psychology. In this we should follow Spearman and henceforth drop the ill-fated word from our scientific vocabulary, or use it only in quotes, to remind ourselves that it is not only scientifically unsatisfactory but wholly unnecessary.

Formal definitions, however, are essential in science. But they themselves do not address the nature of a phenomenon or claim the status of empirical fact. Nor do they imply any particular theory or require logical or experimental proof. Formal definitions are theoretically neutral conventions that scientists agree upon in order to get on with their job. It makes no sense to disagree over such conventional definitions. It is important only that a definition be sufficiently clear and explicit to serve its pragmatic purpose.

To put the study of mental ability on a firm scientific footing, we must begin by using theoretically neutral, objective, operational definitions. From this position "intelligence" (or any synonym or conceptual substitute for it) never needs to enter the discussion. Just blot out whatever this word with all its ambiguities and emotional baggage may mean to you (or your dictionary). (Nor shall I try to provide another word or concept as a verbal substitute.)

Science begins by first recognizing certain objective realities and asking questions about them. In the domain of human abilities, what are these realities? To answer this, we must first become familiar with the technique known as factor analysis. The purpose of factor analysis is to explain the intercorrelations among variables in terms of a more limited number of hypothetical or latent variables termed *factors*. Factor analysis thus makes it possible to sort out the main sources of variance (i.e., factors) that are common to a variety of mental tests. But first, so that it will not seem arcane, it is important for readers to understand the basic concepts that underlie this analytic method.

ESSENTIAL DEFINITIONS AND CONCEPTS

The reader should not skip over the following definitions, even if the words themselves look familiar. They are used here in a special and precise way, and it would be cumbersome to have to define these terms repeatedly throughout the book to ensure that readers understand just how I am using them. By first agreeing on this specialized vocabulary and methodology we can proceed to a scientific analysis of mental ability.

Objective. In the present context, "objective" simply means *agreement* among observers of an external event, or between measurements or recordings of events registered by some device, and agreement among persons who read these records. The degree of agreement needed for any given purpose is another consideration. Degree of agreement can be quantified by the correlation between different observers or between repeated measurements by the same observer. When a correlation coefficient is used this way, it is termed a *reliability coefficient*, symbolized r_{xx}. The difference between the reliability coefficient and unity (i.e., $1 - r_{xx}$) represents the proportion of the total variance of the measurements that is attributed to *measurement error.*

It is a common misconception that psychological measurements of human abilities are generally more prone to error or inaccuracy than are physical measurements. In most psychological research, and especially in psychometrics, this kind of measurement error is practically negligible. If need be, and with proper care, the error variance can usually be made vanishingly small. In my laboratory, for example, we have been able to measure such variables as memory span, flicker-fusion frequency (a sensory threshold), and reaction time (RT) with reliability coefficients greater than .99 (that is, less than 1 percent of the variance in RT is due to errors of measurement). The reliability coefficients for multi-item tests of more complex mental processes, such as measured by typical IQ tests, are generally about .90 to .95. This is higher than the reliability of people's height and weight measured in a doctor's office! The reliability coefficients of blood pressure measurements, blood cholesterol level, and diagnosis based on chest X-rays are typically around .50.

Item Performance (IP). This term, henceforth abbreviated IP, refers to any distinct voluntary behavioral act. It can be any such overt action provided it is also observable or recordable in some way. Saying (or writing) "four" (or any other response) to the question "what is two plus two?", if the response can be agreed upon by observers, is an IP. Doing a triple axel, writing one's name, hitting middle C on the piano, performing the Tchaikovsky violin concerto, solving (or failing) an attempted math problem, jumping over a two-foot hurdle, cutting an apple in half, hitting a baseball into left field, and parking parallel— these are all IPs. An IP may be a discretely classifiable act (e.g., either hitting or missing a target) or some action that can be graded on a continuum (e.g., speed of response to a signal, time taken to complete a task, distance run in a given time). The universe of possible IPs is obviously unlimited. The definition of IP also includes, of course, a voluntary response to an item in any kind of test or to any laboratory procedure that measures, for example, reaction time, sensory threshold, speed of rote learning, or memory span.

Excluded from the category of IPs are unconscious, involuntary, or accidental acts, such as tripping on a stair, eye blinks, facial tics, unconditioned and conditioned reflexes, reactions of the autonomic nervous system, somnambulistic actions, drug reactions per se, fainting, and the like. Organismic events that are not strictly *behavioral* acts are also excluded, such as changes in brain waves, glandular secretions, pulse rate, blood pressure, skin conductance, and pupillary dilation, although these phenomena may be correlated with certain IPs. Most importantly, it should be noted that an IP is not an inference, or an abstraction, or an interpretation. It is a single objective raw datum—some overt act, directly observable by other persons or immediately recordable by an apparatus.

Ability. Going from an IP to an *ability* is going from a direct observation to an abstraction or inference, although of the lowest order. The universe of abilities is open-ended but bounded by certain qualifications.

An *ability* is an IP that meets the following three criteria:

(1) it has some specified degree of *temporal stability* (consistency or repeatability); (2) it can be reliably classified, measured, ranked, rated, graded, or scored in terms of meeting some objective *standard of proficiency*; and (3) it has some specified degree of *generality*.

Stability. For an IP to qualify as an *ability*, it must be evident that the IP can occur more dependably than chance probability, or pure luck, would allow under constant external circumstances. Holding a winning lottery ticket, for example, is not an ability. Because there is often some random variability in a person's IP from one point in time to another, some *average* IP has to be determined. *Temporal stability* implies that the IP can be elicited repeatedly at better than chance frequency under the same external conditions within a specified time interval, the length of which could range anywhere from seconds to months or (rarely) years. The consistency or repeatability of a *single individual's* IP can be quantified by the mean and standard deviation of the individual's IPs measured in some specified number of trials within a specified time interval. The consistency of *individual differences* in the IP among a group of persons can be quantified by the correlation of the IP measures across a given number of trials. (In psychometrics this is termed the *test-retest reliability*.)

Proficiency. An essential element in the definition of *ability* is that the IP must be an act that can be objectively classified, ranked, graded, or scored in terms of an objective *standard of proficiency*. This standard implies no judgment about the personal, moral, social, or economic value of the IP. For example, a particular person at a given point in time either *can* (score = 1) or *cannot* (score = 0) lift a 200-pound barbell and hold it one foot above the floor for ten seconds. A reaction time (RT) of 400 milliseconds is a quicker response than a RT of 450 milliseconds. The answer "four" to the question "2 + 2 = ?" is correct; the answer "five" is incorrect. Repeating a series of nine random digits after hearing them spoken once is to recall more digits than recalling only seven random digits under the same conditions. If an IP cannot be rated reliably or scored in terms of some such objective standard, it cannot be called an ability. Ratings or rankings with a specified degree of agreement among several judges (as quantified by the intraclass correlation or the coefficient of concordance) can also qualify as an objective standard and may serve to rate IPs that do not lend themselves to direct measurement, such as performance in figure skating, playing a musical instrument, singing, art work, influencing people, and the like.

Generality. Some degree of *generality* is also a necessary condition for an IP to be considered an ability. The critical question is, how much generality? The answer is that the essential features of the IP must be preserved while its nonessential features vary. For example, a person can repeat a string of seven digits (say, 7164835) after hearing them spoken once, at the rate of one digit per second. This is an IP, to be sure. And we may decide that its essential feature is the number of digits. But this person's IP cannot be called an ability at this point, because the person's recalling as many as seven digits could have been peculiar to just this particular string of digits; for example, it might have been his own well-memorized telephone number. If given ten more trials at recalling different strings of seven digits under the same conditions, the person possibly might not be able to repeat any of them correctly. He could not then be said to have the *ability* to repeat seven digits under these conditions. For any given IP to be regarded as an ability, an objective criterion of generality must first be defined. For example, we may decide that a digit span memory for, say, seven digits has to be demonstrated in any three out of four consecutive trials, all given under the same conditions, varying only the seven digits (randomly selected from 1 to 9) on each trial. Such a procedure can be applied to most other kinds of IPs. (This is called *equivalent forms reliability* in psychometrics.)

The generality of an IP, say, repeating (or failing to repeat) seven digits, can be inferred by its being significantly correlated (in a group of persons) with some other IP. This is because the correlation would not differ significantly from zero if a particular IP were just a random occurrence for every person in the group. Randomness, or pure chance, dilutes correlation to near zero. Significant correlation between IPs indicates that the correlated IPs qualify as *abilities*, at least for some of the people in the group for which the correlation was determined. To establish whether an IP is an ability with respect to any particular person, however, it is necessary to demonstrate its consistency and generality over a specified number of trials for that person, as explained above.

Mental Ability. The distinction between *physical* abilities and *mental* abilities is more difficult, and there may be a "zone of ambiguity" between these classes. There are two criteria for distinguishing a *mental ability*:

1. An ability (as defined above) is a *mental* ability if, with respect to information transmission per se, the receptor and effector mechanisms are nonspecific. In other words, an individual's performance is not essentially dependent on any *particular* sensory or motor system. Persons with a severe sensory handicap can still receive information in ways that circumvent their nonfunctional channel; and similarly, persons with a severe motor handicap can communicate information by some alternate route.

2. An ability is a *mental* ability if, within a group of people who have no major sensory or motor handicap (as independently determined), individual differences in the ability are insignificantly correlated with measures of sensory acuity, physical strength, endurance, agility, or dexterity (as independently assessed). If there is a significant correlation, one other correlational criterion must be met, based on factor analysis. The ability in question is *not* a mental ability if its largest factor loading (in a factor analysis of a wide variety of abilities) is found on a group factor defined as "physical." (That is, a group factor whose

largest loadings are found on measures of sensory acuity, physical strength, agility, endurance, and similar types of performance.) This last criterion assumes, of course, that a wide enough variety of ability measures are included in the factor analysis that both physical and mental abilities are represented, even if at the outset we are not certain of each one's classification as physical or mental.

Based on my study of the known physical correlates of mental abilities, I am confident that the above criteria for distinguishing between mental and physical abilities leave few of them in the "zone of ambiguity." This is not to say, however, that we should expect to find no correlations at all between certain unambiguously classified mental and physical abilities. But any such correlations will seldom represent an "intrinsic" or "functional" (i.e., directly causal) relationship between the two kinds of ability. (Full explication of these terms is postponed to Chapter 6.) Finding an "intrinsic" correlation between a physical and a mental trait, however, may provide important clues about the causal underpinnings of individual differences in the correlated traits.

As the rest of this book deals primarily with mental ability, I will henceforth use just the word "ability" to mean *mental ability*, as defined above, unless otherwise qualified.

Test and Item. A test is any collection of *items* (tasks, problems, questions, etc.) that elicit abilities when persons are asked to respond to the items in a particular way. The items may be anything the test maker chooses, so long as each one elicits an ability.

It is important not to confuse the three distinct meanings associated with the term "item." First, there is the *physical item* itself—a spoken or printed question, or problem, or task to be performed (but not including the person's performance). Second, there is the *item response*—the record or *score* of a person's adequacy of performance on the item. Third, there are the *item statistics*—the mean and variance of the scores on an item taken by a group of persons. (Other item statistics used in test construction are not so germane here.) In most contexts, the word "item" implies the item score or an item statistic, not the physical item itself. The expression "item variance," for example, means the variance of the scores on the item for a group of persons who attempted the item. Saying that two items are correlated means that the *item scores* are correlated in a group of persons who attempted both items.

If an item response is scored in a binary fashion, such as *right/wrong* or *pass/fail* (quantitized as 1/0), the *item mean* is the percentage (P) of persons who "passed" the item. The item's P value is an index of how easy it is for the group of persons who attempted it. Conversely, $100 - P$ is an index of *item difficulty*. The *item variance* of a single binary-scored item is $p \times q$ where p is the proportion of persons who pass the item and q is the proportion who fail the item (assuming $p + q = 1$).

Item Intercorrelation. It so happens—not because the test constructor makes it happen, but because it is an observed fact of nature—that all mental abilities are positively correlated with each other. Stated more exactly, if two or more items each reliably elicits an ability, the item scores obtained in a large and representative sample of the general population will be positively correlated to some degree. These *item intercorrelations* may vary considerably in magnitude. For example, most people who can repeat a string of 7 digits on at least 3 out of 4 trials can also repeat a string of 6 digits on at least 3 out of 4 trials; but most people who, under the same conditions, *cannot* repeat 6 digits also cannot repeat 7 digits. This fact creates a correlation between these two items—a 6-digit item and a 7-digit item. The correlation between any two items, each scored either pass (1) or fail (0) can be calculated from a 2 × 2 *contingency table* (see below) showing the number of persons who passed or failed each item.

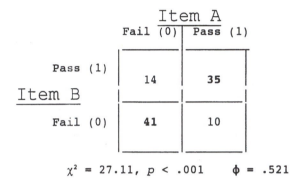

The value of the statistic known as chi squared (χ^2), can be calculated from the frequencies in the four cells of this contingency table. If it is large enough, it indicates a statistically significant correlation. That is, the probability (*p*) that a value of χ^2 this large would occur by pure chance is less than one in a thousand (thus $p < .001$). (If the four cells had nearly equal frequencies, the correlation would not be significant.) The correlation between Item A and Item B in the example above (technically termed a phi coefficient, ϕ, when calculated on a 2 × 2 contingency table) is +.521. (This is atypically large for item correlations.[4])

A test (composed of three or more items) can also be measured for its degree of *homogeneity*. One index of homogeneity is the average correlation among all of the items. Imagine that we pick 100 items at random from a very large pool of items that elicit a wide variety of abilities. The 100 items are administered to a thousand people, and from these data we calculate all the interitem correlations. (There will be a total of 100 (100 − 1)/2 = 4,950 correlation coefficients.) Say the average of the interitem correlations is only .10. We can create a number of shorter, but more homogeneous, tests from this collection of 100 items by making up small groups of items in which every item is correlated, say, at least .20 with every other item in the same group. (Leftover items that are correlated less than .20 with any other items are assigned to the group of items with which they have the highest average correlation.) So then we will have a number of small but relatively homogeneous subtests. The average of the item correlations *within* each of the homogeneous subtests will be larger than the average correlation between items drawn from different subtests.

Items within a given homogeneous subtest are generally of a similar type. That is, they resemble each other considerably more in their type of information content than they resemble the types of items in other subtests. Each of the homogeneous groups of items usually turns out to be largely composed of, say, either numerical items, verbal items, memory span items, figural items, or mechanical items. Thus the process of grouping items by their degree of intercorrelation tends to bring together items with similar features and content. Yet even items that are grouped in this manner (or any other manner) are still positively correlated, though perhaps only slightly, with the items in any other subtests.

A Test's Raw Score. The *raw score* on a test is the sum of all the item scores, which are the numerical values used to grade an individual's response to each of the items. Typically, a response on each item of a test is scored as either 1 or 0 (for pass or fail, according to some specified objective standard), and the sum of the item scores constitutes the person's *raw score* on the test as a whole.

The total variance of the raw scores on a test is really an abstraction, at least a step or two removed from the observable item performances that constitute an ability. While the variance of a single item is $p \times q$ (see above), the *variance of total scores on a test* (which by definition is composed of three or more items) *is the sum of the item variances plus twice the sum of the item covariances.*[5]

Item covariance per se is not an observable act or a sample of behavior. It is, however, a natural phenomenon. The largest part (typically 90 to 95 percent) of the total variance in mental test scores consists of the sum of all the item covariances. If the covariance between items is not itself directly observable or measurable *behavior*, then what is it? There is only one answer: It is a *factor*, as technically defined below.

Factor. The word "factor" has a number of dictionary definitions, but the term as used here has a very restricted, specialized meaning. A *factor* is a hypothetical variable that "underlies" an observed or measured variable. Thus a factor is also referred to as a *latent* variable. It is best thought of initially in terms of the mathematical operations by which we identify and measure it.

Although a factor is identifiable and quantifiable, it is not directly observable. It is not a tangible "thing" or an observable event. So we have to be especially careful in talking about factors, lest someone think we believe that we are talking about "things" rather than hypothetical and mathematical constructs. But one can say the very same thing about the many constructs used in the physical sciences (gravitation, magnetism, heat, valence, and potential energy, to name a few). They are all *constructs*. This does not imply, however, that scientists cannot inquire about the relationship of a clearly defined construct to other phenomena or try to fathom its causal nature. Nor is a construct "unreal" or "chimerical" or less important than some directly observable action or tangible object. Certainly the force of gravity (a hypothetical construct) has more widespread importance than the particular chair I am sitting in at the moment, and is every bit as real. A lot of pointless arguments can be avoided by consistently maintaining a clear distinction between the purely mathematical definition, identification, or measurement of factors, on the one hand, and theories about their causal nature, on the other. (In this chapter, I am not saying anything at all about the causal nature of factors.)

Factors arise only from the reliable or nonchance correlation between abilities. Now, if it were the case that tests were constructed of only those items that happened to be correlated with one another (and items that did not were discarded), factors would indeed be mere psychometric *artifacts*. That is, factors would be no more than a product of the arbitrary way that ability items are devised or selected for inclusion in psychometric tests. If so, it should be possible in theory to devise mental ability tests in which the items did not correlate more than could be expected by pure chance. Such a test could not be analyzed into factors. Its total variance would consist only of the sum of the separate item variances plus a little random error variance due to the small chance correlations among items.

In reality, this has never happened, so long as our open-ended definition of a *mental ability* is used to select the test items. It is important to note that there is nothing circular or in any way tautological in this observation, because our definition of a *mental ability* is completely independent of the condition of a correlation between abilities. By this definition, abilities could just as well be uncorrelated or negatively correlated as being positively correlated.

The striking empirical fact, however, is that, as far as has yet been determined, mental abilities *are* all positively intercorrelated beyond chance to some degree. I have yet to find a bona fide exception. For a century psychologists have made countless attempts to discover even a small number of mental test items that are truly uncorrelated. All have failed. This does not mean that zero or negative correlations never occur. In various studies of item intercorrelations, based on subject samples of varying size, the relatively small number of interitem correlations found to be zero or negative is inversely related to the range of ability in the sample and to the size of the sample. Further, the mean of the negative correlations is always very much smaller than the mean of the positive correlations. This indicates that nonpositive correlations between items are merely flukes due to sampling error. The finding of ubiquitous positive correlations between mental abilities is not a psychometric artifact, but an empirical fact, a natural phenomenon.

Because of this phenomenon of ubiquitous positive correlations among all items in the practically unlimited universe of mental abilities, we can proceed to determine the various *factors* (or latent variables) that "account for" these intercorrelations. I put "account for" in quotation marks to indicate that it is just a manner of speaking in this field; it does not imply an explanation of *why* abilities are correlated, which is another issue. Some factor analysts say that the factors "explain" the correlations between abilities, that is, certain abilities may have certain factors in common. But this is merely a semantic quibble as long as one recognizes that a factor per se is itself a phenomenon that needs to be explained. The methods of factor analysis permit us to identify and quantify a factor, but they cannot tell us what is responsible for the emergence of the factor. As Spearman said, we can identify factors only by site (i.e., the tests in which they are loaded) and not by nature (i.e., the physiological conditions that cause their emergence). This is because factors are only mathematical transformations of a matrix of correlation coefficients.[6] The methodology for performing these transformations is called *factor analysis*.

THE GIST OF FACTOR ANALYSIS

Factor analysis involves a whole class of complex mathematical techniques. Textbooks on factor analysis usually assume some knowledge of statistical concepts and matrix algebra. Sidestepping the mathematics, I will here provide some idea of what factor analysis is and does without explaining its mathematical basis or exactly how it is performed in practice. For that, readers should refer to one of the several modern textbooks on factor analysis.[7] While a technical knowledge of factor analysis is not required to understand the rest of this book, a few points are quite important. This book is largely about *g*, and because *g* is a *factor* in the technical sense, it would remain virtually undefinable and conceptually meaningless without some *conceptual* understanding of factor analysis.[8]

The purpose of a factor analysis of a set of *n* variables is to transform the *correlation matrix* of all of the variables' intercorrelations (called the *R* matrix) into a *factor matrix* of *p* factors. In factor analysis, $p < n$. That is, the number of factors is less than the number of variables. There are two main ways that a set of variables can be factor-analyzed: from the bottom up, or from the top down. By "top" is meant the highest degree of factorial commonality or generality; "bottom" is the lowest degree of generality or the most specificity. A factor's "generality" refers to the number of variables that it encompasses, as shown by their having significant loadings on the factor.

Let me first illustrate the logic of a factor analysis from the bottom up. (This isn't the actual mathematical procedure used in doing a factor analysis, but it gives a fairly clear idea of what it does.) Typically, factor analysis begins with scores on relatively homogeneous tests. It ordinarily assumes standardized variables, which is accomplished as part of the formula for computing the Pearson correlation coefficients with which the factor analytic procedure begins. Here it will be more instructive to start a step lower in the hierarchy of abstraction than the tests. We will start with the single items that compose the tests.

Figure 3.1 will make the explanation easier to follow. Note that the levels of

5

4

3

2
1

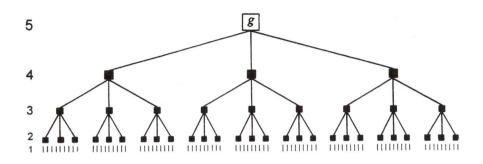

Figure 3.1. Hypothetical example of a hierarchical factor analysis (with components of variance represented as squares) of 243 test items (Level 1, at bottom of hierarchy). Level 2 = tests; Level 3 = first-order factors; Level 4 = second-order factors; Level 5 = third-order factor, or the general factor, *g*. The lines connecting the squares represent correlations greater than some specified magnitude.

the hierarchy are labeled 1 (lowest) through 5 (highest), as shown in the left margin of Figure 3.1.

Level 1: At the very "bottom" of the whole process are the ability *items*. So we begin with a large number (say, 243) of diverse items, each one measuring an ability. Any one of these ability items is exceedingly *narrow* in generality. That is, it has only very low correlations with all other ability items except those that are very much like itself. For example, the ability to repeat a string of six digits after *hearing* them spoken correlates much more with the ability to repeat them after *reading* them than with, say, the ability to do simple arithmetic. We administer the items to a large sample of, say, 1,000 adults randomly selected from the general population. From our inspection of the total matrix of 29,403 (i.e., $[n^2 - n]/2$, where n is the number of items) correlations among all of these *item scores*, we group together sets of items that are the most highly correlated with each other.

Level 2: Each such group of items constitutes a *homogeneous test*. There are, say, twenty-seven such tests, each containing about three items. (This small number of items is only a concession to the space limitation of Figure 3.1; in practice each homogeneous test would typically be composed of ten to twenty items). The commonality among the items in each test makes it broader (more general) than any of its narrower constituent items. (Inspection of the contents in each homogeneous group of items may permit us to give descriptive names to the various constituted tests, such as spelling, mechanical arithmetic, vocabulary, perceptual speed, visual form perception, figure analogies, digit memory span, word memory span, block counting, and the like.) We obtain the persons' total *raw scores* on each of the tests and use these scores to calculate the correlations among the twenty-seven tests. This yields a test correlation matrix that contains 351 correlation coefficients.

Level 3: From inspection of this matrix of test correlations, we group the tests that are the most highly correlated with each other together. Say we get nine such relatively homogeneous groups, each containing three tests. (Most researchers agree that each factor should be defined by a minimum of three experimentally independent variables or tests.) These groups of tests are *first-order factors* (also called *primary* factors, or *primaries*). The sum of a person's score on each of the tests in a group is here called a *factor score*. (This statement, intended here for the simplest possible explanation, is not accurate, as factor scores are actually weighted sums with certain statistical properties based on regression analysis. The various rather technical methods for obtaining factor scores are explained in the textbooks on factor analysis.) Factor scores are broader, or more general, than the score on any of the constituent tests, for each factor score here encompasses three tests. Just as the different *tests* are more highly correlated with each other, on average, than are the *items* that compose the tests, so the different *factors* may be (but are not necessarily) more highly correlated with each other, on average, than are the different tests that compose the factors.

Level 4: The same process is applied to the first-order factors. Those primary factors most highly correlated with each other are grouped together to form the *second-order* factors. There are three of these in Figure 3.1. The second-order factors are more general than the first-order factors.

Level 5: The correlations among the second-order factors form a single third-order factor, g, which is the most general (highest level) factor of all.

The hierarchy of generality, from the least general to the most general is: (1) items, (2) tests, (3) first-order factors, (4) second-order factors, and (5) g, the single most general factor. When the number of tests is not large and the abilities they sample are not highly diverse, g usually emerges as a second-order factor. It is exceedingly rare, however, to find more than a single third-order factor (namely, g). In hundreds of factor analyses of ability tests, g always emerges as either a second-order or a third-order factor.[9]

But now we must backtrack, to make this simplified explanation more technically correct. Factors are not items, or tests, or scores. It will be more correct if we think of them as "pieces" of the total true-score variance of all of the items at the base of the hierarchy. You will recall that the total variance of a number of measurements (in this case item scores on a large number of items) can be sliced up into a number of parts. Factor analysis is one way of slicing up the total variance, each slice representing a factor.

So referring back to Figure 3.1, we can think of all of the black rectangles in the hierarchy as different sized pieces of the total variance that exists in the pool of items at the base of the hierarchy (**Level 1**). At each level of the hierarchy, the variance is cut into a different number of slices. The variance in each of the tests (**Level 2**) consists of the sum of the variances of its constituent items plus twice all of the item covariances.

The first-order factors (**Level 3**) are created from the correlations among tests; that part of each test's total variance that is uncorrelated with any other test is left out of the first-order factors. This uncorrelated part of a test's total variance, which does not go into one (or more) of the first-order factors, is the test's *uniqueness*. It is composed of the sum of the test's item variances (called the item's *error* variance) and the part of the test's true-score variance that is not common to any other test (called the test's *specificity*). The first-order factors, therefore, are slices of variance that three or more tests all have in common.

The second-order factors (**Level 4**) are created by the correlations between first-order factors. What is left behind in each first-order factor is that part of its variance that it does not have in common with any other first-order factor. Since whatever variance the first-order factors had in common has been removed to form the second-order factors, the resulting first-order factors are uncorrelated with one another. And since each first-order factor has now lost whatever variance it had in common with any other factor, it is also uncorrelated with every second-order factor as well. Such uncorrelated factors are said to be *orthogonal*.

Finally, the third-order factor, *g* (**Level 5**), is created from the correlations among the second-order factors, whose residual variance consists of whatever variance they do not have in common with each other. They are uncorrelated with each other and with *g*. So the whole factor hierarchy (i.e., **Levels 3, 4, 5** in Figure 3.1) has been *orthogonalized*. At this point it is possible, by a mathematical algorithm (the Schmid-Leiman orthogonalization transformation[10]) to determine the correlation between each test and each of the orthogonal factors in the hierarchy. The correlations of a test with each of the orthogonal factors are called *factor loadings*. A table that shows each test's loading on each factor is called a *factor matrix*.

Another aspect of this simplified explanation of factor analysis should now be made clear. I said that by inspecting the matrix of correlations among all of the tests we can group together those tests that are the most highly correlated with each other. Actually we don't have to do this by inspection. With a very large number of correlations it would be an exceedingly difficult task. In practice, the mathematical procedures of factor analysis objectively determine which tests should be grouped together to form a factor and also provide objective criteria to determine the number of common factors among the variables in the analysis.

The number of factors extracted represents the number of dimensions in the *factor space* needed to accommodate the factor structure of the data. Although we spatially visualize only three dimensions in our everyday world, it is mathematically possible to deal with an *n*-dimensional space, where *n* is the number of dimensions needed to accommodate *n* straight lines (factors), each one at right angles to each of the others. For example, take four match sticks. Lay one of them down on the table; it occupies one dimension. Lay down another stick at right angles to it; this pattern occupies two dimensions. The third stick must be placed perpendicular to the table top jutting up in the air in order to be at right angles to the other two. Now three dimensions are occupied. Where can we put the fourth match stick and yet preserve right angles between all of the sticks? To do so, we need to go beyond our everyday three-dimensional space to a four-dimensional space. And so on. The sticks are here analogous to orthogonal (i.e., uncorrelated) factors.

If the correlated variables all have unit variance (as is the case in a factor analysis), we can represent each correlation spatially as an angle, where the correlation coefficient is equal to the cosine of the angle theta (θ) (that is, $r = \cos \theta$). For example, the cosine of a right angle (cos 90°) = r_0 = 0; cos 0° = $+1$ = r_{+1}; and cos 180° = -1 = r_{-1}. This transformational equivalence of correlations and angles allows another use of the idea of dimensionality. All angles can be displayed in two dimensions, but it is possible that three or more angles, when considered simultaneously, may not be accommodated in two dimensions. That is, three or more angles may not be shown accurately on a plane surface. (See Figure 3.2.) Consider the three angles (and their corresponding correlations shown above each angle) formed by the unit length vectors **A, B,** and **C.** We see (directly below) that the three angles can all be put together in the same plane; all of the vectors and their angles add up exactly to the largest angle (AC = 75°), so they can be represented simultaneously in one plane (a two-dimensional space). In contrast, consider the lower set of angles formed by the vectors **X, Y,** and **Z.** There is no way that we can put these three angles together in one plane (i.e., 60° + 30° ≠ 70°); they can be represented only in a three-dimensional space, as illustrated in the lower figure.[11]

A simple real-life example may intuitively illustrate how dimensionality underlies factor analysis. Suppose that three people, named Tom, Dick, and Harry, are tested every day for a month on their abilities to do these things: lift a barbell (**B**), do a shotput (**S**), and throw a javelin (**J**). B is measured as the maximum weight that can be lifted; S and J are measured by the distances that the shot and the javelin, respectively, are thrown. For all three tests we find on more than 90 percent of the trials that Tom did better than Dick, who did better than Harry (i.e., on **B, S, J**: Tom > Dick > Harry). All the performances on **B, S,** and **J** can, therefore, be ranked (or graphed) on just one dimension. In other words, one factor adequately accounts for the data. (That is, little or none of the original information is lost by performing the transformation from three dimensions to one.) We might label this factor as "general strength," as it determines the individual differences in performance on every test. Tom scores higher on this "general strength" factor than Dick and Harry, and Dick scores higher than Harry.

But suppose we had found that on more than 90 percent of the trials the following occurred:

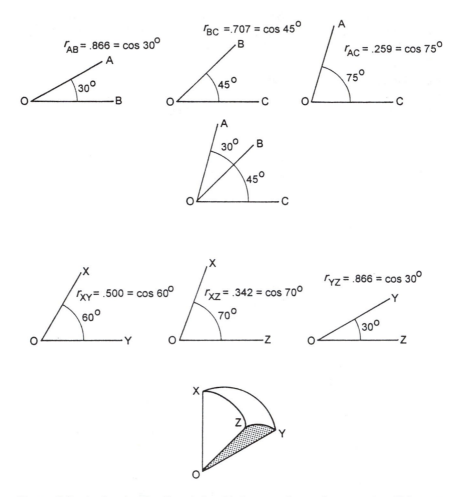

Figure 3.2. Angles showing the relationship between the angular separation (θ) between two line segments (e.g., A and B) with the same origin (O) and the coefficient of correlation (r) between them: $r = \cos\theta$. The top three angles (or correlations) can be represented together in two-dimensional space. The three lower angles (correlations) can be represented together only in three-dimensional space.

On **B** and **S**: Tom > Dick > Harry
On **J**: Harry > Tom > Dick

B and **S** are much alike, ranking people in one dimension (that is, graphing them on a single line), but **J** doesn't rank people the same way. **J** evidently involves some specific skill that is not required for **B** and **S**. To represent these data accurately, then, we must have two dimensions: one on which we can rank the subjects on **B** and **S**, the other on which we can rank them on **J**. If we had found the following:

> On **B**: Tom > Dick > Harry
>
> On **S**: Dick > Tom > Harry
>
> On **J**: Harry > Tom > Dick,

we would need three dimensions on which to rank-order the subjects. Each task, then, would evidently measure some distinct ability not shared by the other two tests. We would therefore have to posit three separate factors to account for the three tests. Of course this is only a didactic example. In reality, a greater number and variety of tests, and a great many more subjects, would be required for a proper factor analysis. The analysis would define the dimensionality of the factor space needed to represent the correlations among the n tests. Each dimension is a factor axis. A test's loadings on each of the factors maps its location in the n-dimensional factor space. The factors are thus somewhat analogous to the lines of latitude and longitude on a globe of the world that permit us to specify the exact location of any city.

Each test can be represented in factor space as a *vector*, that is, a straight line segment having magnitude and direction, where the length of the line represents its magnitude and its direction is represented by the line's orientation in space. The six arrows shown in Figure 3.3 are the vectors of six positively correlated tests labeled A, B, C, X, Y, Z. As the test scores all have unit variance (hence are depicted in Figure 3.3 as vectors all having the same length), the correlation between any pair of tests is equal to the cosine of the angle between them. The cosine relation between angles and correlations thus allows us to represent the matrix of correlations among all of the tests geometrically as an array of vectors. Since all of the vectors in our example can be represented on a plane, we can represent the common factor variance of these six tests in terms of their projections on two uncorrelated axes (i.e., a 90° angle between them, hence called *orthogonal*).[12]

These axes are orthogonal *factors*, labeled I and II in Figure 3.3. One method by which they are precisely determined mathematically is termed *principal factor analysis*, in which case the derived factors are called *principal factors*.[13] Each factor axis passes through the origin of all the test vectors at their zero point (0). The position of the first principal factor, labeled Factor I, is determined mathematically such that it lies closer to *all* of the test vectors (A, B, C, etc.) than does any other straight line. Hence it maximizes the sum of the squared loadings of all the variables on the factor. Because the first principal factor is the largest factor (that is, it accounts for more of the total variance than does any other single factor), this is a "top-down" method of factor analysis. The second principal factor, Factor II, is located so as to pass through the origin (0) and be at right angles to Factor I.

For orthogonal factors, the projection of a test vector on a factor is the test's

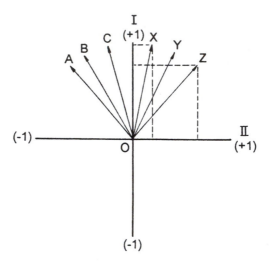

Figure 3.3. Six test vectors (arrows) and the two orthogonal axes, Factors I and II, needed to account for their common variance.

loading on that factor. In Figure 3.3, the dashed lines show the projections of Tests X and Z on Factor I and Factor II. One can see that Test X has a very large (about +.99, or 99% of the way from the origin to the top of the axis) projection (or loading) on Factor I and a quite small (about .15) projection on Factor II. Test Z has a loading of about +.80 on Factor I and of about +.60 on Factor II. Note that each of the six tests has its largest projection on Factor I and all of these projections are *positive*. Therefore, Factor I is interpreted as the *general factor* in this set of tests. It qualifies as the general factor, not because it is the first principal factor, but because it is more highly correlated with each and every one of the tests than is any other factor and the correlations (loadings) are all positive.

Because the projections of Tests A, B, C on Factor II are *negative*, while Tests X, Y, Z have *positive* projections, Factor II is called a *bipolar* factor. If we added to this set of six tests three or more other tests whose intercorrelations with the first six could not be represented in the same plane, we would need yet another factor axis projecting out into the third dimension. Factor III would then pass through the origin (0) at right angles to Factors I and II. The test vectors for this set of three new tests would slant away from the surface of the page into this three-dimensional space and they would have projections on Factor III and possibly also on Factors I and II. If still another three (or more) tests were added to the set and their intercorrelations could not be accommodated in a three-dimensional space, another factor axis at right angles to the first three (Factor IV) would be needed. In order to be at right angles to the first three factors, it would have to exist in the fourth dimension. Vectors that project into a space of more than three dimensions are said to exist in *hyperspace*.

Rotation of Orthogonal Factors and the Principle of "Simple Structure." There is nothing intrinsically sacrosanct about the original position of the factor axes given by the computational procedure in factor analysis. One is completely free to *rotate* the original factors around their origin in any way that might produce a theoretically clearer or more meaningful picture of the factor structure of the tests. For example, since the tests themselves are all positively correlated with one another, it might seem sensible that they should all have positive factor loadings on each of the two factors that describe their location in the factor space. It might also seem sensible if the two factors had more equal weight, in terms of the proportions of the total variance that each one accounts for, than is seen in the original position of the factor axes. This can often be achieved by rotating the axes to another position, while still keeping them orthogonal (that is, at right angles).

Louis Leon Thurstone (1887–1955), the chief developer of multiple factor analysis, proposed an important principle for factor rotation, which he termed *simple structure*. The aim of simple structure is to rotate the factors to a position that maximizes the number of very large factor loadings and the number of very small loadings, with as few intermediate-sized loadings as possible, while maintaining the orthogonality of all the factors. The main consequence of employing this criterion, hopefully, is that each test has a large loading on only one factor and near-zero loadings on every other factor. This makes it fairly easy to give a psychological interpretation and a clear-cut label to each factor simply by examining the kinds of information or mental processes called for by the tests that have large loadings on the factor. For example, if all of the verbal tests, in contrast to spatial and numerical tests, have large loadings on one factor and small or zero loadings on all other factors, we would identify this factor as "verbal ability."

No matter how one rotates the factor axes, the test vectors always remain invariant (that is, in the exact same positions) in relation to one another. The test vectors shown in Figure 3.3, for example, are reproduced exactly in Figure 3.4, but the factors have been rotated to a position that approximates simple structure as closely as possible for this set of tests. Notice the results of this rotation: (1) All of the test vectors are located in the positive quadrant of the factor space (both Factor I' and Factor II' are positive) and therefore all of the tests now have positive projections (i.e., factor loadings) on each factor. (2) Half of the tests (A, B, C) are brought much closer to Factor I' (I' is the rotated Factor I), while the other tests (X, Y, Z) are brought closer to Factor II'. Tests A, B, C therefore have large loadings on I' and relatively small loadings on II', and just the opposite is true for tests X, Y, Z. Test A, whose vector nearly coincides with the axis labeled Factor I', is therefore an almost perfect *marker* for Factor I'. Similarly, Test Z is an almost perfect marker for Factor II'. If tests A, B, and C consisted, respectively, of vocabulary, synonyms-antonyms, and verbal analogies, we might label Factor I' as verbal ability. And if tests X, Y, and Z consisted, respectively, of number series completion, arithmetic reasoning,

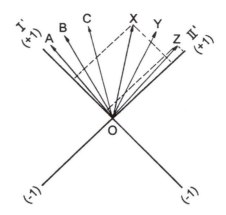

Figure 3.4. The same test vectors as in Figure 3.3, but here the factor axes (Factors I' and II") have been *rotated* so that all of the test vectors have positive projections on both factors and approximate the *simple structure* criterion (defined in the text). The factor axes remain orthogonal (i.e., at a 90° angle, hence uncorrelated, since $r = \cos 90° = 0$).

and mechanical arithmetic, we might label Factor II' as numerical or quantitative ability.

But what has happened to the general factor, which was so prominent in Figure 3.3? It best represented the fact that the tests are all positively correlated and therefore all had some factor in common—a general factor, or *g*. The general factor that was so prominent in the analysis depicted in Figure 3.3 seems to have disappeared from Figure 3.4 as a result of rotating the factor axes. Actually, it has simply been dispersed (or redistributed) among the rotated factors. Notice that even though the rotation to simple structure has maximized each test's loadings on one factor and minimized its loading on the other factor, some of the tests (B, C and X, Y) still have some significant, though unequal, loadings on each factor. So if you ask where the *g* went, the answer is that it has been divided up and lies "hidden" among all of the tests' smaller loadings on all of the orthogonally rotated factors. Its variance has not disappeared, it has simply been obscured by being dispersed throughout the whole factor matrix. The price paid for the clarity afforded by simple structure in identifying and labeling the factors psychologically is the loss of the clear evidence of the tests' loadings on the general factor. In the past, some factor analysts mistakenly argued that this supposed "disappearance" of the general factor after rotation proved its nonexistence.

In many analyses, some tests (like Test X in Figure 3.4) load almost equally on two (or more) factors. This violates the criterion of simple structure. Application of the simple structure principle in the early history of factor analysis led to futile debates over whether there is or is not a general factor in the analyzed tests. British psychologists, following Burt, did not rotate and claimed there was a general factor. American psychologists, following Thurstone, rotated and claimed there was no general factor. It was probably the most fatuous and futile argument in the history of psychometrics. It was finally settled by Thurstone himself, to the delight of Spearman, the unwavering champion of g. The essential fact is that, in the mental abilities domain, where unavoidably all tests are positively correlated, it is virtually impossible to rotate *orthogonal* factors to achieve an optimal approximation to simple structure. An empirical fact of nature, demonstrated repeatedly—positive correlations among all mental tests—contradicts Thurstone's principle of simple structure. But this contradiction exists only if one insists that all of the factor axes must be orthogonal. Yet there is no compelling reason to maintain orthogonality if it prevents the aim of achieving simple structure.

Oblique Factors. Thurstone, therefore, invented the use of *oblique* factors, that is, factor axes that have angular separations of less than 90°. The factor axes are positioned at oblique angles to one another in such a way as to minimize their distances from various clusters of test vectors. Using the same set of test vectors as in Figures 3.3 and 3.4, Figure 3.5 shows the "best fit" of the two oblique factor axes to the test vectors. Each factor axis goes right through each cluster of tests. Now we see that tests A, B, and C all have large projections on Factor I" (our original Factor I, now in oblique rotation) and relatively small projections on Factor II". (The projection indicates the correlation of the test with the factor.) Allowing the factors to be oblique makes it possible for rotation to more closely approximate the criterion of simple structure and therefore provides a "cleaner" picture of the factor structure of the tests, because the tests, on average, will lie closer to the oblique factors than to the orthogonally rotated factors (in Figure 3.4).

What now has happened to the general factor in the oblique situation? It still exists but is now accounted for by the correlation between the oblique factors. The angle between I" and II" is 55°, so the correlation between these factors is $r_{I''II''} = \cos 55° = +.57$. The correlation between the first-order oblique factors constitutes a *second-order* (higher-order) factor, which in this case is the *general factor*, or g. With only two first-order factors in this simple didactic example, however, the loadings of the first-order factors on the second-order factor are indeterminate, although we know that their product is equal to $+.57$. We would actually need to know the correlations between at least three first-order factors to be able to calculate their loadings on a second-order factor. It is considered improper to present second-order factors without also reporting the correlation(s) between them, otherwise not all of the common factor variance in the original correlation matrix is represented by the oblique factor structure.

The extraction of a higher, second-order factor from the correlations among the oblique first-order factors constitutes a *hierarchical factor analysis*. (With a large and diverse battery of tests, a third-order factor may also emerge from the correlations among three or more second-order factors. But it is an empirical

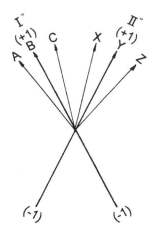

Figure 3.5. The same test vectors as in Figures 3.3 and 3.4, but here the factor axes (Factors I" and II") are no longer orthogonal, but *oblique*, at an angular separation of 55°, hence $r = +.57$. The oblique factors more closely approximate simple structure than the rotated orthogonal factors in Figure 3.4.

fact that fourth-order factors virtually never emerge in the mental abilities domain.) It is important to note that the extraction of higher-order factors from the oblique first-order factors does not affect the proportion of the total test variance accounted for by all of the factors or each test's communality,[12] which are identical for both the rotated and the unrotated factors, whether they are orthogonal or oblique, hierarchical or nonhierarchical.

NOTES

1. Published as "Intelligence and its measurement: A symposium." *Journal of Educational Psychology*, 1921, *12*, 123–147, 195–216, 271–275.

2. Sternberg & Detterman, 1986.

3. I have written more extensively elsewhere on the intractable problem of the definition of "intelligence" and the abandonment of this term in scientific discourse (Jensen, 1987b; 1993a; 1994c).

4. Because the size of the phi coefficient (ϕ) as a measure of correlation between two items is affected by the item variances when they are unequal for the two items, a correction (known as ϕ/ϕ_{max}) for unequal variances is often applied to obtain the expected correlation if both items had equal variances. [Note: The item variance (σ_i^2) is directly related to the proportion (p) of persons passing the item: $\sigma_i^2 = p(1 - p)$.] A *tetrachoric* correlation (r_t) is also used for item intercorrelations, particularly if the sample size is very large and the correlations are to be factor analyzed, in which case the r_t has important technical advantages over the phi coefficient. These points are fully explicated in many statistical and psychometric textbooks.

5. The covariance between two items, *a* and *b*, is $Cov_{ab} = \phi_{ab}\sigma_a\sigma_b$. (In the contin-

gency table shown in the text, the covariance between items A and B is .521 × .497 × .500 = .129.)

6. Factor analysis can also be applied to a covariance matrix, although factor analysis of a correlation matrix is the much more usual procedure. A correlation coefficient is simply a standardized covariance, that is, a correlation coefficient (unlike a covariance) is completely independent of the particular variables' scale of measurement and of their means and variances. It is thus a pure index of relationship. The *covariance* of variables X and Y, where X and Y are the raw measurements, is $\text{Cov}_{xy} = \Sigma(X-\overline{X})(Y-\overline{Y})/N$. The *correlation* of X and Y is $r_{xy} = \Sigma(X-\overline{X})(Y-\overline{Y})/N\sigma_x\sigma_y$. (*Note:* $\overline{X}$ and $\overline{Y}$ are the means of variables X and Y; σ_x and σ_y are their respective standard deviations.)

7. The three great classics of factor analysis are by Burt (1941), Thomson (1951), and Thurstone (1947). The best-known modern textbooks are by Cattell (1978), Comrey & Lee (1992), Gorsuch (1983), Harman (1976), and Mulaik (1972).

8. There are two main purposes of factor analysis—*exploratory* factor analysis (EPA) and *confirmatory* factor analysis (CFA), which differ in methodology. But this distinction is not important for understanding the gist of factor analysis. CFA is in fact a quite recent development in the history of factor analysis, and probably most factor analyses seen in the present literature are still EFA. EFA is used to analyze a set of variables when there are no definite hypotheses about the factor structure of the set of variables, although we may have some speculations or intuitions about this based on prior experience or theoretical considerations. One begins without any definite idea about the number of factors or the degree to which each of the variables is loaded on each factor. Whatever factor structure is latent in the set of variables will emerge from the analysis. In CFA, on the other hand, one begins with a definite hypothesis (or a number of competing hypotheses) about the factor structure (i.e., the number of factors and the magnitudes of their loadings in each variable) and the method of CFA statistically tests the "goodness of fit" of the data to the hypothesized factor structure, or *model*, as it is also called. Thus CFA permits rigorous statistical evaluation of competing models or theories concerning the "covariance structure" of the domain of variables under study. CFA usually comes into the picture at a later stage of research, after EFA has been used to map out the territory, so to speak, and when competing theories about details of the map are in contention. CFA and its cousin, path analysis, are specialized methodologies in a broad class of statistical methods for the analysis of covariance structures. An excellent introduction to these topics (including EFA) is provided by Loehlin (1992).

9. Carroll (1993a), in an encyclopedic study of the results of the factor analysis of cognitive abilities, has performed factor analyses on some 460 different sets of mental ability tests, encompassing almost every kind of cognitive ability that has been psychometrically assessed, and has found that *g* is always either a second-order or third-order factor in a hierarchical factor analysis. Below *g*, only some seven or eight broad second-order factors have been reliably established. The total number of first-order factors in the whole abilities domain is undoubtedly very large. But in principle the number of theoretically possible first-order factors is indeterminate, and each successive new first-order factor becomes harder to discover reliably. To date some fifty to sixty are claimed to have been identified.

10. Schmid & Leiman (1957). Wherry (1959) presented a computationally different but mathematically equivalent method for arriving at the same factor matrix as is yielded by the Schmid-Leiman procedure. For more discussion of the comparison of these methods with other types of factor analysis, see Jensen & Weng (1994).

11. It is possible to obtain "impossible" correlations among a set of three (or more) variables, if each of the correlations was not obtained in one and the same subject sample. The "impossible" correlations are a result of the sampling error of the correlations. For example, the correlations (necessarily obtained in different samples) between variables X, Y, and Z of $r_{xy} = .90$, $r_{xz} = .80$, and $r_{yz} = .20$, are "impossible" estimates of the true correlations in the population. If X is highly related to Y and to Z, then it is impossible for Y to have such a low degree of relationship to Z. A test of whether any three correlation coefficients are "impossible" estimates of the true correlations in the population is that the following equation (known as the *consistency relation* among correlation coefficients) is violated (from Walker & Lev, 1953, p. 344):

$$1 - r^2_{xy} - r^2_{xz} - r^2_{yz} + 2r_{xy}r_{xz}r_{yz} > 0$$

12. For didactic simplicity, this example assumes that none of the tests' variances contains any unique variance (i.e., specific variance + error variance), and therefore each test's *communality* (i.e., the proportion of a test's total variance that is common to other tests in the analysis) is unity, or 1. This is represented in Figure 3.3 by all the test vectors having unit length. When the tests' variances contain uniqueness (in addition to common factor variance) and the tests' communalities are therefore less than 1 (usually by various amounts), then the correlation between two tests (say, X and Y) in the factor space has the following relation to the angular separation of the tests' vectors: $r_{xy} = h_x h_y \cos \theta$, where h is the square root of the test's communality (h^2). The symbol h^2 for communality comes from the word *hypotenuse*. Referring back to Figure 3.3, note the projection of vector Z on Factor II; it forms a right triangle, of which the vector Z is the hypotenuse. Similarly, the projection of Z on I forms a right triangle, of which Z is the hypotenuse. By the Pythagorean theorem, the square of the hypotenuse is equal to the sum of the squares of the two sides. The two sides of each triangle in this case are the loadings of test Z on Factors I and II. These loadings are .8 and .6, so $h^2 = .8^2 + .6^2 = .64 + .36 = 1.00$. Therefore, a test's communality (h^2) is the sum of its squared loadings on each orthogonal common factor. In a factor analysis, a test's communality is an important item of information, as it tells us the proportion of the test's total variance that is accounted for by the factors. The proportion of variance unaccounted for by the common factors is the test's *unique* variance (i.e., $u^2 = 1 - h^2$). A given test's communality cannot be known until the factor analysis is completed, but it can usually be closely estimated by the squared multiple correlation (SMC) between the test and all the other tests in the matrix. The computational procedure in factor analysis usually begins with these computable SMC estimates of the communalities in the main diagonal of the correlation matrix. An iterative procedure then converges the estimated h^2 values toward the tests' true communalities. Largely because of this tedious iteration, the computations of a single factor analysis, which in the days of electrical calculators could take a skilled technician a full forty-hour week, can now be performed by high-speed electronic computers in just a second or so after the data have been entered into the computer.

13. *Principal factor analysis* (PFA) should be clearly distinguished from *principal components analysis* (PCA). In the present example (Figure 3.3) all of the test vectors are of unit length and therefore each has a communality equal to 1. In this case, all of the variance in the tests is accounted for by the factors, so there is no specificity or error variance in any of the tests. Therefore, this didactic example is both a PFA and a PCA. The distinction between PCA and PFA arises when the tests' variances include uniqueness as well as common factor variance, making the tests' communalities less than unity.

The distinction between PFA and PCA is that PFA analyzes only the common factor variance of the tests, whereas PCA analyzes the tests' total variance into orthogonal axes, or components. (These may also be rotated in the same ways as principal factors.) Therefore, tests' (squared) factor loadings in a PFA do not contain the tests specificity or error variance. In a PCA, each of the tests' squared component loadings contains some small part of the variance attributed to the tests' specificity and measurement error in addition to their common factor variance. In principal components (PCs), the specificity and error are rather evenly spread throughout all of the components, and because PCA analyzes all of the variance in the tests, the number of components that can be extracted is the same as the number of tests. In PFA, however, the number of factors will be less, usually much less, than the number of tests, because only the common factor variance enters into the analysis. Assuming that the PFA has been done properly and all of the common factors have been extracted, the sum of the tests' communalities indicates the proportion of the total variance accounted for by common factors. The mathematical procedures of PFA can be thought of as first separating the total variance into common factor variance and unique variance and then performing a PCA on just the tests' common factor variance.

For theoretical purposes, such as generating hypotheses about the factor structure of a set of tests (as in "exploratory factor analysis"), there is no question that PFA is preferable to PCA. But if one's only purpose is to transform a set of n correlated variables into a set of n perfectly uncorrelated variables (i.e., principal component scores) which retain the total variance of the original variables, then PCA is the proper method. PCA is used in this manner in quantum mechanics and in other fields, where working with uncorrelated variables is mathematically simpler than working with correlated variables.

Because each successive PC extracted accounts for a smaller proportion of the total variance, it is often possible to account for a large proportion of the total variance by extracting many fewer PCs than the total number of tests without much loss of information. Therefore, if one's purpose does not demand the degree of precision that would be afforded by the total variance in many tests, a relatively small set of PCs that will account for some usefully large proportion of the variance can be used to obtain component scores. For example, if scores on a battery of a dozen tests (entered into a multiple regression equation) are a good predictor of some criterion, a PCA may reveal that only three components account for nearly all of the variance in the dozen tests and that the simple sum of the (uncorrelated) PC scores (derived from the three PCs) predicts the criterion with nearly the same degree of accuracy as if one had used the full dozen test scores in a multiple regression equation to predict the criterion. PCA is often used to gain this kind of efficiency.

A PCA is often used preliminary to a PFA to determine the number of PFs that should be extracted from a correlation matrix. This can be determined from the PCA in several ways, which are discussed in textbooks of factor analysis. Probably the most commonly used criterion is the Kaiser-Guttman rule: the number of factors should be equal to the number of PCs with *eigenvalues* larger than 1. (When important theoretical issues are at stake, it is usually advisable to get a consensus between the eigenvalues > 1 rule and other criteria, such as R. B. Cattell's scree test and the Humphreys-Montanelli procedure, which are described in most modern textbooks of factor analysis. The "number of factors" issue, however, is now most definitively settled by confirmatory factor analysis, implemented by the LISREL computer programs [for references to this see Loehlin, 1992].) Eigenvalues (also termed *latent roots*), which are an inherent property of a correlation matrix, are determined exactly by a PCA. PCs' eigenvalues decrease rapidly in size, from the first PC to the nth PC (where n is the number of tests = the number of PCs). The logic of the Kaiser-Guttman rule is essentially this: Since each test's standardized variance = 1, the total variance of the n tests in a correlation matrix is equal to n, and the sum of the eigenvalues of all of the PCs extracted from a correlation matrix = n. If the correlation matrix is random (i.e., the correlations are derived from random numbers), there are of course no true common factors. If such a random correlation matrix were subjected to a PCA, all of the resulting eigenvalues would be very close to 1; the first few PCs would have eigenvalues just slightly greater than 1, due to small, purely chance correlations; the remaining eigenvalues would be slightly less than 1. Therefore, in factor analyzing a real, or nonrandom, correlation matrix, the eigenvalues of some of the PCs will be considerably greater than 1, and the cutoff for the number of authentic factors should be equal to the number of PCs with eigenvalues greater than 1.

Chapter 4

Models and Characteristics of *g*

The general factor, *g*, can be extracted from the correlation matrix of a battery of mental ability tests by a number of different methods of factor analysis and according to different models of the factor structure of abilities. Provided the number of tests in the analyzed battery is sufficiently large to yield reliable factors and the tests are sufficiently diverse in item types and information content to reflect more than a single narrow ability, a *g* factor always emerges. The only exception occurs when orthogonal rotation of the principal axes is employed. That method expressly precludes the appearance of a *g* factor. With orthogonal rotation, the *g* variance remains in the factor matrix, but is dispersed among all of the group (or primary) factors. This method of factor analysis (for which the most common factor rotation method is known as *varimax*) is not appropriate to any domain of variables, such as mental abilities, in which substantial positive correlations among all the variables reveal a large general factor.

Among the various methods of factor analysis that do not mathematically preclude the appearance of *g* when it is actually latent in the correlation matrix, a hierarchical model is generally the most satisfactory, both theoretically and statistically. In a hierarchical analysis, a number of correlated group factors (first-order factors) are extracted first. The *g* factor then emerges as a second-order factor (or as a third-order factor in some very large and diverse batteries) from the correlations among the first-order factors (or among the second-order factors when *g* is at the third order).

The *g* factor is found to be remarkably invariant across all the various methods of factor analysis except those that mathematically preclude the appearance of a general factor.

The *g* factor is found to be relatively invariant across different batteries of diverse tests of mental ability. This fact justifies the postulation of a *true g* (analogous to *true score* in classical measurement theory), of which the *g* obtained in any empirical study is an estimate.

The *g* factor is also found to be ubiquitous and relatively invariant across various racial and cultural groups.

The form of the population distribution of *g* is not known, because *g* cannot yet be measured on a ratio scale, but there are good theoretical reasons to assume that the distribution of *g* approximates the normal, or bell-shaped, curve.

The *g* factor is ubiquitous in all mental ability tests, and tests' *g* loadings are a *continuous* variable, ranging from values that are slightly greater than zero on some tests to values that are near the reliability coefficient of some tests.

Although certain types of tests consistently show higher *g* loadings than other tests, it is conceptually incorrect to regard characteristics (e.g., relation eduction and abstract reasoning) of such tests as the "essence" or "defining characteristic" of *g*.

These features of tests may indicate the site of *g*, but not its nature. Unlike the group factors, the *g* factor cannot be described in terms of the item characteristics and information content of tests. Nor is *g* a measure of test difficulty; a test's *g* loading and its difficulty are conceptually separate.

It is wrong to regard *g* as a cognitive process, or as an operating principle of the mind, or as a design feature of the brain's neural circuitry. At the level of psychometrics, ideally, *g* may be thought of as a distillate of the common source of individual differences in all mental tests, completely stripped of their distinctive features of information content, skill, strategy, and the like. In this sense, *g* can be roughly likened to a computer's central processing unit. The knowledge and skills tapped by mental test performance merely provide a *vehicle* for the measurement of *g*. Therefore, we cannot begin to fathom the causal underpinning of *g* merely by examining the most highly *g*-loaded psychometric tests. At the level of causality, *g* is perhaps best regarded as a source of variance in performance associated with individual differences in the speed or efficiency of the neural processes that affect the kinds of behavior called mental abilities (as defined in Chapter 3).

The previous chapters have demonstrated the essential basis of the *g* revealed by factor analysis—the correlations between mental tests of every kind are all positive. But factor analysis also reveals other factors, although they are less general than *g*. The most general are the second-order group factors. The first-order, or primary, factors are of still lesser generality.

The terminology "models" of *g* refers to the different ways that the relationship between *g* and the other factors can be represented. Each representation is derived from the factor analysis of the matrix of correlations among a variety of tests. Critics of *g* argue that, because there are different methods for factor analyzing a correlation matrix, these differing methods, even when applied to one and the same matrix, necessarily yield quite different factors, including different *g* factors, or even no *g* at all.

If this criticism were true, and especially if there were no theoretically compelling basis for preferring one of the various methods of factor analysis over the others, then the importance of *g* as a scientific construct would surely be questionable, at least insofar as *g* is determined by any type of factor analysis. Indeed, if the data supported this criticism, I would not have written this book. The counterargument against the criticism, however, is technically quite complex and has two parts—the mathematical principles underlying factor analysis (or the related technique of principal components analysis [see Chapter 3, Note 13]) and the empirical evidence from a wide variety of studies of human performance.

With the help of experts on the mathematical foundations of factor analysis, I examined this issue in detail and reported the results in a lengthy technical editorial in the journal *Intelligence*.[1] The conclusions can be explained fairly simply, however, with the aid of some diagrams.

The Spearman Model. This is the simplest possible factor structure (Figure 4.1). The nine variables (V1 through V9) in the factor analysis are tests and *u* is the variable's correlation with whatever the variable measures uniquely, that is, whatever the variable measures that is not measured by any of the other variables in the factor analysis. (This quantity, *u*, termed the variable's *uniqueness* consists of specificity + random error.) We see that *g* is in all nine Vs and is the only factor that they have in common. It is possible to find sets of a relatively small number of mental tests that, when factor-analyzed, conform to this simple model of a single common factor. This is not generally the case, however. Spearman's method of factor analysis (which is now obsolete) can extract a proper *g* from such a set of tests, and so can other, more modern methods. The disadvantage of Spearman's method is that if his tetrad criterion shows that more than one common factor exists in the tests, his method of factor analysis will not work.[2] If used, it gives an incorrect *g*. The degree of incorrectness depends on the nature of the matrix to which it is applied.

The Thurstone Model. This is a multifactor model (see Figure 4.2).

As shown here it has three group factors, without any general factor common to all of the variables. The method used to estimate the factors in Thurstone's model is typically principal factor analysis with orthogonal rotation of the factor axes to simple structure. The most widely used method of rotation is Kaiser's *varimax* criterion, which tries to achieve *simple structure* by orthogonal rotation

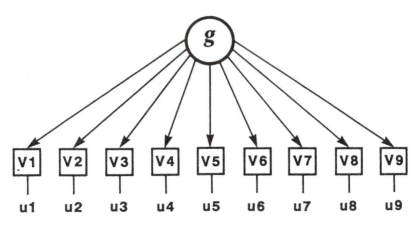

Figure 4.1. Spearman Model. The simplest possible factor model: A single general factor, originally proposed by Spearman as a *two-factor* model, the two factors being the general factor (*g*) common to all of the variables (V) and the "factors" specific to each variable, termed *specificity* (*s*). Each variable's *uniqueness* (*u*) comprises *s* and measurement error. (From Jensen & Weng, 1994. Used with permission of Ablex.)

of the factor axes to a position that maximizes the variance of the squared factor loadings on each factor. This has the effect of giving each test a large loading on only one of the first-order factors and small loadings on all of the other first-order factors. The following idealized hypothetical factor matrix illustrates a perfect simple structure of orthogonal (uncorrelated) factors, in which all of the variance on a given test is explained by a single factor.

Tests	Factors		
	I	*II*	*III*
a	1	0	0
b	1	0	0
c	1	0	0
d	0	1	0
e	0	1	0
f	0	1	0
g	0	0	1
h	0	0	1
i	0	0	1

This orthogonal simple structure model, it turns out, has proved inappropriate in the abilities domain, and in fact Thurstone (1931) himself early on used *oblique* rotation of the factor axes to achieve the best possible approximation to simple structure. (Oblique factors are correlated with each other.) He only subsequently advanced orthogonal rotation to avoid some of the complications as-

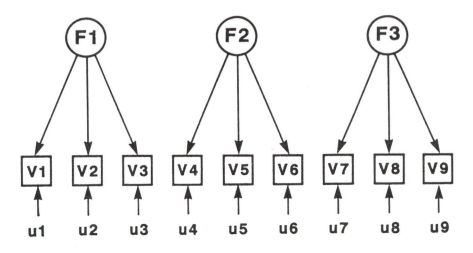

Figure 4.2. Thurstone Model. A multiple-factor model with three independent _group factors_ (F1, F2, F3), without a _g_ factor common to all of the variables—a model originally proposed by Thurstone. (From Jensen & Weng, 1994. Used with permission of Ablex.)

sociated with oblique rotation. But it was apparent that, in the abilities domain, a good fit of the data to a simple structure model could not be achieved with orthogonal rotation, because a general factor permeates all of the primary abilities. Orthogonal rotation would achieve simple structure only if Thurstone's original theory were true. (That is the theory that mental ability consists of a number of distinct, uncorrelated abilities represented by the primary factors, and that there is no general factor in the abilities domain.) But that theory has long since been proven false. Thurstone assiduously attempted to devise tests that would provide factor-pure measures of what he called the _primary mental abilities_ revealed by his method of multiple factor analysis.[3] But it proved impossible to devise a test that was a pure measure of any primary factor. In samples of the general population, Thurstone's tests of the ''primary mental abilities'' always showed quite large correlations with each other. This was because they all measured _g_ in addition to whatever ''primary ability'' they were intended to measure as purely as possible. The primary abilities were not pure at all. Although it was possible to devise tests that would measure any one of the primary mental abilities and no other primary ability, the test always measured _g_ as well. And usually the test's _g_ variance was larger than the variance of the particular primary ability factor it was specially devised to measure. In other words, _g_ accounted for more than the primary ability. Thurstone therefore returned to his earlier position and proposed oblique rotation of the primary factor axes to achieve the best possible approximation to simple structure. The correlations between the primary factors could then be factor analyzed to yield _g_ as a higher-

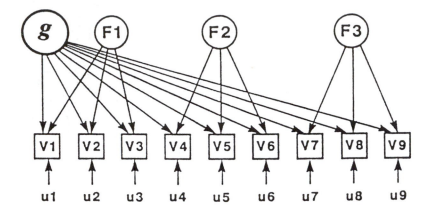

Figure 4.3. Bifactor Model. Each variable (V) is loaded on one of the three group factors (F) and is also loaded on *g*, but the variables' *g* loadings are not constrained by their loadings on the group factors (as in the case of the hierarchical model); variables' correlations with F and with *g* are independent of one another. (From Jensen & Weng, 1994. Used with permission of Ablex.)

order factor. This method is known as a hierarchical factor analysis. But before we discuss it, there is one other model that should be considered.

The Bifactor Model. This model was proposed by Karl Holzinger, a student of Spearman's, who later became a professor in the University of Chicago, where Thurstone was also a professor. Holzinger's method of bifactor analysis, in effect, combines the Spearman model with the Thurstone model. It yields both Spearman's *g* factor and Thurstone's group factors, but without deriving *g* from the correlations among the obliquely rotated primary factors. The procedure consists essentially of first extracting *g* from the correlation matrix in such a way as to leave all-positive correlations in the *residual matrix* (i.e., the correlation matrix after the *g* factor has been removed). With *g* removed from the correlation matrix, a Thurstone-type of factor analysis (or a principal factor analysis) can then obtain quite clean-cut orthogonal primary factors that closely conform to simple structure. The bifactor model, shown in Figure 4.3, therefore reveals both *g* and the group (or primary) factors, which are all orthogonal to each other.[4]

 The Orthogonalized Hierarchical Model. As this has become the generally preferred model, it should be explicated in somewhat more detail than the others.[5] An actual correlation matrix will be subjected to a hierarchical analysis to illustrate how it works. The hierarchical model is shown in Figure 4.4 in terms of nine variables (V1 through V9), three first-order factors (F1, F2, F3), and the second-order factor, *g*. The *correlation* matrix that has been subjected to the hierarchical analysis is shown in Table 4.1. The end result of the computational procedure (Schmid-Leiman, 1975) is the *factor* matrix shown in Table 4.2.

 The correlation matrix (Table 4.1) simply shows the correlation coefficients

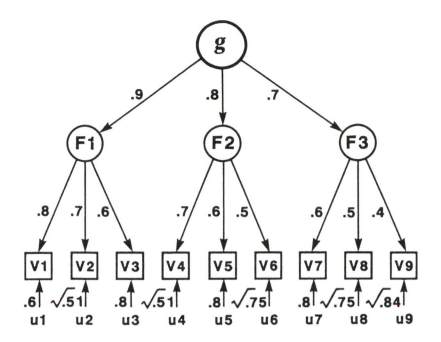

Figure 4.4. Hierarchical Model. The first-order factors (F) are correlated, giving rise to a second-order factor, *g*. Variables (V) are correlated with *g* only via their correlation with the three first-order factors. (From Jensen & Weng, 1994. Used with permission of Ablex.)

of every variable with every other variable. The factor matrix (Table 4.2) shows the loadings of each of the nine variables on *g* and on each of the three first-order factors. Here we see a perfect simple structure of the first-order factors. Variables V1, V2, and V3, for example, measure only *g* + F1, with zero loadings on F2 and F3; variables V4, V5, and V6 measure only *g* + F2; and so on. The *communality* (h^2) is the proportion of the variable's total variance that is attributable to the common factors; it is the sum of the variable's squared factor loadings on *g* and the first-order factor(s) [e.g., $(.72)^2 + (.3487)^2 = .64$]. The *uniqueness* ($u^2$) is the variance not accounted for by common factors. It consists of *specific* variance and *error* variance. The sum of h^2 and u^2 for each variable is the variable's total standardized variance and therefore must equal 1. The bottom of Table 4.2 shows the variance of each factor (i.e., the sum of the squared factor loadings) and (in the final row) the percentage of the total variance on all of the variables that is attributable to each factor.

Typically, *g* accounts for a larger proportion (i.e., a higher percentage) of the total variance than any other factor and often accounts for more of the variance than all of the other factors combined. The sum of the communalities (3.36, or 37.33% of the total variance) is relatively small and indicates that these variables possess a high degree of uniqueness, which accounts for 62.67% of the total

Table 4.1
Correlation Matrix[a] for Hierarchical Factor Analysis

					VARIABLES				
	V1	V2	V3	V4	V5	V6	V7	V8	V9
V1		5600	4800	4032	3456	2880	3024	2520	2016
V2	5600		4200	3528	3024	2520	2646	2205	1764
V3	4800	4200		3024	2592	2160	2268	1890	1512
V4	4032	3528	3024		4200	3500	2352	1960	1568
V5	3456	3024	2592	4200		3000	2016	1680	1344
V6	2880	2520	2160	3500	3000		1680	1400	1120
V7	3024	2646	2268	2352	2016	1680		3000	2400
V8	2520	2205	1890	1960	1680	1400	3000		2000
V9	2016	1764	1512	1568	1344	1120	2400	2000	

[a]Decimals omitted.

variance in these variables. (Since we do not know the reliability coefficients of these nine variables, we cannot determine how much of the uniqueness for each variable consists of specificity and how much consists of error.)

From the information given in Table 4.2, it is possible to calculate the direct (nonresidualized) correlation coefficients shown alongside each of the arrows in Figure 4.4. For example, *g* is correlated .9 with F1, and F1 is correlated .8 with V1. The correlation between V1 and *g*, therefore, is the product of the two correlations that connect *g* with V1, that is, .8 × .9 = .72, which is the *g* loading of V1. V1 and V2 are connected only by F1, so their correlation is .8 × .7 = .56. But V1 and V4 are connected by F1, *g*, and F2, so the correlation between V1 and V4 is [.8 × .9] × [.8 × .7] = .4032. (The correlations between the first-order factors are calculated the same way; for example, F1 and F2 are correlated .9 × .8 = .72.)

We could proceed in this way to reconstitute all of the correlations in Table 4.1 from the factor structure shown in Table 4.2 and Figure 4.4.[6] It can be done with perfect exactitude here, because this correlation matrix was specially made up for this demonstration. In reality, the reconstituted matrix always shows slight random deviations from the exact values of the original correlation matrix. If the factor analysis was done properly, the residual matrix (i.e., the matrix of

Table 4.2
Factor Matrix for Orthogonalized Hierarchical Model

Variable	2nd Order	First Order			Communality	Uniqueness
		Factor Loadings				
	g	F1	F2	F3	h²	u²
V1	.72	.3487	0	0	.64	.36
V2	.63	.3051	0	0	.49	.51
V3	.54	.2615	0	0	.36	.64
V4	.56	0	.42	0	.49	.51
V5	.48	0	.36	0	.36	.64
V6	.40	0	.30	0	.25	.75
V7	.42	0	0	.4284	.36	.64
V8	.35	0	0	.3570	.25	.75
V9	.28	0	0	.2856	.16	.84
Var.	2.2882	.283	.396	.3925	3.36	5.64
% Var.	25.42	3.15	4.40	4.36	37.33	62.67

original correlations minus the matrix of reconstituted correlations) would consist of only the test specificity and random error.

HOW INVARIANT IS *g* ACROSS DIFFERENT METHODS OF FACTOR ANALYSIS?

This is one of the crucially important questions in our present inquiry. Obviously the simplest way to answer it is to simulate a variety of correlation matrices that are similar to those found for actual mental test data but for which we already know the true factor structure exactly, and then see how accurately different factor analytic models and methods can estimate[7] the "true" factors known to exist in these artificial matrices.

This is just what I did, in collaboration with Dr. Li-Jen Weng, at that time a postdoctoral research scholar at the University of California, Berkeley, and a specialist in factor analysis and mathematical statistics. Besides applying six different methods of factor analysis to four simulated matrices for which the factors were exactly known, we also applied nine different methods of factor analysis to a real correlation matrix based on twenty-four tests administered to 145 students in grades 7 and 8. Of course, we used no type of factor analysis that is expressly designed to preclude the appearance of a general factor (such as orthogonal rotation of the primary factors). We were concerned here exclusively with the amount of variation in the *g* factor when it is extracted by the various methods most commonly described in modern textbooks of factor analysis.

Since we knew exactly the true *g* loadings of the variables in the artificial correlation matrix (because we had initially generated the correlation matrix from the "true" factor loadings), it was simply a matter of comparing these true loadings with each of the various sets of *g* loadings extracted from the artificial matrix by the six different methods of factor analysis. A set of factor loadings (such as the ones shown previously in the columns of Table 4.2) is called a *column vector*. We compared the column vector of true *g* loadings with the column vector of the *g* loadings obtained by each method of factor analysis. The degree of similarity of the two vectors was measured by the *coefficient of congruence*[8] (r_c) between the two vectors. The amount of discrepancy between the loadings was measured by the average absolute difference between the true and obtained *g* loadings (calculated as the *root mean square difference*).[9]

The result of this analysis was that every one of the methods of factor analysis estimated the true *g* so closely that there was hardly any basis for choosing between them. The congruence coefficients between the true *g* factor and the *g* factor obtained by the various methods ranged from +.997 to +.999, with an average of +.998. This is especially remarkable because some of the artificial matrices were specifically designed to "trick" particular methods into yielding estimates that would deviate markedly from the true values, for example by simulating tests of highly mixed factor composition (e.g., each test having substantial loadings on all of the primary factors). The root mean square difference between the true *g* and the estimated *g* averaged .047 (ranging from .031 to .059) for the various methods, which is negligible compared to the average size of the factor loadings (about .50). In brief, when estimating the true *g*, the various factor analytic methods were all remarkably and similarly robust and arrived at estimates that deviated very little from the true values.

For the real data obtained on twenty-four tests administered to students, of course, we do not know the true *g*, but we can compare the estimates of it obtained from ten different methods of factor analyses. Given the results of the previous analyses of artificial correlation matrices, finding a high degree of agreement among the ten column vectors of *g* loadings based on a real correlation matrix would permit the reasonable inference that the hypothetical true *g* for the matrix was closely approximated by all of the various factor analytic methods. Again, we found remarkably high agreement. The forty-five congruence coefficients between the ten *g* vectors ranged from +.991 to 1.000, averaging +.995.

Another study[10], conducted at Brooks Air Force Base with 9,173 recruits, investigated the invariance of *g* obtained from the ten tests of the Armed Services Vocational Aptitude Battery (ASVAB). The ASVAB was factor analyzed by 14 different methods, and *g* factor scores for every subject were calculated from the results of each of the 14 methods. The average correlation between the 14 sets of *g* factor scores was .984, indicating that the different methods of factor analysis resulted in very little variation among the obtained *g* factors.

The gist of these various analyses is that whatever variation exists among the myriad estimates of *g* that have been reported since the beginning of factor analysis, exceedingly little of it can be attributed to differences in the methods of factor analysis employed. However, there are several other possible sources of deviance of an obtained *g*.

STATISTICAL SAMPLING ERROR

The size of *g*, that is, the proportion of the total variance that *g* accounts for in any given battery of tests, depends to some extent on the statistical characteristics of the group tested (as compared with a large random sample of the general population). Most factor analytic studies of tests reported in the literature are not based on representative samples of the general population. Rather, subject samples are usually drawn from some segment of the population (often college students or military trainees) that does not display either the mean level of mental ability or the range of mental ability that exists in the total population. Because *g* is by far the most important ability factor in determining the aggregation of people into such statistically distinguishable groups, the study groups will be more homogeneous in *g* than in any other ability factors. Hence when the *g* factor is extracted, it is actually smaller than it would be if extracted from data for the general population. Relative to other factors, *g* is typically underestimated in most studies. This is especially so in samples drawn from the students at the most selective colleges and universities, where admission is based on such highly *g*-loaded criteria as superior grades in high school and high scores on scholastic aptitude tests.

Many factor analytic studies have been based on recruits in the military, which is a truncated sample of the population, with the lower 10 percent (i.e., IQs below 80) excluded by congressional mandate. Also, the various branches of the armed services differ in their selection criteria based in part on mental test scores (rejecting the lowest-scoring 10 to 30 percent), with consequently different range restrictions of *g*.

The samples most representative of the population are the large samples used to standardize most modern IQ tests and the studies of elementary schoolchildren randomly sampled from urban, suburban, and rural schools. Because the dropout rate increases with grade level and is inversely related to IQ, high school students are a somewhat more *g*-restricted sample of the general population.

A theoretically interesting phenomenon is that *g* accounts for *less* of the variance in a battery of tests for the *upper* half of the population distribution of IQ than for the lower half, even though the upper and lower halves do not differ in the range of test scores or in their variance.[11] The basis of *g* is that the correlations among a variety of tests are all positive. Since the correlations are smaller, on average, in the upper half than in the lower half of the IQ distribution, it implies that abilities are more highly differentiated in the upper half of the ability distribution. That is, relatively more of the total variance consists of group factors and the tests' specificity, and relatively less consists of *g* for the upper half of the IQ distribution than for the lower half. (For a detailed discussion of this phenomenon, see Appendix A.)

Specificity (*s*) is the least consistent characteristic of tests across different factor analyses, because the amount of specific variance in a test is a function of the number and the variety of the other tests in the factor analysis. Holding constant the number of tests, the specificity of each test *increases* as the variety of the tests in the battery increases. As variety decreases, or the more that the tests in a battery are made to resemble one another, the variance that would otherwise constitute specificity becomes common factor variance and forms *group factors*. If the variety of tests in a battery is held constant, specificity *decreases* as the number of tests in the battery is increased. As similar tests are added, they contribute more to the common factor variance (*g* + group factors), leaving less residual variance (which includes specificity).

As more and more different tests are included in a battery, each newly added test has a greater chance of sharing the common factor variance, thereby losing some of its specificity. For example, if a battery of tests includes the ubiquitous *g* and three group factors but includes only one test of short-term memory (e.g., digit span), that test's variance components will consist only of *g* plus *s* plus *error*. If at least two more tests of short-term memory (say, word span and repetition of sentences) are then added to this battery, the three short-term memory tests will form a group factor. Most of what was the digit span test's specific variance, when it stood alone in the battery, is now aggregated into a group factor (composed of digit span, word span, and repetition of sentences), leaving little residual specificity in each of these related tests.

Theoretically, the only condition that limits the transformation of specific variance into common factor variance when new tests are added or existing tests are made more alike is the reliability of the individual test scores. When the correlation between any two or more tests is as high as their reliability coefficients will allow (the square root of the product of the tests' reliability coefficients is the mathematical upper bound), they no longer qualify as separate tests and cannot legitimately be used in the same factor analysis to create another group factor. A group factor created in this manner is considered spurious. But there are also some nonspurious group factors that are so small and inconsistently replicable across different test batteries or different population samples that they are trivial, theoretically and practically.

PSYCHOMETRIC SAMPLING ERROR

How invariant is the _g_ extracted from different collections of tests when the method of factor analysis and the subject sample remain constant? There is no method of factor analysis that can yield _exactly_ the same _g_ when different tests are included in the battery. As John B. Carroll (1993a, p. 596) aptly put it, the _g_ factor is "colored" or "flavored" by its ingredients, which are the tests or primary factors whose variance is dominated by _g_. The _g_ is always influenced, more or less, by both the nature and the variety of the tests from which it is extracted. If the _g_ extracted from different batteries of tests was not substantially consistent, however, _g_ would have little theoretical or practical importance as a scientific construct. But the fact is that _g_ remains quite invariant across many different collections of tests.

It should be recognized, of course, that in factor analysis, as in every form of measurement in science, either direct or indirect (e.g., through logical inference), there are certain procedural rules that must be followed if valid measures are to be obtained. The accuracy of quantitative analysis in chemistry, for example, depends on using reagents of standardized purity. Similarly, in factor analysis, the extraction of _g_ depends on certain requirements for proper psychometric sampling.

The _number of tests_ is the first consideration. The extraction of _g_ as a second-order factor in a hierarchical analysis requires a minimum of nine tests from which at least three primary factors can be obtained.

That three or more primary factors are called for implies the second requirement: a _variety of tests_ (with respect to their information content, skills, and task demands on a variety of mental operations) is needed to form at least three or more distinct primary factors. In other words, the particular collection of tests used to estimate _g_ should come as close as possible, with some limited number of tests, to being a representative sample of all types of mental tests, and the various kinds of tests should be represented as equally as possible. If a collection of tests appears to be quite limited in variety, or is markedly unbalanced in the varieties it contains, the extracted _g_ is probably contaminated by non-_g_ variance and is therefore a poor representation of true _g_.

If we factor-analyzed a battery consisting, say, of ten kinds of numerical tests, two tests of verbal reasoning, and one test of spatial reasoning, for example, we would obtain a quite distorted _g_. The general factor (or nominal _g_) of this battery would actually consist of _g_ plus some sizable admixture of a numerical ability factor. Therefore, this nominal _g_ would differ considerably from another nominal _g_ obtained from a battery consisting of, say, ten verbal tests, two spatial reasoning tests, and one numerical test. The nominal _g_ of this second battery would really consist of _g_ plus a large admixture of verbal ability.

The problem of contamination is especially significant when one extracts *g* as the first factor (PF1) in a principal factor analysis. The largest PF1 loadings that emerge are all on tests of the same type, so a marked imbalance in the types of tests entering into the analysis will tend to distort the PF1 as a representation of *g*. If there are enough tests to permit a proper hierarchical analysis, however, an imbalance in the variety of tests is overcome to a large extent by the aggregation of the overrepresented tests into a single group factor. This factor then carries a weight that is more equivalent to the other group factors (which are based on fewer tests), and it is from the correlations among the group factors that the higher-order *g* is derived. This is one of the main advantages of a hierarchical analysis.

Empirical Estimates of the Consistency of *g* across Different Test Batteries. How consistent is the *g* loading of a given mental test when it is factor analyzed among several different sets of tests when both the method of analysis and the subject sample are held constant? This important question has received surprisingly little empirical investigation. In his encyclopedic survey of factor analytic studies, Carroll (1993a, pp. 591–597) examined 153 hierarchical *g* loadings in 142 data sets and surmised that "if it were possible to obtain factor scores for each of these factors in some appropriate population, these factor scores might be highly correlated, especially after correction for attenuation. But it is unlikely that they would be perfectly correlated, because the *g* factor for a given data set is dependent on what lower-order factors or variables are loaded on it" (p. 596).

Carroll made no attempt to estimate the size of the average correlation between the *g* loadings of a given variable when obtained in different test batteries, and I can think of no way of doing so from the available data. Many of the data sets that he reviewed were not intended to meet the psychometric sampling criteria (i.e., *variety* and *balance*) needed to obtain a good *g*. My estimate of the standard deviation of the *g* factor loadings of a given variable obtained in these data sets is about .08. This value is only about one-sixth the average size of the loadings themselves, which indicates a considerable degree of consistency of a variable's *g* loadings across different data sets. In other words, approximately two-thirds of a variable's *g* loadings in these various data sets falls within $\pm.08$ of the overall average *g* loading for that variable.

A much more ideal determination of the consistency of *g* across different data sets was obtained by the psychometrician Robert L. Thorndike (1987), in a study expressly designed for this purpose. Thorndike began with 65 highly diverse tests used by the U.S. Air Force. From 48 of these tests, he formed six non-overlapping batteries, each composed of eight randomly selected tests. The 17 remaining "probe" tests were inserted, one at a time, into each of these six batteries. Thus each of the six batteries was factor-analyzed 17 times, each time with a different one of the 17 probe tests. (Principal factor analysis was used; *g* was represented by the first principal factor.) The six *g* loadings obtained for each of the 17 probe tests were then compared against one another. The *g* loadings for any given test proved to be highly similar across all six batteries, although the average *g* loadings of the different tests varied considerably. The average correlation between *g* loadings across the six batteries was .85. If each battery had contained more tests from the same general test pool, it is a statistical certainty that the average cross-battery correlations between *g* loadings would have been even higher.

Thorndike's finding, which is consistent with Carroll's surmise, constitutes strong evidence that a very similar *g* emerges from most collections of diverse cognitive tests. This analysis also indicates that the invariance of *g* across test batteries does not depend on their having "identical elements" (in the sense of elements of test content) in common. Even highly dissimilar tests (e.g., vocabulary and block designs) have comparably high loadings on one and the same *g* factor.

The Concept of a "True" *g*. Just as we can think statistically in terms of sampling error of a statistic when we randomly select a limited group of subjects from a population, or of measurement error when we obtain a limited number of measurements of a particular variable, so too we can think in terms of *psychometric sampling error* in factor analysis. In making up any collection of cognitive tests, we do not have a perfectly representative sample of the entire universe of all possible cognitive tests. So any one limited sample of tests will not yield exactly the same *g* as another limited sample. The sample values of *g* are affected by subject sampling error, measurement error, and psychometric sampling error. But the fact that *g* is very substantially correlated across different test batteries implies that the differing obtained values of *g* can all be interpreted as estimates of a true (but unknown) *g* (in the same sense that, in classical test theory, an obtained score is viewed as an estimate of a true score).[12]

Cross-Cultural and Cross-Racial Consistency of *g*. Here we are not referring to differences between groups in the average *level* of *g* factor scores, but rather to the similarity of the *g* factor obtained when different groups are given the same battery of tests. Most of the relevant studies have been reviewed and referenced elsewhere.[13] The general finding, even when quite disparate cultures are included (e.g., North America, Europe, and various Asian and African subpopulations), is that there is a remarkable degree of consistency in the factor structure across different racial and cultural groups. All-positive correlations among ability tests, a large *g* factor, and most of the well-established primary mental abilities all show up in virtually every cross-cultural factor analysis. The *g* factor is certainly the most ubiquitous and invariant feature of all these analyses.

The precise degree of cross-cultural similarity of *g* in highly dissimilar cultures, measured by correlations or congruence coefficients, depends considerably on the particular combination of tests factor analyzed. We know, for example, that the Japanese translation of the Wechsler scales given to large samples of the population in Japan shows a *g* whose congruence coefficient with the *g* obtained in the American standardization sample is so high (+.99) as to indicate virtual identity.[14] The congruence coefficient between two large Japanese samples (in Hiroshima and Nagasaki) was also +.99. Many studies, based on various batteries of tests, have shown a similarly high degree of congruence, or even virtual identity, between the *g* factors obtained in large samples of the black and white populations in the United States. The white and black standardization samples for the Wechsler Intelligence Scales for Children (WISC), for example, show a *g* congruence of +.995.[15] (The Verbal, Performance, and Memory factors, independently of *g*, were almost as congruent as *g*.) The percentages of the total WISC variance accounted for by *g* in the black and white standardization samples were 31.7 and 29.7, respectively; a trivial difference.

THE FORM OF THE POPULATION DISTRIBUTION OF *g*

The form of the population distribution of *g* as a measure of individual differences is not known, and at present there is no way of determining it. The form of a distribution can be known directly only if the raw measurements of the variable constitute a true ratio scale, and the measurement of individual differences in *g* is based on a weighted composite of mental test scores, which are not a ratio scale. There are plausible reasons, however, for assuming that individual differences in *g* have an approximately normal, or Gaussian ("bell-shaped"), distribution, at least within the range of $\pm 2\sigma$ from the mean. That range is equivalent to IQs from 70 to 130 on the typical IQ scale (i.e., $\mu = 100$, $\sigma = 15$). Individual differences in general mental ability are usually measured by some test or combination of tests that are highly *g* loaded, and such tests are purposely constructed to have an approximately normal or bell-shaped distribution in the standardization population. Although the normal distribution of test scores is usually accomplished by means of certain psychometric artifices, it has a quite defensible rationale.[16]

The *g* factor as a theoretical construct will probably never be measured in individuals as simply and directly as we can measure a person's height with a ruler. However, a rigorously testable and empirically substantiated theory of *g* would itself dictate the form of its population distribution, and our empirical measures of *g* can then be scaled so as to yield such a distribution. The necessary kinds of experimental research and theory development have been taking shape rapidly in recent years (see Chapters 6 and 8). One major development is the use of mental chronometry in psychometric theory and research, that is, using *real time* as the fundamental scale for the measurement of mental ability.

THE RELATION OF *g* TO IQ AND SIMILAR TESTS OF ABILITY

The term *intelligence quotient* (IQ) refers to a score on a test that has certain characteristics. The test's raw score distribution has typically been standardized in a large random or representative sample of a certain specified population. The standardization is done within narrow age intervals, so that the standardized scores, called IQ, will have the same mean and standard deviation (*SD*) at every age level. IQ is conventionally scaled to a mean of 100 and a *SD* of 15. The form of the IQ distribution closely approximates the normal curve within the range of ±2.5 *SD* of the mean.

The chief characteristic of IQ tests, from Binet on, is that they all are highly *g* loaded. This is true even when the test constructors never used factor analysis, or even had *g* in mind, or even disbelieved in the existence of *g*. The purely pragmatic, criterion-oriented process of composing and selecting those test items that, in combination, show the largest range of individual differences in the population also shows the highest predictive validity for a broad variety of practical criteria. The attainment of these psychometric desiderata unavoidably results in a test that is highly *g* loaded.

The first "IQ test" (the term "IQ," however, had not yet come into being) was invented by Binet in 1905. It was highly *g* loaded, even though, at the time, Binet had never heard of factor analysis or of *g*. Twenty years before Binet, the German psychologist Hermann Ebbinghaus (1850–1909) invented a "sentence completion" test (the testee fills in an omitted word to make sense of the sentence). Scores on the test agreed with teachers' judgments of pupils' "brightness." Sentence completion has since been found to be among the most highly *g*-loaded tests.

After innumerable factor analyses had clearly established what types of test items are most *g* loaded, test constructors deliberately composed and selected items so as to maximize the *g*-ness of their IQ tests. The most *g*-loaded items are those that involve some form of *inductive* or *deductive* reasoning (i.e., Spearman's "eduction of relations and correlates"), problems that involve *spatial visualization, quantitative* reasoning, and *verbal* knowledge and reasoning (such as word meanings, distinctions between related words, antonyms-synonyms, verbal analogies, and reading comprehension). The best *g* items make minimal demands for specialized or esoteric knowledge.

One may wonder why tests of vocabulary and of general information are typically found to be highly *g* loaded when subjects have had similar opportunity to acquire vocabulary and many bits of general information. The reason is that most words in a person's vocabulary are learned through exposure to them in a variety of contexts that allow inferences of their meaning by the "eduction of relations and correlates." The higher the level of a person's *g*, the fewer encounters with a word are needed to correctly infer its meaning. Therefore, over a period of years, the amount of vocabulary acquired by adolescence shows large individual differences, even between full siblings brought up together. These significant differences in vocabulary are highly correlated with comparable differences in *g*-loaded tests that have no verbal content. A vocabulary test that is factor-analyzed in a battery made up exclusively of nonverbal tests still shows a large *g* loading. The same is true of tests called "general information."

Another characteristic of most IQ tests is that the types of items that serve as media or vehicles for relation eduction are rather evenly balanced among verbal, spatial, and numerical (or other) contents. This serves, in effect, to "average out'' the group factors associated with these differing types of content and allows most of the variance in the total score to represent a *g* that is relatively uncontaminated by group factors. The IQ obtained from such tests, therefore, is a quite good, though slightly diluted, stand-in for *g*.

A very few nonverbal, nonspatial visualization, and nonnumerical tests (such as Raven's Progressive Matrices and Cattell's Culture-Fair Test of *g*), which are based entirely on figural materials, have been expressly devised to maximize relation eduction and to minimize group factors. When factor analyzed among a wide variety of other tests, they do, in fact, have among the highest *g* loadings, and they usually have nonsignificant loadings on any less general factors. The Raven Matrices is sometimes moderately loaded on a broad spatial group factor, but always far less than on the *g* factor. Also, the Raven has some specificity (5 to 10 percent) arising most probably from the matrix format of all its items. Cattell's test largely "averages out" such specifics by including a variety of figural item types.

The *g* Loading of IQ Tests. Here it is important to distinguish between two things: (1) the proportion of the total variance attributable to *g* when we factor analyze the set of various subtests that compose the IQ test, and (2) the *g* loading of the IQ itself (derived from the total of the standardized scores on all of the subtests) when the IQ is factor-analyzed among a large collection of diverse cognitive tests.

1. Probably the most typical example is the Wechsler Intelligence Scale for Children (WISC) and for Adults (WAIS). The Wechsler battery consists of twelve subtests (Vocabulary, Similarities, Information, Comprehension, Arithmetic, Digit Span, Digit Symbol, Picture Completion, Block Design, Picture Arrangement, Object Assembly and Mazes). When this battery is factor analyzed in various age groups of the standardization population, the percentage of the total variance in all the subtests accounted for by *g* averages about 30 percent in a hierarchical analysis and about 37 percent when *g* is represented by the first principal factor. The average percentage of variance accounted for by each of the three group factors in a hierarchical analysis is: Verbal 6 percent, Performance (largely spatial ability) 6 percent, and Memory 4 percent. Some 40 percent of the total variance is *specific* to each subtest, and about 10 percent is measurement error (unreliability). The *g* factor scores obtained from the whole Wechsler battery are correlated more than .95 with the tests' total score (called Full Scale IQ). With such a high correlation between the factor scores and the IQ scores, it is pointless to calculate factor scores.[17]

2. Factor analyses of the composite scores (or IQs) of a number of standard IQ tests are exceedingly rare, because the total IQ is an amalgam of various factors that does not lend itself to factor analysis with much expectation of finding more than one significant factor, namely, *g*. Also, it is rare that more than two or three IQ tests are administered to a sample large enough to allow a proper factor analysis. Such a large study, which promises a virtually foregone conclusion yielding no new information of theoretical interest or practical use,

would hardly justify the effort. However, one can make a good estimate of the _g_ loadings of IQ tests from the correlations between various IQ tests reported in the literature, even when no more than two or three tests were administered to the same sample. I have summarized many such correlations elsewhere.[18] The correlations between various IQ tests average about +.77. The square root of this correlation ($\sqrt{.77}$ = .88) is an estimate of the average _g_ loading of IQ tests, since the correlation between two tests is the product of their factor loadings. This value (.88) is an overestimate of the average _g_ loading if it is assumed that various pairs of tests also have certain group factors in common (for example, two purely verbal IQ tests). If we look at just those tests that appear to have no group factors in common (e.g., the Raven and the Peabody Picture Vocabulary), the average correlation between them is +.69, which estimates an average _g_ loading of $\sqrt{.69}$ = .83. It would seem safe to conclude that the average _g_ loading of IQ as measured by various standard IQ tests is in the +.80s.

So-called aptitude tests used in selection for employment, training programs, and college admissions, such as the General Aptitude Test Battery (GATB), the Armed Services Aptitude Battery (ASVAB), and the Scholastic Assessment Test (SAT), are nearly as highly _g_ loaded as IQ tests. For example, the GATB _G_ score (a composite of verbal, numerical, and spatial tests) has an average correlation of +.76 with various IQ tests, suggesting an average _g_ loading of .87. Aptitude tests, however, typically include items of scholastic knowledge or job information intended to reflect educational attainments or work skills relevant to the criteria the test is designed to predict (such as scholastic performance, or job performance, or success in a training program for a particular job). These sources of variance tend to dilute the test's _g_ loading if the item content merely requires direct recall of information without involving relation eduction. The more similar the educational background of the persons tested, however, the larger is the proportion of _g_ variance in their scores on such tests. Those higher on _g_ will have acquired more knowledge and skills from the same amount of schooling or work experience than persons who are lower on _g_.

SOME COMMON MISCONCEPTIONS ABOUT _g_

_g_ Cannot Be Described in Terms of Test Characteristics. Unlike group factors, _g_ cannot be described in terms of the superficial characteristics or information content of the tests in which it is loaded. All mental tests have some degree of _g_ loading and even extremely dissimilar tests (e.g., sentence completion and block designs) can have nearly equal _g_ loadings. Group factors, on the other hand, are labeled and described in terms of the obvious characteristics of the kinds of tests that load on them (such as verbal, numerical, spatial visualization, memory, mechanical, to name a few of the established group factors).

Further, _g_ is not describable in terms of any pure or unique behavior. Verbal ability cannot be demonstrated without the person's engaging in some form of behavior involving verbal material—read, heard, spoken, or written. And so it is for every other group factor. But not for _g_. There is no single distinct type or class of behavior or materials required for the manifestation of _g_.

Of course, neither _g_ nor the group factors are properties of tests per se. Rather, they are components of variance in test scores obtained in some defined group of persons. Tests don't "contain" _g_, but some tests are better indicators of it than others. One might say that the _g_ factor emerges only after analysis has "filtered out" those characteristics of each test that make for group factors and specificity.

It is also a mistake to describe _g_ (or, as one often hears, the "essence" of _g_, or its "defining characteristic") in such terms as relation eduction, abstract reasoning, capacity for complex thinking, problem solving, or similar descriptive terms. These terms describe characteristics of certain test items, but they cannot describe _g_. As Spearman aptly noted, these descriptions of test characteristics merely identify _g_ by site, not by nature. Or as David Wechsler put it, _g_ is not really an ability at all, but a property of the mind. It is true that tests that measure some form of relation eduction are the most highly _g_ loaded, but they represent only the upper segment of the whole _continuum_ of _g_ loadings. Many tests that categorically show none of the characteristics of tests based on relation education are also _g_ loaded, although to a lesser degree. However, a composite score based on a number of such tests, none of which displays any of the above-named features mistakenly said to characterize the "essence" of _g_, can have as large a _g_ loading as the type of test that displays the supposed "defining characteristics" or "essence" of _g_. (The evidence for this, based on elementary cognitive tasks, is discussed in Chapter 8.)

The fact that a certain class of tests measures _g_ more efficiently than other tests does not qualify the characteristics of the former tests to be considered the "essence" or "defining characteristics" of _g_. Because a measuring tape is a more efficient and reliable device than a yardstick for measuring the circumference of tree trunks does not make a measuring tape the defining characteristic of circumference. The salient characteristics of the most highly _g_-loaded tests are not essential or definitional, but are empirical phenomena in need of theoretical explanation in their own right. As will be seen in Chapter 8, the critical question is why the physiological substrate of _g_ is expressed or aggregated more fully in the variance of some types of tests than it is in others.

A General Factor Is Not Inevitable. Factor analysis is not by its nature bound to produce a general factor regardless of the nature of the correlation matrix that is analyzed. A general factor emerges from a hierarchical factor analysis if, and only if, a general factor is truly latent in the particular correlation matrix. A general factor derived from a hierarchical analysis should be based on a matrix of positive correlations that has at least three latent roots (eigenvalues) greater than 1.

For proof that a general factor is not inevitable, one need only turn to studies of personality. The myriad of inventories that measure various personality traits have been subjected to every type of factor analysis, yet no general factor has ever emerged in the personality domain. There are, however, a great many first-order group factors and several clearly identified second-order group factors, or "superfactors" (e.g., introversion-extraversion, neuroticism, and psychoticism), but no general factor. In the abilities domain, on the other hand, a general factor, _g_, always emerges, provided the number and variety of mental tests are sufficient to allow a proper factor analysis. The domain of body measurements (including every externally measurable feature of anatomy) when factor analyzed also shows a large general factor (besides several small group factors). Similarly, the correlations among various measures of athletic ability show a substantial general factor.

Ability Variation between Persons and within Persons. It is sometimes claimed that any given person shows such large differences in various abilities that it makes no sense to talk about _general_ ability, or to attempt to represent it by a single score, or to rank persons on it. One student does very well in math, yet has difficulty with English composition; another is just the opposite; a third displays a marked talent for music but is mediocre in English and math. Is this a valid argument against _g_? It turns out that it is not valid, for if it were true, it would not be possible to demonstrate repeatedly the existence of all-positive correlations among scores on diverse tests abilities, or to obtain a _g_ factor in a hierarchical factor analysis. At most, there would only be uncorrelated group factors, and one could orthogonally rotate the principal factor axes to virtually perfect simple structure.

A necessary implication of the claim that the levels of different abilities possessed by an individual are so variable as to contradict the idea of general ability is that the differences between various abilities _within_ persons would, on average, be larger than the differences _between_ persons in the overall average of these various abilities. This proposition can be (and has been) definitively tested by means of the statistical method known as the analysis of variance. The method is most easily explained with the following type of "Tests × Persons" matrix.

Persons	Tests										Mean P
	A	B	C	D	E	F	G	H	I	J	
1	z_{A1}	z_{B1}	z_{C1}	·	·	·	·	·	·	z_{J1}	z_1
2	z_{A2}	z_{B2}	z_{C2}	·	·	·	·	·	·	z_{J2}	z_2
3	·	·	·	·	·	·	·	·	·	z_{J3}	z_3
4	·	·	·	·	·	·	·	·	·	·	·
·	·	·	·	·	·	·	·	·	·	·	·
·	·	·	·	·	·	·	·	·	·	·	·
·	·	·	·	·	·	·	·	·	·	·	·
N	z_{AN}	z_{BN}	z_{CN}	·	·	·	·	·	·	z_{JN}	z_N
Mean T	z_A	z_B	z_C	·	·	·	·	·		z_J	

It shows ten hypothetical tests of any diverse mental abilities (A, B, . . . J) administered to a large number, N, of persons. The test scores have all been standardized (i.e., converted to z scores) so that every test has a mean $z = 0$ and standard deviation $= 1$. Therefore, the mean score on every test (i.e., Mean T in the bottom row) is the same (i.e., Mean $= 0$). Hence there can be only three sources of variance in this whole matrix: (1) the differences *between* persons' (P) mean scores on the ten tests (Mean P [z_1, z_2, z_3, etc.] in last column), and (2) the differences between test scores *within* each person (e.g., the z_{A1}, z_{B1}, z_{C1}, etc., are the z scores on Tests A, B, C, etc., for Person 1). Now, if the average variance *within* persons proves to be as large as or larger than the variance *between* persons, one could say there is no overall general level of ability, or *g*, in which people differ. That is, differences in the level of various abilities *within* a person are as large or larger, on average, than differences *between* persons in the overall average level of these various abilities. In fact, just the opposite is empirically true: Differences in the average level of abilities *between* persons are very significantly greater than differences in various abilities *within* persons.

It should be remembered that *g* and all other factors derived from factor analysis depend essentially on variance between persons. Traits in which there is very little or no variance do not show up in a factor analysis. A small range of variation in the measurements subjected to factor analysis may result in fewer and smaller factors. A factor analysis performed on the fairly similar body measurements of all the Miss Universe contestants (or of heavyweight boxers), for example, would yield fewer and much smaller factors than the same analysis performed on persons randomly selected from the general population.

Difficulty Level of a Test and *g* Are Separate Concepts. A test's level of difficulty and its *g* loading are conceptually distinct; they may be empirically related, but not necessarily. A test's difficulty level depends on the ability level of the persons taking the test and is typically indexed by the proportion of the test items that are failed in a sample of some specified population. The closer that proportion is to 0.50, the greater the variance in test scores. Because the size of the correlations between tests is affected (positively) by the range of ability (hence the variance) in the population tested, the size of the *g* extracted from the intercorrelations among the tests is correspondingly affected. When the difficulty level of a wide variety of tests is held constant, however, the various tests show a wide range of *g* loadings. Tests that involve some form of reasoning or relation eduction, for example, have considerably higher *g* loadings than tests of rote memory, even though both types of tests are perfectly matched in their level of difficulty and have the same variance. So we see that a test's *g* loading is not intrinsically related to the test's level of difficulty. An appropriate level of difficulty for a given population is merely a psychometric requirement for the reliable measurement of individual differences.

The Confusion of *g* with Mental Processes. It is important to understand that *g* is *not* a mental or cognitive process or one of the operating principles of the mind, such as perception, learning, or memory. Every kind of cognitive performance depends upon the operation of some integrated set of processes in the brain. These can be called cognitive processes, information processes, or neural processes. Presumably their operation involves many complex design features of the brain and its neural processes. But these features are not what *g* (or any other psychometric factor) is about. Rather, *g* only reflects some part of the *individual differences* in mental abilities (as defined in Chapter 2) that undoubtedly depend on the operation of neural processes in the brain. By inference, *g* also reflects individual differences in the speed, or efficiency, or capacity of these operations. But *g* is not these operations themselves.

A simple distinction between *process* and factor is that a process could be discovered by observing one person, whereas a factor could be discovered only by observing a number of persons. For example, one person is observed throwing darts at a target, trying on each trial to hit the bull's-eye. In the course of fifty trials, the person gradually improves in his level of proficiency, from at first being able to hit the bull's-eye only once in every ten trials to finally hitting the bull's-eye on nine out of every ten trials. This observable change in the person's level of proficiency over the course of practice represents a *process*, in this case *learning*. Many of its characteristics could be discovered by means of experiments on a single person. (In fact, Ebbinghaus discovered some of the basic facts of learning and memory by experiments using only himself as a subject.) But now we observe another person performing the same dart-throwing task. We see that it takes this person 200 trials to attain the same level of proficiency as was attained by the first person in only fifty trials. So here we see *individual differences* in the process of learning, in this case, a difference in the *rate* of learning. Obviously, this discovery that learning rates for this task can differ could only have been discovered by observing more than one individual. We could then devise several other diverse tasks in which learning (i.e., improvement with practice) can be seen to occur. We may then find that on every task these two persons differ consistently in their rate of learning. If so, this would mean that all the tasks are positively correlated. At this point, a *factor*, call it "general learning ability," has been discovered. Simply stated, we have demonstrated the existence of a single dimension of individual differences that cuts across a variety of learning tasks.

NOTES

1. Jensen & Weng, 1994. The late Professor Henry F. Kaiser (1927–1992), one of the world's leading experts on factor analysis, made a valuable contribution to our effort through the extensive discussions that Weng and I were privileged to have with him about the fundamental issues dealt with in our article.

2. There are five alternative methods that do not have these problems, but the first two of these, at least, have certain problems of their own.

i. Principal components analysis. The first principal component (PC1) in a principal components analysis is often interpreted as *g*. Indeed, the PC1 usually looks like *g*, as all of the variables usually have substantial loadings on the PC1. But the PC1 has two shortcomings as an estimate of *g*.

First, it slightly overestimates the *g* loadings of each of the variables and therefore also the total proportion of variance attributable to *g*. This is because the PC1 includes some small part of each variable's uniqueness, which is unrelated to *g* (or any other common factor) and the PC1 is therefore an inflated and contaminated estimate of *g*.

Second, the PC1 may give the expected appearance of a *g* factor because of its all-positive loadings on every variable, even when there is no general factor in the matrix. Although the PC1 may give a reasonably good, but slightly inflated and slightly contaminated, estimate of *g* when there is, in fact, a *g* in the matrix, the PC1 can also fool us into thinking there is a *g* in the matrix by showing substantial positive loadings on all of the variables, even when, in fact, there is no *g* in the matrix. The reason for this is that principal components analysis was never devised to estimate the general factor of a correlation matrix, and the PC1 should really not be defined as the general factor. The PC1 is accurately defined only as the weighting factor that maximizes the variance of a linear (i.e., additive) combination of all of the variables. That is, if we multiply each person's standardized score (z) on each test by the test's loading on the PC1, and then obtain the sum (Σ) of these weighted scores (ΣzPC1) for each person, the values of ΣzPC1 (over all persons) will have a larger variance than any other weighted combination of the test scores. The mathematical procedure of principal components analysis determines for each variable whatever weight is needed to accomplish this single purpose. But this does not guarantee that the weights given by the PC1 are accurate estimates of the variables' *g* loadings. However, if there really is a *g* in the matrix, the PC1 will not be very far off the mark as estimates of the variables' true *g* loadings. But if there really is no *g* in the matrix, or if the *g* accounts for only a small part of the total variance, the PC1 can be misleading. This is unlikely in the case of mental ability tests, however, simply because it is extremely hard to make up a set of diverse mental tests that does not have a large *g* factor.

Principal components analysis has one legitimate and useful feature as a preliminary to other analyses. It is useful in determining the number of independent factors in the correlation matrix. As pointed out in Chapter 3, each principal component has an associated eigenvalue, and, as a rule, the number of significant common factors in a matrix is equal to the number of principal components that have eigenvalues larger than 1. (However, there are alternative, and often better, ways to determine the number of common factors, such as the goodness of fit indices in confirmatory factor analysis.)

A little-known feature of the PC1 is that its eigenvalue (λ) can be used to obtain the best estimate of the *average correlation* (r_{ave}) in a square correlation matrix of *p* variables by the following formula (Kaiser, 1968): $r_{ave} = (\lambda - 1)/(p - 1)$.

ii. Principal factor (PF) analysis. This is much like principal components (PC) analysis, except that in PF analysis only the *common factor* variance is analyzed into linearly independent components (then called *factors*). (PC analyzes the total variance, i.e., the common factor variance plus the unique variance.) Therefore, the first principal factor (PF1) in a PF analysis is preferable to the PC1 as an estimate of *g*, because it is not spuriously inflated by the variables' uniqueness, as is the PC1. But the PF1 has the same drawback as the PC1, in that it can give the appearance of a general factor even when a general factor does not exist in the matrix. In practice, its only real risk is that it can make a weak general factor look stronger than it really is. For example, it is possible for two (or more) uncorrelated variables, which actually have no factor in common, to deceptively show substantial loadings on the PF1, in which case the PF1 is not really a general factor. Like the PC1, the PF1 is accurately defined only as the weighting factor that maximizes the total variance of the set of variables, in this case, after all the variables have been stripped of their uniqueness.

iii. Tandem criteria rotation. This method, which is not used as much as it probably should be, gets around the risk of a "deceptive" *g*, as pointed out in connection with the PC1 and PF1. The method begins with a principal factor analysis. The factor axes are then rotated in such a way as to meet two criteria (called *tandem criteria* because they are used in tandem) which ensure that a "deceptive" *g* cannot appear and that if there really is a *g* in the matrix, it will show up. The tandem criteria are based on the following two principles: (I). *If two variables are correlated, they should appear on the same factor.* (II). *If two variables are not correlated, they should not appear on the same factor.* A principal factor rotated to these criteria and that has significant positive loadings in every variable qualifies as a general factor. (Invented by Andrew L. Comrey, the tandem method of factor rotation is fully described in the textbook by Comrey & Lee [1992, pp. 194–204]. The authors also provide a computer program for it, available from the publisher of their textbook.)

iv. Confirmatory factor analysis. This method permits one to hypothesize any particular factor model, for example, models that do or do not have a general factor, and to test statistically how well the observed correlations fit the model. Competing models (e.g., one with a *g* factor and one without) are compared in terms of an index of the data's "goodness of fit" to the hypothesized model. The presence or absence of a general factor can be tested in this way, as can hypotheses about the number of factors in the matrix and precisely which variables should have substantial loadings on each factor. The procedure yields estimates of all the factor loadings within the constraints of the particular hypothesized model.

v. Hierarchical factor analysis. All of the above methods are sensitive to "psychometric sampling error," i.e., having quite unequal numbers of tests that represent different factors in the test battery. A test battery composed of, say, ten memory tests, three verbal reasoning tests, and three spatial reasoning tests, would not yield a very good *g* if it were extracted by any of the methods mentioned so far. The overrepresentation of memory tests would contaminate the *g* factor with memory ability (M); the PC1 would really be *g* + *k*M, where *k* is some fraction of the memory factor. Hierarchical factor analysis (HFA) largely overcomes this problem by rotating the factor axes (obtained from a principal factor analysis) so as to obtain as clear-cut oblique group factors (in this case, *numerical, verbal,* and *spatial*) as possible, and then extracting *g* from the correlations among the group factors. If there is no general factor in the matrix, the group factors will not be correlated and therefore cannot yield a *g*. For these reasons, a hierarchical factor model is generally preferred for estimating the *g* factor and representing the other factors in the matrix. A two-strata hierarchical analysis is not feasible, however, unless there are enough different kinds of tests to produce at least three group factors (with a minimum of three tests per factor). A correlation matrix that is suitable for the Spearman model, for example, would not lend itself to a hierarchical analysis.

3. The seven primary mental abilities that were well identified by Thurstone's factor analyses of a great many tests and for which he devised "factor-pure" tests were: verbal comprehension, reasoning, word fluency, numerical ability, spatial visualization, perceptual speed, and associative memory. Since Thurstone's time, many more primary ability

factors have been identified. (See Carroll, 1993a, for the most comprehensive coverage of this subject.)

4. Although the bifactor model superficially may seem to resemble the hierarchical model, there are certain important differences involving the rank of the correlation matrix represented by each model (the rank of the correlations represented by the hierarchical model is one less than that of the bifactor model). Also, the bifactor model, because it derives *g* directly from the original correlation matrix, has fewer mathematical constraints than the hierarchical model, which derives *g* from the correlations among the first-order factors (see Jensen & Weng, 1994). Thus the bifactor model can be called a "top-down" factor analysis, whereas the hierarchical model is a "bottom-up" factor analysis. The computational procedures of the bifactor model are now most easily done by means of the LISREL-VII computer program, and as both the bifactor and hierarchical models can be specified in LISREL, the goodness of fit index can be used to determine which model better represents the factor structure of the variables.

5. Although hierarchical factor analysis with the Schmid-Leiman (1957) orthogonalization is the most appropriate form of exploratory factor analysis and has been widely used in the last two decades, it (like virtually all other exploratory factor models) is rapidly being supplanted by confirmatory factor analysis implemented by the computer software package LISREL (an acronym for **LI**near **S**tructural **REL**ations) devised by the Swedish statistician Karl Jöreskog (Jöreskog & Sörbom, 1989). Essentially the same orthogonalized hierarchical factor model can be obtained with LISREL, with the added advantage of an objective statistical comparison (for goodness of fit to the data) with other factor models, such as the bifactor model, that may be more suitable, depending on the nature of the correlation matrix. In analyzing a variety of artificially devised correlation matrices in which all the factors are known exactly, we have found that the LISREL method of estimating the factors seems to show the best overall batting average.

6. The original correlation matrix can also be reconstituted from the factor loadings given in Table 4.2, by the rule that the correlation between any two variables is the sum of the products of their loadings on each factor. For example, the correlation between V1 and V2 (in Table 4.1) is reconstituted from their factor loadings (in Table 4.2) as follows: $(.72 \times .63) + (.3487 \times .3051) = .56$.

7. Readers should be warned against misinterpreting the meaning of the word "estimate" when it is used in the context of empirical science, statistics, or factor analysis. In popular parlance "estimate" usually means merely a guess or a rough calculation, as when a building contractor quotes an estimate of the final cost of a construction job. In science, however, it refers to a measurement that inevitably has some associated probable degree of inaccuracy, which is true of all measurements in empirical science, although of course measurements differ in their degree of accuracy. But the hypothetical *true* measurement always remains unknown and is in principle unknowable. It is usually possible, however, to determine the probable error of a measurement and to state whether or not the measurement is sufficiently accurate for its intended purpose. Comparing the weights of different atoms obviously requires a very different degree of precision than comparing the weights of hogs. The term "estimate" can be dispensed with only in pure mathematics, in which a quantity can be defined exactly but does not pertain to any reality outside of itself. In statistics (and factor analysis) the concept of estimate presupposes a true measurement or value that can be estimated with some specified degree of accuracy (or "probable error"). In statistics, the true value is that which would be found if every element (i.e., person, item, object, or whatever) in the total population of such

elements had been measured, rather than just a sample of these elements. In the factor analysis of abilities, the sampled "elements" are of two kinds: a defined population of persons (e.g., all American-born, English-speaking ten-year-olds) and a defined population of mental ability tests (e.g., the more than 200 published tests classified as mental ability tests listed in the ninth edition of the Buros _Mental Measurements Yearbook_). The "estimate" obtained from the analysis of a sample of the population itself is not in the least inexact (assuming the calculations were done correctly), and therefore it is not an estimate of some characteristic of the sample per se. However, the precise value of a characteristic (e.g., a mean, a correlation coefficient, or a factor loading) obtained from the sample (called a _statistic_) is an estimate of that characteristic in a population (called a _parameter_). A statistic has a precisely known _standard error, SE_ (or _probable error, PE_, which is .6745 _SE_), which is a function of the sample size. The sample value (or statistic) has a 50 percent chance of falling within ±1 _PE_ of the population value (or parameter). In the case of factor analysis, the estimated parameters (the factors themselves and the variables' factor loadings) are also subject to one other source of variation (or error) in addition to sampling error (both for subjects and for tests, as sampled from specified populations of people and tests), namely, the particular method of factor analysis that is used. The results of different methods of factor analysis vary when they are applied to one and the same correlation matrix. (This is the main subject of the article by Jensen & Weng, 1994.)

8. The congruence coefficient (r_c) is an index of factor similarity. Like the Pearson correlation coefficient (r), it is scaled to range from -1 to 0 to $+1$. A value of r_c of $+.90$ is considered a high degree of factor similarity; a value greater than $+.95$ is generally interpreted as practical identity of the factors. The r_c is preferred to the Pearson r for comparing factors, because the r_c estimates the correlation between the _factors_ themselves, whereas the Pearson r gives only the correlation between the two column vectors of factor loadings. Pearson r is based on standardized deviations from the mean of each variate, whereas r_c is based on raw deviations from zero. Comparing the definitional formulas for r and r_c side-by-side shows how they differ. Say we wish to assess the similarity of two factors, here labeled **X** and **Y** (e.g., suppose the same battery of n tests was given to subject samples drawn from two different populations [called X and Y] and after factor analyzing the battery within each sample, we wish to know how similar a particular factor in one sample is to the presumably corresponding factor in the other sample). So the n factor loadings of each of the n tests for each sample can be arrayed as two-column vectors (i.e., a column of the n factor loadings for each sample). The separate loadings are here called X and Y, with standardized values z_x and z_y.)

Pearson $r = \Sigma(z_x z_y)/n$

Congruence coefficient $r_c = \Sigma XY / \sqrt{\Sigma X^2 \Sigma Y^2}$.

Showing the formulas for r and r_c in terms of the original measurements, X and Y, will make the difference between the two coefficients more apparent, showing that r is based on the deviation of the factor loadings from the local mean, whereas r_c is based on the factor loadings' deviations from zero:

$$r = \frac{\Sigma(X - \overline{X})(Y - \overline{Y})}{\sqrt{\Sigma(X - \overline{X})^2 \, \Sigma(Y - \overline{Y})^2}}$$

$$r_c = \frac{\Sigma(X - 0)(Y - 0)}{\sqrt{\Sigma(X - 0)^2 \, \Sigma(Y - 0)^2}} = \frac{\Sigma XY}{\sqrt{\Sigma X^2 \, \Sigma Y^2}}$$

It should be noticed that the Pearson r, being based on standardized factor loadings, cannot reflect a difference between the means of the loadings, whereas the r_c does so. That is one advantage of r_c over r. One reason that r_c is used instead of r to compare factors is illustrated in the following example. Consider the following two sets of factor loadings on hypothetical factors X and Y, which are hardly similar factors, much less the same factor. To save space on this page, the loadings are here presented as a _row_ vector rather than as a _column_ vector (which is the conventional form in a factor matrix.)

Factor Loadings

Factor X:	.9	.8	.7	.6	.5	.4	.3	.2	.1
Factor Y:	.4	.3	.2	.1	.0	−.1	−.2	−.3	−.4

The Pearson $r = 1.00$ gives the very misleading impression that the factors are identical. The coefficient of congruence $r_c = .46$. A r_c of this size indicates that the factors are distinctly different factors, though not absolutely unrelated.

The main virtue of r_c, however, is that it estimates the theoretical correlation (Pearson r) between the true _factor scores_ of each of the compared factors. (It is mathematically the exact correlation in the case of principal components.) Gorsuch (1983) states: "In the case of orthogonal components where the factor scores have means of zero and variances of one, the result of calculating coefficients of congruence on the factor pattern is identical to correlating the exact factor scores and is, indeed, a simplified formula for that correlation" (p. 285). (I have tested this empirically and found it to be accurate within the limits of rounding errors in the third decimal place. The approximation of r_c to the actual correlation between estimated factor scores in the case of principal factors and a hierarchical g is almost as good as for the exact solution given for principal components.)

Another way of defining the congruence coefficient is in terms of the locations of the factor axes based on the same set of variables (tests) obtained in two subject samples. Say we calculate and then plot on graph paper the first principal axis of a set of tests given to Group A, and then superimpose upon this graph a plot of the first principal axis based on the same set of tests given to Group B. The cosine of the angle between these two principal axes, then, is the congruence coefficient. With perfect congruence the angle between the axes has 0 degrees, and the cosine of 0 equals 1. The cosine of 90 degrees is 0 (no congruence); and the cosine of 180 degrees is −1. A congruence coefficient of +.99 corresponds to an angle of 8.1 degrees.

9. The _root mean square difference_ (RMSD) between two vectors is simply the square root of the mean of the squared differences between each pair of factor loadings. In the above example (Note 8), the RMSD = 0.5, which is a very large value compared to the sizes of the factor loadings. It, too, indicates that these factors are quite different.

10. Ree & Earles, 1991a.

11. Detterman & Daniel, 1989.

12. By analogy with the concept of "true"-score in classical test theory and the formulation of the correlation r_{ot} between obtained scores (o) and true-scores (t), the correlation between the obtained g and the true g is given by the following formula (Kaiser & Caffrey, 1965):

$$r_{ot} = \sqrt{[(n/(n-1)(1 - 1/\lambda)]},$$

where n is the number of tests and λ is the eigenvalue of the first principal component of the correlation matrix. Accordingly, the reliability of the factor is r_{ot}^2. (See Jensen & Weng, 1994, for further discussion of this formula.)

13. Irvine & Berry (1988); see particularly Chapter 5, by Royce, who summarizes the main findings, giving references to most of this literature; also see "factor analysis" and "g" in the index of the Irvine & Berry book for other references to cross-cultural factor analytic studies.

14. Jensen, 1983.

15. Jensen, 1985a; Jensen & Reynolds, 1982.

16. Nothing of fundamental empirical or theoretical importance is revealed by the frequency distribution per se of the scores on any psychometric test composed of items. This is true regardless of whether we are dealing with raw scores or standardized scores or any otherwise transformed scores. Therefore, it would be trivial and pointless to review the empirical test literature regarding the form of the distribution of mental test scores.

In a given population, the form of the distribution of raw scores (i.e., number of items passed) is entirely a function of three interrelated item characteristics: (1) the average probability of getting the correct answer by chance, i.e., by pure guessing, (2) the average level of difficulty of the items (as indexed by the percentage of the population that fails them), and (3) the average correlation between items. Item difficulty is completely under the test constructor's control. Score increments due to chance guessing are a function of the number and quality of the alternatives in multiple-choice items and the nature of the instructions to subjects regarding the penalty for guessing at the answer instead of omitting response when uncertain (e.g., total score based on number of right minus number of wrong answers). The item intercorrelations can be controlled to a considerable degree (but never completely) through item selection. Hence, in constructing a test it is possible, within broad limits, to produce almost any desired form of frequency distribution of the raw scores in a given population.

If we have no basis for arguing that the obtained scores have true measurement properties in addition to merely having a rank-order correlation with the latent trait that they measure—and this seems to be typically the case for psychometric test scores—the precise form of the obtained score distribution is essentially arbitrary. The very most that we can say in this case is that (within the limits of measurement error) our test scores have some monotonic relation to whatever the test really "measures." If we could truly measure whatever latent variable, such as g, accounts for the variation in the obtained scores on an absolute scale (i.e., one having a true zero and additivity of scale intervals), the form of its population distribution could turn out to be quite different from that of the test scores we have actually obtained.

Certain forms of distribution are simply more useful than others, psychometrically and statistically, and it is this consideration that mainly determines the form of the distribution test constructors decide to adopt. The aims of maximizing the statistical discriminability of scores throughout a fairly wide range of talent and of obtaining a fair degree of internal consistency reliability (i.e., interitem correlation) are what largely dictate item selection. The test scores that result under these conditions of item selection typically (and necessarily) have a symmetrical and more-or-less "bell-shaped" frequency distribution. It is not truly the normal (or Gaussian) curve, although it usually resembles it closely. By juggling item characteristics the test constructor can get a distribution that reasonably approximates the normal curve. Or the scores can be transformed mathematically to approximate a normal distribution. (Such "normalized" scores are obtained by converting the raw scores to ranks, then converting these to percentile ranks, and then, by reference to a table of the areas under the normal curve, converting these to normal deviates, i.e., normalized z scores.) The reason for thus normalizing a score distribution is not mainly theoretical, but statistical. The normal curve has certain mathematical properties that make it extremely useful in statistical analysis and interpretation.

The argument is often made on theoretical grounds, however, that the main latent trait reflected by most complex cognitive tests—namely *g*—should be normally distributed in the general population. This argument, if accepted, justifies and indeed demands that IQs (or any other type of scores on any highly *g*-loaded tests) should be purposely scaled so that the form of their population distribution closely approximates the normal distribution. What can be said for this argument? There are three main facets:

First, there is the argument by *default*: Unless there is some compelling reason to suppose that the form of the distribution of *g* is something *other* than normal, we might as well assume that it is normal, which is at least statistically convenient.

Second, there is the argument from the *Central-Limit Theorem* in mathematical statistics, which essentially states that the distribution of a composite variable representing the *additive* effects of a number of independent elements (components, causes, or influences) rapidly approaches the normal distribution as the number of elements increases. This should be the case for *g*, to the extent that we can argue on various theoretical and empirical grounds that individual differences in *g* are the result of a great many different additive effects: for example, individual differences in the efficiency of a number of different cognitive processes, each of which is somewhat independently conditioned by polygenic inheritance interacting with a multitude of different environmental influences encountered throughout the course of development since the moment of conception. The population distribution of any variable with such multiple additive determinants, theoretically, should approximate the normal curve.

Third, there is the argument by *analogy* with human characteristics that actually *can* be measured on an absolute scale, such as height, brain weight, neural conduction velocity, sensory acuity, choice reaction time, and digit span memory (i.e., the number of digits that can be recalled entirely correctly after one presentation on 50 percent of the trials). We may reasonably presume that individual differences in each of these variables has multiple determinants, just as in the case of *g*. Indeed, we find that in very large samples of the general population the distribution of each of these variables (measured on an absolute scale) approximates the normal curve. Marked deviations from the normal curve usually occur in the regions beyond $\pm 2\sigma$ from the mean of the distribution. These deviations from normality can usually be explained in terms of certain rare genetic or environmental effects that override the multiple normal determinants of variation. This line of argument by analogy makes it quite plausible that *g* (or any other complexly determined trait) is normally distributed, but it cannot prove it. Also, the argument by analogy is weakened by the fact that not all complexly determined biological variables that can be measured on an absolute scale necessarily conform to the normal distribution. Age at death (beyond five years), for example, has a very negatively skewed distribution, because the mode is close to 75 years and the highest known limit of human longevity is about 113 years. (Below age five, the age of death is distributed as a so-called J curve, with the mode immediately after birth.)

Fourth, the assumption of a normal distribution of *g* reveals a remarkable consistency between various population groups that show a given mean difference (in σ units) on highly *g*-loaded tests, such as IQ tests. By knowing the means and standard deviations of two population groups on such a measure, and by assuming that the latent trait, *g*, reflected by the measurements has a normal distribution in each group, one can make fairly accurate estimates of the *percentages* of each group that fall above or below some criterion that is not measured by any psychometric technique but is known to be correlated with *g* to some extent, such as number of years of education, occupational level, or as being judged by nonpsychometric criteria as mentally retarded or as intellectually gifted. Even though these percentages may vary widely from one criterion to another, when the percentages are transformed to normal deviates (obtained from tables of the normal curve), the differences between the groups' normal deviates on various *g*-related criteria show a considerable degree of constancy. This could not happen if the distribution of *g* were not approximately normal.

Probably the best answer at present concerning the distribution of *g* is that, although we cannot determine it directly by any currently available means, it is a reasonable inference that it approximates the normal curve and there is no good reason for assuming that the distribution of *g* is *not* approximately normal, at least within the middle range of about four standard deviations. Most psychometricians implicitly work on the statistically advantageous assumption of normality, and no argument has yet come forth that it is theoretically implausible or adversely affects any practical uses of *g*-loaded tests. But the question is mainly of scientific interest, and a really satisfactory answer to it cannot come about through improved measurement techniques per se, but will become possible only as part and parcel of a comprehensive theory of the nature of *g*. If we have some theoretical conception of what the form of the distribution should be in a population with certain specified characteristics, we can use random samples from such a population to validate the scale we have devised to measure *g*. The distribution of obtained measurements should conform to the characteristics of the distribution dictated by theoretical considerations.

17. The *g* factor scores are simply the linear weighted sum of an individual's standardized subtest scores, each subtest score weighted by its *g* loading. The Full Scale IQ is based on an unweighted sum of the standardized subtest scores. With as many as twelve subtests entering into the composite, the weighted and unweighted sums will be highly correlated. A theorem put forth by Wilks (1938) offers a mathematical proof that the correlation between two linear composites having different sets of (all positive) weights tends toward 1 as the number of positively intercorrelated elements (e.g., subtests) in the composite increases. For this reason, practically nothing is gained by obtaining *g* factor scores (instead of unweighted composite scores) from a multitest battery such as the Wechsler scales, the General Aptitude Test Battery (GATB), and the Armed Services Vocational Aptitude Battery (ASVAB). When *g* factor scores were obtained on the ASVAB (with ten subtests) for 9,173 recruits, they were correlated +.991 with the unweighted composite scores (Ree & Earles, 1991a).

One occasionally encounters an erroneous interpretation of the "percentage of variance" (or "proportion of variance") attributed to the *g* factor in a factor analysis of a battery of subtests, for example, the Wechsler battery consisting of twelve subtests. The "proportion of variance" attributed to a given factor in this case refers only to the average of the variances (the squared factor loadings) of each of the separate subtests. The square root of the average proportion of variance due to (say) *g* in the *n* subtests is simply the best representation of the average of the *g* loadings of the separate subtests. The *g* loading of the *composite* score (i.e., the sum of the subtest scores), if it could be included in the same factor analysis with all the subtests without affecting their *g* loadings, would be much larger than the average of the *g* loadings of the separate subtests, assuming a fair number of subtests. Spearman (1927, Appendix, pp. xix–xxi) derived the formula for the g loading of the total, or composite, score based on a number of subtests for each of which the g loading has been determined by factor analysis:

$$r_{tg} = \{1 + \{\Sigma[r^2_{sg}/(1-r^2_{sg})]\}^{-1}\}^{-\frac{1}{2}}$$

where

r_{tg} = the correlation between total score (composite of all subtests) and g (i.e., the g loading of the total score).

Σ = the sum of . . .

r^2_{sg} = each subtest's squared correlation with g (i.e., each subtest's squared g loading).

For example, applying this formula to the g loadings of the nine variables (V1 . . . V9) in Table 4.2 (p. 81), whose average is only $\sqrt{.2542}$ =.504, the g loading of a composite score based on all nine variables is .883.

18. Jensen, 1980a, pp. 314–315.

Chapter 5

Challenges to *g*

Viewpoints and theories antithetical, or in some cases mistakenly thought to be antithetical, to the large body of psychometric evidence supporting the presence of a predominant general factor, *g*, in the domain of mental abilities are reviewed. The proponents of the specificity doctrine, which holds that mental tests measure only a collection of bits of knowledge and skills that happen to be valued by the dominant culture in a society, as well as those who hold that individual differences in mental abilities reflect only differences in opportunities for learning certain skills, largely of a scholastic nature, or the contextualists who claim that mental ability is not general but is entirely specific to particular tasks and circumstances, have not produced any empirical evidence that contradicts the existence of the ubiquitous *g* factor found in any large and diverse collection of mental tests. There are, however, more rigorous critiques of *g*.

Guilford's Structure-of-Intellect (SOI) model, which claims 150 separate abilities, is supported only by a type of factor analysis that mathematically forces a large number of narrow factors to be uncorrelated, even though all the various ability tests that are entered into the analysis are correlated with one another. Guilford's claim of zero correlations between ability tests is unsupported by evidence; the few zero and negative correlations that are found are attributable to sampling error and other statistical limitations.

Cattell's theory of fluid intelligence (Gf) and crystallized intelligence (Gc) is reflected as second-order factors in tests that are either highly culture-reduced (Gf) or highly culture-specific (Gc) and is particularly valid in culturally and educationally heterogeneous populations. The greater the homogeneity in the population, however, the higher is the correlation between Gf and Gc. The correlation between these second-order factors is represented in a hierarchical factor analysis as a single third-order factor, namely *g*. Typically there is a near-perfect correlation between Gf and *g*, so that when the second-order factors are residualized, thereby subsuming their common variance into *g*, the Gf factor vanishes. In other words, Cattell's Gf and the third-order factor, *g*, turn out be one and the same.

Guttman's radex model, a multidimensional scaling method for spatially representing the relations between diverse mental tests, perfectly parallels the relationships shown in a hierarchical factor analysis. Tests' *g* loadings derived from factor analysis are displayed spatially in the radex model by the tests' proximity to the center of the circular array, with the most highly *g*-loaded tests being closest to the center.

Gardner's theory of seven independent "intelligences" is contradicted by the well-established correlations between at least four of these "intelligences" (verbal, logical-mathematical, spatial, musical, all of which are substantially *g* loaded; the factorial structure of two of the "intelligences" (interpersonal and intrapersonal) has not been determined, so their *g* loadings remain unknown; and one ability (kinesthetic) probably does not fall into the mental abilities domain as defined in Chapter 3. There is no incompatibility between *g* and the existence of neural modules that control particular abilities.

Sternberg's componential and triarchic theories, which are sometimes mistakenly thought to be incompatible with *g* theory, are shown to be entirely consistent with it. Sternberg's theory explains the existence of *g* in terms of information-processing components and metacomponents rather than in terms of any unitary process or property of the brain, a subject to be considered in Chapter 8.

Virtually all present-day researchers in psychometrics now accept as a well-established fact that individual differences in all complex mental tests are positively correlated and that a hierarchical factor model, consisting of a number of group factors dominated by *g* at the apex (or the highest level of generality), is the best representation of the correlational structure of mental abilities.

The previous chapter documented the evidence in support of the concept of a general factor as the most important source of individual differences in mental ability. The fact that *g* can be extracted in a hierarchical analysis from any large and diverse battery of mental tests itself proves the existence of *g*, at least at the level of factor analysis. Moreover, certain reliable empirical phenomena that are intrinsically related to *g* call for explanation, for example: (1) the existence of positive correlations among all mental tests however diverse; (2) tests differ with some consistency in their average correlation with many other tests, and the rank order of various tests' average correlations with other tests is roughly similar to the rank order of the tests' g loadings. In fact, a test's g loading is a more refined and more accurate measure of the test's average correlation with every other test, stripped of the correlation the test has with other tests that are like itself in type of information content and skill required, that is, the features from which the first-order group factors arise.

Given these empirical corollaries of g, one might ask why there is any argument at all over either the existence or the meaning of g. While g theory is far and away the prevailing view among the majority of practicing psychometricians and authorities on human intelligence, agreement is not universal.

The arguments against g theory can be grouped into two broad categories: (1) verbal arguments, and (2) mathematical and statistical arguments. The first category has produced little if anything in the way of an alternate research program or a body of data to be explained. It will, therefore, be given only a cursory examination. The second category includes important studies, concepts, and analyses. While I will show that none of these arguments disconfirms, or even weakens, g theory, they have provided important tests and additional data and have thereby refined and extended our knowledge of g and its practical usefulness.

VERBAL ARGUMENTS

THE SPECIFICITY DOCTRINE

The viewpoint that I have dubbed the *specificity doctrine*[1] is the belief that "intelligence" consists of nothing other than a learned repertoire of many bits of knowledge and skills, and that environments differ in the opportunity they afford each individual to acquire these various bits of knowledge and skills. Therefore, people's repertoires of knowledge and skills differ to varying degrees. IQ tests are designed to sample some very limited and selected portion of all these environmentally acquired bits of knowledge and skill, particularly those elements to which the socially dominant group attaches special value as requisites for gaining and maintaining their status. A few actual quotations, each from a different source, may reveal the flavor of the specificity doctrine perhaps better than this general definition of it.

> [M]odern science is looking at intelligence as a set of skills and techniques by which a person represents information from the environment and then acts upon that information in such a way as to produce more and more abstract ideas. . . . IQ tests must be recognized as artificial tools to rank individuals according to certain skills.

> IQ tests measure the degree to which a particular individual who takes the test has experience with a particular piece of information, the particular bits of knowledge, the particular habits and approaches that are tested by these tests.

Each person functions in a unique way. The fact that she or he comes out with [an IQ] score that is above average or below average is an artifact of the technique we have used to measure the trait.

Children can be taught to do intelligence tests just as they can be taught to do English, arithmetic, chess, and crosswords.

Intelligence testing is a political expression of those groups in society who most successfully establish behavior they value as a measure of intelligence.

Note especially that the key words the specificity doctrine uses to describe "intelligence" and IQ tests are *skills, techniques*, and *bits of knowledge*. What these terms have in common is not just the implication of particularity, but the idea that intelligence is a learned, taught, or trained *skill* (like doing the manual of arms). Presumably, anyone can acquire such a specific skill through proper training and practice (in the military, basic training is built on precisely that assumption). Therefore, a person's lacking a particular skill or bit of knowledge implies only a failure to have acquired it, either by a fluke, or for lack of exposure to it in the person's culture, or lack of proper education, or of interest, necessity, motivation, or opportunity. This particularistic interpretation of "intelligence" is especially alluring to the egalitarian viewpoint. If "intelligence" consists only of learned skills, and if IQ tests are just contrivances for sampling those skills and bits of knowledge valued by the dominant segment of society, then the implications of observed individual and group differences in "intelligence" are at best minimal or at worst a cry for social action.

At first glance, the premise that the "intelligence" tested by IQ tests is purely learned has obvious commonsense validity. How, one might reasonably ask, can a person possibly answer questions if the answers hadn't been learned, or display skills that hadn't been acquired? A test item and its correct answer are easily conceptualized as the stimulus (S) and the response (R) in the behavioristic theories of S-R conditioning and learning. Neurologically intact organisms presented with a particular stimulus can learn to make a particular response to it after repeated trials of the S-R sequence in which each trial is followed by reward (for the correct response) or punishment (for the incorrect response). The view that all complex human abilities are entirely the result of such conditioning or learning, and thus reflect nothing but the individual's environmental experiences, is the legacy of the "radical behaviorism" school of psychology founded in the 1920s by John B. Watson (1878–1958). One of the historic figures in American psychology, Watson's most famous and often quoted words (from *Behaviorism*, 1924), which will probably outlive anything else he ever wrote, best expresses this point of view: "Give me a dozen healthy infants, well-formed, and my own specified world to bring them up in and I'll guarantee to take any one at random and train him to become any type of specialist I might select—doctor, lawyer, artist, merchant-chief and, yes, even beggar-man and thief, regardless of his talents, penchants, tendencies, abilities, vocations, and race of his ancestors."

"Intelligence" as Learned Behavior. From the 1930s to the 1970s, American psychology was predominantly behavioristic, though not entirely of the "radical" variety espoused by Watson. On the whole, behaviorism did much to help psychology break away from speculative philosophy and to make it a branch of the natural sciences. For his pioneering role in this effort, Watson deserves an honored place in the history of behavioral science. The behaviorist approach unquestionably advanced the science of conditioning and learning, a field in which some of the great figures in the history of behavioral science— Ivan Pavlov, E. L. Thorndike, Clark Hull, and B. F. Skinner—earned their fame. Behaviorism has especially dominated that branch of psychology generally known as experimental psychology. It also contributed methods and tools that are now used in such diverse research areas as pharmacology and neurophysiology.

But there were some psychological phenomena that behaviorism proved unable either to explain or to understand. Behaviorism's greatest inadequacy was its unwillingness even to consider the field of differential psychology. Largely as a result of the behaviorism that so pervaded American psychology for almost half a century, and its conspicuous inability to provide a coherent account of the main phenomena associated with individual differences, differential psychology was virtually excluded from mainstream psychology for at least three decades.

Meanwhile, the main research tools of differential psychology—mental tests— developed independently into what became another major branch of psychology in its own right, namely, psychometrics. Psychometrics developed as a substantively nontheoretical technology for reliably measuring individual differences and validating the practical use of the measurements for making decisions and predictions about individuals. The genuine success of psychometric technology in achieving its practical aims was amply demonstrated by the utility of psychometric tests in the diagnosis of school learning problems, college admissions, personnel selection, and the assignment of recruits to different specialized training schools in the armed services. No other branch of psychology could claim practical applications with such conspicuously consequential and economically demonstrable impact.

Psychometric technology, however, was not expressly concerned with the nature of just what it is that is measured by mental tests (as, for example, Spearman was). It focused on proving the reliability and practical predictive validity of the measurements. Traditionally this purely practical orientation has emphasized the manifest features of tests and their measurement properties per se, rather than the latent traits that contribute to their variance. By latching on to the former aspect of mental tests and ignoring the latter, a few latter-day Watsonians still try to explain "intelligence" or IQ and the psychometric data strictly in terms of behavioristic theories of learning.[2]

The behavioristic approach attempts to understand IQ (or other mental test scores) in purely behavioral terms by applying the methods of experimental psychology to a "task analysis" of the specific behavior called for by single test items or a very narrow class of similar items. When subjects are trained on one type of task typical of certain mental test items, there is a "transfer of training" (that is, an increased proficiency in performance on similar tasks that have not been specifically trained). This is one of the principles of learning that is invoked to account for the correlation between various test items. However, it is a further principle that the amount of transfer decreases sharply as the similarity between the trained and untrained task requirements decreases. Transfer of training cannot, therefore, explain the substantial correlations repeatedly found between highly dissimilar items. To explain the correlations between different kinds of items or tests, behavioristic theorists invoke yet another principle—the learning of general strategies, or systematic procedures, for solving broad classes of problems. The learned strategies that are invoked to explain high correlations between very dissimilar tasks must be made so all-encompassing as to be predictively vacuous. Most often, however, the cause of interitem correlations is simply ignored, because it cannot be explained convincingly in strictly behavioristic terms.

If the only source of individual differences is past learning, it is hard to explain why individual differences in a variety of tasks that are so novel to all of the subjects as to scarcely reflect the transfer of training from prior learned skills or problem-solving strategies are still highly correlated. Transfer from prior learning is quite task-specific. It is well known, for example, that memory span for digits (i.e., repeating a string of *n* random digits after hearing them spoken at a rate of one digit per second) has a moderate correlation with IQ. It also has a high correlation with memory span for random consonant letters presented in the same way. The average memory span in the adult population is about seven digits, or seven consonant letters. (The inclusion of vowels permits the grouping of letters into pronounceable syllables, which lengthens the memory span.) Experiments have been performed in which persons are given prolonged daily practice in digit span memory over a period of several months. Digit span memory increases remarkably with practice; some persons eventually become able to repeat even 70 to 100 digits without error after a single presentation.[3] But this developed skill shows no transfer effect on IQ, provided the IQ test does not include digit span. But what is even more surprising is that there is no transfer to letter span memory. Persons who could repeat a string of seven letters before engaging in practice that raised their *digit* span from seven to 70 or more digits still have a *letter* span of about seven letters. Obviously, practicing one kind of task does not affect any general memory capacity, much less *g*.

What would happen to the *g* loadings of a battery of cognitive tasks if they were factor analyzed both before and after subjects had been given prolonged practice that markedly improved their performance on all tasks of the same kind? I know of only one study like this, involving a battery of cognitive and perceptual-motor skill tasks.[4] Measures of task performance taken at intervals during the course of practice showed that the tasks gradually lost much of their _g_ loading as practice continued, and the rank order of the tasks' pre- and post-practice _g_ loadings became quite different. Most striking was that each task's _specificity_ markedly increased. Thus it appears that what can be trained up is not the _g_ factor common to all tasks, but rather each task's specificity, which reflects individual differences in the specific behavior that is peculiar to each task. By definition a given task's specificity lacks the power to predict performance significantly on any other tasks except those that are very close to the given task on the transfer gradient.

The meager success of skills training designed for persons scoring below average on typical _g_-loaded tests illustrates the limited gain in job competence that can be obtained when specific skills are trained up, leaving _g_ unaffected. In the early 1980s, for example, the Army Basic Skills Education Program was spending some $40 million per year to train up basic skills for the 10 percent of enlisted men who scored below the ninth-grade level on tests of reading and math, with up to 240 hours of instruction lasting up to three months. The program was motivated by the finding that recruits who score well on tests of these skills learn and perform better than low scorers in many army jobs of a technical nature. An investigation of the program's outcomes by the U.S. General Accounting Office (G.A.O.), however, discovered very low success rates. Only a small percentage of the training program's enrollees completed the program successfully, in terms of achieving the level of competence required for adequate performance of many jobs. But to remedy the problem, the G.A.O. suggested more highly specific forms of skills training. It recommended that the Army carry out task analyses to determine the specific skills required for each particular military job and provide training for just those skills.[5] The outcome of this approach was not reported, but as will be seen in Chapter 9, there is massive evidence that _g_ is reflected even in individual differences in the outcome of training highly specific skills.

In jobs where assurance of competence is absolutely critical, however, such as airline pilots and nuclear reactor operators, government agencies seem to have recognized that specific skills, no matter how well trained, though essential for job performance, are risky if they are not accompanied by a fairly high level of _g_. For example, the TVA, a leader in the selection and training of reactor operators, concluded that results of tests of mechanical aptitude and specific job knowledge were inadequate for predicting an operator's actual performance on the job. A TVA task force on the selection and training of reactor operators stated: ''intelligence will be stressed as one of the most important characteristics of superior reactor operators. . . . intelligence distinguishes those who have merely memorized a series of discrete manual operations from those who can think through a problem and conceptualize solutions based on a fundamental understanding of possible contingencies.''[6] This reminds one of Carl Bereiter's clever definition of ''intelligence'' as ''what you use when you don't know what to do.''

It is also interesting that the conception of "intelligence" as a mere repertoire of learned skills conflicts absolutely with the notion of "intelligence" that is implicit in common language usage. For example, try substituting the word "intelligence" in place of the italicized word in each of the following sentences: "He learned *math* in school." His mother taught him *music*." "Although she was at the top of her class in *Latin*, she has since forgotten most of it." "She picked up her *accent* from her Scottish grandmother." Obviously, the word "intelligence" has evolved in common language to mean some quality or attribute, however ill-defined, that is essentially different from learning per se or from the acquisitions of learning in the form of knowledge and skills.[7] However, people often *infer* a person's "intelligence" from their impression of the person's knowledge and skills. The idea of *learning ability* (e.g., characterizing someone as a "fast learner") is closely associated with "intelligence" in common expression. While the *acquisitions of learning* (knowledge and skill) and *learning ability* are commonly perceived as correlated, they also remain conceptually distinct. (The relation of learning ability to *g* is discussed in Chapter 9.)

Closely related to the notion of "intelligence" as a repertoire of specific skills is the idea of *competence*. Some psychologists disparage or belittle the concept of *g* and the use of highly *g*-loaded tests, and argue that tests of "competence" should be used instead. No one denies the reality or value of competence, loosely defined though it is. But to the extent that actual examples of competence involve something much more general than demonstrated capability in a specific situation calling for well-learned skills, its main ingredient is probably *g*. Competence is not a unitary trait, but a combination of traits: mostly *g* plus certain personality factors plus resourcefulness and perseverance in bringing one's acquired skills and know-how to bear in certain situations. Aside from prior demonstrated competence in a fairly broad sphere of activity, by far the best predictor of competence is a highly *g*-loaded test battery. (The predictive validity of *g* for a wide variety of competence in "real life" situations is the topic of Chapter 9.)

The specificity doctrine and theories of individual differences based exclusively on learning principles are contradicted further by several important phenomena in the ability domain.

The most distinctive aspects of mental maturation cannot be explained exclusively in terms of learning. Few children at age five are able to copy a diamond-shaped figure (♦); most five-year-old children cannot even be taught to do it with specific training. Yet by age seven more than 50 percent can do it easily without any prior training. A child cannot copy (much less draw from memory) a figure that he or she cannot conceptualize. It is the abstract conceptualization of the figure that makes it *g* loaded, and that is why this task is used in Binet's test and other tests of children's general ability. Certain figures cannot be adequately conceptualized until the child reaches a certain level of mental maturity related to brain development.

The causal underpinnings of mental development take place at the neurological level even in the absence of any specific environmental inputs such as those that could possibly explain mental growth in something like figure copying in terms of transfer from prior learning. The well-known "Case of Isabel" is a classic example.[8] From birth to age six, Isabel was totally confined to a dimly lighted attic room, where she lived alone with her deaf-mute mother, who was her only social contact. Except for food, shelter, and the presence of her mother, Isabel was reared in what amounted to a totally deprived environment. There were no toys, picture books, or gadgets of any kind for her to play with. When found by the authorities, at age six, Isabel was tested and found to have a mental age of one year and seven months and an IQ of about 30, which is barely at the imbecile level. In many ways she behaved like a very young child; she had no speech and made only croaking sounds. When handed toys or other unfamiliar objects, she would immediately put them in her mouth, as infants normally do. Yet as soon as she was exposed to educational experiences she acquired speech, vocabulary, and syntax at an astonishing rate and gained six years of tested mental age within just two years. By the age of eight, she had come up to a mental age of eight, and her level of achievement in school was on a par with her age-mates. This means that her rate of mental development—gaining six years of mental age in only two years—was three times faster than that of the average child. As she approached the age of eight, however, her mental development and scholastic performance drastically slowed down and proceeded thereafter at the rate of an average child. She graduated from high school as an average student.

What all this means to the _g_ controversy is that the neurological basis of information processing continued developing autonomously throughout the six years of Isabel's environmental deprivation, so that as soon as she was exposed to a normal environment she was able to learn those things for which she was developmentally "ready" at an extraordinarily fast rate, far beyond the rate for typically reared children over the period of six years during which their mental age normally increases from two to eight years. But the fast rate of manifest mental development slowed down to an average rate at the point where the level of mental development caught up with the level of neurological development. Clearly, the rate of mental development during childhood is not just the result of accumulating various learned skills that transfer to the acquisition of new skills, but is largely based on the maturation of neural structures.

Another refutation of the attempt to explain variation in mental ability as purely differences in learned skills is the fact that the size of the correlations between various abilities that are exclusively due to the abilities' _g_ loadings (that is, correlation excluding group factors) cannot be explained in terms of learning and transfer or general problem-solving strategies. These explanations may be idly invoked, but they have no predictive power. Is there any principle of learning or transfer that would explain or predict the high correlations between such dissimilar tasks as _verbal analogies, number series,_ and _block de-_

signs? Could it explain or predict the correlation between pitch discrimination ability and visual perceptual speed, or the fact that they both are correlated with each of the three tests mentioned above?

Finally, to the extent that a theory of mental ability tries to explain individual differences solely as the result of learning, it is doomed to refutation by the evidence of behavioral genetics, which shows that a preponderant proportion of the variance of IQ (even more so of _g_) consists of genetic variance. An individual's genes are certainly not subject to learning or experience. But it is certainly a naïve mistake to suppose that the high heritability of _g_ implies that a great variety of learning experience is not a prerequisite for successful performance on the tests that measure _g_. What high heritability means is that _individual differences_ in test scores are not mainly attributable to individual differences in opportunity for the prerequisite learning. (A review of recent developments in the genetics of mental ability is presented in Chapter 7.)

Contextualism. This is a fairly recent idea—I would call it an ideology—that is mistakenly thought to challenge _g_. It really does nothing of the kind. What it essentially boils down to is little more than another argument about how "intelligence" should be defined. The general answer given by contextualists is that no one cross-cultural definition of "intelligence" is possible in behavioral or psychometric terms, because "intelligence" is just whatever kinds of behavior are typically valued in any particular cultural context. Examples are usually drawn from cultures that are most different and remote from modern Western civilization.

Contextualism argues, for example, that some cultures might consider Einstein "unintelligent" if it were found that he could not throw a spear skillfully enough to fell a wild boar in the bush. That Einstein spent his time scribbling formulas like $E = mc^2$ would probably be seen as a mental disorder in this culture that valued hunting skill above all other abilities. The behavior that one culture values as "intelligent," it is argued, may be seen as maladaptive in some other culture. Beliefs, motives, skills, and actions are perceived as "intelligent" only in terms of what certain persons consider effective or rewarding in a particular context. Thus criminal and antisocial acts, provided they escape the law while seeming to benefit the perpetrator, may be admired as "intelligence" in certain subcultures. Contextualism is trivial from the standpoint of research on mental ability because it provides no answer for the wide range of individual differences that exists even when the total context of performance is held constant (as, for example, among full siblings reared together). The interpretations of "intelligence" offered by cultural relativism and contextualism indeed strengthen my contention in Chapter 2 that attempts to define "the essence" of "intelligence" are scientifically unproductive.[9]

MATHEMATICAL AND STATISTICAL ARGUMENTS

The following challenges to g are considerably more serious and sophisticated than those mentioned thus far. They have had a stronger and more enduring influence on research and theories of mental ability. Although some are quite elaborate theories, only their specific aspects that may seem to pose a challenge to the construct of g are discussed here.

GUILFORD'S "STRUCTURE-OF-INTELLECT" MODEL

While he was director of aviation psychology for the U.S. Air Force during World War II, the eminent psychologist Joy Paul Guilford (1897–1987) developed his widely known Structure-of-Intellect (SOI) model of human abilities.[10] Guilford's thinking was more diametrically opposed to Spearman's than was any other theorist's. Guilford's theory does not recognize the existence of g and formally has no place even for second-order group factors. But it also proved to be an unconvincing and short-lived challenge—one might say pseudo-challenge—to g theory. Carroll's summary of the SOI model fairly represents the viewpoint of most present-day researchers in this field: "Guilford's SOI model must, therefore, be marked down as a somewhat eccentric aberration in the history of intelligence models; that so much attention has been paid to it is disturbing, to the extent that textbooks and other treatments of it have given the impression that the model is valid and widely accepted, when clearly it is not."[11]

The SOI model is termed a *facet* model. The model presupposes three facets of ability, each with several forms: *Contents* (visual, auditory, symbolic, semantic, behavioral), *Products* (units, classes, relations, systems, transformations, implications), and *Operations* (cognition, memory, divergent production, convergent production, and evaluation). Each of the three facets can be represented as one dimension of a rectangular prism containing $5 \times 6 \times 5 = 150$ cells. Each cell is one of the abilities postulated by the SOI. Each of the 150 abilities is thus derived by the intersection of one form of each of the three facets, as shown in Figure 5.1. Guilford found or devised at least 100 tests that he assigned to different cells of the SOI. Some forty or fifty cells remained unfilled by actual tests, but suggested the kinds of tests that would need to be developed to fill them. In the SOI model, separate or independent abilities are simply postulated by the model according to a predetermined scheme. Tests are devised to measure each of the postulated abilities. Many existing tests can be classified into one of the SOI categories.

Auditory digit span memory, for example, would fall into the cell created by the intersection of *Contents*-auditory $\times$ *Products*-units $\times$ *Operations*-memory. Visual digit span memory would fall into a different cell on one facet, namely *Contents*-visual, with the other facets remaining the same. According to the model, the abilities represented in each of the 150 cells are assumed to be

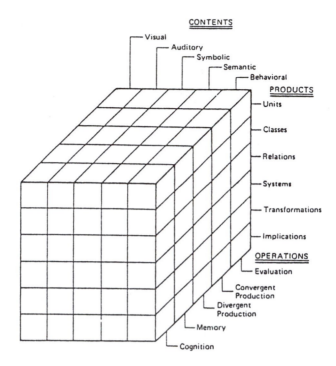

Figure 5.1. Guilford's facet model, known as the Structure-of-Intellect (SOI), in which each cell, created by the intersection of a particular form of each of the three facets (Contents, Products, Operations), defines a distinct ability. The SOI is really a schema for classifying or generating a wide variety of cognitive tests rather than a theory of mental ability. The SOI does not map onto the factors derived from any form of hierarchical factor analysis. (The Structure-of-Intellect model, J. P. Guilford, in B. B. Wolman, ed., *Handbook of intelligence: Theories, measurements, and applications*, Copyright © 1985. Reprinted by permission of John Wiley & Sons, Inc.)

uncorrelated. In fact, however, auditory and visual digit span memory are perfectly correlated (after correction for attenuation) in the normal population.[12] (The correlation is made less than perfect by including persons who have a temporal lobe lesion, which results in a form of aphasia that impairs processing of auditory but not visual information.) Many other tests that are placed in different cells of the SOI are also highly correlated.[13]

Any form of factor analysis that allows the extraction of a general factor has no trouble finding a very robust *g* in any sizable collection of Guilford's tests despite their assignment to distinct cells of the SOI. Guilford nonetheless argued that the 150 cells were orthogonal, or uncorrelated, primary factors. His empirical demonstration of so many orthogonal factors, however, relied on a technique known as *targeted* orthogonal rotation. Aptly named *Procrustes*, this method literally forces tests that were specifically selected or designed to measure the

SOI abilities to have significant loadings only on particular factors, the number and definitions of which are predetermined by the SOI model. This cannot be accepted as evidence that the 150 abilities in different cells of the SOI are not intercorrelated, since Guilford's Procrustes method of orthogonal rotation foreordains uncorrelated factors. In brief, Guilford simply assumed *a priori* that g does not exist, and he eschewed any type of factor analysis that would allow g to appear.

Zero Correlations between Abilities. Guilford's contention that g is untenable probably originated, at least in part, from his observation that some considerable number of cognitive tests showed correlations with each other that are not significantly different from zero. The finding of nonsignificant correlations in Guilford's data based on U.S. Air Force personnel led to his extensive review[14] of the 7,082 correlations among various SOI tests accumulated over some fifteen years. He concluded that about 24 percent of the correlations were not significantly greater than zero. For a good many years, this claim was in fact considered the chief item of evidence against g theory.

Guilford's analysis and conclusion, however, have since been found fallacious. The nonsignificant and near-zero correlations he found in his data were the result of several artifacts: sampling error, restriction of the range-of-talent, attenuation due to measurement error, and the inclusion of some tests of "divergent thinking" that do not qualify as tests of ability as it is defined in Chapter 3. The 7,082 correlations in Guilford's study show a normal frequency distribution, with the number of zero and negative correlations no greater than would be theoretically expected because of chance error. When proper corrections are made for restriction of range and attenuation, all of the correlations are above zero, with a mean of $+.45$.[15] With the collapse of Guilford's claim of zero correlations between mental abilities, there remains no bona fide evidence in the SOI model that contradicts the basic premise of g theory that all mental tests are positively correlated.

SAMPLING THEORIES OF THORNDIKE AND THOMSON

The sampling theories of g do not really question the existence of g as a factor analytic construct, yet it is often mistakenly believed that they somehow challenge or disprove the "true" existence of g. While acknowledging g as a factor, sampling theory interprets it as representing not a unitary property of the mind or brain, such as Spearman's hypothesis of "mental energy," but as the *overlap* of complex mental tests that draw upon different samples of the myriad *uncorrelated* "elements" that, in various combinations, constitute the different mental abilities measured by tests.

Sampling theory, though not called by that name until later, seems to have originated with Edward Lee Thorndike (1874–1949), America's first major abilities theorist. Thorndike was most famous for his theory of learning, which he named *connectionism*. It held that learning consists of "selecting and connect-

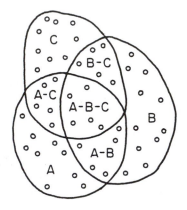

Figure 5.2. Illustration of the sampling theory of ability factors, in which the small circles represent neural elements or bonds and the large circles represent tests that sample different sets of elements (labeled A, B, and C). Correlation between tests is due to the number of elements they sample in common, represented by the areas of overlap. The overlap of A-B-C is the general factor, while the overlaps of A-B, A-C, and B-C are group factors. The non-overlapping areas are the tests' specificities. *Source: Bias in mental testing* by Arthur R. Jensen, Fig. 6.13, p. 238. Copyright © 1980 by Arthur R. Jensen. Reprinted with permission of the Free Press, a Division of Simon & Schuster, and Routledge Ltd.

ing'' stimuli (S) and responses (R). The S-R connections were called *bonds*. Thorndike thought of these bonds in neural terms, presumably as synaptic connections. He hypothesized that individuals differ in the total number of potential bonds they are able to acquire through learning and experience. But as a staunch hereditarian, he believed that individual differences in the number of nerve cells available for acquiring such bonds are innate. Successful performance on any given mental test item would involve the activation of some limited set of the S-R bonds, and any test composed of a wide variety of items would therefore involve a great many S-R bonds. Different tests composed of a variety of items would inevitably tap some of the same bonds, and the fact that various tests sample some of the same bonds in common is what causes the tests to be correlated. The sampling theory can be depicted in terms of the elements sampled by different tests, as shown in Figure 5.2.

Thorndike came to these conclusions even as early as 1903, a year before Spearman's *g* entered the picture. Of course, Thorndike immediately saw the opposition between his connectionist interpretation and Spearman's idea that test intercorrelations reflect some underlying unitary cause.

In 1923, a young British psychologist, Godfrey Thomson (1881–1955), came to spend a year in Thorndike's department at Columbia University. At that time, Thomson was already known as the sharpest critic of Spearman's theory of mental ability as a unitary factor, and it was partly on that basis, along with his expertness in mathematics and statistics, that Thorndike sought him for a position on the Columbia faculty.[16] After a year at Columbia, however, Thomson accepted a distinguished professorship at Edinburgh University and became famous in his own right, being one of the only three British psychologists (along with Sir Frederick Bartlett and Sir Cyril Burt) ever knighted. Thomson and Thorndike were of like mind regarding the interpretation of Spearman's *g*, but because of Thomson's superior understanding of factor analysis, he was able to formalize Thorndike's argument in mathematical terms. It was Thomson's particular formulation that became known as the *sampling theory* of intelligence.

Thomson demonstrated mathematically that various-sized groups of digits randomly sampled from a large pool of digits (each equally represented) could be correlated with each other in terms of the number of digits any two random samples had in common.[17] He showed that the correlations among a number of groups of randomly sampled digits displayed the same kind of hierarchy that Spearman had found for mental tests, and that Spearman's two-factor theory (i.e., a general factor + specific factors) could be demonstrated for the groups of random digits that he generated by tossing dice. The random (hence uncorrelated) digits theoretically correspond to the multitude of neural elements or "bonds" originally hypothesized by Thorndike, while the various-sized groups into which they were randomly selected correspond to mental tests. Thomson correctly argued from this random sampling demonstration that, although Spearman's *g* can indeed be extracted from the matrix of test intercorrelations by means of factor analysis, Spearman's hypothesis that *g* reflects some unitary cause, such as the general level of neural or mental "energy" available to the brain's activity, is not a *necessary* explanation of *g* or of the all-positive correlations among mental tests. These correlations could be explained just as well, and perhaps more parsimoniously, by the overlap of the multiple uncorrelated causal elements that enter into performance on all mental tests. To simulate the results of the factor analysis of mental tests, the sampling model only requires, in Thomson's words, "that it be possible to take our tests with equal ease from any part of the causal background; that there be no linkages among the bonds which will disturb the random frequency of the various possible combinations; in other words, that there be no 'faculties' in the mind. . . . The sampling theory assumes that each ability is composed of *some but not all* of the bonds, and that abilities can differ very markedly in their 'richness,' some needing very many 'bonds,' some only a few."[18] Thomson's formulation appears quite plausible and has attracted many subscribers.[19] On these terms, it seems at least as plausible as Spearman's unitary "mental energy" theory of *g*.

A major criticism of Thomson's version of sampling theory (and the same can probably be said of Spearman's "energy") is that, as originally formulated, it is unsusceptible to falsification and is thus empirically vacuous. The psychometrician Jane Loevinger expressed this view as follows:

> The sampling theory hardly qualifies as a true theory, for it does not make any assertion to which evidence is relevant. Perhaps the large number of adherents to this view is due to the fact that no one has offered evidence against it. But until

the view is defined more sharply, one cannot even conceive of the possibility of contrary evidence, nor, for that matter, confirmatory evidence. A statement about the human mind which can be neither supported nor refuted by any facts, known or conceivable, is certainly useless. Bridgman and other philosophers of science would probably declare the sampling theory to be meaningless.[20]

The plausibility of sampling theory gains its strength from two undeniable observations that are consistent with it. First, it is a fact that the brain is composed of a great many neural elements and some large number of these necessarily play a role in any kind of mental activity. The second is that the degree to which mental tests are correlated with each other is related to the complexity of the mental operations they call for. More complex tests are highly correlated and have larger *g* loadings than less complex tests. This is what one would predict from the sampling theory: a complex test involves more neural elements and would therefore have a greater probability of involving more elements that are common to other tests.

But there are other facts the overlapping elements theory cannot adequately explain. One such question is why a small number of certain kinds of nonverbal tests with minimal informational content, such as the Raven matrices, tend to have the highest *g* loadings, and why they correlate so highly with content-loaded tests such as vocabulary, which surely would seem to tap a largely different pool of neural elements. Another puzzle in terms of sampling theory is that tests such as forward and backward digit span memory, which must tap many common elements, are not as highly correlated as are, for instance, vocabulary and block designs, which would seem to have few elements in common. Of course, one could argue trivially in a circular fashion that a higher correlation means more elements in common, even though the theory can't tell us why seemingly very different tests have many elements in common and seemingly similar tests have relatively few.

Even harder to explain in terms of the sampling theory is the finding that individual differences on a visual scan task (i.e., speed of scanning a set of digits for the presence or absence of a "target" digit), which makes virtually no demand on memory, and a memory scan test (i.e., speed of scanning a set of digits held in memory for the presence or absence of a "target" digit) are perfectly correlated, even though they certainly involve different neural processes.[21] And how would sampling theory explain the finding that choice reaction time is more highly correlated with scores on a nonspeeded vocabulary test than with scores on a test of clerical checking speed? Another apparent stumbling block for sampling theory is the correlation between neural conduction velocity (NCV) in a low-level brain tract (from retina to primary visual cortex) and scores on a complex nonverbal reasoning test (Raven), even though the higher brain centers that are engaged in the complex reasoning ability demanded by the Raven do not involve the visual tract.

Perhaps the most problematic test of overlapping neural elements posited by the sampling theory would be to find two (or more) abilities, say, A and B, that are highly correlated in the general population, and then find some individuals in whom ability A is severely impaired without there being any impairment of ability B. For example, looking back at Figure 5.2, which illustrates sampling theory, we see a large area of overlap between the elements in Test A and the elements in Test B. But if many of the elements in A are eliminated, some of its elements that are shared with the correlated Test B will also be eliminated, and so performance on Test B (and also on Test C in this diagram) will be diminished accordingly. Yet it has been noted that there are cases of extreme impairment in a particular ability due to brain damage, or sensory deprivation due to blindness or deafness, or a failure in development of a certain ability due to certain chromosomal anomalies, without any sign of a corresponding deficit in other highly correlated abilities.[22] On this point, behavioral geneticists Willerman and Bailey comment: "Correlations between phenotypically different mental tests may arise, not because of any causal connection among the mental elements required for correct solutions or because of the physical sharing of neural tissue, but because each test in part requires the same 'qualities' of brain for successful performance. For example, the efficiency of neural conduction or the extent of neuronal arborization may be correlated in different parts of the brain because of a similar epigenetic matrix, not because of concurrent functional overlap."[22] A simple analogy to this would be two independent electric motors (analogous to specific brain functions) that perform different functions both running off the same battery (analogous to *g*). As the battery runs down, both motors slow down at the same rate in performing their functions, which are thus perfectly correlated although the motors themselves have no parts in common. But a malfunction of one machine would have no effect on the other machine, although a sampling theory would have predicted impaired performance for both machines.

Cognitive Process Theories. Sampling theory need not be limited to positing an indefinitely large number of undefined elements or hypothetical neural "bonds" as the units of sampling. The idea of *elementary cognitive processes* (ECPs, also called *information processes*) has also been proposed as a basis for a sampling theory of *g* and the group factors. The advantage of ECPs is that they are few in number, capable of being operationally defined, and can be measured at the behavioral level, though not always directly in an isolated form, by the use of *elementary cognitive tasks* (ECTs). The ECPs are processes such as stimulus apprehension, encoding of stimuli, discrimination, choice, retrieval of information from short-term or long-term memory, transformation or manipulation of information in working memory, and response inhibition or response execution.

The laboratory tasks (ECTs) used to measure these ECPs are so simple that virtually all persons can perform them. The only reliable individual differences are in response times and the degree of consistency of response times over many repeated trials for different individuals. Individual differences in these simple measures of the efficiency of information processing are correlated with scores on various psychometric tests to the degree that the tests are *g* loaded. It has been hypothesized that various psychometric tests involve different subsets of the ECPs to varying degrees and that the most highly *g*-loaded tests are those that call upon a larger number of the ECPs or upon those ECPs that most crucially determine capacity for information processing (analogous to a computer's central processing unit). This line of theory and research is an important recent development in the science of human abilities (see Chapter 8).

Behavioral Repertoire Theory. One of the leading researchers on human abilities, Lloyd G. Humphreys, has long espoused what can be described as a pragmatic behavioristic sampling theory of "intelligence."[23] It represents the purest form of scientific positivism one is likely to find in all of psychology, outside the writings of B. F. Skinner and his most literal disciples. Humphreys favors Thomson's sampling theory, but prefers that the units of sampling be "phenotypic," that is, a repertoire of observable behavior.

Humphreys is not in the least a critic of *g* theory, but he has his own rather unique definition of it, although he seems to prefer the term "general intelligence." He has consistently defined it within the positivism-behaviorist boundaries, as follows:

> Intelligence is the acquired repertoire of all intellectual (cognitive) skills and knowledge available to the person at a particular point in time. Individual differences in intelligence are monotonically related to the size of this repertoire. To avoid circularity, intellectual is defined by the consensus of experts working in the area. The repertoire is acquired during development, but it is acquired, stored, and retrieved by a biological organism. Thus there is both a genetic and an environmental substrate for the trait. . . . A test cannot measure the entire repertoire, but it can measure a broad representative sample of the elements. (1994, p. 180)

I believe that a scientific construct or theory should not have to depend upon a consensus of experts (or of anyone else) for its validity, although there may well be a consensus that certain data or empirically tested predictions are in accord with the construct. This is especially so for a theory that strives so hard to be positivistic. Also, in the advanced sciences, theoretical constructs, as *g* is, are not defined in terms of a "repertoire" of all their multifarious effects, but in terms that account for these effects. As Eysenck noted: "Physicists do not *define* gravitation in terms of its consequences, such as the apple falling on Newton's head, planetary motions, the tides, the shapes of the planets, the movements of the moon, the bulging of the equator, the existence of black holes, the earth's rate of precession, galaxy formation, the movements of comets, or the existence of asteroids. They define gravitation as that which is responsible for all these events, and clearly no agreement would ever be reached if definitions were phrased solely in terms of the consequences of gravitational forces!"[24]

CATTELL'S THEORY OF FLUID AND CRYSTALLIZED ABILITIES

Several years after Raymond B. Cattell (b. 1905) earned his Ph.D. degree (1929) under Spearman, developments in mental testing led him to the hypothesis that Spearman's *g* is not a unitary factor but a composite of two quite different general factors, either of which may dominate depending on the nature of the tests that are factor analyzed. In Cattell's thinking, these two presumably new, semigeneral factors completely replaced Spearman's single overarching *g*. Cattell termed them *fluid* intelligence and *crystallized* intelligence, now conventionally symbolized as *Gf* and *Gc*.[25]

Gf might be called fluid reasoning, or the capacity to figure out novel problems. It is indeed the "eduction of relations and of correlates" as these are demonstrated in mental tests (or life situations) in which specific prior learned knowledge, skills, algorithms, or strategies are of relatively little use. In Cattell's words,[25] *Gf* "is an expression of the level of complexity of relationships which an individual can perceive and act upon when he does not have recourse to answers to such complex issues already stored in memory" (p. 99). *Gf* is most loaded in tests that have virtually no scholastic or cultural content, such as perceptual and figural tests like Raven's matrices, or in verbal tests that depend mainly on figuring out the relationships between certain words when the meanings of all the words themselves are highly familiar.

Gc could be called consolidated knowledge. As described by Cattell[25] *Gc* "arises not only from better educational opportunity but also from a history of persistence and good motivation in applying fluid intelligence to approved areas of learning" (p. 96). *Gc* therefore reflects scholastic and cultural knowledge acquisition. Cattell theorizes that a person's *Gf* is *invested* in the person's learning experiences throughout the life span. As children grow up and their opportunities and interests differentiate, their *Gf* is invested in different subjects to different degrees. But in large part, individual differences in *Gf* determine individual differences in *Gc* among persons with similar educational and cultural opportunities. Persons high in *Gf* tend to acquire more *Gc* (i.e., they reap greater returns on their initial investment) from their opportunities for learning than persons of lower *Gf*. Persons from very different cultural backgrounds, however, may differ markedly in the *Gc* appropriate to any one culture, even though they may be equal in *Gf*. But each person's *Gc* would closely parallel his or her *Gf* in the person's own culture.

Gc is most highly loaded in tests based on scholastic knowledge and cultural content where the relation-eduction demands of the items are fairly simple. Here are two examples of verbal analogy problems, both of about equal difficulty in terms of percentage of correct responses in the English-speaking general population, but the first is more highly loaded on *Gf* and the second is more highly loaded on *Gc*.

1. **Temperature** is to **cold** as **Height** is to
    (a) **hot** (b) **inches** (c) **size** (d) **tall** (e) **weight**

2. **Bizet** is to **Carmen** as **Verdi** is to
    (a) **Aïda** (b) **Elektra** (c) **Lakmé** (d) **Manon** (e) **Tosca**

(Answers: 1, d; 2, a)

Gf and *Gc* typically emerge as higher-order (usually second-order) factors in any large collection of tests given to a highly heterogeneous subject sample in terms of educational or cultural background. In factor analyses based on groups that are quite homogeneous in these respects, such as schoolchildren of the same age and social-cultural background, *Gf* and *Gc* often are not clearly differentiated and amalgamate into a single general factor. But in the general population *Gf* and *Gc* are clearly discerned, and the psychological distinctions that Cattell makes between them are valid. The major exception is Cattell's prediction that the heritability[26] of *Gf* is greater than that of *Gc*. Although this may be true in culturally or linguistically heterogeneous samples for which some of the *Gc*-loaded tests may be inappropriate or culturally biased measures, the usual finding is that *Gf* and *Gc* have about the same heritability. In fact, the heritability of scores on scholastic achievement tests is about the same as that on the best tests of *Gf*. In terms of Cattell's "investment" theory, one could say that persons' standing on tests of *Gc* quite closely reflects the amount of *Gf* they had to invest in the kinds of content that typically compose highly *Gc*-loaded tests.

Since the discovery of *Gf* and *Gc*, Cattell and his former student John Horn have identified a number of other "general" factors (better called *broad* factors) that emerge from large and diverse batteries as second-order factors, such as *Gs* (visual inspection speed), *Gv* (visual-spatial reasoning), *Ga* (auditory thinking), *Gq* (quantitative reasoning independent of Gc), and *Gr* (fluency in recall of learned information, as in speed of naming familiar objects). These broad abilities, though each is labeled *G* (with a distinguishing subscript), are of course not general to the whole matrix of tests. Along with *Gf* and *Gc*, they are correlated second-order factors from which a higher-order factor, or *g*, can be extracted. But Cattell and Horn prefer not to extract the third-order factor, or *g*, contrary to the practice of most factor analysts. The Cattell-Horn model of abilities, therefore, is called a *truncated* hierarchy. That is, it lacks the apex of the hierarchy of factors, which is *g*. Cattell has stated in italics[25] that *"there can be no such thing as a categorical general factor"* (p. 87). (By "categorical" here he presumably means "uniquely determined" or "invariant" across factor analyses of different groups of tests.) But this objection to extracting *g* from the set of second-order factors, such as *Gf*, *Gc*, and all the other second-order factors listed above, provided they are all present in the analyzed battery, does not take into consideration the degree of invariance of the estimates of *g* that would actually be found across different test batteries in which all of these second-order factors could be identified. The departure from perfect invariance would most likely be small.

At the time that only two factors, *Gf* and *Gc*, stood at the highest level of Cattell's "truncated" hierarchy, there was a valid reason not to extract a third-order *g*. The reason is not that *g* doesn't exist in the test battery, but that a third-order hierarchical *g* is mathematically indeterminate when there are no more than two second-order factors. That is, there is only one correlation (i.e., the correlation between the two second-order factors, e.g., *Gf* and *Gc*) and all that can be determined is the geometric mean of the these factors' *g* loadings, which is equal to the square root of the correlation between the two second-order factors. Although we can know the *average* of the two factors' *g* loadings, we can't know the exact *g* loading of each factor separately, and ipso facto we cannot properly calculate the *g* loadings of each of the tests in the battery or calculate the *g* factor scores of the subjects who took the tests.

What happens when a very large battery of tests yielding *Gf* and *Gc*, along with all the other second-order factors listed above (and a good many other second-order factors not listed here), are subjected to a hierarchical factor analysis in which the analysis is carried all the way, allowing a third-order *g* to emerge? This has been done in five independent studies by the Swedish psychometrician Jan-Eric Gustafsson[27] and also by others, all with the same result. Gustafsson found *Gf* and *Gc* and most of the other above-mentioned second-order factors, and quite a few others. But Gustafsson's most interesting and important finding, which was consistent in all five studies, was that the third-order *g* is perfectly correlated with *Gf*, so that when all the second-order factors, including *Gf*, were residualized (i.e., the common-factor part of each second-order factor that went into the *g* factor was removed), *Gf* completely disappeared. *Gf* was subsumed into the single, higher-order *g*. The other second-order factors remained, although their substantial common variance was absorbed into the *g*. The residualized *Gc* remained as an exclusively verbal-numerical-educational factor. The residualized second-order factors represented mostly types of test content, such as verbal and numerical in *Gc* and figural content in *Gv*, but some second-order factors (e.g., auditory perception and memory) represent processes that operate on many types of content. In brief, given a wide variety of tests in the factor analysis, *Gf* and *g* appear to be one and the same factor, or at least to be so highly correlated as to make *Gf* redundant for all practical purposes.

Despite Gustafsson's impressive demonstration, however, some psychologists argue that there are too few large-scale studies at present to permit a definitive conclusion about the equivalence of *Gf* and *g*.[28] There are probably sufficient data in the Cattell-Horn data banks to permit a definitive conclusion if the data were analyzed by confirmatory factor analysis expressly to test this hypothesis. Such an analysis would be well worth performing for its theoretical significance.

Width and Altitude of Intellect. E. L. Thorndike[29] hypothesized the existence of two aspects of mental ability, termed *width* and *altitude*, which are somewhat akin to *Gc* and *Gf*, respectively. *Width* is measured by the *number* of different kinds of things a person knows that are fairly easy to know—for example, common vocabulary and general information items that some 50 to 60 percent of the general population can answer correctly. *Altitude* is measured by various kinds of reasoning problems in which information content is much less important than relation eduction. The items range in complexity, and hence level of difficulty, from problems that can be solved by 95 percent of the general population to items that can be solved by fewer than 5 percent. A person's altitude score reflects the level of complexity of the problems that the person can solve.

Much to Thorndike's surprise, his tests of altitude and width were almost perfectly correlated. They were not distinct aspects of intellect at all, but reflected one and the same general ability, or g. This is very much like the high correlation typically found between Gf and Gc and the near equivalence of Gf and g. It is a safe bet that if tests of a very wide variety of Gc types of items (much like Thorndike's test of "width of intellect") were factor analyzed, they would yield a general factor that is correlated probably as much as $+.90$ with the general factor extracted from tests composed entirely of Gf types of items. In fact, the items of the Verbal and the Performance scales of the Wechsler Intelligence Scale for Children (WISC) correspond rather closely to Gc and Gf types of tests, respectively. In the national standardization sample, a general factor extracted from just the Verbal scale subtests is correlated .80 with the general factor extracted from just the Performance scale subtests. The average g loading of the Verbal and Performance scales is therefore $\sqrt{.80} = .89$. This is almost as high as the reliability of IQ on the WISC, and correction for attenuation would bring this average g very close to unity.

It appears that the g extracted from a wide variety of tests with regard to information content and task demands is in effect a distillate of some relatively small number of basic cognitive processes that enter into performance on this wide variety of test items. The variance associated with the wide variety of knowledge content and specific skills tapped by the many diverse tests is "strained out," so to speak, by the factor analytic procedure, most of it being left in the tests' specificities, while some of it goes into the first-order factors, and less into the second-order factors. Little, if any, gets into the third-order factor, or g, which therefore is like a distillate obtained from many diverse abilities, qualitatively unlike any of them and reflecting individual differences only in the overall efficiency of cognitive processes.

MULTIDIMENSIONAL SCALING AND GUTTMAN'S RADEX MODEL

Louis Guttman (1916–1987), the eminent Israeli psychometrician, devised a method for representing the relationships between various mental tests, which he called a *radex* model.[30] Because Guttman's radex does not use the terminology of factor analysis and appears to have little resemblance to it, especially making no mention of g (or of group factors), some psychologists have mistakenly believed that it contradicts g theory or does away with g altogether.

The radex is obtained by what Guttman called "smallest space" analysis, using nonmetric multidimensional scaling. It is a planar spatial representation of the degree of similarity between tests based on their correlations (or actually the inverse of their correlations). That is, the larger the correlation between any two tests, the smaller is the distance separating them. If each of many tests is

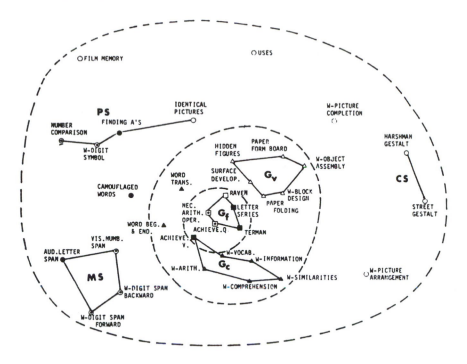

Figure 5.3. A radex representation of various ability tests given to 241 high school students. The factor clusters (**Gf, Gv, Gc, MS, PS, CS**) are superimposed. (From Marshalek, Lohman, & Snow, 1983. Used with permission of Ablex.)

represented as a dot in a spatial array, the dots are scattered over a roughly circular area. In many applications of the radex plot to different batteries of diverse mental tests, the cognitively most complex tests are found to congregate near the center of the circle (i.e., they are the tests that have the highest average correlations with other tests). Radiating out from the center are tests of lesser complexity (and lower average correlations). Proximity to the center, therefore, indicates greater complexity and greater generality (i.e., higher intercorrelations).

The other notable feature of the radex is that tests that are similar in content (such as verbal, numerical, spatial, and memory) fall into different sectors of the circle. The circle can be divided up, like cutting a pie, such that each slice contains a particular type of tests. In other words, the locations of the tests in the circular space (the *radex*) indicate (a) their degree of complexity and generality (i.e., average correlation with other tests), and (b) their degree of similarity to other tests in terms of content. A radex representation of a large battery of tests is shown in Figure 5.3. Note that Raven's matrices test, which is usually the most highly *g* loaded in many factor analyses, lies closest to the center of the radex

In this analysis, as in others, Richard Snow and his co-workers at Stanford

University have found that a hierarchical factor analysis of the same battery of tests almost perfectly maps onto Guttman's radex.[31] That is, every test's degree of proximity to the center of the radex corresponds to the size of the test's (inverse) g loading, and every test's proximity to the midline of the particular sector in which it is located corresponds to the size of the test's (inverse) loading on the group factor. The set of tests that identify a group factor in the hierarchical factor analysis falls within the same sector of the radex. In short, Guttman's radex model amounts to a spatial representation of a hierarchical factor analysis. That a method other than factor analysis orders tests spatially in such close accord with their g loadings as obtained from factor analysis further supports g theory.

GARDNER'S SEVEN "FRAMES OF MIND" AND MENTAL MODULES

Howard Gardner has been perceived as a critic of g theory and of tests that mainly reflect g, such as the IQ. I suspect that this is partly, if not largely, the basis of the popularity accorded Gardner's views, especially in educational circles, as many teachers feel desperate over the wide range of individual differences displayed in their classes. If a child has a low IQ and is doing poorly in school, there are, according to Gardner's theory,[32] several other kinds of "intelligence" in one or more of which the child may excel. Two of the seven "intelligences" claimed by Gardner—*linguistic* and *logical-mathematical*—would considerably overlap the conventional IQ. The remaining five "intelligences" are *spatial, musical, bodily-kinesthetic*, and two kinds of personal "intelligences," *intrapersonal*, or the perception of one's own feelings, and *interpersonal*, or the perception of others' feelings, motives, and the like (also called "social intelligence"). As exemplars of each of these "intelligences" Gardner mentions the following famous persons: T. S. Eliot (linguistic), Einstein (logical-mathematical), Picasso (spatial), Stravinsky (musical), Martha Graham (bodily-kinesthetic), Sigmund Freud (intrapersonal), and Mahatma Gandhi (interpersonal). In an interesting book[33] Gardner gives biographical analyses of each of these famous creative geniuses to illustrate his theory of multiple "intelligences" and of the psychological and developmental aspects of socially recognized creativity. When I personally asked Gardner for his estimate of the lowest IQ one could possibly have and be included in a list of names such as this, he said, "About 120." This would of course exclude 90 percent of the general population, and it testifies to the threshold nature of g. That is, a fairly high level of g is a necessary but not sufficient condition for achievement of socially significant creativity.

Gardner's seven "intelligences" were not arrived at through the factor analysis of psychometric tests, but are identified in terms of several kinds of categorical criteria, such as the extent to which an ability can be impaired or preserved in isolation by brain damage, the existence of idiots savants and prodigies in the particular ability, a common set of information-processing operations, a distinct developmental history, evolutionary plausibility, type of encoding in a symbolic system, modular or domain-specific abilities revealed by laboratory tasks, and the finding that psychometric tests such as IQ have low correlations with at least three of Gardner's seven "intelligences."

The boundaries of these criteria seem vague or elastic and one can easily imagine other "intelligences" that could be admitted by such criteria. Why is there no "sexual intelligence" (Casanova) or "criminal intelligence" (Al Capone)?

Some of Gardner's seven "intelligences" clearly correspond to well-identified group factors, such as linguistic (or verbal), logical-mathematical (or quantitative reasoning), and spatial. Tests of these abilities are all highly g loaded, and many elements of musical aptitude have been found to be moderately g loaded (see Chapter 8, p. 223). Other of Gardner's "intelligences" are not yet quantified or measurable in a way that makes it possible at present to assess their g loadings or their place in the factor analytic hierarchy. Some may not meet the criteria of mental abilities as set forth in Chapter 3, but are rather products of psychometrically identified abilities and certain personality traits (see Chapter 14, pp. 572–578). The completely nonquantitative nature of Gardner's theorizing about "intelligences" makes it impossible to assess their relative importance in terms of variance accounted for in the total range of human variation or in terms of their predictive validity in real-life situations.

As interesting as his theory of "multiple intelligences" may seem from the standpoint of literary psychology, in which Gardner has no betters, it is hard to see that it contributes anything substantively new to the taxonomy of abilities and personality discovered by factor analysis.

In fact, it is hard to justify calling all of the abilities in Gardner's system by the same term—"intelligences." If Gardner claims that the various abilities he refers to as "intelligences" are unrelated to one another (which has not been empirically demonstrated), what does it add to our knowledge to label them all "intelligences"? All of them, of course, are abilities (as defined in Chapter 3), several qualify as group factors, and at least three of the seven are known to be substantially g loaded. To assign to the remaining traits the label "intelligences" makes no more sense to me than regarding chess-playing ability an athletic skill. (After all, playing chess requires some little physical activity, and chess players are jokingly called "wood pushers"). Bobby Fisher, then, could be claimed as one of the world's greatest athletes, and many sedentary chess players might be made to feel good by being called athletes. But who would believe it? The skill involved in chess isn't the kind of thing that most people think of as athletic ability, nor would it have any communality if it were entered into a factor analysis of typical athletic skills. Gardner's analogous extension of the ordinary meaning of "intelligence" probably serves more to make people feel good than to advance the science of mental ability.

In summary, I find nothing in Gardner's writings that could be considered a technically meaningful or coherent criticism of g theory. Gardner is at his best in writing about persons with some unusual accomplishment to illustrate his theory of different kinds of "intelligences." Galton, in his *Hereditary Genius* (1869), recognized that a high level of general ability is a necessary but not sufficient condition for outstanding achievement. Besides an above-average level of g, an exceptionally synergistic combination of special abilities or talents and personality traits is always found in the kinds of outstanding exemplars of Gardner's several kinds of "intelligences," such as the famous persons mentioned above. Most psychomtricians would probably agree with the criticism of Gardner's theory of "multiple intelligences" in a recent textbook[34] on "intelligence": "I have argued that a consideration of several sources of evidence used by Gardner to establish the existence of independent intelligences may be used to support the existence of a superordinate general intelligence factor. Thus I find his taxonomy to be arbitrary and without empirical foundation. Neither his rejection of a superordinate general factor [g] nor the specific subset of intelligences that he postulates appears to have a firm theoretical or empirical basis" (p. 40).

Modular Abilities. Gardner invokes recent neurological research on brain *modules* in support of his theory.[35] But there is nothing at all in this research that conflicts in the least with the findings of factor analysis. It has long been certain that the factor structure of abilities is not unitary, because factor analysis applied to the correlations among any large and diverse battery of ability tests reveals that a number of factors (although fewer than the number of different tests) must be extracted to account for most of the variance in all of the tests. The g factor, which is needed theoretically to account for the positive correlations between all tests, is necessarily unitary only within the domain of factor analysis. But the brain mechanisms or processes responsible for the fact that individual differences in a variety of abilities are positively correlated, giving rise to g, need not be unitary. Whether the neural basis of g is some unitary process or a number of distinct processes is a separate empirical question (see Chapter 8).

Some of the highly correlated abilities identified as factors probably represent what are referred to as *modules*. But here is the crux of the main confusion, which results when one fails to realize that in discussing the modularity of mental abilities we make a transition from talking about individual differences and factors to talking about the localized brain processes connected with various kinds of abilities. Some modules may be reflected in the primary factors; but there are other modules that do not show up as factors, such as the ability to acquire language, quick recognition memory for human faces, and three-dimensional space perception, because individual differences among normal persons are too slight for these virtually universal abilities to emerge as factors, or sources of variance. This makes them no less real or important. Modules are distinct, innate brain structures that have developed in the course of human evolution. They are especially characterized by the various ways that information or knowledge is represented by the neural activity of the brain. The main modules thus are linguistic (verbal/auditory/lexical/semantic), _visuospatial, object recognition, numerical-mathematical, musical_, and _kinesthetic._

Although modules generally exist in all normal persons, they are most strikingly highlighted in two classes of persons, (a) those with highly _localized brain lesions_ or pathology, and (b) _idiots savants._ Savants evince striking discrepancies between amazing proficiency in a particular narrow ability and nearly all other abilities, often showing an overall low level of general ability. Thus we see some savants who are even too mentally retarded to take care of themselves, yet who can perform feats of mental calculation, or play the piano by ear, or memorize pages of a telephone directory, or draw objects from memory with photographic accuracy. The modularity of these abilities is evinced by the fact that rarely, if ever, is more than one of them seen in a given savant.

In contrast, there are persons whose tested general level of ability is within the normal range, yet who, because of a localized brain lesion, show a severe deficiency in some particular ability, such as face recognition, receptive or expressive language dysfunctions (aphasia), or inability to form long-term memories of events. Again, modularity is evidenced by the fact that these functional deficiencies are quite isolated from the person's total repertoire of abilities. Even in persons with a normally intact brain, a module's efficiency can be narrowly enhanced through extensive experience and practice in the particular domain served by the module.

Such observations have led some researchers to the mistaken notion that they contradict the discovery of factor analysis that, in the general population, individual differences in mental abilities are all positively and hierarchically correlated, making for a number of distinct factors and a higher-order general factor, or _g_. The presence of a general factor indicates that the workings of the various modules, though distinct in their functions, are all affected to some degree by some brain characteristic(s), such as chemical neurotransmitters, neural conduction velocity, amount of dendritic branching, and degree of myelination of axons, in which there are individual differences. Hence individual differences in the specialized mental activities associated with different modules are correlated.

A simple analogy might help to explain the theoretical compatibility between the positive correlations among all mental abilities and the existence of modularity in mental abilities. Imagine a dozen factories ("persons"), each of which manufactures the same five different gadgets ("modular abilities"). Each gadget is produced by a different machine ("module"). The five machines are all connected to each other by a gear chain that is powered by one motor. But each of the five factories uses a different motor to drive the gear chain, and each factory's motor runs at a constant speed different from the speed of the motors in any other factory. This will cause the factories to differ in their rates of output of the five gadgets ("scores on five different tests"). The factories will be said to differ in overall efficiency or capacity, because the rates of output of the five gadgets are positively correlated. If the correlations between output rates of the gadgets produced by all five factories were factor analyzed, they would yield a large general factor. Gadgets' output rates may not be perfectly correlated, however, because the sales demand for each gadget differs across factories, and the machines that produce the gadgets with the larger sales are better serviced, better oiled, and kept in consistently better operating condition than the machines that make low-demand gadgets. Therefore, even though the five machines are all driven by the same motor, they differ somewhat in their efficiency and consistency of operation, making for less than a perfect correlation between the rates of output. Now imagine that in one factory the main drive shaft of one of the machines breaks, and it cannot produce its gadget at all (analogous to localized brain damage affecting a single module, but not *g*). In another factory, four of the machines break down and fail to produce gadgets, but one machine is very well maintained because it continues to run and puts out gadgets at a rate commensurate with the speed of the motor that powers the gear chain that runs the machine (analogous to an idiot savant).

STERNBERG'S COMPONENTIAL AND TRIARCHIC THEORIES OF "INTELLIGENCE"

Robert J. Sternberg, an eminent psychologist at Yale University, is an astoundingly prolific contributor to the literature on mental abilities. Because he is also known as a critic of what he has called the *g*-ocentric theory of "intelligence," he has been categorized by some psychologists (and by many journalists in the popular press) as being an anti-*g* theorist. This is wrong, as there is nothing in any of Sternberg's writings that in the least contradicts anything that I am saying about *g*. In the words of Sternberg (and his coauthor M. K. Gardner):[36] "We interpret the preponderance of evidence as overwhelmingly supporting the existence of some kind of general factor in human intelligence. Indeed, we are unable to find any convincing evidence at all that militates against this view" (p. 231).

Sternberg's theory doesn't posit anything *instead* of *g*, but attempts essentially two things: to *explain g* and to *supplement g* (and the major group factors found in psychometric tests) with other broad classes of individual difference variables that contribute to successful coping in "real life" situations.

Sternberg's explanation of *g* falls within the purview of his componential theory of cognition. A component is really a hypothetical construct, defined as an elementary information process that operates upon internal representations of objects or symbols. Metacomponents are higher-order executive processes that govern the deployment and coordination of the more elemental components needed for solving a specific problem. The *g* factor reflects individual differences mainly in the metacomponents; the greater the demand made upon them by a given task, the greater is its *g* loading. This is the gist of Sternberg's theory, albeit oversimplified, but to say more would go beyond the scope and purpose of this chapter.[37]

Sternberg's aim to make ability theory more comprehensive is represented in his _triarchic_ theory, which embraces the componential theory but also includes "social intelligence" and "tacit knowledge" (i.e., practical knowledge about the particular context of one's coping activity that is not acquired through formal instruction). These are really achievement variables that reflect how different individuals invest _g_ in activities as affected by their particular opportunities, interests, personality traits, and motivation (see Chapter 14, pp. 575–578). Beyond this, it would be an injustice to try to describe the triarchic theory in less than a full chapter.[38] What is important to note here is that it is not antithetical to _g_ theory.

NOTES

1. Jensen, 1984a.

2. The most serious and detailed attempt at a theoretical formulation of "intelligence" in terms of "social learning theory" is expounded by Staats and Burns (1981). They call it a "social behaviorism theory" of intelligence. In their words, "The theory states, in summary, that intelligence consists of specific repertoires—systems and skills— learned according to specified learning principles" (p. 241). A classic interpretation of mental abilities in terms of transfer of learning is the presidential address to the Canadian Psychological Association by G. A. Ferguson (1956).

3. Ericsson, 1988.

4. Fleishman & Hempel, 1955.

5. "Army Basic-Skills Program Said Failing," Education Week, July 27, 1983.

6. "IQ Tests for Reactor Operators," _Science_, June 22, 1979, Vol. 204, p. 1285.

7. Derr (1989) has written an entertaining article on the meaning of "intelligence" that is implicit in the common use of language. An excellent survey of laypersons' and experts' conceptions of "intelligence" has been presented by Sternberg, Conway, Ketron, & Bernstein (1981).

8. Davis, 1947. Also see the book by Clarke & Clarke, 1976.

9. A number of authors' views of contextualism can be found in the anthology edited by Fry (1984). Sternberg's (1984a, also included in Fry's anthology) generously tolerant review of contextualist thought is the most comprehensive and comprehensible I have come across in this literature. His view of contextualism from the standpoint of a sympathetic outsider makes it seem more sensible and perhaps less substantively vacuous than the impression one gets from some of the writings by dyed-in-the-wool contextualists.

10. Guilford has written extensively about the SOI model. The most comprehensive accounts, with extensive references that will lead readers to virtually the entire literature on SOI, are Guilford, 1967, 1985.

11. Carroll, 1993a, p. 60. Pp. 57–60 of Carroll's book provide a fairly thorough yet succinct critique of the SOI model.

12. Jensen, 1971a.

13. I spoke to Guilford personally about this several years before he died, mentioning that I had found large correlations between tests that differ on all three facets of the SOI.

He replied that the significant correlations were most likely due to not rigorously controlling for age and "sample heterogeneity" (i.e., including different races or social classes in the same analysis). However, even when these variables are strictly controlled, the tests remain highly correlated. His comment about race and social class, however, led me to look at within-family correlations between tests, which completely rules out variance due to race and social class. I found that within-family correlations between different tests are about the same as the correlations obtained in the general population (see Chapter 7, also Jensen, 1980b).

14. Guilford, 1964.

15. Alliger, 1988.

16. Jonçich, 1968.

17. Thomson (1951) formalized sampling theory as follows: The correlation between tests i and j when there is only one common factor is $r_{ij} = \sqrt{(p_i p_j)}$, where p_i and p_j are the proportions of the total number of available "bonds" sampled by tests i and j, respectively. The correlation between tests i and j when the tests have both a general factor and a group factor in common is $r_{ij} = \sqrt{(p_i p_j)}/t$, where t is some selected subset of "bonds" having the proportion t of the total pool of available "bonds." The correlation between tests i and j due to just the common group factor is $r_{ij} = \sqrt{(p_i p_j)}/t - \sqrt{(p_i p_j)}$. The loadings of tests i and j on the "g" factor are $\sqrt{p_i}$ and $\sqrt{p_j}$. The loadings of tests i and j on the "group" factor are $\sqrt{\{p_i[(1/t_i) - 1]\}}$ and $\sqrt{\{p_j[(1/t_j) - 1]\}}$, respectively.

18. Thomson, 1951, p. 324.

19. Interesting and instructive examples of the application of Thomson's sampling theory to the interpretation of empirical data are provided by one of Thomson's best-known students, A. E. Maxwell (1972a, 1972b) and Maxwell, Fenwick, Fenton, & Dollimore (1974).

20. Loevinger, 1951, pp. 594–595.

21. Jensen, 1987c.

22. Willerman & Bailey, 1987, p. 943. Eysenck (1987a) gives a quite comprehensive account of the deficiencies of sampling theory and contrasts it with Spearman's theory in terms of recent evidence on the brain correlates of g. Much of this evidence is presented in more detail in Chapters 6 and 8.

23. Humphreys, 1971, 1976, 1984, 1989, 1994. These are Humphreys' major statements of his view of "intelligence" and its social importance. I consider them well worth reading for all their important factual information and their great clarity of thought, although I believe his behavioral sampling definition of g does not really qualify as a theory. It seems to me to be purely descriptive, not leading to interesting causal inferences or predictions, and therefore scientifically rather sterile. I have spelled out elsewhere my critical view of Humphreys's insistence on a strictly behavioristic sampling theory (Jensen, 1984b, 1994d). Except for this, which is really a disagreement about the philosophy of science rather than about the facts of mental abilities, I always find myself in agreement with Humphreys on methodological and empirical issues and have learned much from reading his work. I fully agree that a science of mental ability has to begin with objective behavioral description and measurement of the phenomena that need to be explained, but I find little of interest in the theoretical explanation of these phenomena expressed in Humphreys' contributions.

24. Eysenck, 1987a, p. 269.

25. Cattell (1971). This tome is Cattell's major work on abilities and one of the great

works in the history of mental abilities research, probably second only to Spearman's _The Abilities of Man_ (1927). Although Cattell's wonderfully comprehensive book (as of 1971) covers much more than just his own unique contributions, it remains the definitive treatise on his own contributions. His discovery of fluid and crystallized abilities is presented in Chapter 5, and subsequent chapters spell out the details of his "investment" theory of "intelligence." Cattell's line of theorizing has been carried on, extended, and refined by his outstanding student John Horn, now one of the leading ability theorists in his own right. Three major articles by Horn (1985, 1986, 1989) provide a comprehensive account of the more recent theory and research on the Cattell-Horn theory of abilities, particularly as fluid and crystallized abilities are related to the growth and decline of mental abilities across the life span.

26. Heritability is the proportion of population variance in a phenotypic trait that is attributable to genetic factors. It is a major topic in Chapter 7.

27. Gustafsson (1988). This is one of the important articles of the last decade; it summarizes much of Gustafsson's important work on the hierarchical factor analysis of abilities and cites many related studies by other Scandinavian psychometricians and statisticians. It is highly recommended for those with some technical background.

28. Carroll (1993a) has done a Schmid-Leiman hierarchical factor analysis of Gustafsson's data (to which Gustafsson had applied a hierarchical analysis using confirmatory factor analysis [LISREL]) and found that a weakly identified second-order _Gf_ remained after the extraction of the third-order _g_. In a footnote (p. 114), Carroll suggests that his exploratory analysis of Gustafsson's data leaves the question of the equivalence of _Gf_ and _g_ unsettled, but that his analysis of Gustafsson's data "should by no means be taken as a conclusive negative answer to the question of their equivalence." However, the third-order _g_ obtained by Carroll is undoubtedly highly congruent with the _g_ obtained by Gustafsson.

29. Thorndike, 1927, Chapters XI and XII.

30. Guttman & Levy, 1991. This is Guttman's posthumously published summary statement of his thinking about the measurement of "intelligence." It contains references to virtually all of Guttman's publications on the measurement and analysis of mental abilities. Guttman's prescription for mental test construction is a _facet_ approach, which is especially useful in composing classes of tests with similar characteristics in terms of stimulus and response modalities, contents, and other formal features. The radex discussed in the present text, for example, is for "paper-and-pencil" tests, the radex representation of which is one horizontal slice of a vertical cylinder. Other "slices" of the cylinder are radexes for tests that are given orally, and for tests that involve physical manipulation of objects. In every "slice," a test's proximity to the center of the cylinder corresponds to its _g_ loading.

31. Snow, Kyllonen, & Marshalek, 1984. This is probably the most informative and comprehensive discussion of the radex (and related models) I have found in the literature. Also see Marshalek, Lohman, & Snow (1983) for an empirical demonstration of the similarity between the radex and a hierarchical factor model.

32. Gardner, 1983. This is the main exposition of Gardner's theory of "multiple intelligences."

33. Gardner, 1993.

34. Brody, 1992.

35. Fodor, 1983. A book edited by Detterman (1992) contains several interesting papers on the concept of modularity.

36. Sternberg & Gardner, 1982. This is probably the most detailed account of Sternberg's explanation of *g* in terms of the metacomponents in his componential theory.

37. For a fairly succinct explication of the componential theory, see Sternberg (1980), which is followed by a number of critical commentaries. Kline (1991) criticizes the componential aspect of Sternberg's theory on the grounds that the components are *a priori*, or "non-contingent," concepts and hence unamenable to empirical test, a criticism that, if fully justified, would seem to nullify the actual explanatory aim of the componential theory, rendering the theory merely a collection of semantic truisms. The same complaint is echoed by Messick (1992), who has written what is probably the most comprehensive and penetrating critical essay-review of both Sternberg and Gardner, comparing and contrasting their theories with each other and with the hierarchical factor analytic models of Burt, Vernon, and Cattell.

38. The triarchic theory is succinctly explicated in Sternberg (1984b) followed by critiques by twenty-one psychologists. The theory is presented more fully in Sternberg (1985, 1988) and his latest theory and evidence for what he calls "practical intelligence" and "testing common sense" are presented in Sternberg, et al., 1995. In a clever and informative essay, Sternberg (1987) contrasts his theory of intelligence with my own views.

Chapter 6

Biological Correlates of *g*

The fact that psychometric *g* has many physical correlates proves that *g* is not just a methodological artifact of the content and formal characteristics of mental tests or of the mathematical properties of factor analysis, but is a biological phenomenon. The correlations of *g* with physical variables can be functional (causal), or genetically pleiotropic (two or more different phenotypic effects attributable to the same gene), or genetically correlated through cross-assortative mating on both traits, or the nongenetic result of both being affected by some environmental factor (e.g., nutrition). The physical characteristics correlated with *g* that are empirically best established are stature, head size, brain size, frequency of alpha brain waves, latency and amplitude of evoked brain potentials, rate of brain glucose metabolism, and general health.

The general factor of learning and problem-solving tasks in infrahuman animals has some properties similar to the *g* factor in humans, and experimental brain lesion studies suggest that a task's loading on the general factor is directly related to task complexity and to the number of neural processes involved in task performance.

It is clear that *g*, since it is a product of human evolution, is strongly enmeshed with many other organismic variables.

Hierarchical factor analysis has solved the taxonomic problem of dealing with the myriad mental abilities that have been observed and measured. The factors discussed so far, however, concern variables entirely within the realm of conscious, intentional performance on psychometric tests, wherein *g* appears as a predominant and ubiquitous factor.

Is *g* a phenomenon that is entirely confined to the psychometric and behavioral realm in which it was discovered, or does it extend beyond psychometric tests and factor analysis, even beyond behavior, to the broader biological, physical realm? The answer to this question has two important and related aspects.

First, psychometric tests were never intended or devised to measure anything other than purely behavioral variables. Constructors of IQ tests, in fact, have tried to eliminate any source of test item variance that might reflect individual differences in physical attributes such as muscular strength and sensory acuity. Certainly there has never been the least intent that mental tests should reflect any strictly anatomical or physiological variables, which are directly measurable by other methods. It would therefore be most surprising and remarkable if IQ tests were significantly correlated with physical variables. Yet they are. IQ—especially the g factor of IQ tests—is correlated with a variety of physical variables. What does this mean? For the time being, about all one can say with certainty is that whatever is measured by IQ tests—mostly g—is somehow enmeshed in a host of organismic variables and therefore involves something beyond the purely psychological or behavioral. It also proves that g is not just an artifact of the way psychometric tests are constructed, nor is g a mere figment of the arcane mathematical machinations of factor analysis. Obviously, a correlation between psychometric g and a physical variable means that g is somehow connected with underlying biological systems.

The second, and perhaps more important, question for understanding g is much more complicated: How and why is g related to certain physical variables? No single answer can suffice for every physical variable that is related to g, because not all such variables are related to g for the same reason. In each case, the reason may be *ontogenetic*, that is, occurring within the time span of the individual's own development; or it may be *phylogenetic*, that is, having come about during the biological evolution of the species. And the correlation may also be genetic, or environmental, or both. Each of these possibilities invites further analysis and explanation. Although certain analytic methodologies narrow down the type of possible explanations of why a particular physical variable is correlated with g, at this point most explanations are still conjectural.

From a scientific standpoint, it is crucial to distinguish between the two types of correlation that can exist between a behavioral variable (e.g., IQ) and a physical variable (e.g., height). Such a correlation can represent either an *intrinsic* relationship or an *extrinsic* relationship between the variables. The easiest way to show how one "zeroes in" on the nature of the observed correlation between a behavioral and a physical variable is simply to describe the methodology and its rationale.[1]

STATISTICAL METHODS FOR STUDYING BIOLOGICAL CORRELATES OF g

INTRINSIC AND EXTRINSIC CORRELATION

Intrinsic Correlation. A correlation is *intrinsic* if variables X and Y are functionally related. That is, variation in one variable is inexorably related to variation in the other. Provided the correlation is statistically significant, its absolute size says nothing about whether the correlation is intrinsic or extrinsic. (If the correlation is not significant, there is no evidence of any real relationship.) Variable Y may be affected by many other variables besides X (and vice versa), or both variables may have multiple causes, so in either case the correlation between X and Y may be small. The correlation r_{XY} is classed as intrinsic or functional, however, only if there is a causal connection between them. Running speed (a behavioral variable) and leg length (a physical variable), for example, are intrinsically correlated.

An intrinsic relationship cannot be eliminated by selective breeding. If X and Y are intrinsically correlated, genetic selection exclusively for trait X will also affect trait Y as it appears in the offspring. However, some genetic traits are intrinsically correlated in this way without there necessarily being any apparent *functional*, or directly causal, connection between their phenotypes. This phenomenon is called *pleiotropy*, which means that the same gene (or genes) that affects X also affects Y. Even though X and Y may not be functionally related, they are intrinsically related because of their connection with the same gene(s). It is therefore impossible to eliminate the correlation between them by selective breeding.

An intrinsic or functional correlation can also be caused by an environmental factor that affects both traits, assuming individual differences due to the environmental factor. If the correlation between size of biceps and weight-lifting ability is .20 in a class of high school boys none of whom has practiced weight lifting, and then a random half of the class is given a year of daily practice in weight lifting, the correlation between biceps size and weight-lifting performance in the whole class might increase to .40. At least some part of the increase in the correlation from .20 to .40 is environmental. Another hypothetical example: Half of the schoolchildren selected at random are given an optimum daily supplement of vitamins and minerals, which has the dual effect of increasing growth rate (hence greater height at a given age) and reducing the number of days per year that children are absent from school because of illness. In the whole population of this school, therefore, one would find a negative correlation between pupils' height and their amount of absenteeism (i.e., greater height goes with fewer absences). This is an environmentally caused, functional correlation resulting from the fact that some part of the variance in height and in absenteeism is directly attributable to individual differences in nutrition. The negative correlation between height and absenteeism will remain as long as there are differences in the pupils' nutrition.

Extrinsic Correlation. Here there is no functional or directly causal relationship between variables X and Y. Yet they may be phenotypically correlated for either genetic or environmental reasons, or both. There are mainly two ways that X and Y can be genetically correlated in the population: (1) by *pleiotropy*, that is, one gene affecting two (or more) phenotypically different traits, and (2) by *simple genetic correlation* due to the common assortment of the different genes for the different traits.

When there is a spousal correlation between two phenotypically or genotypically distinct traits, it is termed *cross-assortative* mating for the two traits. That is, persons' standing on trait X is correlated with their mates' standing on trait Y. Unlike pleiotropy, a simple genetic correlation can be created or eliminated by selective breeding, but *both* traits have to be selected, because there is no direct causal connection between them. Different sets of genes influence each trait. The genes for the different traits get assorted together in the gametic creation of individuals because of the parents' cross-assortative mating for the traits.

An example will show how cross-assortative mating works. Assume there is zero correlation between height and eye color (blue or brown) in the population, that is, one could not predict people's eye color from a knowledge of their height any better than chance. Then suppose it becomes a general custom for tall people to seek out blue-eyed people as mates (and vice versa) and for short people to seek out brown-eyed people (and vice versa). (This is an example of cross-assortative mating for height and eye color.) After several generations of such cross-assortative mating, we would find that the genes for tallness and the genes for blue eyes would have become sorted together in the offspring of many families, and the same would be true for shortness and brown eyes, so that in the population as a whole there would be a correlation between individuals' height and their eye color. Individuals who have inherited genes for tallness would be more likely also to have inherited genes for blue eyes. But the high association of blue eyes with tallness could just as well have gone in exactly the opposite direction if it had been the custom for tall people to seek out brown-eyed mates and short people to seek out blue-eyed mates. In other words, there is no functional or causal connection between height and eye color. The connection between them could perhaps be called a "cultural" correlation, because a cultural custom in this population influenced mating preferences and so brought about this adventitious or *extrinsic* correlation of height and eye color. Although variation in each trait is highly genetic, the covariation (or correlation) between them is nonfunctional (i.e., neither affects the other) and extrinsic (i.e., they are not caused by the same genes).

The distinction between *intrinsic* and *extrinsic* correlation is very important for interpreting the correlation between a physical and a psychological variable, described in the second part of this chapter. If the correlation is not intrinsic, it provides no clues to the biological underpinning of the psychological variable.

Method of Distinguishing between Intrinsic and Extrinsic Correlation.
This distinction between intrinsic and extrinsic correlation cannot be made if all
we know is the correlation between X and Y in a group of individuals. To
determine that, we also need to know the correlation between X and Y in a
large group composed of pairs of _full siblings_ who were reared together. (Siblings are individuals who have the same two biological parents and thus have,
on average, approximately 50 percent of their segregating genes in common.
Segregating genes are genes that have two or more alleles and contribute to the
genetic variance in the trait; there are about 100,000 such functional gene loci
in the human genome. Dizygotic twins will serve as well, as they are like ordinary siblings except that twins are gestated at the same time.) Every pair of
siblings must come from a different set of biological parents and must have
grown up together in the same family environment.

There is no statistical reason to expect the correlation between traits X and
Y in this group of siblings (taken as individuals) to be significantly different
from the correlation between X and Y obtained in a comparable group composed
entirely of unrelated persons randomly sampled from the same population. The
great advantage of obtaining r_{XY} in a group made up of sibling pairs is that the
obtained r_{XY} is a composite of two distinct correlations, each of which can be
determined: the _between-families_ correlation (BFr) and the _within-families_ correlation (WFr).

The _between_-families correlation of X and Y (BF$r_{X_sY_s}$) is the correlation between X_s (the _sums_ of the siblings' scores in each pair on variable X) and Y_s
(the _sums_ of the siblings' scores in each pair on variable Y).

The _within_-families correlation of X and Y (WF$r_{X_dY_d}$) is the correlation between X_d (the signed _difference_ between the siblings' scores in each pair on
variable X) and Y_d (the signed _difference_ between the siblings' scores in each
pair on variable Y).

Assuming there is a true (population) correlation between X and Y based on
individuals (Ir_{XY}), it is possible for the true values of BFr_{XY} and WFr_{XY} both
to be some absolute[2] value greater than zero, or for either correlation to be zero
while the other correlation is greater than zero.[3]

What can the BF and WF correlations tell us? The answer is rather hard to
explain but important to understand.

A BFr_{XY} = 0 means that if Ir_{XY} > 0 it cannot be attributed to any systematic
influence(s) on both X and Y in which families (here defined as the average of
the siblings in each family) differ from one another. Though BFr_{xy} = 0 and Ir_{xy}
> 0 is theoretically possible, it would seem highly improbable, and in fact, an
instance has not yet been found. Empirically, when the Ir_{XY} is greater than zero,
the BFr_{XY} is always greater than zero.

A WFr_{XY} = 0 means that there is no relation between X and Y _within_ families; that is, there is no systematic tendency for the sibling who is more extreme
in X also to be more extreme in Y. If the hypothesis that WFr_{XY} = 0 cannot
be statistically rejected in a large sample or in a meta-analysis[4] of many inde-

pendent samples, it completely rules out any intrinsic (functional or pleiotropic) correlation between X and Y. The correlation must therefore be attributable to influences on X and Y that exist only *between* families, that is, influences that differ from one family to another. The usual cause of this situation where $BFr_{XY} > 0$ and $WFr_{XY} = 0$ is *population heterogeneity*, whereby two (or more) variables are associated in different subpopulations but the variables are not functionally or pleiotropically related. (Like the hypothetical example given above of a correlation between height and eye color.) The correlation may be due to any genetic or environmental or cultural factors that are related (but not *causally* related) to both X and Y. A clear-cut example: In a heterogeneous population composed of two subpopulations, Anglo-Americans and Chinese-Americans, we would find a correlation between hair color (black vs. not black) and bilingualism (English only vs. English + Cantonese). This correlation would not exist *within* families (assuming most Chinese-American siblings speak both English and Cantonese and most Anglo-Americans speak only English). The correlation would exist only *between* families. Of course, there is no intrinsic (functional or pleiotropic) connection between people's hair color and their tendency to bilingualism. If there were an intrinsic relationship, it would show up as a WF correlation, assuming everyone had equal opportunity to acquire a second language.

Why is a simple genetic correlation between X and Y in the population found only *between* families but not *within* families? The answer is known as Mendel's law of *segregation* and *independent* (i.e., random) *assortment* of genes: Each sibling receives a *random one-half* of each parent's genes, and because the complement received by each sibling is a random assortment of the parental genes, the single genes affecting any two (or more) genotypically distinct traits are not correlated in the individual's genotype any more than would be expected by chance, which by definition is a population correlation of zero. (Just as the heads/tails outcome of tossing one coin is uncorrelated with the outcome of tossing another coin.)

A $WFr_{XY} > 0$ is also an important finding. It implies there is *something* that affects two distinct traits in one (or some) sibling(s) but not in the other(s). This *something* can be either genetic (i.e., pleiotropic) or environmental (e.g., an illness in one sibling, but not in any others, that adversely affects both physical and mental growth and would therefore result in a WF correlation between height and IQ). The WF correlation therefore is *intrinsic*; that is, it represents a functional or a pleiotropic relation.

Most studies of the correlation between IQ and physical variables are based on individuals and do not permit determination of BF and WF correlation. But both BF and WF correlations have also been obtained in some studies. The theoretically more important relationships between psychometric and physical variables are those that are intrinsic, as indicated by a significant WF as well as a BF correlation. In the review that follows, it will be noted whether each correlation is extrinsic, intrinsic, or of unknown status.

But before reviewing the empirical evidence, one other methodological issue must be considered, namely, whether the correlation between a physical variable and a factorially complex psychometric test, such as IQ, is a correlation between the physical variable and the g factor or is a correlation between the physical variable and some psychometric factor *other than g*.

THE METHOD OF CORRELATED VECTORS

Because most of the variance in IQ is g, it is quite improbable that the correlation between IQ and some physical variable (say X) does not involve g. We can generally assume that if X is correlated with IQ, it is also correlated with g. Better evidence would come from a correlation between measurements of X and g factor scores, but even that would not be absolutely definitive, because factor scores are only estimates of the true factor scores and the method of calculating factor scores may leave the scores slightly ''contaminated'' with bits of non-g variance from lower-order factors and specificity. I have proposed a method, called the *method of correlated vectors*, that can determine whether there is a correlation between g and X (or any other factor and X). However, it does not tell us the numerical value of the correlation between g and X (which can only be estimated by the correlation between g factor scores and X). But it can prove that there is a correlation between g and X and it can show whether any other factors (independent of g) are or are not correlated with X.

Explaining how the method of correlated vectors works may possibly seem dauntingly complicated to all but the statistical-minded. (It is explained in detail with a real worked example in Appendix B.) Readers who do not feel compelled to understand the technical details should skip to the next section, in which examples of results obtained by this method are shown graphically for certain biological correlates of g (e.g., evoked brain potentials).

In the present context, a *vector* (V) is defined simply as a *column* consisting of a number (n) of quantitative *elements* (hence it is also called a *column vector*). A vector may be a column composed of each of the n tests' factor loadings on a particular factor; or it may be a column composed of each of the n tests' correlations with some single variable, X, that is experimentally independent of the set of tests from which the factor loadings are derived. (For example, X could be measures of subjects' height, visual acuity, reaction time, socioeconomic status, or whatever, so long as variable X has not entered into the calculation of any elements in the vector of factor loadings.) If the factor is g, for example, the vector of g can be symbolized V_g, and the correlation (r) between V_g and the vector of X would be symbolized rV_gV_X. (The value rV_gV_X is, of course, not the correlation between g and X per se, but the correlation between the parallel column *vectors* of g and X.)

If rV_gV_X is significantly greater than zero, it is proof that g and X are correlated, but only after a possible artifact has been ruled out. This artifact arises if the column vector composed of the tests' reliability coefficients is correlated with either V_g or V_x or both. Each of the elements in both V_g and V_x, of course, is affected by measurement error in the test scores from which each element is derived. The various tests' reliability coefficients may differ considerably, with the consequence that the relative sizes of the elements in the two vectors, and therefore also their rank order, will be partly determined by the differences in their reliability.

Because each test's reliability affects its corresponding elements in both V_g and V_x, there is the possibility that the correlation between V_g and V_x (whether it is significant or not) is an artifactual result of the fact that both vectors are correlated with the vector of the test's reliability coefficients, V_{tt}. This possibility can be ruled out by the statistical device known as partial correlation. (If A and B are correlated with each other, and A or B [or both] are correlated with C, one can statistically remove the effect of C from the correlation between A and B, yielding the *partial* correlation between A and B, written $r_{AB.C}$. Variable C is said to be "partialed out" of the correlation between A and B.)

If the correlation between V_g and V_x with V_{tt} partialed out remains significant, it means that their correlation is not an artifact of the tests' variable reliability coefficients. If, however, the partial correlation between V_g and V_x with V_{tt} partialed out is not significant, a further analysis is needed. Each of the elements in V_g and V_x must be corrected for attenuation, which removes the measurement error from each element, provided there are highly reliable estimates of each tests' reliability coefficient. (A test's *g* loading is corrected by dividing it by the square root of the test's reliability coefficient. A test's correlation with X is corrected in the same way. If the reliability coefficient of X is available, the test's correlation with X can be corrected by dividing it by the square root of the product of the tests' reliability coefficient and the reliability coefficient of X.)

The Pearson correlation (r) between the vectors should be calculated, but it needs to be supplemented by Spearman's rank-order correlation. Because the Pearson r is a parametric statistic based on the assumption that each of the correlated variables is normally distributed in the population, and because this assumption may not be tenable for the correlated vectors, the statistical significance of r cannot be tested rigorously. Therefore, a nonparametric measure of correlation, such as Spearman's rank-order correlation (r_s), must also be calculated between the vectors. Its significance can be determined, as it does not depend upon any assumptions about the population distributions of the correlated variates. The significance of r_s is based simply on what is known as a permutation test. Given that each of the correlated column vectors has n elements, the significance level of an obtained r_s is simply the probability (p) that a value of r_s as large as or larger than the obtained value would occur among all possible permutations of the rank order of the n elements in the correlated vectors. If the obtained value of r_s between the vectors of *g* and X is significant at some specified p value (e.g., $p < .01$), we may conclude that a true correlation exists between _g_ and X, with the probability _p_ that our conclusion is wrong and the probability $1 - p$ that our conclusion is correct.

Researchers should be aware of two conditions that can militate against demonstrating a statistically significant r_s even when there is a true correlation between the vectors. The most obvious pitfall is having too few elements in the vectors, because the significance of r_s depends on the number (_n_) of ranked elements in one vector.[5] (For example, with $n = 10$, the r_s must be at least .648 to be significant at the 5 percent level, or $p < .05$.) Therefore, when _n_ is small, the method of correlated vectors lacks statistical power and incurs considerable risk of wrongly accepting the null hypothesis that the true correlation between the vectors is zero when in fact it is greater than zero. (In statistics this is known as a _Type II error._[6]) The other danger lies in not having a subject sample large enough to ensure highly reliable elements in each vector. The less variation there is among the elements, the more accurate each of them must be to show up in their true rank order. Each of the elements in the vectors, of course, has some sampling error (which is inversely related to the square root of the subject sample size), and the smaller the sampling error, the more accurate will be the obtained correlation between the vectors. (_Note_: The effect of _sampling error_ is entirely distinct from the effect of _measurement error_, which involves the complement of the measurement's reliability coefficient, i.e., $1 - r_{xx}$.) When the true correlation between two vectors is greater than zero, sampling error in the vectors' elements reduces the size of the obtained correlation between the vectors as compared to the size of their true correlation.

What all of this essentially means for using the method of correlated vectors is that when a statistically significant correlation between vectors emerges it has done so against severe odds and is therefore a quite secure phenomenon. But the steep odds against finding a significant correlation between vectors also means that a correlation that falls just short of significance at the .05 level (say, $p < .10$ or $p < .15$) must be interpreted cautiously, mindful of the risk of a Type II error.

RESEARCH FINDINGS ON THE BIOLOGICAL CORRELATES OF g

SPECIFIC BIOLOGICAL CORRELATES OF IQ AND _g_

Because a very comprehensive and detailed review of this subject has been presented elsewhere,[7] it will suffice here to give only a synopsis of the main empirical findings. See the more detailed review for references to the specific studies that support each finding.

In most of the studies described, the physical variable is correlated with scores on an IQ test or other highly _g_-loaded test. In a few studies in which a number of different tests are correlated with the same physical variable, it is possible to apply the method of correlated vectors to determine if the physical variable is correlated specifically with the _g_ factor. The word in parentheses after each heading tells whether the biological correlate of mental ability is _extrinsic, intrinsic_, or _undetermined_. (See discussion earlier in this chapter [and in Appendix B] for definitions of _extrinsic_ and _intrinsic_.)

Body Size (Extrinsic). It is now well established that both height and weight are correlated with IQ. When age is controlled, the correlations in different studies range mostly between +.10 and +.30, and average about +.20. Studies based on siblings find no significant within-family correlation, and gifted children (who are taller than their age mates in the general population) are not taller than their nongifted siblings.

Because both height and IQ are highly heritable, the between-families correlation of stature and IQ probably represents a simple genetic correlation resulting from cross-assortative mating for the two traits. Both height and "intelligence" are highly valued in Western culture and it is known that there is substantial assortative mating for each trait.

There is also evidence of cross-assortative mating for height and IQ; there is some trade-off between them in mate selection. When short and tall women are matched on IQ, educational level, and social class of origin, for example, it is found that the taller women tend to marry men of higher intelligence (reasonably inferred from their higher educational and occupational status) than do shorter women. Leg length relative to overall height is regarded an important factor in judging feminine beauty in Western culture, and it is interesting that the height × IQ correlation is largely attributable to the leg-length component of height. Sitting height is much less correlated with IQ. If there is any _intrinsic_ component of the height × IQ correlation, it is too small to be detected at a significant level even in quite large samples. The two largest studies[8] totaling some 16,000 sibling pairs, did not find significant within-family correlations of IQ with either height or weight (controlling for age) in males or females or in blacks or whites.

Head Size and Brain Size (Intrinsic). There is a great deal of evidence that external measurements of head size are significantly correlated with IQ and other highly _g_-loaded tests, although the correlation is quite small, in most studies ranging between +.10 and +.25, with a mean $r \approx +.15$. The only study using _g_ factor scores showed a correlation of +.30 with a composite measure of head size based on head length, width, and circumference, in a sample of 286 adolescents.[9] Therefore, it appears that head size is mainly correlated with the _g_ component of psychometric scores. The method of correlated vectors applied to the same sample of 286 adolescents showed a highly significant $r_s = +.64$ between the _g_ vector of seventeen diverse tests and the vector of the tests' correlations with head size. The head-size vector had nonsignificant correlations with the vectors of the spatial, verbal, and memory factors of +.27, .00, and +.05, respectively.

In these studies, of course, head size is used as merely a crude proxy for brain size. The external measurement of head size is in fact a considerably attenuated proxy for brain size.

The correlation between the best measures of external head size and actual brain size as directly measured in autopsy is far from perfect, being around +.50 to +.60 in adults and slightly higher in children. There are specially devised formulas by which one can estimate internal cranial capacity (in cubic centimeters) from external head measurements with a fair degree of accuracy. These formulas have been used along with various statistical corrections for age, body size (height, weight, total surface area), and sex to estimate the correlation between IQ and brain size from data on external head size. The typical result is a correlation of about .30.

These indirect methods, however, are no longer necessary, since the technology of _magnetic resonance imaging_ (MRI) now makes it possible to obtain a three-dimensional picture of the brain of a living person. A highly accurate measure of total brain volume (or the volume of any particular structure in the brain) can be obtained from the MRI pictures. Such quantitative data are now usually extracted from the MRI pictures by computer.

To date there are eight MRI studies[10] of the correlation between total brain volume and IQ in healthy children and young adults. In every study the correlations are significant and close to +.40 after removing variance due to differences in body size. (The correlation between body size and brain size in adult humans is between +.20 and +.25.) Large parts of the brain do not subserve cognitive processes, but govern sensory and motor functions, emotions, and autonomic regulation of physiological activity. Controlling body size removes to some extent the sensorimotor aspects of brain size from the correlation of overall brain size with IQ. But controlling body size in the brain × IQ correlation is somewhat problematic, because there may be some truly functional relationship between brain size and body size that includes the brain's cognitive functions. Therefore, controlling body size in the IQ × brain size correlation may be too conservative; it could result in _over_correcting the correlation. Moreover, the height and weight of the head constitute an appreciable proportion of the total body height and weight, so that controlling total body size could also contribute to overcorrection by removing some part of the variance in head and brain size along with variance in general body size. Two of the MRI studies used a battery of diverse cognitive tests, which permitted the use of correlated vectors to determine the relationship between the column vector of the various tests' _g_ factor loadings and the column vector of the tests' correlations with total brain volume. In one study,[10f] based on twenty cognitive tests given to forty adult males sibling pairs, these vectors were correlated +.65. In the other study,[10g] based on eleven diverse cognitive tests, the vector of the tests' _g_ loadings were correlated +.51 with the vector of the tests' correlations with total brain volume and +.66 with the vector of the tests' correlations with the volume of the brain's cortical gray matter. In these studies, all of the variables entering into the analyses were the averages of sibling pairs, which has the effect of increasing the reliability of the measurements. Therefore, these analyses are between-families. A problematic aspect of both studies is that there were no significant within-family correlations between test scores and brain volumes, which implies that there is no intrinsic relationship between brain size and *g*. To conclude that the within-family correlation in the population is zero, however, has a high risk of being a Type II error, given the unreliability of sibling difference scores (on which within-family correlations are based) and the small number of subjects used in these studies. Much larger studies based merely on external head size show significant within-family correlations with IQ. Clearly, further MRI studies are needed for a definitive answer on this critical issue.

Metabolically, the human brain is by far the most "expensive" organ in the whole body, and the body may have evolved to serve in part like a "power pack" for the brain, with a genetically larger brain being accommodated by a larger body. It has been determined experimentally, for example, that strains of rats that were selectively bred from a common stock exclusively to be either good or poor at maze learning were found to differ not only in brain size but also in body size.[11] Body size increased only about one-third as much as brain size as a result of the rats being selectively bred exclusively for good or poor maze-learning ability. There was, of course, no explicit selection for either brain size or body size, but only for maze-learning ability. Obviously, there is some intrinsic functional and genetic relationship between learning ability, brain size, and body size, at least in laboratory rats. Although it would be unwarranted to generalize this finding to humans, it does suggest the hypothesis that a similar relationship may exist in humans. It is known that body size has increased along with brain size in the course of human evolution. The observed correlations between brain size, body size, and mental ability in humans are consistent with these facts, but the nature and direction of the *causal* connections between these variables cannot be inferred without other kinds of evidence that is not yet available.

The IQ × head-size correlation is clearly intrinsic, as shown by significant correlations both between-families ($r = +.20$, $p < .001$) and within-families ($r = +.11$, $p < .05$) in a large sample of seven-year-old children, with head size measured only by circumference and IQ measured by the Wechsler Intelligence Scale for Children.[12] (Age, height, and weight were statistically controlled.) The same children at four years of age showed no significant correlation of head size with Stanford-Binet IQ, and in fact the WF correlation was even negative ($-.04$). This suggests that the correlation of IQ with head size (and, by inference, brain size) is a developmental phenomenon, increasing with age during childhood.

One of the unsolved mysteries regarding the relation of brain size to IQ is the seeming paradox that there is a considerable sex difference in brain size (the adult female brain being about 100 cm^3 smaller than the male) without there being a corresponding sex difference in IQ.[13] It has been argued that some IQ tests have purposely eliminated items that discriminate between the sexes or have balanced-out sex differences in items or subtests. This is not true, however, for many tests such as Raven's matrices, which is almost a pure measure of *g*, yet shows no consistent or significant sex difference. Also, the differing *g* loadings of the subscales of the Wechsler Intelligence Test are not correlated with the size of the sex difference on the various subtests.[14] The correlation between brain size and IQ is virtually the same for both sexes.

The explanation for the well-established mean sex difference in brain size is still somewhat uncertain, although one hypothesis has been empirically tested, with positive results. Properly controlling (by regression) the sex difference in body size diminishes, but by no means eliminates, the sex difference in brain size. Three plausible hypotheses have been proposed to explain the sex difference (of about 8 percent) in average brain size between the sexes despite there being no sex difference in *g*:

1. Possible sexual dimorphism in neural circuitry or in overall neural conduction velocity could cause the female brai to process information more efficiently.

2. The brain size difference could be due to the one ability factor, independent of *g*, that unequivocally shows a large sex difference, namely, spatial visualization ability, in which only 25 percent of females exceed the male median. Spatial ability could well depend upon a large number of neurons, and males may have more of these "spatial ability" neurons than females, thereby increasing the volume of the male brain.

3. Females have the same amount of functional neural tissue as males but there is a greater "packing density" of the neurons in the female brain. While the two previous hypotheses remain purely speculative at present, there is recent direct evidence for a sex difference in the "packing density" of neurons.[15] In the cortical regions most directly related to cognitive ability, the autopsied brains of adult women possessed, on average, about 11 percent more neurons per unit volume than were found in the brains of adult men. The males and females were virtually equated on Wechsler Full Scale IQ (112.3 and 110.6, respectively). The male brains were about 12.5 percent heavier than the female brains. Hence the greater neuronal packing density in the female brain nearly balances the larger size of the male brain. Of course, further studies based on histological, MRI, and PET techniques will be needed to establish the packing density hypothesis as the definitive explanation for the seeming paradox of the two sexes differing in brain size but not differing in IQ despite a correlation of about +.40 between these variables *within* each sex group.

Myopia and IQ (Intrinsic). It has long been known that myopia, or nearsightedness, is related to high IQ. The evidence, reviewed elsewhere,[16] is based on many studies and huge samples. In terms of correlation the *r* is about +.20 to +.25. Myopia is highly heritable and a single gene that controls the shape of the eyeball has been identified as mainly responsible. Myopia in adolescents and adults can be predicted by ocular examination in infants as young as one year of age.

The ''near-work'' hypothesis that myopia is solely caused by excessive use of the eyes for ''near-work'' such as reading, sewing, and the like has been largely discredited by modern researchers. Major chromosomal anomalies, such as trisomy 21 (Down's syndrome), which override the effects of the normal polygenic causes of individual differences in mental ability and result in severe mental retardation, militate against reading and most other forms of ''near-work.'' Yet the incidence of myopia among persons with these conditions is the same as in the general population. Also, myopia has high heritability. As myopia is a continuous trait, it appears that an interaction between a genetic predisposition and at least some slight degree of engagement in ''near-work,'' such as most schoolwork, during childhood are necessary to produce a degree of myopia in adolescence or adulthood that calls for corrective eyeglasses.

Individual differences in degree of myopia and in IQ are positively correlated in the general population. Children in classes for the intellectually gifted (IQ > 130), for example, show an incidence of myopia three to five times greater than the incidence among pupils in regular classes.

The question arises of whether the relation of myopia to IQ is an *intrinsic* or *extrinsic* correlation (as defined on pages 139–40). The correlation could well be extrinsic due to population heterogeneity in both myopia and IQ, because various racial groups differ in the incidence of myopia and also differ, on average, in IQ. To find the answer to this question, the degree of myopia was measured as a continuous variable (refraction error) by means of optical techniques in a group of sixty adolescents selected only for high IQs (Raven matrices) and their less gifted full siblings, who averaged fourteen IQ points lower, a difference equivalent to 0.92σ. The high-IQ subjects differed significantly from their lower-IQ siblings in myopia by an average of 0.39σ on the measure of refraction error.[16] In other words, since there is a *within*-families correlation between myopia and IQ, the relationship is *intrinsic*. However, it is hard to think of any directly *functional* relationship between myopia and IQ. The data are most consistent with there being a *pleiotropic* relationship. The causal pathway through which the genetic factor that causes myopia also to some extent elevates *g* (or vice versa) is unknown. Because the within-family relationship of myopia and IQ was found with Raven's matrices, which in factor analyses is found to have nearly all of its common factor variance on *g*,[17] it leaves virtually no doubt that the IQ score in this case represents *g* almost exclusively.

Electrochemical Activity in the Brain.[18] Neurons are cells that act much like an electrical storage battery with a capacitor that cumulates electrical potential by the unequal concentration of positive and negative ions (Na^+ and Cl^-) on either side of the cell membrane. Nerve impulses are propagated through an electrochemical process that occurs at the cell membrane, whereby the positively and negatively charged ions of common salt, or sodium chloride (sodium Na^+ and chlorine Cl^-), neutralize each other, creating an *action potential* that rapidly progresses down the length of the neuron's tube-like axon at speeds up to about 100 meters per second. This wave of depolarization of ions down the axon is of course extremely slow compared to the flow of electricity in a wire, because the action potential moving through the axon is due to the depolarization of ions (electrically charged atoms), whereas in a wire it is only the atoms' free electrons that flow, and with much less resistance than is met by the ions.

The speed of nerve conduction is a positive function of the diameter of the axon and its degree of myelination. The myelin sheath, composed of fat, surrounds the axon and acts like the insulation on an electric wire. When the neuron is stimulated by a sense organ or at its synaptic connection with an adjacent neuron, it sets off a change in the permeability of the axonal membrane that rapidly moves through the length of the neuron, allowing the positive and negative ions to come together, thereby creating the action potential. The nerve impulse is propagated down the length of the axon. Neurotransmitters at the synaptic connections with other neurons then repeat the process. Neural excitation is thereby transmitted from some part of the body, through the spinal cord, to some region of the brain, and from one region of the brain to another. When this happens simultaneously in millions of neurons, as is always the case in the intact brain, the fluctuating potentials in specific regions of the brain can be detected by electrodes attached to the scalp. These fluctuating potentials are often called brain waves. They can be amplified and recorded on a moving paper tape or photographed on an oscilloscope.

The technical process of recording brain waves is called electroencephalography (EEG). The waves (i.e., electrical potentials) fluctuate above zero amplitude (negative waves, labeled N) and below zero amplitude (positive waves, labeled P). The waves can be described in terms of their *frequency* (measured in Hz, or number of cycles per second) and *amplitude* (measured in microvolts, μV). The number of times the wave crosses the zero point in a specified period of time is a measure of ''zero-crossings.''

EEG waves differ in frequency and amplitude when obtained from different parts of the brain (according to electrode placement) and in different states of the subject, such as deep sleep, dreaming sleep, relaxed wakefulness with eyes closed, wide-awake attentiveness to stimuli, and ongoing purposive thinking or problem solving. Within the differing general characteristics of the brain waves typically obtained under these various conditions there are reliable individual differences in frequency and amplitude. The correlation between these individual measurements of EEG waves and IQ has been the subject of hundreds of studies. It is possible here to give only a brief summary of the typical findings. Excellent detailed reviews[19] of this research are available for anyone who wishes to delve further into the more specialized details of this very complex field.

Two main classes of EEG data have been studied in relation to IQ: (1) natural (termed spontaneous) EEG rhythms occurring in various states of sleep and wakefulness, and (2) the average evoked potential (AEP) to a specific stimulus. EEG waves contain a great deal of background ''noise'' due to random neural activity, and the signal-to-noise ratio is so low that it is hard to obtain very reliable measures of individual differences in normal EEG records for any of the characteristic EEG waves. This drawback is virtually eliminated, however, for the *average evoked potential* (AEP), which consists of the average of usually hundreds of wave samples obtained from one person in response to a specific stimulus. Whatever is consistent (i.e., signal) is enhanced; whatever is random (i.e., "noise") is averaged out. (Similar techniques of signal extraction are used in radar and sonar systems.) Individual differences in the AEP waves are therefore clearly discernible. Various individual difference measurements are obtainable from these AEP records and can be correlated with scores on psychometric tests.

SPONTANEOUS EEG CORRELATES OF *g*

Among the simple, nonaveraged EEG waves, the frequency of the *alpha* wave has most often shown correlations with IQ. These range between zero and about +.60. The alpha rhythm consists of relatively intermediate brain waves, in the range of 7.5 to 12.5 Hz, that occur when the subject is in a state of relaxed wakefulness, with eyes closed. The alpha frequency in Hz is usually averaged over a number of one-second intervals selected at random from an EEG recording that can last several minutes. The studies of the correlation between the alpha frequency and IQ are consistent only in showing a positive relationship, that is, higher IQ is directly related to a higher alpha frequency. This suggests a relationship between alpha frequency and IQ. The cause of the relationship is unknown, but hypotheses, such as more sustained attention in high-IQ subjects, have been suggested. Beyond that fact, however, the literature seems too chaotic to warrant averaging the results of many studies. Their methodologies are far from standardized and the various methodologies are seldom replicated. The results of all these studies probably reflect "method variance" as much as anything else. The unsystematic nature of this particular body of EEG research on alpha waves (and other nonaveraged brain waves) increases the risk of a statistical Type I error in drawing conclusions from a meta-analysis of all the available evidence.

The problem of the excessive "noise" level in nonaveraged EEG records is now being overcome by the application of newly developed nonlinear, mathematical analyses based on deterministic chaos theory, and recent research on the relation of EEG to IQ has become methodologically more sophisticated. This research suggests that it is the *complexity* of EEG waves, more than their frequency, that is positively related to IQ.[20] Complexity here refers to the number of different dimensions needed to describe the waves, which suggests that the more complex waves are determined by the influence of more differentiated processes.

AVERAGE EVOKED POTENTIAL CORRELATES OF *g*

The AEP has shown more consistent and substantial correlations with IQ than have spontaneous EEG waves. In the typical AEP experiment, the subject sits relaxed in a reclining chair. A recording electrode is attached to the scalp at the vertex of the head and reference electrodes are clipped to the earlobes. At random intervals, averaging a few seconds apart, a brief stimulus, such as a sharp "click," occurs and is repeated over a period of several minutes. Each occurrence of the stimulus evokes a momentary change in the electrical potential of millions of neurons in the cortex of the brain. For a given subject, this evoked potential is recorded during a "time-locked" segment of the brain waves that immediately follow the onset of the evoking stimulus. All of the time-locked segments of evoked potentials obtained in this manner during the testing session are averaged by computer over a great many trials. Since each characteristic brain wave in response to the stimulus can be "lined up" precisely with the onset of the stimulus, they can all be neatly averaged by computer, giving a segment of brain waves (the AEP) from which the random neural background "noise" has been virtually eliminated.

Figure 6.1 shows a typical AEP record. The occurrence of the auditory stimulus is indicated by the letter A, which is the zero point on the time line (in milliseconds). The averaged fluctuations in voltage have characteristic peaks (N, for negative deviation from the average baseline [zero] voltage) and troughs (P, for positive deviation). The several distinct waves are thought to reflect the successive stages of the cognitive processing of the stimulus event by the cerebral cortex.

In studying individual differences in the AEP, four of its features are measured: (1) the number of zero-crossings in a specified epoch (time interval from zero), (2) the _latency_, or the time elapsed between the stimulus and one of the peaks or troughs or the average time of two or three such points; (3) the _amplitude_ (in μV) of a peak or trough, or their average; and (4) the _complexity_ of the wave in a specified epoch, that is, the length of the total waveform. This last measure was originally obtained by laying a piece of string over the set of waves and then measuring the length of the straightened string, or by tracing the waves with a map wheel. (This measurement is now performed by a computer.) When a specific person's AEP is obtained several times, it is also possible to compute the _intraindividual variability_ of the AEP latency (or any of the other indices), which is considered a measure of neural transmission errors.

All of these AEP measures have shown significant correlations with IQ. Some critics have claimed that the AEP discriminates only between mentally retarded persons and those in the average and above-average range of IQ. But this claim is disproved by the many studies that show significant correlations _within_ groups whose IQs are in the retarded, average, and gifted ranges of IQ. Higher IQ subjects show _shorter latencies_ (faster neural reaction), _more peaks and troughs_ (more zero-crossings within a specified epoch), _smaller amplitude_ in response to expected stimuli (more efficient expenditure of neural energy, as shown by the positron emission tomography scan studies discussed in the next section), _greater complexity_ (longer "string" measure) of the AEP waves, and _lesser intraindividual variability_ (greater consistency) in each of these indices. Cor-

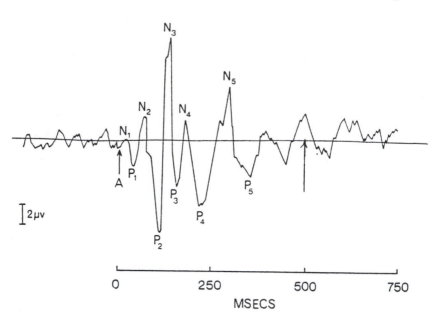

Figure 6.1. The average evoked potential (AEP), showing the waveform of a person with above-average IQ. N and P are negative and positive potentials, respectively, numbered in temporal order. The arrow at **A** indicates the occurrence of the evoking stimulus, which begins (at time 0) the time-locked epoch (of 500 msec), measured in milliseconds (msec). Following point **A** there are twelve _zero-crossings_ (i.e., the wave crossing the baseline) in the 500-msec epoch. The _latency_ of a given wave (say, N_3) is the time interval (measured in msec) between the onset of the evoking stimulus (at time 0) and the peak of the N_3 wave. The _amplitude_ of a wave, measured in microvolts (μv), is the distance of the peak (or trough) of the wave above (or below) the 0 baseline. The complexity of the waveform is the length of the waveline (called the "string" measure) throughout the epoch (in this case 0 to 500 msec).

relations of these AEP variables with IQ typically range between about .30 and .60, with the highest correlations found in the interval between P1 and P2 (see Figure 6.1).

   The latency of the P3 (also called P300, because it occurs on average about 300 msec after the evoking stimulus) shows significant correlations with IQ in some studies. The one study based on _g_ factor scores (derived from the Multidimensional Aptitude Battery, which has ten subtests) found a correlation of −.36 ($p < .05$) between the P300 latency and the _g_ factor scores.[21] The later components of the AEP beyond P300 have not been found to correlate with IQ.

   Even higher correlations between the AEP and IQ can be obtained by combining some of the AEP indices, such as latency and intraindividual variability, or from the difference between AEP indices obtained under different experimental conditions that tap the influence of cognition on the AEP. An example of the latter is the index of "neural adaptability" (NA) invented by pioneer AEP researcher Edward W. P. Schafer.[22] Essentially, the auditory AEP is obtained under two conditions: (1) _self-stimulation_ (SS) in which the subject self-administers the auditory "clicks" by pressing a hand-held microswitch button fifty times at random intervals averaging about two or three seconds; and (2) random _automatic stimulation_ (AS), in which the series of fifty "clicks" that were self-administered by the subject in the previous condition are played back, while the subject remains inactive. The neural adaptability (NA) score is the ratio of the average amplitude of the evoked potential under automatic stimulation (AS) to the amplitude under self-stimulation (SS), that is, NA = AS/SS.

Persons with high IQs show a larger NA score than those with lower IQs. The expectancy of a self-administered "click" results in lower amplitude, the more so the higher the IQ. It appears that stimulus expectancy permits higher-IQ subjects to conserve more brain energy than lower-IQ subjects. In this sense, higher IQ reflects a more efficient use of neural resources. Neural adaptability in humans could have evolved through natural selection for greater efficiency in the brain's utilization of energy as well as selection for the greater cognitive and behavioral capacities associated with increased brain size.

In several studies, the NA index has shown correlations with IQ in the +.50 to +.70 range. In one study,[22] for example, seventy-four normal adults ranging in Wechsler IQ from 98 to 135, with mean IQ of 118, showed a correlation between NA and IQ of +.66. As this subject sample had a restricted range of IQ (the group's standard deviation was only 9.2/15 = .61 as large as the _SD_ in the general population), one can correct the obtained correlation for range restriction to estimate the population correlation, which turns out to be +.82. This is close to the population correlation between two highly _g_-loaded IQ tests (e.g., the Wechsler and the Stanford-Binet).

Another measure derived by Schafer from the average amplitude of the evoked potential (EP) is the _habituation_ of the EP. The amplitude of the EP is recorded for each of 50 auditory "clicks" administered at a stimulus interval of 2 seconds, while the subject relaxes in a reclining chair. It is found that the amplitude of the EP gradually decreases over the 50 "clicks," indicating that "practice" (or expectancy) causes _habituation_, or a diminishing magnitude of the cortical response to the repeated auditory stimulus. A simple measure of the degree of habituation is the difference in average amplitude between the first 25 EPs and the last 25 EPs. This difference score is called the _habituation index_ (HI). Higher IQ subjects show a greater degree of habituation, hence a higher HI.

Schafer used this index to test the hypothesis that a mental test's _g_ loading would predict its correlation with the EP habituation index, or HI, a nonbehavioral, physiological measure.[23] In a group of fifty-two normal adults, ranging in IQ from 98 to 142, the correlation of the HI with the Full Scale Wechsler IQ was +.59; corrected for restriction of IQ range in this group, the correlation rose to .73. Using the method of correlated vectors, the vector of each of the

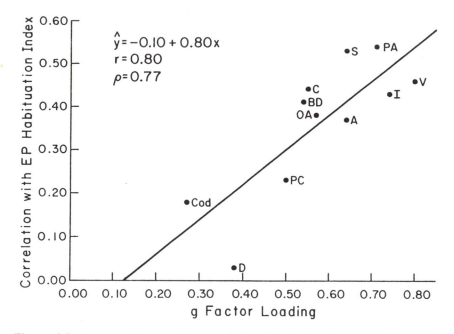

Figure 6.2. A scatter diagram of the correlation of the habituation index of the evoked potential (EP) with the Wechsler Adult Intelligence Scale (WAIS) subtests plotted as a function of the subtests' g loadings. WAIS subtests are Vocabulary (V), Information (I), Similarities (S), Picture Arrangement (PA), Arithmetic (A), Comprehension (C), Block Design (BD), Object Assembly (OA), Picture Completion (PC), Coding (Cod), and Digit Span (DS).

eleven Wechsler subtests' correlations with the HI was correlated with the vector of the subtests' g loadings. (See Appendix B for a detailed explanation of this analysis.) The Pearson correlation (r) between the two vectors is +.80; the Spearman rank-order correlation (r_s) is +.77 (p < .01). The scatter plot of the correlated vectors is shown in Figure 6.2.[24] The analogous plots for the vectors of the three group factors independent of g (Verbal, Spatial, and Memory) that were extracted from the Wechsler battery all showed near-zero correlations with the EP habituation index.

A similar analysis, with the eleven Wechsler subtests and the AEP on 219 normal adolescents, was performed by Eysenck and Barrett.[25] Instead of using Schafer's habituation index, they used a composite measure that reflected both the *complexity* of the AEP (i.e., the "string" measure described on p. 153) and the intraindividual *variance* of the AEP waveform. This composite AEP index correlated .83 with the Full Scale IQ. The method of correlated vectors showed a rank-order correlation of .95 between the vector of the eleven subtests' correlations with the AEP composite score and the vector of the subtests' g loadings. (This correlation falls from .95 to .93 when the vector of the subtests' reliability coefficients is partialed out.)

These studies argue strongly that psychometric *g* is closely related to the electrophysiological information-processing activity of the brain and that *g* is the main, or even the only, cognitive factor represented in the correlation between IQ and the AEP.

Cerebral Glucose Metabolism. The brain's main source of energy is glucose, a simple sugar. Its rate of uptake and subsequent metabolism by different regions of the brain can serve as an indicator of the degree of neural energy expended in various locations of the brain during various kinds of mental activity. This technique consists of injecting a radioactive isotope of glucose (F-18 deoxyglucose) into a person's bloodstream, then having the person engage in some mental activity (such as taking an IQ test) for about half an hour, during which the radioactive glucose is metabolized by the brain. The isotope acts as a radioactive tracer of the brain's neural activity.

Immediately following the uptake period in which the person was engaged in some standardized cognitive task, the gamma rays emitted by the isotope from the nerve cells in the cerebral cortex can be detected and recorded by means of a brain-scanning technique called *positron emission tomography* (or PET scan). The PET scan provides a picture, or map, of the specific cortical location and the amount of neural metabolism (of radioactive glucose) that occurred during an immediately preceding period of mental activity.

Richard J. Haier, a leading researcher in this field, has written a comprehensive review[26a] of the use of the PET scan for studying the physiological basis of individual differences in mental ability. The main findings can be summarized briefly. Normal adults have taken the Raven Advanced Progressive Matrices (RAPM) shortly after they were injected with radioactive glucose. The RAPM, a nonverbal test of reasoning ability, is highly *g* loaded and contains little, if any, other common factor variance. The amount of glucose metabolized during the thirty-five-minute testing period is significantly and *inversely* related to scores on the RAPM, with negative correlations between −.7 and −.8. In solving RAPM problems of a given level of difficulty, the higher-scoring subjects use *less* brain energy than the lower-scoring subjects, as indicated by the amount of glucose uptake. Therefore, it appears that *g* is related to the *efficiency* of the neural activity involved in information processing and problem solving. Negative correlations between RAPM scores and glucose utilization are found in every region of the cerebral cortex, but are highest in the temporal regions, both left and right.

The method of correlated vectors shows that *g* is specifically related to the total brain's glucose metabolic rate (GMR) while engaged in a mental activity over a period of time. In one of Haier's studies,[26b] the total brain's GMR was measured immediately after subjects had taken each of the eleven subtests of the Wechsler Adult Intelligence Scale-Revised (WAIS-R), and the GMR was correlated with scores on each of the subtests. The vector of these correlations was correlated $r = -.79$ ($r_s = -.66$, $p < .05$) with the corresponding vector of the subtests' *g* loadings (based on the national standardization sample).

A phenomenon that might be called "the conservation of *g*" and has been only casually observed in earlier research, but has not yet been rigorously established by experimental studies, is at least consistent with the findings of a clever PET-scan study by Haier and co-workers. The "conservation of *g*" refers to the phenomenon that as people become more proficient in performing certain complex mental tasks through repeated practice on tasks of the same type, the tasks become automatized, less *g* demanding, and consequently less *g* loaded. Although there remain individual differences in proficiency on the tasks after extensive practice, individual differences in performance may reflect less *g* and more task-specific factors. Something like this was observed in a study[26b] in which subjects' PET scans were obtained after their first experience with a video game (Tetris) that calls for rapid and complex information processing, visual spatial ability, strategy learning, and motor coordination. Initially, playing the Tetris game used a relatively large amount of glucose. Daily practice on the video game for 30 to 45 minutes over the course of 30 to 60 days, however, showed greatly increasing proficiency in playing the game, accompanied by a decreasing uptake of glucose and a marked decrease in the correlation of the total brain glucose metabolic rate with *g*. In other words, the specialized brain activity involved in more proficient Tetris performance consumed less energy. Significantly, the rate of change in glucose uptake over the course of practice is positively correlated with RAPM scores. The performance of high-*g* subjects improved more from practice and they also gained greater neural metabolic efficiency during Tetris performance than subjects who were lower in *g*, as indexed by both the RAPM test and the Wechsler Adult Intelligence Scale.

Developmental PET scan studies in individuals from early childhood to maturity show decreasing utilization of glucose in all areas of the brain as individuals mature. In other words, the brain's glucose uptake curve is inversely related to the negatively accelerated curve of mental age, from early childhood to maturity. The increase in the brain's metabolic efficiency seems to be related to the "neural pruning," or normal spontaneous decrease in synaptic density. The spontaneous decrease is greatest during the first several years of life. "Neural pruning" apparently results in greater efficiency of the brain's capacity for information processing. Paradoxical as it may seem, an insufficient loss of neurons during early maturation is associated with some types of mental retardation.

Another study[27] investigated glucose metabolic rate (GMR) as a function of the "mental effort" expended on a task. The investigators did not correlate GMR with the same test for each individual, but compared groups of average- and high-IQ subjects (mean IQ of 104 vs. 123) on easy tasks and on difficult tasks that were equated for the same degree of either "easiness" or "difficulty" within each group. Regardless of the task's objective demands, tasks for which 90% of the responses were correct (within the average group, or within the high-IQ group) were defined as "easy" for each group, and tasks for which only

75% of the responses were correct (within each group) were defined as "difficult." In other words, the level of a task's subjective difficulty was calibrated
relative to each group's ability. For example, the average-IQ group could recall
6 digits backwards on 75% of the trials, whereas the high-IQ group could recall
7 digits on 75% of the trials. The measurements of GMR during these tasks
revealed a significant interaction between IQ level and "mental effort" (i.e.,
level of difficulty relative to the individual's general ability level). Average- and
high-IQ subjects hardly differed in GMR on the "easy" items but differed
markedly on the "difficult" items. The high-IQ subjects brought more "fuel"
to bear on the more difficult task. This increase in GMR by the high-IQ subjects
suggests that more neural units are involved in their level of performance on a
difficult task that is beyond the ability of the average-IQ subjects.

Peripheral Nerve Conduction Velocity. Several studies[28] done in the 1920s
claimed rather surprisingly high correlations between nerve conduction velocity
(NCV) and IQ, but their methods were primitive by modern standards of electrophysiological research, and their results could not be replicated in later studies
in the 1930s. Interest in the subject became almost nonexistent. Then, in 1984,
a geneticist, T. Edward Reed, hypothesized individual differences in NCV as
the mechanism for the heritability of IQ.[29] The well-established heritability of
IQ, of course, implies some physiological basis of IQ differences. Reed suggested that inherited properties of the neuron that govern its conduction velocity
are causally related to IQ. There are now five modern studies that have tested
Reed's hypothesis. Four of the studies are based on the measurement of NCV
in peripheral nerves and one study is based on NCV in a brain tract.

Why should the hypothesis be tested on a peripheral nerve? Located outside
the central nervous system, peripheral nerves are not at all involved in the higher
thought processes or the kinds of problem solving called for by IQ tests. However, it is possible that the properties of neural tissue that are associated with
individual differences in NCV may be more or less similar in all nerve cells
throughout both the peripheral and the central nervous systems. If this were true,
and if individual differences in NCV were related to the cognitive processes
reflected in *g*, then individual differences in NCV in peripheral nerves should
also be related to *g*.

Working from this supposition, Canadian psychologists Vernon and Mori
(1989, 1992) found a significant correlation of +.41 between NCV in the median
nerve of the arm (finger to wrist and wrist to elbow) and IQ (Multidimensional
Aptitude Battery, or MAB) in a sample of eighty-five male and female college
students. A replication of this study, based on eighty-eight students, found a
correlation of +.46. Using the method of correlated vectors, the vector of the
ten MAB subtests' correlations with NCV was correlated +.44 with the vector
of the MAB subtests' *g* loadings.[30a] It was all a very nice picture and bore out
Reed's hypothesis to a tee. Unfortunately, it was at odds with two other studies
that were both performed at about the same time, in London and in Berkeley.

British psychologists Barrett, Daum, and Eysenck (1990), using advanced techniques, measured NCV in the ulnar nerve (finger to wrist) of both the right and left hands of forty-four young adults and found near-zero correlations with IQ (Raven Advanced Progressive Matrices, or RAPM). However, they did find a significant and substantial negative correlation ($-.44$) between IQ and the *variability* of NCV from trial to trial.[30b] (Each trial consists of a brief electrical stimulation of the nerve while recording the speed of its action potential between two points.)

At the same time, Reed and Jensen (1991), at Berkeley, measured IQ (also with the RAPM) and NCV in the median nerve of the arm (from wrist to elbow) in 200 white male college students. The correlation between IQ and NCV was virtually zero, even though the reliability of the IQ and NCV measurements was very high.[30c]

So here was an anomaly. Two apparently solid studies showed a significant IQ × NCV correlation and two equally solid studies did not show any correlation. The studies all had certain minor methodological differences which might account for the contradictory results. But the mystery deepened when the exact same procedures that were used in the two Canadian studies were repeated again, this time with thirty-eight young adult females.[31] The IQ × NCV correlation was virtually zero. This result prompted a reanalysis of the earlier Canadian studies based on samples composed of both males and females. It was found that the correlations for males and females were very different: males had much higher correlations (over $+.60$) than females. This is consistent with the failure to find a correlation in the third Canadian study, based entirely on females, but it is even more at odds with the two contradictory studies (in Britain and in Berkeley). Although these studies were based on largely male samples, they found virtually zero correlations between IQ and peripheral NCV. Still another study, based on twins, also found no significant corrrelation between peripheral NCV and IQ, but did find substantial heritability of NCV.[31b]

The mystery is compounded further by a recent study by a Turkish physiologist, Üner Tan, which found that peripheral NCV measured in the median nerve had a near-zero correlation with IQ (Cattell's Culture Fair Test) in a mixed group of forty-five men and thirty-seven women, but that there was a positive correlation for men ($r = +.63$) and a negative correlation for women ($r = -.55$).[32] Tan suggests that the correlation of NCV with *g* is affected by testosterone level. Clearly, the nature and degree of the relationship between *g* and peripheral NCV remains a puzzle that must be resolved by further research.

Brain Nerve Conduction Velocity. Reed and Jensen (1992) measured NCV in the primary visual tract between the retina of the eye and the visual cortex in 147 college males and found a significant correlation of $+.26$ ($p = .002$) between NCV and Raven IQ. (The correlation is $+.37$ after correction for restriction of range of IQ in this sample of college students.) When the sample is divided into quintiles (five equal-sized groups) on the basis of the average velocity of the P100 visual evoked potential (V:P100), the average IQ in each quintile increases as a function of the V:P100 as shown in Figure 6.3.

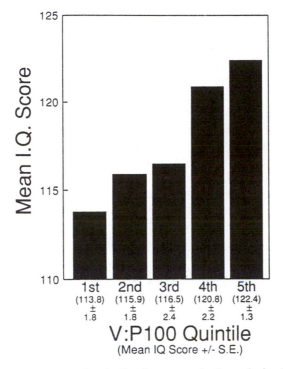

Figure 6.3. Mean IQ in each quintile of nerve conduction velocity (V:P100) as measured in the visual tract in 147 male students. (From Reed & Jensen, 1992. Used with permission of Ablex.)

A theoretically important aspect of this finding is that the NCV (i.e., V:P100) is measured in a brain tract that is not a part of the higher brain centers involved in the complex problem solving required by the Raven test, and the P100 visual evoked potential occurs, on average, about 100 milliseconds after the visual stimulus, which is less than the time needed for conscious awareness of the stimulus. This means that although the cortical NCV involved in Raven performance may be correlated with the NCV in the subcortical visual tract, the same neural elements are not involved. This contradicts Thomson's sampling theory of *g*, which states that tests are correlated to the extent that they utilize the same neural elements. But here we have a correlation between the P100 visual evoked potential and scores on the Raven matrices that cannot be explained in terms of their overlapping neural elements. In the same subject sample, Reed and Jensen found that although NCV and choice reaction time (CRT) are both significantly correlated with IQ, they are not significantly correlated with each other.[33] This suggests two largely independent processes contributing to *g*, one linked to NCV and one linked to CRT. As this puzzling finding is based on a single study, albeit with a large sample, it needs to be replicated before much theoretical importance can be attached to it. There is other evidence that makes the relationship of NCV to *g* worth pursuing. For one thing, the pH level (hydrogen ion concentration) of the fluid surrounding a nerve cell is found experimentally to affect the excitability of the nerve, an increased pH level (i.e., greater alkalinity) producing a lower threshold of excitability.[34a] Also, a study of 42 boys, aged 6 to 13 years, found a correlation of .523 ($p < .001$) between a measure of intracellular brain pH and the WISC-III Full Scale IQ.[34b] Moreover, the method of correlated vectors shows that the vector of the 12 WISC subtests' correlations with pH are significantly correlated with the vector of the subtests' *g* loadings ($r = +.63$, $r_s = +.53$, $p < .05$). This relationship of brain pH to *g* certainly merits further study.

Miscellaneous Physical Correlates of IQ. A number of other physical correlates of IQ have been reported in the literature, as reviewed in detail elsewhere.[35] Although the correlations are generally small, they are nevertheless significant. In most cases, it has not been established whether the correlations are intrinsic or extrinsic.

Among these physical correlates of IQ are certain blood groups and particularly the positive correlation of *g* with the number of homozygous genetic loci (i.e., the same alleles at each locus on both chromosomes) for various blood types, which indicates greater-than-usual genetic similarity of the individual's parents. This would ensure less immunological risk of antigenic incompatibility between mother and fetus, a prenatal factor that can have subtle deleterious effects on brain development in utero. The best-known antigenic incompatibility between mother and fetus with potentially harmful effects on fetal development is that for the Rh factor, which occurs in second-born (and later-born) children when the mother is Rh-negative and the fetus is Rh-positive (having received the Rh+ allele from the father). Dizygotic (DZ) twins who are discordant for the Rh factor (and certain other blood antigens as well) show greater IQ differences than DZ twins who are concordant.

Another blood variable of interest is the amount of uric acid in the blood (serum urate level). Many studies have shown it to have only a slight positive correlation with IQ. But it is considerably more correlated with measures of ambition and achievement. Uric acid, which has a chemical structure similar to caffeine, seems to act as a brain stimulant, and its stimulating effect over the course of the individual's life span results in more notable achievements than are seen in persons of comparable IQ, social and cultural background, and general life-style, but who have a lower serum urate level. High school students with elevated serum urate levels, for example, obtain higher grades than their IQ-matched peers with an average or below-average serum urate level, and, amusingly, one study found a positive correlation between university professors' serum urate levels and their publication rates. The undesirable aspect of high serum urate level is that it predisposes to gout. In fact, that is how the association was originally discovered. The English scientist Havelock Ellis, in studying the lives and accomplishments of the most famous Britishers, discovered that they had a much higher incidence of gout than occurs in the general population.

Asthma and other allergies have a much-higher-than-average frequency in children with higher IQs (over 130), particularly those who are mathematically gifted, and this is an *intrinsic* relationship. The intellectually gifted show some 15 to 20 percent more allergies than their siblings and parents. The gifted are also more apt to be left-handed, as are the mentally retarded; the reason seems to be that the IQ variance of left-handed persons is slightly greater than that of the right-handed, hence more of the left-handed are found in the lower and upper extremes of the normal distribution of IQ.

Then there are also a number of odd and less-well-established physical cor-relates of IQ that have each shown up in only one or two studies, such as vital capacity (i.e., the amount of air that can be expelled from the lungs), handgrip strength, symmetrical facial features, light hair color, light eye color, above-average basic metabolic rate (all these are positively correlated with IQ), and being unable to taste the synthetic chemical phenylthiocarbamide (nontasters are higher both in *g* and in spatial ability than tasters; the two types do not differ in tests of clerical speed and accuracy). The correlations are small and it is not yet known whether any of them are within-family correlations. Therefore, no causal connection with *g* has been established.

Finally, there is substantial evidence of a positive relation between *g* and *general health* or physical well-being.[36] In a very large national sample of high school students (about 10,000 of each sex) there was a correlation of +.381 between a forty-three-item health questionnaire and the composite score on a large number of diverse mental tests, which is virtually a measure of *g*. By comparison, the correlation between the health index and the students' socio-economic status (SES) was only +.222. Partialing out *g* leaves a very small correlation (+.076) between SES and health status. In contrast, the correlation between health and *g* when SES is partialed out is +.326.

A General Factor in Infrahuman Animal Behavior. As there are no fun-damental differences of a qualitative nature between various mammalian species in the anatomy and neurophysiology of the brain, the science of animal behavior generally supports the working hypothesis that interspecies variations in the cognitive abilities inferred from observed differences in behavioral capacities are not discrete gaps but rather quantitative gradations in the complexity of the information-processing systems of mammals. Experimental animal psychology has indeed made important contributions to understanding the basic operating principles of behavioral capacities such as conditioning, learning, perception, and problem solving and in discovering the brain mechanisms underlying these functions. Because most animal behavior research has not focused on individual differences in behavioral capacities *within* a given species, exceedingly few in-frahuman animal studies have been designed that resemble the factor analytic research on *g* in humans. Yet, judging from the three studies described below, animal experimental psychology would appear to be a promising avenue for testing hypotheses concerning the neural basis of g in humans.

The earliest study,[37] by Robert L. Thorndike in 1935, was designed simply to determine whether there is in fact a general factor in the abilities of albino rats. (Coming from twenty different litters of laboratory rats, they were probably a mixture of genetically heterogeneous strains. The highly inbred or isogenic strains used in most research today are virtually the equivalent of monozygotic twins, triplets, etc. If raised in similar laboratory conditions, they would probably be unsuitable for such a study, as they would most likely have a too-limited range of individual differences.) The ninety rats in Thorndike's study were given nine distinct tasks that measured activity level and drive level, as well as speed and accuracy of performance on several more cognitive tasks, such as conditioned responses, learning mazes of various degrees of complexity, and puzzle-box problem solving. With a few exceptions, the performance measures were positively correlated, and factor analysis yielded a general factor that accounted for about two-thirds of the common factor variance and about one-third of the total variance. In this respect, at least, the results were similar to the factor analyses of many psychometric batteries. To distinguish psychometric g from the general factor found in animal studies, the latter is labeled G. Whether G has certain psychological (as opposed to purely statistical) properties similar to g is the open question. Thorndike's analysis is not very enlightening on this point, except that the less "cognitive" measures, such as activity level, drive, and conditioning, had smaller G loadings, on average, than did the somewhat more "cognitive" abilities assessed by mazes and puzzle-boxes. Judging from the tests with the larger loadings on G and his personal observation of the rats' performance on these tests, Thorndike interpreted the G factor as "docility— maze-learning, intelligence, tameness" (p. 63). This modest conclusion was hardly more than suggestive of an interesting hypothesis awaiting investigation, namely, that the G loadings of rat "cognitive" tasks reflect task complexity.

A recent study,[38] by Britt Anderson in 1993, tested this hypothesis using a genetically heterogeneous group of twenty-two male Long-Evans laboratory rats. The rats were given tests selected to measure reasoning and problem solving, in which the rat must deduce a solution (not previously trained) that leads to food reward. The tests required a reasoned (novel), rather than a learned, response. The specific tests involved preference for novelty (which, in human infants, is correlated with later IQ), and speed, accuracy, and response flexibility in maze reasoning problems. Shortly after the completion of testing, each rat was autopsied and its brain removed for weighing. A factor analysis of the test variables yielded a G factor that accounted for 32.3 percent of the total variance. The number of perfect trials on the maze reasoning task had the highest G loading (.70); speed of reasoning was loaded .58; the least demanding task, preference for novelty, had the lowest G loading (.43). Anderson concluded, "[T]he general factor [G] may best be conceived of as relating to individual differences in cognitive ability" (p. 101). Probably the most interesting finding of this study is that the *G* factor scores derived from the rat tests were correlated with brain weight ($r = +.48$) to a degree not unlike that found between *g* and brain size in humans.

A third study, by Francis Crinella and Jen Yu in 1995, used a genetically inbred strain of 120 adult male Sprague-Dawley laboratory rats, in which there are hardly any natural individual differences. Individual differences had to be minimal as the aim of the experiment was to discover how much each specific region of the brain was involved in each of the various behavioral measures. This was done surgically by creating small lesions in 48 specific brain sites selected on the basis of the findings on the rat brain-behavioral correlates found in previous research by Crinella and Yu.[39] In the lesioned group, only one of the 48 sites was lesioned in each pair of rats. A control group of 24 rats was given the same surgical procedure, but without creating a lesion at any site. After full recovery from the operation, all 120 rats were tested in each of seven diverse laboratory tests of learning and problem solving (reasoning). The performance measures from this battery were all positively correlated and yielded a *g* factor that accounted for 34 percent of the total variance in the seven tests. Probably the most important finding is the very high correlation between the various tasks' *G* loadings and the number of brain structures that are significantly involved in task performance—a rank-order correlation of $+.91$. For example, one of the most highly *G*-loaded (.81) tasks (a detour problem, which requires reasoning) is significantly influenced by each of 17 brain structures, whereas a relatively simple conditioned avoidance task, with a lowest *G* loading of only .08, significantly involved only four brain structures. The unlesioned control group performed better on each of the tasks than did the lesioned group. The vector of standardized mean differences between the unlesioned and lesioned (U-L) groups on each of the seven tasks had a significant rank-order correlation of $+.75$ with the vector of *G* loadings for each of the tasks. The *G* factor correlated $-.45$ with the presence of *any* brain lesion—a higher correlation than was found for any single test. In brief, there was a strong relation between a task's *G* loading and its degree of sensitivity to the effects of brain damage in general. The authors suggest that "where the investigator is interested in detecting presence of any type of neuropsychological deficit, as opposed to damage that only affects a particular cognitive/neural system, *g* would be the most sensitive measure" (p. 243). The results of this study lend support to the theory that tests with higher *g* loadings involve proportionately more neural processes than tests with lower *g* loading, even when studied in nonhuman animals.

NOTES

1. The rationale of this methodology is more fully explicated in Jensen, 1980b and in Jensen & Sinha, 1993.

2. The *absolute* value disregards the sign ($+$ or $-$) of the value, hence it is also called an *unsigned* value. Thus $r = +.35$ and $r = -.35$ have the same absolute value, namely $|.35|$. The absolute value of *x* is signified by vertical braces, i.e., $|x|$.

3. The definition of the *true* value of a correlation (symbolized by the Greek letter rho, ρ) is its value in some defined population. The value of ρ is usually unknown or is unknowable. It can only be estimated. A correlation coefficient based on a random sample of the population is an estimate of ρ. The standard error (SE) of this estimate is related to the size of the sample; the larger the sample, of course, the more accurate is the estimate. If $\rho = 0$ (i.e., the null hypothesis), the *standard error* (SE) of the observed correlation in a sample of N subjects is $SE = 1/\sqrt{(N-1)}$. Under the null hypothesis, the frequency distribution of an infinite number of correlation coefficients, each based on a random sample of N subjects, will be normally distributed, with a mean $= 0$ and a standard deviation (SD) $= SE$. When the sample-size is large ($N > 500$), a correlation that differs from 0 by more than $\pm 1.96\ SE$ is said to be *significant* beyond the 5 percent level of confidence (technically written as $p < .05$), meaning that the probability (p) of finding a difference that large by chance (when $\rho = 0$) is less than 5 percent. (Chance, in this case, is technically termed *sampling error.*) Hence we reject the null hypothesis that $\rho = 0$. The 1 percent level of confidence, or $p < .01$, is $\pm 2.58\ SE$. (*Note*: Five percent of the area under the normal curve falls beyond the limits of $\pm 1.96\ SD$ from the mean; 1 percent of the area falls beyond $\pm 2.58\ SD$.) In the technical literature, the correlation coefficient is usually accompanied by the probability that the obtained correlation could have occurred merely by sampling error); for example, $r = .35$ ($p < .01$) would mean that a correlation as large as .35 would be expected to occur by random sampling (of sample size N) less than once in 100 samples if the true correlation (ρ) is zero. Thus one can be at least 99 percent certain that the true correlation is *not* zero. In fact, given only these data, the best *estimate* of the true correlation in this case is .35. (*Note*: For small samples, or if the hypothesized value of ρ is different from zero, somewhat more complicated formulas are needed for an accurate test of the significance of an obtained (sample) correlation or its difference from the hypothesized value (see Fisher, 1970, pp. 194–206).

4. *Meta-analysis* consists of various mathematical-statistical methods that permit one to make statistical estimates of population parameters (e.g., mean, variance, correlation coefficient, along with their significance level or confidence interval) from comparable statistics that were derived from a number of independent studies (i.e., studies based on different subject samples). The results of a proper meta-analysis are generally more valid than the results of any of the single independent studies on which the meta-analysis was based.

5. It is unnecessarily laborious to compute the percentiles of the permutation distribution needed to test the significance of r_s when $n > 10$, or even for smaller values of n. Fortunately, there is a simple method for testing the significance of r_s by means of Student's t test, which gives a very close approximation to the exact p values of the permutation distribution: $t = \{(n-2)r_s^2/(1 - r_s^2)\}^{1/2}$. For a full discussion of the permutation distribution of r_s, see Kendall & Stuart, 1973, Vol. 2, pp. 492–499.

6. The *null hypothesis* states that the true correlation is zero. The more that an empirically obtained value of r departs from zero, the greater is the probability that the null hypothesis is false and therefore should be rejected. A statistical test is specifically aimed at *rejecting* the null hypothesis with a specified level of confidence (e.g., 5 percent chance of being wrong by rejecting the null) when in fact the null hypothesis is *false*. But if the statistical test rejects the null hypothesis when in fact the null hypothesis is *true*, statisticians call this a *Type I error*. If the statistical test does not reject the null hypothesis when in fact the null hypothesis is *false*, it is called a *Type II error*.

7. Jensen & Sinha, 1993. This 100-page chapter is probably the most comprehensive review of the world literature on the physical correlates of mental ability, excluding pathological conditions, electrophysiological brain measurements, and brain biochemistry. The latter two topics are well reviewed in other chapters of the same book, edited by P. A. Vernon (1993b). This is the most up-to-date and comprehensive book on the biological aspects of human mental ability, a "must" for all who wish to delve further into this subject. The chapter by Eysenck (1993) discusses the biology of intelligence in relation to the philosophy of science.

8. Jensen (1980b) and Jensen & Johnson (1994).

9. Jensen, 1994f.

10. (a) Andreasen et al., 1993; (b) Egan et al., 1994; (c) Raz, Torres, et al., 1993; (d) Wickett at al., 1994; (e) Willerman et al., 1991; (f) Wickett et al., 1996; (g) Schoenemann, 1997.

11. Hamilton, 1935.

12. Jensen & Johnson, 1994; also see Johnson, 1991, for additional evidence of a within-families correlation between head size and IQ.

13. Ankney, 1992.

14. Jensen, 1980a, pp. 622–627. This chapter affords a fairly comprehensive review of sex differences in mental abilities and references to much of the literature prior to 1980.

15. Witelson et al., 1995.

16. Cohn, Cohn, & Jensen, 1988.

17. The Raven's _g_ loading when factor analyzed among a large and diverse battery of mental tests is typically about .80. If it were only the Raven's specificity that was involved in its correlation with myopia, one would not expect myopia to be correlated with any other mental tests in which matrix items are absent. In fact, however, myopia is correlated with a wide variety of _g_-loaded tests and various _g_-loaded achievements (Jensen & Sinha, 1993, pp. 212–217).

18. A much more detailed but admirably clear exposition of the basic electrochemistry of the neuron and nerve conduction is given in R. F. Thompson, 1985, particularly Chapter 3 and the Appendix.

19. The most comprehensive and up-to-date general summary I have found is by Deary & Caryl (1993). Earlier, but still worthwhile reviews are by Eysenck & Barrett (1985) and by Haier et al. (1983). Vernon (1993a) offers a briefer, less technical summary, which includes reaction time and other physiological measures in addition to EEG correlates of IQ. More specialized and technical reviews are given by Barrett & Eysenck (1994), who focus entirely on the latest techniques and findings of research on averaged evoked potentials (AEPs), and by Polich & Kok (1995), who focus on only the P300 AEP and all of its reported correlates with individual differences in psychological variables, including memory span and IQ. The extensive lists of references in all of the articles cited above probably encompass some 90 percent of the total literature in this field since about 1960.

20. Lutzenberger et al., 1992.

21. McGarry-Roberts et al., 1992. The P300 latency is generally considered a measure of the time taken for stimulus apprehension and evaluation. Its correlation with IQ, however, is often erratic and therefore not as well established as for the earlier potentials (P100, P200), probably because the P300 is so complexly determined by so many biological variables, most of which are only indirectly related to cognitive ability. For a

comprehensive review of the biological determinants of the P300, see Polich & Kok (1995).

22. Schafer & Marcus, 1973; Schafer, 1982.

23. Schafer, 1985.

24. Partialing out the vector of the subtests' reliability coefficients from the Pearson $r = +.81$ between the EP vector and the *g* vector lowers the *r* to $+.79$. Obviously, the *r* here is not attributable to the tests' differing reliability coefficients.

25. Eysenck & Barrett, 1985, p. 41 and Table 5.

26. (a) Haier, 1993. For other brief reviews of PET studies (also EEG and AEP studies), see Vernon (1990) and Vernon & Mori (1990); (b) Haier et al., 1992.

27. Larson et al., 1995.

.28. These studies are reviewed in Vernon, 1993a, p. 176.

29. Reed, 1984, 1988a, 1988b.

30. (a) Vernon, 1992, 1993a, p. 178; (b) Barrett, Daum, & Eysenck, 1990; (c) Reed & Jensen, 1991.

31. (a) Wickett & Vernon, 1994; (b) Rijsdijk et al., 1995.

32. Tan, 1996.

33. Reed & Jensen, 1993.

34. (a) Lehmann, 1937; (b) Rae et al., 1996.

35. Jensen & Sinha, 1993.

36. Lubinski & Humphreys, 1992.

37. Thorndike, R. L., 1935.

38. Anderson, 1993.

39. Crinella & Yu (1995) provide references to many related studies.

Chapter 7

The Heritability of *g*

Individual differences in mental test scores have a substantial genetic component indexed by the coefficient of *heritability* (in the broad sense), that is, the proportion of the population variance in test scores attributable to all sources of genetic variability. The broad heritability of IQ is about .40 to .50 when measured in children, about .60 to .70 in adolescents and young adults, and approaches .80 in later maturity.

Environmental variance can be partitioned into two sources: (1) environmental influences that are *shared* among children reared in the same family but that differ *between families*, and (2) *nonshared* environmental influences that are specific to each child in the same family and therefore differ *within families*. The shared environmental variance diminishes from about 35 percent of the total IQ variance in early childhood to near zero percent in late adolescence. The nonshared environmental variance remains nearly constant at around 20 to 30 percent from childhood to maturity. That is, virtually all of the nongenetic variance in adult IQs is attributable to *within-family* causes, while virtually none is attributable to the kinds of environmental variables that differ *between families*. The specific sources of much of the within-family environmental variance are still not entirely identified, but a large part of the specific environmental variance appears to be due to the additive effects of a large number of more or less random and largely physical events—developmental "noise"—with small, but variable positive and negative influences on the neurophysiological substrate of mental growth.

More of the genetic variance in test scores is associated with *g* than with any other common factor. Hence the relative *g* loadings of various tests predict their relative heritability coefficients (the proportion of genetic variance in the test scores).

Traits that show genetic dominance provide evidence that they have been subjected to natural selection as a Darwinian fitness character over the course of evolution. IQ, and particularly its _g_ component, manifest the theoretically predictable effects of genetic dominance—inbreeding depression in the offspring of consanguineous parents, and the opposite effect, hybrid vigor (or heterosis), that shows up in the offspring when each parent has a different racial ancestry. Tests' relative _g_ loadings significantly predict the degree to which various tests manifest both inbreeding depression and heterosis. These data support the hypothesis that the _g_ factor of psychometric tests has arisen through natural selection over the course of human evolution and therefore can be regarded as a fitness character in the Darwinian sense.

This chapter is not a detailed explanation of the methodology of behavioral genetics or a review of the extensive research on the genetics of mental ability.[1] Rather, this chapter highlights the developments of the last decade or so that are now well established and are especially important for understanding the biological basis of _g_.

IS _g_ ONE AND THE SAME FACTOR BETWEEN FAMILIES AND WITHIN FAMILIES?

As we shall see, the main factor in the heritability of IQ and other mental tests is _g_. Also, as we shall see, genetic analysis and the calculation of heritability depend on a comparison of the trait variance _between_ families (BF) and the variance _within_ families (WF). (The separation of the total or population variance and correlation into BF and WF components was introduced in Chapter 6, pp. 141–42.) Therefore, before discussing the heritability of _g_, we must ask whether the _g_ factor that emerges from a factor analysis of BF correlations is the very same _g_ that emerges from a factor analysis of WF correlations. Recall that BF is the mean of all the full siblings (reared together) in each family in the population; WF is the differences among full siblings (reared together). In other words, some proportion of the total population variance (V_P) in a trait measured on individuals is variance _between_ families (V_{BF}) and some proportion is variance _within_ families (V_{WF}). Thus theoretically $V_P = V_{BF} + V_{WF}$. Similarly, the population correlation between any two variables reliably measured on individuals can be apportioned to BF and WF. The method for doing this requires measuring the variables of interest in sets of full siblings who were reared together.

Why might one expect the correlations between different mental tests, say X and Y, to be any different BF than WF? If the genetic or environmental influences that cause families to differ from one another on X or Y (or both) are of a different nature than the influences that cause differences on X or Y among siblings reared together in the same family, it would be surprising if the BF correlation of X and Y were the same as the WF correlation. And if there were a large number of diverse tests, the probability would be nil that all their inter-correlations would have the same factor structure in both BF and WF if the tests did not reflect the same causal variables acting to the same degree in both cases.

BF differences can be genetic or environmental, or both. A typical source of BF variance is social class or socioeconomic status (SES). Families differ in SES, but siblings reared in the same family do not differ in SES; therefore SES is not a source of WF variance. The same is true of differences associated with race, cultural identification, ethnic cuisines, and other such variables. They differ between families (BF) but seldom differ between full siblings reared together in the same household.

Now consider two sets of tests: A and B, X and Y. If the scores on Tests A and B are both strongly influenced by SES and other variables on which families differ and on which siblings in the same family do not differ, and if scores on Test X and Test Y are very little influenced by these BF variables, we should expect two things: (1) the BF correlation of A and B (r_{AB}) would be larger than the BF correlation of X and Y (r_{XY}), and (2) the BF correlation of A and B (r_{AB}) would be unrelated to the BF correlation of X and Y (r_{XY}). The greater size of the correlation r_{AB} reflects similarity in the greater effect of SES (or other BF variables) on the scores of these two tests. This could be shown further by the fact that the BF correlation is much larger than the WF correlation for tests A and B. The size of the correlation r_{XY}, on the other hand, reflects something other than SES (or other variables) on which families differ. So if the BF r_{XY} and the WF r_{XY} are virtually equal (after correction for attenuation[2]) and if this is also true of the BF and WF correlations for many diverse tests, it suggests that the same causal factors are involved in both the BF and WF correlations for these tests (unlike Tests A and B).

We can examine the hypothesis that the genetic and environmental influences that produce BF differences in tests' _g_ loadings are the same as the genetic and environmental influences that produce WF differences in the tests' _g_ loadings. If we find that this hypothesis cannot be rejected, we can rule out the supposed direct BF environmental influences on _g_, such as SES, racial-cultural differences, and the like. The observed mean differences _between_ different SES, racial, and cultural groups on highly _g_-loaded tests then must be attributed to the same influences that cause differences among the siblings within the same families. As will be explicated later, these sibling differences result from both genetic and environmental (better called _nongenetic_) effects.

Two large-scale studies have tested this hypothesis. In each study, a _g_ factor was extracted from the BF correlations among a number of highly diverse tests and also from the WF correlations among the same tests.[3] These two factors are referred to as g_{BF} and g_{WF}.

Table 7.1

Congruence Coefficients between the *g* Factor Derived from Between-Family (BF) and Within-Family (WF) Correlations among Seven Diverse Mental Tests in White (W) and Black (B) Samples

	g Factor (2)White WF	(3) Black BF	(4) Black WF
(1) White BF	.987	.993	.991
(2) White WF		.986	.993
(3) Black BF			.985

The first study[4] was based on pairs of siblings (nearest in age, in grades 2 to 6) from 1,495 white and 901 black families. They were all given seven highly diverse age-standardized tests (Memory, Figure Copying, Pictorial IQ, Nonverbal IQ, Verbal IQ, Vocabulary, and Reading Comprehension). Both BF and WF correlations among the tests were obtained separately for whites and blacks, and a *g* factor (first principal component) was extracted from each of the four correlation matrices. The degree of similarity between factors is properly assessed by the coefficient of congruence, r_c.[5] Two factors with values of r_c larger than .90 are generally interpreted as ''highly similar''; values above .95 as having ''virtual identity.'' The values of r_c are shown in Table 7.1. They are all very high and probably not significantly different from one another. The high congruence of the g_{BF} and g_{WF} factors in each racial group indicates that *g* is clearly an *intrinsic* factor (as defined in Chapter 6, p. 139). Also, both g_{BF} and g_{WF} are virtually the same across racial groups. In this California school population, little, if any, of the variance in the *g* factor in these tests is attributable to the effects of SES or cultural differences. Whatever SES and cultural differences may exist in this population do not alter the character of the general factor that all these diverse tests have in common.

The second study[6] is based on groups that probably have more distinct cultural differences than black and white schoolchildren in California, namely, teenage Americans of Japanese ancestry (AJA) and Americans of European ancestry (AEA), all living in Hawaii. Each group was composed of full siblings from a large number of families. They were all given a battery of fifteen highly diverse cognitive tests representing such first-order factors as verbal, spatial, perceptual speed and accuracy, and visual memory. In this study, the *g* factor was extracted as a second-order factor in a confirmatory hierarchical factor analysis. The same type of factor analysis was performed separately on the BF and WF correlations in each racial sample. The congruence coefficient between g_{BF} and g_{WF} was +.99 in both the AJA group and the AEA group, and the congruence across the AJA and AEA groups was +.99 for both g_{BF} and g_{WF}. These results are essentially the same as those in the previous study, even though the populations, tests, and methods of extracting the general factor all differed. Moreover, the four first-order group factors showed almost as high congruence between BF and WF and between AJA and AEA as did the second-order *g* factor. The authors of the second study, behavioral geneticists Craig Nagoshi and Ronald Johnson[6] concluded, "Nearly all of the indices used in the present analyses thus support a high degree of similarity in the factor structures of cognitive ability test scores calculated between versus within families. In other words, they suggest that the genetic and environmental factors underlying cognitive abilities are intrinsic in nature. These indices also suggest that these BF and WF structures are similar across the AEA and AJA ethnic groups, despite some earlier findings that may have led one to expect especially strong between-family effects for the AJA group" (p. 314).

TERMINOLOGY AND FUNDAMENTAL CONCEPTS OF BEHAVIOR-GENETIC ANALYSIS

A phenotype is any observable or measurable characteristic or trait. Many phenotypes, such as height and IQ, vary widely in the population. The total phenotypic variance in a metric trait can be analyzed by the methods of quantitative genetics into a number of components which are labeled according to the different main "sources" of variance that contribute to the total variance. Figure 7.1 shows how the total phenotypic variance is typically analyzed, or subdivided, in behavioral genetic research. While every entry in Figure 7.1 will not be explained (see Note 1), the figure provides a useful framework in which to locate the components of variance that enter into many of the summary conclusions that follow. One other subdivision not shown here, because it cuts across some of the others and would create an extremely confusing diagram if included, is the division of all the genetic variance into *between-families* and *within-families*, just as the total environmental variance is divided.

One of the purposes of quantitative genetics methodology is to determine, for any given phenotype, the proportions of the total phenotypic variance contributed by each of the sources of variance shown in Figure 7.1. This kind of "biometrical analysis," as it is called, depends essentially on correlations between individuals who differ in degree of genetic kinship (e.g., monozygotic, or "identical," twins, who have all of their genes in common; dizygotic twins or siblings, who have on average about one-half of their segregating genes in common; half-siblings, with one-fourth in common; first cousins, with one-eighth; a parent and offspring [one-half]; and unrelated persons, who have no genetic variance in common and whose genetic correlation therefore is zero).

The genetic correlation between relatives corresponds to the proportion of identical segregating genes they have inherited in common from their ancestors. Only segregating genes (i.e., genes that have two or more different alleles each with more than rare frequencies) contribute to genetic variance. Nonsegregating genes, having no variation in alleles (except for rare mutants), are uniformly

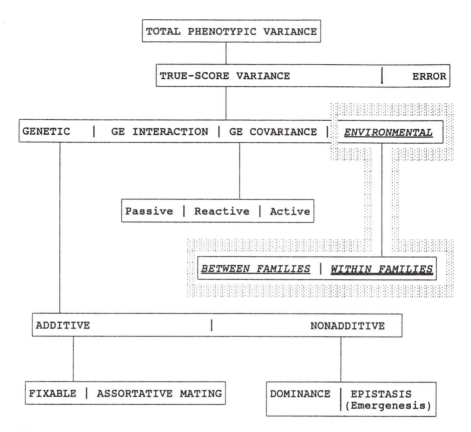

Figure 7.1. Branch diagram partitioning the total phenotypic variance into the components (i.e., sources of variance) that can be estimated by the methods of quantitative genetics. (*Note*: There is no relationship between the areas of the rectangles and the proportions of variance accounted for by the various components.) (From Jensen, 1997a. Used with permission of Cambridge University Press.)

characteristic of a particular species and are usually essential for the individual's viability; hence they are the same for virtually everyone in the population and therefore are not reflected in its total genetic variance. Because these nonsegregating genes are inherited by virtually everyone, they do not cause differences between individuals.

One other requirement, essential for distinguishing genetic from environmental sources of variance, is to have genetically related persons, such as those listed above, some of whom were *reared together* and others who were *reared apart* (ideally in uncorrelated family environments). There are two classes of persons that provide the most valuable data for biometrical analysis. The first is monozygotic (MZ) twins who were reared apart from infancy (identical genes in different environments). The second is genetically unrelated children who were adopted in infancy and reared together in the family environment of their adoptive parents (different genes in the same family environment). More elaborate analyses are possible if one also has data on the trait of interest in the adoptive parents and in one or both of the biological parents of the adopted children (assuming the biological parents are not involved in the adopted child's social environment). If the adopted individual has siblings who were reared by the biological parents or by another adoptive family, they, too, can provide valuable data for genetic analysis.

MZ twins reared apart (MZA) are especially useful, because they are genetically identical and have grown up in different environments. Therefore, the correlation between them is itself a direct estimate of the proportion of genetic variance. All of the phenotypic difference between MZ twins is due to either nongenetic influences or measurement error. On the other hand, persons who are genetically unrelated and grew up together in adoptive families have only their family environment in common, so the correlation between them is a direct estimate of the proportion of BF environmental variance.

From reasonably large samples of data on MZA twins and adoptees, it is possible to obtain estimates of the proportions of total variance contributed by genetic and between-family (BF) environmental factors. Estimation of the other components shown in Figure 7.1 requires data from various other kinships, such as MZ twins reared together and dizygotic (DZ) twins reared together, half-siblings, parent-offspring correlations, the offspring of cousin matings (or other degrees of genetically related parents), and the correlation between the parents of the twins or siblings mentioned above. The mathematical procedures for these kinds of analysis are a complex subject with its own technical literature (it is in fact a major branch of genetics in which one can specialize for a Ph.D. degree). The methods of quantitative genetics are not explained in any detail here (see Note 1 for introductory references on the subject). I will only summarize in almost telegraphic style some of the most secure facts about the biometrical analysis of IQ that have been discovered and replicated in many studies using these methods.

Heritability Defined. Heritability (conventionally symbolized h^2) is roughly defined as the proportion of the phenotypic variance V_P in a trait that is *genetic* variance V_G; in brief, $h^2 = V_G/V_P$. Geneticists use the term *heritability* in two different senses, called *heritability* in the *narrow* sense (h_N^2) and heritability in the *broad* sense (h_B^2). This is an important distinction. Narrow heritability is of interest mainly to animal breeders; broad heritability is of interest mainly to psychologists and behavioral geneticists.

Narrow heritability includes only the *additive* genetic variance V_A, that is, the part of the total genetic variance responsible for the resemblance between parent and offspring. The *fixable* component of the additive variance is the only part of it that "breeds true" (hence it was referred to by R. A. Fisher as the *essential genotype*). Therefore, it is only the *fixable* part of the additive genetic variance that affords the leverage for selective breeding, which can occur either by natural selection or by artificial selection by animal and plant breeders. The *nonfixable* part of the additive variance results from *assortative mating* (some degree of genetic correlation between parents on a specific trait).[7] (The coefficient of assortative mating [also called spousal correlation] for IQ in our present population is between $+.40$ and $+.50$.)

Broad heritability includes *all* sources of genetic variance. Besides the *additive* variance (which is the largest part of broad heritability), there is *genotype × environment* (GE) *interaction*: Different genotypes may react differently to the same environmental factor; an environmental condition that is favorable to the-phenotypic development of a certain genotype is less effective or even unfavorable for a different genotype. Also there is *genotype-environment* (GE) *covariance*, or the correlation between genetic and environmental factors that affect the development of the phenotype: Genotypes that are more favorable than average for the development of a trait are found with greater-than-chance frequency in environments that are also more favorable than average; likewise for genotypes and environments that are less favorable.

Then there is the *nonadditive* genetic variance. It results from two types of genetic interactions: (1) genetic *dominance* (e.g., a dominant and a recessive allele paired at the same locus on the chromosomes might have the same phenotypic effect as two dominant alleles at that locus), and (2) *epistasis* (a gene at one chromosomal locus affects the phenotypic expression of a gene at some other locus). Dominance and epistatis cause lower correlations between direct-line relatives (parents-offspring and full siblings) than would be the case if purely additive genetic effects were the only source of genetic variance.

Distinction between "Hereditary" and "Heritability." These two distinct concepts should never be confused. Heritability (h^2) has been defined above as the proportion of the phenotypic variance in a trait that is attributable to genotypic variance. Heritability never refers to the *amount* of the trait measurement per se that is attributable to genes. (It is a truism that any trait of an individual is necessarily a function of both genes and environment, as both are essential for the very existence of the individual, just as the area of a rectangle depends on its length and its width, and therefore a rectangle cannot even exist without having both dimensions.) Heritability refers only to the observed phenotypic trait *variation* (i.e., measured as the *variance*) among individuals in a defined population. It is also a function of the amount of environmental (i.e., nongenetic) variance among individuals.

The terms *hereditary* and *inherited*, on the other hand, simply mean that a given trait or characteristic of individuals depends on the presence of certain genes or that the gene or genes affecting the trait are transmitted from parents to offspring (whether or not the phenotypic trait appears in the parents). But the term "heritability" is inapplicable (and, in fact, formally meaningless) if applied to hereditary characteristics for which the population variance is zero (or very near zero in the case of variation due to a single rare or mutant gene). Virtually all babies are born with *one* head, *two* hands, and *ten* fingers, for example. As these human characteristics are coded in the genes, they are *hereditary* characteristics. But because these characteristics do not normally vary among individuals, the concept of heritability is simply inapplicable to them.

EMPIRICAL EVIDENCE ON THE HERITABILITY OF IQ

Most behavioral geneticists today agree that the following concatenation of several overwhelmingly well-established facts in behavioral genetics is impossible to explain or understand without invoking a substantial degree of broad heritability of IQ. These facts are: (1) MZ twins *reared together* (MZT) are much more similar in IQ than DZ twins *reared together* (DZT). (2) MZ twins *reared apart* (MZA) are more similar in IQ than DZ twins *reared together*. (3) The IQs of adopted persons who have never known their biological parents are more highly correlated with the IQs of their biological parents than with the IQs of their adoptive parents. (4) Unrelated persons who were reared together from infancy show a much lower IQ correlation with each other in early childhood than do biological siblings, and they show virtually zero IQ correlation in adolescence and adulthood.

Some typical correlation coefficients can be attached to these generalizations based on the average of the IQ correlations found in numerous studies.[8] (These mean correlations are weighted by the number of twin pairs, N_p, in each of the samples that were averaged.)

$$\text{MZ twins reared together } r_{MZT} = +.86 \ (N_p = 4{,}672)$$

$$\text{DZ twins reared together } r_{DZT} = +.60 \ (N_p = 5{,}546)$$

$$\text{MZ twins reared apart } r_{MZA} = +.75 \ (N_p = 158)$$

Note that the correlation r_{MZA} between MZ twins reared apart is a direct estimate of the broad heritability; the weighted mean value of r_{MZA} obtained from all existing studies (with one exception[9]) is +.75. However, the accuracy of the estimate of broad heritability based on r_{MZA} depends on the assumption that the MZ twins were reared in uncorrelated environments, otherwise the r_{MZA} will reflect shared (BF) environmental variance, which would make r_{MZA} a spuriously inflated estimate of the broad heritability, h_B^2. What cannot be ruled out in MZ twins reared apart is their common prenatal, perinatal, and preadoption environments. To the degree that these aspects of shared environment affect later mental development, the correlation between MZ twins reared apart reflects not only the heritability, but, in addition, whatever nongenetic variance may be attributable to the shared component of the twins' prenatal, perinatal, and preadoption environment. Such nongenetic effects are probably not large (most likely less than 10 percent of the total nongenetic variance), but neither would they be expected to be zero. The difference between the IQ correlation of DZ twins and of ordinary siblings (which are about .50 and .60, respectively) is probably attributable in part to prenatal factors (e.g., age, nutrition, and health of the mother, blood antigen incompatibilities, obstetrical procedures, etc.).

Also, due to "placement bias" by adoption agencies the environments of the separated MZ twins in these studies are not perfectly uncorrelated, so one could argue that the high correlation between MZAs is attributable to the similarity of the postadoptive environments in which they were reared. This problem was thoroughly investigated in the MZAs of the ongoing Minnesota twin study,[10] which has a larger sample of MZAs than any other study to date. It is not enough simply to show that there is a correlation between the separated twin's environments on such variables as father's and mother's level of education, their socioeconomic status, their intellectual and achievement orientation, and various physical and cultural advantages in the home environment. _One must also take account of the degree to which these placement variables are correlated with IQ._ The placement variables' contribution to the MZA IQ correlation, then, is the product of the MZA correlation on measures of the placement variables and the correlation of the placement variables with IQ. This product, it turns out, is exceedingly small and statistically nonsignificant, ranging from $-.007$ to $+.032$, with an average of $+.0045$, when calculated for nine different placement variables. In other words, similarities in the MZA's environments cannot possibly account for more than a minute fraction of the IQ correlation of $+.75$ between MZAs. If there were no genetic component at all in the correlation between the twins' IQs, the correlation between their environments would not account for an IQ correlation of more than $+.10$.

Let us now look at the data on ordinary siblings and on genetically unrelated children reared together in adoptive homes. The average correlation of IQ between full siblings reared together is $+.49$, based on over 27,000 sibling pairs.[11] For full siblings reared apart, the correlation is .24 for preadolescents[12] and .47 for adults.[13] The IQs of unrelated persons who were reared together correlate $+.25$ in childhood and $-.01$ in adulthood.[12] What these figures suggest is that during the period between childhood and late adolescence there is a gradual _decrease_ in the influence of the BF or shared environment on IQ and a corresponding _increase_ in the broad heritability of IQ. In other words, the effect of all the aspects of the home environment that are shared by persons reared together becomes a less and less important source of IQ variance as children grow up. By late adolescence these shared (or BF) environmental effects show no detectable contribution to the total variance in IQ. By adulthood, all of the IQ correlation between biologically related persons is genetic. In other words, to the extent that there is a correlation between the IQs of genetically related postpubertal family members, the correlation is entirely due to genetic factors; the environmental contribution to the familial correlations is nil.

Figures 7.2a and 7.2b show the best available estimates of the changes with age in the proportions of the total IQ variance attributable to genetic factors and to the effects of the shared (or BF) and nonshared (or WF) environment.[14] These

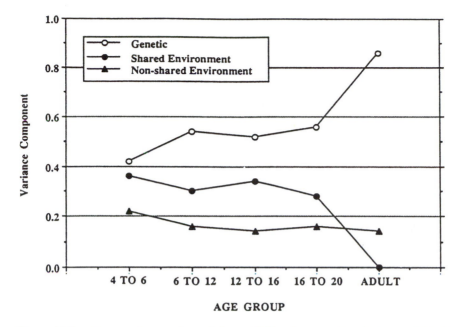

Figure 7.2a. Estimated proportions of the total IQ variance attributable to genetic and environmental (shared and nonshared) effects. Note that only the nonshared (or within-family) environmental variance remains relatively constant across the entire age range. (From McGue et al., 1993, p. 64, Copyright © 1993 by the American Psychological Association. Reprinted with permission of the APA and M. McGue.)

surprising results are among the most striking and strongly substantiated findings of behavioral genetics in recent years.[15]

The diminishing, or even vanishing, effect of differences in home environment revealed by adoption studies, at least within the wide range of typical, humane child-rearing environments in the population, can best be understood in terms of the changing aspects of the genotype-environment (GE) covariance from predominantly *passive*, to *reactive*, to *active*.[16] (See Figure 7.1, p. 174.)

The *passive* component of the GE covariance reflects all those things that happen to the phenotype, independent of its own characteristics. For example, the child of musician parents may have inherited genes for musical talent and is also exposed (through no effort of its own) to a rich musical environment.

The *reactive* component of the GE covariance results from the reaction of others to the individual's phenotypic characteristics that have a genetic basis. For example, a child with some innate musicality shows an unusual sensitivity to music, so the parents give the child piano lessons; the teacher is impressed by the child's evident musical talent and encourages the child to work toward a scholarship at Julliard. The phenotypic expression of the child's genotypic

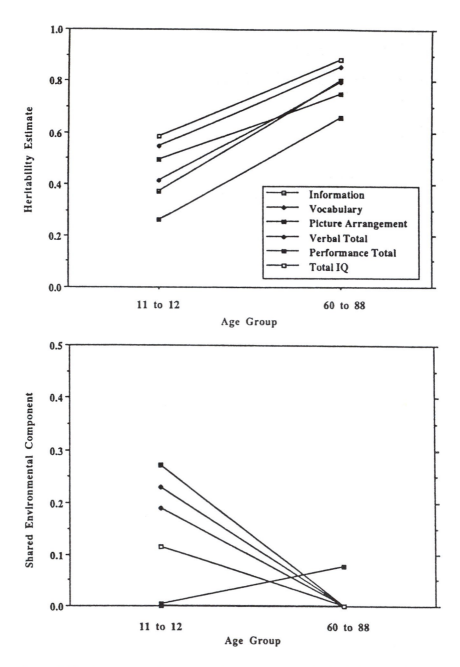

Figure 7.2b. *Upper panel*: Proportion of *genetic* variance in Wechsler IQ and various subtest scores for two age groups. *Lower panel*: Shared (or between-families) *environmental* variance for two age groups. (From McGue et al., 1993, p. 72, Copyright © 1993 by the American Psychological Association. Reprinted with permission of the APA and M. McGue.)

musical propensities causes others to treat this child differently from how they would treat a child without these particular propensities. Each expression of the propensity has consequences that lead to still other opportunities for its expression, thus propelling the individual along the path toward a musical career. This in fact is the abstracted biography of every world-famous musician.

The *active* component of the GE covariance results from the child's actively seeking and creating environmental experiences that are most compatible with the child's genotypic proclivities. The child's enlarging world of potential experiences is like a cafeteria in which the child's choices are biased by genetic factors. The musical child uses his allowance to buy musical recordings and to attend concerts; the child spontaneously selects radio and TV programs that feature music instead of, say, cartoons or sports events; and while walking alone to school the child mentally rehearses a musical composition. The child's musical environment is not imposed by others, but is selected and created by the child. (The same kind of examples could be given for a great many other inclinations and interests that are probably genetically conditioned, such as literary, mathematical, mechanical, scientific, artistic, histrionic, athletic, and social talents.) The child's genotypic propensity can even run into conflict with the parents' wishes and expectations.

From early childhood to late adolescence the predominant component of the GE covariance gradually shifts from *passive* to *reactive* to *active*, which makes for increasing phenotypic expression of individuals' genotypically conditioned characteristics. In other words, as people approach maturity they seek out and even create their own experiential environment. With respect to mental abilities, a "good" environment, in general, is one that affords the greatest freedom and the widest variety of opportunities for reactive and active GE covariance, thereby allowing genotypic propensities their fullest phenotypic expression.

By adulthood, the shared or BF environmental variance has virtually vanished and the total IQ variance is made up of genetic variance (the broad heritability) and the nonshared or WF component of environmental variance, which constitutes about 20 percent of the total adult IQ variance. The causes of the nonshared environmental variance are still somewhat obscure. I have presented analyses of MZ twin data elsewhere which suggest that the nonshared environmental variance is mainly the result of a great many small random effects that are largely of a biological nature.[17] Such effects as childhood diseases, traumas, and the like, as well as prenatal effects such as mother-fetus incompatibility of blood antigens, maternal health, and perinatal effects of anoxia and other complications in the birth process, could each have a small adverse effect on mental development. Such environmental effects could differ randomly among twins or ordinary siblings. Some individuals would have the good luck of being "hit" by very few such adverse random effects, compared to the average, and others would have the bad luck of being "hit" by many more than the average.

Whatever their causes, it turns out that the form of the distribution of these random environmental effects on IQ indicates that the distribution is a composite of two distinct underlying distributions. The largest of these is the normal distribution that would be mathematically expected of any variable that results from the summation of many small random effects—a consequence known as the Central Limit Theorem in mathematical statistics. The smaller distribution, superposed on the normal distribution, reflects the distribution of a few relatively large adverse effects. In the composite or total distribution of environmental effects, then, the feature of the distribution that reflects the large adverse effects, over and above what can be accounted for by the distribution of the many small random effects, probably affects only about 20 percent of the 180 pairs of MZT twins that were studied. Whether this percentage would be appreciably larger or smaller for singletons is unknown and would be very difficult (or probably impossible) to determine. The main point is this: To the extent that the nonshared environment is essentially the same for twins and singletons, it appears to be largely the result of many small random effects, probably acting mostly on the biological substrate of mental ability. Because this is the largest (and, in adulthood, the only) source of nongenetic or environmental variance in IQ, it eludes psychological or educational means of manipulation. This could explain why psychological, educational, and other purely behavioral interventions in the many attempts to raise low IQs (relative to the mean IQ in the population) have had so little success, despite the fact that a fairly large proportion of the IQ variance is "environmental" in the sense of being nongenetic. These largely random environmental effects militate against manipulation of mental development by behavioral means. (Evidence on the malleability of IQ and _g_ through specific environmental interventions is discussed in Chapter 10, pp. 333–44.)

Heritability of Scholastic Achievement. There is no better predictor of scholastic achievement than psychometric _g_, even when the _g_ factor is extracted from tests that have no scholastic content. In fact, the general factor of both scholastic achievement tests and teachers' grades is highly correlated with the _g_ extracted from cognitive tests that are not intended to measure scholastic achievement. It should not be surprising, then, that scholastic achievement has about the same broad heritability as IQ.

Three large-scale studies[18] of the heritability of scholastic attainments, based on twin, parent-child, and sibling correlations, have shown broad heritability coefficients that average about .70, which does not differ significantly from the heritability of IQ in the same samples. The heritability coefficients for various school subjects range from about .40 to .80. As will be seen in the following section, nearly all of the variance that measures of scholastic achievement have in common with nonscholastic cognitive tests consists of the genetic component of _g_ itself.

GENETIC AND ENVIRONMENTAL COMPONENTS OF THE _g_ FACTOR PER SE

Recent evidence shows that by far the most of the heritable component of IQ, as well as of many other mental tests, is carried by _g_. Even though the IQ derived from a battery of tests (such as the Wechsler) is very highly *g* loaded, the *g* factor scores derived from the same battery have slightly higher heritability than the IQ. Several lines of evidence support the conclusion that *g* is the most heritable factor and accounts for more of the variation in the heritability of a wide variety of tests than any other common factor independent of *g*. This is especially remarkable because neither the psychometric tests nor the *g* factor was devised with any thought of heritability or of the kinship correlations that play a part in estimating heritability.

We can apply the method of correlated vectors to kinship data to answer the following question: Is the column vector V_g (composed of the *g* loadings of a set of diverse tests) positively correlated with the column vector V_k (composed of a specific *kinship correlation* on each of the diverse tests)? The correlation between V_g and V_k is a test of the hypothesis that *kinship correlations* differ from one mental test to another largely because of variation in the tests' *g* loadings.

The *spouse correlation* is of interest here because it is the assortative mating coefficient, and assortative mating on a particular trait adds to the population variance of the genotypes for that trait in the offspring generation. The amount of increase in the population variance depends on the degree of assortative mating in the population, which for IQ is a spouse correlation of about +.40. It is worth noting that IQ has a higher spouse correlation than any other behavioral trait and is higher than for most physical traits. (For instance, the spouse correlation is about +.30 for height; it is zero for fingerprint ridge-count.) If there were no assortative mating for whatever is measured by IQ, the population variance of IQ would be decreased by about 10 to 15 percent.

There are five large independent sets of data in which spouse correlations were obtained on a number of diverse tests and in which the tests' *g* loadings are known.[19] In each data set we can look at the correlation between (a) the vector of spouse correlations on each of the tests, and (b) the vector of the tests' *g* loadings. For fifteen tests in three racial/ethnic groups, here are these vector correlations (with one-tailed probability values):

Americans of European ancestry (AEA): $r = +.90$ ($p < .001$)

Americans of Japanese ancestry (AJA): $r = +.32$ ($p < .07$)

Koreans: $r = +.66$ ($p < .01$)

For seven tests (WAIS subtests) in two British groups:

Cambridge: $r = +.75$ ($p < .05$)

Oxford: $r = +.91$ ($p < .03$)

It is exceedingly improbable (in fact, $p < 10^{-10}$) that five independent positive correlations of this size could all have occurred by chance if there were no true correlation between the vector of the tests' *g* loadings and the vector of the tests' spouse correlations.

Kinship Correlations. Now we can look at the correlation between the vector of a specific kinship's correlations V_k on a variety of tests and the vector of these tests' *g* loadings V_g. For fifteen cognitive tests in the AEA and AJA groups[20] here are the $V_k \times V_g$ correlations for specific kinships (with one-tailed *p* values):

	AEA	AJA
Father-son	+.55 (*p* < .025)	+.14 (*p* < .35)
Mother-son	+.69 (*p* < .005)	+.57 (*p* < .025)
Father-daughter	+.59 (*p* < .025)	+.67 (*p* < .005)
Mother-daughter	+.76 (*p* < .0005)	+.74 (*p* < .005)
Brother-brother	+.33 (*p* < .15)	+.35 (*p* < .15)
Sister-sister	+.42 (*p* < .10)	+.76 (*p* < .0005)
Brother-sister	+.26 (*p* < .20)	+.41 (*p* < .10)

Note that all of the correlations are positive and eight of the fourteen meet the conventional criterion of significance, $p < .05$. The joint probability that this whole set of positive correlations could have arisen by chance if there were no true correlation between V_g and V_k is less than one in a billion.

Heritability. Of course, any single kinship correlation (except MZ twins reared apart) does not prove that genetic factors are involved in it. The correlation theoretically could be entirely environmental due to the kinships' shared family environment. To determine whether it is the genetic component of mental tests' variance that is mainly reflected by *g* we have to look at the heritability coefficients of various tests. Again, we can apply the method of correlated vectors, using a number of diverse cognitive tests and looking at the relationship between the column vector of the tests' *g* loadings (V_g) and the column vector of the tests' heritability coefficients (V_h). Each test's heritability coefficient in each of the following studies was determined by the twin method.[21]

Three independent studies[22] have used MZT and DZT twins to obtain the heritability coefficients of each of the eleven subtests of the Wechsler Adult Intelligence Scale. The correlations between V_g and V_h were +.62 ($p < .05$), +.61 ($p < .05$), and +.55 ($p < .10$). A fourth independent study[23] was based on a model-fitting method applied to adult MZ twins reared apart in addition to MZT and DZT to estimate the heritability coefficients of thirteen diverse cognitive tests used in studies of subjects in the Swedish National Twin Registry. The $V_g \times V_h$ correlation was +.77 ($p < .025$). (In this study, the *g* factor scores [based on the first principal component] had a heritability coefficient of .81.) The joint probability[24] that these $V_g \times V_h$ correlations based on four independent studies could have occurred by chance if there were not a true relationship between tests' *g* loadings and the tests' heritability coefficients is less than one in a hundred ($p < .01$).

Mental Retardation. Another relevant study[25] applied the method of correlated vectors to the data from over 4,000 mentally retarded persons who had taken the eleven subtests of the Wechsler Intelligence Scales. The column vector composed of the retarded persons' mean scaled scores on each of the Wechsler subscales and the column vector of the subscales' heritability coefficients (as determined by the twin method in three independent studies of normal samples) were rank-order correlated $-.76$ (one-tailed $p < .01$), $-.46$ ($p < .08$), and $-.50$ ($p < .06$). In other words, the higher a subtest's heritability, the lower is the mean score of the retarded subjects (relative to the mean of the standardization population of the WISC-R).

The study also tested the hypothesis that Wechsler subtests on which the retarded perform most poorly are the subtests with the larger g loadings; that is, there is an inverse relationship (i.e., negative correlation) between the vector of mean scaled scores and the corresponding vector of their g loadings. This hypothesis was examined in four different versions of the Wechsler Intelligence Scales (WAIS, WAIS-R, WISC, WISC-R). Each version was given to a different group of retarded persons. On each of these versions of the Wechsler test the vector of the mean scaled scores and the vector of their g loadings were rank-order correlated, giving the following correlation coefficients:

WAIS	.0
WAIS-R	$-.67$ ($p < .05$)
WISC	$-.63$ ($p < .05$)
WISC-R	$-.60$ ($p < .05$)

The WAIS is clearly an outlier and appears to be based on an atypical group of retarded persons. The vectors of g loadings on all four of the Wechsler versions are all highly congruent (the six congruence coefficients range from .993 to .998), so it is only the vector of scaled scores of the group that took the WAIS that is anomalous. It is the only group whose vector of scaled scores is not significantly correlated with the corresponding vectors in the other three groups, all of which are highly concordant in their vectors of scaled scores. In general, these data show:

1. There is a genetic component in mental retardation.

2. This genetic component reflects the same genetic component that accounts for individual differences in the nonretarded population.

3. The genetic component in mental retardation is expressed in the same g factor that is a major source of variance in mental test scores in the nonretarded population.

Decomposition of Psychometric _g_ into Genetic and Environmental Components. The obtained phenotypic correlation between two tests is a composite of genetic and environmental components. Just as it is possible, using MZ and DZ twins, to decompose the total phenotypic variance of scores on a given test into separate genetic and environmental components, it is possible to decompose the phenotypic correlation between any two tests into genetic and environmental components.[26] That is to say, the scores on two tests may be correlated in part because both tests reflect the same genetic factors common to twins and in part because both tests reflect the same environmental influences that are shared by twins who were reared together. Therefore, with a battery of *n* diverse tests, we can decompose the *n* × *n* square matrix of all their *phenotypic* intercorrelations (the *P* matrix) into a matrix of the tests' *genetic* intercorrelations (the *G* matrix) and a matrix of the tests' environmental intercorrelations (the *E* matrix). Each of these matrices can then be factor analyzed to reveal the separate contributions of genes and environment to the phenotypic factor structure of the given set of tests.

Several studies have been performed using essentially this kind of analysis. I say "essentially" because the analytic methods of the various studies differ depending on the specific mathematical procedures and computer routines used, although their essential logic is as described above. These studies provide the most sophisticated and rigorous analysis of the genetic and environmental composition of *g* and of some of the well-established group factors independent of *g*.

Thompson et al. (1991) compared large samples of MZ and DZ twin data on sets of tests specifically devised to measure Verbal, Spatial, Speed (perceptual-clerical), and Memory abilities, as well as tests of achievement levels in Reading, Math, and Language. They then obtained ordinary MZ and DZ twin correlations and MZ and DZ *cross-twin* correlations. From these they formed separate 7 × 7 matrices of G and E correlations. Three of their findings are especially relevant to *g* theory:

1. The phenotypic correlations of the four ability tests with the three achievement tests is largely due to their genetic correlations, which ranged from .61 to .80.

2. The environmental (shared and nonshared) correlations between the ability tests and achievement tests were all extremely low except for the test of perceptual-clerical speed, which showed very high shared environmental correlations with the three achievement tests.

3. The 7 × 7 matrix of genetic correlations has only one significant factor, which can be called *genetic g*, that accounts for 77 percent of the total genetic variance in the seven variables. (The genetic *g* loadings of the seven variables range from .62 to .99.) Obviously the remainder of the genetic variance is contained in other factors independent of *g*. The authors of the study concluded, "Ability-achievement associations are almost exclusively genetic in origin" (p. 164). This does not mean that the environment does not affect the level of specific abilities and achievements, but only that the correlations between them are largely mediated by the genetic factors they have in common, most of which is genetic *g*, that is, the general factor of the genetic correlations among all of the tests.

Separate hierarchical (Schmid-Leiman) factor analyses of two batteries of tests (eight subtests of the Specific Cognitive Abilities test and eleven subtests of the WISC-R) were decomposed by Luo et al. (1994) into genetic and environmental components using large samples of MZT and DZT twins in a model-fitting procedure. Factor loadings derived from the matrix of phenotypic correlations and the matrix of genetic correlations were compared.

The phenotypic *g* and genetic *g* found by Luo et al. are highly similar. The correlation between the vector of phenotypic *g* loadings and the vector of genetic *g* loadings was $+.88$ ($p < .01$) for the Specific Cognitive Abilities (SCA) tests and $+.85$ ($p < .01$) for the WISC-R.

A general factor which can be called *environmental g* was extracted from the environmental correlations among the variables. Only the environmental correlations based on the twins' *shared environment* are discussed here. (The test intercorrelations that arose from the nonshared environment yielded a negligible and nonsignificant "general" factor in both the SCA and WISC-R, with factor loadings ranging from $-.01$ to $+.35$ and averaging $+.08$.) The correlation between the vector of phenotypic *g* loadings and the vector of (shared) environmental *g* loadings was $+.28$ for the SCA tests and $+.09$ for the WISC-R. In brief, *phenotypic g* closely reflects the *genetic g*, but bears hardly any resemblance to the (shared) *environmental g*.

A similar study of thirteen diverse cognitive tests taken by MZ and DZ twins was conducted in Sweden by Pedersen et al. (1994), but focused on the non-*g* genetic variance in the battery of 13 tests. They found that although genetic *g* accounts for most of the genetic variance in the battery of tests, it does not account for all of it. When the genetic *g* is wholly removed from the tests' total variances, some 12 to 23 percent of the remaining variance is genetic. This finding accords with the previous study (Luo et al., 1994), which also found that 23 percent of the genetic variance resides in factors other than *g*. Pedersen et al. (1994) concluded that "phenotypic *g*-loadings can be used as an initial screening device to identify tests that are likely to show greater or less genetic overlap with *g* . . . if one were to pick a single dimension to focus the search for genes, *g* would be it" (p. 141).

Another study[27] focused on genetic influence on the first-order group factors, independent of *g*, in a Schmid-Leiman hierarchical factor analysis, using confirmatory factor analysis. The phenotypic factor analysis, based on eight diverse tests, yielded four first-order factors (Verbal, Spatial, Perceptual Speed, and Memory) plus the second-order factor, *g*. Using data on large samples of adopted and nonadopted children, and natural and unrelated siblings, the phenotypic factors were decomposed into the following variance components: genetic, shared environment, and unique (nonshared) environment. The variance of phenotypic *g* was .72 genetic and .28 nonshared environmental effects. Although *g* carries more of the genetic variance than any of the first-order factors, three of the first-order factors (Verbal, Spatial, and Memory) have distinct genetic components independent of genetic *g*. (There is no genetic Perceptual Speed factor independent of genetic *g*.) Very little of the environmental variance gets into even the first-order factors, much less the second-order *g* factor. The environmental variance resides mostly in the tests' *specificities*, that is, the residual part

Table 7.2
Phenotypic Correlations (above diagonal) Among Achievement Tests, Their Genetic Components (below diagonal), and the First Principal Component (PF1) of Each Matrix

Test	Eng	Math	Soc St	Nat Sc	PF1
English	--	.65	.71	.70	.83
Mathematics	.48	--	.62	.67	.76
Social Studies	.57	.54	--	.76	.85
Natural Science	.59	.53	.71	--	.87
PF1	.71	.65	.83	.84	

of the tests' true-score variance that is not included in the common factors. It is especially noteworthy that nearly all of the environmental variance is due to *nonshared* environmental effects. Shared environmental influences among children reared together contribute negligibly to the variance and covariance of the test scores.[28] In this study of children who all were beyond Grade 1 in school and averaged 7.4 years of age, *g* and the group factors reflect virtually no effects of shared environment.

Genetic *g* of Scholastic Achievement. As noted previously, psychometric *g* is highly correlated with scholastic achievement and both variables have substantial heritability. It was also noted that it is the genetic component of *g* that largely accounts for the correlation between scores on nonscholastic ability tests and scores on scholastic achievement tests. The phenotypic correlations among different content areas of scholastic achievement have been analyzed into their genetic and shared and nonshared environmental components in one of the largest twin studies ever conducted.[29] The American College Testing (ACT) Program provided 3,427 twin pairs, both MZ and DZ, for the study, which decomposed the phenotypic correlations among the four subtests of the ACT college admissions examination. The four subtests of the ACT examination are English, Mathematics, Social Studies, and Natural Sciences.

Table 7.2 shows the phenotypic correlations and their genetic components. Table 7.3 shows the shared and nonshared components of the correlations. Included in the tables is the general factor of each matrix, represented by the first principal factor (PF1). Note that most of the phenotypic correlation among the achievement variables exists in the genetic components, and the rank order of the PF1 loadings for the phenotypic correlations is the same as for their genetic components. The components due to both the shared and the nonshared environmental effects are relatively small and their first principal factors bear little resemblance to the PF1 of the phenotypic correlation matrix. The general factor

Table 7.3
Components of Shared (above diagonal) and Nonshared (below diagonal) Environmental Influences Among Achievement Tests and the First Principal Component (PF1) of Each Matrix

Test	Eng	Math	Soc St	Nat Sc	PF1
English	--	.12	.09	.07	.36
Mathematics	.05	--	.03	.04	.36
Social Studies	.05	.03	--	.04	.17
Natural Science	.04	.04	.05	--	.21
PF1	.23	.19	.21	.21	

of this battery of scholastic achievement tests clearly reflects genetic covariance much more than covariance due to the shared, or between-families, environmental influences that many educators and sociologists have long claimed to be the main source of variance in overall scholastic achievement.

INBREEDING DEPRESSION AND PSYCHOMETRIC *g*

Inbreeding depression is an especially interesting phenomenon. Its cause is entirely genetic, but it is conceptually distinct from heritability per se, and it is predictable from the most basic and universal genetic principles, which are manifested in all sexually reproducing organisms. It is impossible to explain the observed consequences of inbreeding in other than genetic terms.[30] It is important also because it is the most direct indicator of genetic dominance in a trait.

The genetic cause of inbreeding depression is *dominance*. The presence of dominance also implies *recessiveness*. Every gene locus on the chromosome is occupied by two alleles, which may have different effects on whatever trait is influenced by the gene at the given locus. At every locus, one of the alleles was inherited from the individual's mother, the other from the father. In a polygenic trait, some alleles enhance the trait, or have a positive effect, and some detract from the trait, or have a negative effect, relative to the average value of the trait in the population.

Alleles (whether they have positive or negative effects) may be *additive* in their effects (i.e., their joint effect is simply the sum of the separate effects of each allele) or one allele may be dominant over the other (which is recessive), such that their joint effect is not additive but rather has the same effect as two dominant alleles (this is known as *complete dominance*). For example, say that allele **A** has a positive effect equal to +1 on the development of a person's height and allele **a** has a negative effect equal to −1. If these alleles are *additive*, then all the possible combinations (and their genetic values and relative frequencies) that offspring could inherit from parents who both have the genotype **Aa** is as follows:

		Additive	Dominance	
Genotype	_Genetic Value_	_Relative Frequency_	_Gen. Val._	_Rel. Freq._
AA	+2	1/4	+2	1/4
Aa	0	1/2	+2	1/2
aa	−2	1/4	−2	1/4

If, however, there is complete dominance of allele **A**, then the genetic values of the three genotypes would be **AA** = +2, **Aa** = +2, and **aa** = −2. In this case, three-fourths of the possible genotypes would have a genetic value of +2 and one-fourth would have a genetic value of −2. The genetic value of 0 would not occur at all.

The allelic combinations **AA** and **aa** are called _homozygous_; **Aa** is _heterozygous_. Notice that dominance only affects the genetic value in the heterozygous condition. The difference in genetic values between the heterozygous condition under dominance and under additivity (i.e., +2 − 0 = +2, in the example) is known as _dominance deviation_, and its effect is to increase the total genetic variance.

In our example, the total variance of all the genetic values under additivity is 2. Under complete dominance the total variance is 3. The difference between these two variances is called the _dominance_ variance, which here equals 1. The _additive_ variance (i.e., what remains after dominance variance is accounted for) equals 2. Note that even though there is complete dominance of gene action, only one-third of the total genetic variance is due to dominance in this example. Even when all of the **A** alleles are dominant and all of the **a** alleles are recessive in the population, as long as both types of alleles exist in the population, there will always be some amount of additive genetic variance as well as some dominance variance.

But that is only half of the story of genetic dominance. New and different alleles are constantly being created by natural mutations (changes in the molecular structure of DNA in the existing alleles). The effects of the mutated alleles are highly random and unpredictable. They act as "noise" in the genetic system. Their effects range widely on a continuum of their degree of survival advantage to the individual organism in competition with other individuals who do not possess the particular mutant allele. Every mutant allele must either stand the test of survival or be driven to extinction.

Some mutant alleles have lethal effects; the zygote does not develop normally and is spontaneously aborted, usually at a very early stage of development. (Spontaneous abortions occur in about 25 percent of conceptions in normal, healthy women.) Some mutant genes result in birth defects, physical and mental, which may reduce the infant's chances of surviving to maturity or of eventually reproducing and passing on the mutant allele to his or her progeny. Most of these disadvantageous alleles, therefore, are either eliminated or kept to a very low frequency in the population's gene pool.

If a disadvantageous mutant allele is dominant, it is always expressed in the phenotype and will eventually be eliminated, provided it is expressed before individuals have reached sexual maturity and reproductive capacity. But if the mutant allele is recessive, it will be hidden by dominant alleles in the heterozygous individuals. It will be expressed in the phenotype, and thereby possibly be eliminated, only for homozygotes.

The likelihood is very small that (in random mating) both the father and mother will carry the same rare mutated recessive allele, but if by chance they both are carriers, their progeny will have a one-in-four risk of inheriting a double-recessive. This is why we find that most disadvantageous mutants in the gene pool turn out to be recessive. They are carried in the heterozygous genes and thereby escape phenotypic detection and possible elimination by natural selection.

On the other hand, most alleles that confer some degree of phenotypic advantage tend to be dominant. If the phenotypic advantage of a particular mutant allele is great and its disadvantages, if any, are comparatively small, it will competitively replace any less advantageous alternate alleles, and in a number of generations the trait will rise to complete homozygosity. That is, in our earlier example all the genes eventually will be **AA**. Many of our genes that have survived the "sieve" of natural selection in the course of human evolution thus are homozygous in virtually all biologically normal individuals and therefore do not contribute to individual differences; they are the basic "housekeeping" genes necessary for viability.

Some genes, however, have phenotypic effects that would be disadvantageous to the individual and to the survival of the species, but only if their effects were carried to the extreme of complete homozygosity. A middling position on the continuum of the trait's variation is generally more advantageous than either extreme. Height is an example. For such traits, there is *balanced* rather than *directional* selection. Balanced selection favors the perpetuation of heterozygosity and maintains genetic variance in the trait.

In some cases, the heterozygous condition has advantaging effects not seen in either homozygous extreme. The recessive sickle cell allele (**a**) is a classic example: The common heterozygous condition (**Aa**) confers a degree of immunity to malaria, but the rare homozygous condition (**aa**) results in the serious and often fatal disease known as sickle cell anemia. The recessive allele is therefore maintained in those parts of the world where malaria is prevalent. When malaria is abolished, the heterozygous form of the sickle cell gene no longer confers any advantage to survival and the frequency of the recessive allele gradually diminishes to zero (or to the spontaneous mutation rate).

Genetic dominance of certain traits is itself a product of the evolutionary process. A newly mutated allele that suppresses the phenotypic expression of all other alleles that are disadvantageous to the trait thereby becomes an advantageous dominant allele. It is therefore positively selected and its frequency increases over the course of evolution. Consequently, it is found that traits that are advantageous to survival and reproduction in successive generations (known as "fitness" in the Darwinian sense) show more genetic dominance. That is, more of the trait-enhancing genes become dominant and more of the genes with neutral or disadvantageous effects on the trait become recessive. Artificial selective breeding to enhance a certain trait in the progeny, for example, results in a decrease in the proportion of additive genetic variance (indexed by the narrow heritability) and an increase in the proportion of dominance variance. Additive gene effects show up in the phenotype and thus can be selected for in an artificial breeding program, making it possible to increase the frequency of the trait-enhancing genes and to eliminate the genes with neutral or negative effects.

With complete additivity, the **AA** and **aa** genes can be easily separated and (for the purposes of our example) the less desirable **aa** genes can be eliminated from the strain. The additive genetic variance, therefore, quickly reduces to zero. With complete dominance, however, the homozygous **AA** and the heterozygous **Aa** are phenotypically indistinguishable. In heterozygous individuals, therefore, there is no basis for phenotypical selection against **a**; only the phenotypic effect of **aa** is an infallible guide for culling out the individuals in each generation who carry the recessive **a** allele. The **a** alleles in the heterozygotes escape the grim reaper's scythe.

Thus, as additive genetic variance decreases with selection (because the relative frequency of **AA** increases while **aa** decreases), the dominance variance increases. Considerable dominance variance in a trait is therefore an indication that the trait has undergone genetic selection for a number of generations, either artificial selection or natural selection. If the agent is natural selection, it implies that the trait is (or has been in the past) a "fitness character." That is to say, a certain genetic value (whether it be low, medium, or high) of the allele as expressed phenotypically has been advantageous to survival in the particular environment in which the phenotype developed.

Inbreeding depression is the weakening or diminution of a phenotypic trait in the offspring of parents who are genetically related. The coefficient of inbreeding is equal to one-half the genetic correlation between the mated parents, assuming the parents are not themselves inbred. A zero coefficient between unrelated mates is assumed in the general mating population, although in most racially homogeneous mating populations the average inbreeding coefficient is slightly greater than zero, because much of the population is descended, over many generations, from common stock. Most inbreeding studies are based on marriages of first cousins or second cousins; a few are based on incestuous matings between a parent and its offspring or between full siblings.

All persons carry many recessive alleles and nearly all of the seriously deleterious alleles that all normal persons carry are recessive. The negative effects of the overwhelming majority of these unfavorable recessive alleles are suppressed by the corresponding dominant alleles at the same locus. That is, the deleterious effects of the recessives are hidden by the dominant alleles in the heterozygous condition. In any two genetically unrelated persons, it is unlikely that the same deleterious recessive allele will be carried at the same chromosomal locus by both persons, so if they mate and have offspring there is a very small probability of the double (homozygous) recessive that results in a phenotypic disadvantage.

However, if a person mates with a close relative, they both have many of the same genes inherited from a common ancestor. (For example, first cousins have one pair of grandparents in common.) Consequently, in persons who are related, the "bad" recessives are much more likely to occur at the same loci than in unrelated persons. As a result, the offspring of related persons have a greatly increased probability of receiving a double-recessive gene (with the consequent deleterious effect). This is known as *inbreeding depression.*

Inbreeding can adversely affect any genetic trait that is controlled by both dominant and recessive alleles, where the dominant allele is the more generally advantageous, as is usually the case. Note that inbreeding depression could not occur without genetic dominance, because without dominance the many recessive alleles could not remain hidden in the offspring of unrelated mates, only to later appear as a double dose in the offspring of genetically related mates.

The presence of dominance variance in heritable traits can be detected with biometrical methods that compare the parent-child correlation with the full-sibling correlation and half-sibling correlation. Without dominance the expected parent-child genetic correlation and the full-sibling genetic correlation are exactly the same ($+.50$), and the half-sibling correlation is exactly half the sibling correlation ($+.25$). Differences from these expected values indicate dominance and the magnitude can be used to estimate its amount. Only traits in which some of the total genetic variance includes dominance variance are subject to inbreeding depression in the offspring of genetically related mates.

The inbreeding effect on a given trait is measured by the difference between the mean of a group of inbred offspring and the mean of a group of noninbred offspring, with the two groups matched on age and relevant parental characteristics. Inbred offspring have a somewhat lower mean (when the trait-enhancing allele is dominant) than noninbred offspring.

One other theoretically predictable effect of inbreeding is an increase in variance of the trait in the inbred group. Studies of such inbred offspring have consistently shown the theoretically expected effects of inbreeding on many metric physical traits, such as fetal and infant viability, birth weight, height, head circumference, chest girth, muscular strength, resistance to infectious disease and dental caries, vital capacity, visual and auditory acuity, and rate of physical maturation. Inbreeding depression is also seen in visual and auditory reaction times.[31] When inbreeding is between first cousins, as in most studies, the effect on physical traits is generally quite small, typically averaging about

.05σ to .10σ. Interestingly, the average effect size (.18σ) of inbreeding on re-action times is somewhat greater than for most purely physical traits. The Gal-tonian notion that visual and auditory reaction times were Darwinian fitness characters in the evolution of behavioral capacity in humans is apparently not so far-fetched.

Considering the genetic and evolutionary "fitness" implications of inbreeding depression and the fact that it is manifested in a number of physical traits, it would seem especially interesting to know if inbreeding depression is also man-ifested in the realm of mental abilities. Do IQ tests and other indices of cognitive ability also show inbreeding depression in the offspring of consanguineous par-ents?

Certainly psychometric tests were never constructed with the intention of measuring inbreeding depression. Yet they most certainly do. At least fourteen studies of the effects of inbreeding on mental ability test scores—mostly IQ—have been reported in the literature.[32] Without exception, all of the studies show inbreeding depression both of IQ and of IQ-correlated variables such as scho-lastic achievement. As predicted by genetic theory, the IQ variance of the inbred is greater than that of the noninbred samples. Moreover, the degree to which IQ is depressed is an increasing monotonic function of the coefficient of in-breeding. The severest effects are seen in the offspring of first-degree incestuous matings (e.g., father-daughter, brother-sister); the effect is much less for first-cousin matings and still less for second-cousin matings. The degree of IQ de-pression for first cousins is about half a standard deviation (seven or eight IQ points).

In most of these studies, social class and other environmental factors are well controlled. Studies in Muslim populations in the Middle East and India are especially pertinent. Cousin marriages there are more prevalent in the higher social classes, as a means of keeping wealth in family lines, so inbreeding and high SES would tend to have opposite and canceling effects. The observed effect of inbreeding depression on IQ in the studies conducted in these groups, therefore, cannot be attributed to the environmental effects of SES that are often claimed to explain IQ differences between socioeconomically advantaged and disadvantaged groups.

These studies unquestionably show inbreeding depression for IQ and other single measures of mental ability. The next question, then, concerns the extent to which *g* itself is affected by inbreeding. Inbreeding depression could be mainly manifested in factors other than *g*, possibly even in each test's specificity. To answer this question, we can apply the method of correlated vectors to in-breeding data based on a suitable battery of diverse tests from which *g* can be extracted in a hierarchical factor analysis. I performed these analyses[33] for the several large samples of children born to first-and second-cousin matings in Japan, for whom the effects of inbreeding were intensively studied by geneticists William Schull and James Neel (1965). All of the inbred children and compa-rable control groups of noninbred children were tested on the Japanese version of the Wechsler Intelligence Scale for Children (WISC). The correlations among the eleven subtests of the WISC were subjected to a hierarchical factor analysis, separately for boys and girls, and for different age groups, and the overall average _g_ loadings were obtained as the most reliable estimates of _g_ for each subtest. The analysis revealed the typical factor structure of the WISC—a large _g_ factor and two significant group factors: Verbal and Spatial (Performance). (The Memory factor could not emerge because the Digit Span subtest was not used.) Schull and Neel had determined an index of inbreeding depression on each of the subtests. In each subject sample, the column vector of the eleven subtests' _g_ loadings was correlated with the column vector of the subtests' index of inbreeding depression (ID). (Subtest reliabilities were partialed out of these correlations.) The resulting rank-order correlation between subtests' _g_ loadings and their degree of inbreeding depression was $+.79$ ($p < .025$). The correlation of ID with the Verbal factor loadings (independent of _g_) was $+.50$ and with the Spatial (or Performance) factor the correlation was $-.46$. (The latter two correlations are nonsignificant, each with $p < .05$.) Although this _negative_ correlation of ID with the spatial factor (independent of _g_) falls short of significance, the negative correlation was found in all four independent samples. Moreover, it is consistent with the hypothesis that spatial visualization ability is affected by an X-linked recessive allele.[34] Therefore, it is probably not a fluke.

A more recent study[35] of inbreeding depression, performed in India, was based entirely on the male offspring of first-cousin parents and a control group of the male offspring of genetically unrelated parents. Because no children of second-cousin marriages were included, the degree of inbreeding depression was considerably greater than in the previous study, which included offspring of second-cousin marriages. The average inbreeding effect on the WISC-R Full Scale IQ was about ten points, or about two-third of a standard deviation.[36] The inbreeding index was reported for the ten subtests of the WISC-R used in this study. To apply the method of correlated vectors, however, the correlations among the subtests for this sample are needed to calculate their _g_ loadings. Because these correlations were not reported, I have used the _g_ loadings obtained from a hierarchical factor analysis of the 1,868 white subjects in the WISC-R standardization sample.[37] The column vector of these _g_ loadings and the column vector of the ID index have a rank-order correlation (with the tests' reliability coefficients partialed out) of $+.83$ ($p < .01$), which is only slightly larger than the corresponding correlation between the _g_ and ID vectors in the Japanese study.

In sum, then, the _g_ factor significantly predicts the degree to which performance on various mental tests is affected by inbreeding depression, a theoretically predictable effect for traits that manifest genetic dominance. The larger a test's _g_ loading, the greater is the depression of the test scores of the inbred offspring of consanguineous parents, as compared with the scores of noninbred persons. The evidence in these studies of inbreeding rules out environmental variables as contributing to the observed depression of test scores. Environmental differences were controlled statistically, or by matching the inbred and noninbred groups on relevant indices of environmental advantage.

Hybrid Vigor and *g*. Hybrid vigor (also known as *heterosis*) results from "outbreeding" and has the opposite effect of inbreeding. The same genetic mechanism—dominance—that is responsible for inbreeding depression can work in the opposite direction to cause heterosis. When the alleles that enhance the trait are genetically dominant, the level of the phenotypic trait is raised in outbred individuals. Outbreeding is defined as mating between individuals who are genetically more distant from one another than the average genetic distance between persons picked at random from the mating population. Genetic distance is an inverse function of the number of genes that two persons have in common from the same ancestors. Heterosis results from the creation of more heterozygous genes (e.g., **Aa**), which allows the phenotypic expression of advantageous dominant alleles; and there is a corresponding reduction in the number of phenotypically disadvantageous double-recessive alleles (e.g., **aa**).

Cross-racial mating is an obvious example of outbreeding. However, in humans the possible range of outbreeding effects is not symmetrical with the possible range of inbreeding effects, because the major human races already have such a low average coefficient of inbreeding that cross-racial mating cannot possibly lower the inbreeding coefficient nearly as much as mating between close relatives (i.e., inbreeding) can raise it. Nevertheless, heterosis has been found at statistically significant levels in the offspring of interracial mating. The heterotic effect is strongest, of course, when neither of the outbreeding mates has any similarly outbred ancestors in the historic past.

Because the effects of outbreeding are opposite to those of inbreeding on all the same traits, one should theoretically expect to find the positive effect of heterosis on psychometric *g*, even though the effect may be relatively small compared to the opposite effect, inbreeding depression. This theoretical prediction was tested in a study conducted in Hawaii,[38] where there are many interracial marriages between Americans of European ancestry (AEA) and Americans of Japanese ancestry (AJA). A group of interracial married couples with children and a group of intraracial couples were recruited; the two groups were nearly identical in educational and occupational levels. The children from both groups of parents were given a battery of fifteen highly diverse mental tests. Heterosis was measured by the standardized difference between the mean scores of the interracial (outbred) children and the intraracial (nonoutbred) children. Thirteen of the fifteen tests showed the predicted heterotic effect (i.e., higher scores in the interracial children). (The two tests that showed no heterotic effect were mazes and verbal fluency.) A test well known for its high *g* loading, Raven's Progressive Matrices, showed a heterotic effect of $+.30\sigma$, as compared with the average of $+.12\sigma$ on the other fourteen tests. Factor scores based on the first principal component of the fifteen tests (an estimate of the *g* factor of this battery) showed a heterotic effect of $+.26\sigma$ ($p < .001$).

The method of correlated vectors applied to these data tests whether the different heterotic effects on the various tests are specifically related to the tests' *g* loadings. The column vector of the heterosis index on each of the fifteen tests and the column vector of the tests' *g* loadings show a rank-order correlation (with tests' reliability coefficients partialed out) of $+.52$ ($p < .05$). This finding for heterosis, along with the findings for inbreeding depression, leaves little doubt that a significant part of the genetic basis of psychometric *g* is attributable to dominance of the alleles that to some degree enhance phenotypic mental abilities.

NOTES

1. I have found that many people outside the field of differential psychology (including a majority of psychologists and other social scientists) are very little aware of the presently vast methodological and empirical research literature directly related to the genetics of human mental ability, not to mention many other behavioral traits. Since its inception in 1970, the Behavior Genetics Association has published it own research journal (*Behavior Genetics*), but much of the research in this field also appears in many other psychology and genetics journals (mostly in *Intelligence* and in *Personality and Individual Differences*). It is an almost full-time job just to keep up with the research literature in one specialized area of the whole field of behavior genetics, such as the genetics of mental ability. For those who have not devoted their career to this field, there are fortunately many excellent summaries that describe the essential logic of quantitative genetics methodology and report the main empirical findings derived from these methods in the study of human mental abilities. Various summaries can be recommended according to the amount of specialized background the reader may bring to them.

My own (Jensen, 1981a, Chapter 3, pp. 74–127) attempt to explain the genetics of mental ability as clearly and simply as possible for readers with no technical background whatsoever in this field begins with the earliest study by Galton, introduces the basic concepts of Mendelian and quantitative genetics, and succinctly reviews the main findings regarding the various sources of genetic and environmental variance in IQ. For those who have no prior knowledge of how behavioral genetics "works," this chapter may serve as an essential prerequisite for any of the other items listed below. Another good introduction to behavior genetics methodology, briefer but slightly more technical than Jensen's (1981a), is by Eysenck (1984a). Plomin (1990) offers a more extended elementary treatment. The reading level in Plomin (1994) presents no real technical difficulty for the uninitiated, but its main theme is somewhat specialized and would probably be more appreciated by readers who have some familiarity with the standard material presented in the previously mentioned references. Plomin, DeFries, & McClearn (1990) provide one of the standard introductory textbooks of behavioral genetics. There are also several fairly comprehensive reviews of genetic research on human abilities that assume some knowledge of the terminology and methodology of quantitative genetics (but do not make them absolutely essential for understanding the main conclusions): Bouchard, 1993; Bouchard et al., 1996; Plomin, 1988; Scarr & Carter-Saltzman, 1982; and Vandenberg & Vogler, 1985. A book edited by Plomin & McClearn (1993) presents elementary accounts of specialized topics in human behavioral genetics, although the first two chapters introduce the most basic general principles of quantitative genetics. Accounts of the historical and controversial aspects of the so-called "nature-nurture" debate in modern times are well dealt with by Bouchard, 1987; Plomin, 1987; Loehlin, 1984; and Snyderman & Rothman (1988), who also provide good explanations of the key concepts in behavior genetics. The most recent (but highly technical) text on the statistical methodology of quantitative genetic research using twin and family data is by Neale and Cardon, 1992. The many citations found in all of the above-listed references probably include virtually the entire literature on the genetics of mental ability since about 1970.

2. Because a WF correlation is based on differences between siblings, it could, for that reason alone, be smaller than the BF correlation, which is based on the mean of the siblings. This is because a difference between two positively correlated variables, say X − Y, always has a lower reliability coefficient than the reliability of either X or Y. The sum or mean of two positively correlated variables, X + Y, always has higher reliability than that of either variable alone. Only if X and Y are measured with perfect reliability will the values X−Y and X+Y both have perfect reliability. The correlation between sibling differences and the correlation between sibling sums (or means) can be corrected for attenuation (unreliability) by methods explicated in Jensen, 1980b, p. 158.

3. The BF correlation of X and Y is the correlation between the *sums* of the siblings in each family on variable X and on variable Y. The WF correlation of X and Y is the correlation between the *signed difference* between pairs of siblings on variable X and on variable Y. (For further discussion, see Chapter 6, p. 141.)

4. Jensen, 1980b.

5. According to Gorsuch (1983), "In the case of orthogonal components [i.e., principal components] where factor scores have means of zero and variances of one, the result of calculating coefficients of congruence on the factor patterns is identical to correlating the exact factor scores and is, indeed, a simplified formula for that correlation" (p. 285).

6. Nagoshi & Johnson, 1987.

7. Jensen (1978) provides a comprehensive review of the effects of assortative mating (and inbreeding) on behavioral traits, with detailed explication of the genetic mechanisms through which these effects occur.

8. Bouchard et al.(1990) summarizes the findings of the Minnesota study of MZ twins reared apart. Bouchard & McGue (1981) is a summary of all every kind of kinship correlation for IQ and similar cognitive measures reported in the world literature, comprising over 100 studies and some 40,000 kinship pairs. Estimates of IQ heritability based on all of these kindship correlations, using the latest methods in modeling techniques, place the broad heritability between about .50 and .60, the narrow heritability between about .30 and .40 (Loehlin, 1989; Plomin & Rende, 1991). It should be noted that the world literature on kinship correlations is based largely on mental measurements obtained from samples of children and adolescents, and it is known that heritability increases from early childhood to later maturity. Therefore, if adult kinships were equally represented in this meta-analysis, the overall heritabilities would be slightly higher.

9. The fifty-three twin pairs (MZA) reported by Cyril Burt (1966) five years before his death in 1971 have routinely been omitted from all meta-analyses of twin data ever since their accuracy and authenticity were first brought into question (see Jensen, 1974a). Jensen (1992b) has reviewed virtually the entire literature on the so-called Burt scandal, and an authoritative analysis of the main substantive elements of the Burt affair can be found in a book by several experts, edited by Mackintosh (1995). Although there is no reputable evidence that Burt's data on MZA were falsified, errors and ambiguities in Burt's reports of these data make it unwise to include them in summaries of research on

MZA. However, Burt's results ($r_{MZA} = +.771$) are so closely in line with those of other studies, inclusion of his data would make little difference. Whereas the *N*-weighted mean r_{MZA} based on all studies but *excluding* Burt's data is +.749, the *N*-weighted mean r_{MZA} based on all studies *including* Burt's data is +.755—a difference of .006.

10. Bouchard et al. (1990); Bouchard (1993), pp. 40–43.

11. Paul, 1980.

12. McGue et al., 1993, pp. 60–67; Scarr, 1989, pp. 103–105; Segal, 1997; Teasdale & Owen, 1984.

13. McGue et al., 1993, pp. 60–67; Scarr, 1989, pp. 103–105; Segal, 1997.

14. It is important to be clear about what is meant by the *shared* and the *nonshared* environment. (Other paired terms with exactly the same meaning are: *between-family* (BF) and *within-family* (WF), *common* and *specific, systematic* and *random*.) The *shared* environment is whatever aspects of the environment that cause individuals (of a given degree of genetic kinship) who are reared together to be more alike, on average, than individuals (of the same degree of kinship) who were not reared together. The *nonshared* environment are those aspects of the environment that cause differences between individuals who are reared together. To say that the effect of the shared environment is nil is not to say that there are no environmental differences between families, but rather that these family differences in environment, whatever they may be, are not reflected in phenotypic differences in the trait in question, e.g., *g*. Nonshared environmental influences that cause differences between persons who are reared together in the same family are unique to each individual in the family.

15. There is now a considerable literature on this phenomenon of the vanishing effect of the shared environment on IQ. Nearly all of it is referenced in the following major reviews of this subject: Jensen, 1997a; McGue at al., 1993; Plomin, 1994; Plomin & Daniels, 1987: Plomin & Bergeman, 1991; Rowe, 1994; Scarr, 1989, 1996, 1997; Scarr & McCartney, 1983. Since virtually all of the studies of the effect of shared environment on IQ are based on adopted children, and since adoptive parents certainly do not provide an environment that is at all typical of the poorest or underclass segment in our society, it is questionable whether the present evidence on the disappearing effect of shared environment would generalize to the total population if its underclass were included. Aspects of the biological environment, prenatal and postnatal, that are unfavorable for normal brain development, such as poor maternal nutrition, alcohol or drug abuse, and physical or psychological child neglect, are likely to be common to all of the offspring of a given mother and would therefore constitute a between-families source of environmental influence on mental development. These conditions are considered in more detail in Chapter 12, pp. 500–509.

16. These concepts were introduced in a now classic paper by Plomin, DeFries, & Loehlin, 1977.

17. Jensen, 1997a. This article is mainly an analysis of the form of the distribution of the IQ differences found *within* pairs of MZ twins reared together (MZT). MZT provide the only data from which nonshared environmental effects can be directly measured, as this is the only part of the total variance in which they differ (except for random error of measurement, which can be determined by knowing the measurement's reliability coefficient). The IQ correlation between MZ twins reared together reflects all of the genetic variance and all of the shared environmental variance; the difference between MZ twins reflects only nonshared environmental effects.

18. Gill, et al., 1985; Heath et al., 1985; Martin, 1975.

19. These are found in two studies: (1) the Nagoshi & Johnson (1986) study, based on fifteen tests given to large samples (1,816 pairs) of spouses in three racial/ethnic groups: Americans of European ancestry (AEA), Americans of Japanese ancestry (AJA), and Koreans; (2) the study by Mascie-Taylor (1989), based on spouse correlations on seven subtests of the Wechsler Adult Intelligence Scale in two British samples totaling about 343 pairs.

20. From Nagoshi & Johnson, 1986, p. 205. Koreans were omitted because of incomplete kinship data for siblings; however, the $V_k \times V_g$ correlations for the parent-offspring kinship averaged $+.45$.

21. The twin method of estimating heritability consists essentially of either obtaining the correlation between MZ twins reared apart (MZA), which is a direct estimate of broad heritability, or using the correlations of MZ twins reared together (MZT) and of DZ twins reared together (DZT). The simplest formula for heritability (h^2) is known as the Falconer formula (after Desmond S. Falconer, Professor of Genetics in Edinburgh University and author of a classic textbook on quantitative genetics [Falconer, 1981, p. 185]): $h^2 = 2(r_{MZT} - r_{DZT})$. This formula does not take account of assortative mating and slightly underestimates h^2 when the twins' parents are assortatively mated on the trait in question. Assortative mating has no effect on the MZ twin correlation but increases the DZ correlation. When the degree of assortative mating is known, the theoretical genetic correlation (ρ) between DZ twins (or any full siblings) can be estimated and used in the following formula to obtain a more accurate value of the heritability:

$$h^2 = (r_{MZT} - r_{DZT})/(1 - \rho).$$

(This formula and the formula for obtaining ρ are fully explicated in Jensen, 1967, 1976.) These formulas for h^2 are now seldom used, since confirmatory or statistical hypothesis testing methods for fitting models based on LISREL programs are used for estimating the components (and subcomponents) of genetic and environmental variance from twin and other family data. (See textbook on these methods by Neale & Cardon, 1992.) The modern model-fitting procedures mainly have statistical hypothesis-testing advantages over the simple heritability formulas mentioned above, although the estimates of the heritability coefficient per se obtained by the different methods (assuming all of the same data are taken into account) scarcely differ.

22. Block (1968); Segal (1985); Tambs et al. (1984).

23. Pedersen et al, 1992, 1994. An important sequel to this paper with reference to *g* is by Plomin, Pedersen, Lichtenstein, & McClearn, 1994.

24. The method for calculating the joint probability of obtaining by chance (i.e., assuming the null hypothesis is true) the set of *N* *p* values obtained in *N* independent studies is given by R. A. Fisher (1970, pp. 99–101).

25. Spitz, 1988.

26. The genetic correlation between variables X and Y can be obtained from the *cross-twin* correlation (r_{MXxy}) of MZ twins reared apart, in which case the average cross-twin correlation estimates the genetic covariance between X and Y, and the genetic correlation (r_G), therefore, is the genetic covariance divided by the total genetic variance in the two variables, which is the geometric mean of the heritability coefficients of the two variables, i.e., $r_G = r_{MXxy}/\sqrt{h_X^2 \cdot h_Y^2}$. More frequently the genetic correlation is determined from the cross-twin correlations of MZ and DZ twins. Say the two members of a pair of twins are called 1 and 2, and the scores of twin 1 on variables X and Y are X_1 and Y_1 and of twin 2 are X_2 and Y_2. The cross-twin correlation between variables X and Y is obtained

separately for MZ and DZ twins. For each twin type, the average (via the geometric mean) of the two cross-twin correlations, $X_1 \times Y_2$ and $\times X_2 \times Y_1$, is the best estimate of the cross-twin correlation between X and Y. Given the average cross-twin correlations (r_{MZ} and r_{DZ}) for MZ and DZ twins and the heritability coefficients (h_X^2 and h_Y^2) of X and Y, the genetic correlation of X and Y (r_G) is: $r_G = 2(r_{MZ} - r_{DZ})/\sqrt{h_X^2 \cdot h_Y^2}$. The environmental correlation, r_E, can be obtained from the phenotypic correlation (r_P) of X and Y, their genetic correlation (r_G), the heritability coefficients of X and Y, and the environmental variances of X and Y, i.e., ($r_{XX} - 1$) and ($r_{YY} - 1$), where r_{XX} and r_{YY} are the reliability coefficients of X and Y. The environmental correlation of X and Y, then, is:

$$r_E = (r_P - \sqrt{(h_X^2 \cdot h_Y^2)} r_G / \sqrt{(r_{XX} - h_X^2)(r_{YY} - _Y^2)}.$$

These are the two simplest methods for determining the genetic and environmental correlations between two variables. When MZA in addition to MZT and DZT or other kinships or adoptees are included in the data set, they all can be analyzed simultaneously to estimate some of the specific subcomponents of the genetic and environmental correlations. The methodology for doing this makes use of highly complex computer routines which today are of major interest to experts and advanced students in quantitative genetics. They are described in the textbook by Neale & Cardon (1992).

27. Cardon et al., 1992.

28. Amount of total phenotypic variance accounted for by common factor variance (i.e., g + group factors) = 47%. Phenotypic common factor variance accounted for by g = 52%. Phenotypic common factor variance accounted for by all group factors (independent of g) = 48%. Phenotypic common factor variance due to genetic influences = 85%; due to nonshared environmental influences = 15%; due to shared environmental influences $\approx$ 0%. Common factor genetic variance contained in phenotypic g = 44%. Common factor genetic variance contained in all phenotypic group factors (independent of g) = 56% (Verbal =19%, Spatial = 19%, Memory = 17%, Perceptual Speed$\approx$ 0). Variance in phenotypic g due to genetic influences = 72%; due to nonshared environmental influences = 28%; due to shared environmental influences $\approx$ 0. From the analyses given in Cardon et al. (1992), it is possible to calculate a rough estimate of the congruence coefficient between the vector of phenotypic g loadings and the vector of genetic g loadings; it is +.955, which implies that the phenotypic g factor closely reflects the genetic g factor—not surprising when the heritability of the phenotypic g is .72. The correlation between phenotype and genotype is the square root of the heritability, which in this case is $\sqrt{.72}$ = .85.

29. Page & Jarjoura, 1979.

30. A detailed explanation of the genetic mechanism that causes inbreeding depression and a review of some of the most striking empirical studies of it, particularly the effect of incestuous mating on the offspring, can be found in Jensen, 1978. Some of the evolutionary implications of genetic dominance, which is reflected in inbreeding depression, are discussed in Jensen, 1983.

31. Much of the evidence on inbreeding depression has been reviewed by Daniels et al., 1982. Gibbons (1993) reviews a recent conference on the incidence of inbreeding in different parts of the world.

32. Adams & Neel, 1967; Afzal, 1988; Afzal & Sinha, 1984; Agrawal et al., 1984; Badaruddoza & Afzil, 1993; Bashi, 1977; Böök, 1957; Carter, 1967; Cohen et al., 1963;

Inbaraj & Rao, 1978; Neel, et al., 1970; Schull & Neel, 1965; Seemanova, 1971; Slatis & Hoene, 1961.

33. Jensen, 1983.

34. Bock & Kolakowski, 1973. The hypothesis that spatial ability is affected to some degree by an X-linked recessive allele is consistent with the well-established finding of a large sex difference (favoring males) in spatial visualization ability. (Only about one-fourth of females exceed the male median in tests of spatial ability.) The hypothesis of X-linkage, however, also predicts different parent-offspring correlations in spatial ability depending on the sex of each member of the correlated pair, and the X-linkage hypothesis for spatial ability has not consistently met this test in several studies. It now appears that hormonal factors, particularly testosterone, may affect spatial ability. It is also possible that X-linkage plays a part but acts as a threshold variable, with its expression depending on the individual's testosterone level. This is still an unsettled issue in behavioral genetic research; a more definitive answer must await further research.

35. Badaruddoza & Afzal, 1993.

36. Another study of all-male adolescent offspring of first-cousins in Rajasthan, India, using the highly *g*-loaded Standard Raven Matrices test, showed a noninbred-inbred difference of 0.55σ, equivalent to about eight IQ points (Agrawal, Sinha, & Jensen, 1984). There were 86 inbred and 100 noninbred subjects.

37. A Schmid-Leiman hierarchical factor analysis of the WISC-R, separately for whites and blacks, is given in Jensen & Reynolds, 1982, Table 3.

38. Nagoshi & Johnson, 1986.

Chapter 8

Information Processing and *g*

Psychometric *g* can be studied more analytically by means of elementary cognitive tasks (ECTs) than is possible with the conventional IQ tests with items based on past acquired knowledge, reasoning, and problem solving requiring the concerted action of a number of relatively complex cognitive processes. A particular ECT is intended to measure a few relatively simple cognitive processes, independently of specific knowledge or information content. Each ECT is devised to tap a somewhat different set of cognitive processes, and performance on two or more different ECTs yields data from which individual differences in distinct processes can be measured, such as stimulus apprehension, discrimination, choice, visual search, scanning of short-term memory (STM), and retrieval of information from long-term memory (LTM).

ECTs typically involve no past-learned information content, and in those that do, the content is so familiar and overlearned as to be common to all persons taking the ECT, as can be shown on a nonspeeded version of the ECT. Most ECTs are so simple that every person in the study can perform them easily, and individual differences in performance must be measured in terms of response time (RT). The theoretically most interesting ECTs are those with RTs of less than one second and with response error rates close to zero. The subject's median RT (over *n* number of trials) and the subject's intraindividual variability of RTs (measured as the standard deviation of RT, or RTSD, over *n* trials) are of particular interest. Another type of ECT, known as Inspection Time (IT), measures sheer speed of perceptual discrimination (visual or auditory) independently of RT.

Measures of RT, RTSD, and IT derived from the various ECTs

are correlated with IQ. For single ECTs, the correlations average about −.35, ranging from about −.10 to −.50, depending on the complexity or number of distinct processes involved in the ECT. Some processes are more strongly correlated with IQ than others. ECTs that strain the capacity of working memory generally have larger correlations with IQ. A composite score based on the RTs and RTSDs from several different ECTs, thereby sampling a greater number of different processes, typically correlates between −.50 and −.70 with IQ. (Recall that the average correlation between various standard IQ tests is about .80.) Factor analysis and the method of correlated vectors show that it is the *g* component of IQ (or of any other kind of cognitive test) that is almost entirely responsible for the correlations between ECTs and conventional psychometric tests. RT and RTSD show only negligible loadings on group factors independent of *g*.

The RT × *g* correlation is not explained by speed-accuracy trade-off, use of strategies, or motivation. Nor can the correlation be attributed to correlating RT with speeded psychometric tests. Most studies of the RT × *g* correlation are based on untimed or non-speeded IQ tests. Moreover, the RTs of ECTs have near-zero loadings on the speed-of-test-taking factor that emerges from some factor analyses of test batteries that include speeded tests.

The RT × *g* correlation reflects individual differences in the speed and efficiency (i.e., trial-to-trial consistency of RT, as measured by RTSD) of information processing. As there is a general factor of speed of processing common to virtually all ECTs, and as this general speed-of-information-processing factor is highly loaded on psychometric *g*, it is hypothesized that *g* is explainable, at least in part, in terms of the speed and efficiency of information processing.

The physiological properties of the brain that might account for the speed-of-processing aspect of *g* are not yet known completely, but it seems safe to say that they would have to be properties that are common to all regions and modules of the brain that subserve cognitive functions in which there are reliable individual differences in the neurologically normal population. One obvious candidate is individual differences in nerve conduction velocity (NCV). Brain NCV increases along with measurements of mental growth from childhood to maturity and decreases along with mental decline in old age. NCV is also significantly correlated with IQ (Raven matrices) in college students. (The great theoretical importance of this finding, based on a single study, absolutely demands its replication.) Periodic oscillation of the synchronized action potentials of groups of neurons has been hypothesized to account for intraindividual variability (RTSD) in ECTs. It is also hypothesized that random biological "noise" in the neural transmission of information in the brain causes slower and less efficient information processing, individual differences in which constitute some part of _g_. NCV and "noise" in neural transmission are related to the degree of myelination of nerve fibers, which may be the major physiological variable underlying _g_. Considerable empirical evidence indicates a relationship between myelin and other physiological and behavioral phenomena that are correlated with _g_. Structural, neural-net, or "design" features of the brain have scarcely been investigated in relation to _g_ in normal persons and cannot be evaluated in this respect at present.

At the level of complex psychometric tests the _g_ factor is unitary. But it now appears most unlikely that _g_ is unitary at the level of its causal underpinnings, as indicated by the timed measurements of performance on various ECTs and by neurophysiological measurements of variables such as NCV, rate of glucose metabolism (PET scan), and degree of myelination (MRI) of nerve fibers.

The well-established fact that there is a large genetic component in individual differences in mental ability, especially concentrated in the _g_ factor, is itself sufficient proof that the observed population variance in scores on highly _g_-loaded tests, such as IQ, reflects something other than the acquired bits of knowledge, skills, and strategies called for by such tests. It is most implausible that these specific aspects of mental test items would be encoded in the DNA. Biological "information" transmitted in the genetic code of DNA is a prerequisite condition for the heritability of any characteristic, including mental test scores. The human characteristics coded in the DNA are products of the evolutionary process. They existed aeons before the specific information content of conventional mental tests came into existence. Obviously, the genetically established brain mechanisms involved cannot be described simply in terms of the information content and other obvious features of psychometric tests. Further, the _g_ factor itself, which accounts for most of the genetic variance in mental abilities, manifests itself in such a wide variety of tests, differing greatly in the kinds of knowledge and skills required for successful performance, as to be inexplicable in strictly psychometric or psychological terms.

INFORMATION PROCESSING

To get at least one step closer to understanding the biological substrate of individual differences in mental ability (particularly its general factor, _g_), we can investigate _information processes_. Information processes are essentially hypothetical constructs used by cognitive theorists to describe how persons apprehend, discriminate, select, and attend to certain aspects of the vast welter of stimuli that impinge on the sensorium to form internal representations that can be mentally manipulated, transformed, related to previous internal representations, stored in memory (short-term or long-term memory), and later retrieved from storage to govern the person's decisions and behavior in a particular situation.

The term "information" in this context has a more specialized and generic meaning than the word "information" usually connotes in common usage. "Information" here does not refer to any specific fact or a particular item of acquired knowledge. It refers generally to any stimulus that *reduces uncertainty* in a given situation. Information is measured in *bits* (for *binary digits*). A bit is the amount of information that reduces uncertainty by one-half. For instance, I am thinking of a number from 1 to 16 and ask you to arrive at this number in the most efficient way possible, by asking me a series of questions to which I can give a binary answer (e.g., "Yes" or "No"). You ask, "Is it a number from 1 to 8?" I reply "Yes" (or "No") and thereby give you one bit of information, which reduces your uncertainty by one-half. Because there are three more such questions to which the binary answers will each reduce your uncertainty by one-half, we can say that the total uncertainty posed by this task is reduced to zero by four bits of information. Note that the number of bits of information called for by the task in order to reduce its uncertainty to zero is the binary logarithm ($\log_2$) of the number of initial choices or alternatives (i.e., $\log_2 16 = 4$).

Although it is possible to devise simple tests with known amounts of information measured in bits, typical cognitive tests are too complex to allow us to quantify the amount of information precisely. But this limitation does not alter the utility of the concept of information as that which reduces uncertainty. We use the term "information processing" here to describe the hypothetical processes that depend, presumably, on the structural and physiological properties of the brain that are activated whenever uncertainty is perceived and we work to reduce it.

The many theories (or models) of information processing proposed in recent years are all fairly similar. Investigating them has become the most prolific branch of experimental psychology. The various models all have two tenets in common: (1) the idea that information processing occurs in stages, most often serially but also at times simultaneously in parallel, and (2) information processing occurs in real time, with each step in the process taking a certain amount of time. *Time* itself therefore is the natural scale of measurement for the study of information processes. Time is also the scale used to measure individual differences in the speed or efficiency of these information processes. Because time is measured on an absolute, or ratio, scale[1] with international standard units, it has certain theoretical and scientific advantages over ordinary test scores. Test scores are based on the number of items answered correctly on a particular test and therefore must be interpreted in relation to the corresponding performance in some defined "normative" population or reference group.

Psychologists interested in the nature of the general factor common to psychometric tests of ability have therefore recently and increasingly turned to theories of information processing for research paradigms and their associated methodology. Hardly anyone disputes the idea that performance on IQ tests and the like depends on information processing. The problem is that the typical item in these kinds of tests is much too complex to allow one to measure their component information processes. Too many cognitive processes are involved in the subject's arriving at a response to a test item to permit any kind of analysis of just how the subject did so. All we know is whether the person passed the item or failed, which gives no clue as to the nature of the difference between those who pass and those who fail the item. A person could have failed the item because of a lack of some specific knowledge, or because a particular skill called for by the item had never been acquired, or because the knowledge or skill, though it had been acquired, couldn't be recalled, or because of a failure to process the information given in the item or retrieved from long-term memory. Trying to determine why a given test item is hard for one person but easy for another is unfeasible when so many possible variables can affect performance.

ELEMENTARY COGNITIVE TASKS

What we need are tests that are so simple and so lacking in any specific skill or knowledge content as to greatly limit the possibilities of exactly what the subject must do to perform successfully. Yet, despite the test's extreme simplicity, if it is to be a useful analytic tool it must reveal individual differences in performance. Such a simple task is called an *elementary cognitive task*, or ECT. In experimental work with ECTs it is important that the ECT be so simple that every subject included in the study can perform the required responses very easily, with few, if any, errors. An error should not result from the subject's not understanding the task requirements. Nor should errors result from the subject's lacking some particular knowledge that would have had to be learned prior to performing the ECT.

The main source of individual differences on such ECTs, then, is not the correctness of response (since everyone "gets it" eventually), but response *time*—the amount of time taken to complete the ECT performance. (The reciprocal of the time taken indicates the subject's *speed* of performance.) The technology of measuring response times in performance on ECTs to infer the time-course of information processing in the human nervous system is called *mental chronometry*. It has a venerable history, beginning about 1860, when the Dutch physiologist F. C. Donders first used a person's reaction time (RT) to a visual stimulus to measure the time taken for such simple mental processes as stimulus apprehension, discrimination, decision, and response execution.

Not long after Donders, Sir Francis Galton began measuring individual differences in visual and auditory RT, along with various measures of sensory discrimination, in hopes of deriving a composite "score" that would reflect the biological aspect of general ability. While Donders (and later Wilhelm Wundt,

the father of experimental psychology) used RT to discover the general principles of mental chronometry that would characterize all human beings, Galton
was interested in RT mainly as a possible indicator of individual differences in
human mental capacity. But Galton's effort was largely unsuccessful, for reasons
unknown to him and his immediate followers. They found so little apparent
correlation between their measurements of RT and "real life" indicators of
mental ability, such as educational attainments and occupational status, that
shortly after the turn of the century the whole effort was abandoned. What was
considered an especially crucial study at the time used students at Columbia
University.- As there were no "intelligence" tests at that time, general mental
ability was assessed only by course grades in classics and mathematics.

We now know why these early attempts failed: (1) the RT measurements had
exceedingly low reliability, with test-retest correlations around .20; (2) subjects
were selected from groups (e.g., university students) with a very restricted range
of ability; and (3) investigators lacked the modern statistical methods that could
determine whether or not the results were statistically significant.

In fact, it has turned out that Galton's own massive data (over 1,000 persons),
when subjected to statistical methods that had not yet been invented in his time,
have proved to be highly significant.[2] A number of studies following in the
wake of Galton's seemingly unimpressive results were considerably more successful. But they were so overshadowed by the failure of the then most prestigious laboratories to demonstrate important relationships between RT and
commonsense criteria of intelligence that the few promising successes were almost completely ignored and never made their way into the most influential
textbooks.[3] The prevailing conclusion was that reaction time is not related to
"intelligence."

Then, too, the practical success of Binet's famous test, after 1905, turned the
study of mental ability in a quite different direction. The Binet test, based on
the summation of pass-or-fail scores on a number of relatively complex mental
tasks, had readily demonstrable practical utility. But the tasks' complexity precluded analytic investigation of the nature of the general ability represented by
success or failure on this collection of tasks. The terms used by Binet to describe
what his test measured, such as "judgment," "plan of action," "following
directions," "problem solving," and the like, spark few theoretical insights and
afford scant analytic clues to the nature of individual differences in test performance. The ensuing emphasis on psychometrics per se, though highly worthwhile for practical purposes, did little to advance understanding of the causal
nature of variance in mental abilities.

Only within the last twenty years or so have more than a few behavioral
scientists pursued a theory-driven search for the elementary processes that underlie _g_. The new models of information processing and techniques of mental
chronometry are clearly descended from those early attempts by Donders and
Galton more than a century ago.[4] Before reviewing the main findings from these
recent studies as they relate to _g_, it will be helpful to give brief descriptions of

some of the most frequently used ECTs and the variables typically derived from them.[5]

General Features of ECTs. ECTs are made especially simple so that every subject in the study can easily understand and perform the task requirements. If any particular knowledge content is required to perform the task, such as understanding alphanumeric symbols, it is first determined that this knowledge is possessed by all subjects. Preliminary practice trials are given to ensure that subjects can do the task. Nothing in the instructions to the subject is intended to disguise the purpose of the task, which is always represented as a test to determine how quickly and accurately the subject can respond. Subjects are explicitly asked to respond as fast as they can, consistent with accuracy of response. In some tests, inaccurate responses are eliminated and the trial is "recycled," so that all subjects in the study have the same number of "good" trials. Subjects are given repeated trials on any ECT to ensure high reliability of the composite measurement of RT.[6] (Subjects typically perform six to ten trials per minute.)

"Outlier" trials are usually eliminated. Response times less than about 150 milliseconds are considered outliers. Such outliers are excluded from analysis because they are faster than humans' "physiological limit" for the time required for the transduction of the stimulus by the sense organs, through the sensory nerves to the brain, then through the efferent nerves to the arm and hand muscles, These fast outliers most often result from "anticipatory errors," that is, the subject's initiating the response just before the onset of the reaction stimulus. At the other extreme, slow response times that are more than three standard deviations slower than the subject's median response time are also considered outliers. They usually result from a momentary distraction or lapse of attention. As outliers are essentially flukes that contribute to error variance, omitting them from the subject's total score improves the reliability of measurement.

Subjects are tested individually in a sound-protected room free of distractions. The subject typically responds to an ECT by either releasing or depressing a key or push button with the index finger of the preferred hand. Usually, each trial begins with a warning signal (or preparatory stimulus), such as a high-pitched "beep," to alert the subject that the reaction stimulus is about to occur (within a random interval of, say, one to four seconds after the beep). Subjects are prescreened for any sensorimotor handicaps that could affect performance, and all stimulus and response materials are sufficiently large and clear as to be easily perceived by all persons who do not have a major visual, auditory, or motor disability. The motor response requires only minimal physical strength and small hand movements.

Variables Derived from ECTs. Many ECTs are subject-paced. A trial cycle begins by the subject's pressing down a "home" button. After a delay of about one second, a preparatory stimulus ("beep") occurs, and after a brief (one to four seconds) random interval the reaction stimulus, or task, appears on a screen or computer monitor. The subject then releases the home button and touches the response button called for by the reaction stimulus. Three variables are recorded (usually automatically by computer) on each trial: (1) *reaction time* (RT)—the time interval between the onset of the reaction stimulus and the subject's releasing the home button, (2) *movement time* (MT)—the time interval between releasing the home button and touching the response button, and (3) *error score*—whether the response was correct or incorrect (1 or 0). The RT and MT are measured in milliseconds. These three measures—RT, MT, and errors—are obtained on each set of *n* trials. From these *n* × 3 basic measurements, five individual difference variables are derived for each subject: (1) median[7] RT, (2) the standard deviation of the subject's RTs over *n* trials (RTSD, a measure of intraindividual variability in RT), (3) median MT, (4) the standard deviation of the subject's MTs over *n* trials (MTSD, a measure of intraindividual variability in MT), and (5) total number of error responses in *n* trials. The timed measurements are the variables of primary interest in ECTs. The error responses usually are of least interest, as their total number is usually small and generally has low test-retest reliability.

SOME SPECIFIC ECTs AND THEIR TYPICAL RESULTS

Simple and Choice RT. These are the first ECTs ever used in psychological research. Donders used them to measure the time needed for certain mental processes.

In simple RT (SRT), the subject depresses a telegraph key with the index finger; then a preparatory stimulus is given to alert the subject to the imminent appearance of the reaction stimulus. The reaction stimulus may be visual (e.g., a light going "on" or "off") or auditory (a tone, loud click, or bell). When it occurs, the subject releases the key as quickly as possible. RT is the time between the appearance of the stimulus and the time the subject releases the key. Since RT is measured on a large number of trials, the subject's median RT will be highly reliable. (This is where Galton and his immediate followers went wrong; they gave too few trials to achieve reliable measurement.)

SRT consists of three main components of processing time—two distinct *peripheral* components and a *central* component. The peripheral components are: (1) sensory lag and stimulus transduction from sense organ through the afferent nerve fibers to the brain, and (2) effector time, comprising the efferent nerve impulses from brain to the muscles and muscle lag. The central component is the brain processing time taken for apprehension of the stimulus and mediating between the two peripheral systems. Note that in SRT the subject does not have to make any *discrimination* between different stimuli or any *choice* between different response alternatives. Only a single possible response to the apprehension of the expected occurrence of a single stimulus is all that is called for in SRT. In normal young adults, the average SRT under these conditions is about one-fifth of a second, or 200 milliseconds (msec). RT is slightly shorter to an auditory than to a visual stimulus, because the sensory lag is less in the auditory receptor (a mechanical reaction) than in the retina (a chemical reaction). RT is affected by a number of specific features of the procedure, such as the length of the preparatory interval, the modality and intensity of the reaction stimulus, and other experimentally manipulable conditions.[8]

In pure *discrimination* RT (DRT), the subject is confronted with the possible occurrence of either of two (or more) different reaction stimuli—for example, either a yellow light or a blue light goes on. One or the other colored light appears on each trial in a purely random order. The subject is instructed to respond to only one of the stimuli, say, the yellow light. Responding to the blue light here would constitute an error. The DRT consists of all of the processing components of the SRT *plus* the additional time required to *discriminate* the yellow and blue light—a central process. Donders (and many others following him) found that DRT is greater than SRT. He argued that by subtracting SRT from DRT one could measure the time required for *discrimination* per se, over and above the time needed for simple *apprehension* of a stimulus. This procedure has become known as Donder's *subtraction method*. It has been widely used in studying the time required for various cognitive processes, such as discrimination, choice or decision, and retrieval of information from memory. Discrimination time (the DRT-SRT difference) varies, on average, from about 30 msec to over 100 msec, depending on the difficulty of the discrimination. There is a wider range of individual differences in DRT than in SRT, which implies that people differ more in the central information-processing component of performance on ECTs than on the sensorimotor component.

Choice reaction time (CRT) includes both stimulus *discrimination* (as in DRT) and making a choice between two (or more) different response alternatives, each keyed to a different reaction stimulus. Either stimulus **A** or stimulus **B** appears (at random) and the subject must release (or press) button A (on the left) or button B (on the right) accordingly. Having to make a *choice* (or any decision) in responding to the reaction stimulus is another cognitive process that adds to the total time over and above pure discrimination. So by subtracting DRT from CRT, Donders could measure the time taken for choosing between the possible response alternatives.

Later studies of individual differences in SRT, DRT, and CRT revealed that each is negatively correlated with IQ and also with scholastic achievement (negatively because lower RTs go with higher IQs.) The correlations are generally quite small, but what is important is that they increase in size, going from SRT < DRT < CRT, with average correlations close to −.10, −.20, −.30, respectively. As the ECT becomes more *complex* (that is, it requires more different cognitive processes so more time) individual differences become more highly correlated with IQ. As will be shown presently, the "active ingredient" in these correlations is *g*.

The Hick Paradigm. In 1952, the British experimental psychologist John Hick formulated a precise relationship between two variables: (1) the amount of information (measured in *bits*) conveyed by the reaction stimulus of the ECT

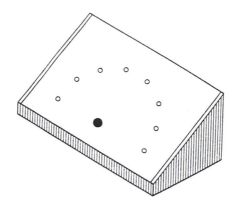

Figure 8.1. The subject's response console of the RT-MT apparatus. The panel is 13 in. × 17 in., painted flat black, and tilted at a 30° angle. At the lower center is the home button (black, 1 in. diameter), which the subject depresses with the index finger while waiting for the reaction stimulus. The semicircle of 8 small circles represent translucent push buttons (green, ½ in. diameter, each at a distance of 6 in. from the home button); each button can be lighted independently. Touching a lighted button turns off the light. Various plates can be placed over the console to cover some of the buttons, leaving either 1, 2, 4, or all 8 buttons exposed to view, making for four different ECTs, each with a different number of equally likely response alternatives. The binary logarithms of 1, 2, 4, and 8 exposed buttons are equivalent to 0, 1, 2, and 3 bits of information, respectively. A trial begins with the subject depressing the home button; 1 sec. later a preparatory stimulus ("beep") of 1 sec. duration occurs; then, after a 1-to-4-sec. random interval, one of the buttons lights up, whereupon the subject's index finger leaves the home button and touches the underlighted button. RT is the interval between a light button going "on" and the subject's lifting the index finger from the home button; MT is the interval between releasing the home button and touching the underlighted button. On each trial only one of the buttons lights up, entirely at random from trial to trial.

and (2) the RT to the ECT. This relationship has since become known as *Hick's law*.[9] It states that RT increases linearly with the binary logarithm of the number (n) of equally likely response alternatives in the ECT. (That is, $\Delta RT = K \log_2 (n + 1)$, where K is the slope constant, or proportional increase in RT as a function of the logarithmic increase in response alternatives.)

Hick's law is most easily explained in connection with an apparatus I devised in 1976 to study individual differences. (It has been dubbed "Jensen's button box" in some of the RT literature; it is more properly called the RT-MT apparatus.) The subject's console is shown in Figure 8.1. It is interfaced with a microcomputer, so the entire procedure can be programmed and run automatically; the subject's RT and MT on every trial are registered and stored in the computer, which also calculates and prints out the subject's median RT and MT, the RTSD and MTSD, and the number of errors. The intercept and slope of the

Hick function are also automatically calculated. Hence the testing procedure is uniform for all subjects.

The subject's median RTs and MTs to 1, 2, 4, and 8 buttons (i.e., response alternatives corresponding to 0, 1, 2, and 3 bits of information) are obtained. When RT is plotted as a function of bits, the linear relation known as Hick's law is clearly evident for the vast majority of subjects in the IQ range from 50 to 150. A few subjects do not show it, for unknown reasons; they probably process the information in some idiosyncratic way or adopt a strategy that overrides Hick's law. Severely retarded persons (IQs below 50) who are able to perform the task usually do not manifest Hick's law beyond one or two bits of information, and their average RTs are very much slower than those of normal persons.[10] The fact that chimpanzees obey Hick's law[11] as perfectly as most humans (with RTs comparable to normal eight-year-old children) suggests that severely retarded persons may fail to do so because of some brain pathology or abnormality. Most mildly retarded persons (IQs 50 to 75) conform to Hick's law as well as persons of above-average IQ, although their RTs are much slower.

Figure 8.2 shows a plot of RT and MT. It illustrates Hick's law for RT. MT does not show Hick's law; that is, MT does not vary significantly as a function of the information in the reaction stimulus. It is also much shorter than RT. Most subjects apparently do not release the home button until information processing is virtually complete and the appropriate response has been "programmed"; the MT then is virtually independent of the information processing per se. MT thus appears to be more a motor function than a cognitive function.

More than thirty studies have shown correlations between the timed parameters of the Hick task and IQ. The largest correlations are for intraindividual variability in reaction time (RTSD); the lowest (and nonsignificant) correlation is for intraindividual variability in movement time (MTSD). RT correlations with IQ increase slightly, as information goes from 0 to 3 bits. But this task encompasses an extremely small range of task difficulty, as indicated by the range of RTs. The average RT in 27 studies comprising 1,850 subjects ranges from 335 msec at 0 bits to 439 msec at 3 bits, or approximately 35 msec of RT for processing one bit of information. The average rate of information processing, therefore, is about 30 bits per second.

Theoretically, one might expect the _slope_ of RT (which represents the increase in RT per bit of information) in the Hick function to have the largest negative correlation with IQ. This has not proved to be the case. The average correlation over all studies, after correction for attenuation, is highly significant ($p < .001$), but small—about $-.17$, or about the same as the RT $\times$ IQ correlation for zero bits. There can be no doubt that the relationship is real, however, as various groups that differ in mean IQ always show significant differences in mean slope of the Hick function, the higher-IQ group always having the lesser slope. This means that higher IQ is associated with a faster rate of information processing. The multiple correlation between all of the timed Hick parameters and IQ is between .35 and .50.

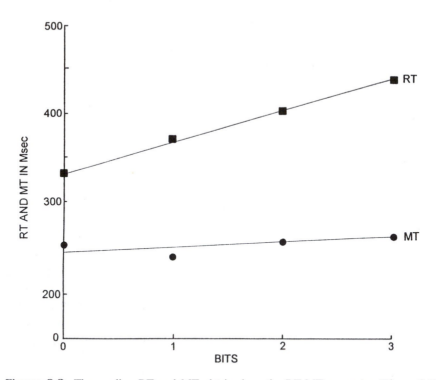

Figure 8.2. The median RT and MT obtained on the RT-MT apparatus (Figure 8.1) averaged over more than 1,500 individuals. Note the significant positive slope of RT (RT = 336 + 34 BIT, r = .998), demonstrating Hick's law, which predicts a linear relationship of RT to the amount of information measured in BITs. In marked contrast is the nonsignificant slope of MT (MT = 245 + 4.3 BIT, r = .641). (Data from Jensen, 1987d, Tables 3 and 7.)

Odd-Man-Out Paradigm. This ECT was introduced by Frearson and Eysenck (1986) to increase the *discrimination* component over what it is in the Hick task, using the same RT-MT apparatus shown in Figure 8.1. They hypothesized that the increase in the information-processing demand of the tasks should significantly increase the RT × IQ correlation. The odd-man task uses all eight buttons and the procedure is identical to the Hick procedure described above, except that instead of a single light going "on," three lights go "on" simultaneously. Their locations are random and unpredictable on each trial, except that two of the lights are always in closer proximity to one another than the third light—the odd-man-out. For example, if the buttons are numbered 1 to 8 from left to right, an odd-man pattern could be lights 1, 2, and 5 on; or 2, 4, 8, or 3, 6, 8. (With 8 buttons, there are 45 such odd-man patterns.)

The discrimination demand of the odd-man task requires about 200 msec more processing time than the single-light (1 out of 8) Hick paradigm. The odd-man

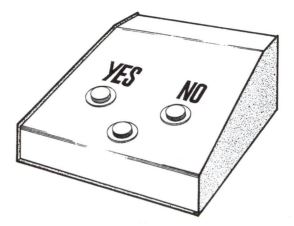

Figure 8.3. A binary response console (6 ½ in. × 10 in.) used in all ECTs that call for a binary response (Yes-No, True-False, Same-Different, etc.). The push buttons are all 1 in. in diameter. The lower one is the home button, which the subject depresses with the index finger until the reaction stimulus occurs. On each trial the subject responds by pressing either the left or right button, here labeled YES and NO. (The magnetized labels can be quickly and easily changed.) The programmed reaction stimuli appear on a computer monitor directly behind the response console.

RT shows significantly larger (approximately doubled) correlations with IQ than the 3-bit condition in the Hick paradigm.[12] Moreover, experimentally increasing the complexity of the discrimination increases RT and also increases the correlation of both RT and RTSD with IQ.[13]

Memory-Scan Paradigm. This ECT originated with Saul Sternberg, an experimental psychologist with the Bell Telephone Laboratories.[14] It measures the time taken to scan short-term memory for a particular item of information. The apparatus used for this in my chronometric laboratory includes a binary response console, shown in Figure 8.3, and a computer display, both interfaced with a microcomputer, which runs the trials automatically and records the subject's RT and MT and errors, just as in the Hick paradigm. A trial begins with the subject depressing the home button. Following shortly after the preparatory stimulus ("beep"), a _set_ of from 1 to 7 digits (in a random order) appears simultaneously on the display for 3 seconds, during which the subject memorizes the set of digits. The screen then goes blank for 1 second and a single _probe_ digit appears. The subject immediately responds (YES or NO on the response buttons) whether the probe was (YES) or was not (NO) present in the displayed set. (It is present on a random 50 percent of the trials.) The RT and MT are measured as described earlier.

Two striking results are found in virtually all subjects: (1) RT increases as a linear function of set size (i.e., the number of digits in the set), and (2) it takes some 30 to 50 msec longer to respond NO than to respond YES. Typical results

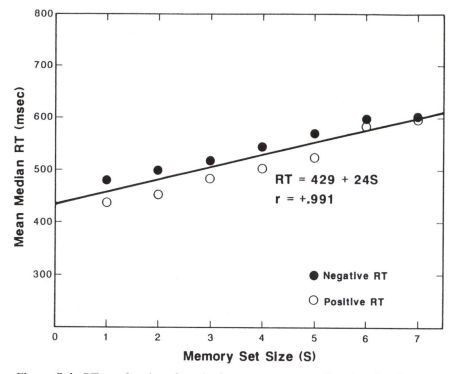

Figure 8.4. RT as a function of set size in memory-scan paradigm, based on forty-eight university undergraduates. (From Jensen, 1987f. Used with permission of Ablex.)

are shown in Figure 8.4. For college students, the average slope of RT as a function of set size is 25 to 30 msec per digit, which is a short-term memory-scanning rate of about 35 digits per second. The median RT and intraindividual variability in RT on this task show correlations with IQ larger than −.30.[15]

Visual-Scan Paradigm. This is just the reverse of the memory-scan paradigm. The same apparatus is used, but virtually no demand is made on memory. After the preparatory stimulus, a single *target* digit appears on the screen for 3 seconds. The display screen goes blank for 1 second and then a set of anywhere from 1 to 7 digits appears. The subject responds (by pressing either the YES or the NO button) according to whether the target digit is present or absent in the displayed set. The results are identical in almost every feature to those for memory scan, as are the correlations between RT and IQ.

In a sample of university students, the disattenuated correlation between individual differences in median RT on memory scan and visual scan was +.998. This is an example of two ECTs that are perfectly correlated even though they involve different processing mechanisms: one ECT depends on the speed of *mentally* scanning a set of digits held in short-term memory; the other depends on the speed of *visually* scanning the set of digits as they are displayed. Although the mechanisms are different, the basic factor that determines the speed of both, and hence individual differences in both, is apparently the same. (A rough analogy would be two distinct mechanisms that perform different functions, but both mechanisms are powered by one and the same motor.) When median RTs and MTs from the memory scan and the visual scan are combined with those from the Hick paradigm, the multiple correlation with Raven's matrices in a college sample is .40. The corresponding multiple correlation for RTSD and MTSD (intraindividual variability) is .50.[15]

Coincidence Timing. This is one of the simplest ECTs. Throughout all the trials, a thin vertical line remains in the middle of a computer display screen, extending from top to bottom. A trial begins with a small square appearing at either the left or right side of the screen, halfway between the top and bottom of the screen. It moves horizontally at a constant speed (e.g., ten centimeters per second), crosses the vertical line, and goes to the opposite side of the screen. (In some conditions, the square may move at an angle or along a curved trajectory.) The subject's task on every trial is simply to press a key the moment the moving square meets the vertical line.

Coincidence timing measures something more than simple RT; information of the reaction stimulus (the coincidence of the moving square and the vertical line) is conveyed by the speed and path of the moving square. Two scores are obtained from the subject's performance on all trials: (1) the mean absolute distance between the vertical line and the position of the square when the subject presses the key, and (2) the intrasubject standard deviation of the distances over trials. These combined measures correlate about −.40 with scores on the highly *g*-loaded Raven Standard Progressive Matrices.[16]

Posner Paradigm. This ECT, originated by Michael Posner,[17] measures the speed of accessing long-term memory for simple, highly learned items of information. It is based on contrasting the speed of response to a reaction stimulus that calls for retrieval of information from long-term memory (LTM) and the speed of response to a reaction stimulus that does not require memory retrieval.

The procedure uses a binary response console like that in Figure 8.3. RT is measured on two separate tasks, called *physical identity* (PI) and *name identity* (NI).

In the *PI task*, a pair of letters appears on the computer display; the subject responds on the binary console, pressing the button labeled SAME (if the two letters are *physically* identical) or pressing the button labeled DIFFERENT (if the two letters are not physically identical). For example, AA = SAME and Aa = DIFFERENT, AB = DIFFERENT, and bB = DIFFERENT. RT is the interval between the onset of the letter pair and the subject's finger leaving the home button.

In the *NI task*, the same letter pairs occur, but now the subject is instructed to respond according to the *name* identity or nonidentity of the two letters, rather than to their physical identity. Thus AA = SAME and Aa = SAME; but AB = DIFFERENT.

The PI task does not call on memory; pairs of completely meaningless or novel symbols that are either the same or different could just as well be substituted for the letters. The NI task, however, requires that the name codes for the letters must be retrieved from long-term memory, where they have been stored since childhood, when the names of upper-case and lower-case printed letters were learned. The difference between the median RT to the NI task and the median RT to the PI task (NI-PI), therefore, measures the time required to access the letter names from LTM.

For college students, the NI-PI difference in RT is about 50 to 75 msec. There are reliable individual differences in the NI-PI difference, and the NI-PI difference in RT is correlated with IQ. The first study of this kind showed that college students with SAT-Verbal scores in the lower quartile had larger NI-PI differences than did students in the upper quartile.[18]

In my lab we have used a version of this task, modified so as to increase the memory retrieval time and its correlation with IQ. Instead of letters, we have used highly familiar words. The PI condition is pairs of words that are physically the same or different, regardless of their meaning, e.g., DOG-DOG = SAME, DOG-BOG = DIFFERENT. The NI condition is word pairs that have similar or opposite meanings (synonyms or antonyms); that is, they are semantically "same" or "different," a distinction that requires access to the words' meanings, stored in LTM. When these items are presented to college students as a nonspeeded paper-and-pencil test, they show error-free performance, indicating that the students possess the requisite information; it is only their speed of retrieving the information that matters. Many studies have been done with this paradigm, which consistently shows significant correlations with IQ, averaging about −.35.[19]

Semantic Verification Test. The SVT uses the binary response console (Figure 8.3) and a computer display screen. Following the preparatory "beep," a simple statement appears on the screen. The statement involves the relative positions of the three letters A, B, C as they may appear (equally spaced) in a horizontal array. Each trial uses one of the six possible permutations of these three letters chosen at random. The statement appears on the screen for three seconds, allowing more than enough time for the subject to read it. There are fourteen possible statements of the following types: "A after B," "C before A," "A between B and C," "B first," "B last," "C before A and B," "C after B and A"; and the negative form of each of these statements, for instance, "A *not* after B." Following the three-second appearance of one of these statements, the screen goes blank for one second and then one of the permutations of the letters A B C appears. The subject responds by pressing either the TRUE or FALSE button, depending on whether the positions of the letters does or does not agree with the immediately previous statement.

Although the SVT is the most complex of the many ECTs that have been tried in my lab, the average RT for university students is still less than 1 second. The various "problems" differ widely in difficulty, with average RTs ranging from 650 msec to 1,400 msec. Negative statements take about 200 msec longer than the corresponding positive statements. MT, on the other hand, is virtually constant across conditions, indicating that it represents something other than speed of information processing.

The overall median RT and RTSD as measured in the SVT each correlates about −.50 with scores on the Raven's Advanced Progressive Matrices given without time limit. The average RT on the SVT also shows large differences between Navy recruits and university students,[20] and between academically gifted children and their less gifted siblings.[21] The fact that there is a within-families correlation between RT and IQ indicates that these variables are intrinsically and functionally related.

One study[20] reveals that the average processing time for each of the fourteen types of SVT statements in university students predicts the difficulty level of the statements (in terms of error responses) in children (third-graders) who were given the SVT as a nonspeeded paper-and-pencil test. While the SVT is of such trivial difficulty for college students that individual differences are much more reliably reflected by RT rather than by errors, the SVT items are relatively difficult for young children. Even when they take the SVT as a nonspeeded paper-and-pencil test, young children make errors on about 20 percent of the trials. (The few university students who made even a single error under these conditions, given as a pretest, were screened out.) The fact that the rank order of the children's error rates on the various types of SVT statements closely corresponds to the rank order of the college students' average RTs on the same statements indicates that item difficulty is related to speed of processing, even when the test is nonspeeded.

It appears that if information exceeds a critical level of complexity for the individual, the individual's speed of processing is too slow to handle the information all at once; the system becomes overloaded and processing breaks down, with resulting errors, even for nonspeeded tests on which subjects are told to take all the time they need. There are some items in Raven's Advanced Matrices, for example, that the majority of college students cannot solve with greater than chance success, even when given any amount of time, although the problems do not call for the retrieval of any particular knowledge. As already noted, the scores on such nonspeeded tests are correlated with the speed of information processing in simple ECTs that are easily performed by all subjects in the study.

Dual Tasks and Working Memory. As we have seen, the RT elicited by most single ECTs has a rather modest correlation with IQ, typically with *r* in the range of −.20 to −.40. It is experimentally possible, however, and theoretically informative, to increase slightly an ECT's correlation with IQ by making it a part of a *dual* task. In a dual task, two different ECTs are run in tandem and the RT is measured separately for each. The two important results are (1) the RT is longer for both tasks, and (2) the RT on each task has a higher correlation with IQ than either one has when given as a single task.

To understand how a typical dual task works, we can combine two of the ECTs described earlier: *memory scan* and *synonym-antonym* (S-A). Here is an example of the sequence of events the subject sees on the screen:

Preparatory signal ("beep")	1 sec.
Blank screen	1 sec.
7 2 5 1 3 [digit set appears]	3 sec.
HOT - COLD	
Subject presses button A	RT_1 and MT_1
Blank screen	1 sec.
5 [probe digit appears]	
Subject presses button YES	RT_2 and MT_2

The subject must hold the digit set (**72513**) in memory while processing the synonym-antonym item (e.g., **HOT-COLD**), and, when the probe digit (e.g., **5**) appears, must scan the digit set in memory to determine if it was included in the digit set. Both RT_1 and RT_2 are about 50 to 100 msec longer than the RT to either task presented singly. And their correlations with IQ are reliably increased by .05 to .10 correlation points. Apparently, the amount of strain on Working Memory slows RT_1 and the degradation of the memory trace of the digit set over time (during the interpolated synonym-antonym task) slows RT_2.

The reason for the increased RT and its increased correlation with IQ seems to be that IQ reflects, among other things, not only the *speed* of information processing, but also the *capacity* of *working memory* (WM) for the short-term retention of information. WM is the active aspect of short-term memory (STM), the process that retains recently input information until it can be processed further, by being mentally manipulated to arrive at a decision, codified and stored in long-term memory (LTM), or associated with related material retrieved from LTM.

Working memory has been likened to the central processing unit, or CPU, of a computer. It has also been called the "mind's scratch pad." It is short-term, because the neural traces of recently input information rapidly decay, with corresponding loss of the information, unless time is taken to get the information into LTM by immediate repetition or rehearsal. But WM is a single-channel processor, and while it is actively rehearsing the latest input, it cannot process new input. Thus when there is a quick succession of input, there is a trade-off between processing and storage, and a faster speed of information processing becomes a definite advantage. Because dual tasks put a somewhat greater burden on WM than single tasks and create more contention for the channel, they better reflect individual differences in *g*.

Digit span[22] memory, for example, is moderately correlated with *g*, but individual differences are revealed only if all subjects are tested to the limits of their digit span. The functional relationship between digit span and RT is shown by the fact that immediate memory span for any given kind of items (digits, letters, words, nonsense syllables, colors, etc.) is highly related to the processing rate for such items, as measured in the memory scan paradigm described above.[23]

Forward digit span (FDS) can be made into a dual task, in effect, by making it into backward digit span (BDS). In BDS the subject has to retain the input digits (task 1) while reversing them (task 2) before recall. The result of task 2 is that WM is strained and some information is lost (always measured by number of digits here, not time, BDS < FDS) and BDS shows a much higher correlation with IQ than FDS. The correlations of FDS and BDS with IQ are about .30 and .60, respectively.

The more information that has to be held in WM while other information is being processed, the greater is the ECT's *g* loading. When information input exceeds the capacity of WM, even some of the information already held in WM is "crowded out" and lost. Most persons who can recall all 7 digits when 7 digits are presented can't recall 8 or even 7 digits when 8 are presented, but can recall only 5 or 6. We all have had this experience: You look up a telephone number in the directory, and just as you are about to dial it, someone asks you a simple question; if you answer it, you then have to look up the phone number again. WM has a very limited capacity and the information in WM rapidly fades beyond retrieval. So central is the role of WM capacity in individual differences in information processing that some cognitive theorists equate WM capacity with *g* itself. Some empirical evidence tends to support this idea.[24] A theory of the possible neural basis of individual differences in WM capacity is explained later in the section on theories of the RT-*g* connection.

Inspection Time (IT). As mentioned earlier, RT has both peripheral and central processing components, and it is only the central component that is correlated with *g*. Variance associated with the peripheral components merely attenuates the RT-*g* correlation. The IT paradigm completely eliminates the efferent or motor part of the peripheral sensorimotor component, with the consequence that although IT is less complex than most ECTs based on RT, it generally has higher correlations with *g*-loaded tests than does RT. IT measures the speed with which a simple sensory discrimination can be made. In the past decade or so, IT research has accrued a large and impressive literature.[25]

IT can be tested in both the visual and auditory modalities. Here is how visual IT is usually measured. The subject is told to fixate on a target point (small red dot) in the center of a display screen. After three seconds the red dot disappears and the *test figure* (Figure **a**, following page) appears immediately in the center of the screen. After an interval of *t* msec, the *masking figure* (Figure **b**, following page) appears in exactly the same location as the test figure, completely covering

a   b

it. The subject then indicates (by pressing one of the two thumb buttons held in each hand) whether the long leg of the test figure was on the left side (i.e., subject presses button held in left hand) or the right side. The subject can take as much time as necessary to make this decision. The time interval *t* between the appearance of the test figure and of the masking figure varies systematically from trial to trial, as the computer program is reactive, taking account of the subject's correct and error responses on each trial and automatically making the interval between the test stimulus and the mask longer or shorter until it stabilizes at the point where the subject responds correctly on 97.5% of the trials. (This high level of accuracy of the subject's responses ensures that the subject is fully able to understand and perform the task.) The length of the *t* interval at the point of 97.5% response accuracy is the subject's inspection time, or IT.

Another method for measuring IT is exactly the same as the method described above, but the test figure consists of a hollow square with one side completely missing; the masking figure is a full square of exactly the same size as the test figure. The subject has to indicate whether the missing side of the test square was at the top, bottom, left side, or right side. It is important to note than in the IT tasks, the time taken by the subject to respond is irrelevant. The crucial variable is the IT itself, that is, the exposure time needed for the subject to perceive the test figure correctly on 97.5 percent of the trials. The IT for young adults is between 100 and 200 msec.

Auditory IT has been made even simpler in some ways than visual IT. Here is one version that has proved effective.[26] Prior to the test itself, subjects are first given a high-pitch tone followed by a low-pitch tone; the difference in pitch is easily discriminated by all subjects on 100 percent of the trials when each tone is presented singly. Subjects are also practiced in identifying a masking tone, with a pitch halfway between the low and high tones. The IT task, then, consists of the brief presentation of the test tone (high or low) followed after an interval *t* by the masking tone. The subject then reports, without time pressure, whether the test tone was high or low. The auditory IT is very slightly shorter than the visual IT, just as auditory RT is slightly faster than visual RT. But this slight difference of about 10 to 20 msec seems to be a peripheral effect, attributable to the visual receptor being a biochemical reaction, which is slower than the mechanical reaction of the auditory receptor.

Both kinds of IT show highly reliable individual differences, which are substantially correlated with IQ and other _g_-loaded tests throughout the full range of biologically normal mental ability. There are highly significant differences, for example, between university students from the upper and lower quartiles of SAT scores. A meta-analysis[27a] of all studies up to 1988 shows an average correlation between IT and "IQ" of −.54. This is a remarkably large correlation, considering the extreme difference between the IT procedure and conventional psychometric tests.

Is it the _g_ factor of IT that is responsible for its correlation with IQ and other psychometric tests, or does the correlation reflect the loadings of IT on other, non-_g_ factors that also constitute some part of the variance in most psychometric tests? The answer is found by a factor analysis of visual IT among a battery of eleven tests consisting of the Raven's Advanced Progressive Matrices and the ten diverse subtests of the Multidimenional Aptitude Battery, administered to 101 college students.[27b] The largest factor loading of IT shows up on the _g_ factor of this psychometric battery by each of three methods for extracting a general factor. Independently of _g_, IT has a small loading on a spatial factor and a virtually zero loading on a verbal factor.

There are many other kinds of simple tasks that do not resemble the contents of conventional psychometric tests but that have significant correlations with IQ. Many studies have confirmed Spearman's finding that pitch discrimination is _g_-loaded, and other musical discriminations, in duration, timbre, rhythmic pattern, pitch interval, and harmony, are correlated with IQ, independently of musical training.[28] The strength of certain optical illusions is also significantly related to IQ.[29] Surprisingly, higher-IQ subjects experience certain illusions more strongly than subjects with lower IQ, probably because seeing the illusion implies a greater amount of mental transformation of the stimulus, and tasks that involve transformation of information (e.g., backward digit span) are typically more _g_ loaded than tasks involving less transformation of the input (e.g., forward digit span). The positive correlation between IQ and susceptibility to illusions is consistent with the fact that susceptibility to optical illusions also increases with age, from childhood to maturity, and then decreases in old age—the same trajectory we see for raw-score performance on IQ tests and for speed and intraindividual consistency of RT in ECTs. The speed and consistency of information processing generally show an inverted U curve across the life span.

SOME EMPIRICAL GENERALIZATIONS FROM RESEARCH ON ECTs

A comprehensive review of the research literature on the relation between speed of information processing in ECTs and IQ would fill a book at least as large as the present one. I am forced, therefore, to select and summarize all too briefly a few of the major findings in ETC research that seem most germane to understanding the nature of their relation to *g*. The points mentioned here have important implications for a theory of the causal basis of *g*. Such a theory, in empirically testable form, is now taking shape, though it is still embryonic.

RT and Speeded Versus Nonspeeded Psychometric Tests. Early on, doubters of the RT-IQ correlation tried to explain it away by arguing that RT correlated with psychometric tests because the latter were themselves given to subjects under speeded conditions, and that one is simply measuring the same speed factor in both kinds of tests. This notion has died hard because true-blue psychometricians and paper-and-pencil testers have been reluctant to admit that general mental ability could be assessed by means other than conventional tests. Their superficial interpretation of the RT-IQ correlation, however, has been thoroughly refuted by experiments specifically designed to put it to a rigorous test.[30] They show that speeding psychometric tests by imposing severe time limits slightly *decreases* the test's correlation with RT as compared with the same test given without time limit.

In most RT-IQ studies, and always in those conducted in my lab, the psychometric tests are given either without time limits or with very liberal time limits. We have emphasized the "power" nature of the test and always instruct subjects to take all the time they need to attempt every item in the test (usually Raven's matrices). Also, subjects are tested alone in a quiet room so they cannot be influenced by observing the time taken by other subjects. Yet their test scores are correlated with RT in a wide variety of ECTs.

Some psychometricians have mistakenly believed that RT measures the same speed factor that is measured by highly speeded psychometric tests, such as clerical checking, number series comparisons, and simple arithmetic. In fact, such tests have lower correlations with RT than do nonspeeded power tests. The two most speeded subtests out of the ten subtests of the Armed Services Vocational Aptitude Battery (ASVAB), for example, have repeatedly shown the lowest correlations with RT, yet these tests are typically identified with the speed factor that appears in factor analyses of various speeded and nonspeeded psychometric tests.

The fact is that psychometric speed—better called *test-taking speed*—is something entirely different from the speed of information processing measured by RT or IT. RT and IT have their highest correlations with pure power tests. The explanation for this seeming paradox is that the speed of information processing is a large part of *g*, whereas test-taking speed is not—it is more a personality factor than a cognitive factor. One of my studies found that the time taken by university students to complete the Raven's matrices, when instructed to take all the time they need and to attempt every item, was not significantly correlated with their Raven scores (number right), nor was test-taking time significantly correlated with RT, but it was significantly correlated ($r = -.45$) with Extraversion as measured by the Eysenck Personality Inventory, which was not significantly correlated with RT. The personality trait of "conscientiousness" is probably also related to test-taking speed, but this has not yet been investigated. In all such correlations involving time, the variable of age must be controlled, as both test-taking speed and RT gradually change for the "worse" with increasing age beyond early adulthood.[31] There is, of course, a wide range of individual differences in the rates of this change with aging, which has the effect of increasing the correlations between all speeded tests in elderly people.

RT and Latency of Conscious Awareness. We have found that subjects cannot normally "fake" RT on simple ECTs such as the Hick or the Odd-Man-Out paradigm. Obviously, persons cannot fake faster responses than the fastest they are able to perform. But can they consistently fake slower RTs than their average RT when they are trying to respond as quickly as possible? Their conscious attempt to slow their RTs typically results in RTs that are so exceedingly slow as to fall outside the normal range of RTs, or even outside the range of RTs produced by the mentally retarded. Given a lot of practice with informative feedback following every trial, college students can gradually learn to produce RTs that are about as slow, on average, as those of mentally retarded persons.

We wondered why it should be so difficult to "fake bad" without producing RTs that are so far out from the mean as to be even outside the range of the mentally retarded. The apparent answer to this puzzle came to us in the remarkable researches of the neurophysiologist Benjamin Libet,[32] who measured "reaction times" (i.e., neural reaction potentials) through electrodes placed directly inside the brain. He was able to determine that the time required for conscious awareness of a stimulus is, on average, about 500 msec. The subject claims to be consciously aware of the stimulus at the instance of its occurrence, but this is only the result of subjective referral of the sensory experience backward in time. As William James (1894) noted much earlier, "The whole succession [of the RT process] is so rapid that perception seems to be retrospective and the time order of events to be read off in memory rather than known at the moment" (p. 88).

Clearly, subjects in our RT studies had to be responding _before_ they were consciously aware of the reaction stimulus, because the RTs usually averaged _less_ than 500 msec. In the Hick paradigm, for example, the median RTs for zero to three bits of information average between 300 and 400 msec. Apparently the reason that subjects without special training are unable to fake believable slow responses is that they do not have intentional or conscious control over their RTs. The response is triggered by the reaction stimulus and is completed before the subject is even consciously aware of the reaction stimulus. This shows how exceedingly little RTs in these simple ECTs involve anything that could be called thinking, cogitation, or problem solving in any meaningful sense of these terms. RTs appears to reflect activity at a basic neural level that occurs prior to the full activation of consciously guided processes.

Intraindividual Variability in RT (RTSD). This is the standard deviation of a subject's RTs over _n_ trials. It is a rare study in which RTSD does not have a larger (negative) correlation with IQ than does RT itself. In other words, higher-IQ persons have more *consistent* RTs from trial to trial when performing an ECT. Persons of varying levels of IQ, from the mildly retarded (with IQs around 70) to the brightest university students (with IQs above 130), differ surprisingly little in their shortest RTs, but differ markedly in their longer RTs. Retarded persons produce a small percentage of RTs that are almost as fast as the fastest RTs of high-IQ subjects and faster than the median RT of high-IQ subjects. But high-IQ subjects virtually never produce RTs that are as slow as most of the RTs produced by retarded persons. Yet even in the highly restricted IQ range of university students, there is a significant negative correlation between RTSD and IQ, and the correlation is nearly always larger than the correlation between RT and IQ.

Intraindividual variability per se is not a prima facie indicator of the "goodness" of performance and can hardly be considered an ability. Yet it is correlated with IQ and with *g*. Although RTSD is quite highly correlated with RT, RTSD is significantly correlated with *g* independently of RT (as shown by partial correlation). That is, RT and RTSD have both overlapping components and nonoverlapping components that are independently correlated with *g*, and RTSD has the larger *g* component.[33] These facts must be accounted for by a theory of the RT-*g* correlation.

Two studies[34] have revealed that it is the individual's longer RTs that are most highly correlated with IQ. When subjects' RTs obtained in *n* trials are rank-ordered from the fastest to the slowest and the RT × IQ correlation is calculated within each of the *n* ranks, the *n* correlation coefficients show a steady rise from the speediest to the slowest rank. This was found both in Navy recruits and in university students.

RT and Ability-Group Differences. Individual differences in RT and mean group differences in RT are perfectly consistent. By this I mean that ECTs that show a negative correlation between IQ and RT for individuals also show a negative correlation between the IQ means and the RT means of various groups that differ in IQ. In fact, the IT × IQ correlation for group means is unity. Also, the negative correlation between RT and IQ (and RTSD and IQ) exists *within* groups at every level of IQ, from the severely retarded, to university students, to members of Mensa (the organization that requires a minimum IQ of 132 for membership). The correlations are slightly higher in low-IQ groups than in high-IQ groups, even when corrections have been made for restriction of range of IQ within groups.

There is some independent evidence that at lower levels of IQ, more of the test variance is attributable to *g* than to group factors, as compared with higher levels of IQ. This phenomenon, which Spearman dubbed the "Law of Diminishing Returns," is more fully discussed in Appendix A. It would be of considerable theoretical importance if it were firmly established as generalizable to all test batteries.

Large RT (and RTSD) differences and IT differences are seen between the severely retarded and the mildly retarded, and between mildly retarded and non-

retarded groups.[35a,b,c] More important from a theoretical standpoint is the finding of a fairly constant proportional RT difference between retarded and
nonretarded groups on a wide variety of ECTs, which suggests that a single
factor determines the group differences in RT on a variety of superficially different tasks. This phenomenon has been specifically investigated by Robert
Kail,[35d] with striking results. The mean RT of a retarded group (RT_R) on a
great many types of timed performance can be expressed as $RT_R = KRT_N$, where
K is the constant of proportionality and RT_N is the mean response time of a
group with normal or average IQ. The value of K varies from about 1.6 to 2.0,
depending on the mean level of IQ of the retarded group (in the IQ range 50
to 70). The main implication of this finding is that individual differences in
some global mechanism, undoubtedly related to _g_, affect virtually every kind of
ECT in the same way, despite the varied task demands of the different ECTs,
which possibly lend themselves to different strategies.

Kail has also shown[35e] that RT differences between younger and older age
groups behave in the same way and can be expressed in terms of a constant of
proportionality that holds for a wide variety of ECTs. That is, children's RTs
can be expressed as a constant multiple of adults' RTs regardless of the specific
task demands of the ECT in which RT is measured. Kail draws the following
apt analogy: "If two computers have identical software, but one machine has a
slower cycle time (i.e., the time for the central processor to execute a single
instruction), that machine will execute all processes more slowly, by an amount
that depends on the total number of instructions to be executed. . . . Speed of
cognitive processing might be limited by the speed with which the human information processor can execute a fundamental cognitive instruction" (p. 179).
Kail further argues: "Just as the central processing unit of a microcomputer can
run programs in different languages that accomplish an incredible variety of
tasks, the fundamental processes of cognition are almost certainly the same for
all humans, despite the fact that the organization of these fundamental processes
to perform more complex acts is strongly culture-bound. A working assumption
in my research is that the speed with which fundamental cognitive processes
can be executed may well be one of those aspects of cognition that is universal
rather than culture bound" (p. 155).

The constant proportionality of RT also applies to mean RT differences between young and elderly adults.[35f] The same phenomenon also is strikingly
evident in comparisons of mean RTs of average and of gifted children on a
variety of ECTs.[35g,h,i] Highly gifted youths averaging thirteen years of age who
were enrolled in university courses in math and science were compared with
typical junior-high-school age-mates and with regular university undergraduates
on eight different ECTs. The profile of mean RTs on the eight ECTs was nearly
identical for all three groups (average $r = +.96$). However, the gifted group's
profile coincided with the university students' profile, whereas the junior-high
students' profile, though closely resembling that of the other two groups, had
mean RTs that were almost twice as long. University students and Navy recruits

show highly similar ($r = +.97$) profiles of RT over the fourteen different forms of the Sentence Verification Test, but the groups differ about 300 msec in average RT (equivalent to a standardized mean difference of 0.67σ).[35j]

The consistency of all these findings makes it most implausible that these group differences in average RT could result from each group's adopting a different strategy for approaching the various ECTs. Rather, the evidence is most consistent with Kail's argument (quoted above) that individual and group differences in RT on a wide variety of ECTs largely reflect some global mechanism that affects the speed of mental operations in all cognitive tasks. It is *global* in the sense that it cuts across the specific knowledge, skill, and task requirements of the great variety of ECTs, showing a constant proportionality of group differences in processing speed. We may go a step further and suggest that this "global" mechanism, whatever its neurophysiological nature, is either wholly or partly the basis of *g*.

RT Correlations across Different Test Contents. The late Robert L. Thorndike and his co-workers expressly designed a study to examine whether correlations between RT and psychometric test scores cut across different kinds of contents (verbal, quantitative, spatial) in both the conventional tests and the ECTs based on these contents.[36] The conventional tests were the Cognitive Abilities Tests (CogAT), a widely used set of paper-and-pencil tests composed of contents designed to yield separate measures of the three most well-established ability factors in addition to *g*: verbal, quantitative, and visuospatial. The speed-of-processing tests consisted of six ECTs, in which the reaction stimuli consisted either of verbal, or of quantitative, or of spatial material. The separate RT scores therefore were based on responses to either verbal, quantitative, or spatial stimuli.

The ECTs were quite simple; children in the fourth, seventh, and tenth grades had RTs averaging 1.7 sec; the fourth-graders' mean RT was exactly double the mean RT of tenth graders. The RT × CogAT correlations when the type of content was the *same* for both were compared with the RT × CogAT correlations when the type of content was *different*. The main finding was that the RT × CogAT correlations hardly differed between *same* or *different* contents, although the correlation was slightly larger for *same* content ($-.27$ versus $-.22$). All of the correlations in this study mainly reflect the large general factor common to both the CogAT and RT measures.

The RTs on all six ECTs along with the CogAT Verbal, Quantitative, and Spatial scores were subjected to a hierarchical factor analysis. The second-order factor (i.e., the general or *g* factor of this matrix) loadings of the six RT variables (averaging $-.40$) are quite comparable in magnitude to the loadings of the three CogAT tests (averaging $+.43$). (The correlations have opposite signs, of course, because shorter RTs go with higher CogAT scores.) The factor analysis also revealed a large RT factor independent of *g*. As we shall see in a later section on the factor analysis of RT, this fact sets an inexorable ceiling on the size of the correlation that can be obtained between RT based on any single ECT and psychometric _g_.

The Correlation between Composite RT Measures and IQ. Reaction time measures based on any single ECT are rarely more than moderately correlated with IQ. Correlations are typically in the range from −.20 to −.40, sometimes less, but rarely more. It is important to understand why there should be this apparent correlational ceiling, and we will get to that point in the next section. But it is also important to understand the related issue of why it is possible to increase the correlation markedly by combining[37] subjects' median RTs from a number of different ECTs. This has been done in many studies, and the result has always been a significant rise in the RT-IQ correlation.

It is sufficient here to note that the combined RTs from a number of ECTs and IQ or other highly _g_-loaded measure approach the correlations typically found between various psychometric power tests, ranging up to correlations of about .70. A review[38] of several studies in which RTs (and RTSDs) from four or five different ECTs were combined shows _multiple correlations_ (_R_) ranging from .431 to .745, with an average _R_ of .61 for RT, .60 for RTSD (i.e., intra-individual variability in RT), and .67 for RT + RTSD.[39] (All these values of R have been corrected for bias [i.e., "shrunken"] to take account of the number of independent variables.) These correlations, based on college students, have not been corrected for attenuation or for the restricted range of IQ in the college samples. If so corrected, they would be larger by at least .10. It should be noted that these correlations closely approach the average value of the heritability estimates of IQ in the adult population, the square root of which probably approaches the maximum possible correlation of IQ with any physiological variables. The combined RTs from a number of different ECTs therefore predict some 50 to 70 percent of the heritable part of the variance in IQ.[40]

Why should the composite RT from two or more different ECTs show higher correlations with IQ than the RT from any single ECT? A small part of the increase is merely a result of increased reliability of the RT measurement. An increased _R_ would result even if one and the same ECT were given a number of times and their RTs were combined. But if the RT measures are quite reliable to begin with, this increase in correlation with IQ attributable only to improving the reliability of the RT measure by combining RTs from repeated testing on the same ECT is a relatively small gain, and the gains from repeated testing rapidly diminish. The observed effect we are concerned with here is much greater than can be accounted for by a simple increase in reliability, although it has an analogous basis.

Every ECT, besides reflecting a global speed of information processing, has a certain amount of uniqueness; that is, it also reflects other sources of variance in addition to the global speed of information processing. These sources of variance may arise in part from individual differences in the noncognitive or purely sensorimotor functions differentially called for by different ECTs and in part from different processes called for by different tasks. Individual differences in the distinct information processes called upon by a particular ECT are not perfectly correlated with individual differences in the distinct information processes called upon by other ECTs, although all of the different processes also share in each individual's global or general speed of processing. Hence by summing (or averaging) the RTs of a number of different ECTs, the global speed is added in by every RT, while the specific processing speed unique to each ECT gets added in only once. So the more ECTs that are included in the composite RT, the larger is the variance (individual differences) of the global speed component relative to the variance of any of the specific speed components. This is the same psychometric principle that explains why including a greater variety of items in a test increases the test's correlations with other tests, even tests that have no specific contents in common.

In summary, no single ECT affords as good a measure of the global speed of information processing as a composite measure of speed from a variety of ECTs. But it should be emphasized that the composite RT is still based only on ECTs that bear no resemblance to conventional, complex psychometric tests. The important and theoretically interesting phenomenon is that even though none of the ECTs calls for what one normally thinks of as cogitation or mental power (as each ECT can be performed in usually less than one second), their composite score is very substantially correlated with unspeeded psychometric tests designed to measure the level of a person's mental power or complex reasoning ability. An explanation of the cause of this remarkable correlation would be a large step indeed toward understanding the nature of *g*. As yet we have only a few tentative but promising hypotheses of how this correlation comes about. But before looking at these, we should consider three other empirical aspects of the RT-*g* correlation.

Factor Analysis of ECTs along with Nonspeeded Psychometric Tests. A Schmid-Leiman hierarchical factor analysis of a correlation matrix that includes both timed measures (RT, MT, and IT) from a number of ECTs and scores on a number of unspeeded psychometric power tests reveals four important features.[41] These are seen in the generalized didactic factor model in Table 8.1: (1) Both the psychometric power tests and the RTs of the ECTs are substantially loaded (indicated by +) on the second-order general factor, *g*. (2) The MTs (movement times) of the ECTs generally are not significantly loaded on the *g* factor, but give rise to a separate factor whose major loadings are exclusively on the MT for various ECTs. (3) The non-*g* variance of the psychometric tests (PT) splits into the well-established independent group factors such as verbal and spatial. (4) Most important, the RT variance is divided between *g* and an independent group factor, which could be called the non-*g* component of RT.[42]

This latter observation is theoretically important for the interpretation of ECT × psychometric test correlations. RT reflects at least two major components: a cognitive, or *g* component, which is *information-processing* speed and a noncognitive, or non-*g* component, which is *sensorimotor* speed. But the non-*g* component of RT is not unique to each and every ECT in which RT is measured.

Table 8.1

Generalized Hierarchical Factor Analysis of a Matrix of Psychometric Tests (PT) and Elementary Cognitive Tasks (ECT)

Variables	*g*	PT-Verbal	PT-Spatial	ECT-RT	ECT-MT
			Factors		
PT-Verbal 1	+	+			
PT-Verbal 2	+	+			
PT-Verbal 3	+	+			
PT-Spatial 1	+		+		
PT-Spatial 2	+		+		
PT-Spatial 3	+		+		
ECT-RT 1	+			+	
ECT-RT 2	+			+	
ECT-RT 3	+			+	
ECT-MT 1					+
ECT-MT 2					+
ECT-MT 3					+

Note: Salient (large) factor loadings are indicated by +. Small or nonsignificant loadings are omitted. All of the chronometric variables (RT and MT) have been reflected (i.e., signs changed) so that "goodness" (+) of performance on the ECTs and on the psychometric tests are positively correlated. The numbered boxes are keyed to explanations in the text.

Various ECTs have some part of the non-*g* component of RT in common, which creates a group factor in its own right. For this reason there is a ceiling considerably below unity on the correlation that the composite RTs from any number of ECTs can have with *g* or any other psychometric variable. Inspection time (IT) has a higher ceiling than RT, most likely because it has no psychomotor component. These relationships are shown in the schematic factor model in Figure 8.5.

The sensorimotor component in simple RT (SRT), and hence its non-*g* component, is relatively large compared to its *g* component. Choice RT (CRT) and the RTs of other more complex ECTs have a relatively larger cognitive component. Therefore, by subtracting SRT from CRT (or other complex RT) it is possible to rid CRT of some of its sensorimotor component and thereby increase its *g* loading.[43]

Genetics of the RT × *g* Correlation. Response times in ECTs have not yet been subjected to extensive genetic analyses, although there are now several studies[44] that clearly indicate significant heritability for a number of ECTs. The heritability coefficients for RT range widely for different ECTs, from close to

PSYCHOMETRIC TESTS

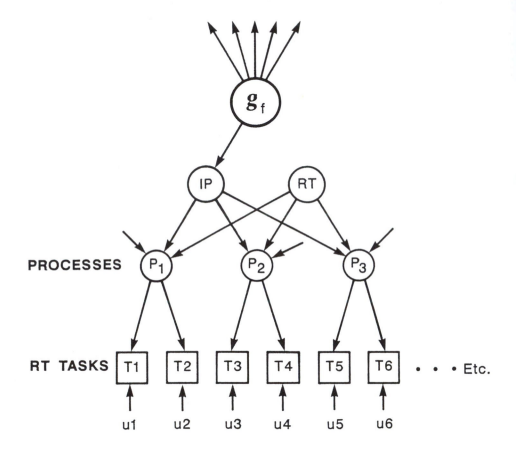

Figure 8.5. Representation of the factor structure of RTs on various ECTs. The correlations of the RTs on various ECTs (T1, T2, etc.) with the *g* of psychometric tests is mediated by *processes* (P_1, P_2, P_3) that are involved in different ECTs, and by a general speed of information-processing factor (IP) common to all RT tasks. The RT tasks and their common processes also have in common a non-*g* factor (labeled RT in the model), which is a sensorimotor speed factor that is distinct from the speed of information processing (IP). (The letter u stands for the square root of the *uniqueness* of each task.) (From Jensen, 1994c. Used with permission of Ablex.)

zero to values approaching the heritability of standard psychometric tests. A first principal component RT factor score based on several ECTs showed a correlation of .456 between MZ twins reared apart (MZA),[44a] which can be taken as an estimate of broad heritability. The heritability of principal component RT scores (labeled "basic speed" by the authors) estimated from both MZA and DZA was .54.[44b] In another study,[44c] using eleven ECTs (many of those previously described), the "general speed" factor scores (based on the RTs from all of the ECTs) showed a heritability coefficient [i.e., $h^2 = 2(r_{MZ} - r_{DZ})$] of .57. Intraindividual variability of RT had a heritability of .70.

Two other findings are especially noteworthy in this context. First, just as the RTs on the more complex ECTs have higher correlations with IQ, they also show higher heritability. In view of the fact that mean RT of an ECT closely reflects subjective estimates of its complexity[45] relative to other ECTs, it is interesting that the heritabilities of the various ECTs were correlated .676 with their mean RTs. Second, the degree to which the RTs of the various ECTs are correlated with the Wechsler Full Scale IQ (a good proxy for *g*) predicts the ECTs' heritability coefficients with a correlation of .603. When the same relationship was determined using *g* factor scores from the Multidimensional Aptitude Battery instead of Wechsler IQ, the resulting correlation was .604.

These studies leave little doubt that individual differences in RT, or speed and consistency of information processing, have a substantial genetic component and that the genetic component of RT is related to *g*. But more important, theoretically, than the heritability per se of RT is the degree of *genetic correlation*[46] between RT and *g* (or its proxies such as IQ or scores on the most highly *g*-loaded tests). Even though RT and IQ each may have a substantial genetic component, it is conceivable that all or most of their correlation results from *nongenetic* factors that affect both variables.

Two independent quantitative genetic studies[47] based on MZ and DZ twins were designed to determine the relative roles of genetic and environmental effects in mediating the correlation between speed of information processing and IQ. In the first study,[47a] the *genetic correlation* between speed of processing and IQ was .84. Common (between-family) environmental effects contributed virtually nothing to the phenotypic correlation. In the second study,[47b] the genetic correlation between RT and *g* was virtually unity. That is to say, whatever variance RT and IQ have in common is almost entirely genetic. The findings of these two studies are succinctly summarized by their authors:

> Our results indicate that the phenotypic relationship between the measures of general intelligence [*g*] and the measures of speed of processing [RT] employed are due largely to correlated genetic effects. While correlated specific environmental effects were less important, correlated common environmental effects were negligible. In general, the findings support the notion of some common biological mechanism(s) underlying both general intelligence and speed-of-processing measures.[47a] (p. 247)

The common factor [between RTs and IQs] was influenced primarily by additive genetic effects, such that the observed relationships among the speed and IQ measures are mediated entirely by hereditary factors. There was additional specific genetic variance for Verbal IQ and specific shared-twin environmental variance for Performance IQ. However, twin similarity for general speed of processing was explained entirely by genetic factors related to intelligence. The results emphasize the importance of common, heritable, biological mechanisms underlying the speed-IQ association.[47b] (p. 351)

Proof of the Relationship between Speed-of-Processing and g. Finally, we should be assured that the correlation between IQ tests (or other g-loaded psychometric tests) and speed-of-processing as measured by RT in various ECTs actually reflects the tests' g factor and not some non-g source of variance in the test scores with which RT may be correlated. An explicit demonstration that RT in fact reflects psychometric g is crucially important for theories that accord a prominent role to mental speed. Therefore, we must consider the studies that directly address this point.

First, it is important to note that mental processing speed (measured by RT) is correlated with crystallized intelligence (Gc) independently of fluid intelligence (Gf), and RT is correlated with Gf independently of Gc. As Gc and Gf are highly correlated with each other, this means that RT is correlated with a higher-order factor that both Gf and Gc have in common; that factor of course is g.[48a] This is also further evidence that in the hierarchy of psychometric ability factors, Gf and Gc are subordinate to g, the highest-order common factor. This arrangement is in fact necessary to comprehend the independent correlations of Gf and Gc with RT.

Vernon[48b] summarized the results of five studies in each of which a g factor was extracted from a test battery (the Wechsler Intelligence Scale for Adults [WAIS] + Raven Advanced Progressive Matrices [RAPM] or the Multidimensional Aptitude Battery [MAB]), which he labeled IQ$_g$; and a general factor was extracted from the RTs of a battery of ECTs, labeled RT$_g$. IQ$_g$ factor scores were correlated with RT$_g$ factor scores. The results are summarized in Table 8.2. The N-weighted average IQ$_g$ × RT$_g$ correlation is −.52.

Vernon[48c] also found that when the g factor was partialed out of the WAIS + RAPM, none of the twelve subtests was significantly correlated with RT$_g$. Interestingly, the RAPM, a nontimed test that shares no face content in common with any of the RT tests, has the largest g loading of any of the psychometric tests and also has the largest correlation with RT$_g$. In contrast, Digit Symbol, which is the least complex and the most speeded of all the WAIS subtests, has the smallest g loading and also the smallest correlation with RT$_g$.

Another study,[48d] not included in Table 8.2, showed a correlation of .44 (.56 after correction for restricted range of IQ in the university sample) between g factor scores (from the MAB + RAPM) and a composite unit-weighted measure of speed and efficiency of processing on six ECTs.

Table 8.2
Correlations between IQ$_g$ and RT$_g$ in Five Studies[48b]

Study	Sample	N	IQ Test(s)	Variance accounted for by:		Correlation between IQg and RTg
				IQg (%)	RTg (%)	
Vernon (1983)	University students	100	WAIS + RAPM	55.4	65.5	−0.406
Vernon and Jensen (1984)	Vocational college students	106	ASVAB	45.4	65.5	−0.260
Vernon, Nador and Kantor (1985)	University students	81	MAB (timed)*	42.4	71.4	−0.503
			MAB (untimed)	39.0	71.4	−0.357
Vernon and Kantor (1986)	High school students	58	MAB (timed)*	46.0	76.3	−0.446
		55	MAB (untimed)	49.7	77.3	−0.462
Vernon (1989a)	MZ twins	100	MAB	60.9	83.4	−0.673
	DZ twins	104	MAB	49.6	68.5	−0.550
	MZ and DZ twins and non-twin siblings	274	MAB	55.5	76.9	−0.628

*See original references for the time/untimed distinction.

The mere size of the simple correlation between RTs and various psychometric tests is much less important to theories of mental ability than establishing the fact that the correlations are dependent on the relationship of RT to g. Definitive evidence for this relationship is provided by the method of *correlated vectors*, whereby the column vector of various psychometric tests' g loadings (V_g) is correlated with the column vector of the tests' correlations with RT (V_{RT}). (See Appendix B for an example of this method.) The data from several studies[49] that report the g factor loadings of a number of diverse psychometric tests and the tests' correlations with RT (or other chronometric variables derived from RT) permit the application of this method.

Smith and Stanley[49a] correlated scores on eight psychometric tests separately with the RTs and RTSDs from the 2, 4, and 8 button conditions (1, 2, and 3 bits, respectively) of the Hick paradigm. The correlation coefficients constitute the column vector V_{RT} (or V_{RTSD}). The g loadings of the eight psychometric tests constitute the column vector V_g. For RT, the $V_g \times V_{RT}$ correlations (r) for 1, 2, and 3 bits were $-.765$, $-.160$, and $-.966$, respectively (the 2-bits condition, with $r = -.160$, is obviously anomalous; the rank-order correlation is only $-.270$). For RTSD, or intraindividual variability in RT, the $V_g \times V_{RTSD}$ correlations for 1, 2, and 3 bits were $-.687$, $-.410$, and $-.772$, respectively (again, the 2-bits condition, with $r = -.410$, seems anomalous, but here Spearman's rank-order correlation r_s is $-.714$.) The authors concluded, "It was clearly shown that the profile of the PT's [psychometric tests'] g loadings could be well predicted from the RT-PT correlations for four of the RT measures. It can be concluded that RT tasks do measure general intelligence. Analysis of the errors in prediction suggested that the RTs may correlate more with fluid than crystallized intelligence" (p. 291).

An important point in the authors' Table 1, but not mentioned by them, is seen in the correlations of all the RT and RTSD variables with g (the first principal component) and also with the next largest psychometric component (the bipolar verbal vs. spatial second principal component), which is perfectly uncorrelated with g and could be called a non-g factor. The average of all the $g \times$ RT and $g \times$ RTSD correlations is $-.24$ $(p < .01)$, whereas the average of all the non-$g \times$ RT and non-$g \times$ RTSD correlations is $+.02$. This indicates that RT and RTSD are not correlated with any significant common factor in this psychometric battery other than g. In fact, I have not found an example of RT and RTSD being significantly correlated with any psychometric factor that is orthogonal to g.

Eleven ECTs (RTs and IT) given to seventy-three Navy recruits were used in a multiple correlation (R) to predict scores on each of the ten subtests of the Armed Services Vocational Aptitude Battery (ASVAB), the Raven Matrices (Advanced), and g factor scores derived from the ASVAB.[49b] The individual Rs ranged from .61 (for g factor scores) to .29 (for both Numerical Operations and Coding, the two most speeded tests in the ASVAB battery). The thirty-six-item Raven Matrices, with a forty-minute time limit, had the second largest

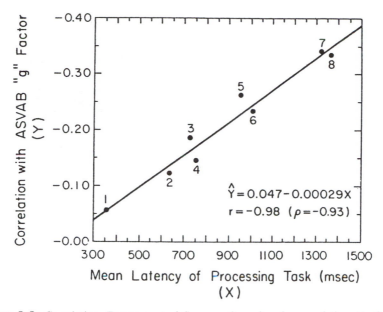

Figure 8.6. Correlation (Pearson *r* and Spearman's rank-order correlation ρ) of eight ECTs with ASVAB *g* factor scores as a function of task complexity as indicated by mean response latency (RT in msec) on each task. (The ECTs numbered 1 to 8 are described in the original article.[49c]) Reprinted from *Personality and Individual Differences, 5*, P. A. Vernon & A. R. Jensen, Individual and group differences in intelligence and speed of information processing, 411–423, Copyright 1984, with kind permission from Elsevier Science Ltd, The Boulevard, Langford Lane, Kidlington 0X5 1GB, UK.

correlation ($R = .55$). The correlation between the column vector of the twelve variables' *g* loadings and the vector of the variables' multiple *R*s with the ECTs is $r = .78$.

The *g* loadings of RTs on various ECTs are clearly related to the complexity of the cognitive operations they call for. The mean RT of each of eight different ECTs in a sample of 106 vocational college students was used as an objective index of each ECT's cognitive demand. The mean RTs of the eight ECTs ranged from 355 msec to 1,400 msec. The students also took the ASVAB, from which the *g* factor was extracted. The correlation between the eight RT means (on the ECTs) and the ECT's correlations with *g* factor scores (from the ASVAB) is $r = -.98$ ($r_s = -.93$), as shown in Figure 8.6.

A composite speed measure (based on RT, IT, and the Coding speed subtest of the WAIS) was obtained from 102 elderly persons (aged fifty-four to eighty-five).[49d] Partial correlations (with age partialed out) were obtained between this speed measure and each of eleven diverse psychometric tests. The vector of these correlations and the vector of the tests' *g* loadings are correlated $r = .95$, $r_s = .72$ ($p < .01$).

In the Hick paradigm (previously described), RT increases as a linear function of task complexity measured in bits of information. The rate of this increase in RT with increases in task complexity (that is, the *slope* of the linear regression of RT on bits) is negatively related to the speed of information processing. The increment in RT with each increase in task complexity is less for high-IQ than for low-IQ individuals.

RT in the Hick paradigm is itself a function of both the *intercept* and the *slope* of the regression of RT on bits. Slope has generally shown only weak and often nonsignificant (negative) correlations with IQ, especially in college samples. The reason for this is its usually low reliability, which makes slope a poor measure of individual differences. When Hick paradigm data are aggregated over many subjects, however, the slope of the mean RTs is much more reliable than the slope for any individual. Groups that differ in mean IQ also show highly significant differences in the mean slope of their RTs as a function of bits. The higher-IQ group always shows the lesser slope. So there can be little doubt that the slope of RT as a function of task complexity (measured as bits of information) is related to IQ. A study of the Hick paradigm based on 59 school-children (aged 6 to 11) obtained partial correlations (age partialed out) between RT *slope* and each of the 12 subtests of the Wechsler Intelligence Scale for Children-Revised (WISC-R). The vector of these 12 correlation coefficients and the vector of the 12 WISC-R subtests' *g* loadings are correlated $r = -.80$, $r_s = -.83$ $(p < .01)$.[49e]

These findings amply establish the relationship between psychometric *g* and speed of information processing. So now we can proceed to consider hypotheses that attempt to explain the causal basis of this relationship.

BLIND ALLEY EXPLANATIONS OF THE RT-*g* RELATIONSHIP

The term RT-*g* is used here in a generic sense to include the correlation of any speed-of-information processing measure with psychometric *g*. Before taking up the more promising leads for a theory of the RT-*g* correlation, it may be helpful to dismiss those hypotheses which evidence indicates are theoretical blind alleys. We have already examined the discredited notion that the RT-*g* correlation results from the speededness of psychometric tests. But there are several other, almost equally unfruitful, explanations that, when fully examined, are contradicted by a preponderance of evidence.

The fact that any particular explanatory element can be demonstrated to have an effect in some particular experiment does not establish it as a primary cause of the RT-*g* correlations seen across many experiments. No one has claimed that it is impossible to manipulate certain experimental conditions that are essentially extrinsic to the RT-*g* correlation in ways that may affect RT or even the RT-*g* correlation, although, in fact, it is surprising how few experimental manipulations produce any significant effect. Although, for the extenuating reasons already pointed out, the RT-*g* correlation may not be especially large, it is in fact remarkably robust across a wide variety of laboratory techniques and procedures and shows up within every age group from preschoolers to the elderly and within subject samples selected from every segment of the distribution of IQ in the population, from the severely retarded to the exceptionally gifted. The RT-_g_ correlation has proved to be one of the most dependable phenomena in the behavioral sciences. With that in mind, here are the failed explanations of the RT-_g_ correlation.

Speed-Accuracy Trade-Off. While it is true that the degree to which either the speed or the accuracy of responding is emphasized in the preliminary instructions to subjects can affect the speed of response and the error rate (in opposite directions), it cannot really explain the RT-_g_ correlation. The idea was that higher-IQ persons would opt for the strategy of maximizing their quickness of response at the expense of making more errors, while lower-IQ persons would sacrifice speed for accuracy of response. Hence the negative correlation between RT and IQ. But if this were the true explanation of the RT-_g_ correlation, one should predict two things: (1) a *positive* correlation between errors and IQ; and (2) a *negative* correlation between RT and errors. What is typically found, however, is just the opposite of both predictions. Higher-IQ subjects are faster and more accurate than lower-IQ subjects, and fast responders make fewer errors than slow responders. Also, at any given level of accuracy, high-IQ subjects have faster RTs than low-IQ subjects. These facts are not explained by the speed-accuracy trade-off theory.

The Strategy Deficit Hypothesis. This is the idea that higher-IQ persons are better at discovering more efficient strategies for solving particular problems and that even simple ECTs lend themselves to different strategies that are more or less efficient. Alderton and Larson[50a] have defined strategy use as "some goal-directed, purposeful use or allocation of intellectual resources . . . guided by the individual's knowledge of the structure of the task or problem" (p. 48). A simple analogy would be two cars each starting out at the same time, fueled with the same grade of gas; they drive from town A to town B at the same average speed, but the car whose driver discovers a shortcut (i.e., a more efficient strategy) arrives at the destination half an hour before the other car. This is causally a quite different phenomenon from the case where both cars take the same route but arrive at different times because they average different speeds, perhaps because one is a racing car and the other is a jalopy.

It is likely that people differ in their "strategic" tendencies, with some persons better able than others to discover, learn, or use acquired strategies in novel situations. The important question with respect to ECTs, however, is whether individual differences in RT and IT (and intraindividual variability in RT) simply reflect individual differences in the use of strategies that are more or less efficient (or individual differences in the number of trials needed to discover a more efficient strategy). If using a more efficient strategy is a general characteristic of higher IQs, that would explain the RT-_g_ correlation. An alternative possibility is that individual differences in IQ and in efficiency of strategies both reflect individual differences in a more basic physiological substrate that could be called something like "neural efficiency."

Several lines of evidence help in deciding between these alternatives. If highly reliable individual differences in the RTs to a particular ECT could be demonstrated over a wide range, such that the number of significant differences between subjects is almost as great as the number of subjects, it would seem improbable that all these differences could represent an equal number of unique strategies, all differing in efficiency. And if it were the case that all the subjects changed from less to more efficient strategies at different points in the course of practice, it would contradict the very high intertrial consistency of individual differences in RT and IT that it is in fact possible to attain on many ECTs. Also, various ECTs based on different task requirements would each evoke a different strategy, and one would have to conclude that all of these strategies have some variance in common, because all ECTs, like all psychometric tests, are positively correlated. So far, nothing that could be called a "general strategy factor" has been discovered that is not just *g* in another guise. Despite its lack of compelling empirical support, the strategy hypothesis of the RT-*g* correlation appeals to some psychologists, I believe, because it accords with their ideology of explaining behavior in strictly behavioral terms and viewing individual differences purely in terms of learning, without implying any "hard-wired" brain processes. Such Behaviorism with a capital "B" insists upon "debiologizing" the RT-*g* correlation and denying individual differences in basic processes.

The research conducted to test the strategy hypothesis of the RT-*g* correlation is rather complex, but quite conclusive in its negative verdict. In perhaps the most clever study[50a] of this issue, fairly simple computerized ECTs, given to 243 Navy recruits, were specially devised so as to elicit different strategies. At certain points in the sequence of trials, the stimulus features of the ECTs were altered in ways that would allow subjects to discover the possibility of a more efficient strategy. The ECTs were purposely much more liable to elicit different strategies than are most of the previously described ECTs typically used in research on individual differences. This paradigm allowed the investigators to determine from the resulting RT data which particular strategy each subject had adopted, and if there was a change in strategy over the course of many trials, it was possible to determine the exact trial on which the subject adopted a different strategy.

Here is what was found. As usual, the RT-*g* correlation appeared, based on the *g* (or *Gf*) factor derived from nineteen diverse psychometric tests. As usual, the RTs were positively correlated across the different ECTs. However, individual differences in the strategy measures derived from these ECTs were unique to each ECT, that is, they were uncorrelated across the different ECTs. They were also uncorrelated with any of the psychometric test scores or the tests' *g* factor. The study's authors, U.S. Navy research psychologists Alderton and Larson, concluded the following:

[T]here was uniformly no evidence supporting cross-task consistency in strategy use, which conflicts with the theoretical conjecture that effective strategy use is general across tasks and an explanation for the statistical phenomenon of general intelligence. Admittedly, the current tasks were simple, require few cognitive operations, and thus are restricted in terms of possible strategy variations. However, although there was no evidence for cross-task consistency in strategy use, global performance on these tasks was highly intercorrelated and broadly dependent upon aptitude, including general intelligence. Thus, although high intelligence individuals did not consistently optimize strategy use across tasks, they certainly optimized overall performance across tasks. This returns us to our central conclusion: Alternatives to strategy theories of *g* must be pursued if progress is to be made in explaining general intelligence. (p. 74)

Strategy use has also been examined in the inspection time (IT) paradigm, which is probably the least complex of all ECTs. IT has a quite large *g* component in common with psychometric tests and with RTs from other ECTs. It also has a speed component, independent of psychometric *g*, which is also common to RT in certain ECTs that reflect quickness of visual perception, such as the Visual Scan test (described on p. 216).[50b]

There is one possible strategy (if it can even be called a strategy) that is used by some subjects in one form of the IT task, in which the tachistoscopically presented test stimulus consists of two vertical lines side-by-side, one line only half as long as the other; the subject has to decide whether the longer line appeared on the right or the left side of the display. Some subjects, for reasons that are still unclear, report being able to see an illusion of "apparent movement" of the shorter line after the backward mask has covered the test stimulus. This apparent movement often cues the correct answer and subjects try to use it in hopes of improving their IT performance.

In several studies[50c] subjects were questioned after the IT test to find out whether or not they had used the apparent movement cue. When all the tested subjects were included, the IT-IQ correlations were in the range of $-.30$ to $-.40$. After excluding the subjects who reported using the apparent movement strategy, the IT-IQ correlations increased in magnitude to $-.60$ to $-.70$. In other words, individual differences in strategy use actually *decreased* the correlation of IT with IQ. Subjects who were able to use the strategy were compared with those who did not, and there was no significant difference between the two groups either in mean IT or in mean IQ.

Motivation, Effort, Drive, and Arousal. Some psychologists have invoked this class of variables to explain the RT-*g* correlation and even *g* itself. The idea is that individual differences in performance on both psychometric tests and ECTs reflect mostly individual differences in subjects' motivation and effort expended in the test situation. According to this theory, higher-scoring subjects are simply those who are more highly motivated to perform well. This explanation, though plausible, is contradicted by the evidence.

First, much is known empirically about the effects of these variables on cognitive performance, and the general principles derived from all this evidence appear to make this class of motivational variables an exceedingly weak prospect as an explanation of either *g* or the RT-*g* correlation. The Yerkes-Dodson law is most pertinent here. This is the well-established empirical generalization that the optimal level of motivation or drive (*D*) for learning or performance of a task is inversely related to the degree of complexity of the task; that is, a *lower* level of *D* is *more* advantageous for the performance of more complex tasks. In this respect, *D* is just the *opposite* of *g*. The *g* loading of tasks increases with task complexity, and persons who score highest in the most *g*-loaded tests are more successful in dealing with complexity. This is inconsistent with what is known about the effects of *D* on the performance of simple and complex tasks.

If individual differences in *g* were primarily the result of individual differences in *D*, we should expect, in accord with the Yerkes-Dodson law, that simple RT should be more correlated with *g* than two-choice RT, which should be more correlated with *g* than Odd-Man-Out RT. But in fact the correlations go in the opposite direction. Another point: The very low correlation between individual differences in RT and MT (movement time), and the fact that in factor analyses RT and MT have their salient loadings on different factors, would be impossible to explain by the motivational hypothesis without invoking the additional implausible ad hoc hypothesis that individual differences in motivation differentially affect RT and MT. As noted previously, RT is highly sensitive to differences in the complexity or information load of the reaction stimulus, while MT scarcely varies with task complexity. Despite this, subjects perceive RT and MT not as separately measured acts, but as a single ballistic response. It is most unlikely that a motivational effect would shift during the brief unperceived RT-MT interval.

The assessment of drive level and its attendant effort is not a function of subjective reports or of the experimenter's merely assuming the effectiveness of manipulating subjects' level of motivation by instructions or incentives. Drive level is reflected in objectively measurable physiological variables mediated by the autonomic nervous system. One such autonomic indicator of increased drive or arousal is pupillary dilation.

Pupillary diameter can be continuously and precisely measured and recorded by a television pupillometer while the subject is attending to a task displayed on a screen. This technique was used to investigate changes in effort as subjects were given relatively simple tasks (mental multiplication problems) that differed in complexity and difficulty.[51a] The subjects were two groups of university students; they had been selected for either relatively high or relatively low SAT scores, and the score distributions of the two groups were nonoverlapping on an independent IQ test. The whole ETC procedure was conducted automatically by computer; subjects responded on a microswitch keyboard. Here are the main findings: (1) pupillary dilation was directly related to level of problem difficulty (indexed both by the objective complexity of the problem and by the percentage of subjects giving the correct answer), and (2) subjects with higher scores on the psychometric tests showed less pupillary dilation at any given level of difficulty. The UCLA investigators, Sylvia Ahern and Jackson Beatty, concluded: "These results help to clarify the biological basis of psychometrically-defined intelligence. They suggest that more intelligent individuals do not solve a tractable cognitive problem by bringing increased activation, 'mental energy' or 'mental effort' to bear. On the contrary, these individuals show less task-induced activation in solving a problem of a given level of difficulty. This suggests that individuals differing in intelligence must also differ in the efficiency of those brain processes which mediate the particular cognitive task" (p. 1292).

Another study[51b] in this vein, based on 109 university students, measured two autonomic effects of increased motivation (heart rate and skin conductance) as well as a self-report questionnaire about the student's subjective level of motivation and effort. The purpose was to determine if increasing motivation by a monetary incentive ($20) would improve performance on three computerized ECTs or affect the ECTs' correlations with a composite score based on two highly *g*-loaded tests (Raven and Otis-Lennon IQ). Subjects were randomly assigned to either the incentive or the no-incentive conditions. Each subject was tested in two sessions; only those in the incentive group were offered $20 if they could improve their performance from the first to the second session. The incentive group reported a significantly ($p < .01$) higher level of motivation and effort than was reported by the no-incentive group. But the physiological indices of arousal recorded during the testing showed no significant effect of the incentive motivation. Processing speed (RT or IT) was not significantly affected by the incentive condition on any of the ECTs, although on a composite measure based on all three ECTs, the incentive group showed a small, but significant ($p < .05$) improvement from the first to the second session, as compared to the no-incentive group. The correlation of the combined ECTs with the composite IQ averaged .345 for the no-incentive condition and .305 for the incentive condition (a nonsignificant difference). Although both groups showed a significant practice effect (improvement) from the first to the second session on each ECT, the average ECT × IQ correlation was not affected. The authors concluded, "In no case . . . did incentives affect the overall IQ-performance correlation for the tests used in the battery. These results support the view that correlations between information processing scores and intelligence reflect common mental capacities, rather than some affective variable such as motivation"[51b] (p. 25).

RT as a Learned Skill. This hypothesis holds that individual differences in learning ability are related to *g* (which is certainly true) and that the faster learners, who have a higher level of *g*, learn more quickly how to cope with various ECTs and to improve their RTs than do slower learners. High-*g* persons even begin the task with faster RTs, supposedly because they have a better immediate mental representation of the nature and requirements of the RT task. There is little doubt that learning ability, RT, and *g* are all related to one another. But they are related because they all depend on the basic speed and efficiency of information processing, not because individual differences in learning ability are the essential cause of individual differences in RT on various ECTs.

Systematic improvement of performance over the course of practice is evidence of learning. The learning hypothesis of the RT-_g_ correlation is contradicted by evidence that shows that the RTs in certain ECTs are correlated with _g_, yet show either no improvement with practice, or so slight a degree of improvement as to acccount for only a fraction of the individual differences variance. After prolonged practice, improvement in ECT performance still shows reliable individual differences between subjects at the asymptotic level of performance (that is, at the point beyond which the effects of practice have nearly leveled off and will show little further improvement for a given individual).[52]

It has been suggested that when all subjects have been allowed sufficient practice to reach their asymptotic level on the RT task, the RT-_g_ correlation would be reduced almost to zero. A study[53] expressly designed to investigate the effects of prolonged practice on the RT-IQ correlation measured two kinds of RT on a sentence-picture verification test in sixty university students over the course of more than 2,500 trials and nine hours of practice. The RTs showed significant declines in RT-IQ correlations early in practice, but during approximately the last 1,200 trials the RT-IQ correlations stabilized at an asymptotic level. Initially the RT-IQ correlation was $-.46$. After more than 2,500 trials and nine hours of practice, the sentence verification RT correlated $-.39$ with IQ. The authors concluded, "If RTs in an ECT still correlate with psychometric intelligence after more than 2000 trials of training (as was demonstrated), then top-down explanations of this relationship on the basis of metaprocesses . . . or controlled vs. automatic processing . . . seem largely implausible. Instead, from our findings we infer a strong support for the biologically based bottom-up explanations of the 'mental speed' theory of intelligence" (p. 214). Some of the terms in this quote, though highly familiar to specialists, are so important for understanding the argument here as to warrant some explanation for the general reader.

Top-down versus _bottom-up_ distinguishes between two theoretical possibilities: (1) _Top-down_ means that the causal direction of the RT-_g_ correlation arises from individual differences in "higher," or more complex, mental processes, which are deemed responsible for individual differences in the "lower," or less complex, speed of processing reflected in RT. (2) _Bottom-up_ means that individual differences in the speed of processing, reflected in RT, are the causal basis of individual differences in the higher, more complex mental processes of the kind involved in abstract reasoning, problem solving, and knowledge acquisition.

The top-down theory holds that higher mental functions, such as the subject's ability fully to grasp the task requirements, to discover and use more effective strategies, to transfer past learning and allocate the most appropriate "cognitive resources" to the particular task, and the like, all determine the person's RT in any ECT. As these kinds of complex mental functions are what are assessed by

IQ and the most highly _g_-loaded tests, and, as these higher mental processes supposedly influence RT, it is little wonder that we should find a correlation between RT and _g_.

The bottom-up theory, on the other hand, holds that individual differences in performance of these higher mental functions are themselves a manifestation of individual differences at a simpler, more basic, and more general level of brain activity, namely, neural and synaptic attributes that determine the speed and efficiency of information processing. (There is an operational distinction between speed and efficiency; efficiency refers to the moment-to-moment _consistency_ of speed of processing information, as reflected by the amount of variability [measured by the standard deviation] of a person's RTs over a number of trials.)

The fact that RTs and evoked brain potentials to a reaction stimulus can occur within a lesser time interval than it takes for the neural effects of the stimulus to reach the higher brain centers or conscious awareness of the stimulus would seem to be much more in accord with the bottom-up than with the top-down theory. Besides, it is hard to imagine how a person's complex, higher-level capabilities typically displayed in IQ tests (e.g., defining words, solving analogies, copying block designs, doing mental arithmetic, and the like) would give the person any advantage in producing faster RTs in the comparatively simple ECTs that show correlations with IQ or _g_. On the other hand, it is easy to conceive how greater speed and efficiency of information processing could be an advantage in the performance of complex cognitive tasks such as those that constitute IQ tests. This is described in greater detail below in the section titled "Makings of a Theory of the RT-_g_ Correlation."

Why does RT in most ECTs show so little improvement with practice and only a slight shrinkage of its correlation with _g_? Other evidence indicates that some other tasks lose much, or nearly all, of their _g_ loading after prolonged practice. Why not ECTs? The answer seems to be that very few features of most ECTs lend themselves to automatization of responses; they are explicitly designed to demand controlled processing. For a task to become automatized over the course of prolonged practice, all of the task's stimulus-response elements ($S^1 - R^1$, $S^2 - R^2$, etc.) and chained responses ($R^1 - R^2$) must be highly consistent throughout practice.

Automatization consists of the overlearning of these consistent aspects of the task through practice long beyond the point of initial mastery of the task, until the routine is thoroughly "entrenched," to use Robert Sternberg's apt term. Automatization of the key aspects of RT tasks, however, is usually intentionally prevented by randomization of the S-R conditions, which constantly maintains the subject's uncertainty of the moment of occurrence, or the location, or the properties of the reaction stimulus throughout the course of practice. RT tasks in which the reaction stimuli occur in a purely randomized or unpredictable order are essentially nonautomatizable; they depend almost entirely on controlled processing. The distinction between controlled and automatic processing has become an important concept in cognitive psychology.

Controlled Processing. The distinguishing characteristics of controlled processing of information are that it demands the individual's focused attention, requires conscious mental effort, is relatively slow as compared to automatic processing, deals with information input sequentially, and therefore is able to deal with only very limited amounts of information at one time, and is unable to execute different mental operations simultaneously. These characteristics are, of course, those associated with working memory. In some circumstances the input demand on controlled processing may approach the maximum capacity of working memory; any faster rate of input overloads the system and results in "breakdown" or "turn-off." Solving novel problems, learning new knowledge or skills, and consciously monitoring an unpredictably changing situation that calls for varied responses all involve controlled processing.

Not surprisingly, tasks that demand controlled processing are *g* loaded, the more so the greater the demands made on working memory. If everything we did mentally had to depend entirely on controlled processing, life would be intolerably burdensome indeed, and our efficiency would be greatly impaired. Fortunately, the evolution of the brain has provided us with the means for escape from such a fate, namely, the development of automatic processing. It is the mechanism for what might be called "the conservation of *g*."

Automatic Processing. Practice, if sufficiently long-term, can automatize certain information-processing routines, which frees up working memory to be used for the controlled processing of other information. In contrast to controlled processing, automatic processing does not demand one's entire attention; it is relatively effortless and can deal with large amounts of information and perform different operations on it simultaneously.

The degree to which task performance can become automatized depends on how consistent, predictable, or routine the information-processing demands of the task are. Automatization is easier the more consistent the required sequence of operations between input and output. In learning to send Morse code, for example, there is an invariant one-to-one relationship between letters of the alphabet and their corresponding dot-and-dash codes. The act of sending and receiving messages becomes completely automatized for expert telegraphers.

Most skills, however, involve both controlled and automatic processing. Driving a car is a good example. In the early stage of learning to drive, controlled processing predominates. To minimize external distractions, the learner must practice in a quiet street. The learner's full and undivided attention is required to execute smoothly the simultaneous operations of the clutch, the gear shift, the gas pedal, the steering wheel, and the brake, and also remember to make the appropriate hand signals at the right times. While doing all this the learner finds it impossible to converse, listen to the radio, or think about other things, without risk of grinding gears, killing the engine, running off the road, or worse.

With more and more practice, driving skill becomes increasingly automatic.

The seasoned driver performs all these operations without having to think about them at all. Controlled processing is still necessary, however, to deal with constantly changing traffic conditions. We have to relinquish conversation or other attention-demanding activity momentarily when traffic conditions change suddenly or look complicated and unpredictable. The working memory is then briefly occupied to full capacity. That is controlled processing. If all of the driver's operational skills were not fully automatic, they would encroach on the capacity of working memory and thereby impair the efficiency of the controlled processing needed to get through the traffic crisis without a mishap.

A perfect example of the combined roles of controlled and automatic processing is sight-reading an unfamiliar piece of music—an essential requirement of professional orchestra players. The controlled processing aspect of this feat occupies a considerable part of the capacity of working memory, especially if the performer must play up-to-tempo and at the same time be highly responsive to the conductor's expressive signals. Yet it would be utterly impossible for controlled processing to accomplish this kind of performance were it not for the fact that for professional musicians both the reading of musical notation and its execution on their instruments are about 99 percent automatized. Scarcely any thought at all need be given to those aspects of the musical notation per se that normally demand so much of the novice's attention, or to the incredibly complex combinations of perfectly coordinated muscular movements required to produce the correct sequences of notes on a musical instrument. The sequence of notes on the printed score is automatically translated into the sequence of muscular movements that produce the required sounds on the player's instrument.

Indeed, many complex skills can never be mastered at all without a high degree of automatization of many of their components, because just the absolutely irreducible demand on controlled processing alone takes up the full capacity of the working memory, making it necessary that other components of the skill occur automatically. A high degree of automatic processing is not just a greatly speeded-up form of controlled processing. It is most characterized by simultaneity of different processes and "pattern thinking." Duffers at chess, for example, think only one move ahead, at most. Excellent chess players often think several moves ahead. But world-class chess masters work quite differently.

Research on the nature of the skill of chess masters has discovered that they instantly perceive a whole pattern on the chessboard, and the properties of the pattern largely dictate the optimal move in light of the player's particular strategy. The greatest difference between duffers and masters is not how many moves ahead they plan, but the patterns of possible combinations they perceive on the board at any given move and the relative advantages and disadvantages of any particular change in the pattern. All this depends of course upon the master's vast store of information gained from years of practice. Chess masters easily memorize entire chess games in terms of such patterns, much as we can recall a sentence we have just read, without any conscious attention to the sequence of all the individual letters it contains. Yet studies have shown that chess masters do not have an exceptional memory in general. Given various memory tests unrelated to chess, they perform on a par with most college students. The difference is that the chess master's long-term memory is extraordinarily well stocked with chess rules, strategies, positions, combinations, and the like, which are automatically accessed the moment the chess master looks at a particular configuration of pieces on the chessboard. The phenomenon is akin to literacy in one's native language. A similar phenomenon is seen in experts in many other fields.[54]

The speed of controlled processing and the capacity of working memory are of great importance because of their heavy contribution to variance in *g*. Recent research on persons who show truly exceptional performance in any field, however, indicates that the critical difference between them and the average person is not raw *g* but depends essentially on a much greater than ordinary amount of automatization of certain knowledge and skills in their field of achievement.

The road to automatization—apparently the only road—is practice, and plenty of it, accompanied by conscious effort to improve performance. Few people realize the exceeding amount and consistency of practice that recent studies have revealed to be the indispensable precursors of surpassing skill or expertise in any field. Paderewski, who routinely practiced the piano ten hours a day in his youth, when later acclaimed a genius, remarked, "Yes, and before I was a genius I was a drudge."

MAKINGS OF A THEORY OF THE RT-*g* CORRELATION

At present, any theory of the neural basis of *g* has to be tentative and incomplete. Enough is already known, however, to permit some inkling of what a proper theory might look like, or at least to indicate some of the main phenomena it must encompass. Much is already known about the workings of neurons and synapses and about the brain localization of sensory and motor functions and certain cognitive functions.[55] However, we are still far from knowing precisely what goes on in the brain's neural circuits when we "think" or execute a *g*-loaded task. Our incomplete knowledge of these design features of the neural circuitry has made it necessary for psychologists to invent purely cognitive theories which make no reference to the specific physiological mechanisms involved.

Cognitive theorists posit hypothetical processes, such as apprehension, discrimination, working memory, short-and long-term memory, and the like, that are inferred from the experimental analysis and mental chronometry of people's responses to specially contrived tasks. A given stimulus sets off a sequence of unspecified neural activity in the brain and the end results are interpreted in terms of the hypothetical cognitive constructs. The information gained from this approach is most valuable for determining the phenomena that we hope can eventually be explained in terms of what actually goes on in the brain.

In recent years we have seen increasing rapprochement between cognitive and neurological theorizing. Some cognitive theorists aim for theories that are explicitly compatible with neurological knowledge and even couch their cognitive theories as much as possible in neurological terms. And some neuroscientists have turned their attention to cognitive processes.[56]

It is useful in this respect to distinguish between _general_ properties of the nervous system that affect nearly every aspect of its functioning and _specific_ or _localized_ brain mechanisms that subserve specialized functions. Whatever else a neurological theory of _g_ might entail, it would have to include those aspects of neural activity that are common to all parts of the central nervous system involved in cognition per se. This general property of the nervous system's cognitive functions would also have to show individual differences, as _g_ reflects individual differences.

The notion of a general property of the nervous system has been expressed by theorists in terms such as neural adaptability, cortical conductivity, neural connectivity (or dendritic arborization), neural efficiency, and neural conduction velocity. Some of these terms represent hypothetical constructs inferred from behavior while others are directly measurable phenomena. But the need for some generality of neural function to account for correlated individual differences in various functions seems inescapable. For example, even though the neural mechanisms that subserve verbal and spatial abilities are localized in different parts of the brain, these parts presumably have some property in common that accounts for the correlation between individual differences in verbal and spatial abilities. Another possibility is that the normal operation of both the verbal and the spatial areas depends on their communicating with the same central processing unit—the working memory—which provides the correlational link between them. All cognitive tasks that involve working memory show individual differences and are _g_ loaded.

Partly because of the ubiquitous correlations of reaction time and inspection time with _g_, the most often hypothesized common neural source of individual differences is the _speed_ of neural activity, or neural conduction velocity (NCV), including both synaptic transmission and propagation of the action potential along the axon. Individual differences in the speed of neural transmission could be either a general property throughout the brain or could be concentrated only in the area involving working memory, which seems to be located in Area 46 and other parts of the prefrontal cortex.[57] Even relatively simple information processing involves considerable communication between widely separated regions of the brain, so nervous impulses involved in any cognitive activity travel considerable distances between the brain's sensory projection areas and the efferent or motor system. With a finite nerve conduction velocity, of course, all this neuronal communication between different areas of the brain takes time, with individual differences measurable in milliseconds.[58] However, other neural properties in addition to conduction velocity are needed for even the simplest theory of the RT-_g_ correlation, as will be noted shortly.

But before taking up that part of the story, it should be noted that direct temporal connections have been demonstrated between RT in ECTs and brain activity measured by the EEG. The brain activity that accompanies a person's RT is wholly involuntary and unconscious. For example, with the identical "button box" apparatus used in my lab for measuring RT in the Hick paradigm, measurements of the subjects' evoked potentials were obtained while they were doing the RT task for 1, 4, and 8 light buttons (corresponding to 0, 2, and 3 bits of information). The latencies of the average evoked potentials (AEP) were measured from the onset of the reaction stimulus (i.e., one of the lighted buttons going "on"). Just like the RTs, the latencies of the AEPs displayed Hick's law, increasing linearly as a function of bits. Rank-order correlations between RTs and AEPs ranged between .58 and .65.[59a]

Also, differences between correct and erroneous RTs in binary-choice RT tasks of differing complexity were recorded at the physiological level in a study of the trial-by-trial correlation between the subjects' overt RTs and the latencies of the P300 cortical potential evoked by the reaction stimulus (RS) on the same trial.[59b] Three binary-choice RT tasks varying in the complexity of the hypothesized processes involved in the evaluation of the RS were administered under two conditions of speed/accuracy instructions. Correlations between the latencies of the P300 wave of the EP and the RTs on correct responses ranged from +.48 to +.66, but the correlations based on *both* correct and incorrect RTs were considerably lower (+.26 to +.61). More important for understanding the nature of error responses in RT tasks, however, is the finding that not only are the correct RTs relatively more closely coupled with their corresponding P300 latencies than are the incorrect RTs, but with remarkably few exceptions, the correct RTs are longer than their corresponding EP latencies, while the incorrect RTs are almost invariably much shorter. This indicates that on the incorrect RT trials the overt reaction process was initiated long before the process associated with P300 was terminated.

This research provides clear evidence of the dual nature of RT, which consists of a stimulus evaluation process (reflected by the P300 evoked potential) and the efferent process involved in executing the overt response. As there is independent evidence that P300 reflects completion of the most central evaluative discrimination or decision aspect of information processing, it appears that RT response errors occur when the depth of information processing of the reaction stimulus required for a correct response is incomplete. Hence the more complex the reaction stimulus, as indexed by bits of information or by the mean RT of correct responses, the greater is the probability of erroneous response. From such studies, it is evident that RT and IT are probably closer to the interface of brain and behavior than any other purely behavioral *g*-loaded measure in experimental psychology's armamentarium.

Basic Elements of the Information-Processing System. As working memory (WM) is so central to understanding the RT-*g* correlation, its relation to other elements of the information-processing system should be mentioned. Many models and flow diagrams of the processing system have been proposed. They

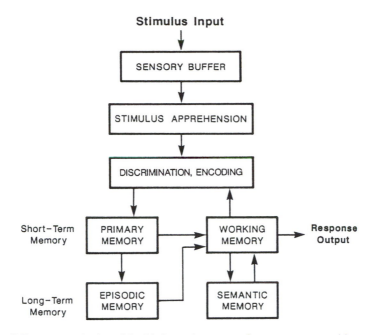

Figure 8.7. Hypothetical model of information-processing components, with arrows indicating the direction of information flow. (From Jensen, 1993a. Used with permission of Kluwer Academic Publishers.)

are all quite similar. Because they have many elements in common, and because no particular model has yet been generally adopted as the preferred one, I have made up the simplest generic model that incorporates the common elements of most of the others, as shown in Figure 8.7. It should be remembered that all such cognitive processing models are really analogical rather than physiological, although the various hypothesized cognitive processes presumably have structural and physiological counterparts in the brain. Each of the boxes represents a cognitive process; the arrows indicate the direction of information flow between the elements of the processing system.

The *Sensory Buffer* protects the processing system from being overloaded by the welter of sensory stimulation that impinges on the total sensorium at any given moment. It acts as a gatekeeper or filter, allowing only certain stimuli to be salient to consciousness at any given time. This is an essential condition for the mental state known as *attention*, or focused awareness, without which no particular aspect of the total stimulus input could be salient.

Stimulus Apprehension is the perception of a change in a salient stimulus.

Discrimination is objectively indicated by consistently differential responses to different stimuli. *Encoding* may or may not accompany discrimination; it is the assignment of a name or label or some tag of recognition or identification to the particular stimulus. The perception of familiar stimuli (e.g., the letter **A**, a cat, a chair, a man) usually involves both discrimination and automatic encoding. Unfamiliar stimuli (e.g., ⁊ ⌊ ⌊ ⌊ ⌊ め ⌊) may be discriminated but not encoded, although repeated exposures usually result in idiosyncratic encoding.

Short-Term Memory (STM) comprises *Primary Memory* (PM) and *Working Memory* (WM). STM is characterized by limited capacity and rapid decay of the information input. In the absence of rehearsal of the information held in STM, the memory trace fades, typically in a few seconds, to the point that it is no longer accessible to awareness or retrieval (with the exception of certain episodic memories, noted below). PM is a short-term passive holding station. PM does not rehearse, transform, manipulate, or otherwise act on the information input, which, however, may be transferred to WM, which may perform all of these active functions. Some of these processing functions of WM can be bypassed in performing certain complex tasks through extensive practice, which leads to automatization of the invariant aspects of the task, as pointed out previously (p. 246). WM is also the temporary stage from which information is transferred into long-term Semantic Memory. This filing and storage function of WM consumes some of its available capacity, thus reducing its capacity for processing incoming information.[60]

Long-Term Memory (LTM) comprises *Episodic Memory* and *Semantic Memory*, both of which are accessible to WM. LTM has practically unlimited storage capacity. Episodic Memory is a nonabstracted or nonsymbolic contextualized representation of spatial-temporal experiences and is generally less accessible to recall than to recognition, such as recognizing some previously encountered person, a particular place or scene, a particular strain of music, a scent, or an emotional experience. Especially vivid or emotional experiences enter directly into Episodic Memory without the intervention of WM.

In contrast, Semantic Memory is the repository of abstracted and symbolically encoded information, including past-learned meanings, relationships, rules, and strategies for operating on certain classes of information (such as words, syntax, numbers, arithmetic operations, musical notation, chess combinations, and the like). The information in Semantic Memory is usually decontextualized; that is, unlike Episodic Memory, there is not necessarily recollection of a specific occasion or experience that accompanied the acquisition of the particular information recalled from Semantic Memory.

Each stage of processing takes a finite amount of time, which accumulates between Stimulus Input and Response Output and can be inferred from measures of RT or IT. Cognitive tasks differ in the extent of their demands on the various processing elements and therefore take different amounts of time. The Inspection Time test makes minimal demands on memory retrieval and maximal demands on speed of apprehension and discrimination. Simple RT reflects Stimulus Apprehension more than Discrimination; the opposite is true for choice or discrimination RT. Backward digit span involves Working Memory more than forward digit span does. RT in the S. Sternberg memory scan task involves Short-Term

Memory more than Long-Term Memory; the reverse is true for the Posner name identity task. The fact that timed measurements from all of these tasks are positively correlated indicates, of course, that they all have something in common, namely speed of operation. This common factor is also correlated with the *g* factor of nonspeeded psychometric tests involving complex reasoning and problem solving. A reasonable prima facie case can therefore be made for individual differences in mental speed (and, by inference, neural conduction velocity) as a causal basis of *g*.

The Importance of Processing Speed in Working Memory. RT on the kinds of ECTs that involve the functions that cognitive theorists ascribe to WM are always *g* loaded, usually more so than tasks that make less demand on WM. Hence an important part of the connection between RT on ECTs and performance on untimed psychometric tests in which item responses are scored as correct or incorrect seems to center on the functions ascribed to WM. The connection can be accounted for theoretically in terms of individual differences in the processing *capacity* of WM, which is a function of the speed of its information-processing operations, in addition to another variable to be discussed shortly.

Two properties of WM make speed of operation crucial: (1) its *limited capacity* (i.e., the amount of information WM can hold at one time), and (2) the short *duration* of information in WM (i.e., the rapid rate of loss of information in WM). The operations performed on incoming information by WM must occur before the information is lost. Otherwise it has to be entered again. Hence we need to jot down long phone numbers and work most arithmetic problems with paper and pencil. If the amount of newly input information exceeds the capacity of WM, it has to be transferred to LTM in successive stages, so all of it can be retrieved in WM for answering the question or solving the problem that was posed. The transfer from WM to LTM itself occupies some of the WM capacity, so there is a necessary trade-off between processing and storage of incoming information.

If the amount of information that must be processed overloads the WM's capacity for performing these functions, there is a breakdown of processing and some essential information is lost. Incomplete processing of the incoming information results in erroneous output, or response. Speedier processing, therefore, is advantageous because more information can be processed or stored before it decays beyond retrieval.

RT is more highly correlated with *g* when WM capacity is strained to or near the point of breakdown. In very easy tasks response errors are few and are largely flukes, hardly correlated with *g*. As a task becomes more complex and demands more information processing, RTs increase and the rate of response errors increases and becomes more *g* loaded. As the ratio of errors to RT increases, the ratio of the errors' *g* loading to the RT's *g* loading also increases. In other words, in easy tasks that do not "threaten" the capacity of WM, the RT × *g* correlation is large relative to the error × *g* correlation; the opposite is true for more complex tasks that strain the capacity of WM to the point of breakdown.[61]

Computerized testing can zero-in on the particular test items that a given person has a slightly better than chance probability of answering correctly under nonspeeded conditions; these are generally the items that best discriminate individual differences in *g*. Their difficulty level is very near the threshold of the person's information-processing capacity. Much easier items, which elicit few if any errors, are correlated with *g* only via their response latencies, or RT. Task or test complexity is positively related to *g* loading not because *g* per se is an exclusive property only of the higher mental processes engaged in complex tasks involving reasoning and problem solving, but because complex tasks involve more elements of the whole processing system and so strain the capacity of WM. The efficiency of the whole information-processing system is more fully sampled by more complex tasks, thereby cumulatively yielding a more reliable indicator of individual differences in the totality of neural processes that make for *g*.

The Capacity of WM. Scientists Lehrl and Fischer at Erlangen University, Germany, have formulated capacity (C) in terms of the speed (S) and duration (D) of neural traces:

$$\text{C bits} = \text{S bits/sec} \times \text{D sec.}$$

Using chronometric methods for measuring S and D, Lehrl and Fischer[62a] have operationalized and tested this formulation. Each of the variables in the formula is substantially correlated with an untimed vocabulary test (which is highly *g* loaded), but C had the largest correlation: +.67 in a study of 672 subjects and +.88 in a study of 66 subjects. A team of British psychologists headed by the psychometrician Paul Kline[62b] has replicated the Erlangen scientists' essential finding, though with smaller correlations on individual tests in a restricted college sample. Kline's group used the Erlangen techniques for measuring C, S, and D, but using the Raven Matrices ("fluid intelligence" or *Gf*) and the Mill Hill Vocabulary Test ("crystallized intelligence" or *Gc*) as the measures of *g*. When all the chronometric and psychometric tests were factor analyzed together and *g* (first principal factor) was extracted, the result was quite impressive, causing the authors to comment, "Factor I [*g*] would have to be interpreted as biological intelligence with its huge loading on S [also C] and high loadings on the Mill Hill [vocabulary] and Raven's matrices scores. This is striking confirmation of the claims made by Lehrl and Fischer" (pp. 534–535).[62c] It is noteworthy that C, S, and D are correlated at least as high or higher with *Gc* (vocabulary) as with *Gf* (Raven).[62d]

The Hypothesis of Neural "Noise" in Information Processing. Elsewhere I have made a distinction between the *speed* and the *efficiency* of information processing.[63] High-*g* and low-*g* persons differ not only in their *speed* of information processing (as indicated by median RT), but also in their *consistency*, as indicated by intraindividual variability of RT (measured as the standard deviation of RT [RTSD] over many trials). RTSD hypothetically reflects (negatively) the *efficiency* of processing, because it is probably manifested in the course of information processing at many points in the system prior to making the overt response from which RT is measured. There is a periodicity or rhythm in the excitatory potential of neurons. (The synchrony of this rhythm in large groups of neurons is registered by the EEG as brain waves.) The speed of transmission of neurally encoded information is assumed to depend not only on the speed of axonal and synaptic conduction, but also on the probability that impulses are delayed by oscillation of neurons' excitatory potentials. As the phase of excitatory potential, oscillating below and above the threshold of excitation by a given stimulus intensity, is random with respect to the onset of the stimulus, the probability that the stimulus will be immediately propagated varies depending on whether the potential is above or below the threshold of excitability. The faster the oscillation, the shorter is the average difference in time between the quickest and slowest reactions to a stimulus. We know in the case of RT, for example, that high-*g* persons show much less difference than low-*g* persons between their slowest and quickest RTs and that the high and low groups differ only slightly in their fastest RTs but differ greatly in their slowest RTs.[64]

This neuronal oscillation model is rather analogous to viewing a moving object through an aperture with an oscillating (repeatedly opening-closing) shutter. If the frequency of the oscillations is fast, the viewer sees the scene with little delay even if the shutter is closed when viewing begins, and throughout the viewing little "information" is missed, because the open-close oscillations of the shutter create hardly more than a repeated flicker in the image. With a slowly oscillating shutter, however, the first glimpse may be either immediate or delayed, depending on whether the shutter is open or closed when the viewer first looked into the aperture, and in the course of viewing with a very slow shutter some information may be lost to the viewer during the closed phases.

The neural oscillation model is consistent with the findings that there are reliable individual differences in the oscillation (i.e., trial-to-trial variability) of RT,[65a,b] latency of the evoked potential,[65c] and neural conduction velocity,[65d] and that these individual differences are even more highly related to *g* than are measures of speed per se (i.e., greater variability = lower *g*). The hypothesized neural oscillation can also be called "neural noise," likened to the static and cross talk on a bad telephone line, which reduces the efficiency of communication and thereby increases the time of the callers' conversation, because many words and phrases have to be repeated to get the message across. The fact that RTSD (and other measures of intraindividual variability) is correlated with *g*, independently of median RT, suggests that it should be incorporated into the Erlangen (Lehrl & Fischer) model of information processing.

Myelination of Neurons Related to Speed of Information Processing. A prime candidate for the physiological basis of *g* as a reflection of individual differences in the speed and efficiency of information processing is individual differences in the degree of myelination of neurons in the brain. Myelin is a fatty substance that forms a thin covering, or sheath, around the neuron's axon. The axon conducts nerve impulses from the cell neuron cell body to the synaptic terminals that connect with other neurons.

The brain's "gray matter" consists of the unmyelinated cell bodies of the neurons. The "white matter," underlying the cerebral cortex, consists of the cortical neurons' myelinated axons, the association fibers that transmit neurally encoded information (as electrochemical action potentials) from one part of the brain to another and also connect the left and right cerebral hemispheres. The myelin sheath surrounding the nerve fibers acts as an insulator, similar to the insulation on an electrical wire. A large part of the brain, by weight and volume, consists of white matter, or myelinated neurons. Compared to other species, humans have a larger proportion of white matter in relation to cortical gray matter.

The degree of myelination of nerves in the brain increases steadily from birth to maturity. Gradually, in later maturity, and more rapidly in old age, demyelination occurs. This growth and decline of myelin has important implications for the observed relatively rapid growth and slower later decline of mental ability over the individual's lifetime. For any particular type of neuron, nerve conduction velocity (NCV) is directly related to the degree of myelination. Hence RT and RTSD, as well as all other indices of speed or efficiency of information processing, including NCV, markedly improve over the years from early childhood to maturity and decline in the later years.

The amount of neural "noise," as explained above, could be a function of the incompleteness of myelination, the insufficient insulation resulting in impulses crossing between axons nonsynaptically, causing interference, like cross talk on a bad telephone connection. The degree of myelination, therefore, could theoretically account, at least in part, for both the speed (via NCV in axons) and consistency, or relative lack of neural "noise" (via insulation of axons), of information processing. Edward Miller has written a detailed review of the many types of evidence relating myelin to mental ability, offering highly plausible hypotheses for future research on the evolutionary and physiological basis of *g*.[66]

Design Features of the Brain in Relation to *g*. The design aspects of the brain, that is, the neural circuitry, specialized modules, localization of functions, and the like, is the major focus of research in present-day neuroscience. However, very little is known about individual differences in these features or whether they are in any way related to *g*. The working assumption seems to be that all biologically normal persons have the same neural "hardware," so to speak, and that individual differences are not structural but rather a matter of how efficiently the "hardware" functions. The individual differences possibly result from differences in prior environmental experience or differences in brain chemistry.[67] Nevertheless, the possibility cannot yet be ruled out that there may be some normal individual differences in the brain's structural mechanisms.

These structural design features of the neural substrate of information processing are probably more related to psychometric group factors independent of _g_ rather than to _g_ itself. One example of a design feature involved in a specific ability is pitch discrimination. Spearman originally found that pitch discrimination is _g_ loaded to some extent, as is every cognitive ability, a finding that has been confirmed in many later studies. But pitch discrimination also has a substantial specific factor, and it is noteworthy that few persons, regardless of their level on _g_, are able to acquire what is known as absolute pitch, that is, the ability to sing or identify a specific musical note without reference to any other note. It is therefore called a "special" ability. Absolute pitch has been found in some mentally retarded persons, yet is lacking in some of the world's greatest musicians. Such individual differences seem impossible to explain in terms of sheer speed of processing. Neuroscientists Willerman and Raz[68] put forth the following hypothesis of pitch discrimination, based on a type of neural mechanism already established in visual discrimination:

> Neurons varying in central frequencies and band-widths can be organized to produce many features of intelligent functioning as indexed by our discrimination experiments. In the auditory domain, one neuron might be especially sensitive to hair cells that have a modal firing frequency of 800 to 810 Hz, another sensitive to frequencies of 805 to 815 Hz. In addition, their conjoint activation could trigger a third neuron, . . . referred to as a "grandmother" cell. An activated grandmother cell indicates that the specific frequency of the sensory signal must have been between 805 and 810 Hz. By adding increasing layers to the hierarchy of neurons, for example, great-grandmother cells that fire only when two grandmother cells are simultaneously activated, the frequency of the original signal can be retrieved with increasingly greater precision. Therefore, it seems reasonable to propose the theory that intelligent people have a greater number of cortical elements arranged in some hierarchical order which permits finer analysis of signals. (p. 9)

There may well be other such hierarchical neural structures, probably of common epigenetic origin and hence correlated with individual differences, that play a part in many other forms of information processing besides auditory and visual discrimination. But as yet these ideas are only speculation at the cutting edge of cognitive neuroscience. We have a number of suggestive neurological correlates of _g_, but as yet these have not been integrated into a coherent neurophysiological theory of _g_. There are still too many missing pieces of the jigsaw puzzle to be able to assemble a complete picture.

Another mechanism that is coming into prominence in the study of information processing and has been proffered as an element in _g_ is the _inhibition_, or suppression, of irrelevant associations and reaction tendencies.[69] For example, reading comprehension, which is highly _g_ loaded, is hindered if irrelevant associations to ambiguous or double-meaning words (e.g., "bear" or "lean") are not inhibited by the context in which they occur. It is not yet clear, however, whether this type of inhibition is generally related to _g_ per se or to some narrower group factor.

Brain Mechanisms in Psychometric Group Factors. We know more about the neural substrate of specialized functions, some of them corresponding to the major group factors established by factor analysis, particularly the verbal and spatial visualization factors. Research on these specialized functions is made possible by using persons with localized brain injuries and persons with rare genetic defects. It is most interesting that these localized abnormalities in the brain, when they affect mental abilities, usually produce behavioral effects that coincide with one or another of the main mental ability group factors identified in the normal samples by factor analysis. Verbal ability and visual-spatial ability are prime examples. They are primarily localized in the left (verbal) and right (spatial) cerebral hemispheres, yet in normal persons performance on tests of verbal ability and of spatial ability is highly correlated, because the actual expression of these abilities in normal persons always involves *g*. Their separation from *g* in biologically normal persons is made possible only by factor analysis, but then they are not really observable abilities but are hypothetical independent verbal and spatial group factors which, along with other factors (especially *g*), are loaded in the behaviorally manifested abilities. The existence of the group factors, of course, necessarily implies that there are individual differences (either innate or acquired) in their causal underpinnings. Localized damage to the brain areas that normally subserve one of these group factors can leave the person severely impaired in the expression of the abilities loaded on the group factor, but with little or no impairment of abilities that are loaded on other group factors or on *g*.

A classic example of this is females who are born with a chromosomal anomaly known as Turner's syndrome.[70] Instead of having the two normal female sex chromosomes (designated XX), they lack one X chromosome (hence are designated XO). Provided no spatial visualization tests are included in the IQ battery, the IQs of these women (and presumably their levels of *g*) are normally distributed and virtually indistinguishable from that of the general population. Yet their performance on all tests that are highly loaded on the spatial-visualization factor is extremely low, typically borderline retarded, even in Turner's syndrome women with verbal IQs above 130. It is as if their level of *g* is almost totally unreflected in their level of performance on spatial tasks.

It is much harder to imagine the behavior of persons who are especially deficient in all abilities involving *g* and all of the major group factors, but have only one group factor that remains intact. In our everyday experience, persons who are highly verbal, fluent, articulate, and use a highly varied vocabulary, speaking with perfect syntax and appropriate expression, are judged to be of at least average or probably superior IQ. But there is a rare and, until recently, little-known genetic anomaly, Williams syndrome,[71] in which the above-listed characteristics of high verbal ability are present in persons who are otherwise severely mentally deficient, with IQs averaging about 50. In most ways, Williams syndrome persons appear to behave with no more general capability of getting along in the world than most other persons with similarly low IQs. As adults, they display only the most rudimentary scholastic skills and must live under supervision. Only their spoken verbal ability has been spared by this genetic defect. But their verbal ability appears to be "hollow" with respect to *g*. They speak in complete, often complex, sentences, with good syntax, and even use unusual words appropriately. (They do surprisingly well on the Peabody Picture Vocabulary Test.) In response to a series of pictures, they can tell a connected and fully elaborated story, accompanied by appropriate, if somewhat exaggerated, emotional expression. Yet they have exceedingly little ability to reason, or to explain or summarize the meaning of what they say. On most spatial ability tests they generally perform on a par with Down syndrome persons of comparable IQ, but they also differ markedly from Down persons in peculiar ways. Williams syndrome subjects are more handicapped than IQ-matched Down subjects in figure copying and block designs.

Comparing Turner's syndrome with Williams syndrome obviously suggests the generalization that a severe deficiency of one group factor in the presence of an average level of *g* is far less a handicap than an intact group factor in the presence of a very low level of *g*.

The Relationship between Brain Modules and *g*. It is now well established that the brain has many differentiated modules for various specialized functions, including certain forms of information processing. The modules associated with some abilities in the cognitive domain are sources of individual differences that are statistically independent of the common source of individual differences attributable to *g*. In other words, individual differences in functions associated with various modules are not perfectly correlated across modules. But there is no inherent contradiction whatsoever between the existence of *g* and the existence of distinct brain modules for certain abilities.

Largely on the basis of such functional and neurological assemblies, Howard Gardner has proposed a model of the mind, referred to as "multiple intelligences," that includes seven distinct "intelligences": *linguistic, logical-mathematical, spatial, musical, body-kinesthetic, interpersonal* (understanding and influencing others), and *intrapersonal* (understanding oneself).[72a] Gardner has written a fascinating book[72b] of psychobiographical sketches of seven illustrious twentieth-century geniuses he regards as exemplars of each of these "intelligences": T. S. Eliot, Albert Einstein, Pablo Picasso, Igor Stravinsky, Martha Graham, Mahatma Gandhi, and Sigmund Freud.

The first three of Gardner's "multiple intelligences" (linguistic, logical-mathematical, and spatial) have repeatedly emerged from factor analyses performed over the last fifty years or so as major group factors. Measures of musical ability have been included in too few factor analyses with a wide enough variety of other psychometric tests to definitely characterize its status in the total hierarchical factor structure of human abilities. However, as some of the basic components of musical aptitude are known to be correlated with highly *g*-loaded tests, it seems a safe prediction that a battery of musical aptitude tests, such as the Seashore battery, if factor analyzed among a large number of other non-musical cognitive tests, would emerge either as a first-order or second-order group factor (called "musical aptitude") and would be substantially loaded on *g*.

Little is known about the factor structure of the three remaining "intelligences" (body-kinesthetic, interpersonal, and intrapersonal) and it is even arguable from a factor analytic viewpoint whether they should even be included in the cognitive domain, so calling them "intelligences" may be a misnomer. But it hardly matters, because "intelligence" has no proper scientific meaning anyway. This is not to deny the undoubted behavioral reality of these individual characteristics, but "body-kinesthetic" may be more appropriately considered as aspects of motor skills and coordination, and "interpersonal" and "intrapersonal" may be aspects of personality rather than abilities. It has not yet been objectively determined where these qualities fit into the factorial structure of human traits.

A question largely neglected by Gardner concerns the extent to which a high level on any of these abilities would be advantageous to an individual in the absence of some fairly high threshold level of *g*. Gardner has stated that the manifestation of one of his multiple "intelligences" at a level of scientific, artistic, or social significance such as illustrated by his list of famous exemplars depend on a threshold IQ of at least 120. This minimum IQ cutoff of 120, of course, excludes the 90 percent of the population who are below this level. (Many psychologists would probably set the threshold at IQ 130 or more, thus excluding 98 percent of the population.) It is noteworthy that so-called idiots savants who manifest one of the multiple "intelligences" despite having a very low IQ are never considered as outstanding mathematicians, musicians, artists, or dancers; and exceedingly few, if any, are able to earn a living by their special talent. An average or above-average level of *g* seems an essential condition for the intellectually or artistically significant expression of any special talent in the cognitive domain.

The Question of the Unity or Disunity of *g*. The question of whether *g* is the result of individual differences in some single process or in a number of different processes[73] is probably answerable only if one takes into consideration different levels of analysis. At the level of conventional or complex psychometric tests, *g* appears to be unitary. But at some level of analysis of the processes correlated with *g* it will certainly be found that more than a single process is responsible for *g*, whether these processes are at the level of the processes measured by elementary cognitive tasks, or at the level of neurophysiological processes, or even at the molecular level of neural activity. If successful performance on every complex mental test involves, let us say, two distinct, uncorrelated processes, A and B (which are distinguishable and measurable at some less complex level than that of the said tests) in addition to any other processes that are specific to each test or common only to certain groups of tests, then in a factor analysis all tests containing A and B will be loaded on a general factor.

At this level of analysis, this general factor will forever appear unitary, although it is actually the result of two separate processes, A and B.

To show that the general factor involves individual differences in two independent processes, A and B, and is therefore not fundamentally unitary would require that individual differences in A and B be measured separately and that A and B are each independently correlated with the general factor of the psychometric tests. The more difficult condition to satisfy (which has been the basis of contention on this issue) is that it must be assumed that the empirical _g_ factor scores derived from the tests are "pure" _g_ uncontaminated by any non-_g_ "impurities" that constitute some of the variance in the measures of processes A or B. Because it is virtually impossible to prove definitively that the _g_ factor scores are "pure" in this sense, the issue retreats from the scientific arena, and it then becomes a purely metaphysical question whether _g_ is or is not unitary. However, the fact that _g_ has all the characteristics of a polygenic trait (with a substantial component of nongenetic variance) and is correlated with a number of complexly determined aspects of brain anatomy and physiology, as indicated in Chapter 6, makes it highly probable that _g_, though unitary at a psychometric level of analysis, is not unitary at a biological level.

NOTES

1. The defining criteria of a ratio scale are that it has: (1) a true zero point and (2) units of measurement that represent equal intervals or increments of the thing or dimension being measured. An ordinary thermometer (whether centigrade or Fahrenheit), for example, is an equal-interval scale, but it is not a ratio scale, because it lacks a true zero point. In the case of the centigrade thermometer, the $0°$ C point is arbitrarily set at the freezing point of distilled water at sea level; $100°$ C is set at the boiling point. The true zero point is $273°$ below $0°$ C, which is the absolute limit of "coldness." The Kelvin thermometer, which is a ratio scale, measures temperature from its absolute zero point, so that the freezing point of water is $273°$ K. Ratios between the measurements are meaningless on any scale that is not a true ratio scale. For example, $100°$ C does not represent twice as much heat as $50°$ C, because on the absolute Kelvin scale these temperatures are $373°K/323°K = 1.15$, not 2. Similarly, an IQ of 100 does not represent twice as much "intelligence" as an IQ of 50. Statements often seen in the popular press, such as "children have developed half of their adult level of intelligence by the age of four," are wholly nonsensical unless "intelligence" can be measured on one and the same equal-interval ratio scale at age four and at maturity. At present there is no psychometric test that has the ratio scale properties that could justify such a statement. The actual shape of the mental growth curve (beyond saying that it is an increasing monotonic function of age, from infancy to maturity) cannot be known without ratio scale measurements of mental ability. However, a true growth curve of increasing ability could be plotted from measurements based on time (e.g., "X milliseconds to process one bit of information"). The question then is whether the ratio scale measurements based on time adequately represent a construct of scientific or practical importance as indicated by significant relations to other phenomena of interest, such as psychometric _g_.

2. Johnson et al. (1985) analyzed virtually all of Galton's data by means of the

analysis of variance and found significant differences in RT (and various measures of discrimination) according to educational and occupation level. Though significant, the differences are trivial and unimpressive in themselves, but if their statistical significance had been known earlier it would have alerted investigators to the possibility that more reliable measurements might reveal theoretically important relationships between RT and various commonsense criteria of high, medium, and low levels of mental ability.

3. For a brief review of the history of research on reaction time (and references to the historical literature), see Jensen, 1982a. Deary (1994a) has reviewed the early history of tests of sensory discrimination and RT in the study of intelligence and has corrected some of the most common misconceptions about this work that have long been perpetuated in many psychology textbooks. It is a remarkable demonstration of how the scientific and academic zeitgeist can act as a sieve in determining which kinds of research, methodologies, and empirical evidence can get into the basic textbooks in the field, or be fairly assessed if it is mentioned at all. The typical textbook misrepresentation of the Galtonian approach to the study of human mental ability gave it virtually an outcaste status for at least half a century during which empirical research in this vein remained in the doldrums. As a consequence, the Galtonian line of investigation has had to overcome enormous prejudice to gain its recent ascendance.

4. The most prominent figures in the first decade of the revival of chronometric, information-processing approaches to the study of individual differences are here listed chronologically according to their first influential publication on the subject: H. J. Eysenck (1967), Earl Hunt et al. (1973), John B. Carroll (1976), and Robert J. Sternberg (1977). Eysenck (1987b) provides an overview of the theoretical and empirical status of research on speed of information processing in the recent study of individual differences.

5. An introduction to chronometric techniques and descriptions of the elementary cognitive tasks most widely used (ECTs) in research on individual differences in information processing is given in Jensen, 1985c. Studies of the relationship between reaction time and IQ are reviewed by Jensen (1982a, 1982b). A variety of ECTs and the results of some of the studies using them are presented in the collection of articles edited by Vernon (1987a).

6. In ECTs, the reliability of the total score (either mean or median RT over all trials) as a function of the number of trials conforms remarkably well to the reliability coefficient predicted by the Spearman-Brown prophecy formula. Therefore, the observed reliability of the total score based on a given number of trials permits one to determine (via the Spearman-Brown formula) the number of trials that would be needed to achieve any desired level of reliability.

7. Because the frequency distribution of a person's single-trial reaction times is always skewed (positively), the median RT (or MT) is a better measure of the distribution's central tendency than the mean RT. Studies in my chronometric laboratory have shown that the median RT has slightly higher internal consistency reliability and higher test-retest reliability than the mean.

8. A highly technical and mathematically sophisticated treatment of the experimental conditions affecting RT is given in the book by mathematical psychologist Duncan Luce (1986), which also contains the most extensive bibliography available on the experimental psychology of RT. This literature impresses one that the experimental study of RT has become as much an exact science as physics or chemistry. The topic of individual differences in RT, however, is not considered in Luce's monograph or its bibliography.

A comparable monograph on this subject would be a worthwhile contribution to psychological science.

9. Hick, 1952. A succinct explanation of Hick's formulation and a comprehensive review of the literature on individual differences in the variables derived from the Hick paradigm and their correlations with IQ are provided in Jensen, 1987d.

10. Jensen, Schafer, & Crinella, 1981.

11. Morris & Hopkins, 1995.

12. Frearson & Eysenck (1986); Jensen, 1992d; 1993d; Jensen & Whang, 1993.

13. Diascro & Brody (1994); Jensen, 1987e, pp. 111–118.

14. Sternberg, S. (1966, 1969).

15. Jensen, 1987f.

16. Smith & McPhee, 1987.

17. Posner, 1978, pp. 35–49.

18. Hunt et al., 1975.

19. Vernon, 1983. This and many subsequent studies by P. A. Vernon have used this version of the Posner paradigm.

20. Jensen, Larson, & Paul, 1988.

21. Jensen, Cohn, & Cohn, 1989.

22. Digit span is measured by the largest number of digits a person can repeat without error on two consecutive trials after the digits have been presented at the rate of one digit per second, either aurally or visually. Recalling the digits in the order of presentation is termed forward digit span (FDS); recalling the digits in the reverse order of presentation is termed backward digit span (BDS). Digit span is a part of the Stanford-Binet and of the Wechsler scales. Digit span increases with age, from early childhood to maturity. In adults, the average FDS is about 7; average BDS is about 5. I have found that Berkeley students, whose average IQ is about 120, have an average FDS of between 8 and 9 digits.

23. Cavanagh (1972); Kail, 1994.

24. Kyllonen & Christal, 1990. This article issues from the large-scale program of research on individual differences in speed of information processing being conducted at the Brooks Air Force Base; it has references to much of the other important research from this program. Later important studies in this research program are by Kyllonen, 1993, 1994. A study by Roberts et al. (1988) shows how changes in task complexity experimentally introduced into the Hick paradigm by the dual-task method increase its correlation with Raven's matrices.

25. Brand & Deary (1982) and Nettelbeck (1987) review most of the literature on the methods and findings of IT research; their references will lead readers to more than 90 percent of the IT literature. An excellent integrative overview of IT and its relation to RT, evoked potentials, and IQ is provided by Deary & Stough (1996).

26. Raz, Willerman, et al., 1983.

27. (a) Kranzler & Jensen, 1989. (b) The correlations used in this analysis are in Kranzler & Jensen (1991a, Table A-7) and in Carroll (1991b, Table 5).

28. Lynn, Wilson, & Gault, 1989. A study by Deary (1994b) obtained correlations between the nontimed Seashore pitch discrimination test (PD), auditory inspection time (AIT), the Mill Hill Vocabulary test (MHV), and Raven's Standard Progressive Matrices (SPM) on 108 thirteen-year-old students. (The score on AIT was a factor-score composite of two different methods of measuring AIT.) The *g* loadings (here represented by the first unrotated principal component) of these four variables are as follows (AIT is re-

flected so that "goodness" of performance is positively correlated between all variables): PD = .36, AIT = .72, MHV = .77, SPM = .78. Although there are too few variables here to permit a hierarchical factor analysis, a principal factor analysis would have been preferable to the principal components analysis used by Deary. I have performed a principal factor analysis on the correlations given by Deary. The first principal factor (i.e., the "*g*" of this matrix) is the only significant factor (i.e., eigenvalue > 1). Its loadings in the four variables are as follows: PD = .21, AIT = .58, MHV = .65, SPM = .66.

29. Holt & Matson, 1974; Beer et al., 1989.

30. Vernon & Kantor, 1986; Vernon, Nador, & Kantor, 1985.

31. Cerella, 1985; Salthouse, 1985.

32. Libet, 1985, 1987; Libet et al., 1991. These papers are probably the best introduction to Libet's work and they provide references to much of his other work on the neural basis-of conscious experience.

33. Jensen, 1992d.

34. Larson & Alderton, 1990; Kranzler, 1992.

35. (a) Nettelbeck, 1985; (b) Jensen, Schafer, & Crinella, 1981; (c) Vernon, 1981a, 1987c; (d) Kail, 1992; (e) Kail, 1991; (f) Cerella, 1985; (g) Jensen, Cohn, & Cohn, 1989; (h) Cohn, Carlson, & Jensen, 1985; (i) Kranzler, Whang, & Jensen, 1994; (j) Jensen, Larson, & Paul, 1988.

36. Levine, Preddy, & Thorndike, 1987.

37. Two methods for combining RTs have been used: multiple regression and simple summation. In multiple regression, a different weight is given to each of the RT variables before they are summed for each subject; the weights (obtained by multiple regression analysis) are such as to maximize the correlation (now called a *multiple correlation, R*) between the weighted sum of the several RT variables and IQ (or whatever is the criterion or dependent variable). When the sample size is very large and the number of predictor variables (also called independent variables) is small, there is very little bias in the multiple *R*. (*R* is always biased upward.) The smaller the subject sample size and the larger the number of predictor variables, the more that the true *R* is overestimated. On the other hand, there is no such bias (or "capitalization on chance") in a simple sum of the predictor variables, although the simple sum will not yield quite as large a correlation (*r*) as the multiple *R*. In most studies using multiple *R*, however, the *R* is corrected for bias. When the RTs from different ECTs have significantly different means, their combination in effect gives differential weights to the various ECTs. This may or may not be desirable, depending on the researcher's purpose and the nature of the hypothesis being tested. When it is not considered desirable, it is preferable either to use multiple regression analysis to obtain the multiple *R*, or to assign unit weights to the RTs of the various ECTs. This is done by transforming all of the RTs (separately for each ECT) to standardized (*z*) scores and averaging these to obtain each subject's unit-weighted RT *z* score.

38. Vernon, 1988.

39. The multiple *R* is not signed because it can never be less than zero. The multiple *R*s shown here, however, represent negative correlations, because each of the predictor variables (RT or RTSD) entered into the multiple regression equation is negatively correlated with the dependent variable (IQ).

40. It should be recalled that the proportion of IQ variance accounted for by RT is the square of the correlation between IQ and RT. Because the heritability coefficient is the proportion of (IQ) variance accounted for by genetic factors, we must compare the

RT × IQ correlation *squared* with the heritability coefficient. Taking the upper-range RT × IQ correlation, for example, as .70 and the heritability as .70, one can say that the RT measure accounts for $100(.70^2/.70) = 70$ percent of the heritable variance in IQ, assuming the genetic variance of IQ is the only variance in common between IQ and RT. (*Note*: If the heritability coefficient for, say, IQ is h^2, then the correlation between the phenotypic and genotypic IQ is $\sqrt{h^2} = h$.)

41. Probably the simplest and clearest factor analysis of combined ECTs and psychometric tests is the study by Levine et al. (1987), in which verbal, quantitative, and spatial psychometric tests were analyzed along with RTs from ECTs based on verbal, quantitative, and spatial contents. The largest single factor analysis of this kind was performed by John B. Carroll (1991b; see also Carroll, 1993a, pp. 484–485) on data from the Berkeley chronometric laboratory (described in Kranzler & Jensen, 1991a). Carroll entered 38 variables into the hierarchical factor analysis—27 from ECTs (of the types described earlier in this chapter) and 11 psychometric tests (Raven's Advanced Progressive Matrices and the 10 diverse verbal and nonverbal subtests of the Multidimensional Aptitude Battery). The subjects were 101 Berkeley undergraduates whose average IQ was 120, with a *SD* of about 10, or only two-thirds of the population *SD* of 15; therefore, one must bear in mind the restricted range of ability in this sample. Carroll's factor analysis, fully presented in his article, is quite complex because of the large number of ECT variables, and possibly also because some of the ECT variables (e.g., median RT and RTSD) are not experimentally independent, a condition that is problematic in factor analysis.

42. In Carroll's (1991b) factor analysis of twenty-seven chronometric variables and eleven psychometric tests, for example, the average loading of the chronometric variables (RT and RTSD) on the *g* factor is .47; their average loading on the non-*g* RT factors is .51. This implies that the average squared *uniqueness* (i.e., the proportion of variance due to specificity + error) of the RT and RTSD variables is about $(1 - .47^2 - .51^2) = .52$. (In the battery of mostly ECTs, the eleven psychometric tests have an average *g* loading of .35; their average loadings on the verbal [or *Gc*] and spatial factors are .61 and .47, respectively. The average squared uniqueness of the psychometric tests therefore is only .28.)

43. Jensen & Reed (1990) showed that simple RT (SRT) can act as a suppressor variable when it is entered into a multiple correlation with RTs based on more complex ECTs, such as choice RT (CRT) and Odd-Man-Out, to predict IQ. It should be noted, however, that when SRT is subtracted from the RT of a more complex ECT, say CRT, the difference has lower reliability than either of the original measurements. It is a general psychometric principle that the reliability of a difference score, say X − Y, is a function of the reliability coefficients of X and Y and the correlation r_{XY}:

$$r_{(X-Y)(X-Y)} = (r_{XX} + r_{YY} - 2r_{XY}) / (2 - 2r_{XY}).$$

Therefore, there is a trade-off (usually unequal) between two opposing effects: (1) the increased correlation of the difference CRT-SRT with *g* (as compared with the CRT × *g* correlation), and (2) the decreased reliability of the difference, CRT-SRT, which lowers the correlation of CRT-SRT with *g*. All this is fully explained, with empirical examples, in Jensen & Reed, 1990.

44. (a) McGue et al., 1984; (b) McGue & Bouchard, 1989; (c) Vernon, 1989a.

45. Jensen, Larson, & Paul, 1988.

46. The correlation between two phenotypic traits can be partitioned into genetic and environmental components. The genetic correlation indicates the degree to which the two correlated variables are pleiotropic or influenced by the same genes. The environmental (or better-called "nongenetic") correlation indicates the extent to which both variables have been subject to the same nongenetic influences. (The method for calculating the genetic correlation between two phenotypic variables is explained in Note 26 of Chapter 7.)

47. (a) Ho, Baker, & Decker, 1988; (b) Baker, Vernon, & Ho, 1991.

48. (a) Jenkinson, 1983; (b) Vernon, 1989b; (c) Vernon, 1983; (d) Kranzler & Jensen, 1991a.

49. (a) Smith & Stanley, 1987; (b) Larson, Merritt, & Williams, 1988; (c) Vernon & Jensen, 1984, (d) Nettelbeck & Rabbitt, 1992; (e) Hemmelgarn & Kehle, 1984.

50. (a) Alderton & Larson, 1994; (b) Chaiken, 1994; (c) Chaiken & Young, 1993. Brand (1987b) presents a trenchant critique of strategy theories of g.

51. (a) Ahern & Beatty, 1979; (b) Larson, Saccuzzo, & Brown, 1994.

52. Jensen (1987d, pp. 126–133) examined practice effects on the Hick paradigm in ten university students who were tested on nine occasions. The variance due to the regular downward trend in RT in the course of prolonged practice, though statistically significant, was much smaller than the variance due to individual differences; and the rank order of individual differences is fairly constant over the course of practice sessions distributed over nine days, as shown by the high reliability of individual differences in the RTs summed over all nine practice sessions for each of the ten subjects.

53. Neubauer & Freudenthaler, 1994. This study used the well-known sentence verification test (SVT) introduced by Baddeley, known as the "star above plus" test. Various statements of this type are presented, followed by a picture of a star (*) above (or below) a plus sign (+), to which the subject responds by pressing buttons labeled **T** (true) or **F** (false). The terms **star** and **plus** are randomly interchanged, and the intermediate words, also occurring at random, are **above, below, not above, not below**. This experiment permits measurement of two kinds of RT: Comprehension RT and Verification RT. After the appearance of the "statement," the subject, having read it, presses a button to bring up the picture on a display screen. (The interval between onset of the "statement" and pressing the button is the *Comprehension* RT, or CRT.) The subject evaluates the picture and "verifies" it as either true or false by pressing the appropriate button. (The interval between the onset of the picture and pressing the "verification" button is the *Verification* RT, or VRT.) The effects of practice on the RT-IQ correlation follow different (downward) trajectories and asymptotes at different points for CRT and VRT. Both are correlated with IQ after nearly 2,700 practice trials, with rs of $-.22$ and $-.39$ for CRT and VRT, respectively.

54. Ericsson & Charness, 1994.

55. Thompson's (1985) primer gives an excellent overview of this subject.

56. Excellent examples of neurological approaches to understanding cognitive phenomena are seen in the articles by Gazzaniga (1989) and Posner et al. (1988). Also coming into prominence is the field of *artificial neural networks* (ANN), in which various neural models suggested by research in the neurosciences can be computerized. The interplay between neuroscience and ANN should prove valuable in testing theoretical models of the neural design features of the brain proposed to explain certain cognitive phenomena (Freedman, 1994).

57. Goldman-Rakic (1994) reviews evidence from bilateral prefrontal ablation studies

in monkeys and from human performance on working memory tests in persons with lesions in the prefrontal area, the part of the brain that is larger and more highly developed in humans than in any other species. They both show marked impairment of the normal functions associated with working memory (a part of the short-term memory system). Long-term memory (LTM), however, remained perfectly intact in these cases. Impairment of consolidating (or later retrieving) recently acquired information in LTM is associated with lesions of the hippocampus, located near the base of the brain far from the frontal lobes. The short-term and long-term memory systems are quite distinct, both in brain localization and in function.

58. The speed of nerve impulses was unknown until the mid-nineteenth century, when Hermann von Helmholtz (1821–1894) measured nerve conduction velocity (NCV), first in frogs, later in humans. Earlier it was generally believed that nerve conduction had infinite velocity. On the basis of this belief, Immanuel Kant (1724–1804) even argued that mental activity could never come under scientific measurement or investigation. Shortly before Helmholtz's discovery, a leading physiologist of the time, Johann Müller (1823–1900), was more optimistic than Kant. He argued that the speed of nerve conduction was not infinite but cautiously claimed its velocity was sixty times greater than the speed of light! We now know it actually averages closer to one-third the speed of sound. NCVs are highly variable, depending on the location of the neuron, its diameter, the amount of myelination (fatty insulation surrounding the axon), temperature, and certain biochemical conditions. Hence NCVs range from a few miles per hour to nearly 200 miles per hour—quite a bit slower indeed than the speed of light (186,282 miles per second).

59. (a) Schafer et al., 1982; (b) Kutas et al., 1977.

60. A useful analogy for WM is of a juggler who can juggle, say, 5 balls (e.g., bits of information). That is, his *capacity* is 5 balls (or bits). If, while he is juggling 5 balls, someone tosses him another ball, he must drop a ball to catch the new ball and in the act of catching the new ball may even drop another ball, thereby ending up with only 4 balls. (Like a person with a digit span of 5 being given 6 digits and being able to recall only 4.) If, while juggling 5 balls, the juggler tries to place 1 ball on a table (e.g., get it into LTM), this action causes him to drop another ball, so he is left with 1 ball on the table and only 3 still being juggled; the fourth ball is "lost." WM seems to operate in much the same fashion. But this analogy shouldn't be carried any further.

61. Jensen, 1992c, 1992e, 1993c.

62. (a) Lehrl & Fischer, 1988, 1990. I have translated the symbols used by these German authors, which are antimnemonic for readers of English, to the initial letters for Capacity, Speed, and Duration. (b) Kline, Draycott, & McAndrew, 1994. (c) The g (principal factor I) loadings of the variables were C = .92, S =.84, D = .49; Raven = .44, Vocabulary = .52. The latter two loadings are smaller than would normally be expected, most likely because these relatively easy tests have a more restricted range in a college sample than the timed tests used for measuring S and D. Personality factors were also measured in this study, but were negligibly related to the cognitive factors. A measure of LTM (discriminative recognition memory) for past-presented nonsense syllables showed a loading of only .18 on the PFI. This is consistent with the general finding that tests of rote memory of material of low meaningfulness have little g loading. (d) More recently, Draycott & Kline (1994) published another study of the Erlangen theory and methodology and found that the S measure was highly loaded on Gc (mainly defined by verbal ability in an obliquely rotated factor analysis) but had a negligible

loading on *Gf*. This study, based on an unusually small sample size (65) in relation to the number of tests (20) entered into the factor analysis and the number of factors extracted (4) calls for replication. Also, it is essential that a *g* factor (not just *Gc* and *Gf* as rotated primary factors) be extracted. It also seems likely that the Erlangen measure of S (processing speed) is factorially too narrow, containing a specific verbal factor, causing it to load more on *Gc* than on *Gf*. A composite measure of speed derived from tasks of varied content would almost certainly be more highly loaded on *Gf* and on *g*.

63. Jensen, 1992d, 1993b.

64. Anderson (1994) has proposed a different neural model to explain this particular phenomenon. Using a neural network type of model based on the specific pattern of the connections between neurons, data simulated by computer showed a good fit to the empirically observed differences typically found between retarded and average persons in the non-Gaussian characteristics of the frequency distribution of an individual's RTs obtained over many trials. Like the neural oscillation model, it attempts to explain the striking phenomenon that retarded persons' fastest RTs differ much less from the fastest RTs of average persons than the difference between the slowest RTs of retarded and average persons. This phenomenon is evident between higher- and lower-IQ subjects within every segment of the range of IQs we have examined, from IQs of 50 to 150. Graphic plots of such data can be seen in Jensen, 1982a, Figures 17, 18, 19.

65. (a) Fairbank et al., 1991; (b) Jensen, 1992. (c) Callaway, 1979; (d) Barrett, Daum, & Eysenck, 1990. To the best of my knowledge, there has been no explicit study of intraindividual variability in IT (inspection time), probably because of the difficulty, perhaps even impossibility, of measuring the kind of intraindividual variability in IT that can be measured as RTSD in studies of reaction time.

66. Miller, 1994. The summary from Miller's lengthy article indicates the wide variety of lines of evidence he has surveyed relating myelin to *g*:

Many observations concerning intelligence could be explained if much variance in intelligence reflects myelination differences. More intelligent brains show faster nerve conduction, less glucose utilization in positron emission tomography, faster reaction times, faster inspection times, faster speeds in general, greater circumference and volume, smaller standard deviation in reaction times, greater variability in EEG measures, shorter white matter T^2 relaxation times, and higher gray-white matter contrast with magnetic resonance imaging. Also explainable are peculiarities of the increased reaction times and standard deviations with number of choices and complexity, reaction time skewness, the shorter latencies in evoked potentials, shorter latencies to the P300 wave, the high glial to neuron ratio in Einstein's brain, less glucose utilization per unit volume in large brains, certain results related to lipids, essential fatty acids, and cholesterol in adults and premature babies, and the survival of genes for lower intelligence. Children's improved performance with maturation might result from myelination. The slowing of response times with age, the decline in intelligence, and increased T^1 relaxation times could be explained. Differential myelination in the mouse brain might be able to explain the heterosis observed for myelination, brain size, caudal nerve conduction velocity, and maze performance observed. (p. 803)

Consistent with this theory are the intriguing findings by Benton (1995, 1996), based on very large samples, that amount of fat in the diet and cholesterol level are related to faster choice RT. The relationship is apparent in both "blue collar" and "white collar" adults.

67. Certain ions (e.g., K^+ and Ca^{++}) are ubiquitous in all forms of chemical neurotransmission and variations in their concentrations and transport could be among the physiological processes involved in *g*. Specific neurotransmitters, which vary widely and are keyed to localized regions and specialized functions, would be less likely candidates for explaining *g*.

68. Willerman & Raz, 1987.

69. Dempster & Brainerd (1994) have edited a collection of articles on theory and research on the construct of central inhibition in cognitive processing.

70. Bender, Linden, & Robinson, 1994.

71. Bellugi, Wang, & Jernigan, 1994.

72. (a) Gardner, 1983; (b) Gardner, 1993. Gardner's books are well worth reading, although he largely ignores the psychometric research literature, and I disagree with his apparently intentional but entirely unjustified exclusion of *g* in his theoretical system. Including *g* would, of course, subtract considerably from the variance accounted for by most of his other "intelligences" that are most highly *g* loaded. Critiques of Gardner's theory of "multiple intelligences" are provided by Brody (1992, pp. 34–40) and Carroll (1993a, pp. 641–642).

73. See the rather fruitless debate on the methodological problems of proving the "unity" or "disunity" of *g* in the series of articles by Kranzler & Jensen (1991a, 1991b, 1993) and Carroll (1991b, 1991c, 1993b).

Chapter 9

The Practical Validity of *g*

Practical validity is indicated by a significant and predictively useful correlation of a measurement with some educational, economic, or social criterion that is deemed important by many people. The *g* factor (and highly *g*-loaded test scores, such as the IQ) shows a more far-reaching and universal practical validity than any other coherent psychological construct yet discovered. It predicts performance to some degree in every kind of behavior that calls for learning, decision, and judgment. Its validity is an increasing monotonic function of the level of cognitive complexity in the predicted criterion. Even at moderate levels of complexity of the criterion to be predicted, *g* is the *sine qua non* of test validity. The removal of *g* (by statistical regression) from any psychometric test or battery, leaving only group factors and specificity, absolutely destroys their practical validity when they are used in a population that ranges widely in general ability.

The validity of *g* is most conspicuous in scholastic performance, not because *g*-loaded tests measure specifically what is taught in school, but because *g* is intrinsic to learning novel material, grasping concepts, distinctions, and meanings. The pupil's most crucial tool for scholastic learning beyond the primary grades—reading comprehension—is probably the most highly *g*-loaded attainment in the course of elementary education.

In the world of work, *g* is the main cognitive correlate and best single predictor of success in job training and job performance. Its validity is not nullified or replaced by formal education (independent of *g*), nor is it decreased by increasing experience on the job.

Although *g* has ubiquitous validity as a predictor of job performance, tests that tap other ability factors in addition to *g* may improve the predictive validity for certain types of jobs—tests of spatial ability for mechanical jobs and tests of speed and accuracy for clerical and secretarial jobs.

Meta-analyses of hundreds of test validation studies have shown that the validity of a highly _g_-loaded test with demonstrated validity for a particular job in a particular organizational setting is generalizable to virtually all other jobs and settings, especially within broad job categories.

The _g_ factor is also reflected in many broad social outcomes. Many social behavior problems, including dropping out of school, chronic welfare status, illegitimacy, child neglect, poverty, accident proneness, delinquency, and crime, are negatively correlated with _g_ or IQ independently of social class of origin. These social pathologies have an inverse monotonic relation to IQ level in the population, and show, on average, nearly five times the percentage of occurrence in the lowest quartile (IQ below 90) of the total distribution of IQ as in the highest quartile (IQ above 110).

So far, _g_ has been discussed strictly in terms of its psychometric and statistical features, its correlation with biological variables, its genetic and environmental determinants, and its relation to information-processing theory. These aspects of _g_ would be of little interest outside the strictly scientific realm if _g_ did not also have substantial correlations with variables that are of direct practical importance, both to individuals and to the welfare of society. This chapter presents the main evidence that _g_ is indeed the chief active ingredient responsible for the observed correlations between various widely used mental tests and many criteria of universally acknowledged importance in all civilized societies.

This chapter is not a detailed exposition of the statistical techniques for establishing test validity or a comprehensive review of the evidence for the predictive validity of the tests most commonly used for selection in education, employment, and the armed forces. (Entrée to the extensive literature on this can be found elsewhere.[11]) Rather, the focus is restricted to the role of _g_ per se in practical predictive validity.

Most validity studies have concerned particular tests, which often were constructed to yield predictive validity coefficients as high as possible for a particular criterion, such as success in college, or in certain types of jobs, or in specialized training schools in the armed forces. Such tests are typically loaded substantially with _g_ in addition to other factors intended to enhance their validity for some particular purpose. Surprisingly little of this applied literature on test validity, however, examines the degree to which _g_ itself, as compared to other factors and specificity, contributes to tests' validity. Fortunately, the few studies that focus specifically on this question have been conducted mostly by the armed forces and by the U.S. Employment Service of the Department of Labor. These studies, based on huge samples, are technically excellent.

PSYCHOMETRIC PRINCIPLES OF VALIDITY

THE ASSESSMENT OF PREDICTIVE VALIDITY

A test's practical validity is measured by its correlation with performance on some criterion that is external to the test. Such a correlation is termed a *validity coefficient*, and since it is a correlation coefficient, it of course has all the statistical properties of a correlation coefficient. It is simply the correlation, r_{xc} between a test score (x) and a measure of some criterion (c), such as college grade-point average, a rating of job performance, or a work sample.

Validity is said to be *predictive* if the test is administered *prior* to the assessment of the criterion performance. A college selection test such as the SAT, for example, may be used to predict a student's grade-point average at the end of the freshman year, or to predict how likely the student is to graduate.

Many types of correlation coefficient can be used to measure validity. The Pearson r is the most commonly used. A multiple correlation coefficient (R) is used when two or more test scores (or other kinds of quantified variables) are used in combination to predict the criterion.

The particular value of a given validity coefficient should *not* be thought of as an intrinsic property of a test. Conceptually, a validity coefficient is *specific* to the conditions under which it was determined. These include the nature of the criterion, the reliability of the test, the reliability of the criterion measurement, and the range of individual differences in test-related ability in the subject pool for which prediction of the criterion variable is made. The degree of *generalizability* of a given test's validity for predicting a variety of different criteria, and its generalizability across different subject pools (e.g., males, females, and different ethnic or cultural groups) is an empirical issue that has great importance for the practical use of tests in selection. (It is discussed later in this chapter.)

The most fundamental fact about test validity is that the magnitude, or numerical value, of a test's validity coefficient results from the degree of congruence between the factor composition of the test and the factor composition of the criterion. The validity coefficient is also affected to some degree (often negligible) by a kind of specificity that usually does not show up in the factor composition of a test battery, namely, common *method* variance. This is some feature of the measurement procedure per se that is common to both the test and the criterion. For example, the predictor variable X may be a paper-and-pencil aptitude test and the criterion may be a paper-and-pencil test of job knowledge. Some part of the correlation r_{xc}, then, could be the result of the method variance (i.e., use of paper-and-pencil tests). Whatever part of the correlation r_{xc} is the result of measuring both the predictor and the criterion by the common method therefore spuriously inflates the validity coefficient to some degree. Such spurious inflation of the validity coefficient occurs only if there are reliable individual differences in whatever constitutes the method variance; otherwise the particular method variance does not even exist and therefore is not reflected in the validity coefficient.

The validity coefficient is also affected by the reliability of the test and the reliability of the criterion. It is also affected by the range of ability in the subject pool, as reflected both in the test and in the measure of the criterion. If the variance observed in the criterion measurement does not include some of the same ability factors measured by the test, of course, there is no possibility of the test's having any predictive validity. The reliability of the test and the range of ability in the subject pool, both of which affect the size of the validity coefficient, can be determined independently of validity, and the observed validity coefficient can be precisely corrected for attenuation (unreliability) and for restriction of range.

Correction of the validity coefficient for restriction of range is essential when the correlation (i.e., the raw validity coefficient) between the test and the criterion is determined in a subject sample that was not randomly selected from a larger unselected subject pool but rather was selected on the basis of test scores. The test-selected group will have a restricted range of ability compared to the total subject pool, and the validity of the test in the total pool will be underestimated by the observed correlation between test scores and criterion performance in the selected group. Correction for range restriction of the validity coefficient obtained in a selected sample provides an estimate of the validity coefficient in the unrestricted subject pool. The corrected validity coefficient estimates the test's validity in preselecting persons who are the most likely to succeed on the criterion measure at a later time.

What exactly does a validity coefficient, r_{xc}, tell us in quantitative terms? There are several possible answers,[2] but probably the simplest is this: When test scores are expressed in standardized form (z_x) and the criterion measures are expressed in standardized form (z_c), then, if an individual's standardized score on a test is z_{xi}, the individual's predicted performance on the criterion is $z_{ci} = r_{xc} \times z_{xi}$. For example, if a person scores two standard deviations above the group mean on the test (i.e., $z_{xi} = +2$) and the test's validity coefficient is $+.50$ (i.e., $r_{xc} = +.50$), the person's predicted performance on the criterion would be one standard deviation above the group mean (i.e., $z_{ci} = r_{xc} \times z_{xi} = +.50 \times 2 = +1$).

Prediction is never without some margin of error (except in the unrealistic case where $r_{xc} = 1$). The lower the validity coefficient, the greater is the error of prediction. Errors of prediction (technically termed the *error of estimate*[3]) are random and hence evenly divided between overestimates and underestimates of the criterion. (Errors of prediction that are systematic, or nonrandom, and cause consistent over- [or under-] estimation of the criterion performance of certain identifiable groups relative to other groups in the population, constitute *test bias*.[4])

EDUCATION AND *g* VALIDITY

THE RELATION OF *g* TO LEARNING ABILITY

Strangely, the study of learning and the study of "intelligence" have advanced along quite different tracks throughout the history of psychology. Learning has been a province of experimental psychology, while "intelligence" is a province of psychometrics and differential psychology. Yet definitions of "intelligence" often include learning ability as perhaps second only to reasoning ability. Learning and "intelligence" have had separate research "genealogies" only because they are *conceptually* distinct phenomena, even though they are closely related in everyday reality.

Learning per se can be studied in an individual organism. All organisms with a nervous system, however rudimentary, are capable of learning. Learning is manifested as a change in behavior, or response tendency, as the result of prior experience or practice. More precisely, learning may be defined as an experientially acquired change in the strength or probability of occurrence of a particular overt or covert response in the presence of a particular stimulus. (Excluded from the definition of learning are changes in response tendency attributable to physical maturation of the nervous system, fatigue, illness, drug effects, brain damage, emotional state, or level of motivation.)

Memory is the retention, over some period of time, of the behavioral changes that resulted from learning. Forgetting is a lessening or loss of, or the momentary inability to retrieve, the changes that were acquired through learning. Theories of learning are mainly concerned with the nature of the experimentally manipulable conditions that affect the rate of change in a particular response tendency in an individual organism and the experimental conditions that affect the retention of what has been learned. Learning theorists have seldom shown any interest in the wide range of differences in learning rates across individuals subjected to the very same experimental conditions.

When we focus our attention on individual differences in *rate* of learning (under conditions of learning that are the same for all individuals), we move into the field of differential psychology. It is well known that different individuals need very different amounts of time to learn something to the same level of mastery, and some individuals are able to learn certain things that other individuals, given the same conditions of learning, are not able to learn at all.

All the knowledge possessed by any individual, of course, has had to be acquired through learning. It is obvious that there is a wide range of individual differences both in the rate of learning, the amount learned, and the upper level of complexity and abstractness of what can be learned at all. Hence, at any given age, people (even full siblings who are reared together) differ in the amount of knowledge and skills they possess. Some people acquire knowledge (i.e., learning *what*) and skills (i.e., learning *how*) some ten to twenty times faster than others.[5] In a typical school classroom, the fastest learners acquire knowledge and skills some five times faster than the slowest learners. By the time students reach their last year in high school there are some who are still having seemingly insurmountable trouble with long division and fractions while some others are learning calculus. These differences cannot be attributed merely to differences in opportunity, interest, or motivation. Laboratory experiments, in which the conditions of learning are highly controlled, have shown that individuals differ in the upper limit of complexity of the tasks or concepts that they are able to learn to a criterion of mastery, given any amount of time.

The question that concerns us here is the degree to which such individual differences in rate of learning per se are a function of *g*. As I have written a detailed article[6] on this subject, with references to virtually the entire literature on the relationship between learning and IQ, I will here only summarize the main conclusions, and then present some especially informative new research that was not available when I wrote my review.

There is ample evidence of a wide range of individual differences in time to learn (TTL) a given amount of material to a uniform level of mastery, and that TTL is correlated with IQ.[7] For some years, however, psychologists believed that IQ and TTL were almost totally unrelated. This misconception came about as a result of studies performed in the 1940s that looked for correlations between IQ and each of a variety of single learning tasks of the simple type used in laboratory experiments on human learning. In these studies, tasks were selected for which the tested subjects had no prior experience, and the content to be learned consisted of meaningless material, such as nonsense syllables (e.g., cev, gok, jex). The material had to be learned by rote, and an individual's learning rate was measured as either the amount learned in a set number of learning trials or the number of trials needed to learn the material to a criterion of mastery (i.e., the first trial on which every element in the task is performed without error). The typical measure of an individual's learning was a *gain score*, that is, the difference between a measure of the level of performance taken on the last trial (of a uniform number of learning trials given to every individual) and a measure of performance level on the initial trial.

These measures of learning indeed had surprisingly low correlations with IQ, especially when *gain scores* were used. In some studies there was even a negative correlation between gain scores and IQ. Since performance levels on both the first trial and the last trial are often correlated with IQ, a gain score created by taking the difference between the two eliminates much of the variance in scores attributable to individual differences in IQ. Hence the correlation between the gain-score measure of learning ability and IQ is spuriously deflated.

The chief cause of the low correlation between IQ and learning scores, however, is that most laboratory learning tasks are so narrowly specialized in the ability they call upon that their factor composition consists mostly of specificity. In this respect, a particular learning task is much like a single item in an IQ test. The variance of a single item consists mostly of specificity, and the correlations among single test items are typically between .10 and .20. The correlations between measures obtained from various laboratory learning tasks are scarcely larger than the correlations between the single items of IQ tests. However, when the correlations among a large number of learning tasks are factor analyzed, a general factor common to all of the learning tasks is revealed. This common factor could be called "general learning ability."

The important point is that this general learning ability factor is highly correlated with the *g* factor extracted from psychometric tests, and seems to be essentially nothing other than *g*. When a number of learning tasks and a number of psychometric tests of mental abilities are all entered into the same correlation matrix and factor analyzed, they are found to share a large common factor which is indistinguishable from psychometric *g*. In fact, there is no general learning factor (that is, a factor common to all learning tasks) that is independent of psychometric *g*. The general factor of each domain—learning and psychometric abilities—is essentially one and the same *g*.

Certain kinds of learning tasks, of course, are more *g* loaded than others. Concept learning and the acquisition of learning sets (i.e., generalized learning-to-learn), for example, are more *g* loaded than rote learning, trial-and-error learning, and perceptual-motor skills learning. Attempts to devise tests of "learning potential" in which the subject is first tested on some task (or set of tasks), then given some standard instruction, coaching, or practice on the same or a similar task, and then retested to obtain a measure of the gain in task performance resulting from the interpolated coaching have proved to be a poor substitute for ordinary IQ tests. Standard IQ has higher validity for predicting scholastic achievement.[8] The existing tests of "learning potential," when used in conjunction with an IQ test, add virtually nothing to the predictive validity of the IQ when it is used alone, probably because the chief active ingredient in predictive validity is *g*, and tests of learning potential have not proved to be as good measures of *g* as conventional IQ tests.

Correlated Vectors Analysis of *g* and Learning Ability. Two large-scale studies[9] conducted by the U.S. Air Force provide the data needed to establish the central role of *g* in learning, as shown by the method of correlated vectors (which is explained in Chapter 6, p. 143, and Appendix B, p. 589). The experimental learning task consisted of a brief course intended to teach a basic knowledge of "logic gates."[10] Such knowledge is an essential element in troubleshooting failures in electronic equipment. The training program on this limited and clearly defined subject matter was entirely computerized and lasted about two hours. Having the training program completely computerized ensured uniform instruction for all subjects.

After completing the training program, the subjects were given a test devised to measure their accuracy in specifying the outputs of the various kinds of logic gates that were taught in the instructional program. A subject's performance on this test is here called his *learning score*. The subjects were also given the Armed Services Vocational Aptitude Battery (ASVAB), which consists of ten separately scored subtests (General Science, Arithmetic Reasoning, Word

Knowledge, Paragraph Comprehension, Numerical Operations, Coding Speed, Auto and Shop Information, Mathematical Knowledge, Mechanical Comprehension, Electronic Information).

The *validity* coefficients, or correlations of each of the separate ASVAB subtest scores with the learning scores (i.e., number correct on the "gates" test), ranged from +.39 (for both Auto and Shop Information) to +.65 (for Arithmetic), with an overall average validity coefficient of +.53. (The Electronic Information subtest had a validity coefficient of +.53, interestingly not as high as that for Arithmetic.)

Correlated Vectors. The correlation between the column vector composed of the ten ASVAB *validity* coefficients and the corresponding column vector of the ten ASVAB subtests' *g* loadings was +.82 in Study 1 and +.87 in Study 2. (The ASVAB subtests' *g* loadings were based on the nationally representative 1980 population sample of $N = 25,408,193$ youths; the validity coefficients were corrected for range restriction so as to be representative of the same population sample.) These data clearly indicate that individual differences in the amount learned during a course of instruction of uniform duration is related mostly to *g*.

SCHOLASTIC ACHIEVEMENT

The purpose of the first "intelligence" test, devised by Binet and Simon in 1905, was to assess elementary school children and identify those most likely to fail in the regular instructional program. These children would learn better with more specialized and individualized instruction suited to their below-average level of cognitive development. Since Binet's invention, there have been countless studies of the validity of mental tests for predicting children's scholastic performance. The *Psychological Abstracts* contains some 11,000 citations of studies on the relation of educational achievement to "IQ." If there is any unquestioned fact in applied psychometrics, it is that IQ tests have a high degree of predictive validity for many educational criteria, such as scores on scholastic achievement tests, school and college grades, retention in grade, school dropout, number of years of schooling, probability of entering college, and, after entering, probability of receiving a bachelor's degree. With equality of educational opportunity for the whole population increasing in recent decades, IQ has become even more predictive of educational outcomes than it was before the second half of this century.

The evidence for the validity of IQ in predicting educational variables is so vast and has been reviewed so extensively elsewhere[11] that there is no need to review it in detail here. The median validity coefficient of IQ for educational variables is about +.50, but the spread of validity coefficients is considerable, ranging from close to zero up to about .85. Most of the variability in validity coefficients is due to differences in the range of ability in the particular groups being tested. The less the variability of IQ in a given group, of course, the lower is the correlation ceiling that the IQ is likely to have with any criterion variable. Hence we see an appreciable decrease in the average validity coefficient for each rung of the educational ladder from kindergarten to graduate or professional school. Several rungs on the educational ladder are the main junctures for either dropping out or continuing in school.

The correlation of IQ with grades and achievement test scores is highest (.60 to .70) in elementary school, which includes virtually the entire child population and hence the full range of mental ability. At each more advanced educational level, more and more pupils from the lower end of the IQ distribution drop out, thereby restricting the range of IQs. The average validity coefficients decrease accordingly: high school (.50 to .60), college (.40 to .50), graduate school (.30 to .40). All of these are quite high, as validity coefficients go, but they permit far less than accurate prediction of a specific individual. (The standard error of estimate is quite large for validity coefficients in this range.)

Achievement test scores are more highly correlated with IQ than are grades, probably because grades are more influenced by the teacher's idiosyncratic perceptions of the child's apparent effort, personality, docility, deportment, gender, and the like. For example, teachers tend, on average, to give higher course grades to girls than to boys, although the boys and the girls scarcely differ on objective achievement tests.

Even when pupils' school grades are averaged over a number of years, so that different teachers' idiosyncratic variability in grading is averaged out, the correlation between grades and IQ is still far from perfect. A strong test of the overall relationship between IQ and course grades was provided in a study[12] based on longitudinal data from the Berkeley Growth Study. A general factor (and individual factor scores) was obtained from pupils' teacher-assigned grades in arithmetic, English, and social studies in grades one through ten. Also, the general factor (and factor scores) was extracted from the matrix of intercorrelations of Stanford-Binet IQs obtained from the same pupils on six occasions at one- to two-year intervals between grades one and ten. Thus we have here highly stable measures of both school grades and IQs, with each individual's year-to-year fluctuations in IQ and teachers' grades averaged out in the general factor scores for IQ and for grades.

The correlation between the general factor for grades and the general factor for Stanford-Binet IQ was +.69. Corrected for attenuation, the correlation is +.75. This corrected correlation indicates that pupils' grades in academic subjects, although highly correlated with IQ, also reflect consistent sources of variance that are independent of IQ. The difficulty in studying or measuring the sources of variance in school grades that are not accounted for by IQ is that they seem to consist of a great many small (but relatively stable) sources of variance (personality traits, idiosyncratic traits, study habits, interests, drive, etc.) rather than just a few large, measurable traits. This is probably why attempts to improve the prediction of scholastic performance by including personality scales along with cognitive tests have shown little promise of raising predictive validity appreciably above that attributable to IQ alone. In the noncognitive realm, no general factor, or any combination of broad group factors, has been discovered that appreciably increases the predictive validity over and above the prediction from IQ alone.

Although IQ tests are highly _g_ loaded, they also measure other factors in addition to _g_, such as verbal and numerical abilities. It is of interest, then, to ask how much the reported validity of IQ for predicting scholastic success can be attributed to _g_ and how much to other factors independent of _g_.

The psychometrician Robert L. Thorndike[13] analyzed data specifically to answer this question. He concluded that 80 to 90 percent of the _predictable_ variance in scholastic performance is accounted for by _g_, with 10 to 20 percent of the variance predicted by other factors measured by the IQ or other tests. This should not be surprising, since highly _g_-loaded tests that contain no verbal or numerical factors or information content that resembles anything taught in school (the Raven matrices is a good example) are only slightly less correlated with various measures of scholastic performance than are the standard IQ and scholastic aptitude tests, which typically include some scholastic content. Clearly the predictive validity of _g_ does not depend on the test's containing material that children are taught in school or at home. Pupils' grades in different academic subjects share a substantial common factor that is largely _g_.[14]

The reason that IQ tests predict academic achievement better than any other measurable variable is that school learning itself is _g_-demanding. Pupils must continually grasp "relations and correlates" as new material is introduced, and they must transfer previously learned knowledge and skills to the learning of new material. These cognitive activities, when specifically investigated, are found to be heavily _g_ loaded. It has also been found that various school subjects differ in their _g_ demands. Mathematics and written composition, for example, are more _g_-demanding than arithmetic computation and spelling. Reading comprehension is so _g_ loaded and also so crucial in the educational process as to warrant a separate section (p. 280).

The number of years of formal education that a person acquires is a relatively crude measure of educational attainment. It is quite highly correlated with IQ, typically between $+.60$ and $+.70$.[15] This correlation cannot be explained as entirely the result of more education causing higher IQ. A substantial correlation exists even if the IQ is measured at an age when all persons have had the same number of years of schooling. Validity coefficients in the range of .40 to .50 are found between IQ at age seven and amount of education completed by age 40.[16]

Equally important is the fact that the correlation between IQ and years of education is also a _within-family_ correlation. A within-family correlation (explained in Chapter 6, pp. 139) cannot be the result of differences in social class or other family background factors that siblings share in common. This is evident from a study[17] in which _g_ factor scores (derived from the first principal component of fifteen diverse mental tests) were obtained for adult full siblings (reared together). The *difference* between the siblings' g factor scores and the *difference* in their number of years of education was +.50 for brothers, +.17 for sisters, and +.34 for brother-sister pairs. (Similar correlations were found for siblings' differences in g and the differences in their occupational status.)

There is also a *between*-families component of the correlation between IQ and years of education associated with socioeconomic status (SES). More children at a given IQ level from high-SES families tend to be "overeducated" (i.e., are more likely to enter college) as compared with middle-SES and especially with low-SES children, who are less apt to enter college, given the same IQ as middle- and high-SES children.

Correlated Vectors. I have found only one study[18a] that provides the necessary data for a correlated vectors analysis of the relationship between tests' g loadings and their predictive validity for school and college grades. The Wechsler Adult Intelligence Scale (WAIS) was given to high school juniors and each of the eleven subtests was correlated with the students' class rank in grades at graduation. The WAIS Full Scale IQ was correlated +.62 with class rank. The column vector composed of the eleven WAIS subtests' g loadings (based on an independent comparable sample[18b]) was correlated +.73 with the column vector of the subtests' validity coefficients ($r = +.51$ after partialing out the vector of the subtests' reliability coefficients). The corresponding rank-order correlation is .68, $p < .05$.

The WAIS was also administered to entering college freshman. The Full Scale IQ correlated +.44 with the students' Grade Point Average (GPA) at the end of the first semester. (The correlation is lower for college students than for high school students, because of restriction of range of IQ in the college sample.) In the college sample, the vector of the WAIS subtests' g loadings (the same vector as above) was correlated +.91 with the vector of the subtests' correlations with freshman GPA ($r = +.83$ after partialing out the vector of the tests' reliability coefficients). The corresponding rank-order correlation is .92, $p < .01$.

Although the WAIS Full Scale IQ validity is lower for college freshman than for high school students (because of the greater restriction of range of IQ and of grades in the college sample), the correlated vectors suggest that college grades reflect g more than do high school grades.[19] This is probably because the college-level subject matter is more cognitively demanding and course grades are based more on examinations that reflect intellectual performance and less on teacher-perceived student characteristics that are less correlated with g, such as effort and classroom deportment.

Reading. It is common knowledge in psychometrics that a standardized test of reading comprehension is a good proxy for an IQ test. But this is true only if the persons tested are already skilled in *word reading*. In the psychology of reading, it is important to distinguish between the processes of *decoding* the symbols that constitute written or printed words (also known as "word reading") and *comprehension*, or understanding sentences and paragraphs.

The acquisition of decoding skill in young children is highly related to mental age (and to IQ in children of the same chronological age). But after word reading skill is fairly mastered, it is only weakly diagnostic of IQ or _g_. Children with average or above-average IQ who, with the typical reading instruction in the elementary grades, are still having trouble with word reading by age eight or nine are usually regarded as having a specific reading disability and are in need of expert diagnosis and special instruction.

Some 10 to 15 percent of school children are found to have a developmental reading disability. There are two main causes of reading problems, varying in severity and amenability to remediation. One is a slow rate of mental development (manifested as low IQ on nonverbal tests); the other is various forms of dyslexia, in which the reading disability is highly specific and unrelated to _g_. Children diagnosed as dyslexic may, in fact, obtain very high scores on _g_-loaded tests if the test does not require reading. Specific reading disabilities show up almost entirely in the decoding aspect of reading, and decoding per se is not highly _g_-demanding. However, unless the decoding process becomes highly _automatized_ (as described in Chapter 8, p. 246), it occupies _working memory_ (the central information-processing unit) to some extent, thereby hindering full comprehension of the material being read.

People differ much more in reading comprehension than in decoding skill. And it is reading comprehension that is the most unavoidable of the _g_-loaded activities in the whole educational process. The educational psychologist Edward L. Thorndike, as early as 1917, likened the process of reading comprehension to that of reasoning. He well described the aspects of reading comprehension that demand the full use of working memory and cause it to be highly _g_ loaded: "The mind is assailed as it were by every word in the paragraph. It must select, repress, soften, emphasize, correlate and organize, all under the influence of the right mental set or purpose or demand."[20] Every one of the verbs used here by Thorndike describes a _g_-related function.

It is probably because of the _g_ demand of reading comprehension that educators have noticed a marked increase in individual differences in scholastic performance, and its increased correlation with IQ, between the third and fourth grades in school. In grades one to three, pupils are _learning to read_. Beginning in grade four and beyond they are _reading to learn_. At this latter stage, a deficiency in decoding skills becomes a serious handicap for comprehension. The vast majority of pupils, however, acquires adequate decoding skill by grade four, and from there on, the development of reading comprehension, with its heavy _g_ saturation, closely parallels the pupil's mental age (as measured by IQ tests). Except for the small percentage of persons with specific reading disabilities, the level of reading comprehension of persons who have been exposed to four or more years of schooling is very highly related to their level of _g_, as measured by both verbal and nonverbal tests.

Unless an individual has made the transition from word reading to reading comprehension of sentences and paragraphs, reading is neither pleasurable nor practically useful. Few adults with an IQ of eighty (the tenth percentile of the overall population norm) ever make the transition from word reading skill to reading comprehension. The problem of adult illiteracy (defined as less than a fourth-grade level of reading comprehension) in a society that provides an elementary school education to virtually its entire population is therefore largely a problem of the lower segment of the population distribution of *g*. In the vast majority of people with low reading comprehension, the problem is not word reading per se, but lack of comprehension. These individuals score about the same on tests of reading comprehension even if the test paragraphs are read aloud to them by the examiner. In other words, individual differences in oral comprehension and in reading comprehension are highly correlated.[21]

THE VALIDITY OF g IN THE WORLD OF WORK

Virtually every type of work calls for behavior that is guided by cognitive processes. As all such processes reflect *g* to some extent, work proficiency is *g* loaded. The degree depends on the level of novelty and cognitive complexity the job demands. No job is so simple as to be totally without a cognitive component. Several decades of empirical studies have shown thousands of correlations of various mental tests with work proficiency. One of the most important conclusions that can be drawn from all this research is that mental ability tests in general have a higher success rate in predicting job performance than any other variables that have been researched in this context, including (in descending order of average predictive validity) skill testing, reference checks, class rank or grade-point average, experience, interview, education, and interest measures.[22] In recent years, one personality constellation, characterized as "conscientiousness," has emerged near the top of the list (just after general mental ability) as a predictor of occupational success.

My purpose here, however, is not to provide a comprehensive review of this vast body of research on the practical validity of mental tests.[23] Instead, the focus is on the role of *g* per se in the practical validity of tests used in personnel selection. The discussion is best divided into three main topics: job training, job performance, and occupational level.

VALIDITY OF g FOR PREDICTING SUCCESS IN JOB TRAINING

A person cannot perform a job successfully without the specific knowledge required by the job. Possibly such job knowledge could be acquired on the job after a long period of trial-and-error learning. For all but the very simplest jobs, however, trial-and-error learning is simply too costly, both in time and in errors. Job training inculcates the basic knowledge much more efficiently, provided that later on-the-job experience further enhances the knowledge or skills acquired in prior job training. Because knowledge and skill acquisition depend on learning, and because the rate of learning is related to *g*, it is a reasonable hypothesis that *g* should be an effective predictor of individuals' relative success in any specific training program.

The best studies for testing this hypothesis have been performed in the armed forces. Many thousands of recruits have been selected for entering different training programs for dozens of highly specialized jobs based on their performance on a variety of mental tests. As the amount of time for training is limited, efficiency dictates assigning military personnel to the various training schools so as to maximize the number who can complete the training successfully and minimize the number who fail in any given specialized school. When a failed trainee must be rerouted to a different training school better suited to his aptitude, it wastes time and money. Because the various schools make quite differing demands on cognitive abilities, the armed services employ psychometric researchers to develop and validate tests to best predict an individual's probability of success in one or another of the various specialized schools.

The best-known test battery that has evolved from this research effort so far is the *Armed Services Vocational Aptitude Battery* (ASVAB). It consists of ten distinct paper-and-pencil tests: Arithmetic Reasoning, Numerical Operations, Paragraph Comprehension, Word Knowledge, Coding Speed, General Science, Mathematics Knowledge, Electronics Information, Mechanical Comprehension, Automotive-Shop Information.

The Air Force has developed its own test battery, the *Air Force Officer Qualifying Test* (AFOQT), which includes, in addition to six of the ASVAB subtests, ten others: Verbal Analogies, Data Interpretation, Electrical Maze, Scale Reading, Instrument Comprehension, Block Counting, Table Reading, Aviation Information, Rotated Blocks, and Hidden Figures. The Air Force probably has the largest number (over 150) of technical training schools, and the most varied and specialized, of any branch of the armed services.

Let me summarize, therefore, the Air Force research[24] on the role of *g* in the validity of its selection tests for predicting success in training, as measured by final grades based on written tests of job *knowledge* and ratings of performance of the specific job *skills* that had been taught.

One study,[24a,b] based on 24,000 subjects in training for thirty-seven diverse jobs, used the method of correlated vectors, in which the vector of *g* loadings of the ten ASVAB subtests was correlated with the vector of ten validity coefficients of each of the ASVAB subtests for predicting training success. The rank-order correlation between the two vectors was $+.75$; this correlation increased to $+.98$ when the effect of the subtests' differing reliabilities was statistically controlled. In brief, the larger a test's *g* loading, the better it predicts training success. The study was replicated[24b] on a sample of 78,000 subjects across 150 different job training courses, yielding a correlation of $+.96$ (controlling the subtests' reliabilities) between the subtests' *g* loadings and their validity coefficients.[25]

Incremental Validity of Non-*g* Variance. The term *incremental validity* refers to the magnitude by which the validity coefficient is increased by adding another variable to predict the criterion measure. A variable's incremental validity is determined by multiple regression analysis, in which each predictive variable is entered into the multiple regression equation in a stepwise fashion, and the size of the increment in the multiple correlation (R) is noted as each predictor variable is successively included in the regression equation. An example will make this clearer. Suppose we have three tests, X, Y, and Z, each of which has some correlation with the criterion C. If X, Y, and Z are not correlated with each other, then each will contribute its total predictive validity to the multiple correlation. But if X, Y, and Z are correlated with each other (hence they have overlapping predictive power), then the first variable (say, X) entered into the regression equation contributes all of its predictive power, the second variable (Y) contributes only that part of its predictive power that it does not share with X, and the third variable (Z) entered contributes only that part of its predictive power that it does not share with X and Y. By entering each variable in the regression equation in a different order, one can determine its unique (or _incremental_) contribution to the predictive validity of the combined set of variables (X, Y, and Z). In combining the predictor variables (e.g., test scores), the variables are each weighted so as to maximize the correlation (R) between their weighted sum and the criterion measure (C). The _regression equation_ (in terms of our example) is $C = b_{cx}X + b_{cy}Y + b_{cz}Z$, where C is an individual's _predicted_ performance on the criterion measure, b is the optimal predictive weight for each test (called a _regression coefficient_), and X, Y, and Z are the individual's scores on each of the three tests. We will be concerned here with the incremental validity of a test battery after the amount of validity contributed by the battery's _g_ factor is accounted for. The incremental validity in this case is associated with only the test variance that is _not g_, here called non-_g_. The reliable non-_g_ variance typically consists of _group factors_ (e.g., verbal, numerical, spatial, all residualized from _g_) and test _specificity_ (e.g., general information, vocabulary, verbal analogies, synonyms-antonyms, sentence completion, and the like, all residualized from both _g_ and the group factors).

A study[24b] of the incremental validity of non-_g_ (i.e., all sources of variance in the ten ASVAB subtests remaining after _g_ has been removed) was based on 78,049 airmen in eighty-nine technical job training courses. The _g_ factor scores had an average validity coefficient of +.76 (corrected for restriction of range due to prior use of the test for selection); the non-_g_ portion of the ASVAB variance had an average predictive validity of +.02. The highest non-_g_ validity for any of the eighty-nine jobs was +.10. Non-_g_ had no significant validity for one-third of the jobs. Moreover, the relation between _g_ and training success was practically the same for all jobs. When an overall average prediction equation for all eighty-nine jobs was compared against using a unique optimal prediction equation for each job, the total loss in predictive accuracy was less than one-half of 1 percent.

In the same study, the average _g_ validity was lower (+.33) for actual performance measures than for course grades or a measure of job knowledge, but it was still appreciably higher than the corresponding average non-_g_ validity, which was only +.05.

A study[24c] based on 1,400 navigator trainees and 4,000 pilot trainees used the sixteen subtests of the AFOQT to predict success in achieving a number of training criteria measured in actual performance of the required skills at the end of training. The _g_ score validity (cross validated, range corrected) for the composite criteria was +.482 for navigators and +.398 for pilots. The corresponding incremental non-_g_ validity coefficients were +.020 and +.084, respectively. Again, _g_ proved to be the chief factor responsible for the AFOQT's predictive validity.

The very small predictive validity of the ASVAB's non-_g_ component, it might be surmised, could result if each of the subtests measured scarcely anything other than _g_, despite the subtests' quite different knowledge content. Empirically, however, this is clearly not the case. The _g_ factor accounts for only 40 to 60 percent (depending on the range of ability in various samples) of the total variance of the ten ASVAB subtests. The remaining variance comprises group factors, test specificity, and measurement error (about 10 to 15 percent). Therefore, theoretically there is enough reliable non-_g_ variance (about 30 to 50 percent) in the ASVAB for it to have an incremental validity almost as high as that for _g_.

Ratings based on structured interviews (which systematically assess subject attributes including educational background, self-confidence and leadership, flying motivation) were also found to have significant predictive validity for success in pilot training.[26] However, when the interview ratings were included in a multiple correlation along with the ASVAB to predict training success, the interview ratings proved to have no incremental validity over the ASVAB score. This finding indicates that whatever predictive validity the interview had was due to its overlapping variance with the predictive component of the ability factors tapped by the ASVAB, which is largely _g_.

VALIDITY OF _g_ FOR PREDICTING JOB PERFORMANCE

Test validity for predicting actual job performance criteria is somewhat lower (by about .20, overall) than for job training criteria. Although _g_ overshadows the validity of the non-_g_ components of test variance slightly less than it does in the prediction of training success, _g_ is still the main component of test validity for predicting job performance.

The General Aptitude Test Battery (GATB) developed by the U.S. Employment Service is more varied in its factor composition than either the ASVAB or the AFOQT. In addition to paper-and-pencil tests (for measuring Verbal, Numerical, Spatial, and Clerical aptitudes), the GATB also includes several performance tests that measure perceptual and motor abilities (form perception, motor coordination, finger dexterity, and manual dexterity). The predictive validity coefficients of the GATB have been determined and cross-validated re-

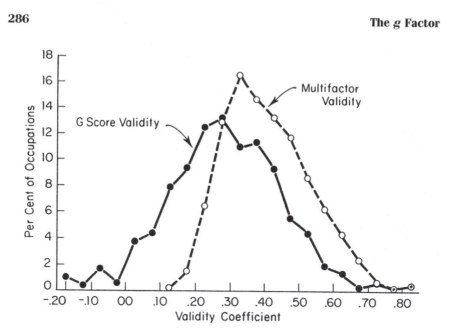

Figure 9.1. Frequency distribution of 537 validity coefficients for the General Aptitude Test Battery (GATB) for 446 different occupations. The *G*-score is a single measure of general mental ability; multifactor validity is based on an optimally weighted composite of nine GATB aptitudes (including *G*) for each job category. The median validity coefficients are +.27 for *G* and +.36 for the multifactor composite. If *G* is partialed out (i.e, removed), the validity coefficient (multiple *R*) of the residual multifactor composite is +.24. *Source: Bias in mental testing* by Arthur R. Jensen, Fig. 8.8, p. 349. Copyright © 1980 by Arthur R. Jensen. Reprinted with permission of The Free Press, a Division of Simon & Schuster, and Routledge Ltd.

peatedly and are reported for approximately 500 different occupations, ranging from unskilled manual laborer to Ph.D. mathematician. Correlations of each of the GATB scales with supervisor ratings of job performance or with objective work samples are reported in the GATB Manual. Using data in the GATB Manual, I have applied the method of correlated vectors to the GATB subscales. The vector of the subscales' *g* loadings (i.e., the first principal factor of the eight GATB aptitudes) correlated +.65 with the subscales' mean validity coefficients across 300 occupations. This shows that *g* is the ubiquitous agent of predictive validity over an extremely wide variety of jobs.[27]

This conclusion is further substantiated by the data presented in Figure 9.1, which shows the frequency distributions of validity coefficients obtained for 446 different occupations. *g-score validity* here is based on a single score (*g*) representing general cognitive ability (the GATB g-score is a composite of Verbal, Numerical, and Spatial aptitudes), and is measured by a Pearson *r. Multifactor validity* is a multiple correlation (*R*), which is the correlation between the measure of job performance (called the *dependent* variable) and an optimally weighted composite of all eight of the GATB aptitudes (called the *independent variables*), each independent variable so weighted as to yield the highest possible correlation with the dependent variable for each specific job. (Mathematically, R can never be less than zero, while the Pearson r may have any value from -1 to $+1$. Also, when the regression weights derived for a given sample are used to calculate the multiple R for the same sample, the R can never be smaller than the largest correlation of the dependent variable with any one of the independent variables.) The median *g*-score validity is $+.27$; the median multifactor validity is $+.36$. Hence the incremental validity of the non-*g* predictors is $\sqrt{(.36)^2 - (.27)^2} = .24$. This is a slight overestimate of the incremental validity of the non-*g* component, as R is statistically biased (inflated) because of its "capitalization on chance." (When the regression weights determined in one subject sample are cross-validated on a different sample, the R is always smaller in the second sample, the more so the smaller the samples.) It should be noted that the validity coefficients in Figure 9.1 are generally underestimates of the potential validity of the GATB, because they have not been corrected for range restriction in the applicant pool. The applicants for most of the jobs for which validity coefficients were obtained were self-selected, which considerably narrows the range of ability in the applicant pool for any given job. If applicants for every job were randomly selected from the general population, the *g* validity coefficients would be much higher, probably averaging at least $+.50$.

A study[28] of the validity of the ASVAB for predicting work-sample job performance criteria in seven varied Air Force jobs compared *g* factor score validity coefficients with the multiple correlation (R), which optimally combines the scores obtained from each of the ten ASVAB subtests. The obtained value of R (which is uniquely determined for each job) sets the upper limit of the possible correlation between the ASVAB subtests and the criterion measure of performance for each job. (To permit proper comparison with the single *g*-score validity coefficient, the R validity was statistically "shrunken" to adjust for degrees of freedom.) For predicting the overall work-sample performance criteria, averaged over the seven jobs, the *g*-score validity was $+.42$; the adjusted R validity was $+.44$. Thus the total ASVAB has a practical predictive validity that is only $+.02$ greater than its *g* validity alone.

Further evidence of the potency of *g* and the relative impotence of other factors in tests' predictive validity is demonstrated in a series of analyses by R. L. Thorndike.[29] Three different multiple aptitude batteries (Differential Aptitude Test [DAT], Army Classification Test [ACT], and General Aptitude Test Battery [GATB]) were used to obtain validity coefficients for training criteria and for actual job performance in sixty-three highly diverse jobs. In one-half of the subject sample, the validity of each test battery for predicting performance within each job classification was measured by the multiple R between the battery's set of subtests and the performance measure. The regression weights for the obtained R were then cross-validated on the other half of the subject sample to obtain the cross-validated R for each battery and each job.

Thorndike asked, How does the cross-validated R (which is uniquely determined for each job) compare with the validity of g factor scores obtained from each test battery? (For a given test battery, a common set of g loadings, based on the entire subject pool, was used to calculate the g factor scores of subjects in every job category.) For the three batteries (DAT, ACT, GATB), the validity coefficients based on g scores accounted for approximately 85, 90, and 120 percent, respectively, as much criterion variance as the cross-validated multiple Rs. (If you are puzzled by the 120 percent, see Note 29 for explanation.) Thorndike called this "a rather startling result" and concluded, "[F]or a wide range of criterion variables the major role in validity appears to be played by a common general factor" (p. 241).

Incremental Validity of Spatial and Psychomotor Aptitudes. The factors that provide the largest incremental validity over and above the criterion variance predicted by g are spatial and psychomotor abilities, which often contribute to the validity for predicting success in jobs requiring technical or motor skills. Physical scientists, for example, are well above average not only in g but also in spatial ability. Although most spatial tests are also quite g loaded, they can significantly enhance predictive validity for certain job categories.

Tests of psychomotor abilities also enhance validity for some jobs that depend on manual dexterity and muscular coordination. Considering how very different in form and content psychomotor tests are from the paper-and-pencil tests typically used to measure cognitive ability, it may seem surprising how relatively small the incremental validity contributed by psychomotor tests actually is, compared to the g validity even for jobs where psychomotor ability is relevant.[30] The apparent reason for this is that the psychomotor tests are themselves largely tests of g, showing true-score correlations with g even as high as .70 after correction for range restriction in Air Force samples. Usually g accounts for most of the validity of psychomotor tests, thus allowing comparatively little incremental validity.[31] (The expectation that a test's appearance necessarily indicates what latent traits it measures has been called the "topographical fallacy.")

Major efforts to discover other psychometric variables that add appreciable increments over and above g to predictive validity for "core job performance" have not proved fruitful.[32] Of course there are many other aspects of success in life besides g or spatial and psychomotor factors, such as physical and mental energy level, effort, conscientiousness, dependability, personal integrity, emotional stability, self-discipline, leadership, and creativity. These characteristics, however, fall into the personality domain and can be assessed to some extent by personality inventories. A person's interests have little incremental validity over g or other cognitive abilities, largely because a person's interests are to some degree related to the person's abilities. People generally do not develop an interest in subjects or activities requiring a level of cognitive complexity that overtaxes their level of g. Specialized talents, when highly developed, may be crucial for success in certain fields, such as music, art, and creative writing. The individual's level of g, however, is an important threshold variable for the socially and economically significant expression of such talents. Probably very few, if any, successful professionals in these fields have a below-average IQ.

Job Complexity and g Validity. In order to demonstrate the validity of a predictor variable, the criterion being predicted must vary. It is a fact that when various jobs are rank-ordered from low to high according to their complexity, or information-processing demands, there is a corresponding increase in the variance, or range of individual differences, in performance.[33] There is also a corresponding increase in the validity of g for predicting job performance as jobs increase in their information-processing demands. This phenomenon, which seems to have extremely broad generality, apparently holds throughout the entire range of job complexity. As noted in Chapter 8, even when going from simple reaction time to choice reaction time, there is an increase in individual differences in the standard deviation of the RT and a corresponding increase in the correlation between RT and g.

Linearity of Regression. The regression line, in terms of validity, is the line that best fits the relationship between the predicted criterion and the predictor test. In nearly all studies of the predictive validity of highly g-loaded tests, this regression line is linear (i.e., a straight line). This is illustrated, for example, in Figure 9.2, from a study where the Scholastic Aptitude Test (SAT) was used to predict college grade-point average (GPA) for students just entering college. The regression line per se is not shown in this graph, but the mean GPAs at equal intervals on the scale of SAT scores all fall on a single straight line, from the lowest possible SAT score (200) to the highest possible score (800). In other words, the regression of the criterion measure (GPA) on the predictor measure (SAT score) is *linear* throughout the entire range of GPAs and SAT scores. A similar picture emerges in hundreds of studies of the prediction of training success and job performance with various g-loaded tests.[34ab]

One of the mistaken beliefs about the predictive validity of IQ (and other g-loaded tests) is that beyond a certain threshold level, g has no practical validity, and individuals who score at different levels above the threshold will be effectively equivalent in criterion performance. This is another way of saying that the linear regression of the criterion on g does not hold above some point on the scale of g and beyond this point g-level is irrelevant. This belief is probably false. I have not found any study in which it has been demonstrated, except where there is an artificial ceiling on the criterion measure.

This is not to deny that as variance in g is decreased (owing to restriction of range in highly g-selected groups), other ability and personality factors that were not initially selected may gain in relative importance. But studies have shown that the linearity of the relation between g and performance criteria is maintained throughout the full range of g for all but the least complex performance criteria. Individual differences in IQ, even within groups in which all individuals are above the ninety-ninth percentile (that is, IQ > 140), are significantly correlated

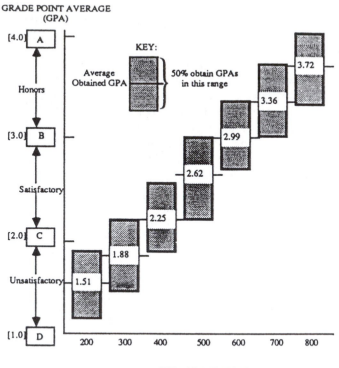

Figure 9.2. Average college grade-point average (GPA) for students with different SAT scores. (*Source*: Manning & Jackson, 1984. Used with permission of Plenum Publishing and W. H. Manning.)

with differences in a variety of achievement criteria such as earning a college degree, intellectual level of college attended, honors won, college GPA, attending graduate school, and intensity of involvement with math and science. Since these are statistical trends to which there are many exceptions, prediction based on a g measure *for a given individual* is only probabilistic, with a wide margin of error. When individuals of a given level of g are aggregated, however, and there are several such aggregate groups, each at a different level of g, the correlation between the group means on g and the group means on the criterion measure approaches unity.[34c] Since many idiosyncratic subject variables are averaged out in the group means, the linear relationship of the criterion measure to g is clearly revealed.

Effect of Job Experience on Predictive Validity. There is no argument that job knowledge and performance skills increase with actual experience on the job. But it is a common misconception that the correlation between g-loaded test scores and job performance measures washes out after people have gained a certain base level of job experience. The idea here seems to be that learning the knowledge and skills needed to do the job is the most important thing and that once these are acquired through experience on the job, individual differences in whatever was measured by the selection test (mostly g) quickly become irrelevant.

Large-scale studies have proven that this notion is false. Job knowledge is the strongest predictor of work-sample performance, and the rate of acquisition and the asymptotic level of job knowledge gained through experience are both positively related to g. For jobs of moderate complexity, periodic assessments of job knowledge, work samples, and supervisor ratings, after four months to five years of experience on the job, show no systematic decrease in the predictive validity of g.[35] Five years of experience is simply the limit that has been tested to date, but there is no evidence to suggest that performance levels would be unrelated to g at any point in time beyond that limit. For jobs of greater complexity and autonomy, it is likely that individual differences in g would be reflected increasingly in performance with increasing experience.

Residual Validity of Amount of Education. Some employers use number of years of education or other educational credentials as a basis for selecting workers. These measures are usually valid predictors, though seldom as valid as tests of general ability, except for a specialized job where specific educational qualifications are intrinsic and essential. Educational credentials derive almost all of their predictive validity from their substantial correlation with g. In general, the number of years of education, for example, is correlated .60 to .70 with IQ. Since the applicants for many jobs are self-selected in terms of educational qualifications, the true correlation of educational level with ability is even higher. It may seem surprising, but in most selection situations the validity coefficient for years of education is typically not more than .10 to .15 versus a g validity of .40 to .50 in similar situations. Further, the incremental validity of education over a measure of g is practically nil. This is largely because the variance in educational level (measured by the highest school grade completed) is less than the variance in actual ability in the applicant pool and also because there is a wide range of ability at every level of education. On tests of general ability, such as IQ, and even on tests of scholastic achievement, there is considerable overlap between the score distributions of high school graduates and college graduates.[36]

VALIDITY GENERALIZATION

The reported validity coefficients of cognitive tests vary greatly. The same (or highly similar) tests show highly variable validity across different jobs, or across nominally the same job in different work settings, in different organizations, and in different populations. Similarly for a given battery of tests, the specific set of regression weights that maximize the battery's predictive validity varies greatly, not only across different jobs, but across different situations for the same job. These observations led to a long-held belief that a test's predictive validity is not general, but specific to each and every situation in which the test is used. This outlook implied that a given test's validity must be proved over and over again, whenever it is to be used in a different situation.

Recent meta-analyses of hundreds of test validation studies carried out over the past two decades have proved this belief to be largely false.[37] It remains true, however, that test validity varies to some degree across broad job categories, depending mostly on job complexity, as previously explained.

The *observed variability* in validity coefficients across different studies (in which sample sizes are typically small) performed in different employment situations is almost entirely the result of various artifacts. A test's *true validity* (within broad job categories) has virtually no variability across different situations. A test's true validity is its validity coefficient after the irrelevant or nonessential components of its variation across studies conducted in different situations have been statistically removed. Observed situational specificity can largely be explained in terms of statistical sampling error, criterion unreliability, test unreliability, range restriction, different factor structures of tests and test batteries, and the use of non-Pearsonian (e.g., biserial, triserial, or tetrachoric) measures of correlation.

When all such artifacts are accounted for, the variance of the observed validity coefficients is reduced to about .01. (Sampling error alone accounts for some 60 percent of validity variation.) Hence the best indicator of a test's *effective* predictive validity for any given job (within a broad category of jobs or training programs) is the average of its observed validity coefficients obtained in many validation studies performed within the relevant broad job category.

OCCUPATIONAL LEVEL AS A FUNCTION OF *g*

The research literature on this subject has been so comprehensively reviewed elsewhere[38] that I will simply summarize the main conclusions for highly *g*-loaded measures such as standard IQ tests and the *g*-scores of the General Aptitude Test Battery (GATB).

There is a high degree of agreement among people when they are asked to rank occupational titles according to their impression of (1) the occupation's socially perceived prestige, (2) the desirability (for whatever reason) of being employed in the occupation, and (3) the estimated level of "intelligence" needed to succeed in the occupation. When a number of people rank a large number of different occupational titles, from highest to lowest, on each of these standards, the mean rank for each occupation remains fairly constant. The overall rank-order correlations in various studies fall between .95 and .98. This high consistency of rank order holds up across rankings by people from different occupations, social class backgrounds, industrialized countries, and generations. This high degree of agreement in people's subjective impressions of the status of different occupations means that this status hierarchy is associated with people's impression of the "intelligence" demands of the various occupations.

The objective validity of such average subjective judgments is shown by the correlation between the mean ranks of occupations and the rank order of the actual mean IQ within each occupation, which is between .90 and .95. Thus there is no question that socially perceived occupational status is intimately related to IQ. Because IQ in the general population is correlated around .90 with *g*, the occupational hierarchy obviously reflects *g* more than any other psychometric factor.

Another way to demonstrate the overall relative magnitude of *g* differences between occupations is by analysis of variance. I have performed this analysis on all 444 occupational titles used by the U.S. Employment Service. The General Aptitude Test Battery (GATB) Manual presents the mean and standard deviation of GATB *G*-scores for large samples of each of the 444 different occupations. An analysis of variance performed on these data shows that 47 percent of the total *G*-score variance is *between* occupations (i.e., differences between the mean *G*-scores of the various occupations) and 53 percent of the variance is *within* occupations (i.e., differences between the *G*-scores of individuals within each occupation). Since about 10 percent of the within-occupations variance is attributable to measurement error, the true within-occupations variance constitutes only 43 percent of the total *G*-score variance. From these figures one can compute[39] the true-score correlation (based on individuals, not group means) between occupations and *G*-scores. It is .72, which closely agrees with the average correlation of .70 found in other studies in which individual IQs were directly correlated with the mean rank of people's subjective ranking of occupations. The correlation of individuals' IQs with occupational rank increases with age, ranging from about .50 for young persons to about .70 for middle-aged and older persons, whose career lines by then are well established.

The relation of IQ to occupational level is not at all caused by differences in individuals' IQs being determined by the differences in amount of education or the particular intellectual demands associated with different occupations. This is proved by the fact that IQ, even when measured in childhood, is correlated about .70 with occupational level in later adulthood.

Two statistically related features of the data on IQ and occupations afford an insight into the nature of their relationship. The first is the observed negative correlation between the means and standard deviations (*SDs*) of IQ across occupational levels. The higher the mean IQ of an occupation, the smaller is the range of IQs within the occupation.

The second is that high IQs are found in almost every occupation, but the lowest IQ found in each of the various occupations rises markedly, going from lower to higher occupational levels. This means that IQ (or *g*) acts as a variable threshold for different occupations, first because of the level of educational attainment required, and second because of the *g* demands of successful performance. For example, the U.S. Employment Service data show that the *lowest* IQ found among persons employed with the occupational title "mathematician" was 115 (the eighty-fifth percentile of the general population); the mean IQ was

143. However, IQs this high are found within the total range of IQs reported for even unskilled jobs that have a mean IQ below the general population average. Of course, there is a range of individual differences in *g* within every occupation, differences that are often accommodated by the variety of tasks that can be performed by different workers in the same nominal occupation.

The findings reviewed here indicate that *g* plays an important role in occupational level, as well as in level of performance within occupations. This fact, however, does not imply that a host of other factors in addition to *g*—special abilities, various personality traits, energy level, motivation, ambition, persistence, education, and experience—are not also important, or even crucial, for success in many occupations. But none of these other factors is so potent as to completely override the threshold aspect of *g* in predicting an individual's probable success in a particular occupation.

SOCIAL CORRELATES OF g

The well-established correlation of IQ and similar cognitive measures with a number of social variables, such as poverty, crime, illegitimacy, and chronic welfare status, makes it almost a certainty that *g* itself is the major cognitive component in the relationship. However, I have not found a study that directly addresses the extent to which just *g* itself, rather than IQ or other highly *g*-loaded measures, is related to social variables. The repeated finding that verbal test scores are somewhat more highly correlated with delinquent and criminal behavior than are nonverbal performance tests (generally loaded on the spatial factor) suggests that other cognitive factors in addition to *g* are probably responsible for the correlation of IQ with these most common forms of antisocial behavior.

It must be recognized that the social variables known to be correlated with IQ are also correlated with other, noncognitive variables, such as age, gender, social class, cultural background, and education, to name a few. Because IQ is also correlated with most of these variables, the causal matrix is highly problematic. Therefore, even the most well-established correlation of IQ with any complexly determined social variable must be viewed simply as a raw empirical datum, without implying the direction of causality. The nature of the causal connections between all these variables is open to theoretical speculations, on which, so far, there has been little agreement among the experts. The complex statistical techniques applied to deciphering the causal pathways among the set of independent variables (including IQ) that are correlated with the targeted social variable are at least capable of establishing whether or not IQ makes any independent contribution to the targeted variable, over and above the contribution of the other correlated variables. Usually it does.

Though the independent contribution of IQ to any given social variable is typically small (a raw correlation generally less than .30), it can have striking consequences in certain segments of the IQ distribution in the population. Although the correlation coefficient can establish that a statistically significant relationship exists, it does not provide the best representation of the relationship between IQ and some form of social behavior that is manifested by only a small fraction of the population and on which persons can be "scored" only dichotomously (e.g., convicted felon = 1, nonfelon = 2). In such cases, there is a severe restriction of range (or variance) on the social variable, which mathematically limits the magnitude of the correlation coefficient.[40]

Most forms of social phenomena that are generally considered undesirable are heavily concentrated in the relatively small segment of the population distribution of IQ that falls below the tenth percentile (i.e., IQs below 80). The relationship of IQ to social phenomena is often large enough to have considerable social and economic consequences. Because the majority of people in the lower range of the IQ distribution are not involved in antisocial phenomena or in conditions often referred to as "social pathology," and an even much smaller percentage of those of higher IQ are involved, there is a severe "restriction of range" on the social variable. Moreover, the form of the relationship between IQ and social behavior is often significantly nonlinear. Therefore, the Pearson correlation coefficient cannot fully convey the degree of relationship between IQ and the particular form of social behavior. The relationship can be most clearly depicted, not by any single statistical index, but by a table or graph that shows the percentage of people within each segment (e.g., intervals of ten or fifteen IQ points) of the entire IQ distribution who manifest the particular social condition. Since many social variables, besides being related to IQ, are also related to age and to socioeconomic status (SES), it is possible statistically to control the effects of age and SES, thereby revealing the relationship of IQ to the particular social variable independently of age and SES. (Also, the relationship of the social variable to SES can be shown independently of IQ and age.)

This type of analysis was carried out by Herrnstein and Murray[41] for non-Hispanic whites from the nationally representative sample (N = 11,878) of young adults (aged eighteen to twenty-three) in the 1990 survey of the National Longitudinal Study of Youth (NLSY). Subjects were grouped into five categories on the basis of their scores on the Armed Forces Qualification Test (AFQT), a highly g-loaded battery. For the analyses summarized here, the AFQT scores were transformed to an IQ scale (mean = 100, SD = 15). The personal-social variables related to IQ all represent a dichotomous (Yes/No) classification of subjects. Table 9.1 shows the probability (percentage) of persons in each of the five segments of the total IQ distribution who manifested one of the listed personal-social outcomes. The first two variables (A and B) are generally positively valued in our society; all the remaining variables (C through S) are typically considered socially or personally unfortunate or undesirable. It is clearly evident that there is a consistent monotonic relationship between IQ level and the probabilities of these outcomes. Note that for most of the social variables, the effects of age and SES have been statistically controlled, so that, in effect, all subjects

Table 9.1

Probability of Various Personal-Social Outcomes as a Function of IQ Level in White Sample of NLSY[1]

Outcome	IQ Level[2]				
	I	II	III	IV	V
A. Earning a bachelor's degree	75	38	8	1	0
B. Middle-class values[3]	75	63	47	32	22
C. Below poverty line*	1	4	7	14	26
D. High school dropout*	0	1	6	26	64
E. Unemployed 1 month during year[4] (males)*	4	6	8	11	14
F. Disability on job (males)	13	21	37	45	62
G. Divorced in first 5 years of marriage*	12	17	21	26	32
H. Mother with illegitimate first birth*	4	8	14	22	34
I. Ever had illegitimate child	2	4	8	17	32
J. Mother below poverty line first child illegitimate*	13	25	37	45	70
K. Chronic (>5 years) welfare recipient after birth of first child	0	2	8	17	31
L. Mother went on welfare after birth of first child**	1	4	12	21	55
M. Chronic welfare recipient*	7	10	14	20	28
N. Mother of low birthweight baby*	1.5	2.3	3.5	5.0	7.2
O. Mother, child in poverty first 3 years after birth of child*	0	2	5	15	32
P. Mother, with child living in bottom decile of HOME index*	2	3	5	10	17
Q. Mother whose child is in bottom decile on developmental indicators*	6	7	10	13	16
R. Mother whose child is in bottom decile of IQ (IQ<80).*	1	3	6	16	30
S. Ever interviewed in correctional facility (males)*	<1	1	3	6	13
Column Means[5]	4.3	7.5	12.7	20.0	33.8

[1]Data from National Longitudinal Study of Youth (NLSY) as reported by Herrnstein & Murray (1994).

[2]IQ range at each level: (I) above 125, (II) 110–125, (III) 90–110, (IV) 75–90, (V) below 75.

[3]Subjects indexed as having middle-class values were those who: (for men) obtained high school degree (or more), were in labor force throughout year (1989), had never been interviewed in jail, were still married to their first wife; (for women) obtained a high school degree, had never given birth out of wedlock, had never been interviewed in jail, were still married to their first husband.

[4]Persons in school or college not included.

[5]Column means include only variables C through S.

*Effects of age and socioeconomic status of subject's rearing environment statistically controlled.

**Effects of age, marital status, and poverty status at time of first birth statistically controlled.

were statistically set equal to the average age and the average SES level of the total sample.

Replacing IQ by the subject's SES of origin (with IQ and age controlled) reveals that SES is generally much less related to the various social outcomes than is IQ. (Herrnstein and Murray graphically show the independent effects of IQ and of SES on each of these variables.) IQ per se is a more potent variable than SES per se in relation to this set of socially important variables. The data clearly indicate that _g_ is in some way implicated, however complexly, in these seemingly noncognitive social outcomes. As shown by the column means in the last row of Table 9.1, the probability of unfortunate personal-social outcomes rises sharply for the two lower IQ levels (IQs below ninety and below seventy-five).

DELINQUENCY AND CRIME

The last social outcome (labeled S in Table 9.1) indicates that getting into trouble with the law is related to IQ. Because of the social importance of delinquency and crime, their relationship to IQ has been studied more extensively than probably any other social variable except SES.[42] The studies show that nearly all forms of antisocial behavior, especially crimes against persons or property and crimes that reflect impulsiveness, physical threat, or violence, are more apt to be committed by persons in the lower half of the IQ distribution. Such persons are, on average, about ten to twelve IQ points below the average IQ of the general population. The more important fact is that the negative correlation between IQ and delinquency exists _within_ families. That is, criminals average about ten IQ points lower than their own full siblings with whom they were reared.[42a] Since the delinquents and their siblings were brought up together in the same family with the very same socioeconomic and cultural background, these environmental background variables cannot explain the independent role of IQ in antisocial behavior.

A large-scale longitudinal study of delinquency showed that among boys, then thirteen years of age, the relationship between delinquency and IQ remains even when social class, race, and test motivation were statistically controlled.[43] An important finding of this study was that the degree of seriousness of self-reported delinquent behaviors is inversely monotonically related to IQ.

When the circumstantial differences in the conditions often claimed as the instigating causes of criminal behavior are fairly uniform and controlled, as among Army recruits living together under highly similar conditions, the same relationship between IQ and delinquency as found in civilian life still exists. Among 1,780 enlisted men in the Army, delinquent behavior serious enough for court-martial conviction showed a (biserial) correlation of .31 with the AFQT, a highly _g_-loaded test. Other studies conducted in the armed forces show a similar relationship between mental test scores and delinquency.[44]

Although there is no generally accepted theory of the IQ-delinquency relationship, various hypotheses have been suggested. One hypothesis is that having a lower IQ than one's siblings and classmates results in comparatively fewer experiences of success and more experiences of failure in the kinds of performance that are typically rewarded in school. This leads to frustration, alienation, rejection of commonly accepted social values, and aggression. Repeated experiences of being unable to settle disagreements or win disputes though verbal argument finally lead to the use of physical threat. Another view is that IQ is related to all forms of reasoning, and that low-IQ persons have not reached the developmental level of moral reasoning generally attained by adults of average and higher IQ. Other hypotheses invoke the mediation of IQ-related traits that are found to characterize some criminals, such as impulsiveness, inability to delay gratification, and a "present-orientation"—failing to consider the long-term consequences of one's behavior. Probably all of these hypothesized causes work together in causing the IQ-delinquency correlation. But whatever its cause, the correlation itself is a well-established empirical fact. Research on the causes (and prevention) of crime and delinquency, therefore, cannot dismiss the effects of low g. In fact, path models that take account of IQ and various other social and personal variables in analyzing their relationship to delinquency support the hypothesis that a moderately low level of g is probably one of the most direct causal factors.[43]

ACCIDENT PRONENESS AND MORTALITY RATE

Large-scale epidemiological studies[45] of accident and death rates conducted in Australia have shown that these variables are related to g, independently of other psychometric abilities and of personal and demographic variables that predict accident proneness and mortality. In the study cohort of 46,166 men, aged twenty to thirty-four, who had previously served in the Australian armed forces and for whom the study data had already been obtained, a total of 523 men died of causes other than combat in the armed forces. The Army General Classification (AGC) test and other tests measuring speed-and-accuracy and mechanical comprehension were obtained on all subjects in addition to fifty-four other variables classifiable into three categories: level of education, personal conduct (alcohol use, arrests, AWOL in army, and other personality and behavioral traits considered risk factors for accidents), and health records (number of days in hospital, etc.). A complex multiple regression analysis of all fifty-seven variables was used to predict mortality (i.e., being alive or dead at the time of the study) in this cohort of twenty-to-thirty-four-year-old adults.[45a] The analysis was designed to reveal which of the fifty-seven variables made a statistically significant *independent* contribution to the prediction of mortality. The AGC, which is the most highly g loaded of the psychometric tests used, was the only test that made an independent contribution. It was considerable—a one standard deviation rise in the AGC test score was associated with a 16 percent decrease

Table 9.2
Death Rate per 10,000 due to Motor Vehicle Accidents for Australian Men Aged 20 to 34

IQ Level[a]	Death Rate
Above 115	51.3
100 - 115	51.5
85 - 100	92.2
80 - 85	146.7

[a]Based on Army General Classification test, with raw scores transformed to IQ scale (mean = 100, *SD* = 15).
Source: O'Toole, 1990.

in mortality rate. Surprisingly, individuals' health records were not as good a predictor.

Most of the deaths in this age group (twenty to thirty-four years) were attributable to external causes, particularly vehicular accidents. A separate analysis[45b] was performed for those who had died in motor vehicle accidents. The results are shown in Table 9.2. (It should be noted that, because all subjects had been accepted into the armed forces, the IQ distribution in this cohort was truncated at IQs below eighty.) The author of the study, Brian O'Toole, interpreted the result as follows: "[P]eople with lower intelligence may have a poorer ability to assess risks and, consequently, may take more poor risks in their driving than more intelligent people. That is, their driving may not be any riskier in terms of follow-on distance, running amber lights, speeding, and so on, but they may take such risks under conditions that a more intelligent person would avoid" (p. 220).

MISCELLANEOUS CORRELATES OF *g*

Many variables besides those previously mentioned in this book have been reported in numerous studies to be significantly correlated with *g*.[46] All of these variables (including those previously mentioned) are listed in Table 9.3. These are presented here simply as empirical correlates, without attempting to determine their causal nature. For most of these *g*-correlated variables the causation almost certainly comes about quite indirectly and *g* accounts for only a small part of the variance. The causal network in most cases is undoubtedly complex and largely unknown, although plausible speculative hypotheses may easily come to mind. The theoretically important point is that so many of these *g*-correlated variables are unrelated to any of the purposes for which mental tests were originally devised, or were at all in mind when factor analysis was first invented and *g* was discovered. This shows that *g* is a dimension of individual

Table 9.3
Variables Correlated With *g*

Positive Correlation

Achievement motivation	Practical knowledge
Altruism	Psychotherapy, response to
Analytic style	Reading ability
Aptitudes, cognitive abilities,	Regional differences
'abstractness of' integrative	Social skills
complexity	Socioeconomic status
Artistic preferences	of origin
and abilities	Socioeconomic status
Craftwork	achieved
Creativity; fluency	Sports participation
Dietary preferences	at university
(low-sugar, low-fat)	Supermarket shopping
Educational attainment	ability
Eminence, genius	Talking speed
Emotional sensitivity	Values and attitudes
Extra-curricular attainments	
Field-independence	
Height	Negative Correlation
Health, fitness, longevity	
Humor, sense of	
Income	Accident proneness
Interests, depth and breadth of	Acquiescence
Involvement in school activities	Aging
Leadership	Alcoholism
Linguistic abilities	Authoritarianism
(including spelling)	Conservatism (of social
Logical abilities	views)
Marital partner, choice of	Crime
Media preferences	Delinquency
Memory	Dogmatism
Migration (voluntary)	Falsification ("Lie"
Military rank	scores)
Moral reasoning and development	Hysteria (versus other
Motor skills	neuroses)
Musical preferences and abilities	Impulsivity
Myopia	Infant mortality
Occupational status	Psychoticism
Occupational success	Racial prejudice
Perceptual abilities	Reaction times
Piaget-type abilities	Smoking
	Truancy
	Weight/height ratio

Source: Brand, 1987a.

differences that enters into many aspects of human behavior besides those narrowly conceived of as scholastic or intellectual.

NOTES

1. Jensen, 1980a (Chapter 8); Jensen, 1993a. The most detailed and advanced treatments of validity are by Cronbach (1971) and Messick (1989).

2. Another way of conceptualizing the meaning of a validity coefficient (r_{xc}) is in terms of the following formula:

$$r_{xc} = (T - R) / (P - R),$$

where **T** is the average level of performance on the criterion for persons selected with the test, **R** is the mean level of criterion performance for persons selected at random, and **P** is the mean criterion performance for perfectly selected persons, as if $r_{xc} = 1$. Hence r_{xc} is a direct measure of the proportional gain in the mean criterion performance that results from the use of the test for selection as compared to what the mean level of criterion performance would be with random selection. In other words, the validity coefficient is a direct indicator of the effectiveness of the test's predictive accuracy, such that, for example, a validity coefficient of .50 provides just half as accurate prediction as a validity coefficient of 1.00, which indicates perfect prediction. Even a quite modest validity coefficient has considerable practical value when a great many binary (i.e., yes-no, pass-fail, win-lose) decisions are made. For example, the casino at Monte Carlo reaps large sums of money every day from its roulette games, because of course the house always has better odds for not losing than the gamblers have for winning, yet the house advantage is, in fact, equivalent to a predictive validity coefficient of only +.027! The practical value of a validity coefficient of +.27, therefore, is certainly not of negligible value where a large number of selection decisions must be made.

3. The *standard error of estimate* (SE_{est}) is related to the validity coefficient (r_{xc}) as follows: $SE_{est} = s_c (1 - r_{xc}^2)^{1/2}$, where s_c is the standard deviation of the criterion measure. The ratio SE_{est}/s_c measures the proportional error of predicting individuals' point values on the criterion. The percentage gain in accuracy of point predictions as compared with purely random selection is equal to $100(1 - SE_{est}/s_c)$, which is termed the *index of forecasting efficiency*. The use of this index is now in disfavor when the overall value of test-based selection is being considered, because the index of forecasting efficiency is not directly related to the overall mean gain in criterion performance afforded by test-based selection. The validity coefficient itself, however, is a direct indicator of the proportional gain in mean criterion performance of individuals who were selected by means of a test with a certain validity coefficient (see Note 2). The common habit of squaring the validity coefficient to obtain the proportion of variance in the criterion accounted for by the linear regression of criterion measures on test scores, although not statistically incorrect, is an uninformative and misleading way of interpreting a validity coefficient for any practical purpose.

4. There are several types, definitions, and statistical criteria of test bias. For a comprehensive discussion, see Jensen, 1980a, Chapter 9.

5. Some psychologists distinguish between two types of knowledge: *declarative* knowledge, which is knowing *about* something (e.g., Fe stands for iron in the periodic table of elements; Plato wrote *The Republic*; yeast is used in making bread), and *procedural* knowledge, which is knowing *how* to go about doing something (e.g., trouble-

shooting a stalled car; playing a musical instrument; solving a quadratic equation; writing an essay). A *skill* is some fairly specific and usually highly practiced form of procedural knowledge.

6. Jensen, 1989a.

7. Gettinger, 1984.

8. Glutting & McDermott, 1990.

9. Christal, 1991.

10. A "gate" is an electronic component or logical element that makes an electronic circuit operative or inoperative until another signal is received. A "logic gate" is an electronic component that has one output which is activated only by a certain combination of two or more inputs.

11. Jensen, 1980a, Chapter 8; Jensen, 1991b, 1993a; Matarazzo, 1972, Chapter 12; Snow & Yalow, 1982. These citations also contain extensive references of other reviews of the relationship of IQ to educational variables.

12. Gedye, 1981.

13. Thorndike, 1984.

14. A factor analysis of pupils' grades in six academic subjects yielded a general factor accounting for 58 percent of the total variance in grades, with factor loadings averaging .76 and ranging from .65 to .86. I performed this principal factor analysis on the correlation matrix given in an article by Rushton & Endler, 1977, p. 301. The correlations between six academic subjects (English, spelling, mathematics, geography, history, and science) ranged from .25 to .86, with a mean correlation of .56, for ninety-one pupils, aged ten to twelve. Besides the large common factor (i.e., the 1st PF) there was only one other factor with an eigenvalue > 1. It accounted for 9% of the total variance.

15. Matarazzo, 1972, p. 289. Although the g factor in IQ is the cause of the correlation between IQ and level of educational attainments, there is also evidence that amount of education has some causal effect on IQ scores per se, although probably not on g itself (Ceci, 1991). This issue is discussed further in Chapter 10, p. 302.

16. Occupational status at age forty has a similar correlation with IQ measured at age seven (details of these studies given in Jensen, 1980a, pp. 333–335).

17. Nagoshi, Johnson, & Honbo, 1993.

18. (a) Conry & Plant, 1965; (b) Silverstein, 1982.

19. The vector of the validity coefficients for the eleven WAIS subtests for high school grades and the corresponding vector of validity coefficients for college grades are correlated $+.84$ (rank-order correlation $+.74$).

20. E. L. Thorndike, 1917, p. 329. (Cf. R. L. Thorndike, 1973–74.)

21. Sticht et al., 1981.

22. Hunter, 1989.

23. Ghiselli (1966) is a classic text on the validity of job selection tests, but it predates the application of meta-analysis to the study of test validity. Recent references on modern methods of studying the predictive validity of tests for personnel selection and summaries of the large-scale researches (which go well beyond Ghiselli's review) can be found in Gottfredson (1986), Gottfredson & Sharf (1988), Hunter, J. E. & Hunter, R. F. (1984), Schmidt & Hunter (1981), Schmidt, Ones, & Hunter (1992). Lubinski & Dawis (1992) provide an exceptionally keen discussion, at a fairly advanced level, of a number of cutting-edge issues and recent developments in the study of validity. It is recommended as probably the most up-to-date and comprehensive entrée to the research literature on test validity.

24. Technical details of these studies are contained in unpublished reports of the Armstrong Laboratory at Brooks Air Force Base. Various studies are well summarized in the following journal articles: (a) Ree & Earles, 1992a (also 1991b), (b) Ree & Earles, 1994, (c) Olea & Ree, 1994, (d) Earles & Ree, 1992, (e) Ree & Earles, 1992b.

25. I have computed the correlation between the *g* vector and the vector of validity coefficients (corrected for restriction of range and controlling reliability) of the ten AS-VAB subtests, using data reported in three other Air Force studies[24c,d] of navigator and pilot trainees, and the combined samples from 150 other different technical training schools. (A large part of these samples are included in the other reports described in the text.) The total $N = 90,548$. The *N*-weighted mean of the correlation between the vector of ASVAB subtests' *g* loadings and the vector of the ASVAB subtests' validity coefficients (averaged across schools) was $+.95$. All these results, taken together, leave no doubt that *g* is the chief active ingredient in ASVAB's predictive validity for training success.

26. Walters, Miller, & Ree (1993).

27. Details of this analysis are given in Jensen (1980a, pp. 735–36).

28. Ree, Earles, & Teachout, 1994.

29. Thorndike (1985). *Note*: In the initial validation sample, the regression weights for calculating the multiple *R* are mathematically determined such that they will yield the maximum possible *R* obtainable with the given set of predictor variables (tests). The magnitude of this *R* capitalizes to some extent on "sampling error," that is, characteristics peculiar to the particular sample, but not to the population from which it was selected. Therefore, when the set of tests is *cross-validated* on a different subject sample, using the very same regression weights that were determined in the first sample, the weights will not yield the maximum possible *R* in the second sample. (Only a set of weights based on the second sample could do that.) The cross-validated *R* is somewhat smaller (in statistical terms, "shrunken") by an amount related to the sample size and to the number of independent variables in the regression equation. But the cross-validated *R* is a better estimate of the true *R* (i.e., the value of *R* in the population) than the *R* obtained in the first sample. (And, of course, the only weights available for prediction in a new sample are those that were previously derived in another sample.) For example, suppose the *R* validity coefficient in the first sample is .50, the cross-validated *R* is .40, and the *g* validity of the test battery in either sample is .48 (based on the subtests' *g* loadings determined in a large independent sample of job applicants comprising all job categories.) The *g* validity then would be $.48/.50 = 96\%$ of the initial R validity and $.48/.40 = 120\%$ of the cross-validated *R* validity.

In his last, posthumous publication, Thorndike (1994) gives a most interesting testimonial and summary of his views on *g* and its practical predictive validity.

30. Ree & Earles, 1994, p. 131; Ree & Earles, 1993.

31. Ree and Carretta (1994) performed a confirmatory hierarchical factor analysis of four highly *g*-loaded subtests of the ASVAB along with eight psychomotor tests used in selection for pilot training in the Air Force (e.g., two-hand coordination in pursuit tracking, complex coordination, time-sharing tracking and monitoring, vertical and horizontal tracking). The best-fitting hierarchical factor model showed five first-order factors, a second-order psychomotor factor (common to all the psychomotor tests), and a *g* factor common to all of the tests, both cognitive and psychomotor. The *g* accounted for 39% of the variance in the whole battery; the psychomotor factor accounted for 29%. The *g* loadings of the eight psychomotor variables ranged from $+.22$ to $+.51$, averaging $+.34$.

But the most important finding in this study, from the standpoint of *g* theory, is the comparison of the four ASVAB subtests' *g* loadings when factor analyzed along with the psychomotor tests compared against their *g* loadings when they are factor analyzed separately from the psychomotor tests. The two sets of *g* loadings were almost identical; the largest difference between them was .04. I have compared the *g* loadings obtained on the four ASVAB subtests when factor analyzed among the psychomotor tests (in the sample of Air Force pilot trainees) with the *g* loadings of the same four ASVAB subtests when factor analyzed among the whole ASVAB battery of ten subtests (using data from a representative sample of about 12,000 American youths). The average difference between these two sets of *g* loadings was .025, the largest difference being .030. These findings (like those of Thorndike, 1987) contradict the claim that tests' *g* loadings are highly erratic and vary markedly depending on the particular collection of tests among which they are factor analyzed. The four ASVAB subtests showed only very slight fluctuations in *g* loadings when factor analyzed among such contrasting test batteries as the total battery of ASVAB paper-and-pencil tests or the battery of hands-on mechanical devices used for measuring motor abilities.

32. McHenry et al., 1990.

33. Hunter, Schmidt, & Judiesch (1990) have demonstrated the relationship of variability in employee output to job complexity. Their measure of variability of employee output was the coefficient of variation ($CV = \sigma/\mu$), that is, the ratio of the standard deviation of employee output to the mean output for all employees, expressed as a percentage (i.e., $CV \times 100$). This measure was found to increase from below 20%, to 30%, to above 50%, going from jobs of low, to medium, to high complexity, respectively.

34. (a) Hawk, 1970; (b) Toomepuu, 1986; (c) Lubinski & Dawis, 1992, pp. 41–45; Coward & Sackett, 1990. Also see Lubinski & Humphreys (1996) on the use of aggregation (group means) in correlation analysis.

35. Schmidt et al., 1986, 1988.

36. The validity of education in employment selection, its relation to general ability, and its contribution to maintaining the occupational hierarchy in modern society are all penetratingly discussed by Gottfredson (1985).

37. The following publications, besides summarizing the essential methodology and research on validity generalization, provide comprehensive references to most of this extensive literature: Hunter & Schmidt, 1990; Schmidt, 1992; Schmidt, Law, et al., 1993.

38. Dawis, 1994; Jensen, 1980a, pp. 339–347.

39. The intraclass correlation (r_i) calculated from these data (corrected for error, assuming *G*-score reliability of .90) is $r_i = .47/.90 = .52$. The r_i is a measure of the similarity (in *G*-scores) between individuals in the same occupation. The correlation of individuals' *G*-scores with occupations, therefore, is $\sqrt{r_i} = \sqrt{.52} = .72$.

40. When a variable is dichotomous, with binary "scores" (e.g., unemployed = 1, employed = 2), the variable's variance is $p \times q$, where *p* is the proportion of individuals scored 1 and *q* is the proportion scored 2 (and $p + q = 1$). It is apparent, therefore, that the largest variance exists when $p = q = .50$, and the variance decreases as *p* and *q* depart from .50. Hence the relative frequencies in the two parts of the dichotomized variable affect the size of the dichotomous variable's correlation with another variable (whether the variable is continuous, dichotomous, trichotomous, or whatever). Departure from a .50/.50 split on the dichotomized variable imposes a constraint on the size of its correlation with another variable. The obtained correlation can be mathematically corrected for restriction of variance, but then the corrected correlation has no realistic or

practical meaning, although it may be of theoretical interest. The corrected correlation would indicate, for example, how much might be gained by changing (if possible) the dichotomous variable to a continuous variable or to several categories (scored, say, one to five) instead of just two.

41. Herrnstein & Murray, 1994. Details of the NLSY sample are given in their Appendix 2. The major part of their book (Chapters 5 to 12) presents detailed analyses, graphical presentations, and psychological interpretations of the NLSY data briefly summarized here.

42. In addition to Chapter 11 in Herrnstein & Murray (1994), key reviews and references to the research on the relationship of antisocial behavior to IQ are (a) Hirschi & Hindelang, 1977, (b) Gordon, 1975, 1987a, (c) Wilson & Herrnstein, 1985, (d) Levin, 1997, Chapter 9.

43. Lynam et al., 1993; this study's finding of a negative monotonic relation between the severity of delinquent acts and IQ has since been replicated twice (once in Pittsburgh and again in New Zealand) among males and females, blacks and whites, using several different measures of delinquency (Moffitt, et al., 1981, 1995). Levin (1997) provides a discussion of the relationship between cognitive ability and the comprehension of moral principles, particularly with reference to racial differences in crime rates.

44. Bayroff, 1963.

45. (a) O'Toole & Stankov, 1992; (b) O'Toole, 1990.

46. References to these studies are listed by Brand (1987a).

Chapter 10

Construct, Vehicles, and Measurements

As a *construct*, the g factor can be represented with varying degrees of convenience, efficiency, and validity by a wide variety of *vehicles* (psychometric tests, laboratory techniques, physiological indices) that yield *measurements* that have different scale properties. These three key concepts are related to one another, but do not all represent one and the same thing. It is important to recognize the distinctions between them when considering the nature of empirically observed changes in objective mental measurements. These may be spontaneous changes in test scores within an individual, or a secular trend in the mean of a population, or score gains induced by training or other interventions.

The critical question, then, is the locus of the change. Does it represent a change in the construct itself? Or is the change more attributable to properties of the vehicle, or to properties of the scale of measurement? The item content of the Stanford-Binet IQ tests, for example, differs from one age level to the next. Several different highly g-loaded tests (e.g., Stanford-Binet, Wechsler, Raven) differ in other factors unrelated to g. What exactly has changed—the level of g or the non-g sources of variance? Is a unit change in one range of the measuring scale equivalent to a unit change in another range, that is, are the measurements an interval scale throughout their range? A change in the measurement is not necessarily a change in the level of the construct; it could reflect any one (or a combination) of several different sources of variance in the measurements.

Evidence for an authentic change in the construct g requires broad transfer or generalizability across a wide variety of cognitive performance. Anything less implies changes in lower-order factors, or in test specificity, or in conditions peculiar to the tests, or the conditions of administration, or the measurement scales.

The practice effect from taking a given g-loaded test, as indicated by the amount of test-retest gain in score, appears to be unrelated to g. Test-retest gains probably reflect only the source of variance known as the test's *specificity*.

Some persons show large, apparently spontaneous changes in IQ from one testing to another. They are a small minority of all persons who have been tested. All but about 10 percent of this group showing large changes in IQ (or in other g-loaded test scores) can be accounted for by the normal distribution of measurement errors. The 10 percent or so not so accounted for by measurement error are not attributable to any specific systematic causes and are statistically unpredictable for any given individual. The kinds of events and life experiences typically invoked post hoc to explain large IQ changes are in fact *not* significantly correlated with IQ change but occur with the same frequency among persons who have shown little or no change in IQ.

A secular upward trend in IQ averaging three IQ points per decade has been observed over the past half-century or so in many first-world countries. The gain has been greater on tests of fluid abilities (Gf) than of crystallized abilities (Gc), and it is generally greater in the lower than in the upper half of the IQ distribution. It is uncertain to what extent the rise in IQ represents a real change in g itself. Several different theories have been propounded to account for the secular rise in IQ, involving changing attitudes (e.g., risk taking, guessing tendencies) toward mental tests, effects of extended schooling and more widespread education throughout all strata of society, and improvements in nutrition and medical and health care. That many such biological factors could be a major cause of the IQ gains is suggested by the fact that, over the same period of time, the average physical stature of the population has shown a comparable increase (measured in standard deviation units).

Experimental attempts to raise IQ have not produced large or lasting effects. The most intensive and extensive psychological interventions, beginning shortly after birth and continuing until five or six years of age, when the treated children enter regular schools, have produced gains of twenty to thirty or more IQ points above that of a control group at the peak of their effectiveness. But these large gains diminish greatly over time. Moreover, the almost negligible generalizability, or transfer, of the training effect to scholastic performance during the years following treatment suggests that it is not the level of g, but only the test *scores* that were raised, and suggests that most of the training effect resulted from "teaching to the test." The IQ gain is thus "hollow" with respect to g. However, the most recent and best-conducted intensive intervention experiment showed a lasting gain equivalent to about five IQ points (at age twelve), and a significant transfer to scholastic achievement and to unconventional g-loaded Piagetian tests, which suggest that the expected outcome is a real change in the level of g. The long-term persistence of this gain, which some experts question, could be established by a follow-up study, perhaps when the subjects are high school seniors.

This chapter concerns three classes of phenomena: (1) the natural variability in the measurements of g for the same individual, (2) the intentional malleability of g measurements for individuals, and (3) the secular stability (or instability) of the mean level of g measurements in a population across generations or for different same-age cohorts tested years or decades apart. These phenomena have been viewed as methodologically and empirically problematic for psychometrics and theories of mental ability. Before discussing the empirical findings, however, several basic concepts are essential background.

Three distinct concepts must be considered: (1) the *construct* of primary interest (i.e., g, in this case); (2) the *vehicle* used to elicit the construct, such as a test or an apparatus and the specific procedures for using it; and (3) the *measurement* derived from the vehicle. Although these concepts are theoretically related, they can each vary independently. ("Vehicle" is used here in the sense of a means of conveyance, as a bus is a vehicle for passengers or *Hamlet* is a vehicle for Sir Laurence Olivier's talent.)

Construct. The construct, g, can be elicited in many different ways, as I have already pointed out. It is not a function of any particular vehicle, but is a source of variance (i.e., individual differences) that is evidenced by the correlations between a number of diverse tests, each of which reflects g to some extent but may also reflect group factors and specificity. If individuals differ from one another in whatever innate or acquired properties or processes of the brain are reflected by the g factor, as must necessarily be the case for g even to emerge from the factor analysis of a correlation matrix, then individuals can be rank-ordered in terms of g, at least in theory. A hypothetical pure test of g could rank-order individuals perfectly in terms of whatever it is that creates the variance in performance on mental tests reflected in a factor analysis as g. And, in a manner of speaking, one could then say that certain individuals have more (or less) g than others. But to actually achieve such a ranking of individuals would require first having some test or device for registering each individual's standing on g. Simply identifying g by factor analysis and knowing each test's g loading can tell us nothing at all about the g level of any given individual. Factors and factor loadings are derived entirely from correlation coefficients, which are pure numbers. That is, they are completely divested of any information about the level of performance of individuals or of the overall mean of the group used for the factor analysis. This is a purely mathematical consequence of any factor analysis based on correlations. When a Pearson correlation coefficient r_{xy} between any two variables, say X and Y, is computed, the actual means and standard deviations of the variables are completely lost, because the correlation is based on standardized scores (z_x and z_y), for which the means and standard deviations are deliberately set to mean = 0 and $SD = 1$ for each variable (i.e., $r_{xy} = \Sigma(z_x \cdot z_y)/N$). Therefore, to rank individuals on their level of g requires a *vehicle* for eliciting and indicating an individual's *level* of g.

Vehicles. Because g is manifested in so many kinds of behavior that involve mental abilities, an individual's level of g can be elicited and assessed in many ways. The psychometrician's aim is to devise a vehicle that will most accurately and efficiently measure an individuals' standing on the construct.

As no pure test of g exists, the traditional solution has been to obtain a composite score from a number of substantially g-loaded tests that are highly diverse in the specific kinds of knowledge and skills required. Most of the variance due to the unique demands made by each test is averaged out. The greater the number of such diverse (but g-loaded) tests that enter into the composite score, the more the unwanted sources of variance are averaged out and the more accurately the composite scores indicate individual differences in g level. In the best standardized test batteries currently in use, some 75 percent or more of the variance of the composite scores consists of g, which means that the correlation between the obtained scores and the construct g approaches $\sqrt{.75} = .87$. This is typical for the most widely used individual IQ tests. Factor scores, based on an optimally weighted composite of the subtests, are somewhat more highly correlated with the "true" g. But since the gain in precision is trivial or irrelevant for practical purposes, g factor scores are rarely calculated, except in research work.

Accurate measurement requires a prescribed standardized procedure. In mental testing, this includes the instructions to be given by the examiner, the preparatory practice given on typical test items, the precise time limits (if any), and the ambience of the testing conditions.

What is most important to realize, but not easy to grasp, is the conceptual distinction between the particular *vehicle* of g and the g construct per se. *The vehicle is not the construct; the construct is not the vehicle.* For example, Mount Everest has a "true" height, which can be measured (i.e., estimated with some degree of accuracy) by a variety of means—by the altimeter in an airplane flying alongside Everest at a level even with its peak, or with a surveyor's transit, or by the time it takes a cannonball shot out horizontally from the peak to reach the ground level, or by the oxygen content of the air sampled at the peak. All of these measurements, if properly done, would be in close agreement.

Likewise, two test batteries with quite different item contents can each be a good vehicle of g. However, under certain conditions one test may be better than the other. In a group of persons who have had the same schooling, for example, scores on a test containing many items of scholastic knowledge could be as highly correlated with a hypothetical true *g* as scores on a test containing only nonverbal items with no dependence at all on scholastic content. But in a group of much more heterogeneous educational background, the two types of tests probably would not be equally good vehicles of *g*.

Each test score reflects both the level of *g and* the properties of the *vehicle* of *g* (the latter being largely unrelated to *g*). One would predict, for example, that the *g* factor, which is highly and equally loaded in batteries of verbal and nonverbal tests when given to monolingual children, would have much smaller *g* loadings on the verbal tests (given in English) than on the nonverbal tests when that battery is given to bilingual children. For the bilingual group the verbal tests would reflect the degree of second-language acquisition more than they would reflect *g*.

An individual's *raw score* on a test is simply the number of test items answered correctly. The difficulty level of an item (termed the *P* value) is the percentage who pass the item in a representative sample of the normative population for which the test is to be used. Variation in item *P* values provides the basic units of an individual's score on the test. In composing items for a test, the idea is to have a wide enough range of item difficulty, from very easy to very hard items, to be able to register the full range of individuals' ability levels in the particular population for which the test is intended. A test in which the easiest items are failed by some persons is said to produce a "floor" effect; a test in which the hardest items are passed by some persons is said to produce a "ceiling" effect. Floor and ceiling effects truncate the range in test scores, which then underestimate the full range of individual differences in the population. Floor and ceiling effects are eliminated by including easier items or more difficult items, respectively.

Various tests, each having a quite different range of item difficulty, could yield equally valid measures of *g* provided each test's difficulty level were appropriate (i.e., without floor or ceiling effects) for the range of ability in the group to which it is administered. It sacrifices accuracy and wastes testing time to use a test containing item difficulty levels appropriate for the entire range of ability in the general population when only a select segment of the ability distribution in the total population is to be tested. Hence there are different tests, each measuring mostly *g*, that are best suited for use with groups that have a restricted range of ability. But the scores on all these different tests are usually not on a common scale, so a person's score on Test A cannot be directly compared with another person's score on Test B. An analogy is the different types of thermometers we use for measuring temperatures in different ranges, as in a refrigerator, a room, the human body, a kitchen oven, or a blast furnace. They all measure temperature, but you wouldn't want to use a clinical thermometer in a blast furnace.

There is, however, an essential difference between the specialized thermometers and the various tests of g. The temperatures measured by all the different thermometers can be represented on one and the same scale of measurement, and the distances between scale points on each thermometer correspond to the same equal intervals of differences in the amount of the thing being measured, namely, heat. Also, different temperature scales, such as Fahrenheit (F) or Celsius (C), can each be transformed by a linear equation into each other or into Kelvin (K), the absolute measure of temperature having a true zero point, equal intervals on the scale representing equal increments of heat, and physically meaningful ratios (e.g., 50°K is in fact one-half as much heat as 100°K, whereas 50°F/100°F $\neq$ 50°C/100°C $\neq$ one-half the amount of heat).

Mental Measurements. Very few mental test scales, on the other hand, have these advantageous scale properties of physical measurements. Raw scores on a test are a function of two things: the number of items composing the test and the items' difficulty levels as determined in a random sample of persons from some appropriate reference population, or "norm" group. Raw scores typically constitute only an ordinal, or rank-order, scale. The score by itself is not at all interpretable.[1] (The percentage of items answered correctly is equally uninterpretable.)

To have any meaning at all, a test has to be "normed" on a subject sample of some defined population. A raw score (X) then can be transformed to a *standardized* score (called a z score), which is expressed as a deviation from the mean of the norm group in units determined by the standard deviation of the raw scores (i.e., $z = [X - \text{mean}]/SD$). The distribution of raw scores can even be "normalized," that is, made to fit the normal curve perfectly, first by rank-ordering the raw scores, then converting the ranks to percentile ranks, and finally assigning to each percentile rank the standard score (z) corresponding to the percentile of a normal deviate, that is, all values of z distributed as the normal, or Gaussian, curve. (The IQ scale, with mean = 100 and SD = 15, is simply $100 + 15z$.) An individual's score on such a standardized or normalized scale only indicates that individual's standing relative to the particular norm group. Most important: an individual's test score (in either raw or standardized form) is *not* a measure of the *quantity* of the latent trait (e.g., g) per se possessed by that individual.

When a new test is created, or a test is revised and some of the original items are replaced by new items, the test must be renormed on a new sample for the scores to be interpretable. By giving the new norm group both the old test and the new (or revised) test, it is possible to *equate*[2] the two tests' scores so an individual's standardized score on either test indicates the same percentile rank (within the new norm group) on both tests. Obviously, these norm-derived scores do not measure an absolute level of ability, nor can they be transformed to an absolute or ratio scale (as temperatures on Fahrenheit or Celsius thermometers can be transformed to Kelvin, the absolute scale of heat). Modern techniques of constructing and scaling tests, known as *item response theory*[3] (IRT), however, have gone beyond the scaling methods of classic test theory by making it possible to scale item difficulty independently of the ability level of any norm group and to measure both item difficulty and individual differences in ability on one and the same equal-interval scale. However, the most widely used IQ tests today, such as the Stanford-Binet and Wechsler scales, are not based on IRT. In any case, although the methods of IRT scaling would be a technical boon to the measurement aspect of research on the temporal fluctuations of test scores known to occur both for individuals and for populations, it could not by itself answer the main question as to the meaning or causes of the observed fluctuations. Are they fluctuations in *g* itself, or only in the vehicle or measurement of *g*?

A rough analogy may help to make the essential point. Suppose that for some reason it was impossible to measure persons' heights directly in the usual way, with a measuring stick. However, we still could accurately measure the length of the shadow cast by each person when the person is standing outdoors in the sunlight. Provided everyone's shadow is measured at the same time of day, at the same day of the year, and at the same latitude on the earth's surface, the shadow measurements would show exactly the same correlations with persons' weight, shoe size, suit or dress size, as if we had measured everyone directly with a yardstick; and the shadow measurements could be used to predict perfectly whether or not a given person had to stoop when walking through a door that is only 5½-feet high. However, if one group of persons' shadows were measured at 9:00 A.M. and another group's at 10:00 A.M., the pooled measurements would show a much smaller correlation with weight and other factors than if they were all measured at the same time, date, and place, and the measurements would have poor validity for predicting which persons could walk through a 5½-foot door without stooping. We would say, correctly, that these measurements are biased. In order to make them usefully accurate as predictors of a person's weight and so forth, we would have to know the time the person's shadow was measured and could then add or subtract a value that would adjust the measurement so as to make it commensurate with measurements obtained at some other specific time, date, and location. This procedure would permit the standardized shadow measurements of height, which in principle would be as good as the measurements obtained directly with a measuring stick.

Standardized IQs are somewhat analogous to the standardized shadow measurements of height, while the raw scores on IQ tests are more analogous to the raw measurements of the shadows themselves. If we naïvely remain unaware that the shadow measurements vary with the time of day, the day of the year, and the degrees of latitude, our raw measurements would prove practically worthless for comparing individuals or groups tested at different times, dates, or places. Correlations and predictions could be accurate only within each unique group of persons whose shadows were measured at the same time, date, and place. Since psychologists do not yet have the equivalent of a yardstick for measuring mental ability directly, their vehicles of mental measurement—IQ scores—are necessarily "shadow" measurements, as in our height analogy, albeit with amply demonstrated practical predictive validity and construct validity within certain temporal and cultural limits.

Many possible factors determine whether a person passes or fails a particular test item. Does the person understand the item at all (e.g., "What is the sum of all the latent roots of a 7×7 **R** matrix?")? Has the person acquired the specific knowledge called for by the item (e.g., "Who wrote *Faust*?"), or perhaps has he acquired it in the past and has since forgotten it? Did the person really know the answer, but just couldn't recall it at the moment of being tested? Does the item call for a cognitive skill the person either never acquired or has forgotten through disuse (e.g., "How much of a whole apple is two-thirds of one-half of the apple?")? Does the person understand the problem and know how to solve it, but is unable to do it within the allotted time limit (e.g., substituting the corresponding letter of the alphabet for each of the numbers from one to twenty-six listed in a random order in one minute)? Or even when there is a liberal time limit does the person give up on the item or just guess at the answer prematurely, perhaps because the item looks too complicated at first glance (e.g., "If it takes six garden hoses, all running for three hours and thirty minutes to fill a tank, how many additional hoses would be needed to fill the tank in thirty minutes?")? [*Answer*: thirty-six.]

Obviously, there is almost no limit to the possible idiosyncratic reasons for failing a given item. It is probable, however, that some part of the reason for failing a particular item is the person's standing on the general ability measured by the test as a whole (composed of, say, 100 items), even absent the particular item in question. Thus it is possible to state the probability that any given item will be passed (or failed) by a person selected at random from all persons who obtained the same g score (derived from the whole test). In a well-constructed test to measure g, *the probability that a given person will pass any given item is a positive monotonic function of the person's standing on* g. A plot of this "S"-shaped function is called the *item characteristic curve* (ICC).

The ICCs for each of two items are shown in Figure 10.1. The location of the zero point and the slope parameter of the ICC may differ for every item in the test. This general monotonic relationship between a person's ability level and the probability of the person's passing a given item holds even when the items differ as much as or more than those in the earlier list of why items are failed.

Item types can vary greatly, and the ICC's baseline g scores can even be derived from a battery of exclusively nonverbal tests such as Raven matrices, block designs, number series, and figural analogies and yet yield typical ICC functions for vocabulary items (such as "What is an *amanuensis*?") or general information items (like "What is the capital of India?"). Obviously, some latent trait has to exist on which persons differ and which can be distilled from a large pool of items such that the more of the trait that a person possesses, the greater is the probability that the person will pass any given item. A test that does not manifest this relationship between persons' ability level and items has in fact

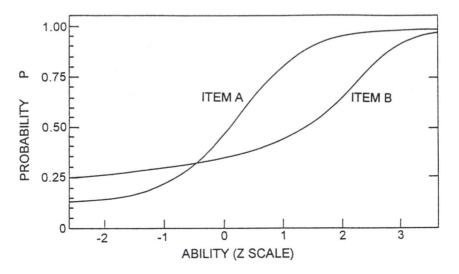

Figure 10.1. Typical item characteristic curve (ICC) for each of two test items. Item A is a quite "easy" item; Item B is relatively "difficult." The standard error of P, the probability of passing the item at any given score on the latent trait or ability factor (e.g., g), is inversely related to the size (N) of the sample used to determine the ICC at that region: $SE_P = \sqrt{[P(1 - P)/N]}$.

little external validity for predicting "real life" criteria and is not a practically useful test.

These points are necessary in order to address the real question: What is it that changes when test scores fluctuate, for individuals or for populations—the construct, the vehicle, or the measurement? Does a change in a person's IQ (or a group's mean IQ) represent a real change in the *construct*—the efficiency of information processing reflected by g and its neural substrate? Or is it just a change in the vehicle—the increased general familiarity of certain items' information content attributable to education, TV, or previous experience in taking similar tests? Or is it a change in IQ on a renormed test—the result of a sampling artifact whereby the new norm group does not represent the same population, but has a different absolute level of ability from the previous norm group whose raw scores were used for the original standardized of the IQ scale?

TEST-RETEST CHANGE IN SCORES

When the same test, or an equivalent or parallel form of the test, is administered to persons on two separate occasions, days, weeks, or even months apart, there is usually an increase in scores, called a "practice effect." It affects performance on the particular test and on highly similar tests.[4] Subsequent retesting on the same (or similar) tests, however, shows ever smaller gains. Typically

Table 10.1

Spearman's Rank Correlation between the Column Vector of Mean Test-Retest Increments on GATB Aptitude Scores for Various Retest Intervals and the Column Vector of the Aptitudes' g Loadings[a]

	Rank Correlation	
Test-Retest Interval	Males	Females
1 Day	-.526	-.381
2 Weeks	-.397	-.619
6 Weeks	-.529	-.500
13 Weeks	-.387	-.108
26 Weeks	-.462	-.180
1 Year	-.791	-.548
2 Years	-.861	-.707
3 Years	-.860	-.695

[a]All the g loadings (first principal factor) of the GATB subscales were corrected for attenuation.

the initial gain amounts to almost one-third of a standard deviation (about three to six points on the IQ scale).

The increment in scores due to the practice effect, however, has little effect on the rank order of individuals' scores. For intervals of less than one year, the test-retest correlations are generally above .90. This indicates that the test measures essentially the same factors on both occasions, despite the average increment in scores. It would be interesting to know, however, whether the increment in scores due to the practice effect reflects an actual increase in g itself or an increase in group factors or test specificity that are independent of g.

My search of the literature turned up a data set that lends itself to the kind of analysis appropriate to answer this question.[5] Large samples were given the General Aptitude Test Battery (GATB) on two occasions, separated by intervals of 1 day, 2 weeks, 6 weeks, 13 weeks, and 26 weeks. Other large groups had test-retest intervals of either 1, 2, or 3 years. Each of the eight distinct aptitude[6] scores yielded by the GATB subtests showed a retest increment (ranging over all aptitudes and test-retest intervals from about .08σ to 0.5σ). I then correlated the column vector of score increments on each of the eight aptitudes with the column vector of the g loadings of each of the aptitudes, based on the total GATB standardization sample ($N = 23,428$; Table 10.1). Note that the test-retest increments in the aptitude scores for all intervals are *negatively* correlated with the aptitude tests' g loadings.[7]

The higher a test's g loading, the less susceptible it is to a practice effect. That is what these data indicate about the relation of the practice effect to g. If there were a *positive* correlation, it would mean that the more that a test is g

loaded, the greater is the increment in test scores with practice, whether or not the increment is also *g* loaded. But a *negative* correlation, as was found here, means that the more *g* loaded a test is, the less susceptible it is to practice gains, whether or not the score increment due to practice is also *g* loaded. In other words, a test's *g* loading predicts the magnitude of the practice effect on that test relative to other tests, but tells us nothing about the degree to which the increment in scores is *g* loaded.

Since the observed score increments could just as well reflect gains in test specificity rather than in *g* or any other common factors, a further analysis is required. A principal components analysis of the mean practice gains over all test-retest intervals on each of the GATB aptitudes reveals two significant components (eigenvalues > 1) that together account for 78 percent of the variance. However, neither one bears any resemblance to the aptitudes' *g* loadings (Spearman rank correlations of $-.048$ and $-.024$, respectively). This tells us that the common factors in the score increments are not related to the *g* factor of the GATB. Probably subtest specificity, rather than any common factors, is the main constituent reflected in the score increments due to a practice effect. This interpretation is consistent with the general finding that practice effects, or even gains from specific training, on a given test show remarkably little transfer to other tests. The inverse relationship between *g* loadings and practice effects, and the relative absence of *g* in the increments themselves, may explain the low external validity of the IQ gains that result from specific training in the various cognitive skills assumed to be measured by IQ tests. The training-induced gains in IQ scores fail to predict external criteria (e.g., scholastic achievement) to the degree that would be expected if the induced gain in IQ represented a true gain in *g*, rather than merely a gain in the test's specificity. This "hollow IQ" phenomenon is discussed more fully in a later section on the attempts to raise IQ by special educational interventions.

"SPONTANEOUS" CHANGES IN IQ ARE MOSTLY IDIOSYNCRATIC CHANCE

Individuals' IQs fluctuate over the age range from early childhood to maturity and from later maturity to old age and death. IQ is relatively unstable in early childhood, but from age two to age ten it becomes increasingly stable and more highly predictive of individuals' IQs in early adulthood. The correlation between IQ at age 10 and at age 18 is between .70 and .80; IQ measured at successive ages beyond age 10 gradually approaches a correlation of .90 with IQ at age 18.[8] Much of the variability in mental growth rates from early childhood to maturity is genetically programmed, as shown by the fact that monozygotic twins have nearly identical mental growth curves, with the same spurts and plateaus, while dizygotic twins show less similar growth curves, with spurts and plateaus occurring at different ages.[9] The decreasing stability of IQ in old age is related to increasing individual differences in general health and physical fitness and probably inherited differences in the rate of mental decline.

Developmental psychologists and psychometricians alike have puzzled over the occasionally large and seemingly spontaneous changes in some individuals' IQs and the fact that IQ has proven so resistant to change by means of psychological and educational interventions. If the cause(s) of the seemingly spontaneous changes could be discovered, perhaps they then could be intentionally manipulated to produce desired changes in IQ.

The most thorough study[10] analyzing spontaneous IQ changes that I have found in the literature is based on a representative sample of 794 children who were tested on the Wechsler Intelligence Scale for Children (WISC-R) at ages 7, 9, 11, and 13. The correlations of IQ at every age with every other age range from .74 to .84, indicating some instability in the children's relative standings on IQ from one testing time to another. The magnitude of changes, in IQ points, was rather normally distributed, with a mean near zero and a slight positive skew (i.e., more extreme upward than extreme downward changes). The mean intraindividual standard deviation of IQ over all four test occasions was 3.35 points. At each testing interval, about 10 percent of the sample changed more than fifteen IQ points. For the vast majority of children, the fluctuations in IQ were small enough to be accounted for by the unreliability of measurement, but the IQ changes shown by that 10 percent of the sample were too large to fall within the range of normally distributed measurement errors, given the reliability and standard error of measurement of the WISC-R. Concerning this group with real and marked IQ changes, the authors stated, "[T]his change is variable in its timing, idiosyncratic in its source and transient in its course" (p. 455).

In an attempt to discover possible causes of the larger than chance IQ changes, the 107 most erratic testees were compared against the 687 relatively stable members of the sample on a set of thirty-seven family and child characteristics that have been theoretically or empirically related to IQ (such as perinatal problems, central nervous system syndromes, impaired vision or audition, motor development, behavior problems, family size, maternal health, family relations, socioeconomic status, moving location, changing caretakers, and the like). Only three of the thirty-seven variables showed a significant difference ($p < .05$) between the erratic and stable groups in frequency of occurrence (mean address changes by age thirteen, percent boys, motor development score). Out of thirty-seven such comparisons, one should expect about two significant ones to occur by chance alone. Therefore, it is quite possible that the two groups did not really differ overall more than chance expectancy in the variables thought to influence mental development.

Other variables were also examined, such as parental separation or remarriage, nervous system trauma or illness, emotional problems, and the like. But for every child for whom a life event was linked to a marked IQ change, it was possible to find several other children who had experienced the same life event but who showed no detectable effect on IQ. The authors suggested that "the causes of marked IQ change may be unique events that occur in the lives of individual children; 'the slings and arrows of outrageous fortune' '' (p. 489). Also, they concluded, ''[W]e cannot yet predict in advance whether or not a child's IQ will change in response to any perturbing event, no matter how strong'' (p. 491). The IQ is described as ''elastic'' rather than ''plastic,'' because marked changes in the trajectory of a child's mental development are typically followed later by a return to the initial trajectory for that child. The finding that the reliable change in IQ that does take place is idiosyncratic and not associated with any identifiable environmental change is entirely consistent with the finding, based on the correlation of mental growth curves of MZ and DZ twins, that the observed spurts and plateaus in mental growth, as indicated by IQ, are about as genetically determined as individual differences in IQ measured on any one occasion during middle childhood and adolescence.[9]

THE SECULAR INCREASE IN IQ

One of the most puzzling phenomena is the increase in raw scores on various IQ tests in many populations over the last sixty years or so. This phenomenon has been under investigation since the mid-1980s. Most of the evidence for the upward trend comes from the many past studies where various tests that were originally normed at one time on a representative population sample were renormed many years later on a different, but supposedly equivalent, population sample.

This upward trend in the population's mean test scores has been aptly dubbed the ''Flynn effect,'' after James R. Flynn, a professor of political science at the Otago University in New Zealand, who was responsible for amassing most of the evidence for what he has referred to as ''massive IQ gains.''[11] The bulk of this evidence comes from the period between 1930 and 1980.

Before summarizing this evidence, it should be noted that when a test is normed or renormed, the IQ (which is a standardized score) is always scaled such that the population mean is 100 and the standard deviation is fifteen. Population trends in actual test performance, as indicated by raw scores (number right), therefore, are not reflected by the IQ, except to some degree as the trend proceeds between the original norming and the renorming of the same test. Actual gains in test performance over long periods are adequately measured only by raw scores.

In measuring these raw-score gains two problems must be considered: (1) The change in raw scores must be demonstrated on the identical test administered on both occasions. Changes in test items (e.g., dropping some old items and substituting new ones) may alter the overall difficulty level of the test, causing a spurious rise (or fall) in the mean raw score of the more recently tested sample; (2) a much more problematic condition in renorming tests (or in comparing the same test on different samples that were tested at widely separated times) is the assumption that the two norm samples are truly equivalent. A number of factors militate against obtaining equivalent and representative samples of a population. The most obvious are population changes over decades or generations, due to changing demographics, such as birth rates in different socioeconomic segments of the population, rates of immigration and emigration, regional changes in the types of employment available, and the like.

Although the supposed equivalence of samples taken at different times is often open to doubt, changing demographics should not cause changes in test scores that are consistently in one direction for every test in every study conducted with many different population samples. Flynn's compilations of changes in test scores over decades and generations were drawn from fifteen economically advanced nations in North America, Europe, and Asia. In addition, since the publication of Flynn's major reviews, other investigators have reported highly similar results based on data from other countries and on tests not included in Flynn's reviews. The overwhelming consistency of virtually all of the data with respect to the direction of the trend in test scores leaves little doubt of the reality of the "Flynn effect." Whatever inconsistencies exist are all in the details.

Descriptive Statistics on Increase in Scores. Although all of the score increases discussed here are based on raw scores, they have been standardized and expressed as IQ differences, as the IQ scale ($\mu = 100$, $\sigma = 15$) is the most familiar. Because different data sets span different time intervals, the change in test scores is always expressed here in terms of the amount of *IQ change per decade*, henceforth labeled ΔIQ ("delta IQ").

The reported values of ΔIQ for twenty-five tests in fifteen countries range from 1.8 to 12.5, with an overall mean of 5.0 ($SD = 2.9$). ΔIQ varies rather erratically across different countries, across different studies within the same country, across studies, across different tests, and across different time periods between 1930 and 1990. All these variables are utterly confounded with one another in the available data.

The most frequently reported test data on secular trends are for the Raven Matrices (nonverbal) and the Wechsler (both verbal and performance scales). The Raven's overall average ΔIQ is 5.69 ($SD = 3.49$); the Wechsler's ΔIQ is 5.20 ($SD = .271$). (*Note*: getting just one additional correct item on the Raven makes for two to three points increase in IQ.) More of the secular increase in the Wechsler IQ is on the Performance scale (ΔIQ = 7.8) than on the Verbal scale (ΔIQ = 4.2). In the United States between 1932 and 1978, ΔIQ $\cong$ 3.0, averaged over the Wechsler and Stanford-Binet tests. Culture-reduced tests and tests of fluid g (Gf) show somewhat larger ΔIQ than verbal tests or tests of crystallized g (Gc). Strangely, despite the trend over the same period toward universal education in all economically advanced countries, tests that emphasize scholastic content show the least gain. The several studies in Great Britain[12] show ΔIQ values ranging from about 1.5 to 3.0, which is probably the smallest gain of all the countries in which studies have been done, with the possible exception of Denmark. Also in the British and Danish studies, the increase in scores is largely concentrated in the lower segment of the IQ distribution. What-ever causes the rise in IQ, it has its greatest effect on those at the lower end of the scale, with a corresponding shrinkage of the standard deviation.

The best studies available on the secular increase in test scores, published after Flynn's 1987 review, were based on five large cohorts of males (born between 1939 and 1969), who were tested at age eighteen as part of the com-pulsory conscription for military service in Denmark.[13] Each of the five cohorts of eighteen-year-olds selected from different years (at five-year intervals) was so selected as to constitute at the time a truly random sample of Denmark's male population of the same age. Moreover, the test was ideal in its construction and in its scaling of item difficulty.[14] Each of the four highly *g*-loaded subtests (letter matrices, verbal analogies, number series, and geometric figures) consti-tutes a unidimensional scale, and the composite score is an excellent measure of *g*.

The increase in mean raw scores in this study was equivalent to a ΔIQ of 2.5. Although the test used has almost no scholastic content, the observed in-crease is related to the average increase in the level of education going from the earlier to the later cohorts. Since the cohorts were randomly selected to represent the entire male population at age 18, the correlation ($r = +.71$) be-tween ΔIQ and the rising educational level probably indicates a direct causal relationship.[15]

Components of Secular Change in Population Means. I have not found any study of the factor composition of the secular increase in test scores. Has the level of *g* and of other common factors changed, or does the increase in scores reflect only properties of the vehicles of these factors, because of people's greater sophistication in taking tests, as a result of their increasing use?

What has been determined is that the mean scores on highly *g*-loaded tests (e.g., Raven Matrices, Wechsler, Stanford-Binet) all show secular change, but the tests' *g* loadings are not highly correlated with the amount of secular change in scores. A study[16] in Scotland of the average gains on the six verbal subscales of the WISC from 1961 to 1983/84 permits a rank-order correlation of the column vector of gains on each of the subtests with the column vector of each of the subtests' *g* loadings (obtained from the U.S. standardization sample). The rank correlations are +.22 and +.40 for ten-year-olds and thirteen-year-olds, respectively. (The high reliability of the vector of subtest gains is indicated by its +.96 correlation between the two age groups.)

The Seattle Longitudinal Study[17] compared twelve age cohorts with birth years from 1889 to 1966, all tested at the same age as adults, at seven-year intervals, on five of Thurstone's Primary Mental Abilities. The largest gains were on the two most highly *g*-loaded tests (Inductive Reasoning [*g* = .84] and Word Meaning [*g* =.67]), the next highest gain was for Spatial Orientation (*g* = .33), while there was no overall gain for Number (*g* = .60) and Word Fluency (*g* = .68). The rank-order correlation between the degree of secular increase (over seventy-seven years) in each of the five PMA scores and their *g* loadings is only +.30. Hence the mean rise in test scores largely reflects something other than the degree to which the scores measure g, although we cannot rule out that some increase in the level of g may also be one of the constituents in the overall trend.

Another study,[18] of secular changes (1978 to 1988 in Northern Ireland) on five of Thurstone's PMA tests given to children nine to eleven years old, showed the following values of ΔIQ: Verbal 0.24, Reasoning 1.30, Numerical 2.58, Spatial 6.18, Perceptual Speed 8.88. (There was no appreciable decrease in *SD* for any test.) Here there is an inverse relationship between the tests' g loadings and their ΔIQ. The Spatial Relations and Perceptual Speed tests, which are the least g loaded of the PMA battery, show the largest gains, while the Reasoning and Verbal abilities, which are the most g loaded, show the least gains. On the other hand, research by the Educational Testing Service[19] on various national samples of United States high school seniors found a decline in spatial/visual skills between 1960 and 1980. Both male and female high school seniors in 1980 performed on spatial tests at the level of high school freshmen in 1960. (The male-female difference on the spatial tests decreased by one-third during this period.) The most likely explanation for the decline among seniors is the decrease in high school dropout rates between 1960 and 1980, creating a less select group of seniors. (Their reading scores also declined between 1960 and 1980.) This well illustrates the possible artifact associated with population sampling, which probably accounts for much of the inconsistency in studies of secular change. It is likely that a large part of the variation in the magnitudes of the observed effects in different studies results from the failure to obtain equivalent population samples when the samples are selected at widely separated points in time, such as a decade or more.

Spearman's "Law of Diminishing Returns" (see Appendix A, pp. 585–88) states that less of the variance in a collection of diverse mental tests consists of g within a high-ability group than it does within a low-ability group. A corollary of this "law" is that the average intercorrelation among diverse tests is smaller for a high-ability group than it is for a low-ability group. The mounting evidence that this is an authentic phenomenon suggests a possible test of the hypothesis that the secular increase in IQ involves to some extent an increase in the actual *level* of g in the population. It would be supported by finding a secular *decrease* in the average intercorrelation among tests (and hence a decrease in their g loadings). This hypothesis, first advanced by Richard Lynn,[20] was tested on the French and Japanese versions of the WISC (and WISC-R) in France (for a sixteen-year interval) and Japan (for a twenty-five-year interval). Increases in test scores had already been found in these countries. The hypothesis *appears* to be borne out in both data sets; that is, the average correlation between the Wechsler subtests decreased in the more recently tested group. In France the average subtest intercorrelations decreased from .38 to .29; in Japan, from .41 to .23. Unfortunately, these results cannot be considered definitive, because no account was taken of the possible change in the variances of the subtest scores.

If the subtest variances decreased from one time to the next, their intercorrelations would be diminished from that effect alone, which is incidental with respect to Spearman's "law." Because the subtest variances on each occasion were not reported, I cannot correct the correlations for this possible artifact. It is not an improbable one, since some studies have shown a secular decrease in raw-score variance.[21]

Secular Decline in Scholastic Achievement Scores. During the same period that IQ performance was rising, scores on tests of scholastic achievement were declining, at all age levels. These opposite trends seem paradoxical, because, for students who have had the same amount of schooling, individual differences in scholastic achievement are highly correlated with IQ. When various achievement tests and IQ tests are factor analyzed together, both kinds of tests are highly loaded on a large general factor that is clearly *g*. These results provide a striking example of how the *level* of highly *g*-loaded measurements is influenced by the *vehicle* through which *g* is expressed. When the *g*-loaded test is composed largely of nonscholastic items (e.g., matrices, figure analogies), the raw scores show a secular increase; when an equally *g*-loaded test is composed of scholastic items (e.g., reading comprehension, math) the raw scores show a secular decrease. Obviously, the true level of *g* cannot be changing in opposite directions at the same time. The difference in vehicles must account for the discrepancy. So the extent to which the level of *g* per se has been rising (or falling) over the past few decades remains problematic.

About three-fourths of the decline in the national mean Scholastic Aptitude Test (SAT) score, from 1952 to 1990, is due to the increasing percentage of high school students with college aspirations who take the SAT (rising from about 5 percent in 1952 to about 30 percent in 1968). The pool of applicants, in fact, became increasingly less selective between 1960 and 1985. But even after this decline in test scores due to the changing composition of the college-going population is accounted for, a real SAT score decrement remains. Its cause has been attributed to the "dumbing down" of the school curriculum and slackening attainments in the kinds of academic knowledge and cognitive skills tapped by the SAT, especially by students in the upper quartile.[22] The overall *decline* in SAT scores has been slightly larger than the *gain* in IQ scores; when both are expressed in terms of ΔIQ, they amount to about -5 for the SAT and $+3$ for IQ. (The SAT-Verbal score declined slightly more than SAT-Math.)

Hypothesized Causes of the Secular Increase in IQ Test Performance. Any explanation of the secular change in IQ test raw scores must take account of the fact that, unlike the population means, there are certain properties of the IQ that have remained virtually constant across the past sixty or seventy years. These include its reliability, its correlations with measures of other psychometric abilities, its *g* loading, and its external validity, as indicated by its correlations with variables such as SES, race, scholastic achievement, occupational status, and job performance. Further, there has been no detectable change over the decades in the IQ correlations of MZ twins, or of DZ twins or other kinships, or of the heritability of IQ. The relationship of IQ to each of these variables has in no way been affected by the secular trend of the raw scores themselves. In this respect, the upward trend in scores is like a rising tide that lifts all ships without changing their relative heights. It is as if in each successive year over the past several decades, a small constant value was added to the total raw score obtained by every person who took an IQ test. As a result, the population mean rises steadily, but this does not change the test scores' correlations with any other variables.

At least four distinguishable hypotheses have been put forth to explain what has caused the secular increase in test scores. They are: the *attitude* theory, the *schooling* theory, the *biological-environment* theory, and the *genetic* theory. Although these hypotheses are not mutually exclusive or at all incompatible, their proponents often seem to treat them as if they were. They all seem plausible and I strongly suspect that each is involved to some (as yet undetermined) degree in producing the secular rise in scores. Picking through the many previously mentioned inconsistencies in the details of the extensive and unsystematic data on secular trends, a critic can always find, amid that chaos, some bit of evidence with which to contradict any one (or all) of these causal hypotheses. And the ample possibility for contradictions in this realm has indeed provided ammunition for IQ nihilists. Determining the relative importance of the hypothesized causes of secular trends requires going beyond a piecemeal examination of the existing data. Rather, let's examine the competing hypotheses in detail.

Attitudes. Christopher R. Brand, a psychologist at the University of Edinburgh, has hypothesized[23] that certain general attitudes manifested in the testing room contribute to the secular rise in test scores on timed tests (such as Cattell's culture-reduced tests of g) and on multiple-choice tests (such as the Cattell, the Raven, and many other modern objective group tests). Multiple-choice tests allow subjects to guess at the correct answer. Brand argues that the increasing liberalism, permissiveness, and extraversion (implying a certain risk-taking recklessness) have increased in the modern world's advanced economies in recent decades and these are reflected in a test-taking attitude of quick, intuitive responding that makes for greater speed (hence more items are attempted) and more guessing at the correct answers. These tendencies increase the chances that one or two multiple-choice items, on average, could be gotten "right" more or less by sheer luck. Just one additional "right" answer on the Raven adds nearly three IQ points. This in fact approximates the average gain shown over a whole generation in the Scottish data. Brand goes on to argue that when the supposed intergenerational change in risk-taking attitudes, test sophistication, and cognitive style is taken into account, the modest secular rise on the Raven (and similar tests) is on a par with that seen for the Wechsler Verbal IQ. The Wechsler Verbal IQ is based on untimed tests that call for response *production* rather than multiple-choice response *selection*, thereby making it hardly possible to gain points by simple guessing.

Flynn[24] countered Brand's conclusion with a remarkably indirect and complex estimate of the Scottish gains on the WISC-R Verbal scale of $\Delta IQ \approx 4.4$, which is notably larger than the $\Delta IQ \approx 1.1$ reported by Brand. The main reason for the discrepancy, however, is not in the data themselves, but in the way that the gain-score was calculated. Brand used the median of the gains on each of the separate items on each of the verbal subtests; Flynn based his estimate on the total scores of the subtests. The two methods of measuring the average gain are simply not comparable. For purely statistical reasons, Brand's method (which is improper in this case, as it ignores item intercorrelations and hence under-estimates a possible change in *g*) must inevitably give a much smaller estimate of gain than the method used by Flynn.[25]

Schooling. Over the same time span that IQ has increased, schooling has increased in the general population. More and more people have been exposed to an increasingly standardized educational curriculum extending over more years of schooling, increasing rates of high school graduation, and more people going on to college. Also, first radio, then television, which dispense more general than local information, gradually spread into every segment of the population, finally becoming more universal in the industrialized countries than even indoor plumbing.

Teasdale and Owen,[13] who investigated secular trends in IQ in Denmark, invoke the schooling hypothesis to explain their findings. They discount the attitude or guessing hypothesis as even a partial explanation of their data, since they used tests that did not allow for selecting the correct answer from several multiple-choice alternatives, but rather required subjects to produce the correct answers. They explain their finding that the lower part of the IQ distribution gains the most as the result of the relatively greater increase in amount of education by the lower-scoring segment of the population, the increasing number of "special education" programs, and the lower rate of school dropout.

Although the causal role of increased schooling in producing the secular gains on IQ tests has not been directly investigated, the hypothesis is made highly plausible by strong evidence that schooling does affect IQ and this could be an important causal element in the secular rise of IQ. Stephen J. Ceci, a psychologist at Cornell University, has reviewed virtually the entire research literature on the effects of schooling on IQ.[26a] His analysis leaves little doubt that increased schooling, with more of the population attaining a higher grade, probably accounts for some substantial part, perhaps as much as half, of the observed secular increase in IQ raw scores. But Ceci notes, "Although schooling helps prop up IQ scores, this is not equivalent to claiming that it props up *intelligence*. The latter entails more than the acquisition of certain modes of cognizing that are valued by a test manufacturer, or the acquisition of cultural artifacts—no matter how important some may regard such shared knowledge."[26b] This is just another way of stating the distinction between the construct (i.e., *g*) and any particular vehicle for it (i.e., test content). The construct that Ceci considers to be the sine qua non of "intelligence" is novel problem solving (tests of which are highly *g* loaded). As described later in this chapter, experimental methods that have been successful in raising IQ scores (at least temporarily) also show that the educationally induced gain in test scores is "hollow" with respect to g. The experimentally induced increment in IQ lacks the external validity of highly g-loaded tests.

However, as noted previously, it is the nonverbal and culture-reduced tests, some of which call for novel problem solving, and few of which have item contents that resemble anything explicitly taught in school, that show the largest secular gains of any type of test. At first glance, this appears paradoxical if the schooling hypothesis is true. But perhaps not. One of the well-known by-products of schooling is an increased ability to decontextualize problems. In almost every subject in the school curriculum, pupils learn to discover the general rule that applies to a highly specific situation and to apply a general rule in a wide variety of different contexts. The use of symbols to stand for things in reading (and musical notation); basic arithmetic operations; consistencies in spelling, grammar, and punctuation; regularities and generalizations in history; categorizing, serializing, enumerating, and inferring in science, and so on. Learning to do these things, which are all part of the school curriculum, instills cognitive habits that can be called *decontextualization* of cognitive skills.[27] The tasks seen in many nonverbal or culture-reduced tests call for no scholastic knowledge per se, but do call for the ability to decontextualize novel situations by discovering rules or regularities and then using them to solve the problem.

Biological Environment. During the same period that schooling has increased throughout the industrialized countries there has been a parallel trend in features of the biological environment, particularly nutrition and health care, that have had marked effects on human physical development and well-being. One of the leading researchers on the secular trend in IQ, Richard Lynn, a psychologist at the University of Ulster in Northern Ireland, has hypothesized that these biologically based environmental effects are the major cause of the upward trend of IQ in the populations of the economically advanced countries. The part of the test score gain that is biologically based, in Lynn's view, reflects a real increase in the level of g.[28]

The increase in the biological component of g is viewed as just one among a number of many of the well-known beneficial effects of a nurturing environment on physical development. Others are decreased rates of fetal loss and infant mortality, increased life span, increased stature, and a faster growth rate from infancy to adulthood, with earlier puberty and sexual maturation.

Improved nutrition is probably the main causal agent of the enhanced growth rates and increasing stature, as greater numbers in the population have been receiving more adequate diets over recent decades—milk, breakfast cereals, and other processed foods enriched with vitamin and mineral supplements, along with school lunch programs for children of low-income families, and increased information on nutrition dispensed by schools and the mass media. This has occurred for virtually the entire population of first-world countries (although at somewhat different times and rates), and has brought about an increase of approximately one standard deviation in both adult height and head size over the same period as the secular rise in IQ has taken place. The amount of change in these physical features is fairly comparable to the rise in IQ (equivalent to about three points on the ΔIQ scale). As was noted in Chapter 6 (pp. 146–49), both height and head size (a proxy for brain size) are correlated with IQ. To the extent that there is a direct causal relation between brain size and IQ, and given the correlation between brain size and IQ of approximately 0.40 (as shown in Chapter 6, p. 147), then an increase in brain size of one standardized unit should result in 0.4 of a standardized unit increase in IQ. The effect of improved nutrition on IQ solely via its effect on brain size, therefore, would amount to a ΔIQ = .4 × 3 = 1.2 IQ points. The finding of greater secular gains on nonverbal or performance tests than on verbal tests is consistent with an experiment that added a number of vitamin and mineral supplements to children's diets which produced a significant gain on the Wechsler Performance IQ of 3.7 IQ points over a control group, while the Verbal IQ was unaffected.[29]

There are other environmental factors besides nutrition that have changed throughout this century that probably affect the biological basis of *g*:

- The widespread inoculation of infants against what were formerly the most common childhood diseases, such as scarlet fever, measles, chicken pox, mumps, and whooping cough.

- Advances in obstetrics that have reduced the incidence of prenatal and perinatal risks known as "reproductive casualties," which can affect mental development. For example, the increased use of modern obstetrical techniques and cesarean section to reduce prolonged labor and difficult birth, thus sparing fetuses with larger-than-average head/brain size (and large-headed), has probably contributed to the increase of IQ in first-world countries.

- A decrease in parity (i.e., the number of previous births by a given mother), which reduces the effects of a number of blood-type incompatibilities between mother and fetus, such as kernicterus (the mother is Rh negative and the fetus is Rh positive), a condition that is negatively correlated with the child's later IQ. The increased use of Rh immunoglobulin in second and subsequent pregnancies has lessened the harmful effects of this and other immunoreactive factors in the last two generations.[30]

- The increased hours of exposure to electric lighting and television are also probably responsible for some part of the increased overall rate of maturation, via stimulation of the pineal gland—an effect that has been demonstrated experimentally in animals.[31]

- Because of the remarkably beneficial effect of mother's milk (as contrasted with formulas) on early mental development and later substantial gains in IQ,[32a] the doubling of the percentage of infants who were breast fed[32b] over the past generation has probably contributed to the upward trend of IQ in the population.

Although each one of these different environmental factors alone may have only a small incremental effect on the population level of *g* itself, the summation of many such increments might constitute as much as half of the ΔIQ, while the remainder of ΔIQ reflects the trend toward more universal schooling, wider exposure to the mass media, increased "test-wiseness" from the more frequent use of tests, and similar factors that raise test scores without increasing g.

Genetics. Although IQ is known to have a high heritability, most commentators have assumed that genetics could not be a causal factor in secular gains of the magnitude seen for IQ over such a short time span as just two to three generations. A directional change in the population frequency of genes with additive effects on the phenotypic expression of a trait implies positive selection for the trait. This is the mechanism of biological evolution, in which change by natural selection occurs slowly. The process can be greatly speeded by means of artificial selection, depending on the severity of the selection differential. To produce the observed IQ gain by selection alone would require breeding only by people in the upper half of the IQ distribution. As nothing at all this drastic has happened, genetic selection may be ruled out as the sole or even major cause of the secular trend in IQ.

However, another genetic factor might well have had a small incremental effect on IQ over the last three or four generations. Following the period of the Great Depression in the 1930s, there was an increasing preference by more mature, better-educated, and higher-SES white women (who are mostly in the upper-half of the population IQ distribution) for having more children, shifting away from 2- and 3-child families to 3- and 4-child families as the desired family size in this above-average IQ segment of the population.[33] But the relationship of demographic and birthrate changes within different segments of the IQ distribution to the rising mean IQ of the population has not yet been systematically investigated. It is even possible that genetic and environmental trends have been moving in somewhat opposite directions and that the observable effects on IQ by the one are, to some extent, masked by the other.

Probably a more influential genetic contributor to the rising IQ is heterosis, or hybrid vigor, which results from the mating between persons from different ancestral lines. A purely genetic effect, heterosis enhances all polygenic traits that involve genetic dominance. It is the converse of inbreeding depression. Heterosis results from decreasing the number of double-recessive genes that depress a polygenic trait in relatively inbred populations; inbreeding depression results from an increase in double recessives. Heterosis shows up in the offspring of parents who each came from two separated regions that have long been relatively isolated from each other and who have fewer ancestors in common than two persons from the same region would have. The American "melting pot," which has fostered social contact between many diverse national and ethnic groups, has created the conditions for heterosis on a grand scale. The large-scale relocations of people in the industrialized world during and after World War I and World War II and the vast increases in transportation and travel have contributed to heterotic effects in Europe and Asia, particularly Japan. (A heterotic effect on psychometric g was measured in the offspring of Asian and European crosses in Hawaii.[34])

The only study I have found that investigated whether there has been a secular

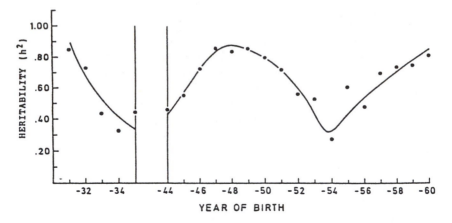

Figure 10.2. The heritability coefficient of the intelligence test used by the Norwegian Army for same-age cohorts born in different years from 1931 to 1960. (From Sundet et al., 1988. Used with permission of Ablex.)

change (over thirty years) in the heritability of *g*-loaded test scores concluded that "the results revealed no unambiguous evidence for secular trends in the heritability of intelligence test scores."[35] However, the heritability coefficients (based on twenty-two same-age cohort samples of MZ and DZ male twins born in Norway between 1930 and 1960) showed some statistically reliable nonlinear trends over the thirty-year period, as shown in Figure 10.2. The overall trend line goes equally down-up-down-up with heritability coefficients ranging from slightly above .80 to slightly below .40. The heritability coefficient was the same for the cohort born in 1930 as for the cohort born in 1960 (for both, $h^2 \approx .80$). The authors offer only weak ad hoc speculations about possible causes of this erratic fluctuation of h^2 across 22 points in time.

Broader Implications of the Secular Rise in IQ. The secular trend in IQ raw scores, despite its great variability across different tests, countries, and time intervals, has been a decidedly upward trend in all economically advanced countries for which data are available. The overall average gain is impressive if measured as differences between generations rather than as increments per decade, or ΔIQ. On average, it amounts to about one standard deviation (fifteen IQ points) per generation (thirty years).

It is improper, however, to extrapolate the trend much beyond one generation. Extrapolation of secular trend lines in either direction beyond the time range of the actual data often leads to absurdity. To make the point, if we extrapolate back to the time to Aristotle, Shakespeare, or Newton (assuming an IQ test standardized in their times gave them each an IQ of 200), their IQs on a test standardized in 1990 would be about −1,000, 0, and 50, respectively! (Even if the secular changes in IQ were not an additive but a proportional progression, these extrapolations backward in time would, of course, still result in ridiculously low [though not below-zero] IQs for these historic geniuses.) The secular gain in IQ is just as limited to a narrow period in modern history as is the secular increase in height (which was marked in the first half of this century but began gradually leveling off after World War II). The extent to which the upward IQ trend is leveling off has not yet been determined.

Flynn uses the secular gain evidence to argue that IQ tests do not measure "intelligence" but rather are a correlate with only a weak causal link to intelligence.[36] His position seems to be that not any part of the intergenerational gain in test scores reflects a gain in "real-world problem solving ability," which surely implies that it doesn't reflect a gain in the level of g, because g is the main factor in mental tests' external validity. Flynn argues that if the intergenerational gain in IQ scores were "real" (i.e., reflected g), the real-life consequences would be conspicuous. For example, the younger generation with average IQs would perceive their parents and grandparents as intellectually dull or borderline retarded. Flynn even suggests that baseball and cricket fans of two or three generations past wouldn't have had enough intelligence to understand the rules of the game. Also, professors whose teaching careers span a generation would have noticed an increase in the number of "geniuses" in their classes, and we would have experienced a renaissance of intellectual creativity in literature and science and invention (as indicated by a marked increase in the number of patents for inventions issued over the past thirty or forty years). If, however, the IQ gain resulted mainly from pulling up the lower end of the IQ distribution, as observed in the exemplary Danish study by Teasdale and Owen,[13] rather than uniformly raising scores throughout the whole distribution, one would not expect the remarkable "renaissance" of intellectual achievements described by Flynn.

That there was a real increase in the functional, or g, component of the approximately one standard deviation gain in the test scores of army draftees between World War I and World War II[37] is attested by the observation that eighteen-year-old draftees in 1942 were able to learn general military and specialty skills more quickly than did their counterparts in 1917, according to Lloyd Humphreys,[38] a leading psychologist who, in World War II, was employed in the armed services to do research on personnel selection and training.

Others have noted, however, that the intergenerational increase in physical stature (which, in standard deviation units, is nearly the same as for IQ) does not invalidate the yardstick as a measure of height or a spring scale as a measure of weight. Nor has it caused people to view their parents or grandparents as midgets. And just as there has been no marked increase in the number of patents, there has been no increase in the number of Olympic gold medals won by the contestants, despite the well-known gains in all athletic records during this century. The standards are more demanding for winning in the Olympics as the performance level of the contestants rises. Likewise, the standard for patents changes. Modern inventions, such as those in electronics and computer hardware, are typically more demanding of scientific and technological ingenuity and research and development than were a great many earlier patented inventions.

In fact, we have no precise and unambiguously interpretable "real life" indices of the intergenerational increase in the level of *g*. Virtually all real-life achievements are much less than perfectly correlated with *g* and depend on other traits and conditions as well, so a standard unit increase in *g* would result in much less than a unit increase in achievement. Flynn's surmise of the dramatic manifest effects of IQ gains if they really reflected *g* (which he denies) would be much less exaggerated if only a fraction (perhaps less than half) of the intergenerational gain in IQ scores were associated with a gain in the level of *g*. This gain in true *g* has probably been brought about largely by secular changes in all the environmental factors that have favorable biological effects.

Flynn argues that the failure of the observed secular gain in IQ to reflect a corresponding increase in real-world achievements requires abandonment, or at least drastic revamping, of the whole Spearmanian theory of *g* (or the Spearman-Jensen theory, as Flynn[36c] prefers to name it).

Whatever its cause(s), the Flynn Effect is important because it does not seem to "fit" in neatly with any existing environmental or genetic theories of mental ability. In science generally, it is such novel facts, when fully investigated, that lead to an increased level of understanding.

What appears counterproductive to me, however, is the extent to which Flynn's argument is used to sidestep the real-world implications of race differences in IQ, particularly the black-white difference. This is even more so for less fair and technically unsophisticated commentators who invoke the Flynn Effect like a mantra in dismissing IQ.

Flynn's research on IQ gains, for example, is the centerpiece of his critique entitled "Race and IQ: Jensen's Case Refuted"[36b] and the same argument is reiterated in most of his publications on secular gains. Flynn hypothesizes that whatever unknown factors are responsible for the intergenerational gain in IQ scores (and are not reflected in "real world problem-solving ability") also operate *within* generations, causing IQ differences between certain contemporary subgroups in the population, in particular the average one standard deviation IQ difference between blacks and whites in the United States. Therefore, Flynn argues, the black-white IQ difference doesn't represent a real functional difference in ability, that is, a difference in *g*, any more than does the IQ raw-score difference observed between successive generations of whites. Psychologist Robert C. Nichols[39] characterized Flynn's argument as a "faulty syllogism":

1. We do not know what causes the test score changes over time.

2. We do not know what causes racial differences in intelligence.

3. Since both causes are unknown, they must, therefore, be the same.

4. Since the unknown cause of changes over time cannot be shown to be genetic, it must be environmental.

5. Therefore, racial differences in intelligence are environmental in origin.

If the Flynn effect is caused by environmental factors, it is most remarkable that a steady rise in the population's average test scores over a period of fifty or sixty years has had no effect on the mean IQ difference between blacks and whites, which has remained at about 1σ since World War I. This era has been one of steadily diminishing disparities between blacks and whites in educational, social, and economic opportunities. Yet the general upward secular trend in the overall population level of mental test scores has not changed the standardized difference between the mean test scores of blacks and whites.

A definitive test of Flynn's hypothesis with respect to contemporary race differences in IQ is simply to compare the external validity of IQ in each racial group. The comparison must be based, not on the validity coefficient (i.e., the correlation between IQ scores and the criterion measure), but on the regression of the criterion measure (e.g., actual job performance) on the IQ scores. This method cannot, of course, be used to test the "reality" of the difference between the present and past generations. But if Flynn's belief that the intergenerational gain in IQ scores is a purely psychometric effect that does not reflect a gain in functional ability, or *g*, is correct, we would predict that the external validity of the IQ scores, assessed by comparing the intercepts and regression coefficients from subject samples separated by a generation or more (but tested at the same age), would reveal that IQ is biased against subjects from the earlier generation. If the IQs had increased in the later generation without reflecting a corresponding increase in functional ability, the IQ would markedly *under*predict the performance of the earlier generation—that is, their actual criterion performance would *exceed* the level of performance attained by those of the later generation who obtained the same IQ. The IQ scores would clearly be functioning differently in the two groups. This is the clearest indication of a biased test—in fact, the condition described here constitutes the very definition of *predictive bias*.[40] If the test scores had the same meaning in both generations, then a given score (on average) should predict the same level of performance in both generations. If this is not the case (and it may well not be), the test is biased and does not permit valid comparisons of "real-life" ability levels across generations.

When this kind of analysis is applied to contemporary black and white groups, the regressions are the same for both groups; that is, blacks and whites with the same test scores perform at the same level on the criterion. Hence it has been concluded that the test scores are not biased; they have the same meaning for each racial group. In hundreds of validity studies, the occasional exceptions to this generalization consist of finding tests that *over*predict the performance of blacks. That is, the black level of real-world criterion performance is, on average, *below* that of whites with the same test score. This discrepancy is usually attributable (correctly) to the imperfect reliability of the test scores (even when the reliability is exactly the same for both racial groups). When the regressions are corrected for attenuation (unreliability), a single regression line predicts individuals' level of performance equally well for each group.[41] This would not happen if the mean difference between the groups' test scores were "hollow" with respect to *g* (and whatever other factors contribute to the test's external validity). The nonexistence of predictive bias for the same test scores obtained by blacks or whites is a strong refutation of Flynn's supposition that the secular trend in test scores explains away the observed average racial differences in IQ (i.e., that there is no real difference in the level of functional ability between races.) As shown by the evidence reviewed in Chapter 9, *g* is the main functional ingredient of tests' practical predictive validity.

Using the method of correlated vectors, we can determine definitively whether the mean differences between any two groups on each of the tests in a battery does or does not reflect a difference in *g*. The battery is factor analyzed, and the column vector of the tests' *g* loadings is correlated with the column vector of the mean group differences on each of the tests. A significant correlation proves that the groups differ on *g* and therefore should also differ on any external, or nonpsychometric, correlates of *g*. This finding in regard to the black-white difference was presaged by Spearman himself and is the subject of the next chapter.

Future Research on Secular Trends in *g*. At present, the most reasonable hypothesis to account for the secular trend in IQ seems to be that the ΔIQ increments consist of two main parts: (1) a functional, *g*-loaded part due to the secular trend in those environmental improvements that produce general biological effects (including brain development) for virtually the entire populations of countries in the industrialized world; and (2) a secular trend in such psychological environmental effects (including increased years of schooling, TV, "test-wiseness," "teaching to the test") that adds an increment to test scores that is slightly, if at all, reflected in a functional increase of real-life problem-solving ability and is largely "hollow" with respect to *g*.

The problem is how to test this surmise rigorously and then determine how much of the secular increment in IQ scores is attributable to each source. I see no way that this can be done with any presently available data. Therefore, if the subject is to be researched in the future, it will call for an innovative methodology and an additional kind of data. As I have suggested elsewhere,[42] conventional psychometric raw scores will need to be *anchored* to measures that presumably are not influenced by the environmental variables that raise test scores without increasing *g*. The anchor variables would consist of measures of reaction time to various elementary cognitive tasks, evoked brain potentials, nerve conduction velocity, and the like, that are demonstrably *g*-loaded. (A composite measure based on the anchor variables should have a reasonably high correlation [say, $r > .50$] with the psychometric test scores.) Mental test raw scores would be regressed on these anchor variables in a representative sample of some population. A later comparable sample would be matched to the earlier sample on the anchor variables. This later sample's raw scores (on the very same psychometric test) then would be regressed on the anchor variables.[43] A significant difference between the regression lines of the earlier and the later tested groups would indicate that the psychometric scores were not measuring the same thing in each group. Thus the secular increment in mean score wouldn't mean simply "more of the same." If the regression lines remained the same, however, it would indicate that any significant observed mean raw-score difference between the groups was a real difference in whatever the test measured at both points in time. That is, the mean gain would be reflected in the anchor variables as well as in the test scores.

EXPERIMENTAL ATTEMPTS TO RAISE MENTAL ABILITY

The question of whether the level of an individual's mental abilities can be improved by psychological or educational means has been investigated systematically ever since mental tests first appeared. The obvious and far-reaching disadvantage of a conspicuously lower level of ability has long motivated efforts to discover ways to raise mental ability by a practically significant amount. Most such attempts, naturally, have been applied to individuals of below-average IQ. On the assumption that mental development is most rapid in early childhood and becomes less malleable with increasing age, attempts to raise mental ability have been applied most frequently to children. Few other topics in the history of behavioral science have resulted in so vast a literature, and no other comes close to it in total research expenditure.

Actually, there are three distinct questions one must ask about any experiment that claims to raise the level of mental ability:

1. Does the indicator (i.e., the measurement obtained on a particular vehicle) of the targeted ability in the treatment group (T) show a significant and practically meaningful gain relative to an untreated control group (C)? This is answered by a statistical test of the significance of the difference between the means of the T group and the C group, along with an evaluation of the *effect size* (i.e., the ratio of the mean difference [T-C] to the averaged standard deviations within the T and C groups). Typically, the indicator is IQ; the vehicle is a particular test, such as the Stanford-Binet or the Wechsler.

2. If there is a significant gain in the indicator of the targeted ability, does it also represent a gain in the latent factor (for example, g) it was intended to measure? Because g (or any other latent ability) cannot be measured directly by a single test, something more than a mean gain in score on a particular test is needed to demonstrate that the level of g itself has been affected by the treatment. What is required, therefore, is a demonstration of what are termed *far transfer* of training or *broad generalizability* of the treatment effect. As all forms of cognitive activity are to some degree saturated with g, the treatment effect, if it really involves g, should be reflected in a wide variety of vehicles that

manifest cognition. Scores based on vehicles that are superficially different though essentially similar to the specific skills trained in the treatment condition may show gains attributable to *near transfer* but fail to show any gain on vehicles that require *far transfer*, even though both the *near* and the *far* transfer tests are equally *g*-loaded in the untreated sample. Any true increase in the level of *g* connotes more than just narrow (or near) transfer of training; it necessarily implies *far* transfer.

One way to test for a far transfer effect following treatment is to compare the T group with the C group on a wide variety of tests and other behavioral correlates of *g* (as demonstrated in untreated samples). If the groups do not differ significantly on all of the varied *g*-saturated criteria, it means that the treatment effect is confined to the particular vehicle or to near transfer to similar vehicles. One can also compare T with an untreated group whose scores on the indicator of the targeted ability match those of the T group after treatment. If these two groups are statistically distinguishable (as by a discriminant analysis) on a wide variety of *g*-saturated criteria, it again means that the treatment had no significant effect on *g* but only on the specificity or lower-order factors in the test on which the two groups were matched. A third method is to apply the method of correlated vectors to determine the correlation between the size of the mean gain (T-C) on a variety of tests and the tests' *g* loadings as determined in an untreated population. If the T group's *gain* in various test scores is unrelated to the tests' *g* loadings, the gains are hollow with respect to *g* and consist only of gains in lower-order factors or, more likely, in test specificity.

3. The last and probably most important question is: Aside from whether or not their level of *g* has been altered by the treatment, was any knowledge or set of skills inculcated that has practical utility for the treated persons in "real life"? Skill training, the acquisition of a useful or employable skill, or of beneficial habits in the conduct of one's life, is valuable in its own right, regardless of any general carry-over to *g*. Although the type and level of skill that can be attained, and the speed of acquisition, may be related to the level of *g* (or other ability factors), acquisition of any useful skill is usually a personal and economic advantage in its own right, regardless of *g*.

The general finding regarding number 1 (proper control group) is that while certain educational-psychological treatments are capable of increasing scores on IQ tests (in a few cases up to as much as twenty IQ points or so) the gains induced by most preschool interventions and special education are typically about 0.3σ, or five IQ points.[44] Even this modest gain, however, typically diminishes to near-zero within one or two years after the intervention. By comparison, the average effect of direct coaching on test taking skills is about 0.25σ.[44] (The coaching effect is also ephemeral.) In both cases the gains probably represent *near transfer*, which in the extreme case is referred to as "teaching to the test."

As for point number 2 (generality of effect), I have found possibly only one bona fide example of an educational-psychological treatment that resulted in test-score gains that appear to be gains in g itself (see Abecedarian Project, below). Most studies, in fact, make no attempt to determine if the treatment actually raised the level of g. The investigators usually assume that a rise in scores on a particular test sufficiently demonstrates the efficacy of the treatment in raising "intelligence," with little or no realization that g is the *sine qua non* of an IQ test's being an indicator of "intelligence."

Others have reviewed this body of evidence and reached similar conclusions. A textbook on intelligence by Nathan Brody,[45] concludes a review of the effects of early interventions on the development of general mental ability as follows: "There is no credible evidence that experimental interventions during the pre-school years will create enduring changes in performance on tests of intelligence" (p. 178). Specifically on the effects of Head Start, Brody writes, "Children exposed to Head Start may have behaved in ways that school authorities found more acceptable than children in the control groups in these investigations. These changes, however, were not accompanied by enduring changes in cognitive functioning either as assessed by intelligence tests or by the ability to acquire the skills that constitute the standard curriculum in the public schools" (p. 179). The final summary chapter[46] of a book in which twenty-three psychologists and educators addressed the issue of how intelligence might be increased by psychological methods concluded: "We now return to the contrast made in the title between training cognitive skills and raising intelligence. We would argue that although the participants may eventually be quite successful at raising cognitive skills, their present papers are silent on the issue of intelligence and its modifiability" (p. 226).

The training of specific skills (referred to under question number 3, above) has generally proven successful, when the degree of complexity of the particular skill and the method of instruction are properly geared to the learner's level of g. Skill training, though essential and valuable in its own right, demonstrates most clearly that g per se is not a skill, nor any combination of skills, nor can it be characterized in the psychological terms used to describe the nature of skill. Learned skills are, of course, every bit as important as g for getting along in life, but they are not a substitute for g (any more than g is a substitute for skills). The operative difference is that skills can be inculcated, within limits, by psychological means, while the level of g, as such, cannot be permanently raised by training, as far as we know. Skill acquisition depends mostly on the contingencies of instrumental learning—essentially, the person's making specific responses to a given situation, receiving immediate feedback as to adequacy of the responses, and being allowed repeated practice. These are the basic psychological variables involved in acquiring any skill, from tying one's shoelaces to playing a Tchaikovsky violin concerto. On the other hand, the preponderance of evidence argues that variance in the level of g is not a psychologically manipulable variable, but rather a biological phenomenon under the control both of the genes and of those external physical variables that affect the physiological and biochemical functioning of the central nervous system, which mediates the behavioral manifestations of *g*.

In a well-researched book on the history of attempts to raise the intelligence of retarded persons, Herman Spitz, an expert in this area, concluded as follows:

> Much of the evidence from basic psychological research suggests that mild and moderate mental retardation [IQ < 70] is not primarily a deficiency in learning and memory except to the extent that thinking enters into learning and memory. Mental retardation is, rather, a *thinking* disability, and intelligence is synonymous with thinking. Although it is possible to educate mentally retarded persons and to train them to perform many tasks, up to a point, we do not yet have the means of raising their general level of intelligence. We have no prescription that will change their capacity to think and to reason at the level of persons of average intelligence, to solve novel problems and real-life challenges of some complexity, and to respond effectively to an infinite variety of circumstances, but just to those used in training.[47]

The level of mental retardation described by Spitz is not of a type distinct from the total distribution of *g* in the general population, rather it reflects a level of *g* lying on the same continuum as the average and higher levels. Mental retardation is the lower tail of the whole range of *g* represented by the bell-curve distribution of IQ in the population. The differences in *g* (reflected by IQ) are manifested continuously throughout the entire scale covered by the bell curve. That is, they are not differences of kind but of degree. For example, a positive correlation between individual differences on the highly *g*-loaded mathematics subtest of the SAT and academic achievement exists within every decile of the SAT scale and has been shown to predict later achievement even within a large sample of individuals who were tested in grades seven and eight and scored in the top 1 percent of the SAT distribution.[48] Aggregated data most clearly show a monotonic increase in socially desirable behavior and achievements, when indices of these are plotted as a function of group means for every decile of the IQ range.

The conditions and general findings described in the preceding paragraphs regarding the effects of training or other educational interventions on abilities can be most neatly summarized in terms of what Carroll[49] refers to as the three-stratum hierarchical factor model of mental abilities, such as shown in Figure 10.3. At the base of the triangle-shaped hierarchy are a great many tests, different clusters of which are each dominated by a different first-stratum factor. Smaller groups of the first-stratum factors are each dominated by several second-stratum factors, all of which are dominated by the single third-stratum factor, or *g*. As Carroll notes, the efficacy of special interventions is most clearly manifested on specific tests that most resemble the trained skills. The training effect is still evident at the level of certain first-stratum factors, depending on the nature of the training. However, it all but disappears at the level of second-stratum factors, and is altogether undetectable at the third-stratum of factor generality,

General Factor

Second-Order Factors

Primary Factors

Tests

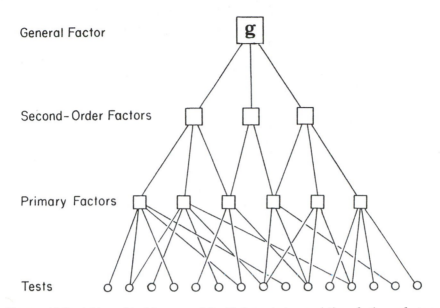

Figure 10.3. A hierarchical factor model with three strata, consisting of primary factors, second-order factors, and a general factor, *g*. *Source: Bias in mental testing* by Arthur R. Jensen, Fig. 6.9, p. 212. Copyright © 1980 by Arthur R. Jensen. Reprinted with permission of The Free Press, a Division of Simon & Schuster, and Routledge Ltd.

which is *g*. This implies that training effects show the most transfer across tests or tasks that are all dominated by one particular first-stratum factor. Transfer is almost nil across tasks dominated by different second-stratum factors, and it is sifted out completely before reaching the level of *g* derived from any large and diverse battery of tests. The few tests that are most similar to the trained skills, and therefore most likely to reflect the specific training effect, tend to diminish in *g* loading after training, when compared to their *g* loadings before training. That is, after training, these particular tests reflect the effect of the specific training more than the general ability factor that accounts for their correlation with many superficially dissimilar tests.

We can now use the three questions posed above to examine critically specific intervention programs, which are often claimed to raise IQ.

Head Start. The federal preschool intervention known as Head Start, which has been in continual existence now since 1964, is undoubtedly the largest-scale, though not the most intensive, educational intervention program ever undertaken, with an annual expenditure over $2 billion. The program is aimed at improving the health status and the learning and social skills of preschoolers from poor backgrounds so they can begin regular school more on a par with children from more privileged backgrounds. The intervention is typically short-term, with various programs lasting anywhere from a few months to two years.

The general conclusion of the hundreds of studies based on Head Start data is that the program has little, if any, effect on IQ or scholastic achievement that endures beyond more than two to three years after exposure to Head Start. The program does, however, have some potential health benefits, such as inoculations of enrollees against common childhood diseases and improved nutrition (by school-provided breakfast or lunch). The documented behavioral effects are less retention-in-grade and lower dropout rates. The cause(s) of these effects are uncertain. Because eligible children were not randomly enrolled in Head Start, but were selected by parents and program administrators, these scholastic correlates of Head Start are uninterpretable from a causal standpoint. Selection, rather than direct causation by the educational intervention itself, could be the explanation of Head Start's beneficial outcomes.

The most penetrating statistical analysis[50] of Head Start outcomes that I have found in the vast literature on this subject controls many family background factors, including mothers' ''IQ'' (measured by the Armed Forces Qualification Test). The analyses are based on within-family data, that is, children who were enrolled in Head Start were compared on a number of variables against their siblings who were not in Head Start. Also, mothers who themselves had been enrolled in Head Start as preschoolers were compared against their adult sisters who had not experienced Head Start.

Groups were also analyzed separately by ethnicity: white, black, and Hispanic. This is important, because different factors influence the selection of children into Head Start according to ethnicity. White children who attend Head Start, for example, were the most disadvantaged in academic potential, but showed larger and more lasting effects of Head Start on cognitive measures than did the black children. (In marked contrast, white children who attended a preschool other than Head Start were more privileged and scored above the average white child on IQ tests.) Hispanic children, whose Head Start programs emphasized English language acquisition, also manifested significant and enduring gains in mental test scores and especially in scholastic performance. The gains in cognitive skills for whites and Hispanics, in fact, were still detectable in their test scores as adults. Blacks, who constituted the largest proportion of Head Start enrollees, did not perform better on IQ tests or in school as a result of Head Start, although they grew to be significantly taller than their siblings who did not attend. It is uncertain whether the gain in height is attributable to Head Start (possibly its nutritional component) or was a result of a difference in children's characteristics that may have governed parental selection of particular children to be enrolled in Head Start.

One of the most important findings is that the effectiveness of Head Start increased as a function of the mother's IQ (AFQT score). Also, children from the most advantaged backgrounds (in terms of family income, maternal IQ, and education) gained more from Head Start than did children from less advantaged backgrounds. Simply lumping together all the results and not examining these moderating variables tends to obscure the possibly beneficial aspects of Head Start for improving cognitive and scholastic outcomes.

The disappointing outcome for the most disadvantaged, and for blacks in particular, is often attributed to the short-term treatment afforded by Head Start. Therefore, it is important to examine the most intensive and prolonged intervention programs that have so far been tried.

Adoption. Adoption of a child in infancy who is then reared by caring adoptive parents in a middle-class or upper-middle-class home is an intensive and prolonged kind of intervention open to study. This is especially so if the level of IQ and the environmental status of the adopted child's biological parent(s) are predictably less advantageous for a child's mental development than the conditions provided by the adoptive parents.

Adopted children's IQs are generally more highly correlated with their biological mothers' IQs than with their adoptive mothers' IQs, even when the child has had no contact with the biological mothers since birth or early infancy. This fact should not be misinterpreted as meaning that adopted children's level of IQ is, on average, closer to that of their biological mothers than to that of their adoptive mothers. A correlation coefficient, by its mathematical nature, cannot reflect the size of the mean difference between the correlated groups, in this case, mothers and their children. A correlation coefficient indicates the degree to which the *rank order* of the measurements on one variable (e.g., the mothers' IQs) is similar to the rank order of another variable (e.g., their children's IQs), regardless of the average difference in the absolute level of IQ between the mothers and the children. In assessing the malleability of IQ, therefore, one must take account of the mean difference between the biological mother and her adopted child and compare this difference with the mother-child difference in IQ for mothers of the same IQ and socioeconomic level who did not put their child up for adoption. Another informative comparison is between the mean IQ of adopted children and the theoretically predicted mean IQ of children born to mothers whose average IQ is the same as the average IQ of the biological mothers of the adopted children.[51] Adoption studies are most valuable for assessing the malleability of IQ when there is a large disparity between the IQ levels of the biological and adoptive parents. (The IQ of the biological father is unknown in most studies of adopted children.)

The famous study by Skodak and Skeels has long been cited as one of the most striking examples of the estimated effect of adoption on IQ. The biological mothers of the adopted children had an average IQ of 92.7. If the children had been reared by their biological mothers, their average expected IQ would be about 97. But presumably because the children had been adopted into much more privileged homes than are typically provided by parents whose IQs average 92, the children in fact averaged 105.5, or about nine IQ points above their expected mean value if they had been reared by their biological mothers.[52] This estimated gain in IQ is fairly close to the typical maximum effect of adoption on IQ found in other studies.

A detailed and methodologically expert review[53] of adoption studies best suited for determining the maximum estimated gain in IQ that resulted from markedly contrasting environments found the best estimate of the limit of IQ malleability to be about ten to twelve IQ points. It concluded: ''Simply put, there appear to be limits to the extent to which even the most substantial environmental changes can affect IQ. The clarity of this conclusion depends precisely on the failure to find evidence of higher malleability where it should most easily be seen—in studies of contrasted environments. This is not to imply that malleability is insignificant in these studies, only that is seems relatively modest where it might in theory be far more impressive given the potential for change provided by the adoptive environments'' (p. 290).

Three main additional points should be kept in mind when interpreting these findings. First, they are based, as they only could be, on existing environmental conditions. Obviously, they can tell us nothing about other, but as yet nonexistent, environmental conditions that might possibly have a greater effect. Second, they do not tell us the precise cause of the adoption effect (which could be better nutrition and other conditions for health, greater cognitive stimulation and educational advantages, or uncontrolled selection factors in final adoption placements that might favor healthier, more energetic, or alert-looking infants). Environmental effects on IQ seem to be highly multifactorial, resulting from the cumulative effects of a great many small, largely random or unrelated, microenvironmental events.[54] Third, the adoption studies, though showing beneficial effects on IQ per se, are not informative about the extent to which the IQ gain reflects a gain in *g*. I am not aware of adoption data that can answer that question. This would require assessing the similarity of groups of adopted and nonadopted children on the *g* loadings derived from a large battery of highly diverse cognitive tests. It would also be valuable to compare the subsequent life histories and achievements of groups of adopted and nonadopted individuals of approximately the same IQ.

However, it could be argued that although adoption is undoubtedly a *long-term* ''treatment,'' extending from infancy to early adulthood, it is not necessarily the most intensive treatment that could be devised to promote cognitive development. Therefore, it would pay to look at the two most intensive and prolonged experimental intervention programs for raising IQ ever attempted.

The Milwaukee Project. Aside from Head Start, this is the most highly publicized of all intervention experiments. It was the most intensive and extensive educational intervention ever conducted for which the final results have been published.[55] It was also the most costly single experiment in the history of psychology and education—over $14 million. In terms of the highest peak of IQ gains for the seventeen children in the treatment condition (before the gains began to vanish), the cost was an estimated $23,000 per IQ point per child.

The intensive treatment phase lasted from 1966 to 1973. Periodic follow-up testing and assessment of scholastic performance continued through 1981, when the subjects approached fifteen years of age.

The experiment was expressly intended to determine whether children, without intervention, were predictably at risk for mental retardation because they were born in poor environments to mothers whose IQs were seventy-five or below. All the mothers were black and from the poorest inner-city section of Milwaukee. They were selected while pregnant, prior to the birth of the proband children. Forty mothers volunteered for the experiment. The main inducement to participate was the offer of regular pediatric examinations and medical care throughout the duration of the study.

The study sample was divided into fairly equivalent treatment (T) and control (C) groups, each with twenty infants. Subject attrition during the long course of the study resulted in final samples of T = 17 and C = 18, on which all of the statistical analyses were based. Both the T and C groups received the same periodic IQ testing with the Stanford-Binet and the Wechsler (WISC) tests throughout the duration of the study.

Before the infants were six months old, those in the T group were removed from their homes every weekday to spend several hours in what was called the Infant Stimulation Center, established in the "high risk" neighborhood in which the children lived. This regimen lasted until the children were six years of age. At the beginning, each child had a private tutor trained in child development. As the children grew, the child-tutor ratio of 1:1 was increased to 2:1 and later to 3:1.

The program of cognitive stimulation and training received by the children was intensive. It incorporated virtually every kind of play and didactic activity ever suggested in the child psychology literature as having a beneficial effect on children's mental development. The founder and director of the program, Rick Heber, once quipped that compared to the cognitive development regimen provided in the Stimulation Center, the childhood environments of such famous prodigies as John Stuart Mill and Sir Francis Galton appear educationally deprived.

This intensive treatment, extending continuously over six years, indeed raised the T group's mean IQ well above that of the C group, with the thirteen testings over that interval showing an average T-C difference of about thirty IQ points. The treatment program ended when the children entered first grade in the public schools. At that time the T-C difference in IQ was 119 − 87 = 32 points on the Stanford-Binet. From age six to age fourteen there was a gradual decrease in the T-C difference, falling from 119 − 87 = 32 to 101 − 91 = 10 IQ points—still a statistically significant difference, larger and of longer duration than the typical IQ gains produced by less intensive intervention.

But why the eighteen-point decline in IQ scores for the T group? The most plausible explanation is that the prolonged, intensive training in cognitive skills given to the children during their first six years closely resembled the skills demanded by the assessment tests used in each of the periodic testings. Much of the cognitive training activity promoted the acquisition of the kinds of knowledge and skills that psychologists would glean from a task analysis of the items typically found in a variety of standard intelligence tests. The T children's performance was thus probably based on narrow transfer of the trained skills to the IQ tests. In other words, it was an indirect form of "teaching to the test." Consistent with this interpretation is the fact that, in subsequent testings on more advanced IQ tests during the period of decline after age six, those subtests whose contents least resembled the kinds of material on which the children had been trained (and tested) showed the greatest decline. These tests, evidently, showed the least transfer of training. It should be noted that the IQ tests' item contents differ somewhat at each age level, so in each subsequent year after age six, when the children entered regular school, the contents of the subsequent IQ tests became less and less similar to the materials they had been trained on in the Stimulation Center. Therefore, as the transfer of training effect gradually diminished, the tests increasingly reflected the children's true level of *g*.

This interpretation is most impressively underlined by the annual assessments of the children's scholastic performance as they progressed through regular school. Even by the end of grade one, the T-C difference in scholastic achievement scores was not significant, although T still scored somewhat higher than C. For all school years up to the end of grade four there was no significant difference between the T and the C groups. The T group scored near the tenth percentile on the math problem-solving section of the Metropolitan Achievement Test, which is the most *g*-loaded subtest in the MAT. (The tenth percentile of the standardization sample for the IQ scale is eighty, which is the mean of the C group's IQ.) In short, the T group's scholastic achievement fell far below the level normally predicted for children of the same nominal IQ as the T group. The T group, despite having a ten-point higher IQ than the C group, still performed in school very much like the C group. That is, both the E and C groups performed in school much as would be expected for children with an average IQ of eighty. The evident lack of generality, or broad transfer, of the effects of the T group's previous cognitive treatment indicates that the T-C gain in IQ was "hollow" with respect to *g*.

The Abecedarian Early Intervention Project. This project, begun in 1972 at the University of North Carolina, is similar to the Milwaukee Project in its intent and essential methodology. It differs, however, in its subject selection procedure. The infants were selected on a number of criteria known to be predictive of risk for mild (i.e., familial or sociocultural) mental retardation, such as low family income, low level of parents' education and occupation, welfare status or recipient of special social services, and mother's low IQ (i.e., below ninety-one). No single criterion was critical for selection, which was based on a composite score on all of the criteria. A mother with above-average IQ could volunteer her infant for participation in the Project provided the required "high risk" score was met by other selection criteria. Whereas all of the mothers whose infants took part in the Milwaukee Project had IQs below seventy-five, the average IQ of the mothers in the Abecedarian Project averaged eighty-four. Most of the subjects (98 percent) were black. Both the experimental (E) and control (C) groups were provided pediatric care and nutritional supplements, as well as family support services by social workers.

The Abecedarian Project, from its beginning, has been conducted in a model fashion as a scientific experiment, in terms of frequency of reporting results in peer-reviewed journals and in the openness and completeness of reporting results. Benefiting from a knowledge of the methodological questions raised by the Milwaukee Project and avoiding the excessive hype given earlier claims by the mass media, the Abecedarian Project is now generally regarded by experts as a larger, less questionable, educational experiment with statistically more definitive results than the Milwaukee Project.

From as early as six weeks of age, infants in the T group attended a day-care center six to eight hours a day, five days a week, fifty weeks a year, for five years, and then entered regular kindergarten in the public schools. In addition to pediatric surveillance and good nutrition, they were given a specially designed curriculum for cognitive development, with pupil-teacher ratios of 1:1 to 6:1 at various stages of the program, which appears to have been as intensive as the Milwaukee Project in its aim to stimulate mental development.

Both the T and C groups (each with about fifty subjects) were given age-appropriate mental tests (Bayley, Stanford-Binet, McCarthy, WPPSI) at six-month intervals from age six months to sixty months. The important comparisons here are the mean T-C differences at each testing. (Because the test scores do not have the same factor composition across this wide age range, the absolute scores of the T group alone are not as informative of the efficacy of the intervention as are the mean T-C differences.) At every testing from six months to five years of age, the T group outperformed the C group, and the overall average T-C difference ($103.3 - 95.5 = 7.8$ IQ points) was highly significant ($p < .001$). Peculiarly, however, the largest T-C differences (averaging fifteen IQ points) occurred between eighteen and thirty-six months of age and then declined during the last two years of intervention. At sixty months, the average T-C difference was 7.5 IQ points. This decrease might simply reflect the fact that with the children's increasing age the tests become increasingly more g-loaded. The tests used before two or three years of age measure mainly perceptual-motor functions that have relatively little g saturation. Only later does g becomes the predominant component of variance in IQ. In follow-up studies at eight and twelve years of age, the T-C difference on the WISC-R was about five IQ points,[57] a difference that has remained up to age fifteen. At the last reported testing, the T-C difference was 4.6 IQ points, or a difference of 0.35σ. Scholastic achievement test scores showed a somewhat larger effect of the intervention up to age fifteen.[57] The intervention effect on other criteria of the project's success was demonstrated by the decreased percentage of children who repeated at least one grade by age twelve (T = 28 percent, C = 55 percent) and the percentage of children with borderline or retarded intelligence (IQ < 85) (T = 12.8 percent, C = 44.2 percent).[56]

Thus this five-year program of intensive intervention beginning in early infancy increased IQ (at age fifteen years) by about five points. Judging from a comparable gain in scholastic achievement, the effect had broad transfer, suggesting that it probably raised the level of *g* to some extent. The finding that the T subjects did better than the C subjects on a battery of Piaget's tests of conservation, which reflect important stages in mental development, is further evidence. The Piagetian tests are not only very different in task demands from anything in the conventional IQ tests used in the conventional assessments, but are also highly *g* loaded.[57] The mean T-C difference on the Piagetian conservation tests was equal to 0.33σ (equivalent to five IQ points). Assuming that the instructional materials in the intervention program did not closely resemble Piaget's tests, it is a warranted conclusion that the intervention appreciably raised the level of *g*.

As in the other studies reviewed here, the specific causal agent has not yet been isolated. Perhaps it never will be, because the intervention effect is most likely the result of a great many small, varied, and unrelated events with beneficial effects that saturate the child's experience throughout an extended period during early development. And perhaps the critical factor is a certain *combination* of such events. Anything less than very early and intensive intervention, including medical and nutritional advantages, during the preschool years (and also prenatally), is probably inadequate to cause a lasting increase in the child's level of *g*.

NOTES

1. A certain type of test, called a *criterion-referenced* test, which is most often intended to assess specific achievements (usually scholastic or job-related knowledge and skills) does not need to be normed. The subject's performance is described strictly in terms of identifying the types of items that the subject passes or fails. Hence assessment of the subject's performance need make no reference to the level of performance in any reference group (as would a norm-referenced test). A criterion-referenced test of arithmetic, for example, would tell us that a given pupil can solve problems that call for dealing with addition, subtraction, multiplication, or short division of whole numbers, but cannot solve problems that call for dealing with long division, fractions, or decimals.

2. The technique for equating test scores is fully described by Angoff (1984).

3. Hambleton (1989) provides an excellent introduction and extensive references to the literature on item response theory.

4. A detailed discussion of the stability of test scores is presented in Jensen, 1980a, Chapter 7.

5. U.S. Department of Labor (1970), pp. 251–276.

6. The eight distinct aptitudes measured by the 16 GATB subtests are Verbal, Numerical, Spatial, Form Perception, Clerical, Motor Coordination, Finger Dexterity, Manual Dexterity.

7. The mean test-retest increments in the aptitude scores are quite reliable, as indicated by the average correlation of +.73 between the vector of increments on the eight

GATB aptitudes for any one of the test-retest intervals and any other interval within the range of intervals in this study (one day to three years).

8. Research on the stability of IQ across the age range from childhood to maturity is reviewed in detail in Jensen, 1980a, Chapter 7.

9. Wilson (1983).

10. Moffitt, Caspi, Harness, & Silva, 1993.

11. Flynn, 1884, 1987a, 1994.

12. Lynn & Hampson, 1986; Lynn, Hampson, & Mullineux, 1987.

13. Teasdale & Owen, 1987, 1989.

14. The Danish conscription test (the *Børge Prien Prøve*) was devised to conform to the strict criterion of a unidimensional test imposed by selecting and scaling items for difficulty in accord with the Rasch model. The item contents emphasize the kinds of relation eduction that maximize *g*. The Rasch one-parameter logistic model dictates the nature of the item characteristic curve (for a brief exposition, see Hambleton, 1989, pp. 156–157).

15. It should be noted that the reported correlation of +.71 is what is called an "ecological" correlation, that is, a correlation based not on the measurements of individuals, but on the *means* of a number of large groups, each group measured on two or more variables. Since a group mean averages out all of the idiosyncratic factors that cause the scores of individuals to vary besides the factor(s) the test was intended to measure, and that attenuate the test's correlation with other variables, ecological correlations are invariably much larger than correlations based on individual scores. For example, the correlation between children's IQs and their parents' socioeconomic status (SES) is about .40. But if we group children into several nonoverlapping groups by IQ level and group parents into several nonoverlapping groups by SES level, the correlation between the means of the two sets of groups (assuming the groups are large) will be close to one (assuming a linear relationship throughout the range on both variables).

16. Brand, Freshwater, & Dockrell, 1989.

17. Schaie (1994), Figure 7, p. 308. The PMA tests' *g* loadings mentioned in the text are based on Thurstone's 1938 standardization data for the PMA (given in Jensen, 1980a, p. 215, Figure 6.11).

18. Lynn, 1990a.

19. *ETS Developments*, 1986. (ETS, Princeton, NJ).

20. Lynn & Cooper, 1993 (France); 1994 (Japan).

21. Lynn & Hampson (1986); Teasdale & Owen, 1989.

22. Detailed analyses and explanations of the secular decline of scores on the SAT and other measures of scholastic achievement are provided by Jones (1981), Murray & Herrnstein (1992), and in a multiauthored book edited by Austin & Garber (1982).

23. Brand, 1987c; Brand et al., 1989.

24. Flynn, 1990.

25. The statistical reason that the average increase in performance on individual items greatly underestimates the average increase in total scores (based on a large number of items) is that single-item performance is far from perfectly correlated with the total score, the typical correlation being +.20 to +.30. Thus the regression of item scores on total scores would predict that a difference between two groups on a single item will be only about 20 or 30 percent as large as the group difference on the total score. The average item difference and the total score difference between groups could be approximately equal only under one of the two following unrealistic conditions: (1) all of the item

intercorrelations averaged zero (in which case the items would have zero correlation with the total score and the internal consistency reliability of the test would be zero, that is, the item scores and total scores would be purely random error), or (2) all the item intercorrelations were unity (in which case a single item would serve as well as the whole test). Neither of these extreme conditions applies to any actual mental test.

26. (a) Ceci, 1991; (b) Ceci, 1992, p. 8.

27. A simple example of this is that in first grade children are taught, say, that 2 + 3 is the same as 3 + 2. Later, when the child learns algebra, the rule is made more abstract and general: a + b = b + a. All algebraic formulas and equations are decontextualized statements. Syllogisms can be decontextualized: Which statement (1 or 2) is false? (1) All Xs are Y; all Ys are Z; therefore all Xs are Z. (2) All Ps are Q; all Ns are Q; therefore all Ps are N. Now notice how much easier equivalent syllogisms seem when they are contextualized: (1) All men are persons; all persons are human; therefore all men are human. (2) All chickens are fowl; all ducks are fowl; therefore all chickens are ducks. A person who is unable to decontextualize a syllogism would most likely declare the following syllogism to be false, although in terms of pure logic (but not experience) it is true: All apples are fruit; all fruits are green; therefore all apples are green. Syllogisms are no longer used in IQ tests, because syllogisms are uniformly easy for persons who solve them by using Venn diagrams. Since knowing or not knowing the "trick" of using a Venn diagram is the main determinant of passing or failing a syllogism, syllogisms are poor items for an IQ test. Different persons with the same IQ differ much too markedly on "syllogism ability," a difference often attributable to their either having learned or not having learned the "trick" of using Venn diagrams for verifying syllogisms. However, syllogisms would be suitable items in an achievement test, to determine whether a student had mastered the use of Venn diagrams after receiving instruction.

28. Lynn, 1987a, 1987b, 1989, 1990a, 1990b; Lynn & Pagliari, 1994.

29. Schoenthaler et al., 1991. A good, though far from comprehensive, article on the effects of nutrition on IQ (Ricciuti, 1994) offers a somewhat more conservative assessment than the articles by Lynn[28] and by Schoenthaler. Eysenck (1995) discusses the use of nutrients as a means of sudying intelligence differences experimentally. Eysenck and Schoenthaler (1997) provide the most recent and comprehensive review of experimental studies of the effects of nutrition on IQ.

30. Jensen (1997a) reviews much of the recent literature on the effects of the biological environmental factors (including mother-fetus immunogenic incompatibility factors) on mental development. Most of the environmental variance in IQ is attributable to the cumulative effect of such biological factors. Jensen (1996a) replies to an article by Flynn (in the same book) and summarizes the specific environmental factors hypothesized to play some part in the secular rise in IQ.

31. Modern mass-production poultry farms make use of this phenomenon, by keeping chicks under bright electric lighting twenty-four hours a day, to hasten their rate of growth and the time needed to reach their maximum egg-laying capacity.

32. (a) Lucas et al., 1992; (b) Ryan et al., 1991.

33. Blake, 1966.

34. Nagoshi & Johnson, 1986.

35. Sundet, Tambs, Magnus, & Berg, 1988, p. 47.

36. (a) Flynn, 1984; (b) 1987b; (c) 1987c; (d) 1996.

37. Tuddenham, 1948.

38. Humphreys, 1989, p. 198. Humphreys cites no specific study in connection with this statement, which may be based on his personal observations.

39. Nichols, 1987a, p. 234.

40. Suppose Group A took a mechanical aptitude test in 1930 and Group B (at the same age as Group A was in 1930) took the same test thirty years later, in 1960. Also, suppose both groups were measured on the same external criterion (e.g., some job performance, say, widgets produced per hour) at about the same time that they took the test. The regression of the criterion measures on the test raw scores for Group B is indicated by the regression line $\hat{Y}_B$. For any subject in Group B, it gives the best prediction of the criterion value, that is, how many widgets he will in fact produce in an hour, given that subject's raw score on the mechanical aptitude test (X). If Group A had the same regression line as Group B, then a subject in Group A who scored, say, fifty on the mechanical aptitude test will have the same predicted widgets per hour production as a subject in Group B who also scored fifty on the test. But if Group A has lower scores, on average, than Group B, and if the B-A difference in mean scores is nonfunctional (i.e., ''hollow'', lacking g) then a member of Group A with a test score of, say,

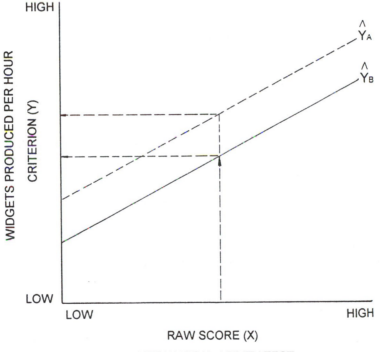

Figure 10.N. Regression lines of criterion measures (Y), (e.g., widgets produced per hour) on raw test scores (X) (e.g., a mechanical ability test) for Groups A and B, with arrows showing the predicted values ($\hat{Y}_A$ and $\hat{Y}_B$) of the criterion for a given raw score (e.g., fifty). (See Note 40 for explanation.)

fifty will predictably produce more widgets than will a member of Group B who also has a test score of fifty. This means that Group A has a different regression line $(\hat{Y}_A)$ from Group B and that Group B's regression line, $\hat{Y}_B$, *under*predicts the widget-producing performance by members of Group A.

41. Jensen, 1980a, Chapter 10 ("Bias in Predictive Validity"); Wigdor & Garner, 1982.

42. Jensen, 1991a.

43. See explanation of "regression line" in Note 40.

44. Lipsey, M. W., & Wilson, D. B., 1993, Table 1.

45. Brody, 1992.

46. Brown & Campione, 1982.

47. Spitz, 1986, p. 215.

48. Benbow, 1992.

49. Carroll, 1993a. See pp. 669–672.

50. Currie & Thomas, 1995.

51. A child's statistically expected IQ $(_E IQ_c)$ is given by the regression equation $_E IQ_c = r_{pc}(IQ_p - \overline{X}_{IQ}) + \overline{X}_{IQ}$, where r_{pc} is the parent-child correlation for IQ, IQ_p is the parent's IQ, and $\overline{X}_{IQ}$ is the mean IQ of the population from which the child's parent was sampled. The median IQ correlation between a parent and a child (when reared by the parent) in thirty-two studies reported in the literature is $r_{pc} = +0.42$. For example, assuming $IQ_p = 80$ and $\overline{X}_{IQ} = 100$, the child's statistically expected IQ is $.42(80 - 100) + 100 = 91.6$. This predicted value has a considerable standard error of estimate for any individual child whose IQ is predicted by this equation. For a large sample of parents all of whom had an IQ of eighty, however, there would be little discrepancy between the predicted value (91.6) and the actual mean IQ of all their children.

52. The original study by Skodak and Skeels (1949) used two different editions of the Stanford-Binet IQ test based on different standardization samples (separated by fourteen years) for testing sixty-three of the biological mothers and for testing all of the children. Flynn (1993) has made the proper adjustments in the mean IQ of mothers and of children to correct for the differing norms in the two standardizations. This adjustment had the effect of considerably reducing the size of the mother-child IQ difference originally reported by Skodak and Skeels (from 20.55 IQ points to 12.87 IQ points). My calculation of the children's average expected IQ (see Note 51) is based on Flynn's adjusted means, a mother-child correlation of +.42, and a population mean of 100.

53. Locurto, 1990.

54. Bouchard & Segal, 1985. This is the most comprehensive review and interpretation of evidence on environmental influences on mental development and IQ in the psychological literature.

55. Garber's (1988) book is a large monograph describing the entire Milwaukee Project and reporting all of its final results. The originator and first director of the project, Rick Heber, died in an airplane crash and was not involved in the production of the final report. An extensive analytic review of Garber's monograph (including references to virtually all of the literature on the project) is provided by Jensen (1989b); four other critical reviews (by D. Guthrie, D. L. MacMillan & K. Widaman, H. Spitz, and R. A. Weinberg) and a reply by Garber and his co-workers appear in the *American Journal on Mental Retardation*, 1991, *95*, 447–524.

56. Campbell & Ramey, 1990, 1994, 1995.

57. A general description of the Abecedarian Project, its main results, and key references are given by its principal investigator, C. T. Ramey (1994). Critical reviews of the project are provided by Spitz (1992, 1993a, 1993b). For replies to Spitz, see Ramey (1992, 1993a, 1993b).

Chapter 11

Population Differences in *g*

Because IQ is strictly a phenotype, as is every observable or measurable human characteristic, it does not, by itself, support any inference concerning the cause of either individual or group differences in IQ. Whatever their cause, IQ differences are related to variables of immense practical consequence in the modern world. The substantial correlation of IQ with many educational, economic, and social criteria has been well established. Largely for this reason, there has been a long-standing interest in the IQ differences between various populations in the United States that markedly differ, on average, on these salient criteria. By far the most extensively researched group differences in IQ are those between the two largest populations in the United States: persons of European ancestry who are socially identified as "white" and persons of some African ancestry who are socially identified as "black" or African-American.

The approximately normal distribution of IQ, as measured by nationally standardized tests, shows that, on average, the American black population scores below the white population by about 1.2 standard deviations, equivalent to eighteen IQ points. (Blacks in sub-Saharan Africa score about two standard deviations [approximately thirty IQ points] below the mean of whites on nonverbal tests.)

This statistical mean difference between the American black and white populations has scarcely changed over the past eighty years for which IQ data have been available. However, it varies across different regions of the country, being largest in the Southeast and decreasing in magnitude on a gradient running north and west. The mean difference, which is in evidence by about three years of age, increases slightly from early childhood to maturity. These are simply the phenotypic, psychometric, and statistical facts. The average difference, of course, is relatively small compared to the range of variation within either population and, in fact, is not much greater than the average difference between full siblings reared together in the same family.

The most visible educational, economic, and social consequences of the group difference in IQ arise largely from two effects: (1) the statistical characteristics of the normal curve, and (2) the minimum probable threshold of the level of ability needed for certain socially valued attainments. When two normal distributions of IQ have different means, although the curves largely overlap one another, a given cut-score on the IQ scale can make a very large difference between the proportions of the lower-scoring group and the higher-scoring group that fall below (or above) the cut-score. The further the distance of the cut-score from the mean of the higher-scoring group, the larger is the group difference between the proportion of each group that falls above (or below) the cut-score. Cut-scores on the IQ scale that fall at critical thresholds (mental retardation, passing grades in regular classes, high school graduation, college admission, college degree, high-level occupation, and the like) therefore result in conspicuous disparities between the proportions of the higher-and lower-scoring groups that fall into different social and occupational categories. Therefore it is reasonable to enquire about the nature and causes of these group disparities. Only their strictly phenotypic or psychometric aspects are examined in this chapter.

Extensive research on test bias has shown that no fraction of the white-black (W-B) IQ difference, at least in the United States, is attributable to any cultural bias in the tests. Nor is the magnitude of the difference a function of the formal characteristics of the tests, such as verbal, nonverbal, individual versus group administration, culture-loaded, or culture-reduced. For all of their legitimate, practical, and typical uses, present-day psychometric tests of mental ability have the same reliability and validity for native, English-speaking blacks (and American-born, English-speaking Hispanics and Asians) as they have for whites.

The magnitude of the mean black-white difference, however, varies considerably across tests that have different homogeneous item contents. This variation between tests in the size of the standardized mean W-B difference is not explainable in terms of test bias or in terms of differences in types of item content or other formal or superficial characteristics of the tests. Charles Spearman (1927) suggested that the different relative magnitudes of the W-B differences on various tests are a function of each test's g loading. This hypothesis (now called "Spearman's hypothesis") has since been tested in numerous studies based on large, representative samples of the American black and white populations. The hypothesis is strongly borne out in these studies. The degree to which a particular test is _g_ loaded predicts the magnitude of the standardized mean W-B difference on that test better than does any other psychometric factor yet identified. This implies that the W-B difference consists mainly of a difference in _g_. However, two other factors, independent of _g_, also show a W-B difference: blacks, on average, exceed whites on a short-term memory factor while whites, on average, exceed blacks on a spatial visualization factor. The effects of these factors, however, show up only on tests that involve these factors, whereas the _g_ factor enters into the W-B difference on every kind of cognitive test.

Spearman's hypothesis has also been studied using elementary cognitive tasks (ECTs) that measure the time it takes a person to process information presented in tasks that are so simple that all persons in the study sample are able to perform them correctly in only one or two seconds. The chronometric variables derived from such ECTs vary in their _g_ loadings and show significant W-B differences. The extent to which the different ECT variables are _g_ loaded predicts the relative magnitudes of the standardized mean W-B differences on the chronometric variables derived from the ECTs. Spearman's hypothesis is thus confirmed even for tasks that do not call upon previously acquired knowledge or skills and that scarcely resemble conventional psychometric tests.

The _g_ factor is especially germane to the study of group differences in performance on psychometric tests, at least with respect to the populations commonly referred to as black and white. These are the only two groups at present for which we have massive and definitive data specifically related to the _g_ issue. Various psychometric data, including IQ, also exist for Asian and Hispanic populations, but scarcely any of these data have been analyzed with respect to _g_ per se. Our analysis, therefore, is focused on psychometric data obtained from samples of the two largest racial groups in the United States. Blacks presently constitute about 13 percent of the U.S. population and are projected to reach 15 percent by the year 2020.[1]

My aim here is not to review the vast (and readily accessible) literature[2] on racial, ethnic, and cultural group differences in IQ (or other psychometric measures), but to explain why understanding the significance of _g_ is a necessary first step for understanding the nature of the observed W-B differences on a wide variety of cognitive measures. But first I shall summarize the actual data on black and white IQ and indicate the most pertinent conclusions now generally accepted by researchers in psychometrics and differential psychology.

Keep in mind that _all_ of the discussion in this chapter concerns only individuals' _phenotypes_ and the _average phenotypic differences_ between groups. The phenotypes of interest here are test scores (raw or standardized). Test intercorrelations, factor analyses, and factor scores are all based on these phenotypic measurements. As with all measurement and observation in the biological and behavioral sciences, test scores per se are strictly _phenotypic_ data. Phenotypic _variation_, of course, is the result of both genetic and environmental variation. Each of these sources of variance and their interaction (if any) contributes some proportion of the total observed population variance. Given suitable data, the analytic methods of quantitative genetics (explained in Chapter 7) can statistically estimate the proportions of genetic and environmental variance. (For either source of variance, genetic or environmental, a value of either zero or one is possible, depending on the particular phenotype, but intermediate values are the rule for most of the phenotypes of interest to behavioral geneticists.)

There are many important phenotypic differences, both between individuals and between groups, and the cause of such differences is always a topic of interest and controversy. However, discussion of hypothesized causal factors (other than test bias in its strict psychometric sense) is postponed until Chapter 12.

It should be noted that all of the descriptive statistics and studies referred to here are based on the social classification of individuals into racial groups as black or white, although virtually all American blacks have some degree of European Caucasian ancestry (see Chapter 12). American blacks are socially defined simply as persons who have some degree of sub-Saharan African ancestry and who identify themselves (or, in the case of children, are identified by their parents) as black or African-American. Persons of European Caucasoid ancestry are classified as whites.

BLACK AND WHITE IQ DISTRIBUTIONS: STATISTICAL SUMMARY

Mean and Standard Deviation. When IQ is scaled to a mean of 100 and a standard deviation (_SD_) of 15 in the white population, large representative samples of the black population of the whole United States (rather than a local subgroup) show a mean close to 85. For most samples and tests, the range is 80 to 90. The black _SD_ of IQ is approximately 12, ranging in most samples from 11 to 14. There is some slight, nonsystematic variation for different IQ tests and normative samples. For example, the normative sample on one of the most widely used individual IQ tests for school-age children (the Wechsler Intelligence Scale for Children-Revised, or WISC-R), using the same scale (i.e., white mean = 100, _SD_ = 15), the black mean is 84.0, with _SD_ of 13.6. On the same scale, the black normative mean and _SD_ of IQ are 86.5 and 13.5 on another popular IQ test (the 1986 Stanford-Binet-IV).

The mean W-B* differences based on a number of different studies or different tests can be cumulated or averaged most precisely when the mean differences are expressed in units of the averaged standard deviation within each group.[3] This measure is known both as the *sigma* difference (σ diff) or as the *effect size* (*d*). This standardized scale permits direct comparisons of mean differences regardless of the original scale of measurement or the characteristic measured. A meta-analysis of 156 independent studies of the W-B difference, based on many different IQ tests given to American samples, yields an overall mean sigma difference of 1.08σ. The σ differences have a *SD* of 0.36, which means that about two-thirds of the mean W-B differences in these 156 studies fall between 0.72σ and 1.44σ, or roughly equivalent to mean IQ differences between ten and twenty points, with an overall average difference of 16.2.[4]

The meaning of a σ difference might be elucidated by looking at a physical scale that is familiar to everyone, such as human stature. The height (without shoes) of a sample of 8,585 British adult males (measured in 1883) showed a mean of 67.46 inches (5 ft., 7 ½ in.) and a *SD* of 2.57 inches. The distribution of height in this sample is close to normal. Six-footers, therefore, are (72 − 67.46)/2.57 = 1.8σ above the mean. The height of men who are 1σ below the mean is 67.46 − 2.57 ≈ 65 inches (5 ft., 5 in.). The total range in this sample goes from 57 inches (4.1σ below the mean) to 77 inches (3.7σ above the mean). Thus the heights of 57 and 77 inches in this distribution correspond to scores of 39 and 156, respectively, on the IQ scale.

A difference between the means of two population groups has a quite different kind of consequence than does the very same size difference when obtained between two individuals on the same scale. For groups, the most important consequence of a group difference in means is of a statistical nature. This may have far-reaching consequences for society, depending on the variables that are correlated with the characteristic on which the groups differ, on average, and how much society values them. In this statistical sense, the consequences of population differences in IQ (irrespective of cause) are of greater importance, because of all the important correlates of IQ, than are most other measurable characteristics that show comparable population differences.

When two readily distinguishable populations have different means on a socially significant trait (or a trait, like *g*, that correlates with, and therefore reliably predicts, one or more socially significant behaviors), and if that trait has an approximately normal distribution in each population, there are significant social consequences that are readily apparent, even to casual observers who may have no direct method of measuring the trait in question. Because the percentage of individuals who fall in a given σ range decreases so rapidly as one moves away from the mean and toward either tail of the normal distribution (see Figure 11.1),

---

*Throughout the text, W-B or B-W always signifies "white *minus* black" or "black *minus* white," respectively. The two variables are made the minuend and subtrahend so as always to yield a difference with a positive sign.

it quickly becomes obvious that the populations are disproportionately represented in the high ("desirable") and in the low ("undesirable") tails. This can lead to a misconception, or even an institutional policy, that elevates all members of the former population as being "superior" in terms of the desirable trait (or the behaviors that correlate with it) and lowers all members of the latter population as being "inferior." This can in turn result in understandable cries for policies that will redress this statistical inequity.

Consider the fact that the mean difference in IQ between members of the two racial groups (white and black) is little different from the average difference between full siblings reared in the same family. But because "brighter" and "duller" siblings are not immediately recognizable and therefore categorized as such, there has been neither widespread nor institutionalized discrimination against the latter and in favor of the former, nor policies enacted in the hope of redressing the statistical inequity that does in fact exist between these two groups.

This statistical consequence of the mean W-B difference in IQ is seen in Figure 11.1. Although *perfectly* normal curves do not exist in reality, the two curves shown here are made to be perfectly normal to permit precise percentages in each segment of the two curves. It also facilitates explanation to make the *SD* of IQ equal to fifteen in each group and to set the mean difference precisely equal to 1σ. This picture, in fact, comes reasonably close to the actual population statistics and, if anything, slightly underestimates the true statistical consequences of the group difference.

The crucial point in Figure 11.1 is the disparity in percentiles for the two groups, which, given the mean difference of 1σ, is a consequence of the normality of the distributions. To the extent that there are different selection thresholds[5] for the level of IQ needed for certain levels of educational attainment, or for selection into colleges, occupations, or specialized training programs, population groups that differ in mean IQ will be represented unequally in the selection outcome. This is a direct consequence of the correlation between IQ and these socially significant variables within each population. For example, many school systems place children with IQ below seventy in special classes for the "educable mentally retarded" (EMR). The percentages of blacks and whites below IQ seventy are 15.9 percent and 2.3 percent, respectively—a ratio of about seven to one. Highly selective colleges admit students largely from that segment of the population distribution with IQ above 115. Calculated from Figure 11.1, the ratio of white to black percentages above this level is about seven to one. The ratio becomes increasingly disparate the farther above (or below) the IQ level of the selection criterion (or cut-score) is from the mean of the higher-scoring group. Some school systems, for example, place children with IQ above 130 in special classes for the academically gifted. As determined from Figure 11.1, the ratio of percentages of whites to blacks with IQ above 130 is about twenty to one. (Since blacks constitute about 13 percent of the U.S. population, the actual numerical ratio of white/black IQ above 130 is about 150 to

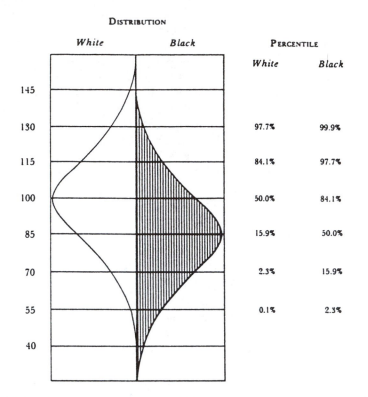

Figure 11.1. IQ distributions in white and black populations shown as normal curves, with the percentile ranks given at each level of IQ marked off at 1σ (=15 IQ points) intervals above and below the white mean (=100). The percentile rank indicates the percentage of the total distribution of IQ that falls below a given cut-score on the IQ scale for the given group.

one.) Ultimately it is these disparate percentage ratios and their commonly perceived consequences for IQ-correlated educational and occupational thresholds that are at the root of the public concern over IQ and race.

The pernicious notion that IQ discriminates mainly along racial lines, however, is utterly false. This can be demonstrated most clearly in terms of a statistical method known as *the analysis of variance*. Table 11.1 shows this kind of analysis for IQ data obtained from equal-sized random samples of black and white children in California schools. Their parents' social class (based on education and occupation) was rated on a ten-point scale.

In the first column in Table 11.1 the total variance of the entire data set is of course 100 percent and the percentage of total variance attributable to each of the sources[6] is then listed in the first column. We see that only 30 percent of the total variance is associated with differences between race and social class,

Table 11.1
Percentage of Variance and Average Difference in IQ Associated Independently with Race (Black or White), Social Class, Between-Families, Within-Families, and Measurement Error

Source	% of Variance		Average IQ Difference
Between races (within social classes)	14		12
Between social classes (within races)	8	30%	6
Interaction of race and social class	8		
Between families (within race and social class)	26		9
Within families (siblings)	39	65%	11
Measurement error	5		4
Total	100		17

whereas 65 percent of the true-score variance is completely unrelated to IQ differences between the races and social classes, and exists entirely *within* each racial and social class group. The single largest source of IQ variance in the whole population exists *within families*, that is, between full siblings reared together in the same family. The second largest source of variance exists *between* families of the same race and the same social class.

The last column of Table 11.1 shows what happens when each of the variances in the first column is transformed into the average IQ difference among members of the given classification. For example, the average difference between blacks and whites of the same social class is 12 IQ points. The average difference between full siblings (reared together) is 11 IQ points. Measurement error (i.e., the average difference between the same person tested on two occasions) is 4 IQ points. (By comparison, the average difference between persons picked at random from the total population is 17 IQ points.) Persons of different social class but of the same race differ, on average, only 6 points, more or less, depending on how far apart they are on the scale of socioeconomic status (SES). What is termed the *interaction* of race and social class (8 percent of the variance) results from the unequal IQ differences between blacks and whites across the spectrum of SES, as shown in Figure 11.2. This interaction is a general finding in other studies as well. Typically, IQ in the black population is not as differentiated by SES as in the white population, and the size of the mean W-B difference increases with the level of SES.

Constancy Over Time. The mean W-B IQ difference has remained fairly constant at about 1σ for at least eighty years, with no clear trend upward or downward since the first large-scale testing of representative samples of blacks and whites in the United States. It is important that the secular increase in IQ

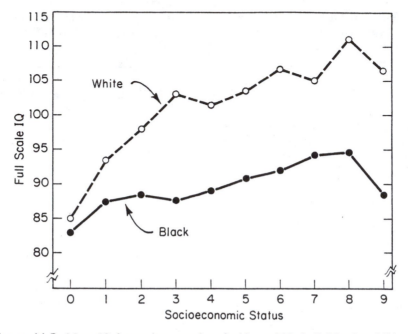

Figure 11.2. Mean IQ for random samples of white and black Californian children in each of ten SES categories (lowest = 1, highest = 9). The *interaction* of race × social class shown in Table 11.1 reflects the increasing B-W difference as the level of SES increases, thus constituting a source of variance (8 percent) associated jointly with race *and* SES. *Source: Bias in mental testing* by Arthur R. Jensen, Fig. 3.1, p. 44. Copyright © 1980 by Arthur R. Jensen. Reprinted with permission of The Free Press, a Division of Simon & Schuster, and Routledge Ltd.

(known as the Flynn effect, discussed in Chapter 10) has affected the black and white populations equally. Although both groups have shown a gradual rise in raw scores on IQ tests over the past several decades, the mean W-B difference of about 1σ has remained virtually constant over the same period.

Regional Variation. The mean IQ of blacks varies between different regions of the country, being generally lower in the Southeastern states, with an increasing gradient of IQ going toward the Northern and Western states. Whites show a similar, though less pronounced, regional gradient. As this gradient already appears in children's IQ measured before school age, it is not entirely attributable to regional differences in the quality of schooling. The regional differences, some as much as ten to fifteen IQ points, are associated with earlier patterns of migration, the population densities in rural and urban areas, and the employment demands for different educational levels in various regions.

Age Variation. Black infants score higher than white infants on developmental scales that depend mainly on sensorimotor abilities. Scores on these infant scales have near-zero correlation with IQ at school age, because the IQ predominantly reflects cognitive rather than sensorimotor development. Between ages three and five years, which is before children normally enter school, the mean W-B IQ difference steadily increases. By five to six years of age, the mean difference is about 0.70σ (eleven IQ points), then approaches about 1σ during the elementary school years, remaining fairly constant until puberty, when it increases slightly and stabilizes at about 1.2σ. The latest (1986) Stanford-Binet IV norms show a W-B difference in prepubescent children that is almost five IQ points smaller than the W-B difference in postpubescent children. (The W-B difference is 0.80σ for ages 2 through 11 as compared with 1.10σ for ages 12 through 23.) This could constitute evidence that the mean W-B difference in the population is decreasing. Or it could simply be that the W-B difference increases from early to later childhood. The interpretation of this age effect on the size of the W-B mean difference remains uncertain in this instance, as it is based entirely on cross-sectional rather than longitudinal data. Both kinds of data are needed to settle the issue. The cause of variation in the mean IQ of different age groups all tested within the same year (a _cross-sectional_ study) may not be the same as the cause of variation (if any) in mean IQ of the same group of individuals when tested at different ages (a _longitudinal_ study).

Types of Tests. The average W-B difference is about the same for verbal and for nonverbal IQ tests, provided the nonverbal tests do not include a substantial spatial-visualization factor (which slightly increases the W-B difference). The mean W-B difference, however, varies considerably across many different kinds of cognitive tests, if each test is composed of homogeneous items (for example, each of the subtests of well-known batteries, such as the Wechsler Intelligence Scales, the General Aptitude Test Battery [GATB], and the Armed Services Vocational Aptitude Battery [ASVAB]). Variation between subtests in the magnitude of the W-B difference is not predictable from simple inspection of the tests as to their item content (e.g., verbal, nonverbal, or performance), or as to the type of test (e.g., paper-and-pencil, free response or multiple-choice, individual or group administration, culture loaded or culture reduced). The magnitude of the W-B difference on a given test is best described in terms of the Spearman hypothesis, discussed later in this chapter.

Generality. The W-B difference in IQ is not confined to the United States, but is quite general and in the same direction, though of varying size, in every country in which representative samples of the white and black populations have been tested. The largest differences have been found in sub-Saharan Africa, averaging about 1.75σ in 11 studies.[7a,b] The largest difference between white and African groups (equated for schooling) is found on the Raven matrices (a nonverbal test of reasoning). In one large study the mean difference averaged about 2.0σ for Africans with no apparent European or Asian (East Indian) ancestry and about 1.1σ for Africans of mixed ancestry.[8] The East Indians in Africa averaged about 0.5σ below Europeans with the same years of schooling.

Studies in Britain have found that the mean IQ difference between the white and the West Indian (mainly African ancestry with some [unknown] degree of Caucasian admixture) populations is about the same as the W-B difference in the United States.[9] Recent immigrant East Indian children score, upon arrival in Britain, about as far below the British mean as do the West Indians, but, unlike the West Indians, the East Indians, after spending four years in British schools, score at about the same level as the indigenous white Britishers. A longitudinal study[10] of this phenomenon concluded, "The most striking result of the longitudinal IQ test results was the declining scores of the West Indians and the rising scores of the Indian children, in comparison to the non-minority children in the same schools. It appeared that the Indian children were acquiring the reasoning skills expected of children in the 8–12-year period, while the West Indians were not keeping pace in reasoning skills with most British children" (p. 40). The most recent British study[11] presents a somewhat different and more complex picture, to the effect that the most recent East Indian and Pakistani immigrants and those born in Britain within the last decade or so have scored less favorably on IQ tests and in scholastic performance than the earlier immigrants from the Indian subcontinent, although the Indian children were still on a par with the British in tests of reasoning and mathematics. It was only in the language area that they tested below the British children. Inexplicably, the Pakistanis performed conspicuously less well than the Indians. As these effects most likely reflect secular shifts in the particular self-selected segments of the home country's population that emigrated to Britain, they would seem to be only of local interest and of questionable general significance.

IS THE W-B DIFFERENCE DUE TO CULTURE-BIASED TESTS?

It is now well established and widely accepted by those familiar with the evidence that the W-B difference on cognitive tests is not attributable to test bias (as defined in psychometrics). This is not to say that the difference couldn't be due to bias, but it so happens that it is not. It is entirely possible to devise tests that are biased, just as it is possible to devise tests that are not biased. It is fair to say that, with respect to all legitimate uses of mental tests, the professionally produced tests in wide use today are not biased for any native-born, English-speaking racial or ethnic subgroups in the U.S. population. A now vast but rather technical body of research literature[12] fully supports this conclusion, and although it has been one of the most critically examined conclusions in all of contemporary psychology, no effective contradiction based on evidence has come forth.

In psychometrics, bias is defined as a *systematic* error of measurement, as contrasted with *random* measurement error. A measurement is said to be biased if it consistently either overestimates or underestimates the true value of the variable that was measured. A number of independent statistical methods are used to detect the presence of bias in mental tests with respect to group differences. These methods are fully capable of revealing such bias if it is in fact present. Each of these methods statistically decides whether the test behaves in the same way for different groups on some essential psychometric property. If the test behaves differently in the two groups on any important psychometric property, it is considered biased. Obviously, since tests are expressly intended to measure individual differences, and because groups are aggregates of individuals, a finding that test scores reveal individual differences or mean differences between groups cannot itself be evidence of bias. Bias is suspected, however, if a test shows signs of not measuring the same thing in different individuals (or in different groups) who differ on some characteristic (such as sex, race, or ethnicity) that has no prima facie relation to the construct nominally measured by the test. If shown, this would imply that the test scores do not have the same meaning for the different groups. Test publishers, such as the Educational Testing Service and the Psychological Corporation, have invested heavily in research on bias detection to ensure that their tests are not biased. In the tryouts of a new (or revised) test, these methods permit any particular source of psychometric bias to be spotted and eliminated. The same is true for the tests developed by the armed services and the U.S. Employment Service.

Countless studies have applied these methods for detecting such bias to the test performance of American blacks and whites, and with overwhelmingly conclusive results. As it would take us too far afield to explain all the technical details of research on test bias, I will only list the main psychometric criteria used to study test bias.

Predictive validity is crucial for assessing bias: Do test scores show the same correlation with some independent criterion variable (e.g., job performance, grade-point average, etc.) in both groups? Does the criterion variable have the same regression on test scores in both groups? (That is, throughout the range of scores and criterion measures does the same test score predict the same level of criterion performance for both groups?) Meta-analyses of innumerable studies based on many different selection tests and a wide variety of criterion measures answer both of these questions in the affirmative. There is no evidence of either _single-group validity_ or _differential validity_ for black and white groups, as would be indicated if a test was valid in one group but had no validity in the other group, or had significantly different degrees of validity for each group. Using these criteria, differential validity is simply nonexistent. Black and white groups not only have the same validity coefficient for a given test, but usually also have the same regression line. When the regression lines for blacks and whites differ significantly, it is usually an artifact of there being the same degree of random measurement error within each group. Typically, the true-score regression is the same for both groups. When there is a real exception to this generalization, it typically consists of what is termed _intercept bias_. In virtually all instances of such bias, however, the test scores for blacks _over_estimate their actual level of criterion performance when prediction is based on either the white regression line or the common regression line (see Figure 11.3). Intercept bias results when the groups differ not only on the factors measured by the test but

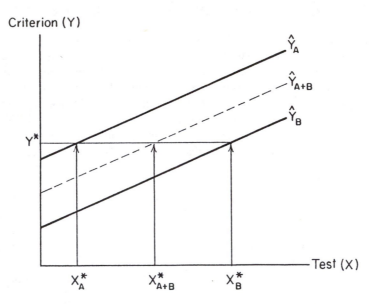

Figure 11.3. An example of intercept bias with respect to hypothetical groups A and B. The asterisk on X and on Y means that these are actually measured variables, in this case test scores (X*) and criterion measures (Y*). Ŷ is the regression line (i.e., the line of best prediction of values of Y* from values of X*) for each group and for the combined groups (A+B). The precise position of the regression lines is determined mathematically from the data on variables X and Y. The regression lines here are parallel (i.e., they have the same slope), but their intercepts are seen to differ (i.e., they cross Y* at different points). As a consequence, for each group (and for the combined groups) the same value on the criterion (Y*) is predicted by a different test score (X*_A, X*_B, and X*_{A+B}). Conversely, a given test score predicts different values of Y* for each group, which means that the common regression line *over*predicts the lower-scoring group (B) and *under*predicts the higher-scoring group (A). The usual remedy for intercept bias is simply to base prediction on each group's own regression line. *Source: Bias in mental testing* by Arthur R. Jensen, fig. 9.10, p. 416. Copyright © 1980 by Arthur R. Jensen. Reprinted with permission of The Free Press, a Division of Simon & Schuster, and Routledge Ltd.

also on other factors that are uncorrelated with the test scores but are correlated with the criterion. These other factors may be abilities not sampled by the test or personality traits such as conscientiousness, dependability, emotional stability, energy level, dominance, and the like.

Order of item difficulty is a completely internal indicator of bias. If the individual items in a test measure the same factor(s) in the black and white groups, then one should expect the rank order of item difficulty levels to be the same for both groups. If item #6 is harder (i.e., more difficult as indicated by the greater percentage of the sample who fail it) than item #5 in one group, item

#6 should also be harder than item #5 in the other group. Thus we can rank the item difficulties in each group and look at the rank-order correlation between the two sets of ranks. This correlation can be compared with the rank-order correlation within each sample (or between two comparable sized samples each selected at random from the same racially homogeneous population). Item bias is indicated if the first correlation is significantly smaller than the second (meaning that the rank ordering of item difficulties is less alike in the two groups than it is in the same group). This method has been applied in many studies based on almost every widely used mental test, including the Wechsler scales and the Stanford-Binet. Invariably, the rank order of item difficulty for blacks and for whites is correlated over +.95 and is as high as the reliability of the rank order within each sample. Hence there is no evidence of bias by this internal criterion.

A stringent test of this criterion was performed[13] on a test intentionally composed of two types of items as judged by a group of psychologists: items judged to be either "culture-loaded" (C) or "noncultural" (NC). The mean W-B difference was actually smaller on the C group of items than on the NC items.

Here is the specific test for item bias: Relative item difficulty, separately for the black and the white groups, and separately for the C and NC items, was expressed for each of the items on an interval scale of difficulty known as the delta (Δ) scale.[14] The results are shown as a scatter diagram in Figure 11.4. The correlation (r) between the black and white Δ values for the 37 C items is +.96, for the 37 NC items $r = +.95$, and for all 74 items $r = +.96$. (The corresponding rank-order correlations are +.98, +.97, and +.97.) Hence, even in a test intentionally made up of items that are commonly expected to accentuate cultural item bias, no evidence of bias was found.

Item $\times$ total score correlation is another internal indicator of item bias. Besides measuring something in common (usually _g_), each of the items in a test also measures some group factors that are shared with only a limited number of other items as well as something that is specific to the particular item. Because the particular mix of these three sources of variance varies across items, there is considerable variation in each single item's correlation with the total test score. If the items are rank-ordered by these item $\times$ total score correlations (designated by r_{IT}) separately for each of two groups that had taken the same test, a correlation between the rank order of r_{IT} values for the two groups close to 1.0 indicates that the items and the test as a whole measure the same factors in both groups, hence ruling out bias. When applied to the W-B difference on various tests this criterion shows no evidence of bias. The rank-order correlation between the item r_{IT} values in black and white samples is typically over +.95.

Similarity of factor structure of diverse tests would be unlikely if a battery of tests measured different things in each group. Factor analyses of different test batteries each composed of highly diverse tests show the same factor structure for blacks and whites when the samples are large and representative of their respective populations. Congruence coefficients (a measure of factor similarity), are typically above .95, indicating virtually identical factors, usually with the

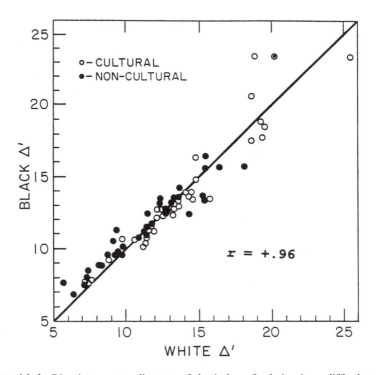

Figure 11.4. Bivariate scatter diagram of the index of relative item difficulty (scaled as Δ) for the thirty-seven "cultural" (C) and thirty-seven "noncultural" (NC) items for the black and white samples. (The Δ values have a mean of thirteen and *SD* of four in each sample for both the C and NC items. The overall scatter diagram of seventy-four data points represents a correlation (*r*) of +.96 between the black and white Δ values. Reprinted from *Personality and Individual Differences, 8,* A. R. Jensen and F. C. J. McGurk, Black-white bias in "cultural" and "noncultural" test items, 295–301, Copyright 1987, with kind permission from Elsevier Science Ltd, The Boulevard, Langford Lane, Kidlington 0X5 1GB, UK.

highest congruence for the *g* factor. This outcome is in fact inevitable if the matrix of test intercorrelations does not differ significantly between blacks and whites, as is generally true. In those cases where there is a significant difference between the black and white correlation matrices, *g* and the large-group factors usually remain unaffected. (The effects of the correlational differences show up only in the smaller principal components, with eigenvalues less than one.)

   Congruence of item characteristic curves (ICC) for different groups is probably the most rigorous means for the fine-grained detection of item bias, although its use is rather restricted to very large samples, such as are available to test publishing firms and the armed services. For each item in a test, the ICC shows the percentage of individuals in a given sample who pass the item, as a function of the total score. (The ICC is shown graphically in Figure 10.1, p. 314.) Item bias is indicated if two groups yield significantly different ICCs. In recent years a variety of methods for detecting item bias has sprung from the ICC approach.[15]

Error distractors in multiple-choice answers are of interest as a method of discovering bias. When a person fails to select the correct answer but instead chooses one of the alternative erroneous responses (called "distractors") offered for an item in a multiple-choice test, the person's incorrect choice is not random, but is about as reliable as is the choice of the correct answer. In other words, error responses, like correct responses, are not just a matter of chance, but reflect certain information processes (or the failure of certain crucial steps in information processing) that lead the person to choose not just any distractor, but a particular one. Some types of errors result from a solution strategy that is more naïve or less sophisticated than other types of errors. For example, consider the following test item:

> If you mix a pint of water at 50° temperature with two pints of water at 80° measured on the same thermometer, what will be the temperature of the mixture? (a) 65°, (b) 70°, (c) 90°, (d) 130°, (e) Can't say without knowing whether the temperatures are Centigrade or Fahrenheit.

We see that the four distractors differ in the level of sophistication in mental processing that would lead to their choice. The most naïve distractor, for example, is D, which is arrived at by simple addition of 50° and 80°. The answer A at least shows that the subject realized the necessity for averaging the temperatures. The answer 90° is the most sophisticated distractor, as it reveals that the subject had a glimmer of the necessity for a weighted average (i.e., 50° + 80°/2 = 90°) but didn't know how to go about calculating it. (The correct answer, of course, is B, because the weighted average is [1 pint × 50° + 2 pints × 80°]/3 pints = 70°.) Preference for selecting different distractors changes across age groups, with younger children being attracted to the less sophisticated type of distractor, as indicated by comparing the percentage of children in different age groups that select each distractor. The kinds of errors made, therefore, appear to reflect something about the children's level of cognitive development.

This kind of developmental trend in choice of distractors shows up distinctly in the Raven matrices test, in which all of the items consist of figures representing different kinds of logical relationships that the subject must induce in order to deduce the correct answer and select it from among a number of distractors. What we have found in analyses of distractor choices in large black and white samples is that both groups show much the same percentages choosing the different distractors, but this is true only when the groups are roughly matched on mental age, not on chronological age. For example, age ten whites and age twelve blacks are much more alike in distractor choices than are white and black children of the same chronological age. The same developmental offset has also been found on tests on which subjects actually produce the answers or responses rather than select the correct response from multiple-choice alternatives. The Gesell Figure Copying test, Piaget's tests of developmental stages, and even free drawing all show highly distinctive performance characteristics at different ages, thus indicating a clear and uniform developmental trend. Although black children show exactly the same age sequence of performance characteristics as whites in these developmental measures, they are on a different time line, reaching each stage of development at a later age. Their lag in attaining these developmental milestones is equivalent to an average cognitive developmental rate (beyond age two) of about 80 percent of that for white children. Thus, on average, a black six-year-old, for example, performs about like a white five-year-old on these developmental tasks. This disparity in developmental level is the basis of the typical W-B difference in school readiness, which, absent tests, is usually brought to light by the cognitive demands of the first-grade curriculum.

Noncognitive correlates of mental tests, if not significantly different between groups, provide ancillary evidence that the test behaves the same in both groups, although it is seldom as compelling as evidence based on cognitive correlates. The noncognitive variables for which the W-B differences in correlations have been studied are the correlation of IQ with chronological age, body measurements (height, weight, head circumference), the IQ correlations between twins and between full siblings, and the coefficient of heritability for IQ.

Unlike IQ itself, which is a standardized score with a mean of 100 and *SD* of fifteen for every age group, the *raw scores* of IQ tests increase steadily and almost linearly with age from early childhood up to about age fifteen years, after which they rapidly approach asymptote at a negatively accelerated rate of increase. The fact that the raw scores on each of the twelve subscales of the WISC-R tests do not show significant differences between blacks and whites in their correlations with age is presumptive evidence that the tests are measuring the same latent variables in both groups.[16] The regressions of scores on age, however, do differ in slope, with blacks showing a lower slope, indicating a slower rate of mental growth, with a lower asymptote.

That the correlation of IQ with either age-adjusted height or weight is not significantly different between very large samples of blacks and whites (approximately 12,000 in each sample) measured at ages four and seven years also suggests that IQ measures the same construct in both groups.[17] In the same samples there was a slight but significant W-B difference (W > B by about .05) in the correlation of IQ with age-adjusted head circumference. (The overall average correlations at ages four and seven years were .12 and .21, respectively.)

A number of studies of the correlation between twins (both MZ and DZ) and between full siblings on a variety of tests show no consistent significant differences between the black and white twin or sibling correlations. From this evidence and a review of the heritability coefficients for IQ, estimated from three studies of black and white MZ and DZ twins, Loehlin et al. concluded there was "appreciable and similar heritability of IQ within the U.S. black and white populations.''[18] However, each of these studies of heritability provides only weak evidence for any conclusion, because of the very large standard errors[18] of h^2 for the sample sizes used, so that even rather large W-B differences in h^2 could not show up as significant. Of course, the obtained differences probably reflect nothing more than the large sampling error associated with the twin method for estimating h^2, but this must remain in doubt until much larger black and white twins samples are obtained. In the four twin studies in which the black and white samples were both part of the same study and took the same tests under the same conditions, the _N_-weighted average values of the h^2 estimates in the black and the white samples (totaling 964 black pairs and 788 white pairs) are .49 and .38, respectively. These values of h^2 are unusually low for IQ generally, but are not much out of line for these samples, which consist mostly of young children. The heritability of IQ, in fact, increases from early childhood to later maturity; that is, the genotypic variance becomes increasingly expressed in the phenotypic variance throughout most of the human life span. (A predominantly environmental theory of IQ variation would have to predict the opposite.)

Race of examiner, for individually or group-administered tests, has no consistent or significant effect on the average level of performance for either blacks or whites.[19]

Two Types of Mental Retardation Mistaken as Test Bias. This is a matter I have not seen mentioned in the literature on test bias. It was brought to my attention in discussions with schoolteachers who have taught classes for the mentally retarded.

Mental retardation is generally defined as an IQ of -2σ or more below the population mean, or IQ below seventy. (Placement in a special class in school depends also on other characteristics in addition to low IQ, such as exceptionally poor progress in regular classes and persistent failing grades in the basic subjects.) What originally drew me into research on test bias was that teachers of retarded classes claimed that far more of their black pupils seem to look and act less retarded than the white pupils with comparable IQ. This was especially apparent in social interactions and playground activities observed by teachers during recess and recreation periods.

Their observations were indeed accurate, as I later confirmed by my own observation and testing of pupils in special classes. In social and outdoor play activities, however, black children with IQ below seventy seldom appeared as other than quite normal youngsters—energetic, sociable, active, motorically well coordinated, and generally indistinguishable from their age-mates in regular classes. But this was not so for as many of the white children with IQ below seventy. More of them were somehow "different" from their white age-mates in the regular classes. They appeared less competent in social interactions with their classmates and were motorically clumsy or awkward, or walked with a flat-footed gait. The retarded white children more often looked and acted generally retarded in their development than the black children of comparable IQ. From such observations, one gets the impression that the IQ tests are somehow biased against the black pupils and underestimate their true ability.

In most of the cognitive tasks of the classroom that call for conceptual learning and problem solving, however, black and white retarded children of the same IQ do not differ measurably either in classroom performance or on objective achievement tests. Trying out a variety of tests in these classes, I found one exception—tasks that depend only on rote learning and memorization through repetition. On these tasks, retarded black pupils, on average, performed significantly better than white pupils of the same IQ.[20]

The explanation for these differences cannot be that the IQ test is biased in its predictive validity for the children's general scholastic learning, because predictive validity scarcely differs between black and white groups. Nor is the test biased according to any of the other standard criteria of bias (reviewed above). Rather, the explanation lies in the fact that IQ per se does not identify the *cause* of the child's retardation (nor is it intended to do so).

There are two distinguishable types of mental retardation, usually referred to as *endogenous* and *exogenous* or, more commonly, as *familial* and *organic*. The lower tail (IQ < 70)) of the normal distribution of IQ in the population comprises both of these types of retardation.

In familial retardation there are no detectable causes of retardation other than the normal polygenic and microenvironmental sources of IQ variation that account for IQ differences throughout the entire range of IQ. Although persons with familial retardation are, on average, lower in IQ than their parents and siblings, they are no lower than would be expected for a trait with normal polygenic inheritance. For example, they score (on average) no *lower* in IQ compared with their first-order relatives than gifted children (above +2σ) score *higher* than their first-order relatives. Parent-child and sibling correlations for IQ are the same (about +.50) in the families of familial retardates as in the general population. In other words, the familial retarded are biologically normal individuals who deviate statistically from the population mean because of the same factors that cause IQ variation among all other biologically normal individuals in the population. Traits that are *not* associated with IQ in the general population do not distinguish the familial retarded from the rest of the biologically normal population. An analogy with stature, also a normally distributed polygenic trait, would be a physically strong, well-proportioned, well-nourished, healthy person of very short height. Such a person is neither a dwarf nor a midget, nor stunted by malnutrition or illness. (In the population distribution of adult male height, −2σ is about 5 ft., 2 in.).

Organic retardation, on the other hand, comprises over 350 identified etiologies, including specific chromosomal and genetic anomalies and environmental prenatal, perinatal, and postnatal brain damage due to disease or trauma that affects brain development. Nearly all of these conditions, when severe enough to cause mental retardation, also have other, more general, neurological and physical manifestations of varying degree. These are in fact among the behavioral and physical signs used for the differential diagnosis of familial and organic retardation. The IQ of organically retarded children is scarcely correlated with the IQ of their first-order relatives, and they typically stand out as deviant in other ways as well. In the white population, for example, the full siblings of familial retarded persons have an average IQ of about ninety, whereas the average IQ of the siblings of organic retardates is close to the general population mean of 100.

Statistical studies of mental retardation based on the white population find that among all persons with IQ below seventy, between one-quarter and one-half are diagnosed as organic, and between one-half and three-quarters are diagnosed as familial. As some 2 to 3 percent of the white population falls below IQ seventy, the population percentage of organic retardates is at most one-half of 3 percent, or 1.5 percent of the population. Studies of the percentage of organic types of retardation in the black population are less conclusive, but they suggest that the percentage of organic retardation is at most only slightly higher than in the white population, probably about 2 percent.[21] However, based on the normal-curve statistics of the distribution of IQ in the black population, about 16 percent fall below IQ seventy. Assuming that organic retardation has a 2 percent incidence in the entire black population, then in classes for the retarded (i.e., IQ < 70) about $2\%/16\% = 12.5$ percent of blacks would be organic as compared to about $1.5\%/3\% = 50$ percent of whites—a white/black ratio of four to one. Hence teachers of retarded classes are more apt to perceive their white children as more generally handicapped by low IQ than are the black children.

VARIABILITY OF THE W-B DIFFERENCE: SPEARMAN'S HYPOTHESIS

IQ tests are seldom composed of homogeneous items. (The Raven matrices is the best-known example of one that is.) For most IQ tests the total score is typically based on an amalgam of heterogeneous item types or of subtests that differ in the particular types of knowledge or skill they demand and in their factor composition. Unfortunately, the almost exclusive emphasis on the black-white IQ difference in discussions of population differences has eclipsed the telling fact that the size of the group difference varies greatly across different (homogeneous) cognitive tests. This is especially regrettable from a research standpoint, because the great variability of the W-B difference across various tests can help us discover the psychometric basis of that difference.

By about 1980, the massive research on test bias had established that the variability of the mean W-B difference cannot be explained adequately in terms of some tests being more culturally biased than others. Besides the lack of objective evidence for bias, there is no connection between the differences in tests' apparent potential for bias and the size of the W-B mean differences on these tests. Nor is the size of the W-B difference systematically related to the test's specific type of information content (e.g., verbal/nonverbal, culture-loaded/ culture-reduced), or to the mode of test administration (e.g., individual/group, subject-produced response/multiple-choice, written/oral, timed/untimed). None of these test characteristics gives a clue as to why the size of the W-B difference varies markedly and consistently across diverse tests. It is on this question especially that all the conjectural explanations of the W-B difference that rely on such broad noncognitive notions as poor motivation in test taking, low self-esteem, vulnerability to racial stereotypes, fear of failure, lower-caste status, and the like, so clearly founder.

Looking for a valid answer to this question, I focused first on the tests of digit span memory found in the Stanford-Binet and the Wechsler Scales. The W-B difference (in standard score units) was almost twice as large for *backward digit span* (BDS) as for *forward digit span* (FDS). Why should there be as large and consistent a difference between the W-B difference on FDS versus BDS? The contents of both tests are identical, namely, single random digits spoken by the examiner at the rate of one digit per second. In FDS, the examiner recites, say, four digits, and the subject is asked to repeat the digits in the same order. Then five digits are given, and so on, until the subject is unable to repeat all *n* digits correctly on two successive trials. The procedure for BDS is exactly the same, except that the subject is asked to repeat the series of digits in the *reverse* order to that presented. (The average adult can recall seven digits forward, five digits backward.)

Several studies[22] showed, in every age group, that the W-B difference on the FDS test is smaller (usually by about 0.5σ) than on the BDS test. Also, when black and white groups were matched on *mental age* (thus the blacks were chronologically older than the whites), the black and white means did not differ, either on FDS or on BDS. These results are not easily explained in terms of a qualitative cultural difference or some motivational factor. Rather, the results are most parsimoniously explained in terms of a difference in the black and white rates of development of whatever abilities enter into FDS and BDS. BDS obviously makes a greater demand on mental manipulation of the input in order to produce the correct output than does FDS. Hence BDS can be characterized as a more complex cognitive task than FDS. Further, a factor analysis of FDS and BDS scores obtained at five grade levels clearly showed (in separate analyses for blacks and whites) that two distinct factors are reflected in these tests, with the most salient loadings of FDS and of BDS found on different factors.

The interpretation of these digit span factors is elucidated by observing the correlations of FDS and of BDS with the WISC-R Full Scale IQ and the Raven IQ.[22] For both tests, the correlation between BDS and IQ is almost twice as large as the correlation between FDS and IQ. A factor analysis of FDS and BDS among a large battery of other tests showed that while both FDS and BDS are loaded on a memory factor and on *g*, BDS has the much larger *g* loading.

Although these findings on the interaction of the W-B difference with FDS and BDS are interesting in their own right, their broader theoretical significance did not strike me fully until a short time later, as I was rereading (after about twenty years) Spearman's major work, *The Abilities of Man*. I came upon a brief passage that had not previously caught my attention enough to have been remembered—undoubtedly because I had not before had in mind the question to which the passage was finally to prove so germane. Following a reference to an early study[23] by psychologists at the University of Indiana that compared 2,000 white and 120 black schoolchildren on a battery of ten diverse tests, Spearman (p. 379) noted that the blacks scored, on average, about two years behind the whites in mental age, but the amount of the W-B difference varied across the ten tests, and was most marked in those tests that were known to be most saturated with *g*.

The key point that struck me, of course, was that the W-B difference not only on digit span tests, but on many other kinds of cognitive tests, possibly on *all* cognitive tests, varies in magnitude directly with the size of the tests' *g* loadings. It seemed as scientifically and aesthetically satisfying an answer to the question as one could imagine. Spearman's hypothesis provides a parsimonious explanation of a wide range of psychometric facts for which previous explanations were purely ad hoc suppositions, most of them mutually inconsistent.

Spearman presented no further analysis of his hypothesis, nor was any possible, since the authors of the cited study did not present the correlations that would have permitted a factor analysis of the tests. Spearman could only have surmised the tests' relative *g* loadings, based on his extensive experience in factor analyzing and examining the *g* loadings of a great variety of tests. The authors of the original study, Pressey and Teter, had also noted that the size of the W-B difference showed distinct variation from test to test; the black children did best in a test of rote memory, poorest in a test of verbal ingenuity (unscrambling disarranged sentences). It was also noted that the rote memory test was the poorest of the ten tests in identifying the mentally retarded, while the disarranged-sentences test was the best. From such sketchy information, apparently, Spearman made the important conjecture that the relative size of the W-B mean difference across a group of diverse tests is a positive function of each test's *g* loading. I have termed this conjecture *Spearman's hypothesis*. Although Spearman may never have intended it to be a formal hypothesis, the potential theoretical implications of his offhand comment called for its being treated as an empirically testable hypothesis—a task I took up immediately.

Why is Spearman's hypothesis so important? Because, if proven true, not only would it answer the question, at least in part, of why the magnitude of the W-B difference varies across different tests, but, of greater general importance, it would tell us that the main source of the W-B difference across various cognitive tests is essentially the same as the main source of differences between individuals within each racial group, namely, *g*. This proposition would imply that a scientific understanding of the nature of the W-B difference in fact depends on understanding the nature of *g*.

Formalizing Spearman's Hypothesis. For a hypothesis to be scientifically useful it must be specified in such a way that it can be rigorously tested. Spearman himself did not formulate his conjecture as a testable hypothesis, and therefore his conjecture implies more than a single form of the hypothesis.

The *strong form* of Spearman's hypothesis states that variation in the size of the mean W-B difference across various tests is *solely* a positive function of variation in the tests' *g* loadings—the larger the *g* loading for a given test, the greater is the mean W-B difference on that test. No factor other than *g* is related to the size of the W-B differences on tests. A corollary of the strong hypothesis is that blacks and whites, on average, should not differ on any factor scores that are statistically independent of *g*. That is, the total score on any battery of diverse subtests from which the *g* factor has been regressed out of all of the subtest scores should not show a significant mean difference between representative samples of the black and white populations. Also, the "profile" of W-B differences on the various subtests, with *g* regressed out, should be flat overall, without any significant peaks or troughs.

The *weak form* of Spearman's hypothesis states that variation in the size of the mean W-B difference across various tests is *mainly* a positive function of variation in the tests' *g* loadings, but certain lower-order group factors (or subtest specificities) may also contribute some smaller part of each W-B difference. A corollary is that when *g* is regressed out of a battery of subtests, the resulting profile of W-B differences on the various subtests will have one or more peaks or troughs. That is, there will remain small but consistent and significant W-B differences on some subtests to the degree that they are loaded on certain non-*g* factors (or on the specificity of one or more of the subtests). (Specificity is that part of a test's true-score variance that is unrelated to the variance of any other test entered into the same factor analysis.)

The *contra* hypothesis to Spearman's hypothesis states that the W-B difference resides entirely or mainly in the tests' group factors and specificity (independently of *g*), while the *g* factor contributes little or nothing to the difference.

The distinctions between the strong, weak, and contra hypotheses are depicted in Figure 11.5.

Methodology for Testing Spearman's Hypothesis. Spearman's hypothesis states, in effect, that the differing size of the W-B difference on various tests is a direct function of (i.e., positively correlated with) the various tests' *g* loadings. The test of Spearman's hypothesis is accomplished by the method of correlated vectors (described in Appendix B). Briefly, one determines the correlation between the column vector of standardized mean W-B differences on a number of tests and the column vector of the tests' *g* loadings. For a proper statistical test of Spearman's hypothesis, the method of correlated vectors ideally must observe several prerequisite conditions:

1. The black and the white samples must be fairly representative of their respective populations and should be sufficiently large that the sampling error

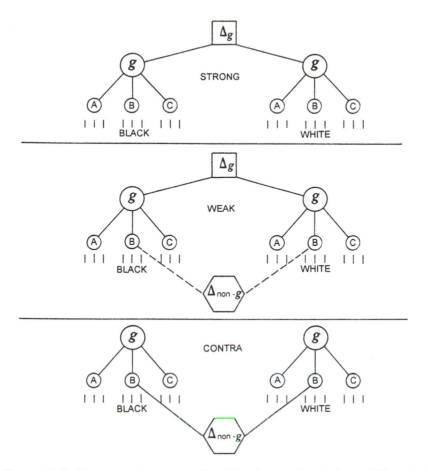

Figure 11.5. Diagrammatic representation of the strong and weak forms of Spearman's hypothesis and the contra hypothesis in terms of the factor structure of nine supposed tests (vertical lines) giving rise to three first-order group factors A, B, C, and a _g_ factor, for both black and white groups. The mean W-B difference is represented by Δ, with its subscript indicating the one (or more) factor(s) that enter into it. Dashed lines signify a weaker relationship of the factor to Δ than do solid lines. In the contra hypothesis, test specificity (of any number of the tests) could also contribute to the Δ_{non-g}.

of the correlations among tests is small enough to yield unambiguous and reliable factors.

2. The black and the white samples should not have been selected on any variables related to cognitive abilities, such as educational or occupational level, that might significantly restrict the range-of-talent (or variance) with respect to performance on the battery of tests subjected to factor analysis.

3. The factor analysis should be based on a large enough number of tests to

permit the extraction of a stable and reliable *g* factor, as would be indicated by a very high coefficient of congruence between the *g* factor obtained in independent samples from the same population.

4. Any test that is demonstrably biased (in the psychometric/statistical sense) with respect to the groups of interest should be excluded.

5. The tests must be sufficiently diverse in content, task demands, and factor structure to allow significant differences between the *g* loadings of the various tests.

6. The tests' reliability coefficients should be known so that each test's *g* loadings (and also the standardized mean group difference) can be corrected for attenuation (i.e., measurement error).

7. The factor analysis must be carried out separately *within* either the white or the black sample or separately for both, but certainly not in the combined samples, so that any psychometric differences between them cannot possibly enter into the factor analysis. (If the factor analysis were performed on the combined group, then, to the extent that the two groups differ on *g*, each subtest's *g* loading would be inflated and there would be a ''built-in'' correlation between the vector of subtests' *g* loadings and the corresponding vector of the mean differences between groups, hence positively biasing the correlated vectors in favor of Spearman's hypothesis.)

8. The vector of *g* loadings extracted separately from each group must be sufficiently similar across groups to assure that the same factor is represented for both, as indicated by a congruence coefficient of above .95 (which is the conventional criterion for virtual identity of the factors). A failure of this condition obviously precludes a test of Spearman's hypothesis, because two groups cannot be compared meaningfully on a nominal factor unless it is, in fact, the *same* factor for both groups.

The statistical test of Spearman's hypothesis, then, is the correlation[24] between the vector of the tests' *g* loadings[25] and the vector of standardized mean differences between the groups on each of the tests, taking the tests' reliability coefficients into account.[26] (Notes 24, 25, and 26 concern technical details on the statistical procedures.)

It should be apparent that Spearman's hypothesis and the method for testing it do not concern the *absolute* magnitude of the W-B difference on any test, but depend only on the *relative* magnitudes of the W-B difference across various tests that differ in their *g* loadings. Therefore, it is conceptually independent of secular trends in absolute test scores, now known as the Flynn effect (discussed in Chapter 10).

Is the *g* Factor the Same in Black and White Groups? This is a basic precondition for testing Spearman's hypothesis and has been observed for every set of data so far used for this purpose. I have calculated the congruence coefficient between the *g* factors obtained in black and white samples in every study that reports the intercorrelations of six or more psychometric tests separately for large representative samples of blacks and whites that I could find in the literature.[27] The number of diverse tests in each factor analysis ranges from 6 to 24, averaging 12.5. The study samples are all independent and the correlation matrices are based on a variety of cognitive tests used in schools, employment selection, and the armed services. The studies were published between 1971 and 1996. All of the g factors are represented either by the first principal factor (in a common factor analysis) or by the highest-order factor of a hierarchical factor analysis.

Over the seventeen studies, the congruence coefficient between the g factors extracted from the black and the white samples ranges from .976 to .999; the mean and median are both equal to .995. Clearly, we must conclude that factor analysis yields essentially the same g factor for both the black and the white samples on each of these seventeen different test batteries. In most cases, the residualized group factors (i.e., lower-order factors independent of g) show nearly as high a degree of black/white congruence, with congruence coefficients over .990 when samples are very large (which decreases the sampling error). In a study[28] of 212,238 white and 32,798 black applicants who took the seventeen diverse subtests of the U.S. Air Force Officer Qualifying Test, a hierarchical factor analysis yielded g and five first-order factors. The black/white congruence coefficients were .99+ for each of the factors. (The Pearson correlations between the vectors of factor loadings ranged between .97 and .99, and the groups did not differ in the average size of the g loadings.)

The g factor of a given battery also remains consistently the same factor across different age groups. Probably the best data that can be examined for this purpose are those based on the Kaufman Assessment Battery for Children (K-ABC), as this battery contains thirteen highly diverse tests representing at least three distinct factors besides g. Using the national standardization data to compare the g factor obtained in two age groups (ages 7 to 8 years versus 11 to 12.5 years), the g congruence coefficient for black children is .991; for white children, .998. (The black/white g congruence *within* each age group is at least .99.) The g factor (first principal component) accounts for about the same percentage of the total variance (averaging 58 percent) among the K-ABC subtest scores for different age groups (between 7 and 12.5 years) and for blacks and whites.[29]

The fact that the g factor (the square of which yields a proportion of variance) is fairly constant across different age groups says nothing, of course, about changes with age in the *level* of performance on highly g-loaded tests. Nor is it informative about possible changes with age in the size of the W-B difference in the *level* of g-loaded performance. There are no data at present that are ideal for answering this question. The best we can do is to compare the size of the W-B difference in IQ across different age groups. To this end I have used the data in Audrey Shuey's compendium[30] of all the published data on W-B IQ differences from 1920 to 1965.

For seventeen studies of young children (aged 3 to 6, averaging 5.2 years) published between the years 1922 and 1965, the mean W-B IQ difference on individually administered IQ tests was 10.76 (*SD* 8.0). The year of the study and the W-B IQ difference are correlated +.55, showing that the W-B difference for this age group has increased over time.

For thirty-three studies of elementary school children (aged 5 to 15, averaging 9.61 years) published between the years 1920 and 1964, the overall mean W-B IQ difference was 14.63 (*SD* 6.8). For thirty-one studies based on nonverbal group tests, the mean W-B IQ difference was 14.32 (*SD* 5.9). For 160 studies of elementary school children based on verbal group tests, the mean W-B difference was 14.51 (*SD* 7.9). For elementary school children, then, the average W-B difference on all three types of tests is 14.5 IQ points. The year of the study and the W-B IQ difference are correlated +.29, showing an increased B-W difference over time for this age group also.

IQ data obtained from students enrolled in high school are no longer very representative of the black and white populations at that age, because of the differing school dropout rates associated with IQ. The probability of a student's dropping out of high school is negatively correlated with IQ, and blacks have had much higher dropout rates than whites[31] during the period covered by Shuey's review. This should produce a decrease in the W-B IQ difference if measured for students actually in high school. In fact, 117 studies of high school students showed a mean W-B IQ difference of 10.40 (*SD* 6.4). A more representative estimate of the IQs of youths between ages eighteen and twenty-six can be obtained from the immense samples of enlisted men in the armed services during World War II. These subjects took the Army General Classification Test (AGCT), which is as highly correlated ($r \approx .80$) with various IQ tests as the IQ tests are correlated with each other. The mean W-B difference on the AGCT was 1.25σ, which is equivalent to 18.7 IQ points. More recent data are provided by the national standardization of the 1986 Stanford-Binet IV, which shows a W-B difference of 1.13σ (or 17.4 IQ points) for youths twelve to twenty-three years of age.[32]

In summary, the cross-sectional data show an increasing mean W-B IQ difference from early childhood (about 0.7σ), to middle childhood (about 1σ), to adolescence and early maturity (about 1.2σ). The same data provide no evidence to indicate a decrease in the mean W-B difference in IQ over the last 20 years or so.[33] There is, however, considerable evidence of a significant decrease in the W-B difference on some scholastic achievement tests, largely due to educational gains by blacks—probably because of blacks' increased attendance rates, years of schooling, and special services in recent decades. (See Chapter 14, Figure 14.2, p. 562.)

Tests of Spearman's Hypothesis. My early research on Spearman's hypothesis is based largely on data that had already been reported in the literature and that reasonably met all of the previously enumerated criteria for testing Spearman's hypothesis, although those data had not been collected for this purpose. Most studies used well-known test batteries that were administered to very large, nationally representative samples of the black and white populations in the

United States. The eleven such independent data sets provide samples totaling 10,783 blacks and 29,712 whites who were given various test batteries of from 6 to 13 diverse subtests (73 different tests in all). Included are all of the subtests of the Wechsler Intelligence Scale for Children-Revised (WISC-R), the Kaufman Assessment Battery for Children (K-ABC), the General Aptitude Test Battery (GATB), the Armed Services Vocational Aptitude Battery (ASVAB), as well as several ad hoc batteries made up of a various published tests. Descriptions and summary tables for all of these tests and data, as well as the statistical results of the tests of Spearman's hypothesis, appear in my "target" article in _The Behavioral and Brain Sciences_, followed by the "peer reviews" by thirty-one commentators selected by the journal's editor, along with my reply.[34a,b] A later issue of this journal contained four more commentaries and my reply.[34f] Since then several new studies (and a few more commentaries and replies) have been added to this collection.[34] Robert Gordon, a sociologist at The Johns Hopkins University, has written what is perhaps the most far-reaching and in-depth critical discussion of my research on Spearman's hypothesis.[34n]

Since the evidence for Spearman's hypothesis and the many commentaries on it have all been published in great detail and are referenced in the notes, I will here only summarize the main findings. In sixteen independent studies (without correction for the effect of differences in the tests' reliability coefficients), the median rank correlation between tests' _g_ loadings and the W-B differences is $+.60$; the mean correlation is $+.59$ (_SD_ .12). With tests' reliability coefficients partialed out, both the median and mean of the correlations are $+.62$ (_SD_ .23). All but three of the correlations are significant beyond the .05 level. Combining the probabilities of the significance levels of all the independent studies, we may reject the null hypothesis (that is, that Spearman's hypothesis is wrong) with an overall probability of less than 10^{-10}. Finally, we can test Spearman's hypothesis on all of the data sets combined. Figure 11.6 shows the scatter diagram for the correlation between the mean group difference (D in σ units) and the _g_ loadings of 149 psychometric tests obtained in fifteen independent samples totaling 43,892 blacks and 243,009 whites. The correlation (with the effects of differences in tests' reliability coefficients partialed out) is highly significant ($t = 9.80$, $df = 146$, $p < .000$). Hence there can be little doubt that Spearman's hypothesis is borne out. Assiduous search of the literature has not turned up a single set of data with six or more diverse tests given to representative samples that contradicts Spearman's hypothesis.[35]

A further validating feature of these data is revealed by the linear regression of the standardized W-B differences on the tests' _g_ loadings. (The regression equation for the W-B difference, shown in Figure 11.6, is $D = 1.47g - .163$). The regression line, which indicates the best estimate of the mean W-B difference on a test with a given _g_ loading, shows that for a hypothetical test with zero _g_ loading, the predicted mean group difference is slightly below zero ($-.163\sigma$), and for a hypothetical test with a _g_ loading of unity ($g = 1$), the predicted mean group difference is 1.31σ. The latter value is, in fact, approached

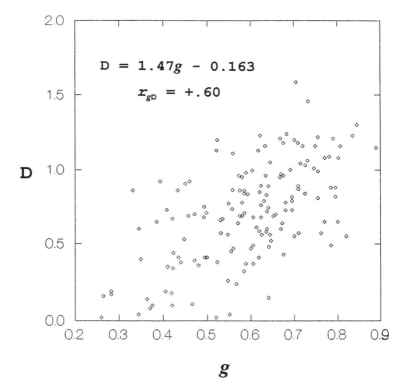

Figure 11.6. Scatter diagram of the correlation (r_{gD}) between the *g* loadings and the standardized mean W-B differences (D) on 149 psychometric tests. With the tests' reliability coefficients partialed out, the correlation is +.63 ($p < .000$).

or equaled by the average difference found for the most highly *g*-loaded test batteries using highly representative samples of black and white Americans twelve years of age and over. In the black and white standardization samples of the Stanford-Binet IV, for example, the mean difference is 1.11σ; for the WISC-R, 1.14σ; and the most precisely representative large-scale sampling of the American youth population (aged fifteen to twenty-three), sponsored by the Department of Defense in 1980, showed a W-B difference of 1.3σ on the AFQT.[36]

The *strong* form of Spearman's hypothesis, however, is not supported by a more fine-grained examination of all the data. That is to say, there are other factors, in addition to *g*, that contribute to the mean group difference, although their contribution is comparatively small next to *g*. There are also certain non-*g* factors that tend to cancel each other to some extent when they are combined in a test battery's total score.

Tests that rather consistently show a *larger* W-B difference (in favor of whites) than is predicted by their *g* loadings are those that, besides being loaded on *g*, are also loaded on a *spatial visualization* factor. Examples are tests such as paper folding, block counting, rotated figures, block design, object assembly, and mazes. When groups of blacks and whites are perfectly matched on the WISC-R Full Scale IQ (which is nearly equivalent to a *g* score), whites still exceed blacks, on average, by as much as $\frac{1}{2}\sigma$ on the most spatially loaded subtests.[34c,i] The tests that rather consistently show a *smaller* W-B difference than is predicted by the tests' *g* loading (and, in fact, favor blacks) are those that are also loaded on a *short-term memory* (STM) factor. Examples are tests such as the Digit Span and Coding subtests of the WISC-R. When black and white groups are matched on Full Scale IQ, blacks exceed whites by as much as 0.62σ on Digit Span and 0.49σ on Coding, the two tests with the highest loadings on the STM factor. In the WISC-R Full Scale IQ, therefore, the whites' average advantage on the spatial factor more or less balances the blacks' advantage on the STM factor. Almost all of the remaining group difference on the test as a whole is therefore attributable to *g*.

To further examine the weak form of Spearman's hypothesis, I compared nine typical test batteries in terms of the amount of the mean W-B difference attributable to *g* versus the amount of the difference attributable to non-*g* common factors (without regard for whatever abilities are reflected by the non-*g* factors).[34f] The aim was not to identify psychologically the abilities represented by these common factors that are independent of *g*, but only to determine just how much they contribute to the W-B difference. The *g* factor alone accounts, on average, for over four times as much of the total between-groups variance as do the three largest non-*g* factors combined.[37] Clearly, in typical test batteries, *g* is the predominant factor in the W-B difference.

The fact that tests that are heavily loaded on either the spatial factor or STM factors consistently cause small but statistically significant deviations from the result predicted by the strong form of Spearman's hypothesis dictates that the strong form of Spearman's hypothesis must be rejected. The weak form of Spearman's hypothesis, however, is confirmed. Rather than being just hypothesis, it is now an empirical fact.

The Effect of Test Specificity. Next we should consider the effect of test specificity on our tests of Spearman's hypothesis. *Specificity*, it will be recalled from Chapter 2, is that proportion of a test's true-score variance that is not accounted for by any common factor. In other words, a test's specificity is whatever that test measures reliably that is uncorrelated with anything measured by any of the other tests included in the same factor analysis. As much as 50 percent or so, on average, of the subtests' variance in some well-known test batteries (e.g., the Wechsler IQ scales) consists of test specificity. This means that, on average, about half of the variance on each subtest is *specific* to that test. This source of variance, of course, does not enter into *g* or any of the group factors.

Within any given battery, specificity (along with measurement error) may be regarded as unwanted "noise." Being uncorrelated with the common factors or with any other sources of variance measured by the subtests, most of the subtests' specificity (like measurement error) tends to "average out" in the total score on the test battery as a whole. It should not be overlooked that the basic units of analysis in the tests of Spearman's hypothesis reviewed so far are the *g* loadings and the standardized mean W-B differences on each of the single, relatively homogeneous subtests in a battery. The single tests' non-*g* common factors (particularly those representing spatial and memory abilities) and their specificities are, in effect, perturbations in our tests of Spearman's hypothesis. Even the weak form of the hypothesis, which recognizes the separate non-*g* effects of the spatial and memory factors on the W-B differences, is not completely accurate. There are still perturbations due to subtest specificity.

In every test battery in which the effect of test specificity has been examined, the vector of specificity coefficients is *negatively* correlated with the vector of mean W-B differences. That is, the larger a test's specificity, the smaller is the W-B difference. Whatever is specific to each of the subtests tends, in general, to reduce the W-B difference, or to favor blacks. On the WISC-R, for example, the average correlation between the W-B differences and the subtest specificities is −.46.[34c] This is not a surprising result, because, in accord with Spearman's hypothesis, *g* accounts for most of the W-B difference, and specificity is simply a residual component of the non-*g* variance. Therefore, a negative correlation between the W-B differences and the specificities of the various tests in a battery is inevitable. Because the roughly complementary relation between *g* and specificity is a mathematical necessity, it would be improper in our test of Spearman's hypothesis to partial out the vector of specificities from the correlation between the vector of *g* loadings and the vector of W-B differences. A better way to virtually eliminate the effects of specificity is to determine the group differences on each of the statistically independent (i.e., uncorrelated) factor scores derived from a test battery. When this was done for the WISC-R, based on the standardization samples of blacks and whites, the standardized mean W-B difference on each of the four factors in this battery of thirteen subtests was: *g* (1.14σ), Memory (−0.32σ), Verbal (0.20σ), and Performance (nonverbal and spatial) (0.20σ). The composite of the scores on all four factors yields a mean W-B difference of 1.22σ.[34c] The *g* component thus accounts for 93 percent of the groups' total factor score difference on the WISC-R. Although the Wechsler tests were not expressly designed to maximize *g* (as was, for example, the Raven matrices test), they have a very large *g* saturation because they were pragmatically constructed so as to have high validity for predicting a wide range of important criteria.[38]

Conditions That Attenuate Tests of Spearman's Hypothesis. Critics have argued that if Spearman's hypothesis (even in its weak form) is true, one should expect much higher correlations between tests' *g* loadings and W-B differences than the correlations that have in fact been demonstrated, which, though fully significant, average only about +.60. This criticism, however, fails to take account of the conditions that markedly attenuate the correlation between these two sets of variables, but are not at all intrinsically related either to tests' *g* loadings or to the magnitudes of group differences. The most critical of these attenuating variables is the restriction of range of *g* loadings in most of the standard test batteries. This results from the fact that the subtests have been expressly selected so as to maximize the *g* saturation of the composite score. The most highly g-loaded batteries, therefore, tend to have the smallest range of variation in the subtests' *g* loadings. Also, in accord with Spearman's hypothesis, if there is a restriction of range of the tests' *g* loadings, there will be a concomitant restriction of range of the W-B differences across the various subtests. A restriction of range of either one or both of two imperfectly correlated variables diminishes the magnitude of the correlation from what it would be without such range restriction.

Because the restriction of range is not at all intrinsic either to *g* or to the group difference on any test, we should correct for the attenuating effect of range restriction on our tests of Spearman's hypothesis. The usual statistical technique for doing this is to correct the obtained correlation for restriction of range. But this procedure presupposes that we have a good population estimate, or some theoretically derived value, of the *unrestricted* standard deviation as a basis for adjusting the *restricted* standard deviation of either one of the observed variables in the correlation. (Correction for restriction of range simultaneously for both of the correlated variables is statistically problematic.) For example, if we made the unwarranted assumption that the *g* loadings in the total universe of all possible psychometric tests ranged from 0 to 1 and were normally distributed, with a mean of .50 and *SD* of .20, the obtained correlation of +.60 in Figure 11.6 after correction for range restriction would be raised to +.75. However, because we have no rationale for assuming the form of the distribution of *g* loadings for the hypothetical universe of all possible cognitive tests from which we could derive the value of the unrestricted standard deviation, we must take a different approach.

We can determine how much the amount of variation in *g* loadings and in group differences in a number of independent studies (based on various batteries) affects each study's degree of conformity to Spearman's hypothesis. Conformity is indicated by the magnitude of the correlation between the vector of *g* loadings and the vector of W-B differences (*d*) for a given battery. (For notational convenience, the correlation between these two vectors, which constitutes the test of Spearman's hypothesis, can be labeled r_{gd}.) In a multiple regression analysis, we can regress the dependent variable, which is the *n* values of r_{gd} (obtained from each of *n* test batteries) on the following two independent variables: (1) the *SD* of the *g* loadings, and (2) the *SD* of the mean W-B differences. The squared multiple correlation (R^2) between the dependent variable r_{gd} (with reliability coefficients partialed out of r_{gd}) and the two independent variables indicates the effect of the independent variables on the test of Spearman's hypothesis. For twelve test batteries, this $R^2 = .22$.[39] In other words, over a fifth of the variance in the statistic r_{gd}, which tests Spearman's hypothesis,

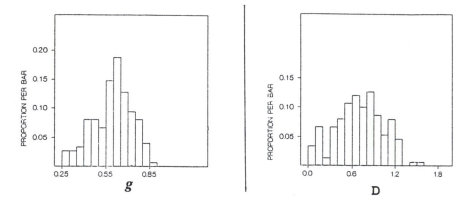

Figure 11.7. Histograms showing the frequency distributions of the *g* loadings (*g*) and of the standardized mean W-B differences (**D**) for 149 subtests from twelve different psychometric batteries each administered to independent black and white samples totaling 286,901 individuals.

is a result of variation that is conceptually unrelated to the hypothesis, but which is unavoidable in any realistic test of the hypothesis based on r_{gd}.

The theoretically ideal conditions for this test of Spearman's hypothesis unfortunately are mutually contradictory: large *g* loadings on the subtests and maximum variation among the subtests' *g* loadings; also, large mean group differences on the subtests and maximum variation among the group differences. Within the necessarily limited range of values from zero to one for *g* loadings, it is impossible to maximize the mean and the standard deviation simultaneously. As is evident from the data I have analyzed, the constructors of test batteries have selected mostly subtests with fairly large *g* loadings in order to maximize the *g* of the battery as a whole, hence a necessarily restricted variation among the subtests' *g* loadings. In the 149 subtests in Figure 11.6, for example, the *g* loadings range from +.26 to +.89, with a mean of +.60 and *SD* of .13; the *g* loadings are concentrated in the upper part of the range, as shown in the left panel of Figure 11.7. The right panel shows the distribution of the standardized mean W-B differences on 149 subtests.

Still another condition that attenuates the r_{gd} test of Spearman's hypothesis is the reliability of the vector of *g* loadings and of the vector of the group differences for a given battery. The vectors are subject to sampling error, as are the statistics on the single subtests. These two sources of sampling error, though statistically somewhat related because they are both based on one and the same subject sample, can be quite different. In large samples (as have been used to test Spearman's hypothesis), the reliability of each of the correlated vectors is generally lower than the reliability of the factor loadings and the group differences on any single subtest.

Since we have data on the twelve subtests of the WISC-R obtained in three large independent representative samples of blacks and whites, we can determine the average correlation between the _g_ vectors obtained for each sample and also the average correlation between the vector of group differences (_d_). The average correlation is an estimate of the reliability of each vector. For the _g_ vector it is .86; for _d_ it is .78. For the test of Spearman's hypothesis based on the WISC-R, if we use these reliability coefficients to disattenuate the average correlation r_{gd} = .61, the correlation is raised to $.61/\sqrt{(.86)(.78)}$ = .74. It seems likely that if the values of r_{gd} obtained for all the other batteries used to test Spearman's hypothesis could be disattenuated in this way, the overall average value of r_{gd} would be increased by some .10 to .20 points, thus putting it somewhere between .70 and .80.

Besides the attenuating effect of _subject_ sampling error, each of the batteries from which a _g_ factor has been extracted is also liable to _psychometric_ sampling error. The _g_ extracted from a given battery is not exactly the same as the _g_ extracted from a similar battery composed of different subtests. Although each battery gives an estimate of the hypothetical "true" _g_ (as explained in Chapter 4, p. 87), estimates of _g_ based on different test batteries typically correlate about +.80 with each other. If one also disattenuated the grand average r_{gd} for the effect of psychometric sampling error (in addition to subject sampling error), the fully corrected r_{gd} would rise to about .90.[40]

Criticisms of Spearman's Hypothesis. The two main technical criticisms that have been made against Spearman's hypothesis or of the method for testing it have been answered in detail elsewhere.[34f,g]

The first criticism is based on the mistaken notion that various psychometric tests either do or do not measure "intelligence," and that the positive outcomes of the tests of Spearman's hypothesis are simply the result of including in the same battery a number of subtests that measure "intelligence" along with a number of subtests that do not. Since blacks and whites are already known to differ on "intelligence" tests, it is argued, the inclusion of tests that do not measure "intelligence" in a battery makes the correlation r_{gd} inevitable. Presumably, it is further argued, if the battery were composed only of subtests that measured "intelligence," any differences in their _g_ loadings would not be correlated with the magnitudes of the W-B differences. These arguments are clearly refuted by three facts: (1) over all subtests there is a perfectly continuous and nearly normal distribution of _g_ loadings, which have an almost perfectly linear regression (_r_ =.97) on their rank order of magnitude; (2) the distribution of standardized W-B differences is perfectly continuous throughout; and (3) there is a linear relationship (_r_ = +.60) between _g_ loadings and W-B differences throughout the entire range of both variables, without the least trace of any nonlinearity. In other words, Spearman's hypothesis holds throughout the entire range of _g_ loadings (+.26 to +.89) used to test it. This has been most strikingly demonstrated in the analysis of various reaction time (RT) measures discussed later in this chapter. These RT measures have quite small _g_ loadings compared to the conventional psychometric tests, but the rank order of their *g* loadings and their W-B differences manifest Spearman's hypothesis to an even higher degree than do most of the psychometric batteries.

The second criticism is the claim that the evidence supporting Spearman's hypothesis is somehow a mathematical necessity or tautology, rather than an empirical discovery, and that confirmation of the hypothesis is an inevitable result of the methodology used to test the hypothesis and is therefore just an artifact. That is to say, it is claimed that a correlation between *g* loadings and groups' differences is guaranteed by the very process of factorization. This claim is fallacious and, in fact, wholly impossible, for the following obvious reason: When Pearson correlations between tests are calculated (always separately for blacks and whites), all information about the means and standard deviations of the tests (or their rank order of magnitudes) is rendered completely absent from the correlations. Consequently, absolutely nothing about the test score means or their rank order of magnitude can possibly be gleaned from the matrix of test intercorrelations. Ipso facto, nothing can be inferred about the rank order of the tests' means from their loadings on *g* (or on any other factors extracted from the correlation matrix). Therefore, the results of the method used here for testing Spearman's hypothesis cannot possibly be a mathematical artifact or merely a tautology. If Spearman's hypothesis is borne out by finding a significant value of r_{gd}, as indeed is the case, it must necessarily be an empirical reality. The only theoretically possible exception to this assertion would be in the unrealistic condition where the total variance of every test in the battery consisted exclusively of variance in *g* and variance due to random errors of measurement, in which case a significant group difference would necessarily be a difference in *g* and any variation in the standardized mean group differences on the various subtests would reflect nothing but variation in the subtests' reliability.

Spearman's Hypothesis with SES Controlled. Countless studies have shown that school-age children's IQs are correlated with their parents' socio-economic status (SES), as determined mainly by their occupational and educational level. Most of the IQ/SES correlations fall in the range of .35 to .45. (This implies a similar degree of correlation between *g* and SES.) Several facts indicate that the causal direction of the IQ/SES correlation is largely from IQ to SES: Adoption studies show near-zero correlations between adoptees' IQs and the SES of their adoptive parents; there is a virtual absence of between-families, or shared, environmental variance in IQ; and IQ is more highly correlated (about .70) with individuals' own attained SES (as adults) than individuals' IQs are correlated with their parents' SES (about .40). In the simplest terms, with arrows indicating the direction of predominant causality,

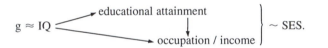

Because blacks and whites differ, on average, in SES, it could be claimed that Spearman's hypothesis simply reflects this fact, and nothing more. The IQ/SES relationship, of course, makes it practically inevitable that (within either racial group) the vector of subtests' correlations with SES would be correlated with the vector of subtests' *g* loadings. In fact, this correlation, based on thirteen subtests of the WISC-R standardization data, is +.84 for whites and +.39 for blacks.[34c] It appears that blacks are much less differentiated in IQ by SES than are whites, which is consistent with the picture in Figure 11.2 (p. 358) based on WISC-R data from an independent sample.

The possibility that Spearman's hypothesis simply reflects the W-B difference in SES was studied with eighty-six matched pairs of black and white fourth- and fifth-graders from three schools.[34h] Each black child was matched with a white child on a five-point scale of SES, and also on age, school, and sex. Each child was individually administered the WISC-R (11 subtests) and the K-ABC (13 subtests). The test of Spearman's hypothesis was based on the combined batteries, 24 subtests in all. A hierarchical (second-order) *g* factor was extracted from this battery and the vector of the 24 subtests' *g* loadings was correlated with the vector of standardized mean W-B differences. The Pearson *r* is +.78, the Spearman r_s is +.75 ($p < .01$), and the partial correlation (with the subtests' reliability coefficients partialed out) is +.85. The scatter diagram is shown in Figure 11.8.

Spearman's hypothesis is substantiated even more clearly by these data on SES-matched groups than by black and white groups that differ in SES. All the other studies that have substantiated Spearman's hypothesis obviously cannot be explained in terms of SES. The SES-matched black and white groups in this study showed the following differences (W-B in σ units) on the orthogonalized factor scores derived from the twenty-four subtests: *g* .77σ, Verbal .20σ, Spatial .39σ, Memory .01σ. (In IQ units these differences are 12, 3, 6, and <1, respectively.) The significant W-B differences on two of the group factors (Verbal and Spatial) independent of *g* is consistent with the weak form of Spearman's hypothesis.

Spearman's Hypothesis in Preschoolers. Only one study[34j] has reported a test of Spearman's hypothesis based on preschoolers. These physically normal, healthy children, drawn from lower, lower-middle, and middle-class areas of Cleveland, were between the ages of 3.0 and 3.4 years. The thirty-three black and thirty-three white children were matched on age, sex, birth order, and mother's education (which averaged 13.58 for the black mothers and 13.24 years for the white). The groups differed significantly in birth weight (B < W), but within each racial group the children's birth weights were not significantly related to their IQs on the Stanford-Binet IV (SB-IV). Despite matching black and white children for maternal education, the children's mean W-B IQ difference was 15.2 IQ points (in terms of the recent SB-IV norms) and 1.39σ in terms of the study group's *SD*. Maternal education was significantly related to IQ inde-

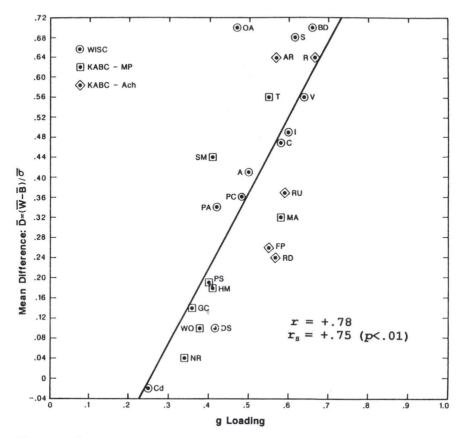

Figure 11.8. Mean B-W differences (expressed in units of the average within-groups standard deviation) on WISC-R and K-ABC subtests as a function of each subtest's loadings on *g*. WISC-R subtests: I—Information, S—Similarities, A—Arithmetic, V—Vocabulary, C—Comprehension, DS—Digit Span, PC—Picture Completion, PA—Picture Arrangement, BD—Block Design, OA—Object Assembly, Cd—Coding. K-ABC Mental Processing (MP) subtests: HM—Hand Movements, GC—Gestalt Closure, NR—Number Recall, T—Triangles, WO—Word Order, MA—Matrix Analogies, SM—Spatial Memory, PS—Photo Series. K-ABC Achievement (Ach) subtests: FP—Faces and Places, Ar—Arithmetic, R—Riddles, RD—Reading/Decoding, RU—Reading/Understanding. (From Naglieri & Jensen, 1987. Used with permission of Ablex.)

pendently of race; that is, maternal education and child's IQ are correlated *within* each racial group.

The groups also differed significantly (B < W) on each of the eight subtests (vocabulary, comprehension, absurdities, pattern analysis, copying, quantitative, bead memory, memory for sentences). The rank-order correlation between the vector of the subtests' disattenuated *g* loadings and the vector of the disattenuated mean W-B differences is $r_s = +.71$ (significant beyond the .05 level), which strongly bears out Spearman's hypothesis among three-year-olds.

Two other features of this study are also relevant to Spearman's hypothesis: (1) The column vector of standardized mean W-B differences on each of the subtests is correlated $r_s = 0.00$ with the column vector of the magnitudes of the standardized difference (averaged within groups) in the effect of maternal education on each subtest.[41] (2) The vector of the subtests' *g* loadings is correlated $r_s = .26$ (nonsignificant) with the vector of magnitudes of the effect of maternal education on the children's performance on each subtest. In other words, there seems to be no relationship between the relative magnitudes of the W-B differences on these subtests and the effects of maternal education on each of the subtests, and no relationship between the subtests' *g* loadings and the effects of maternal education. In accord with Spearman's hypothesis, the subtests' *g* loadings significantly predict the rank order of W-B differences. But the effect of maternal education on the subtests does not predict the rank order of the W-B differences on the subtests or the subtests' *g* loadings.

Spearman's Hypothesis and Criterion Performance. The U.S. Air Force selects pilot trainees partly on the basis of the Air Force Officer Qualification Test (AFOQT). The AFOQT consists of sixteen subtests, twelve of which are from the ASVAB battery. Spearman's hypothesis was tested on AFOQT data from 212,238 white and 32,798 black applicants. The hierarchical (second order) *g* factor for blacks and for whites are virtually identical (congruence coefficient = .999), and therefore were averaged for each of the sixteen subtests. The column vector of average *g* loadings and the column vector of standardized mean W-B differences have a rank-order correlation of .610; with the vector of subtests' reliability coefficients partialed out, the correlation is .603, which is significant ($p < .01$) and consistent with Spearman's hypothesis.[42] We can convert the W-B difference on each subtest to a point-biserial correlation (i.e., the correlation of each subtest scores with race expressed as a dichotomized variable [B = 1, W = 2]), which can then be regarded as the W-B difference factor for the battery. The congruence coefficient between this W-B difference factor and the *g* factor of the battery indicates how similar these two factors are. It is $+.987$, or virtual identity.

But does this fact have any relevance to the training outcome of those applicants who score high enough on the AFOQT to be selected for pilot training? Do the subtests' *g* loadings predict who will or will not make the grade in qualifying as an Air Force pilot? Selectees take a one-year training program in flying, consisting of a ground school phase and a jet plane training phase that includes some 190 hours of aircraft flying. Based on tests of job knowledge and ratings of actual flying performance, the final training outcome (FTO) is graded simply pass or fail. Some 66 to 80 percent of the trainees succeed; most attrition occurs because of deficiencies in actual flying performance.

The overall validity of the composite score on the AFOQT battery for predicting the final training outcome (pass = 1/fail = 0) is about $+.70$ (corrected for range restriction; the uncorrected value is +0.50).[43] To determine the contribution of each of the AFOQT's sixteen subtests for predicting the FTO, the scores on each of the sixteen subtests can be correlated with the FTO. This has been done separately for black ($N = 186$) and for white ($N = 8,955$) trainees to yield the validity coefficients of the separate subtests. The rank-order correlation between the vector of the validity coefficients and the vector of subtests' *g* loadings (with the vector of subtest reliability coefficients partialed out) is +.70 for blacks and +.66 for whites. Hence the various tests' *g* loadings are a strong indicator of the tests' validity for predicting real-life criteria such as the probability of success in pilot training.

Spearman's Hypothesis Tested with Populations Outside the United States. One study[34k] has tested Spearman's hypothesis on groups of secondary school students in South Africa. Each of the three study groups (white, black, and East Indian) had over one thousand students who were given the Junior Aptitude Test (JAT), a group-administered paper-and-pencil test consisting of ten subtests (four verbal, six nonverbal). Factor analysis of the JAT subtests reveals *g* and three group factors: verbal, spatial, and memory.

Unfortunately, an unusually thorough and technically sophisticated study of the JAT with respect to test bias led the study's author (Owen) to conclude that the JAT was not psychometrically satisfactory for black pupils.[44] Three of the subtests had unusually low reliability coefficients(<.34) for blacks as well as extremely large W-B differences (>2.5σ). Two of these subtests call for verbal ability, the other one calls for mechanical knowledge. The problem with these three tests (and to a lesser degree most of the other JAT subtests) for our purposes seems to be that most of the items were overly difficult for most of the black sample, so many items apparently elicited either no response or mere guessing, probably in large part because English was not the primary language of a majority of these children. For this reason (and others that are evident in Owen's highly detailed monograph on bias in the JAT), a test of Spearman's hypothesis based on the JAT in this sample of South African blacks seems questionable. With this caution in mind, the authors' analysis, based on the disattenuated mean differences and *g* loadings, showed the vector of W-B subtest differences to be correlated $r = +.624$ with the vector of subtest *g* loadings for blacks. Because of the problematic psychometric properties of the JAT in the South African black sample, however, this finding can hardly be regarded as a true test of Spearman's hypothesis.[45]

A more unique (and valid) contribution of this South African study is based on the East Indian sample (resident in South Africa). It allows more confidence in its results than do the data on blacks, because the problematic test bias and related psychometric shortcomings of the JAT evident for the black group were not a problem for use of the JAT in the East Indian group, whose subtest reliabilities and subtest intercorrelations were similar to those for the white group. Because the average of the white-Indian difference (W-I) of the JAT subtest scores was 0.96σ, these data can be used to answer the question "Does

Spearman's hypothesis hold for *any* two populations that differ by approximately 1σ on the total score of a test battery?'' With the mean differences and *g* loadings corrected for attenuation, the vector of standardized mean W-I subtest differences and the vector of subtest *g* loadings were correlated $r = +.129$ (for *g* based on the white group) and $+0.081$ (for *g* based on the Indian group). Neither correlation differs significantly from zero. (In fact, the proper test of significance is based on the rank-order correlation with the vector of reliabilities partialed out, which is even a negative correlation $[-.30]$, though nonsignificant.) Evidently some groups may have a test score difference even as large as 1σ that does not consist primarily of a difference in *g*.

SPEARMAN'S HYPOTHESIS TESTED WITH ELEMENTARY COGNITIVE TASKS

Rationale. As explained in Chapter 8, elementary cognitive tasks (ECTs) can be used to measure individual differences in the speed and efficiency of information processing. The subjects being tested find most ECTs so simple that the only aspects of performance that measure individual differences with high reliability are the speed of task performance and the variability in the subject's speed across trials. Much recent research showing that individual differences in these ECT-based measures are systematically related to psychometric *g* (see Chapter 8). Given these findings, it is reasonable to expect that ECTs would also be useful for studying the nature of observed population differences in *g*. ECTs are vehicles of *g*, as are conventional psychometric tests. But ECTs are vastly different vehicles, with virtually no resemblance to ordinary IQ tests beyond the basic requirement that all subjects must attend to the task and respond according to simple instructions.

Advantages of ECTs. The relative simplicity of ECTs is an obvious advantage in testing individuals who differ in cultural and educational background. Virtually all subjects immediately grasp the task requirements. No specialized background knowledge is called for and the ECTs can be performed with little or no practice. Giving subjects a number of practice trials is, however, a routine part of the ECT testing procedure. It allows the subject to learn how to perform on the testing apparatus and allows the experimenter to make certain that the subject fully understands the task. Subjects who, for whatever reason, cannot grasp the essential task requirements or who lack the sensory or motor capability needed for performance are excluded. If the ECT requires any specific prior knowledge, such as the ability to read words or numbers, subjects are given a pretest for this prerequisite knowledge and those who achieve less than perfect performance (regardless of response time) are excluded.

ECTs and Group Differences. It was not until a body of systematic research and generally consistent findings on individual differences in ECTs and their relationship to *g* had accumulated sufficiently to form a somewhat theoretically coherent picture of this domain (see Chapter 8) that mental chronometry could become a useful tool in the study of group differences. As I have reviewed a number of such studies elsewhere,[46] I will here consider only the question whether response time (RT) on various ECTs is related to psychometric *g* in much the same way for different populations as it is for different individuals.

With respect to individual differences, we know, for example, that, within limits, reaction time (RT) is less correlated with *g* for relatively simple ECTs than it is for relatively complex ECTs (such as the difference in information-processing demands even between such easy tasks as simple reaction time and discrimination reaction time). Also, intraindividual variability in RT across a number of trials (*n*) usually reflects individual differences in *g* more strongly than does the median RT over the same *n* trials. RT is more *g* loaded than is movement time (MT), which is the time interval between lifting a finger from a "home" button when the reaction stimulus is first detected (i.e., RT) and pressing another button (typically just a few inches from the home button) that terminates the reaction stimulus (i.e., MT).

Factor analysis reveals that RT and MT reflect different processes, as they have their salient loadings on different factors. Median RT and intraindividual variability in RT (measured by the individual's standard deviation of RT over *n* trials, hence labeled RTSD) reflect, in part, a cognitive or information-processing factor and therefore have their major loadings on the same factor as psychometric *g*. The salient MT loadings, on the other hand, appear on a separate factor best characterized as motor speed and coordination. Since the chronometric apparatus used in some studies does not provide for separate measurements of RT and MT, what is sometimes called RT in these studies is actually a combination of both RT and MT. What I here term RT is often referred to by some researchers as decision time (DT) to distinguish it from MT or from measures that combine RT and MT.

Having separate measurements of RT and MT is especially important in the study of group differences for two reasons: (1) As RT is more related to *g* than is MT, a composite of RT + MT attenuates any correlation with *g*; (2) as RT and MT represent different processes (cognitive and motor, respectively) group differences could go in opposite directions on each variable. If measured as a composite, their effects would cancel each other and obscure the detection of a difference between groups. In fact, there is some evidence for this kind of effect in studies of elementary school children, which show that on tasks more complex than simple RT (SRT), whites have shorter RT than blacks, on average, while blacks have shorter MT than whites.[47] Because this phenomenon does not appear in samples of blacks and whites as young adults,[48] it seems to reflect W-B differences in the rate of cognitive development and of motor development during childhood.

In general, mean W-B differences on various ECTs show effects similar to those found for individual differences within either group. For example, the W-B difference increases with task complexity or difficulty when complexity is objectively measured by the average RT for each task in the combined groups.

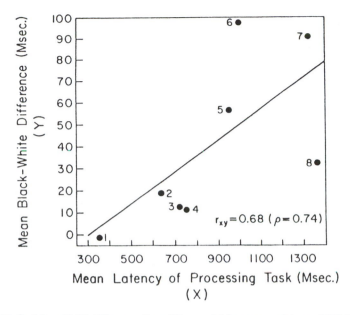

Figure 11.9. Mean B-W difference (in milliseconds) in response latency (RT) to various information-processing tasks as a function of task complexity as indicated by mean response latency on each task in the combined groups. Detailed descriptions of the information processing tasks are given in Vernon & Jensen (1984). Reprinted from *Personality and Individual Differences, 5,* P. A. Vernon & A. R. Jensen, Individual and group differences in intelligence and speed of information processing, 411–423, Copyright 1984, with kind permission from Elsevier Science Ltd, The Boulevard, Langford Lane, Kidlington 0X5 1GB, UK.

In a study[49] based on black and white male students in a vocational college, the mean B-W difference in RT on each of eight ECTs of differing information processing complexity was significantly correlated with the mean RT of each task in the combined groups, as shown in Figure 11.9. Note that even the most difficult of these tasks had a mean RT of only 1.3 to 1.4 seconds. Also there was a high correlation ($r = +.96$, $r_s = +.88$) between the complexity of the eight tasks (as measured by the mean RT for each task in the combined groups) and the tasks' *g* loadings (i.e., their correlation with *g* factor scores derived from the ASVAB battery). The mean W-B difference was 0.7σ on psychometric *g* (derived from the ten ASVAB subtests) and 0.2σ on the general factor of the eight processing tasks. The group difference on the processing tasks was the same as the average difference between two *individuals* (of the same race) who differ by 0.7σ in psychometric *g*. The data of this study bear out the prediction of Spearman's hypothesis: The B-W difference in RT on each of the eight processing tasks has a rank-order correlation with the tasks' *g* loadings of $r_s = +.86$ ($p < .01$).

An African Study. A study by Dutch psychologist Y. H. Poortinga[50] based on white and black African university students (both groups in South Africa) showed virtually no differences on either simple or two-choice RT to visual and auditory stimuli, but showed quite large and significant B-W differences, measured in standard deviation (σ) units, on four-choice and eight-choice RT, as shown below (the mean RT differences are B *minus* W):

	Reaction Stimulus	
	Auditory	*Visual*
Simple RT	0.13σ	0.02σ
2-Choice RT	−0.03σ	0.00σ
4-Choice RT	1.36σ	1.53σ
8-Choice RT	1.30σ	1.26σ

Although the four-choice and the eight-choice auditory RTs were significantly correlated (−.45 and −.38) with the highly *g*-loaded Raven's Advanced Progressive Matrices (APM) for the white sample, there was no significant correlation for the black sample (probably because of the restricted range of scores). The study's author noted that the APM was too difficult for the black students, whose average APM score was 2.2σ below that of the white students. (On two other psychometric tests the groups differed by 2.3σ and 1.5σ.)

The failure of these RT tasks to show significant correlations with highly *g*-loaded psychometric tests in the African sample could indicate either that the RTs do not reflect *g* in this group of African blacks or that these psychometric tests do not accurately measure *g* in this group. The fact that the three psychometric tests are substantially correlated with each other (.64, .73, and .59) indicates a good deal of common variance. But it could be that in the African sample the largest common factor is something other than the *g* factor[51] (which is the largest common factor in such tests for the white sample). As the average correlation between scores on highly *g*-loaded tests and eight-choice RT tasks is about .25 (based on several studies that do not include African blacks), and as the African W-B difference on the APM was 2.2σ, the predicted B-W difference on choice RT would be .30 × 2.2σ = 0.66σ, which is only about half as large as the mean difference actually found between the black and white students in Africa.

The Raven APM therefore greatly *under*predicts the W-B difference in eight-choice RT. This could be because for this sample of African blacks the relation between RT and psychometric *g* is not the same as in the white samples studied. Poortinga suggests his findings were probably a result of using a test that was too difficult for this group of black students. The APM probably has too little variance and too serious a "floor effect" (i.e., a piling up of scores near the chance guessing level) to serve as an adequate measure of *g* in this African group. The mean and *SD* of the APM in the African sample were 9.2 and 5.66, respectively. On American norms, this corresponds to an IQ of 92 (*SD* = 6), but chance guessing on the APM produces a score equivalent to an IQ of 90. Thus the APM scores obtained by the nearly one-half of the black sample who scored below IQ 90 do not reflect reliable variance in _g_. The Standard Progressive Matrices (SPM), which was designed for the middle range of ability, would have been more suitable for the African sample than was the APM, which was designed for testing in the upper half of the distribution of _g_ in the white European and North American populations.[52]

A Critical Test of Spearman's Hypothesis. The following study[53] clearly shows that the phenomenon predicted by Spearman's hypothesis is not restricted to typical psychometric tests. It tested Spearman's hypothesis with variables derived from elementary cognitive tasks (ECTs) at three levels of complexity: (1) simple reaction time (SRT), (2) choice reaction time (CRT), and (3) discrimination reaction time (DRT). The aim was to use ECTs that were so easy to perform that the modal number of errors would be zero in both the black and white samples and the most complex task could be performed without error (i.e., pressing the wrong button) in less than one second. Both of these criteria were in fact realized for every task in this experiment. The computerized apparatus was programmed so that every subject's median RT for each task was based on the same number of error-free trials.

Figure 11.10 shows the subject's response console for each of the three tasks. Console **A** is used for SRT. A trial begins with the subject placing the index finger of the preferred hand on the _home_ button (large black dot at the lower center of the figure). This is followed by a preparatory stimulus (an auditory "beep" of one second duration), to alert the subject of the imminent onset of the _reaction stimulus_ (RS), which occurs at any random time within the next four seconds. The RS is the illumination of a translucent push-button located six inches above the home button. The subject's task is simply to remove the index finger from the home button and touch the illuminated push-button as quickly as possible, thereby turning off the light. Subjects were given eight practice trials and _n_ = 20 error-free test trials.

Console **B** is used for CRT. The procedure is exactly the same as for SRT, except that the subject is here confronted by eight push-buttons, any _one_ of which can illuminate following the preparatory "beep." The uncertainty as to which one of the eight buttons will go "on" increases the subject's RT. Subjects were given eight practice trials and _n_ = 30 error-free test trials.

Console **C**, called the "odd-man-out" paradigm, is used for DRT. The procedure is exactly the same as for CRT, except that three of the buttons light up simultaneously. Two of the lighted buttons are always closer together than is the third lighted button (the "odd-man-out"). The subject's task is simply to touch the "odd" button as quickly as possible, thereby turning off the light. Subjects were given eight practice trials and _n_ = 36 error-free test trials. With eight push-buttons, there are forty-four possible odd-man-out patterns. Because the DRT task requires discrimination of the distances between the lighted buttons, it is more complex and therefore has a longer RT than does the CRT task.

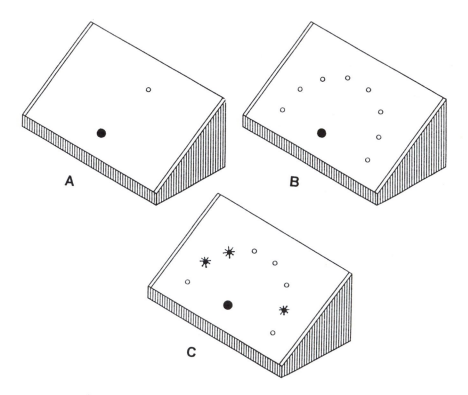

Figure 11.10. The subject's response console for (**A**) SRT, (**B**) CRT, (**C**) DRT (odd-man-out). The black dot in the lower center of each panel represents the *home* button. The open circles, six inches from the home button, are green underlighted, translucent push-buttons. In the SRT and CRT conditions (i.e., **A** and **B**) only one button lights up on each trial; on the DRT task, three buttons light up simultaneously on each trial, with unequal distances between them (shown in **C**), the remotest button from the other two being the odd-man-out, which the subject must touch.

For children of age eleven, the average reaction times (in milliseconds) for these tasks are: SRT~347, CRT~440, DRT~730.

Four different time measurements (in milliseconds) were obtained from each of these tasks:

Reaction Time (RT)—the subject's median value (over *n* error-free trials) of the interval between the onset of the reaction stimulus (RS) and the subject's releasing the home button.

Movement Time (MT)—the subject's median value (over *n* error-free trials) of the interval between releasing the home button and touching the RS.

Intraindividual variability in RT (RTSD)—the standard deviation (*SD*) of the subject's RTs (over *n* error-free trials).

Intraindividual variability in MT (MTSD)—the SD of the subject's MTs (over _n_ error-free trials).

This yields 3 ECTs × 4 types of measurements = 12 ECT variables for each subject.

The subjects were 585 white and 235 black children in regular classes in grades four through six from schools in predominantly middle-class neighborhoods. The black pupils attended white-majority schools. Black majority inner-city schools were not represented in the study sample. Raven's Standard Progressive Matrices (SPM), a highly _g_-loaded nonverbal test of inductive and deductive reasoning, typically shows a mean W-B difference of 1σ (or more) in representative samples. In the present black and white samples, however, the W-B difference was only 0.7σ.

To estimate their _g_ loading, each of the twelve ECT variables was correlated with the subject's score on the highly g-loaded Raven SPM. Each correlation is an estimate of that variable's _g_ loading, uncontaminated by any non-_g_ factors peculiar to the ECT variables.

Because _g_ loadings reflect the cognitive complexity of a task, the cognitively simple ECT variables were expected to have quite small _g_ loadings. The tasks were intentionally made very simple to ensure that the ECTs would be easy and fun to do, as well as being within every child's capability for nearly error-free performance. We also did not want the tasks to look anything at all like conventional psychometric tests. Subjects were told simply that the apparatus measured their reaction speed. However small the ECT variables' _g_ loadings (i.e., their correlations with the SPM), provided they could be reliably rank ordered, they could test Spearman's hypothesis.

Evidence of the reliability of the pattern of the ECT variables' _g_ loadings is the correlation between the vector of _g_ loadings for blacks and the corresponding vector of _g_ loadings for whites. Both the Pearson correlation and the rank-order correlation are +.85; the congruence coefficient is +.97. This shows that the ECT variables represent one and the same _g_ for both the black and the white groups. Therefore, each variable's _g_ loadings could be averaged across the black and white groups, yielding a single vector of twelve _g_ loadings.

The construct validity of the rank order of the ECT variables' _g_ loadings is shown by their correlation with the theoretically expected rank order of their loadings on psychometric _g_. The theoretical rank order of these ECT variables' _g_ loadings is based on a number of general principles derived from many previous studies (which, in fact, correspond to our everyday notions of how "complex" the tests are).[54] Figure 11.11 shows the rank-order correlation of $r_s = +.89$ between the obtained _g_ loadings (averaged over blacks and whites for each variable) and the theoretically expected _g_ loadings. The fit between the theoretical and the obtained rank orders is quite good and is far beyond chance probability ($p < .001$).

As a test of Spearman's hypothesis, then, this column vector of (average) _g_ loadings for each of the twelve ECT variables was correlated with the vector of

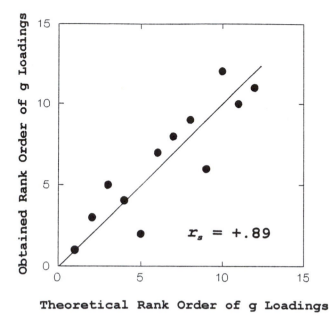

Figure 11.11. Scatter diagram of the rank-order correlation between the obtained *g* loadings of the twelve ECT variables and their theoretically expected rank order.

the twelve standardized mean B-W differences on each of the ECT variables. The Pearson $r = +.81$, the rank-order $r_s = +.79$, $p < .01$. The rank-order correlation scatter diagram between the vector of *g* loadings and the vector of B-W differences is shown in Figure 11.12. It bears out Spearman's hypothesis even more strongly than do most of the studies performed with conventional psychometric tests.

The mean B-W difference on each of the ECT variables increases as a function of the ECT's *g* loading. The SRT and the MT for all three ECTs had the smallest *g* loadings and were among the smallest B-W differences. The three variables with both the largest *g* loadings and the largest B-W differences were DRT, CRTSD, and DRTSD. It is especially noteworthy that intraindividual variability, which is not a speed variable (and strictly speaking, perhaps not even an ability), is the most *g*-loaded variable of all (consistent with many other studies[55]) and also shows the largest B-W difference (with blacks, on average, having the greater variability in RT across trials).

The idea that the B-W difference on these tasks reflects a difference in motivation is disconfirmed by the fact that although the whites had faster RT than the blacks, the blacks had faster MT than the whites. It is implausible that motivation or effort would be thus divided, to work in opposite directions, on the RT and MT phases of a speeded task that can be performed in about one second. Subjects perceive the task as that of making a single ballistic response

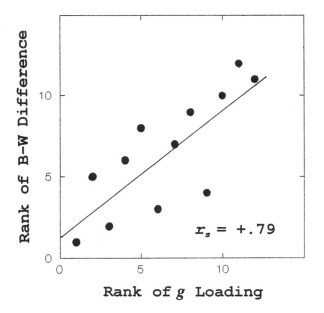

Figure 11.12. Scatter diagram of the rank-order correlation between the rank order of the ECT *g* loadings and the rank order of the mean standardized B-W differences on each of the ECTs.

as quickly as they can, rather than as making two distinct responses—first RT, then MT. The fact that MT is *g* loaded (though to a lesser degree than RT) and that blacks had shorter MT than whites means that blacks performed faster on the motor component of the task than did whites. The RT part of the task also has some slight motor component, which is increasingly outweighed by the task's more highly *g*-loaded information-processing component as the complexity of the task increases (for example, in going from SRT to DRT). We see that even the subject's RT reflects both a cognitive, or *g*, component and a motor component, with the influence of each component being a function of task complexity. SRT and DRT, for example, have about the same motor component, but DRT has a larger cognitive component. Hence the difference score, DRT-SRT, which removes the motor component from the total DRT, is generally more highly correlated with psychometric *g* than is DRT.[56] That is, the motor component in SRT (and also in every type of RT that involves any motor response) has no common variance with the typical psychometric test, and acts as what psychometricians refer to as a suppressor variable in the correlation between RT and scores on psychometric tests.

That RT and MT involve different processes is shown by the fact that when the whole battery of measurements used in the present study is factor analyzed, RT and MT consistently have their salient loadings on different orthogonal factors, which can be characterized as cognitive and motor, respectively. The same kind of clear-cut factorial separation between the cognitive and the motor components of RT and MT and their respective relationships to psychometric _g_ was shown most definitively by John B. Carroll in his hierarchical factor analysis of a large and diverse battery of twenty-seven ECTs and eleven conventional psychometric tests.[57]

Spearman's Hypothesis Tested with South Africans. The very same variables and apparatuses designed to be as much like those used in the previously described study were used by Lynn and Holmshaw[58] to test Spearman's hypothesis on samples consisting of nine-year-old black schoolchildren in South Africa (_N_ = 350) and white schoolchildren of comparable age in Britain (_N_ = 239). The testing procedures were virtually identical to those in the American study based on children averaging about eleven years of age. Because of the difference in subjects' ages in the South African and American studies, a direct comparison on the actual time measurements of RT and MT would not be relevant here. However, the Lynn and Holmshaw study showed much the same pattern of B-W differences (in σ units) across the twelve ECT variables as was found in Jensen's American study, the main difference being in the size of the differences, which are generally much larger in the South African study. The South African blacks were markedly slower than the British whites in RT and also markedly faster in MT. But note that the same phenomenon was present in both studies; that is, whites outperformed blacks on the RT component of the task (which is correlated with _g_) while blacks outperformed whites on the MT component.

The greater B-W differences on the RT and RTSD components of the ECTs in the South African study is best explained by the fact that this group of South African blacks scored, on average, about 2σ below British (or South African) whites, while there is only about 1σ difference between American blacks and whites.[59] In the Lynn and Holmshaw study, the W-B difference on Raven's Standard Progressive Matrices (SPM) was about 2.5σ. But we cannot be very confident of this value, because the SPM appeared to be too difficult for the African blacks. Their mean raw score on the SPM was only about three points above the chance guessing score, which casts doubt on the reliability and validity of the SPM as a measure of individual differences in _g_ for this sample.

The questionable SPM scores for the South African blacks showed much lower correlations and a quite different pattern of correlations with the ECTs than were found in the white sample. Therefore, it is hardly surprising that the data of this study do not accord with Spearman's hypothesis. A proper test of the hypothesis was not even possible, because the vector of the correlations between the ECTs and the SPM, which estimates the _g_ loadings of the ECTs, showed too little congruence between blacks and whites to represent the same vector of factor loadings for the two groups in this study. (The congruence coefficient is only .45, which falls far below the generally accepted minimum value of .90 needed to claim that the factors are similar. The corresponding congruence coefficient in all of the other studies of Spearman's hypothesis ranges from .98 to 1.00, with a mean of .995.)

However, it is noteworthy that the ECTs yielded meaningful data for the South African blacks. The vector of B-W differences on the twelve ECT variables does, in fact, conform to Spearman's hypothesis when it is compared with the vector of *g* loadings based on the American data. (For a highly detailed analysis of the limitations of the statistical data reported in the Lynn and Holmshaw study, see Note 60.)

The ECT Variables in a Chinese-American Sample. Exactly the same tests and procedures as were used in the test of Spearman's hypothesis based on black and white children in California were used in a parallel study of Chinese-American children and white children in elementary school (grades four through six).[61] Most of the Chinese-American children (some of them recent immigrants) were of considerably lower SES than most of the white children, yet the Chinese, on average, outscored the whites by a highly significant 0.32σ (equivalent to five IQ points) on the Raven SPM.

Although Spearman's hypothesis was originally concerned only with W-B differences on psychometric tests, it is of interest to determine if the mean test-score differences between other groups show the same phenomenon. In the case of the Chinese-white comparison, the rank-order correlation of $r_s = +.01$ obtained between the vector of the ECT variables' *g* loadings and the vector of Chinese-white differences on each of the ECT variables is obviously not significantly greater than zero. The vector of the twelve ECT variables' *g* loadings (i.e., their correlations with Raven's SPM) had satisfactory congruence across the two racial groups (congruence coefficient = $+.92$), indicating that the ECT variables were similarly related to psychometric *g* in both groups. The Chinese had as fast or faster CRT and DRT than the whites, but had very markedly *slower* MT than whites on every task. The Chinese were slower than whites on SRT, probably because of its relatively large motor component compared to its cognitive, or *g*, component. It seemed likely that the motor aspect of RT was relatively larger than the cognitive part of RT for the Chinese children. This would attenuate the Chinese-white difference in speed of information processing as measured by RT. To test this conjecture, for every subject, SRT was subtracted from CRT and from DRT, thus ridding CRT and DRT of their motor component. The resulting scores showed the Chinese to be about 0.4σ faster than the whites in information-processing time, a slightly larger difference even than was found on Raven's SPM. The Chinese-Americans were faster than the whites in information-processing time on CRT and DRT by twenty-seven and fifty-two milliseconds, respectively. These seemingly small differences in information-processing speed when brought to bear on much more complex tasks operating over considerable periods of time could result in quite noticeable differences in overall intellectual achievement.

Spearman's Hypothesis Tested with Simple Arithmetic. The ECTs used in the studies reviewed above reflect only three basic information processes—stim-

ulus apprehension, decision (or choice), and discrimination. Another basic process is the retrieval of items of previously acquired information that is stored in
long-term memory (LTM). An important aspect of cognition consists of relating
incoming new information to relevant old information already stored in LTM.
The act of looking up a person's number in the telephone directory, for example,
involves knowledge of how the person's name is spelled, the identification of
alphanumeric symbols, and a knowledge of alphabetic order, all of which are
stored in LTM and must be retrieved for performing this act. Many experiments
(some described in Chapter 8) have shown that the speed with which individuals
can retrieve information from LTM is related to _g_. This is true even when the
information held in LTM is so highly overlearned as to be retrieved automatically on presentation of the eliciting stimuli. Individual differences in the speed
of something so seemingly simple and automatic as recognizing the letters of
the alphabet by name is correlated with highly _g_-loaded nonverbal tests, even
in samples of university students.

   This well-established relationship between _g_ and the speed of retrieval of
information from LTM formed the basis for another test of Spearman's hypothesis. The same variables of RT, RTSD, MT, and MTSD used in the previous
experiments were used to measure the speed of accessing well-learned information held in LTM. The information to be retrieved consisted of what are
called simple number facts (i.e., the knowledge required to answer such questions as $2 + 2 = ?$, or $3 - 2 = ?$, or $2 \times 5 = ?$). The problems always
consisted of the addition, subtraction, or multiplication of the single-digit numbers from one to nine. To permit a binary response to each item by means of
the subject's touching one of two push-buttons labeled YES or NO, each number
fact was presented on the computer monitor with an answer that was either
correct (YES) or incorrect (NO); e.g., $2 + 3 = 5$ (subject should press YES)
or $2 + 3 = 6$ (subject should press NO). This task was therefore called the
Math Verification Test (MVT). Each type of problem (addition, subtraction, or
multiplication) was presented separately in a block of five practice trials and
twenty test trials. The subject's response console is shown in Chapter 8, Figure
8.3 (p. 215). The reaction stimuli appeared on a computer monitor. The task
was self-paced. A trial began with the subject pressing the home button. One
second after the subject pressed the home button, a preparatory stimulus, a small
square, appeared at the center of the monitor screen. In order to direct the
subject's attention, the square occupied the same location that was to be occupied by the mathematical operation sign ($+$, $-$, or $\times$). After a random interval
of one to four seconds, the reaction stimulus appeared (e.g., $2 \times 3 = 8$). The
subject responded by releasing the home button and pressing either the YES or
the NO button. The subject's response was immediately followed by corrective
feedback, which appeared on the screen as **Correct** or **Incorrect.** The simplicity
of the task is attested by the fact that among 191 pupils in grades four to six,
the modal number of errors (in sixty test trials) was zero and the mean number
of errors was less than two.

On each trial, the subject's RT and MT were measured in milliseconds. Each subject's overall scores were the median RT, RTSD, median MT, and MTSD, separately for addition, subtraction, and multiplication, yielding twelve scores in all. Subjects were also tested on Raven's SPM to measure psychometric *g*.

The subjects in this experiment were seventy-three white and 118 black children in grades four through six. The W-B difference on Raven's SPM was 0.72σ. These subjects were selected from a larger number of pupils in regular classes, all of them screened on a test of their knowledge of the very same number facts that were used in the Math Verification Test. The screening test consisted of a group-administered, unspeeded paper-and-pencil test on which subjects wrote the answers to problems presented in the form, for example, $3 + 4 = $ _____. Only those pupils who obtained a perfect score on the screening test were included in the experiment. Thus the MVT was not a test of whether the subject possessed the knowledge of certain arithmetic facts and operations. Rather, it measured only the speed with which the subject accessed this information, which every subject had long since acquired and stored in LTM.

The twelve MTV variables were factor analyzed for the black and the white groups separately. Besides a general factor, only two significant group factors emerged: one on which the RT and RTSD variables were loaded, the other on which the MT and MTSD variables were loaded. The factor structure of the twelve MVT variables was virtually identical for blacks and whites, with congruence coefficients around $+.99$. It should be noted that the three types of arithmetic operations did not emerge as factors in this analysis. The various chronometric variables "read through," so to speak, these purely formal aspects of the problems and mainly reflected individual differences in the speed of accessing whatever knowledge was needed to make correct responses to the MVT. The overall mean RT on the MVT for blacks was 1,800 msec; for whites, 1,480 msec. (In standardized units this is a mean difference of 0.42σ.) There were no appreciable differences between the RTs for addition, subtraction, and multiplication problems within either racial group.

As before, the test of Spearman's hypothesis was the correlation between the vector of the twelve MVT variables' estimated *g* loadings (i.e., each variable's correlation with Raven's SPM) and the vector of B-W differences on each of the MVT variables. The correlation between the two vectors (with the effect of the differing reliability coefficients of the MVT variables partialed out) is the same for the Pearson *r* and the rank-order r_s; both are $+.70$ ($p < .05$). Thus Spearman's hypothesis was borne out by these chronometric data that reflect the speed and efficiency of information *processes* rather than merely the possession of particular items of knowledge.

The Math Verification Test in a Chinese-American Sample. In another study[62] the MVT was applied to samples of Chinese-American ($N = 155$) and non-Hispanic white pupils ($N = 73$) in regular classes of grades four through six. The whites scored 0.32σ below the Chinese-Americans on Raven's SPM.

All of the MVT procedures and variables were the same as in the study of blacks and whites.

All of the RT and RTSD variables had highly significant correlations with the SPM (average $r = -.25$, $p < .001$); none of the MT and MTSD variables was significantly correlated with the SPM (mean $r = +.01$). On RT and RTSD, the overall standardized mean white-Chinese difference was 0.34σ, about the same as the 0.32σ difference they showed on Raven's SPM. (The actual overall mean RT for the whites was 1,480 msec; for the Chinese, 1,204 msec.) But note: The overall average white-Chinese difference on MT and MTSD was in the opposite direction, -0.19σ.

When the vector of the twelve MVT variables' g loadings was correlated with the vector of the white-Chinese standardized mean differences on each of the MVT variables, the Pearson $r = -.93$ and the rank order $r_s = -.90$ ($p < .01$). This indicates that the larger the MVT variable's estimated g loading (i.e., its correlation with the SPM), the more the Chinese outperform the whites on the MVT. On this test, the whites compared with the Chinese in much the same way that the blacks compared with the whites in the previous study. It should be noted that these Chinese children were mostly of lower SES than the white children. The three racial groups—Chinese, white, and black—score in the same rank order both on the SPM and on untimed paper-and-pencil tests of mathematical problem solving.

Conclusion. What these ECT studies clearly demonstrate regarding the group difference on mental tests is that Spearman's hypothesis applies not only to conventional psychometric tests (as proved in many studies using such tests), but also to a quite different type of mental measurement, namely chronometric variables derived from tasks that involve the most elemental aspects of information processing (such as speed and consistency of stimulus apprehension, choice decision, discrimination, and retrieval of information stored in LTM). As shown in many other studies, individual differences in these chronometric variables are correlated to varying degrees with psychometric g. The fact that the relative sizes of these correlations are directly related to the variable sizes of the standardized mean black-white or Chinese-white differences on the chronometric variables means that such differences on conventional g-loaded tests are not solely attributable to one group's advantage in the specific information content of LTM, or to strategies of reasoning and problem solving, or to other metaprocesses of the kind presumably involved in complex mental tests.

NOTES

1. The book edited by Jaynes & Williams (1989) provides comprehensive demographic information and statistics on the social and economic conditions of blacks in America.

2. Entrée to virtually the whole literature on race and IQ, including the descriptive statistics of IQ (and other mental tests) in blacks and whites is accessible through the following key references: Eysenck (1984b), Herrnstein & Murray (1994), Jensen (1973),

Jensen (1980a), Loehlin, Lindzey, & Spuhler (1975), Lynn (1991), Nichols (1987b), Osborne & McGurk (1982), Rushton (1995), Shuey (1966). The literature on the IQ of Asians (Chinese and Japanese) in North America is reviewed by P. E. Vernon (1982); Flynn's (1991) review of the literature on the achievement of Asian Americans in relation to their IQ finds that their level of educational and occupational achievement is higher than would be predicted by IQ alone, when prediction is based on the regression of achievement on IQ in the majority white population.

3. The generalized formula for the σ diff between two groups, A and B, is:

$$\sigma \text{ diff} = (\overline{X}_A - \overline{X}_B)/\sqrt{[(N_A s_A^2 + N_B s_B^2)/(N_A + N_B)]},$$

where $\overline{X}$ is the mean, N is the sample size, _s_ is the standard deviation.

4. Assuming two normal distributions of scores with unequal means, and given the mean and _SD_ deviations of each distribution, Kaiser (1987) gives a general formula for determining the _probability_ that the "score" of a randomly selected individual from the distribution with a lower mean exceeds the "score" of a randomly selected individual from the distribution with the higher mean. This formula shows that for two normal distributions, A and B, where A has a mean = 100 and _SD_ = 15 and B has a mean = 85 and _SD_ = 12 (thus corresponding to typical IQ statistics for the white and black populations) the probability that the "score" of a randomly selected individual from distribution B will exceed that of a random individual from distribution A is precisely 22 percent (i.e., the chances fall between 1 in 5 and 1 in 4). Kaiser found that when forty-seven professional PhD-level psychologists were asked to guess this probability, their guesses ranged from 2 to 27 percent, with a mean of only 13 percent! (If the two distributions had the same mean, of course, the probability would be 50 percent.)

5. It is useful to distinguish between an _explicit_ selection threshold and a _natural_ selection threshold. An explicit threshold is a definite criterion, such as a specific cut-score in the distribution of test scores or grade-point averages, or any other quantified variable. Or it may consist of a specific cut-score on a distribution based on the weighted average of a number of variables. Although an explicit threshold or cut-score may be arbitrary, it may also be justified on statistical grounds, for example, because of its demonstrated predictive validity. A natural threshold is always probabilistic. It is not a point estimate, but a region of the distribution (of the critical characteristic) below which the probability of "success" on a given criterion is so low as to effectively exclude the vast majority of individuals who are below the selection threshold. Examples of such low probabilities of success would be a person under 5'5" aspiring to stardom in professional basketball, a person who can't even "carry a tune" aspiring to sing at the Metropolitan Opera, or a person with an IQ of 100 aspiring to a career in mathematics. The population IQ distribution exerts its influence in education and the world of work more via natural than via explicit selection thresholds.

6. The term "source" in the context of the analysis of variance (ANOVA) is a strictly nominal and neutral term, without any implication of causality. It refers only to the nominal classes of variables that are included in the analysis, from which it is possible to determine the percentage of the total variance associated with (but not necessarily caused by) each of the nominal variables that are listed in an ANOVA table as "sources" of the total variance based on all the measurements that were subjected to analysis.

7. (a) Lynn, 1991a; (b) Zindi, 1994.

8. Owen, 1992.

   9. Mackintosh & Mascie-Taylor, 1983.

   10. Scarr, Caparulo, Ferdman, Tower, & Caplan, 1983.

   11. West, Mackintosh, & Mascie-Taylor, 1992.

   12. Jensen (1980a) gives a comprehensive account of the statistical methodology and findings of research on test bias, with the exception of research based on item response theory, nearly all of which was published after 1980. A précis of this 800-page book is given in Jensen (1981b); also see Jensen (1984b) followed by the commentaries of numerous experts. In Modgil & Modgil (1987, pp. 77–212) four experts (R. A. Gordon, S. Osterlind, J. D. Scheuneman, and L. A. Shepard) debate the issue. Reynolds & Brown (1984) edited a collection of pro and con essays regarding test bias, all of which I have responded to in the same volume. The report of an extensive investigation of test bias by a panel of nineteen experts commissioned by the National Academy of Sciences and the National Research Council is edited by Wigdor & Garner (1982). A completely nontechnical explanation of the methods and research findings on test bias is given by Jensen (1981a, Chapter 4). A more recent and technically advanced general treatment of test bias methodology is by Cole & Moss (1989). Recent methods in item bias research are in books by Camilli & Shepard (1994) and Holland & Wainer (1993).

   13. Jensen & McGurk, 1987.

   14. The Δ scale of item difficulty has a mean of thirteen and a standard deviation of four within each group. It places item difficulties on an interval scale, based on the assumption that the sample percentages of pass and fail on each item divide the normal curve. Thus an item's Δ value is obtained from the z transformation of the percentile of the normal curve that corresponds to the percentage of the subject sample failing the item: $\Delta = 4Z + 13$.

   15. Camilli & Shepard, 1994; Holland & Wainer, 1993.

   16. Reynolds (1980).

   17. Jensen & Johnson (1994).

   18. Loehlin, Lindzey, & Spuhler (1975, p. 133). Formulas for approximating the standard error of h^2 are given on pp. 288–89.

   19. Graziano, Varca, & Levy (1982) review the total literature of over thirty studies on the effect of race of examiner on black and white test scores. (Reprinted in Osborne & McGurk, 1982, pp. 158–188.)

   20. My research on this point, in the 1960s, led me to formulate what became known as the Level I–Level II theory, which is not really a theory but rather a set of generalizations about the nature of the W-B difference on various cognitive tests. The details of Level I–Level II would be an unnecessary digression, as I have since concluded that this formulation is subsumed under the considerably broader generalization I have termed "Spearman's hypothesis," explained later in this chapter. An explanation of the Level I–Level II idea and my reasons for abandoning it can be found in Jensen (1993b, pp. 185–192). In brief, Level I ability requires little mental manipulation of the information input, such as short-term memory (e.g., forward digit span) and rote learning. Level II ability requires mental manipulation or transformation of the information input in order to arrive at a correct response. Especially in mildly retarded groups (IQ fifty to seventy-five), the W-B difference is markedly smaller for Level I than for Level II. Vernon (1981b, 1987b) provides a fairly comprehensive review of the research literature on the Level I–Level II generalization.

   21. Nichols (1984), reporting on the incidence of severe mental retardation (IQ < 50) in the white ($N = 17{,}432$) and black ($N = 19{,}419$) samples of the Collaborative Perinatal

Project, states that at seven years of age 0.5 percent of the white sample and 0.7 percent of the black sample were diagnosed as severely retarded. However, 72 percent of the severely retarded whites showed central nervous system pathology (e.g., Down's syndrome, posttraumatic deficit, Central Nervous System malformations, cerebral palsy, epilepsy, and sensory deficits), as compared with 54 percent of the blacks. Nichols comments, ''The data support the hypothesis that the entire IQ distribution is shifted downward in the black population, so that 'severely' retarded black children with IQs in the 40s are similar to the mildly retarded in terms of central nervous system pathology, socioeconomic status, and familial patterns'' (p. 169).

A recent sociodemographic study by Drews et al. (1995) of ten-year-old mentally retarded children in Metropolitan Atlanta, Georgia, reported (Table 3) that among the mildly retarded (IQ fifty to seventy) without other neurological signs the percentages of blacks and whites were 73.6 and 26.4, respectively. Among the mildly retarded with other neurological conditions, the percentages were blacks = 54.4 and whites = 45.6. For the severely retarded ((IQ < 50) without neurological signs the percentages were blacks = 81.4 and whites = 18.6, respectively; for the severely retarded with other neurological conditions the percentages were blacks = 50.6 and whites = 49.4.

22. Hall & Kleinke, 1971; Herrnstein & Murray, 1994, p. 718, Note 34; Jensen & Figueroa, 1975; Jensen & Osborne 1979; Meeker, 1966.

23. Pressey & Teter, 1919.

24. Both the Pearson _r_ and Spearman's rank-order correlation, r_s, are suitable measures of the degree of relationship between the two vectors. It is most informative to report both; r_s is much less affected by outliers that can spuriously inflate _r_. A statistical test of whether the obtained correlation differs significantly from zero should be based on r_s rather than on _r_, because _r_ is a parametric statistic for which the calculation of its standard error rests on the assumption of normality of the population distributions of each of the correlated variables. But there is no proper basis for assuming anything at all about the form of either the distribution of _g_ loadings or the distribution of standardized mean W-B differences for the total ''population'' of all cognitive tests. In such a case, a nonparametric statistic is called for, as its standard error is not based on any assumption about the population distributions of the correlated variates. Spearman's r_s is such a nonparametric measure of correlation; its level of statistical significance is based simply on a permutation test, that is, the probability that the degree of agreement between the rank orders (from one to _n_) of the two sets of _n_ variates would be as great as (or greater than) the value of the obtained r_s in all possible permutations of the _n_ ranks. (The total possible permutations of _n_ different numbers is _n_!.) The test of significance of r_s is always an exceedingly stringent statistical test of Spearman's hypothesis, because the _n_ (the number of different psychometric measures that can be feasibly administered to groups in any one study) is typically a rather small _n_. (The total range of _n_ in all of the studies of Spearman's hypothesis to date goes from six to seventy-four different psychometric tests.)

The fact that the test of significance of r_s depends only on _n_ (the number of measurements in each of the correlated vectors) does not mean that the number of subjects (_N_) in the study is unimportant. The larger the _N_, the smaller will be the standard error of the _g_ loadings and the larger will be the standardized mean W-B differences, and hence the more reliable will be their vectors and so the more likely that there will be a significant correlation between the two vectors, if Spearman's hypothesis is true.

25. As the tests' _g_ loadings are obtained separately in each group, Spearman's hy-

pothesis can be tested separately for each group's vector of g loadings. However, if the g vector is not virtually identical (i.e., congruence coefficient $> .95$) for both groups, a statistical test of Spearman's hypothesis is precluded. But if the groups show virtual identity of the g factor, the reliability of the vector of g loadings can be increased by combining the two vectors. (*Note*: It is important that the two vectors be obtained separately in each group, so as not to contaminate the factor loadings with any between-groups source of variance.) The two groups' factor loadings (say, a_1 and a_2) on a given test are averaged as follows:

$$\text{Average loading} = \sqrt{(a_1^2 + a_2^2)/2}.$$

It seldom makes a substantial difference whether g is represented by the highest-order factor in a hierarchical factor analysis (the preferred method) or by the first (unrotated) principal factor in a principal factor analysis (also termed principal axes analysis). These typically have a congruence coefficient of .99 or more (Jensen & Weng, 1994). Although the first principal component generally gives highly similar results, it is the least desirable representation of g, because the loadings are slightly (but unequally) inflated by some portion of the variance that is unique to each test, which is by definition a non-g contaminant of the test's true g loading.

26. Test unreliability must be considered because it has the effect of decreasing both the g loadings and the standardized mean W-B differences. If the various tests' reliability coefficients differ significantly, being higher on some tests than on others, then, because they affect each test's factor loading and standardized mean group difference to the same relative degree, a correlation between the vector of loadings and the vector of differences could be entirely an artifact of differences in the reliability of the various tests. On the other hand, if the vector of the tests' reliability coefficients were negatively correlated with either the vector of factor loadings or the vector of mean differences, this fact could obscure or counteract the possibility of a significant correlation between the two vectors for which Spearman's hypothesis predicts a positive correlation. Clearly, the vector of the tests' reliability coefficients has to be dealt with to remove its potentially distorting effect on the test of Spearman's hypothesis. (There would be no problem, of course, if the tests all had the same reliability.)

The two methods for controlling for the effect of the tests' unequal reliability coefficients are *partial correlation* and *correction for attenuation*. They are not mathematically redundant, but complementary, although they both serve much the same purpose.

The *partial correlation* between the vector of g loadings and the vector of mean differences (with the vector of reliability coefficients partialed out) remove the influence of test reliability from the test of Spearman's hypothesis. Whatever the partial correlation is, one knows that it cannot possibly be the result of the two key vectors being in any way linked by common measurement error that affects the paired elements of both vectors. The resulting partial correlation may be larger or smaller than the zero-order (non-partialed) correlation, depending on the sign of the correlation of the key vectors with the vector of reliability coefficients.

Disattenuation of the factor loadings and the standardized mean differences for attenuation (by dividing each test's loading and the standardized mean group difference by the square root of the test's reliability coefficient) is probably less definitive than the partial correlation method, as it depends so much on the reliability of the reliability coefficients themselves. They should be based on a large sample, preferably larger than the study sample used to test Spearman's hypothesis. Otherwise their use may add error to the disattenuated variables. For most tests, the reliability coefficients based on the test's standardization sample are adequate. Usually, when the elements in the key vectors are disattenuated, the correlation between the vectors is made somewhat smaller than before, because the originally smaller _g_ loadings usually are disproportionately increased by disattenuation, thus making all the loadings more alike and restricting the variance among them, which lowers the correlation between the key vectors.

At least one of these methods (partialing or disattenuation) to control for the effect of variation in test reliability was used in all of the tests of Spearman's hypothesis reported in this chapter.

27. Nine of these studies are summarized and referenced in Jensen, 1985a, Table 3, p. 207. Others are: Caretta & Ree, 1995; Fan et al, 1995, Faulstich et al., 1987; Jensen, 1994f; Naglieri & Jensen, 1987; Peoples et al., 1995; Scarr-Salapatek, 1971; Silverstein, 1973.

28. Carretta & Ree, 1995. This study also found that on _g_ and the five residualized group factors extracted from the Air Force Qualifying Test the congruences were all very high (indicating virtual identity of the factors) between males and females, and between different ethnic groups (white, black, Hispanic, Asian-American, and Native-American).

29. Fan, Willson, & Reynolds, 1995.

30. Shuey, 1966.

31. Jaynes & Williams, 1989; see book's Index: "High school dropouts."

32. Thorndike et al., 1986.

33. An article by Vincent (1991), which has gained rather favorable notice recently as a result of its being cited in a popular book, _The Bell Curve_ (Herrnstein & Murray, 1994, pp. 290 and 720, Note 51), suggests that in recent years the W-B IQ gap has been shrinking. Vincent based this surmise on about a dozen previously published studies that seem to show a smaller W-B IQ difference for children tested after 1980, as compared with children tested before 1980 or with persons who were adults when tested. All of the post-1980 groups consist of children of preschool or elementary school age (two to twelve years). But a comprehensive review of earlier data (Shuey, 1966) on this age group indicates a smaller mean W-B IQ difference than is found in older groups, even on IQ tests in the period from 1920 to 1965. Moreover, with the exception of the normative data on the 1986 Stanford-Binet IV, none of the four other studies cited by Vincent is at all suitable for testing the hypothesis in question. The Raven scores cited by Vincent, which were obtained from relatively high SES areas, are not based on representative samples, particularly of the black population (Dr. John Raven, personal communication, July 23, 1995). Other data came from children enrolled in Head Start, for which the black, and especially the white, children are unrepresentative samples of their respective U.S. populations. Still other data were from black and white groups matched on SES and other social and scholastic variables. Yet another data set was based on the K-ABC, a test that is less _g_ loaded than the WISC-R (and probably than most other IQ tests). Therefore, consistent with Spearman's hypothesis, the K-ABC shows a somewhat smaller W-B IQ difference than do other IQ tests (Jensen, 1984c). The only appropriate data for the author's purpose are the Stanford-Binet IV norms, which show the following mean W-B differences, both in IQ units and in σ units for each age group: ages 2 through 6 years: 13.7 IQ, 0.95σ; ages 7 through 11 years: 9.9 IQ, 0.65σ; ages 12 through 18 years: 17.4 IQ, 1.11σ (the last group not reported by Vincent, but in Thorndike et al., 1986, Table 4.5, pp. 34–36). Only the age group 7 to 11 is out of line with all the other data summarized in the text. It is the one and only legitimate item of evidence that

would appear to support Vincent's suggestion that the W-B IQ gap may have narrowed in recent years due to improved educational and economic opportunities for blacks. But if so, why does the even younger group (ages 2 to 6) show a W-B difference of 13.7 IQ points (incorrectly reported by Vincent as 12 IQ points)? It cannot be the effect of schooling on raising the IQ in the school-age blacks, because the black IQ in the pre-school age group is only 1.7 lower than in the school-age group. (The white and black IQ means for ages 2 through 6 are 104.7 and 91.0, respectively; for ages 7 through 11, 102.6 and 92.7, respectively; and for ages 12 through 18, 103.5 and 86.1, respectively.)

Other recent evidence, in fact, suggests that the mean W-B IQ difference is not decreasing but is more probably increasing. Since at least 1970, U.S. Census data have indicated that among *all* women between ages 15 and 44 years (regardless of their marital status) there is a *negative* relationship between years of schooling and number of offspring (Jensen, 1981a, pp. 252–253). This negative relationship is more pronounced for black women than for white women. In 1970, for example, black women with less than 8 years of education had 1.3 more children than black women who graduated from high school and 1.8 more children than black women with 1 to 3 years of college. The corresponding numbers of children for white women were 0.8 and 1.3, respectively. Further, for both blacks and whites, there is a positive correlation between children's IQ and their mother's level of education. In the large representative sample selected for the National Longitudinal Study of Youth (NLSY) the percentage of black children born to mothers with IQ < 90 is 69 percent as compared with 2 percent for mothers with IQ > 110; the corresponding figures for whites are 19 percent and 22 percent. The conjunction of these demographic conditions suggests the widening of the W-B IQ difference in successive generations. This prediction is borne out, so far, by the NLSY data on the IQs of those children (tested at over six years of age) whose mothers were tested in the original NLSY sample. The mean W-B IQ difference for the mothers was 13.2; for their children it was 17.5 IQ points (Herrnstein & Murray, 1994, pp. 352–356). These statistics showing an average lowering of the mean black IQ vis-á-vis the mean white IQ, it should be emphasized, are not necessarily the result of anything that happened directly to the children in the course of their individual development, but rather they probably result from the different birth rates of blacks and whites within different segments of the IQ distribution of the children's parents, as described above. Even supposing there was no racial IQ difference whatsoever in previous generations, then given the continuance of the present condition of birth rates that are differentially associated with IQ within each racial group, the inevitable result would be a racial IQ difference in subsequent generations. The resulting group difference would occur irrespective of the basic cause either of individual differences or of group differences in IQ. Whether the cause is environmental, or genetic, or both, would not alter the well-known educational, social, and economic correlates of IQ differences, which have been most fully spelled out by Herrnstein & Murray (1994).

34. (a) Jensen, 1985a; (b) Jensen, 1985b; (c) Jensen & Reynolds, 1982; (d) Humphreys, 1985a, 1985b; Jensen, 1985d; (e) five critiques by (and exchanges among) six psychometricians (Guttman, Roskam & Ellis, Schönemann, Loehlin, Gustafsson) in *Multivariate Behavioral Research*, 1992, 27, 173–267; (f) Jensen, 1987g; (g) Jensen, 1992f; (h) Naglieri & Jensen, 1987; (i) Reynolds & Jensen, 1983; (j) Peoples et al., 1995; (k) Lynn & Owen, 1994; (l) Jensen & Faulstich, 1988; (m) Jensen, 1994f; (n) Gordon, 1987b, pp. 120–139.

35. In the only analysis (Gustafsson, 1992; reply by Jensen, 1992g) that has claimed

to not support Spearman's hypothesis, the same WISC-R data used in the study by Jensen & Reynolds (1982) were factor analyzed by a method (performed with LISREL) that was not clearly specified. Based on this method, the vector of the subtests' _g_ loadings was not significantly correlated with the vector of W-B differences on the subtests, whereas the correlations reported by Jensen & Reynolds, 1982 (based on a Schmid-Leiman hierarchical factor analysis) were $+.75$ for whites and $+.64$ for blacks (both with $p < .05$). Another type of analysis conclusively shows that the W-B difference on the WISC-R battery is indeed mainly attributable to _g_. The W-B difference on each of the twelve subtests was expressed as a point-biserial correlation (r_{pbs}) between test scores and race (quantitized as white $= 1$, black $= 0$); these point-biserial correlations were entered into the matrix of Pearson correlations among all of the subtests. A principal factor analysis of the whole matrix showed that the loading of race on the _g_ factor (represented as the first principal factor) was much larger than its loading on any of the three next largest factors. The ratio of _g_ variance to non-_g_ variance (the sum of squares of the race loadings on the three next largest factors) was 2.90 when the analysis was based on the correlation matrix for whites and 3.54 when based on the correlation matrix for blacks (Jensen, 1987g, Table 1). This means that most of the between-race variance on the WISC-R is more attributable to _g_ than to all of the other factors combined.

36. Office of the Assistant Secretary of Defense, 1980. The AFQT consists of the four most highly _g_-loaded subtests of the ASVAB (Word Knowledge, Paragraph Comprehension, Arithmetic Reasoning, and Mathematics Knowledge). The AFQT subtests have an average _g_ loading of .84 when factor analyzed among the twelve subtests of the ASVAB. AFQT scores have an approximately normal distribution in the population and are correlated about .80 with standardized IQ tests, which are generally less _g_ loaded than the AFQT.

37. This determination was made by converting the mean W-B differences on each test to a point-biserial correlation, which expresses the W-B difference as a product-moment correlation coefficient between test scores and the racial dichotomy quantitized as black $= 1$, white $= 2$. The point-biserial correlation is monotonically related to the mean difference; in the range of the correlations obtained in the present data, the relation is very nearly linear. The quantitized race variable can then be included in a principal factor analysis with all the other tests in a given battery. The squared factor loadings of the race variable on the _g_ factor (PF1) were compared with the three principal factors that showed the largest non-_g_ loadings on the B/W racial variable. The ratio of _g_/non-_g_ variance averaged over all nine test batteries equaled 4.31; that is, the _g_ factor accounted for more than four times as much of the common factor variance as did the total of all the non-_g_ factors. (Details of this analysis are given in Jensen, 1987g, pp. 513–514 and Table 1.)

38. Matarazzo, 1972; Thorndike & Lohman, 1990.

39. One can also test Spearman's hypothesis by using the mean _g_ and the mean D (i.e., W-B difference) on each of a number of test batteries as the units of analysis. Hence across twelve batteries, the correlation between the mean _g_ loadings of the subtests in each of the batteries and the mean W-B difference on the subtests in each of the batteries is $r = +.53$; partialing out the _SD_s of these variables (_g_ and D) in each battery, the partial correlation is $+.61$. Of course, the batteries as a whole have much less variation in their mean _g_ loadings and mean D values than do the individual subtests within each battery. (For the whole batteries, the _SD_ of the mean _g_ loadings is .07; the mean and _SD_ of the mean D values are .75 and .24, respectively.)

40. Gordon (1987b, pp. 126–131) has argued that the proof of Spearman's hypothesis should be based not on the Pearson or Spearman rank-order correlation coefficient between the vector of *g* loadings and the vector of group differences, but on the congruence coefficient, when the mean group difference on each subtest is expressed as a point-biserial correlation between test score and race (quantized as black = 1, white = 2). The vector of point-biserial correlations can be interpreted as the W-B difference factor. Thus degree of similarity of the W-B difference factor to the *g* factor of the same battery can be assessed by the coefficient of congruence. For the twelve batteries reported in Jensen (1985a), Gordon finds an average congruence coefficient of +.97 between the W-B factor and the *g* factor (whether based on black or on white samples). Thus, Gordon's use of the congruence coefficient would support a conclusion that the black-white difference on mental tests is *almost* entirely a difference in *g*. I believe this conclusion would be true only on the condition that none of the group factors is overrepresented in the battery from which the *g* is extracted; most importantly, neither of the two major group factors on which blacks and whites are known to differ independently of *g* (viz., spatial and memory factors) should markedly predominate in the selection of subtests.

41. Table 3 in Peoples et al. (1995) gives the *F* test for the independent effect of maternal education (dichotomized as *low* $\leq$ 12 years versus *high* > 12 years) on children's scores for each of the eight SB-IV subtests. As *F* is monotonically related to the magnitude of the effect on children's scores of the *high-low* difference in maternal education, the values of *F* for each of the subtests can be used instead of the corresponding mean differences in computing the rank-order correlation r_s between the vector of maternal education effects and the other vectors (subtest *g* loadings and mean W-B differences). This method was necessary because only the *F* values, not the means and *SD*s, for the effect of maternal education on the children's subtest performance were reported by Peoples et al. (1995).

42. The statistics for this study were obtained from three separate articles based on the very same large (black *N* = 32,798, white *N* = 212,238) samples of applicants for the U.S. Air Force who were given all sixteen subtests of the Air Force Qualifying Test battery. The hierarchical factor analyses of these tests are in Carretta & Ree (1995a); the subtest reliability coefficients and the subtests' validity coefficients are in Carretta & Ree (1995b); the means and *SD*s of the black and white samples are in Carretta (1997).

43. The correction for restriction of range is necessary because the trainees were highly selected on the basis of AFOQT score and are therefore an elite group that is not representative of the much wider "range-of-talent" that exists in the total pool of applicants for Air Force training as pilots. The correction of the validity coefficient for range restriction estimates what the validity of the AFOQT would be for predicting the Final Training Outcome if all trainees had been randomly selected from the applicant pool.

44. Owen, 1989.

45. The correlation of +.624 in this case seems to depend more on some of the peculiarly low subtest reliability coefficients used to disattenuate the W-B differences and the *g* loadings than on the intrinsic properties with which Spearman's hypothesis is concerned. For example, on the three subtests with the lowest reliability coefficients for blacks (whose average internal consistency reliability [KR20] was .31) the mean W-B differences (uncorrected) are among the largest, averaging 2.48σ. (The corresponding disattenuated values average 2.81σ.) For blacks, the uncorrected *g* loadings of these three subtests (averaging .467) are smaller than the mean *g* (.525) of all 10 subtests. When disattenuated, however, these three *g* loadings were increased to an average of .834. So

the net effect of disattenuation on the subtests with abnormally low reliability is to greatly increase the W-B mean difference on these subtests and to greatly increase each subtests' g loadings. The effect of disattenuation based on excessively low reliability creates an outcome which, though apparently favoring Spearman's hypothesis, may be considered spurious, because test reliability per se is not intrinsic to Spearman's hypothesis. Measurement error (i.e., unreliability) is merely unwanted ''noise'' that, from a methodological standpoint, should be ''filtered out'' (either by disattenuating the essential variables or partialing out the vector of reliability coefficients). But when the ''noise'' (error variance) is greater than the ''signal'' (true score variance), as is the case for the black group's g loadings on at least three subtests in this study, disattenuation is highly suspect. The effect of disattenuation on the test of Spearman's hypothesis on the South African black group (with a resultant correlation of $+.624$) is revealed by the corresponding correlation when the data are not disattenuated (i.e., measurement error has not been removed); then the Pearson correlation is negligible ($+.011$) and the rank-order correlation is even negative ($-.176$).

46. Jensen (1988a) reviews some of the earlier cross-cultural and cross-racial studies that have used chronometric techniques, and describes recent ECTs that show promise for the study of population differences in information processes.

47. Jensen, 1993d; Lynn & Holmshaw, 1990.

48. Jensen, 1987d, Tables 3 and 7.

49. Vernon & Jensen, 1984.

50. Poortinga, 1971. A brief review of this study is given in Jensen, 1988a.

51. Poortinga (1971) found that a questionnaire designed to assess the Africans' degree of acculturation to a Western European rather than to an African orientation showed a substantial correlation (.59 for the Advanced Progressive Matrices) with three psychometric tests. This further suggests the inappropriateness of the psychometric tests (or at least the particular ones used in Poortinga's study) for the African blacks. However, the degree to which Africans had become psychologically acculturated to European ways might itself be intrinsically related to g. Not all groups that have lacked exposure to Western culture necessarily perform below Western norms on the Raven. Certain groups that show little evidence of acculturation to a European life-style, such as Eskimos living in remote regions above the Arctic Circle, nevertheless perform on a par with European and North American norms on the Raven matrices. (References to these studies in Jensen, 1973, pp. 302–303).

52. In research using the Raven tests in the United States, we have found that the Advanced Progressive Matrices (APM) is usually too difficult (i.e., there is a floor effect, with scores piling up near the chance guessing level) to be a suitable measure for some junior college samples, while the Standard Progressive Matrices (SPM) is wholly satisfactory for groups at this level. On the other hand, we have found that the SPM is unsuitable (i.e., there is a ceiling effect, with scores piling up near the maximum possible score) for students in academically highly selective universities, while the APM is psychometrically satisfactory for these groups. By means of a psychometric procedure known as ''equating,'' it is possible to test various groups that differ rather widely in ability, using the one test (SPM or APM) best suited to each group, and then equating the scores so that they can be represented on a single IQ scale based on national norms for the general population. The equating procedure and tables for converting raw scores on the SPM and APM from one scale to the other and to a common, nationally stan-

dardized IQ scale for the general population are given in Jensen, Saccuzzo, & Larson, 1988.

53. Jensen, 1993d. This article reports two distinct experiments; the second one is described later in this chapter under the heading "Spearman's Hypothesis Tested with Simple Arithmetic."

54. In many previous studies of these and other ECT variables a fairly consistent pattern of relationships between various ECT variables and psychometric g has been observed. On the basis of these regularities, I have induced several generalizations, or rules, from which one can "theoretically" infer each different ECT variable's relative degree of saturation on psychometric g. The relative magnitude of the correlation between psychometric g and various ECT variables is governed by the following rules (where RT > MT, for example, means that the g loading of RT is greater than the g loading of MT):

- More complex task > less complex task.
- Reaction time > movement time (RT > MT).
- Intraindividual variability in RT (or MT) > median RT (or MT).
- As intraindividual variability is measured by the *SD* of the RT (MT) over trials, RTSD > RT and MTSD > MT.

Each of the ECT variables can be rank-ordered theoretically in terms of a simple algorithm for combining the above-listed task characteristics, with each one assigned the following values:

- **Simple** = 1, **Choice** = 2, **Discrimination** = 3
- Median RT = 4, RTSD = 5
- Median MT = 1, MTSD = 2
- For tied ranks, *SD* > median.

The theoretical relative magnitude of a given task's g loading, then, is determined by the product of the ordinal values assigned to these characteristics. For median of simple RT (SRT), for example: $1 \times 4 = 4$. For RTSD of Discrimination (Odd-man): $3 \times 5 = 15$. For median of simple MT: $1 \times 1 = 1$. And so on, for each variable. The resulting values for the twelve ECT variables (which range from 1 to 15) were ranked from 1 (smallest value) to 12 (to permit calculation of their rank-order correlation with observed vectors). The variables with tied ranks (SRT = CMTSD and SMTSD = CMT) are then rank ordered: *SD* > median.

From the above rules, the theoretical rank order of the g saturation of the twelve ECT variables used in this study is (going from highest to lowest g saturation): DRTSD, DRT, CRTSD, CRT, DMTSD, SRTSD, CMTSD, SRT, DMT, SMTSD, CMT, SMT. This theoretical rank order of these variables correlated +0.73 ($p < .01$) with the vector of the mean W-B differences (in σ units) on each of the twelve variables.

55. Jensen, 1992d.

56. Jensen & Reed, 1990.

57. Carroll, 1991b. Carroll's important analysis is described in more detail in Chapter 8, pp. 230–31, 265.

58. Lynn & Holmshaw, 1990.

59. Owen (1992) found a mean difference of 2σ on Raven's Standard Progressive

Matrices in very large and representative samples of blacks and whites, aged fifteen to sixteen, in South Africa. Owen's analyses of the SPM data at the item level show that in this age group the SPM is not biased for blacks in terms of any of the standard statistical criteria for detecting test bias.

60. This note is unfortunately lengthy and quite difficult to read because of the unavoidable complexities of the explication, though it is about as clear and simple as I could make it. And it may be scarcely meaningful to those who do not already have some understanding of principal components (which for this analysis is probably the simplest means to make the argument). Readers who are not inclined to wade through these technical details should skip to the *Conclusion* at the end of this note.

The study by Lynn & Holmshaw (1990), although it was methodologically almost exactly the same as the study by Jensen (1993d), yielded such markedly different results as to call for an attempt at explanation. In fact, the main finding of the Lynn & Holmshaw study appears to be almost the *opposite* of the result of the Jensen (1993d) study. Can this discordance be attributed to an extreme difference between the South African sample of black children and the black children in the American sample, such that these groups do not respond to the elementary cognitive tasks (ECTs) in the same way? To answer this seeming "paradox," as Lynn & Holmshaw call it, we can begin by comparing the correlations between the key vectors, within each study and across the two studies. For economy of notation, the key vectors are labeled as follows:

$\mathbf{G}$ = the column vector of estimated *g* loadings on each of the twelve variables on the elementary cognitive tasks (ECTs) determined separately in the black and in the white samples and averaged (for each ECT) across the black and white samples. (The *g* loading of each variable was represented by the variable's correlation with the highly *g*-loaded Raven's Standard Progressive Matrices, determined separately for black and white samples.) This vector for the black sample is labeled $\mathbf{G_b}$, and for the white sample $\mathbf{G_w}$. Subscripts $\mathbf{J}$(Jensen) and $\mathbf{L}$(Lynn) identify the particular study.

$\mathbf{D}$ = the column vector of standardized mean black *minus* white differences on each of the twelve ECT variables. Subscripts $\mathbf{J}$ and $\mathbf{L}$ identify the study.

The Pearson correlations between the vectors, which indicate the vectors' degree of similarity to each other, are shown in Table 11.N.

Each of the $_L\mathbf{G}$ vectors in the Lynn & Holmshaw study is negatively correlated with all of the vectors in the Jensen study *and* is also correlated $-.87$ with the $_L\mathbf{D}$ vector of Lynn & Holmshaw, which is opposite to the corresponding correlation of $+.83$ between the $_J\mathbf{G}$ and $_J\mathbf{D}$ vectors in the Jensen study. This peculiar discordance between the two studies calls for further examination.

This can be done most efficiently by using the first principal component (PC1) of certain subsets of the variables in the above correlation matrix. In every case the PC1 accounts for a very large proportion of the total variance. (Only those components with eigenvalues > 1 are reported here.) The PC1 in this case clearly reveals the source of the problem. Because $_J\mathbf{G}$ (or $_L\mathbf{G}$) is simply the mean vector of *g* loadings averaged across the white and black groups, they are not included in the principal components analysis. (In the Lynn & Holmshaw study, $_L\mathbf{G_w}$ and $_L\mathbf{G_b}$ should not have been averaged, because these vectors, which have a congruence coefficient of only $+.45$, do not represent the same factor for blacks and whites. A congruence coefficient above $+.90$ is required to claim the factors are the same.) Here is the PC1 of these two sets of only three vectors:

Table 11.N

Correlations between Key Vectors in the Jensen (1993d) and Lynn & Holmshaw (1990) Studies Testing Spearman's Hypothesis with ECTs

	$_JG_w$	$_JG_B$	$_JG$	$_JD$	$_LG_w$	$_LG_B$	$_LG$
$_JG_B$	.85						
$_JG$	.98	.94					
$_JD$	.83	.69	.81				
$_LG_w$	−.14	−.43	−.25	−.32			
$_LG_B$	−.60	−.22	−.47	−.52	−.36		
$_LG$	−.68	−.52	−.64	−.71	.35	.75	
$_LD$	.60	.57	.61	.68	−.68	−.38	−.87

Vector	Jensen PC1	Lynn PC1
G_w	.966	−.903
G_b	.915	−.049
D	.905	.930

Theoretically, to accord with Spearman's hypothesis, all of these PC1 loadings should have the same sign. The PC1 thus highlights a discordance between these sets of vectors in the two studies.

But now let's look at the PC1 and the second principal component (PC2) extracted from the following set of vectors:

Vector	PC1	PC2
$_JG_w$	.916	−.269
$_JG_b$	.853	.130
$_JD$	.908	.104
$_LG_w$	−.453	−.873
$_LG_b$	−.530	.758
$_LD$	.839	.281
Eigenvalue	3.582	1.515

Clearly, it is Lynn's **G** vectors that are inconsistent with Jensen's **G** vectors. Note that Lynn's **D** has a large positive loading on the PC1, as does Jensen's **D**. Theoretically, PC1 should have all large positive loadings, and PC2 should have all negligible loadings (regardless of sign). Hence it appears that Lynn's **G** vectors are peculiar, with negative loadings on PC1 and large loadings (but of opposite sign) on PC2. Lynn's **G**, not his **D**, is contrary to theoretical expectation and seems to be the source of the problem on which to focus further analysis.

A closer look at how the data compare with theoretical expectation can be obtained by correlating the rank order of each of the twelve ECT variables with the theoretically expected rank order of the ECT variables' loadings on psychometric _g_. (The basis for this theoretical expectation is explained in Note 54, above.)

Another clue is afforded by the fact that performance on ECT is related to age, and the effect of the age differences on the twelve ECTs used in the studies by Lynn and by Jensen can be used to examine the data for its consistency with theoretical expectation. Lynn's sample is two years younger (nine years of age) than Jensen's (eleven years of age). Previous research has shown that the magnitude of age changes in performance on a given ECT variable is related to the variable's _g_ loading, reflecting different amounts of mental growth with increasing age, from early childhood to maturity. Therefore, younger and older groups show about the same pattern of differences across a number of ECT variables, as would groups that are matched on age but that differ in mental age, or level of _g_. Based on this, we can then create two new vectors to enter into our analysis: (1) the vector of standardized differences between the mean of the white (_younger_) subjects' scores on each ECT (in Lynn's study) and the mean of the white (_older_) subjects' ECT scores on each ECT in Jensen's study; and (2) the corresponding vector of ECT differences between _younger_ and _older_ black subjects. The first of these vectors is labeled D_{ww}, the second is D_{bb}.

Including the vector of the theoretical rank order of the ECT variables' _g_ loadings (termed ''Theory'') and the vector of standardized mean differences between older and younger white and black groups on each of the ECT variables in the whole matrix of correlations among the other observed vectors, the PC1 and PC2 are:

Vector	PC1	PC2
$_J G_w$	.920	.186
$_J G_b$	.692	.532
$_J D$	.852	.296
$_L G_w$	−.054	−.955
$_L G_b$	−.811	.490
$_L D$	.682	.548
D_{ww}	.844	−.491
D_{bb}	.859	−.353
Theory	.927	−.109
Eigenvalue	5.487	2.235

Again, it is amply clear that it is only the $_L G$ vectors (for both W and B) that are markedly discordant; all of the other vectors have positive loadings on PC1, in accord with Spearman's hypothesis. The theory-derived vector has the largest loading on PC1 and the smallest absolute loading on PC2. The positive PC1 loading of $_L D$ indicates that Lynn's ECT data are in line with Jensen's and with the theory. Further evidence that Lynn's ECT variables are not at fault is that when they are factor analyzed (retaining only the factors with eigenvalues > 1), they have nearly the same communalities as Jensen's ECT variables. (A variable's communality provides a lower-bound estimate of its reliability.) Hence Lynn's ECT data are in fair accord with Spearman's hypothesis; but his Raven scores, used to estimate the _g_ loadings of the ECT variables, are anomalous, especially in the South African (black) sample.

Why are the scores on Raven's Standard Progressive Matrices (SPM) suspect, especially in the South African sample? As seen in Table 11.N, the vector of correlations of each of the ECT variables with the SPM scores for South African blacks (i.e., $_L G_b$) is *negatively* correlated ($-.36$) with the corresponding vector for the British whites (i.e., $_L G_w$). The congruence coefficient between the vectors $_L G_b$ and $_L G_w$ is only $+.45$, indicating that they are very different factors. (A congruence coefficient must be above .90 for the two vectors to be regarded as representing the same factor.) The corresponding congruence coefficient in Jensen's data is $+.97$. (The congruence between $_J G_w$ and $_L G_w$ is $+.80$, indicating barely marginal similarity.) Examination of the statistics on the Raven scores strongly suggests that there exists what is known in psychometrics as a "floor" effect; that is, there are not enough easy items, so the test is much too difficult for many individuals in the sample, and beyond the few easiest items most subjects simply resort to guessing, which, in a multiple-choice test (which the Raven is), causes a piling up of scores near the chance-guessing level of performance. The South African black children had a mean score of only 12.7 (*SD* 4.5), which is at the first percentile (equivalent to an IQ of sixty-five) on the British norms and is only slightly above the chance-guessing score of 8.5. (As there are 6 multiple choices for 24 items and 8 multiple choices for 36 items in the SPM, the expected chance score is $24(1/6) + 36(1/8) = 8.5$ items.) The small *SD* (4.5, as compared to about 10 in other comparable age groups) also suggests a marked "floor" effect in the African sample. Thus the reliability of the African children's scores on the SPM is most probably unacceptably low. (This is not true, however, for older black children in South Africa; Owen [1992] has reported satisfactory reliability coefficients [about .90] for the SPM given to South African blacks of ages 15 to 16 years, whose SPM scores averaged about 28 with a *SD* of about 11.)

Conclusion: If one looks at just the ECT data in the Lynn & Holmshaw (1990) study comparing black schoolchildren in South Africa with white children of about the same age in Britain, the results are in line with the ECT data of the Jensen (1993d) study comparing black and white children selected from the same American schools (even from the same classrooms). Insofar as the ECT data of Lynn & Holmshaw are fairly consistent with Jensen's ECT data and are also concordant with theoretical prediction of the ECT variables' *g* loadings, they lend support to Spearman's hypothesis. The ECT data certainly do not contradict it. What Lynn & Holmshaw refer to as their "paradoxical result" (p. 306) is not attributable to any unusual feature of their ECT data per se, but appears to be a consequence of the questionable validity of the Raven Standard Progressive Matrices test as a measure of *g* for the subjects in this study, especially in the South African black sample, probably because of the "floor" effect on the distribution of test scores (and hence restriction of range) created by most of the SPM items being too difficult for most of the subjects. The nonsignificant negative correlation ($-.14$) between the $_J G_w$ and $_L G_w$ vectors (i.e., the white group's vector of ECT variables' *g* loadings in the Jensen and the Lynn studies), however, is less likely due to a "floor" effect, as the mean SPM score in this group was 36.1 (*SD* 9.6), which is close to the British norm for this age group. Such a discrepancy could be due to the large standard error of the correlation between vectors, because the *N* on which these correlations are based is only twelve. The confidence limits for correlations based on a small *N* are quite wide, so that having only one or two of the values in a different rank order in each of the vectors can rather drastically alter the correlation between them. (The standard error of an observed rank correlation when the null hypothesis is true is $SE_r = 1/\sqrt{N}$; so for $N = 12$, the $SE_r = \pm.29$) For this reason, testing Spearman's hypothesis by means of correlated vectors is an extremely severe test, because in the existing studies the number of variables in each vector is typically about twelve and rarely more than twenty.

61. Jensen & Whang, 1993. This study also refers to three studies by Lynn and co-workers based on groups of the same battery of ECTs given to groups in Japan and Hong Kong and points out similarities and differences in the results obtained in the American Chinese, Hong Kong Chinese, and Japanese samples.

62. Jensen & Whang, 1994.

Chapter 12

Population Differences in *g*:
Causal Hypotheses

The relationship of the *g* factor to a number of biological variables and its relationship to the size of the white-black differences on various cognitive tests (i.e., Spearman's hypothesis) suggests that the average white-black difference in *g* has a biological component. Human races are viewed not as discrete, or Platonic, categories, but rather as breeding populations that, as a result of natural selection, have come to differ statistically in the relative frequencies of many polymorphic genes. The "genetic distances" between various populations form a continuous variable that can be measured in terms of differences in gene frequencies. Racial populations differ in many genetic characteristics, some of which, such as brain size, have behavioral and psychometric correlates, particularly *g*. What I term the default hypothesis states that the causes of the phenotypic differences between contemporary populations of recent African and European descent arise from the same genetic and environmental factors, and in approximately the same magnitudes, that account for individual differences within each population. Thus genetic and environmental variances between groups and within groups are viewed as essentially the same for both populations. The default hypothesis is able to account for the present evidence on the mean white-black difference in *g*. There is no need to invoke any ad hoc hypothesis, or a Factor X, that is unique to either the black or the white population. The environmental component of the average *g* difference between groups is primarily attributable to a host of microenvironmental factors that have biological effects. They result from nongenetic variation in prenatal, perinatal, and neonatal conditions and specific nutritional factors.

The many studies of Spearman's hypothesis using the method of correlated vectors show a strong relationship between the g loadings of a great variety of cognitive tests and the mean black-white differences on those tests. The fact that the same g vectors that are correlated with W-B differences are also correlated (and to about the same degree) with vectors composed of various cognitive tests' correlations with a number of genetic, anatomical, and physiological variables suggests that certain biological factors may be related to the average black-white population difference in the level of g.

The degree to which of each of many different psychometric tests is correlated with all of the other tests is directly related to the magnitude of the test's g loading. What may seem surprising, however, is the fact that the degree to which a given test is correlated with any one of the following variables is a positive function of that test's g loading:

> Heritability of test scores.
>
> Amount of inbreeding depression of test scores.
>
> Heterosis (hybrid vigor, that is, raised test scores, due to outbreeding).
>
> Head size (also, by inference, brain size).
>
> Average evoked potential (AEP) habituation and complexity.
>
> Glucose metabolic rate as measured by PET scan.
>
> Average reaction time to elementary cognitive tasks.
>
> Size of the mean W-B difference on various cognitive tests.

The one (and probably the only) common factor that links all of these non-psychometric variables to psychometric test scores and also links psychometric test scores to the magnitude of the mean W-B difference is the g factor. The critical role of g in these relationships is shown by the fact that the magnitude of a given test's correlation with any one of the above-listed variables is correlated with the magnitude of the W-B difference on that test. For example, Rushton[1] reported a correlation ($r = +.48$) between the magnitudes of the mean W-B differences (in the American standardization sample) on eleven subtests of the WISC-R and the effect of inbreeding depression on the eleven subtest scores of the Japanese version of the WISC. Further, the subtests' g loadings in the Japanese data predicted the American W-B differences on the WISC-R subtests with $r = .69$—striking evidence of the g factor's robustness across different cultures. Similarly, the magnitude of the mean W-B difference on each of seventeen diverse psychometric tests was predicted (with $r = .71$, $p < .01$) by the tests' correlations with head size (a composite measure of length, width, and circumference).[2]

This association of psychometric tests' g loadings, the tests' correlations with genetic and other biological variables, and the mean W-B differences in test scores cannot be dismissed as happenstance. The failure of theories of group differences in IQ that are based exclusively on attitudinal, cultural, and experiential factors to predict or explain such findings argues strongly that biological factors, whether genetic or environmental in origin, must be investigated. Before examining possible biological factors in racial differences in mental abilities, however, we should be conceptually clear about the biological meaning of the term "race."

THE MEANING OF RACE

Nowadays one often reads in the popular press (and in some anthropology textbooks) that the concept of human races is a fiction (or, as one well-known anthropologist termed it, a "dangerous myth"), that races do not exist in reality, but are social constructions of politically and economically dominant groups for the purpose of maintaining their own status and power in a society. It naturally follows from this premise that, since races do not exist in any real, or biological, sense, it is meaningless even to inquire about the biological basis of any racial differences. I believe this line of argument has five main sources, none of them scientific:

- Heaping scorn on the concept of race is deemed an effective way of combating racism—here defined as the belief that individuals who visibly differ in certain characteristics deemed "racial" can be ordered on a dimension of "human worth" from inferior to superior, and that therefore various civil and political rights, as well as social privileges, should be granted or denied according to a person's supposed racial origin.

- Neo-Marxist philosophy (which still has exponents in the social sciences and the popular media) demands that individual and group differences in psychologically and socially significant traits be wholly the result of economic inequality, class status, or the oppression of the working classes in a capitalist society. It therefore excludes consideration of genetic or biological factors (except those that are purely exogenous) from any part in explaining behavioral differences among humans. It views the concept of race as a social invention by those holding economic and political powers to justify the division and oppression of unprivileged classes.

- The view that claims that the concept of race (not just the misconceptions about it) is scientifically discredited is seen as a way to advance more harmonious relations among the groups in our society that are commonly perceived as "racially" different.

- The universal revulsion to the Holocaust, which grew out of the racist doctrines of Hitler's Nazi regime, produced a reluctance on the part of democratic societies to sanction any inquiry into biological aspects of race in relation to any behavioral variables, least of all socially important ones.

- Frustration with the age-old popular wrong-headed conceptions about race has led some experts in population genetics to abandon the concept instead of attempting candidly to make the public aware of how the concept of race is viewed by most present-day scientists.

Wrong Conceptions of Race. The root of most wrong conceptions of race is the Platonic view of human races as *distinct types*, that is, discrete, mutually exclusive categories. According to this view, any observed variation among the members of a particular racial category merely represents individual deviations from the archetype, or ideal type, for that "race." Since, according to this Platonic view of race, every person can be assigned to one or another racial category, it naturally follows that there is some *definite number* of races, each with its unique set of distinctive physical characteristics, such as skin color, hair texture, and facial features. The traditional number has been three: Caucasoid, Mongoloid, and Negroid, in part derived from the pre-Darwinian creationist view that "the races of mankind" could be traced back to the three sons of Noah—Shem, Ham, and Japheth.

The Cause of Biological Variation. All that is known today about the world-wide geographic distribution of differences in human physical characteristics can be understood in terms of the synthesis of Darwinian evolution and population genetics developed by R. A. Fisher, Sewall Wright, Theodosius Dobzhansky, and Ernst Mayr. Races are defined in this context as breeding populations that differ from one another in gene frequencies and that vary in a number of intercorrelated visible features that are highly heritable.

Racial differences are a product of the evolutionary process working on the human genome, which consists of about 100,000 polymorphic genes (that is, genes that contribute to genetic variation among members of a species) located in the twenty-three pairs of chromosomes that exist in every cell of the human body. The genes, each with its own locus (position) on a particular chromosome, contain all of the chemical information needed to create an organism. In addition to the polymorphic genes, there are also a great many other genes that are not polymorphic (that is, are the same in all individuals in the species) and hence do not contribute to the normal range of human variation. Those genes that do produce variation are called *polymorphic* genes, as they have two or more different forms called *alleles*, whose codes differ in their genetic information. Different alleles, therefore, produce different effects on the phenotypic characteristic determined by the gene at a particular chromosomal locus. Genes that do not have different alleles (and thus do not have variable phenotypic effects) are said to have gone to *fixation*; that is, alternative alleles, if any, have long since been eliminated by natural selection in the course of human or mammalian evolution. The physiological functions served by most basic "housekeeping" genes are so crucial for the organism's development and viability that almost any mutation of them proves lethal to the individual who harbors it; hence only one form of the gene is possessed by all members of a species. A great many such essential genes are in fact shared by closely related species; the number of genes that are common to different species is inversely related to the evolutionary distance between them. For instance, the two living species closest to *Homo sapiens* in evolutionary distance, chimpanzees and gorillas, have at least 97 percent of their genes (or total genetic code) in common with present-day humans, scarcely less than chimps and gorillas have in common with each other. This means that even the very small percentage of genes (<3 percent) that differ between humans and the great apes is responsible for all the conspicuous and profound phenotypic differences observed between apes and humans. The genetic difference appears small only if viewed on the scale of differences among all animal species.

A particular gene's genetic code is determined by the unique sequences of four chemical bases of the DNA, arranged in the familiar double-helix structure of the gene. A change in a gene's code (one base pair), however slight, can produce a new or different allele that manifests a different phenotypic effect. (Many such mutations, however, have no phenotypic effect because of redundancy in the DNA.) Such changes in the DNA result from spontaneous mutation. Though mutations occur at random, some gene loci have much higher mutation rates than others, ranging for different loci from less than one per million to perhaps more than 500 per million sex cells—not a trivial number considering that each male ejaculation contains from 200 to 500 million sperm. While natural or spontaneous mutations have largely unknown causes, aptly referred to as biological "noise," it has been shown experimentally that mutations can result from radiation (X-rays, gamma rays, cosmic rays, and ultraviolet radiation). Certain chemical substances are also mutagenic.

The creation of new alleles by spontaneous mutation along with the recombination of alleles in gametogenesis are essential conditions for the evolution of all forms of life. A new allele with phenotypic effects that decrease an individual's fitness in a given environment, compared to the nonmutated allele that would normally occupy the same chromosomal locus, will be passed on to fewer descendants and will eventually go to extinction. The gene is driven out of existence, so to speak, by losing in the competition with other alleles that afford greater fitness. Biological *fitness* (also known as Darwinian fitness), as a technical term in evolutionary genetics, refers only to an individual's reproductive success, often defined operationally as the number of surviving fertile progeny of that individual. (A horse mated with a donkey, for example, might produce many surviving offspring, but because they are all sterile, the horse and donkey in this mating have a fitness of zero.) The frequency of a particular gene in all of an individual's relatives is termed the *inclusive fitness* of that gene. The inclusive fitness of a gene is a measure of its effect on the survival and reproductive success of both the individual bearing the gene and all of the individual's relatives bearing the identical gene. Technically speaking, an individual's biological fitness denotes nothing more than that individual's genetic contribution to the next generation's gene pool relative to the average for the population. The term does not necessarily imply any traits one may deem personally desirable, such as vigor, physical strength, or a beautiful body, although some such traits, to the extent that they are heritable, were undoubtedly genetically selected in the course of evolution only because, we know in retrospect, they enhanced individuals' reproductive success in succeeding generations. The survival of any new allele and its rate of spreading through subsequent generations is wholly a function of the degree to which its phenotypic expression enhances the inclusive fitness of those who inherit the allele. An allele with any advantageous phenotypic effect, in this respect, spreads to an ever-larger part of the breeding population in each successive generation.

New alleles created by mutation are subject to *natural selection* according to the degree of fitness they confer *in a particular environment*. Changed environmental conditions can alter the selection pressure for a certain allele, depending on the nature of its phenotypic expression, thereby either increasing or decreasing its frequency in a breeding population. Depending on its fitness in a given environment, it may go to extinction in the population or it may go to fixation (with every member of the population eventually possessing the allele).[3] Many polymorphic gene loci harbor one or another allele of a *balanced polymorphism*, wherein two or more alleles with comparable fitness values (in a particular environment) are maintained at equilibrium in the population. Thus spontaneous genetic mutation and recombination, along with differential selection of new alleles according to how their phenotypic expression affects inclusive fitness, are crucial mechanisms of the whole evolutionary process. The variation in all inherited human characteristics has resulted from this process, in combination with random changes caused by genetic drift and gene frequency changes caused by migration and intermarriage patterns.

Races as Breeding Populations with Fuzzy Boundaries. Most anthropologists and population geneticists today believe that the preponderance of evidence from both the dating of fossils and the analysis of the geographic distribution of many polymorphic genes in present-day indigenous populations argues that genus *Homo* originated in Africa. Estimates are that our direct distant hominid precursor split off from the great apes some four to six million years ago. The consensus of human paleontologists (as of 1997) accept the following basic scenario of human evolution.

Australopithecus afarensis was a small (about 3'6"), rather ape-like hominid that appears to have been ancestral to all later hominids. It was bipedal, walking more or less upright, and had a cranial capacity of 380 to 520 cm³ (about the same as that of the chimpanzee, but relatively larger for its overall body size). Branching from this species were at least two lineages, one of which led to a new genus, *Homo*.

Homo also had several branches (species). Those that were precursors of modern humans include *Homo habilis*, which lived about 2.5 to 1.5 million years ago. It used tools and even made tools, and had a cranial capacity of 510 to 750 cm³ (about half the size of modern humans). *Homo erectus* lived about 1.5 to 0.3 million years ago and had a cranial capacity of 850 to 1100 cm³ (about three-fourths the size of modern humans). The first hominid whose fossil remains have been found outside Africa, *Homo erectus*, migrated as far as the Middle East, Europe, and Western and Southeastern Asia. No *Homo erectus* remains have been found in Northern Asia, whose cold climate probably was too severe for their survival skills.

Homo sapiens branched off the *Homo erectus* line in Africa at least 100 thousand years ago. During a period from about seventy to ten thousand years ago they spread from Africa to the Middle East, Europe, all of Asia, Australia, and North and South America. To distinguish certain archaic subspecies of *Homo sapiens* (e.g., Neanderthal man) that became extinct during this period from their contemporaries who were anatomically modern humans, the latter are now referred to as *Homo sapiens sapiens* (or *Homo s. sapiens*); it is this line that branched off *Homo erectus* in Africa and spread to every continent during the last 70,000 years. These prehistoric humans survived as foragers living in small groups that frequently migrated in search of food.

GENETIC DISTANCE

As small populations of *Homo s. sapiens* separated and migrated further away from Africa, genetic mutations kept occurring at a constant rate, as occurs in all living creatures. Geographic separation and climatic differences, with their different challenges to survival, provided an increasingly wider basis for populations to become genetically differentiated through natural selection. Genetic mutations that occurred after each geographic separation of a population had taken place were differentially selected in each subpopulation according to the fitness the mutant gene conferred in the respective environments. A great many mutations and a lot of natural selection and genetic drift occurred over the course of the five or six thousand generations that humans were gradually spreading over the globe.

The extent of genetic difference, termed *genetic distance*, between separated populations provides an approximate measure of the amount of time since their separation and of the geographic distance between them. In addition to time and distance, natural geographic hindrances to gene flow (i.e., the interchange of genes between populations), such as mountain ranges, rivers, seas, and deserts, also restrict gene flow between populations. Such relatively isolated groups are termed *breeding populations*, because a much higher frequency of mating occurs between individuals who belong to the same population than occurs between individuals from different populations. (The ratio of the frequencies of *within/between* population matings for two breeding populations determines the degree of their genetic isolation from one another.) Hence the combined effects of geographic separation, genetic mutation, genetic drift, and natural selection for fitness in different environments result in population differences in the frequencies of different alleles at many gene loci.

There are also other causes of relative genetic isolation resulting from language differences as well as from certain social, cultural, or religious sanctions against persons mating outside their own group. These restrictions of gene flow may occur even among populations that occupy the same territory. Over many generations these social forms of genetic isolation produce breeding populations (including certain ethnic groups) that evince relatively slight differences in allele frequencies from other groups living in the same locality.

When two or more populations differ markedly in allele frequencies at a great many gene loci whose phenotypic effects visibly distinguish them by a particular configuration of physical features, these populations are called *subspecies*. Virtually every living species on earth has two or more subspecies. The human species is no exception, but in this case subspecies are called *races*. Like all other subspecies, human races are interfertile breeding populations whose individuals differ on average in distinguishable physical characteristics.

Because all the distinguishable breeding populations of modern humans were derived from the same evolutionary branch of the genus *Homo*, namely, *Homo s. sapiens*, and because breeding populations have relatively permeable (non-biological) boundaries that allow gene flow between them, human races can be considered as genetic "fuzzy sets." That is to say, a race is one of a number of statistically distinguishable groups in which individual membership is not mutually exclusive by any single criterion, and individuals in a given group differ only statistically from one another and from the group's central tendency on each of the many imperfectly correlated genetic characteristics that distinguish between groups as such. The important point is that the *average* difference on all of these characteristics that differ among individuals *within* the group is less than the *average* difference *between* the groups on these genetic characteristics.[4]

What is termed a *cline* results where groups overlap at their fuzzy boundaries in some characteristic, with intermediate gradations of the phenotypic characteristic, often making the classification of many individuals ambiguous or even impossible, unless they are classified by some arbitrary rule that ignores biology. The fact that there are intermediate gradations or blends between racial groups, however, does not contradict the genetic and statistical concept of race. The different colors of a rainbow do not consist of discrete bands but are a perfect continuum, yet we readily distinguish different regions of this continuum as blue, green, yellow, and red, and we effectively classify many things according to these colors. The validity of such distinctions and of the categories based on them obviously need not require that they form perfectly discrete Platonic categories.

It must be emphasized that the biological breeding populations called races can *only* be defined statistically, as populations that differ in the central tendency (or mean) on a large number of different characteristics that are under some degree of genetic control and that are correlated with each other through descent from common ancestors who are relatively recent in the time scale of evolution (i.e., those who lived about ten thousand years ago, at which time all of the continents and most of the major islands of the world were inhabited by relatively isolated breeding populations of *Homo s. sapiens*).

Of course, any rule concerning the *number* of gene loci that must show differences in allele frequencies (or any rule concerning the average *size* of differences in frequency) between different breeding populations for them to be considered *races* is necessarily arbitrary, because the distribution of average absolute differences in allele frequencies in the world's total population is a perfectly continuous variable. Therefore, the number of different categories, or races, into which this continuum can be divided is, in principle, wholly arbitrary, depending on the degree of genetic difference a particular investigator chooses as the criterion for classification or the degree of confidence one is willing to accept with respect to correctly identifying the area of origin of one's ancestors.

Some scientists have embraced all of *Homo sapiens* in as few as two racial categories, while others have claimed as many as seventy. These probably represent the most extreme positions in the "lumper" and "splitter" spectrum. Logically, we could go on splitting up groups of individuals on the basis of their genetic differences until we reach each pair of monozygotic twins, which are genetically identical. But as any pair of MZ twins are always of the same sex, they of course cannot constitute a breeding population. (If hypothetically they could, the average genetic correlation between all of the offspring of any pair of MZ twins would be ⅔; the average genetic correlation between the offspring of individuals paired at random in the total population is ½; the offspring of various forms of genetic relatedness, such as cousins [a preferred match in some parts of the world], falls somewhere between ⅔ and ½.) However, as I will explain shortly, certain multivariate statistical methods can provide objective criteria for deciding on the number and composition of different racial groups that can be reliably determined by the given genetic data or that may be useful for a particular scientific purpose. But one other source of genetic variation between populations must first be explained.

Genetic Drift. In addition to mutation, natural selection, and migration, another means by which breeding population may differ in allele frequencies is through a purely stochastic (that is, random) process termed *genetic drift*. Drift is most consequential during the formation of new populations when their numbers are still quite small. Although drift occurs for all gene loci, Mendelian characters (i.e., phenotypic traits), which are controlled by a single gene locus, are more noticeably affected by drift than are polygenic traits (i.e., those caused by many genes). The reason is purely statistical.

Changes in a population's allele frequencies attributable to genetic drift can be distinguished from changes due to natural selection for two reasons: (1) Many genes are *neutral* in the sense that their allele frequencies have remained unaffected by natural selection, because they neither increase nor decrease fitness; over time they move across the permeable boundaries of different breeding populations. (2) When a small band of individuals emigrates from the breeding population of origin to found a new breeding population, it carries with it only a *random sample* of all of the alleles, including neutral alleles, that existed in the entire original population. That is, the allele frequencies at all gene loci in the migrating band will not exactly match the allele frequencies in the original population. The band of emigrants, and of course all its descendants (who may eventually form a large and stable breeding population), therefore differs genetically from its parent population as the result of a purely random process. This random process is called *founder effect*. It applies to all gene loci. All during the time that genetic drift was occurring, gene mutations steadily continued, and natural selection continued to produce changes in allele frequencies at many loci. Thus the combined effects of genetic drift, mutation, and natural selection ensure that a good many alleles are maintained at different frequencies in various relatively isolated breeding populations. This process did not happen all at once and then cease. It is still going on, but it takes place too slowly to be perceived in the short time span of a few generations.

It should be noted that the phenotypic differences between populations that were due to genetic drift are considerably smaller than the differences in those phenotypic characteristics that were strongly subject to natural selection, especially those traits that reflect adaptations to markedly different climatic conditions, such as darker skin color (thought to have evolved as protection from the tropical sun's rays that can cause skin cancer and to protect against folate decomposition by sunlight), light skin color (to admit more of the ultraviolet rays needed for the skin's formation of vitamin D in northern regions; also because clothing in northern latitudes made dark skin irrelevant selectively and it was lost through random mutation and drift), and globular versus elongated body shape and head shape (better to conserve or dissipate body heat in cold or hot climates, respectively).[5]

Since the genetic drift of neutral genes is a purely random process, and given a fairly constant rate of drift, the differing allele frequencies of many neutral genes in various contemporary populations can be used as a genetic clock to determine the approximate time of their divergence. The same method has been used to estimate the extent of genetic separation, termed *genetic distance*, between populations.

Measurement and Analysis of Genetic Distance Between Groups. Modern genetic technology makes it possible to measure the genetic distance between different populations objectively with considerable precision, or statistical reliability.[6] This measurement is based on a large number of genetic polymorphisms for what are thought to be relatively neutral genes, that is, genes whose allele frequencies therefore differ across populations more because of mutations and genetic drift than because of natural selection. Population allele frequencies can be as low as zero or as high as 1.0 (as there are certain alleles that have large frequencies in some populations but are not found at all in other populations). Neutral genes are preferred in this work because they provide a more stable and accurate evolutionary "clock" than do genes whose phenotypic characters have been subjected to the kinds of diverse external conditions that are the basis for natural selection. Although neutral genes provide a more accurate estimate of populations' divergence times, it should be noted that, by definition, they do not fully reflect the magnitude of genetic differences between populations that are mainly attributable to natural selection.

The technical rationale and formulas for calculating genetic distance are fully explicated elsewhere.[6a] For present purposes, the genetic distance, D, between two groups can be thought of here simply as the average difference in allele frequencies between two populations, with D scaled to range from zero (i.e., no allele differences) to one (i.e., differences in all alleles). One can also think of D as the complement of the correlation coefficient r (i.e., $D = 1 - r$, and $r = 1 - D$). This conversion of D to r is especially useful, because many of the same objective multivariate statistical methods that were originally devised to analyze large correlation matrices (e.g., principal components analysis, factor analysis, hierarchical cluster analysis, multidimensional scaling) can also be used to analyze the total matrix of genetic distances (after they are converted to correlations) between a large number of populations with known allele frequencies based on some large number of genes.

The most comprehensive study of population differences in allele frequencies to date is that of the Stanford University geneticist Luigi Luca Cavalli-Sforza and his co-workers.[6a] Their recent 1,046-page book reporting the detailed results of their study is a major contribution to the science of population genetics. The main analysis was based on blood and tissue specimens obtained from representative samples of forty-two populations, from every continent (and the Pacific islands) in the world. All the individuals in these samples were aboriginal or indigenous to the areas in which they were selected samples; their ancestors have lived in the same geographic area since no later than 1492, a familiar date that generally marks the beginning of extensive worldwide European explorations and the consequent major population movements. In each of the Stanford study's population samples, the allele frequencies of 120 alleles at forty-nine gene loci were determined. Most of these genes determine various blood groups, enzymes, and proteins involved in the immune system, such as human lymphocyte antigens (HLA) and immunoglobulins. These data were then used to calculate the genetic distance (D) between each group and every other group. (DNA sequencing was also used in separate analyses of some groups; it yields finer genetic discrimination between certain groups than can the genetic polymorphisms used in the main analysis.) From the total matrix of $(42 \times 41)/2 = 861$ D values, Cavalli-Sforza et al. constructed a *genetic linkage tree*. The D value between any two groups is represented graphically by the total length of the line that connects the groups in the branching tree. (See Figure 12.1.)

The greatest genetic distance, that is, the largest D, is between the five African groups (listed at the top of Figure 12.1) and all the other groups. The next largest D is between the Australian + New Guinean groups and the remaining other groups; the next largest split is between the South Asians + Pacific Islanders and all the remaining groups, and so on. The clusters at the lowest level (i.e., at far right in Figure 12.1) can also be clustered to show the D values between larger groupings, as in Figure 12.2. Note that these clusters produce much the same picture as the traditional racial classifications that were based on skeletal characteristics and the many visible physical features by which nonspecialists distinguish "races."[7]

It is noteworthy, but perhaps not too surprising, that the grouping of various human populations in terms of invisible genetic polymorphisms for many rela-

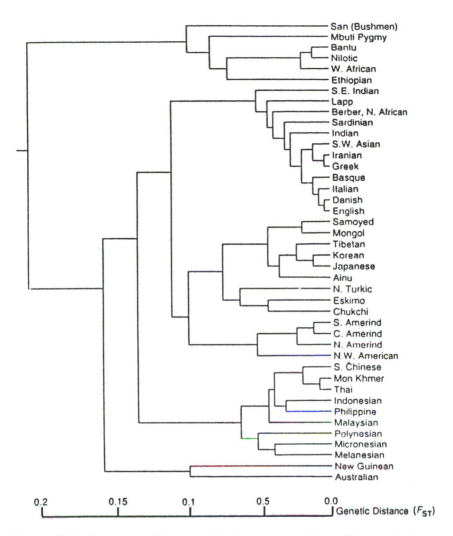

Figure 12.1. The genetic linkage tree for forty-two populations. The genetic distance between any two groups is represented by the total length of the line separating them. (Cavalli-Sforza, L. L., Menozzi, P. & Piazza, A., *The history and geography of human genes*. Copyright © 1994 by Princeton University Press. Reprinted by permission of Princeton University Press.)

tively neutral genes yields results that are highly similar to the classic methods of racial classification based on directly observable anatomical features.

Another notable feature of the Stanford study is that the *geographic* distances between the locations of the groups that are less than 5,000 miles apart are highly correlated ($r \approx .95$) with the respective *genetic* distances between these

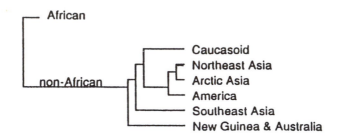

Figure 12.2. A linkage tree based on the average genetic distances between the major clusters among the groups shown in Figure 12.1. (Cavalli-Sforza, L. L., Menozzi, P. & Piazza, A., *The history and geography of human genes.* Copyright © 1994 by Princeton University Press. Reprinted by permission of Princeton University Press.)

groups. This argues that genetic distance provides a fairly good measure of the rate of gene flow between populations that were in place before A.D. 1492.

None of the 120 alleles used in this study has equal frequencies across all of the forty-two populations. This attests to the ubiquity of genetic variation among the world's populations and subpopulations.

All of the modern human population studies based on genetic analysis (including analyses based on DNA markers and sequences) are in close agreement in showing that the earliest, and by far the greatest, genetic divergence within the human species is that between Africans and non-Africans (see Figures 12.1 and 12.2).

Cavalli-Sforza et al. transformed the distance matrix to a correlation matrix consisting of 861 correlation coefficients among the forty-two populations, so they could apply principal components (PC) analysis to their genetic data. (PC analysis is similar to factor analysis; the essential distinction between them is explained in Chapter 3, Note 13.) PC analysis is a wholly objective mathematical procedure. It requires no decisions or judgments on anyone's part and yields identical results for everyone who does the calculations correctly. (Nowadays the calculations are performed by a computer program specifically designed for ·PC analysis.) The important point is that if the various populations were fairly homogeneous in genetic composition, differing no more genetically than could be attributable only to random variation, a PC analysis would not be able to cluster the populations into a number of groups according to their genetic propinquity. In fact, a PC analysis shows that most of the forty-two populations fall very distinctly into the quadrants formed by using the first and second principal components as axes (see Figure 12.3). They form quite widely separated clusters of the various populations that resemble the "classic" major racial groups—Caucasians in the upper right, Negroids in the lower right, Northeast Asians in the upper left, and Southeast Asians (including South Chinese) and Pacific Islanders in the lower left. The first component (which accounts for 27

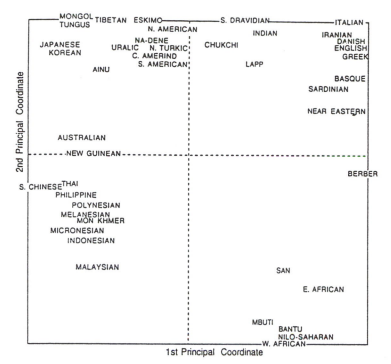

Figure 12.3. A principal components (PC) analysis of the forty-two populations in the Cavalli-Sforza et al. study, showing the bivariate location of each with respect to the coordinates of the first two PCs. The orthogonal dashed lines indicate the mean of each PC. (Cavalli-Sforza, L. L., Menozzi, P. & Piazza, A., *The history and geography of human genes.* Copyright © 1994 by Princeton University Press. Reprinted by permission of Princeton University Press.)

percent of the total genetic variation) corresponds roughly to the geographic migration distances (or therefore time since divergence) from sub-Saharan Africa, reflecting to some extent the differences in allele frequencies that are due to genetic drift. The second component (which accounts for 16 percent of the variation) appears to separate the groups climatically, as the groups' positions on PC2 are quite highly correlated with the degrees latitude of their geographic locations. This suggests that not all of the genes used to determine genetic distances are entirely neutral, but at least some of them differ in allele frequencies to some extent because of natural selection for different climatic conditions. I have tried other objective methods of clustering on the same data (varimax rotation of the principal components, common factor analysis, and hierarchical cluster analysis). All of these types of analysis yield essentially the same picture and identify the same major racial groupings.[8]

African-Americans. The first Africans arrived in North America in 1619 and for more than two centuries thereafter, mostly between 1700 and 1800, the majority of Africans were brought to America as slaves. The end to this involuntary migration came between 1863 and 1865, with the Emancipation Proclamation. Nearly all of the Africans who were enslaved came from sub-Saharan West Africa, specifically the coastal region from Senegal to Angola. The populations in this area are often called West African or North West and Central West Bantu.[9]

Steadily over time, the real, but relatively low frequency of cross-mating between blacks and whites produced an infusion of Caucasoid genes into the black gene pool. As a result, the present-day population of black Americans is genetically different from the African populations from whom they descended. Virtually 100 percent of contemporary black Americans have some Caucasian ancestry. Most of the Caucasian genes in the present-day gene pool of black Americans entered the black gene pool during the period of slavery.[9]

Estimates of the proportion of Caucasoid genes in American blacks are based on a number genetic polymorphisms that have fairly high allele frequencies in the European population but zero or near-zero frequencies in the West African population, or vice versa. For any given allele, the estimated proportion (M) of white European ancestry in American blacks is obtained by the formula $M = (q_B - q_{Af})/(q_W - q_{Af})$, where q_B is the given allele's frequency in the black American population, q_{Af} is its frequency in the African population, and q_W is its frequency in the white European population. The average value of M is obtained over each of twenty or so genes with alleles that are unique either to Africans or to Europeans. The largest studies, which yield estimates with the greatest precision, give mean values of M close to 25 percent, with a standard error of about 3 percent.[10] This is probably the best estimate for the African-American population overall. However, M varies across different regions of the United States, being as low as 4 percent to 10 percent in some southeastern States and spreading out in a fan-shaped gradient toward the north and the west to reach over 40 percent in some northeastern and northwestern states. Among the most typical and precise estimates of M are those for Oakland, California (22.0 percent) and Pittsburgh, Pennsylvania (25.2 percent). This regional variation in M reflects the pattern of selective migration of blacks from the Deep South since the mid-nineteenth century. Gene flow, of course, goes in both directions. In every generation there has been a small percentage of persons who have some African ancestry but whose ancestry is predominantly Caucasian and who permanently "pass as white." The white American gene pool therefore contains some genes that can be traced to Africans who were brought over as slaves (estimated by analyses of genetic polymorphisms to be less than 1 percent).[11]

Genetic Distance and Population Differences in *g*. The preceding discourse on the genetics of populations is germane to any discussion of population differences in *g*. The differences in gene frequencies that originally created different breeding populations largely explain the physical phenotypic differences observed between populations called races. Most of these differences in visible phenotypic characteristics are the result of natural selection working over the course of human evolution. Selection changes gene frequencies in a population by acting directly on any genetically based phenotypic variation that affects Darwinian fitness for a given environment. This applies not only to physical characteristics, but also to behavioral capacities, which are necessarily to some degree a function of underlying physical structures. Structure and function are intimately related, as their evolutionary origins are inseparable.

The behavioral capacities or traits that demonstrate genetic variation can also be viewed from an evolutionary perspective. Given the variation in allele frequencies between populations for virtually every known polymorphic gene, it is exceedingly improbable that populations do not differ in the alleles that affect the structural and functional basis of heritable behavioral traits. The empirical generalization that every polygenic physical characteristic that shows differences between individuals also shows mean differences between populations applies to behavioral as well as physical characteristics. Given the relative genetic distances between the major racial populations, one might expect some behavioral differences between Asians and Europeans to be of lesser magnitude than those between these groups and sub-Saharan Africans.

The behavioral, psychological, or mental characteristics that show the highest g loadings are the most heritable and have the most biological correlates (see Chapter 6) and are therefore the most likely to show genetic population differences. Because of the relative genetic distances, they are also the most likely to show such differences between Africans (including predominantly African descendants) and Caucasians or Asians.

Of the approximately 100,000 human polymorphic genes, about 50,000 are functional in the brain and about 30,000 are unique to brain functions.[12] The brain is by far the structurally and functionally most complex organ in the human body and the greater part of this complexity resides in the neural structures of the cerebral hemispheres, which, in humans, are much larger relative to total brain size than in any other species. A general principle of neural organization states that, within a given species, the size and complexity of a structure reflect the behavioral importance of that structure. The reason, again, is that structure and function have evolved conjointly as an integrated adaptive mechanism. But as there are only some 50,000 genes involved in the brain's development and there are at least 200 billion neurons and trillions of synaptic connections in the brain, it is clear that any single gene must influence some huge number of neurons—not just any neurons selected at random, but complex systems of neurons organized to serve special functions related to behavioral capacities.

It is extremely improbable that the evolution of racial differences since the advent of *Homo sapiens* excluded allelic changes only in those 50,000 genes that are involved with the brain.

Brain size has increased almost threefold during the course of human evolution, from about 500 cm³ in the australopithecenes to about 1,350 cm³ (the present estimated worldwide average) in *Homo sapiens*. Nearly all of this increase in brain volume has occurred in connection with those parts of the cerebral hemispheres associated with cognitive processes, particularly the prefrontal lobes and the posterior association areas, which control foresight, planning, goal-directed behavior, and the integration of sensory information required for higher levels of information processing. The parts of the brain involved in vegetative and sensorimotor functions per se differ much less in size, relative to total brain size, even between humans and chimpanzees than do the parts of the brain that subserve cognitive functions. Moreover, most of the evolutionary increase in brain volume has resulted not from a uniform increase in the total number of cortical neurons per se, but from a much greater increase in the number and complexity of the *interconnections* between neurons, making possible a higher level of interneuronal communication on which complex information processing depends. Although the human brain is three times larger than the chimpanzee brain, it has only 1.25 times as many neurons; the much greater difference is in their degree of arborization, that is, their number of synapses and interconnecting branches.

No other organ system has evolved as rapidly as the brain of *Homo sapiens*, a species that is unprecedented in this respect. Although in hominid evolution there was also an increase in general body size, it was not nearly as great as the increase in brain size. In humans, the correlation between individual differences in brain size and in stature is only about +.20. One minus the square of this relatively small correlation, which is .96, reflects the proportion of the total variance in brain size that *cannot* be accounted for by variation in overall body size. Much of this residual variance in brain size presumably involves cognitive functions.

Bear in mind that, from the standpoint of natural selection, *a larger brain size* (and its corresponding larger head size) *is in many ways decidedly disadvantageous*. A large brain is metabolically very expensive, requiring a high-calorie diet. Though the human brain is less than 2 percent of total body weight, it accounts for some 20 percent of the body's basal metabolic rate (BMR). In other primates, the brain accounts for about 10 percent of the BMR, and for most carnivores, less than 5 percent. A larger head also greatly increases the difficulty of giving birth and incurs much greater risk of perinatal trauma or even fetal death, which are much more frequent in humans than in any other animal species. A larger head also puts a greater strain on the skeletal and muscular support. Further, it increases the chances of being fatally hit by an enemy's club or missile. Despite such disadvantages of larger head size, the human brain, in fact, evolved markedly in size, with its cortical layer accommodating to a relatively lesser increase in head size by becoming highly convoluted in the endocranial vault. In the evolution of the brain, the effects of natural selection had to have reflected the net selective pressures that made an increase in brain size disadvantageous versus those that were advantageous. The advantages obviously outweighed the disadvantages to some degree or the increase in hominid brain size would not have occurred.

The only conceivable advantage to an increase in the size and complexity of the brain is the greater behavioral capacity this would confer. This would include: the integration of sensory information, fine hand-eye coordination, quickness of responding or voluntary response inhibition and delayed reaction depending on the circumstances, perceiving functional relationships between two things when only one or neither is physically present, connecting past and future events, learning from experience, generalization, far transfer of learning, imagery, intentionality and planning, short-term and long-term memory capacity, mentally manipulating objects without need to handle them physically, foresight, problem solving, use of denotative language in vocal communication, as well as all of the information processes that are inferred from performance on what were referred to in Chapter 8 as "elementary cognitive tasks." These basic information processes are involved in coping with the natural exigencies and the contingencies of humans' environment. An increase in these capabilities and their functional efficiency are, in fact, associated with allometric differences in brain size between various species of animals, those with greater brain volume in relation to their overall body size generally displaying more of the kinds of capabilities listed above.[13] The functional efficiency of the various behavioral capabilities that are common to all members of a given species can be enhanced differentially by natural selection, in the same way (though probably not to the same degree) that artificial selection has made dogs of various breeds differ in propensities and trainability for specific types of behavior.[14]

What kinds of environmental pressures encountered by *Homo erectus* and early *Homo sapiens* would have selected for increased size and complexity of the brain? Evolutionists have proposed several plausible scenarios.[15] Generally, a more complex brain would be advantageous in hunting skill, cooperative social interaction, and the development of tool use, followed by the higher-order skill of using tools to make other tools, a capacity possessed by no contemporary species other than *Homo sapiens*.

The environmental forces that contributed to the differentiation of major populations and their gene pools through natural selection were mainly climatic, but parasite avoidance and resistance were also instrumental. *Homo sapiens* evolved in Africa from earlier species of *Homo* that originated there. In migrating from Africa and into Europe and Asia, they encountered highly diverse climates. These migrants, like their parent population that remained in sub-Saharan Africa, were foragers, but they had to forage for sustenance under the highly different conditions of their climatically diverse habitats. Foraging was possible all during the year in the tropical and subtropical climates of equatorial regions, while in the more northern climate of Eurasia the abundance of food that could be obtained by hunting and gathering greatly fluctuated with the seasons. This necessitated the development of more sophisticated techniques for hunting large game, requiring vocal communication and cooperative efforts (e.g., by ambushing, trapping, or corralling), along with foresight in planning ahead for the preservation, storage, and rationing of food in order to survive the severe winter

months when foraging is practically impossible. Extreme seasonal changes and
the cold climate of the northern regions (now inhabited by Mongoloids and
Caucasians) also demanded the ingenuity and skills for constructing more permanent and sturdy dwellings and designing substantial clothing to protect
against the elements. Whatever bodily and behavioral adaptive differences between populations were wrought by the contrasting conditions of the hot climate
of sub-Saharan Africa and the cold seasons of northern Europe and northeast
Asia would have been markedly intensified by the last glaciation, which occurred approximately 30,000 to 10,000 years ago, after *Homo sapiens* had inhabited most of the globe. During this long period of time, large regions of the
Northern Hemisphere were covered by ice and the north Eurasian winters were
far more severe than they have ever been for over 10,000 years.

It seems most plausible, therefore, that behavioral adaptations of a kind that
could be described as complex mental abilities were more crucial for survival
of the populations that migrated to the northern Eurasian regions, and were
therefore under greater selection pressure as fitness characters, than in the populations that remained in tropical or subtropical regions.[15]

Climate has also influenced the evolution of brain size apparently indirectly
through its direct effect on head size, particularly the shape of the skull. Head
size and shape are more related to climate than is the body as a whole. Because
the human brain metabolizes 20 percent of the body's total energy supply, it
generates more heat in relation to its size than any other organ. The resting rate
of energy output of the average European adult male's brain is equal to about
three-fourths that of a 100-watt light bulb. Because temperature changes in the
brain of only four to five degrees Celsius are seriously adverse to the normal
functioning of the brain, it must conserve heat (in a cold environment) or dissipate heat (in a hot environment). Simply in terms of solid geometry, a sphere
contains a larger volume (or cubic capacity) for its total surface area than does
than any other shape. Conversely, a given volume can be contained in a sphere
that has a smaller surface area than can be contained by a nonspherical shape
with the same surface area (an elongated oval shape, for instance). Since heat
radiation takes place at the surface, more spherical shapes will radiate less heat
and conserve more heat for a given volume than a nonspherical shape, and less
spherical shapes will lose more heat by radiation. Applying these geometric
principles to head size and shape, one would predict that natural selection would
favor a smaller head with a less spherical (dolichocephalic) shape because of
its better heat dissipation in hot climates, and would favor a more spherical
(brachycephalic) head to accommodate a larger volume of brain matter with a
smaller surface area because of its better heat conservation in cold climates.
(The dolichocephalic-brachycephalic dimension is related to the head's width:
length ratio, known as the cephalic index.) In brief, a smaller, dolichocephalic
cranium is advantageous for thermoregulation of the brain in a hot climate,
whereas a larger, brachycephalic cranium is advantageous in a cold climate. In

the world's populations, head breadth is correlated about +.8 with cranial capacity; head length is correlated about +.4.

Evidence that the average endocranial volume of various populations is related
to cranial shape and that both phenomena are, in some part, adaptations to
climatic conditions in different regions has been shown by physical anthropologist Kenneth Beals and his co-workers.[16] They amassed measurements of endocranial volume in modern humans from some 20,000 individual crania
collected from every continent, representing 122 ethnically distinguishable populations. They found that the global mean cranial capacity for populations in
hot climates is 1,297 ± 10.5 cm³; for populations in cold and temperate climates
it is 1,386 ± 6.7 cm³, a highly significant ($p < 10^{-4}$) difference of 89 cm³.
Beals also plotted a correlation scatter diagram of the mean cranial capacity in
cm³ of each of 122 global populations as a function of their distance from the
equator (in absolute degrees north or south latitude). The Pearson correlation
between absolute distance from the equator and cranial capacity was $r = +.62$
($p < 10^{-5}$). (The regression equation is: cranial capacity = 2.5 cm³ × |degrees
latitude| + 1257.3 cm³; that is, an average increase of 2.5 cm³ in cranial capacity
for every 1° increase in latitude.) The same analysis applied to populations of
the African-Eurasian landmass showed a cranial capacity × latitude correlation
of +.76 ($p < 10^{-4}$) and a regression slope of 3.1 cm³ increase in cranial capacity
per every 1° of absolute latitude in distance from the equator. The indigenous
populations of North and South American continents show a correlation of +.44
and a regression slope of 1.5; the relationship of cranial capacity to latitude is
less pronounced in the New World than in the Old World, probably because
Homo sapiens inhabited the New World much more recently, having migrated
from Asia to North America only about 15,000 years ago, while *Homo sapiens*
have inhabited the African and Eurasian continents for a much longer period.

RACIAL DIFFERENCES IN HEAD/BRAIN SIZE

Are the climatic factors associated with population differences in cranial capacity, as summarized in the preceding section, reflected in the average cranial
or brain-size measurements of the three broadest contemporary population
groups, generally termed *Caucasoid* (Europeans and their descendants), *Negroid*
(Africans and descendants), and *Mongoloid* (Northeast Asians and descendants)?
A recent comprehensive review[17] summarized the worldwide literature on brain
volume in cm³ as determined from four kinds of measurements: (a) direct measurement of the brain obtained by autopsy, (b) direct measurement of endocranial
volume of the skull, (c) cranial capacity estimated from external head measurements, and (d) cranial capacity estimated from head measurements and corrected
for body size. The aggregation of data obtained by different methods, based on
large samples, from a number of studies tends to average-out the sampling error
and method effects and provides the best overall estimates of the racial group

Table 12.1
Mean Cranial Capacity (cm³) of Three Racial Populations Determined from Four Types of Measurements

Measurement	East Asian	European	African
Autopsy	1351	1356	1223
Endocranial volume	1415	1362	1268
External head measurements	1335	1341	1284
Corrected for body size	1356	1329	1294
Mean	1364	1347	1267

Source: Based on data summarized by Rushton & Ankney, 1996.

means in head/brain size measurements. The results of this aggregation are shown in Table 12.1.

Probably the technically most precise data on brain size for American whites and blacks were obtained from a study of autopsied brains by a team of experts at the Case-Western Reserve University's Medical School in Cleveland, Ohio.[18] It measured the autopsied brains of 811 whites and 450 blacks matched for mean age (sixty years). Subjects with any brain pathology were excluded from the study. The same methods were used to remove, preserve, and weigh the brains for all subjects. The results for each race × sex group are shown in Table 12.2. As the total sample (N =1,261) ranged in age from 25 to 80 years, with a mean of 60 years in both racial groups, it was possible to estimate (by regression) the mean brain weight for each race × sex group at age 25 based on all of the data for each group (shown in the last column of Table 12.2). For the mean height-adjusted brain weight, the W-B difference in standard deviation units is 0.76σ for males, 0.78σ for females. (The actual height-adjusted W-B differences are 102 g for males and 95 g for females.) Neurologically, a difference of 100 g in brain weight corresponds to approximately 550 million cortical neurons.[19] But this average estimate ignores any sex differences in brain size and density of cortical neurons.

Note that for each racial group the sexes differ in brain weight by about 130 g, which is about 30 g more than the average racial difference. This presents a paradox, because while brain size is correlated with IQ, there is little or no sex difference in IQ (even the largest IQ differences that have been claimed by anyone are much smaller than would be predicted by the sex difference in brain size). Attempts to explain this paradox amount to plausible speculations.[20] One thing seems certain: Because of the small correlation (about .20) between brain size and body size, the sex difference in brain volume and weight can be only partially accounted for by the regression of brain size on body size.[21a] The resolution of this paradox may come from the evidence[21b] that females have a higher density of neurons in the posterior temporal cortex, which is the major association area and is involved in higher thought processes. Females have 11

Table 12.2
Mean Brain Weight (in grams) of White and Black Males and Females

Group	N	Height (cm)	Brain Weight	SD of Brain Weight	Brain Weight Ht.Adjusted[a]	Est Brain Weight at Age 25
WM	413	175	1392	130	1392	1570
BM	228	173	1286	138	1290	1375
WF	395	162	1252	125	1252	1339
BF	222	162	1158	119	1158	1291

[a]Brain weight is adjusted by regression based on equating black height with white height.
Source: Data from Ho et al., 1980a, 1980b.

percent more neurons per unit volume than do males, which, if true for the brain as a whole, would more than offset the 10 percent male-female difference in overall brain volume. This sex difference in neuronal packing density is considered a true sexual dimorphism, as are the sex differences in overall body size, skeletal form, the proportion and distribution of body fat, and other secondary sexual characteristics. Sexual dimorphism is seen throughout the animal kingdom and in many species is far more extreme than in *Homo sapiens*. I have not found any investigation of racial differences in neuron density that, as in the case of sex differences, would offset the racial difference in brain weight or volume. Until doubts on this point are empirically resolved, however, interpretations of the behavioral significance of the racial difference in brain size remain tentative. One indication that the race difference in brain weight is not of the same nature as the sex difference is that the allometric ratio of brain weight (in g) to body weight (in kg) is less similar between the racial groups than between the sexes within each racial group.[18c]

Group	Brain Weight / Body Weight (g/kg)	
	Mean	*SD*
WF	22.61	5.29
WM	21.14	4.65
BM	20.65	5.18
BF	19.99	6.22

Also, we must take into account the fact that, on average, about 30 percent of total adult female body weight is fat, as compared to 15 percent for males. Because body fat is much less innervated than muscle tissue, brain size is more highly correlated with fat-free body weight than with total body weight. Statistically controlling for fat-free body weight (instead of total body weight) has been found to reduce the sex difference in head circumference by about 77 percent, or about three times as much as controlling for total body weight.[22] Because head circumference is an imperfect proxy for brain size, the percentage reduction of the sex difference in directly measured brain volume (or weight) that would be achieved by controlling for fat-free weight will be uncertain until such studies are performed. Measuring fat-free body weight should become routine in the conduct of brain-size studies based on autopsied brains or on *in vivo* brain measurements obtained by imaging techniques.

The white-black difference in head/brain size is significant in neonates (about 0.4σ difference in head circumference) and within each racial group head size at birth is correlated (about $+.13$) with IQ at age seven years, when the average within-groups correlation with IQ is $+.21$.[23a] A retrospective study of two groups of seven-year-old children, those with IQ $<$ 80 and those with IQ $>$ 120 were found to have differed by 0.5σ in head circumference measured at one year of age.[23b] Also, small head size measured at eight months has been found to interact most unfavorably with birth weight; infants with very low birth weight who had subnormal head size at eight months had an average IQ about nine points (0.6σ) lower at school age than did infants of comparable birth weight but with normal head size (corrected for prematurity).[23c]

I have not found an estimate of the heritability of directly measured brain size. However, the heritability, h^2, of cranial capacity (estimated by formula from head length, width, and circumference) based on Falconer's formula [$h^2 = 2(r_{MZ} - r_{DZ})$] applied to 107 MZ twin pairs and 129 DZ twin pairs ranged widely for different race $\times$ sex subgroups, for a within-subgroup average of .19. When the estimates of cranial capacity were adjusted for age, stature, and weight, the h^2 values averaged .53.[24a] The narrow h^2 (i.e., the proportion of the total variance attributable only to additive genetic effects) of various head measurements determined in a Caucasoid sample (Bulgarians) by the midparent $\times$ offspring correlation (all offspring over fifteen years of age) were: length .37, height .33, breadth .46, circumference .52.[24b] All of these estimates of the heritability of cranial size [24c] indicate a considerable amount of nongenetic (or environmental) variance, at least as much as for IQ. Moreover, much more of the nongenetic variance is within-families (i.e., unshared among siblings reared together) than is between-families (shared) variance. This implies that shared environmental effects, such as those associated with parents' education, occupation, and general socioeconomic level, are not the major source of variance in cranial capacity as estimated from head measurements. Also, what little evidence we have suggests that the total environmental variance in head measurements is greater for blacks than for whites. (The nature of these environmental influences is discussed later in this chapter.)

Implications of Brain Size for IQ Differences.[25] Chapter 6 reviewed the major evidence showing that head measurements and brain size itself are significantly correlated with IQ. The only available correlations for blacks are based on head length, width, and circumference (and cranial capacity estimated by formula from these measurements); as yet there are no reported correlations between IQ and directly measured brain size for blacks. However, the head measurements are significantly correlated with IQ for age-matched whites and

Table 12.3
Head Circumference (HC) (in cm) of White (W) and Black (B) Groups Matched on IQ at the White Mean IQ and the Black Mean IQ at Two Ages

| | Age 4 Matched on: | | | | Age 7 Matched on: | | | |
| | W Mean IQ | | B Mean IQ | | W Mean IQ | | B Mean IQ | |
Group	N	HC	N	HC	N	HC	N	HC
White males	322	50.59	206	50.34	411	51.93	226	51.67
Black males	216	50.35	335	50.07	221	51.60	438	51.36
WM–BM		0.24		0.27		0.33		0.31
White females	321	49.57	146	49.29	416	51.03	243	50.73
Black females	293	49.94	408	49.81	251	51.34	547	51.04
WF–BF		−0.37		−0.52		−0.31		−0.31
W–B		−0.065		−0.125		0.010		0.000

Note: Both head circumference and IQ were adjusted for age, height, and weight.

blacks, both on raw measurements and on measurements corrected for height and weight, although the correlations are somewhat lower in blacks. Longitudinal data show that the head circumference $\times$ IQ correlation significantly increases between ages 4 and 7, and cross-sectional data indicate that the correlation gradually increases up to 15 years of age, by which time the average growth curves for head size and brain size have reached asymptote.

It is especially important to note that for both racial groups the head size $\times$ IQ correlation exists *within*-families as well as *between*-families, indicating an intrinsic, or functional, relationship, as explained in Chapter 6. Equally important is the fact that within each sex, whites and blacks share precisely one and the same regression line for the regression of head size on IQ. When blacks and whites are perfectly matched for true-score IQ (i.e., IQ corrected for measurement error), either at the black mean or at the white mean, the overall average W-B difference in head circumference is virtually nil, as shown in Table 12.3.

Taken together, these findings suggest that head size and IQ are similarly related to IQ for both blacks and whites. Although matching blacks and whites for IQ virtually eliminates the average difference in head size, matching the groups on head size does not equalize their IQs. This is what we in fact should expect if brain size is only one of a number of brain factors involved in IQ. When matched on IQ, the groups are thereby also equal on at least one of these brain factors, in this case, size. But when black and white groups are matched on head or brain size, they still differ in IQ, though to a lesser degree than in unmatched or representative samples of each population.

The black-white difference in head/brain size is also related to Spearman's hypothesis. A study in which head measurements were correlated (within racial groups) with each of seventeen diverse psychometric tests showed that the column vector of seventeen correlations was rank-order correlated $+.64$ ($p < .01$) with the corresponding vector composed of each test's *g* loading (within groups). In other words, a test's *g* loading significantly predicts the degree to which that test is correlated with head/brain size. We would also predict from Spearman's hypothesis that the degree to which each test was correlated with the head measurements should correlate with the magnitude of the W-B difference on each test. In fact, the column vector of test $\times$ head-size correlations and the vector of standardized mean W-B differences on each of the tests correlate $+.51$ ($p < .05$).

From the available empirical evidence, we can roughly estimate the fraction of the mean IQ difference between the black and white populations that could be attributed to the average difference in brain size. As noted in Chapter 6, direct measurements of *in vivo* brain size obtained by magnetic resonance imaging (MRI) show an average correlation with IQ of about $+.40$ in several studies based on white samples. Given the reasonable assumption that this correlation is the same for blacks, statistical regression would predict that an IQ difference equivalent to 1σ would be reduced by 0.4σ, leaving a difference of only 0.6σ, for black and white groups matched on brain size. This is a sizable effect. As the best estimate of the W-B mean IQ difference in the population is equivalent to 1.1σ or 16 IQ points, then $0.40 \times 16 \approx 6$ IQ points of the black-white IQ difference would be accounted for by differences in brain size. (Slightly more than 0.4σ would predictably be accounted for if a hypothetically pure measure of *g* could be used.) Only MRI studies of brain size in representative samples of each population will allow us to improve this estimate.

Other evidence of a systematic relationship between racial differences in cranial capacity and IQ comes from an "ecological" correlation, which is commonly used in epidemiological research. It is simply the Pearson *r* between the *means* of three or more defined groups, which disregards individual variation within the groups.[26] Referring back to Table 12.1, I have plotted the median IQ of each of the three populations as a function of the overall mean cranial capacity of each population. The median IQ is the median value of all of the mean values of IQ reported in the world literature for Mongoloid, Caucasoid, and Negroid populations. (The source of the cranial capacity means for each group was explained in connection with Table 12.1.) The result of this plot is shown in Figure 12.4. The regression of median IQ on mean cranial capacity is almost perfectly linear, with a Pearson $r = +.998$. Unless the data points in Figure 12.4 are themselves highly questionable, the near-perfect linearity of the regression indicates that IQ can be regarded as a true interval scale. No mathematical transformation of the IQ scale would have yielded a higher correlation. Thus it appears that the central tendency of IQ for different populations is quite accurately predicted by the central tendency of each population's cranial capacity.

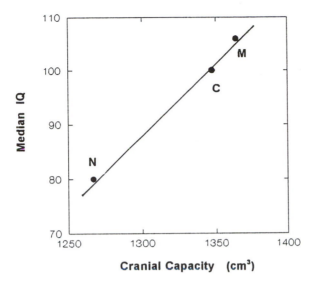

Figure 12.4. Median IQ of three populations (Mongoloid, Caucasoid, and Negroid) plotted as a function of the mean cranial capacity in each population. (Regression: IQ = .262 × cranial capacity − 252.6; r = .998.)

POPULATION DIFFERENCES IN g: THE DEFAULT HYPOTHESIS

Consider the following items of evidence: the many biological correlates of g; the fact that among all of the psychometric factors in the domain of cognitive abilities the g factor accounts for the largest part of the mean difference between blacks and whites; the evolutionary history of *Homo sapiens* and the quantitative differentiation of human populations in allele frequencies for many characteristics, including brain size, largely through adaptive selection for fitness in highly varied climates and habitats; the brain evolved more rapidly than any other organ; half of humans' polymorphic genes affect brain development; the primary evolutionary differentiation and largest genetic distance between human populations is that between the African populations and all others; the intrinsic positive correlation between brain size and measures of g; the positive mean white-black difference in brain size; the positive correlation between the variable heritability of individual differences in various measures of cognitive abilities and the variable magnitudes of their g loadings. All these phenomena, when viewed together, provide the basis for what I shall call the *default hypothesis* concerning the nature of population or racial differences in g.

Although we are concerned here with *variation* between populations, it is also important to keep in mind that, from an evolutionary perspective, it is most unlikely that there are intraspecies differences in the basic structural design and operating principles of the brain. The main structural and functional units of the brain found in any one normal human being should be validly generalizable to all other normal humans. That is to say, the *processes* by which the brain perceives, learns, reasons, remembers, and the like are the same for everyone, as are the essential structures and functions of every organ system in the entire body. Individual differences and population differences in normal brain processes exist at a different level, superimposed, as it were, over and above the brain's common structures and operating principles.

The default hypothesis states that human *individual* differences and *population* differences in heritable behavioral capacities, as products of the evolutionary process in the distant past, are essentially composed of the same stuff, so to speak, controlled by differences in allele frequencies, and that differences in allele frequencies *between* populations exist for all heritable characteristics, physical or behavioral, in which we find individual differences *within* populations.

With respect to the brain and its heritable behavioral correlates, the default hypothesis holds that individual differences and population differences do not result from differences in the brain's basic structural operating mechanisms per se, but result entirely from other aspects of cerebral physiology that modify the sensitivity, efficiency, and effectiveness of the basic information processes that mediate the individual's responses to certain aspects of the environment.[27] A crude analogy would be differences in the operating efficiency (e.g., miles per gallon, horsepower, maximum speed) of different makes of automobiles, all powered by internal combustion engines (hence the same operating mechanisms) but differing in, say, the number of cylinders, their cubic capacity, and the octane rating of the gasoline they are using. Electric motor cars and steam-engine cars (analogous to different species or genera) would have such distinctively different operating mechanisms that their differences in performance would call for quite different explanations.

In brief, the default hypothesis states that the proximal causes of both individual differences and population differences in heritable psychological traits are essentially the same, and are continuous variables. The population differences reflect differences in allele frequencies of the same genes that cause individual differences. Population differences also reflect environmental effects, as do individual differences, and these may differ in frequency between populations, as do allele frequencies.

In research on population differences in mean levels of *g*, I think that the default hypothesis should be viewed as the true "null" hypothesis, that is, the initial hypothesis that must be disproved. The conventional null hypothesis of inferential statistics (i.e., no differences between populations) is so improbable in light of evolutionary knowledge as to be scientifically inappropriate for the study of population differences in any traits that show individual differences. The real question is not whether population differences exist for a given polygenic trait, but rather the *direction* and *magnitude* of the difference.

The question of *direction* of a difference brings up another aspect of the default hypothesis, namely, that it is rare in nature for genotypes and phenotypes of adaptive traits to be negatively correlated. It is exceedingly improbable that racial populations, which are known to differ, on average, in a host of genetically conditioned physical characteristics, would not differ in any of the brain characteristics associated with cognitive abilities, when half of all segregating genes in the human genome are involved with the brain. It is equally improbable that heritable variation among individuals in polygenic adaptive traits, such as g, would not show nontrivial differences between populations, which are aggregations of individuals. Again, from a scientific standpoint, the only real questions about population differences concern their *direction*, their *magnitude*, and their causal mechanism(s). One may also be interested in the social significance of the phenotypic differences. Research will be most productively focused not on whether or not genes are involved in population differences, but in discovering the relative effects of genetic and environmental causes of differences and the nature of these causes, so they can be better understood and perhaps influenced.

The rest of this chapter deals only with the scientific aspect of the default hypothesis. (For a discussion of its social significance, see Chapter 14.) Since far more empirical research relevant to the examination of the default hypothesis with respect to g has been done on the black-white difference, particularly within the United States, than on any other populations, I will focus exclusively on the causal basis of the mean black-white difference in the level of g.

HERITABILITY OF IQ WITHIN GROUPS AND BETWEEN GROUPS

One of the aims of science is to comprehend as wide a range of phenomena as possible within a single framework, using the fewest possible mechanisms with the fewest assumptions and ad hoc hypotheses. With respect to IQ, the default hypothesis relating individual differences and population differences is consistent with this aim, as it encompasses the explanation of both within-group (WG) and between-group (BG) differences as having the same causal sources of variance. The default hypothesis that the BG and WG differences are homogeneous in their causal factors implies that a phenotypic difference of PD between two population groups in mean level of IQ results from the same causal effects as does any difference between individuals (within either of the two populations) whose IQs differ by P_D (i.e., the phenotypic difference). In either case, PD is the joint result of both genetic (G) and environmental (E) effects. In terms of the default hypothesis, the effects of genotype $\times$ environment covariance are the same between populations as within populations. The same is hypothesized for genotype $\times$ environment interaction, although studies have found it contributes negligibly to within-population variance in g.

It is possible for a particular allele to be present in one population but absent in another, or for alleles at certain loci to be turned on in some environments and turned off in others, or to be regulated differently in different environments. These conditions would constitute exceptions to the default hypothesis. But without empirical evidence of these conditions with respect to population differences in g, which is a highly polygenic trait in which most of the variance within (and probably between) populations is attributable to quantitative differences in allele frequencies at many loci, initial investigation is best directed at testing the default hypothesis.

In terms of the black-white IQ difference, the default hypothesis means that the question of why (on average) two whites differ by amount PD in IQ, or two blacks differ by amount P_D, or a black and a white differ by amount PD can all be answered in the same terms. There is no need to invoke any special "racial" factor, either genetic or cultural.

The countervailing *dual* hypothesis contends that: (1) within-group individual differences (WG), on the one hand, and between-group mean differences (BG), on the other, have *different, independent* causes; and (2) there is no relationship between the sources of WG differences and of BG differences. In this view, the high heritability of individual differences in g *within* groups tells us nothing about the heritability (if any) of g *between* groups.

The empirical fact that there is a large genetic component in WG individual differences in g is so well established by now (see Chapter 7) that, with rare exceptions, it is no longer challenged by advocates for the dual hypothesis. The defining tenet of the dual hypothesis, at least as it applies to the phenotypic black-white IQ difference, is that there is no genetic component in the mean BG difference; that is, the causes of the observed BG difference in IQ are entirely environmental. These environmental sources may include nutrition and other biological conditions, as well as socioeconomic, attitudinal, or cultural group differences, to name the most frequently hypothesized causal factors. (Psychometric test bias, as such, has been largely ruled out; see Chapter 11, pp. 360–67.)

Within-Group Heritability of IQ in Black and in White Groups. Before contrasting the dual and the default hypotheses in terms of their formal implications and their consistency with empirical findings, we need to understand what is, and is not, known about the heritability of individual differences in IQ *within* each population.

The many studies of IQ heritability based on white samples are summarized in Chapter 7. They give estimates that range mostly between .40 and .60 for children and adolescents, and between .60 and .80 for adults.

The few studies of IQ heritability in black samples have all been performed in conjunction with age-matched white samples, so that group comparisons would be based on the same tests administered under the same conditions. Only two such studies based on large samples (total Ns of about 300 and 700) of black and white twins of school age have been reported.[28a] The data of these studies do not support rejection of the null hypothesis of no black-white difference in the heritability coefficients for IQ. Nor do these studies show any evidence of a statistically significant racial difference between the magnitudes of the correlations for either MZ or DZ twins. But the sample sizes in these studies, though large, are not large enough to yield statistical significance for real, though small, group differences. The small differences between the black and white twin correlations observed in these studies are, however, consistent with the black-white differences in the correlations between full siblings found in a study[28b] of all of the school-age sibling pairs in the total black and white populations of the seventeen elementary schools of Berkeley, California. The average sibling correlations for IQ in that study were +.38 for blacks and +.40 for whites. (For height, the respective age-corrected correlations were .45 and .42.) Because the samples totaled more than 1,500 sibling pairs, even differences as small as .02 are statistically significant. If the heritability of IQ, calculated from twin data, were very different in the black and white populations, we would expect the difference to show up in the sibling correlations as well.[28c] The fact that sibling correlations based on such large samples differ so little between blacks and whites suggests that the black-white difference in IQ heritability is so small that rejection of the null hypothesis of no W-B difference in IQ heritability would require enormous samples of black and white MZ and DZ twins— far more than any study has yet attempted or is ever likely to attempt. Such a small difference, even if it were statistically reliable, would be of no theoretical or practical importance. On the basis of the existing evidence, therefore, it is reasonable to conclude that the difference between the U.S. black and white populations in the proportion of within-group variance in IQ attributable to genetic factors (that is, the heritability of IQ) is probably too small to be detectable.

The Relationship of Between-Group to Within-Group Heritability. The mantra invoked to ward off any unpalatable implications of the fact that IQ has substantially equal heritability in both the black and the white populations is that "heritability *within* groups does not imply (or prove, or generalize to) heritability *between* groups." Arguing that the fact that there is genetic variance in individual differences *within* groups gives no warrant to generalize to differences *between* groups is, of course, formally equivalent to saying exactly the same thing about environmental variance, which is the complement of the within-groups heritability (i.e., $1 - h^2$). But a little analysis is required to understand the peculiar nature of the relationship between within-group heritability (WGH) and between-group heritability (BGH).

To say there is *no* relationship of any kind between WGH and BGH is wrong. They are mathematically related according to the following equation[29]:

$$BGH = WGH \frac{r_g(1 - r_p)}{r_p(1 - r_g)}$$

where

BGH is the between-group heritability.

WGH is the within-group heritability.

r_g is the genetic intraclass correlation within groups, i.e., r_g = (genetic variance between groups) ÷ (genetic variance between groups + genetic variance within groups).

r_p is the phenotypic intraclass correlation within groups; it is equal to the squared point-biserial correlation between individuals' nominal group membership (e.g., black or white, quantitized as 0 or 1) and the quantitative variable of interest (e.g., IQ).

This is termed the *formal* relationship between WGH and BGH. Although there is no argument about the mathematical correctness of this formulation, it is not empirically applicable, because a single equation containing two unknowns (i.e., BGH and r_g), cannot be solved. (It is also clear mathematically that the formula must assume that WGH is greater than zero and that r_g is less than unity.) The value of r_p can easily be obtained empirically. (For example, if two groups each have the same standard deviation on a given variable and the group means differ by one such standard deviation, the value of r_p = .20). If we knew the value of r_g we could solve the equation for BGH (or vice versa). (If the between-groups difference were entirely nongenetic, as strict environmentalists maintain, then of course r_g would be zero.) But we know neither r_g nor BGH, so the formula is empirically useless.[30]

However, this formula does indicate that for any hypothesized value of r_g greater than zero, BGH is a linearly increasing function of WGH. As I will point out, the hypothesized relationship between WGH and BGH can suggest some useful conjectures and empirical analyses. The formal relationship between WGH and BGH makes no assumptions about the sources of either the genetic or the environmental variance in BGH and WGH, or whether BGH and WGH are qualitatively the same or different in this respect. The default hypothesis, however, posits that the genetic and the environmental factors that cause the between-groups difference exist within each group (but not necessarily in equal degrees). The opposing dual hypothesis is that the environmental factors that cause variance between groups are different not just in degree, but in kind, from the environmental factors that cause individual differences within a group. This conjecture raises problems that I will examine shortly.

The between-groups (BG) versus within-groups (WG) problem can be visualized as shown in Figure 12.5. Assume a population is composed of two equal-sized subpopulations, A and B, and assume that on some characteristic (e.g., IQ) the phenotypic means of these two subpopulations differ, that is, A − B = P_D. (Sampling error and measurement error are assumed to be zero in this didactic diagram.) The measurement of the phenotypic characteristic (P) is standardized in the total population, so its population standard deviation is 1σ and the total variance is the square of the standard deviation, $1\sigma^2$. Any variance can be visualized as the area of a square. The square in Figure 12.5 represents the total phenotypic variance ($1\sigma^2$) of the whole population, and its square root is the standard deviation (1σ) of the phenotypic measurements. The total variance (area of the square) is partitioned horizontally into the variance between groups

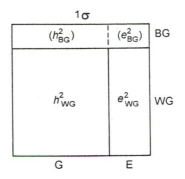

Figure 12.5. The total phenotypic variance (standardized to $1\sigma^2$) shown as a square partitioned vertically into genetic (G) and environmental (E) components and horizontally into between-groups (BG) and within-groups (WG) components. The empirical uncertainty of the division of the BG variance into E and G components is indicated by the dotted line, the position of which as shown here is the representation consistent with the strong form of the default hypothesis. In the weak form of the hypothesis it could be shifted either to the left or to the right.

(BG) and the variance within groups (WG). The total variance is partitioned vertically into the genetic (G) variance, i.e., heritability (h^2) and the environmental (E) variance, i.e., environmentality (e^2). At present, the only variables we are able to determine empirically are the total phenotypic variance, σ_P^2, and the within-group genetic and environmental variances, h^2_{WG}, and e^2_{WG}. The between-group variables, h^2_{BG} and e^2_{BG}, are undetermined (and so are shown in parentheses). As the genetic and environmental proportions of the BG variance have not been empirically determined, they are shown separated by a dotted line in Figure 12.5. This dotted line could move either to the left or to the right, based on new empirical evidence. Its approximate position is the bone of contention between the advocates of the default hypothesis and those of the conventional null hypothesis.

Extreme "environmentalists" argue that both $h^2_{WG} = 0$ and $h^2_{BG} = 0$, leaving environmental agents as the source of all observed phenotypic variance. (Hardly anyone now holds this position with respect to IQ.) A much more common position nowadays is to accept the empirically established WG values, but maintain that the BG variance is all environmental. "Agnostics" would say (correctly) that h^2_{BG} is not empirically known, and some might add that, though unknown, it is plausibly greater than zero.

The strong form of the default hypothesis is represented in Figure 12.5 by the dotted-line extension of the solid vertical line, thus partitioning both the WG and BG variances into the same proportions of genetic and environmental variance. A "relaxed" form of the default hypothesis still posits $h^2_{BG} > 0$, but allows h^2_{BG} to differ from h^2_{WG}. In general, this is closer to reality than is the strong form of the default hypothesis. In both forms of the default hypothesis

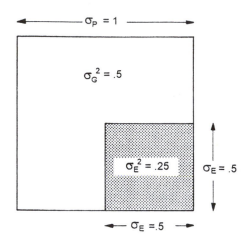

Figure 12.6. The total standardized phenotypic variance (σ_P^2), represented as the area of a square, partitioned into its genetic (G) and environmental (E) variance components, σ_G^2 and σ_E^2, which are shown here as equal to .75 and .25, respectively.

WG variance and BG variance are attributable to the same causal factors, although they may differ in degree. The purpose of hypothesizing some fairly precise value for h^2_{BG} is not because one necessarily thinks it is true, or wants to "sell" it to someone, but rather because scientific knowledge advances by the process that Karl Popper described as "conjectures and refutations"—a strong hypothesis (or conjecture) can permit certain possibly testable deductions or inferences, and can be decisively refuted only if formulated precisely and preferably quantitatively. Any hypothesis is merely the temporary scaffolding that assists in discovering new facts about nature. It helps us to formulate questions precisely and further focuses investigative efforts on research that will yield diacritical results. Beyond this purpose, a hypothesis has no other use. It is not a subject for advocacy.

A clear quantitative statement of the default hypothesis depends upon understanding some important technical points about variance and its relation to linear measurement. The large square in Figure 12.6 represents the total variance (σ^2) of a standardized phenotypic variable (P), with a standard deviation $\sigma_P = 1$. The area of the large square (total phenotypic variance) is partitioned into its genetic and environmental components, corresponding to a heritability of .75 (which makes it easy to visualize). The genetic variance σ_G^2 in Figure 12.6 (unshaded area) is equal to .75, leaving the environmental component σ_E^2 (shaded area) equal to .25. Since the variance of each effect is shown in the diagram as an area, the square root of the area represents the standard deviation of that effect. The linear distances or differences between points on a scaled variable are shown as line segments scaled in standard deviation units, not in variance units. Thus the line segments that form the area in the lower right of the shaded square in Figure 12.6 are each equal to $\sqrt{.25}$ or .5 (in standard deviation units). The linear distances represented by the environmental variance $\sigma w_E^2 = .25$ is $\sqrt{.25} = .50$; and the linear distance represented by the genetic variance $\sigma_G^2 = .75$ is $\sqrt{.75} = .866$. Notice that these two linear measurements (.866 + .500 = 1.366) do not add up to the length of the side of the total square, which is 1. That is, *standard deviation units are not additive.* Before the sum of the standard deviations of two or more component elements can represent the standard deviation of the total of the component elements, you must first take the square root of the sum of the squared standard deviations. Now, with these points in mind, refer back to the values for the standard deviations (σ_G and σ_E) in Figure 12.6. Note that

$$\sqrt{(.866)^2 + (.500)2} = \sqrt{.75 + .25} = \sqrt{1} = 1.$$

We can now ask, "How many units of environmental variance (σ_E^2) are needed to add up to the total phenotypic variance (σ_P^2)? The answer is $\sigma_P^2/\sigma_E^2 = 1/.25 = 4$. This ratio is in variance (i.e., σ^2) units. To express it in linear terms, it has to be converted into standard deviation units, that is, $\sigma_P/\sigma_E = 1/.50 = 2$.

Suppose we obtain IQ scores for all members of two equal-size groups called A and B. Further assume that within each group the IQs have a normal distribution,[31] and the mean of group A is greater than the mean of group B. To keep the math simple, let the IQ scores have perfect reliability, let the standard deviation of the scores be the same in both groups (i.e., $\sigma_A = \sigma_B = 1\sigma$), and let the mean phenotypic difference, P_D, be equal to the average within-group phenotypic standard deviation (i.e., $P_D = A - B = 1\sigma_P$). All of this is depicted by the two overlapping curves in the top half of Figure 12.7.

Now consider the hypothesis that the *between-group heritability* (BGH) is zero and that therefore the cause of the A-B difference is purely environmental. Assume that the *within-group* heritability (WGH) is the same in each group, say, $WGH_A = WGH_B = .75$. Now, if we remove the variance attributable to *genetic* factors (WGH) from the total variance of each group's scores, the remainder (1 − .75 = .25) gives us the proportion of within-group variance attributable to purely *environmental* factors (i.e., 1 − WGH = WGE.) If both the genetic and environmental effects on test scores are normally distributed within each group, the resulting curves after the genetic variance has been removed from each represent the distribution of *environmental* effects on test scores. Note that this does not refer to variation in the environment per se, but rather to the *effects* of environmental variation on the phenotypes (i.e., IQ scores, in this case.) The standard deviation of this distribution of environmental effects (termed σ_E) provides a unit of measurement for environmental effects. (*Note*: It is important to keep in mind throughout the following discussion that σ_E is scaled in terms of the average environmental effect on test scores *within* groups. The mean effect of environmental differences *between* groups can then be expressed on this scale of within-group environmental effects. Hence a mean phe-

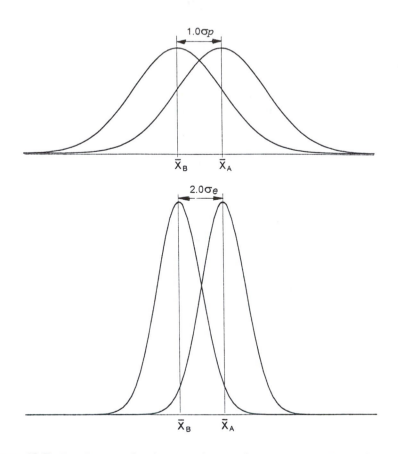

Figure 12.7. *Top*: Two overlapping normal curves for groups A and B showing a mean phenotypic difference $\overline{X}_A - \overline{X}_B = 1.0 \; \sigma_P$. *Bottom*: The two distributions after all of the genetic variance ($h^2 = .75$) has been removed from each one, leaving only the within-group nongenetic, or environmental, variance ($e^2 = .25$). Then, in units of the average within-group σ_E, the group means differ by $2\sigma_E$, showing rather little overlap of the two distributions. The total area (which represents the total frequency) under each curve is the same (in both the upper and lower panels); the upper and lower curves differ only in their degree of dispersion, here measured by the standard deviation (σ_P or σ_E).

notypic difference between groups expressed in terms of the mean within-groups standard deviation of environment effects [σ_E] may be greater than $1\sigma_E$.)

The distribution of just the total environmental effects (assuming WGH = .75) is shown in the two curves in the bottom half of Figure 12.7. The phenotypic difference between the group means is kept constant at $1\sigma_P$, but on the scale of *environmental effects* (measured in environmental standard deviation units, σ_E), the mean environmental effects for groups A and B differ by the

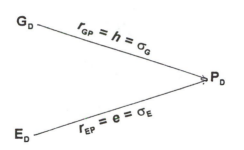

Figure 12.8. Path diagram in which the arrows show the causal relationship of genetic and environmental differences to phenotypic differences.

ratio $\sigma_P/\sigma_E = 1/.50 = 2\sigma_E$, as shown in the lower half of Figure 12.7. What this means is that for two groups to differ phenotypically by $1\sigma_P$ when WGH = .75 and BGH = 0, the two groups would have to differ by $2\sigma_E$ on the scale of environmental effects. This is analogous to two groups in which each member of one group has a monozygotic twin in the other group, thus making the distribution of genotypes exactly the same in both groups. For the test score distributions of these two genotypically matched groups to differ by $1\sigma_P$, the groups would have to differ by $2\sigma_E$ on the scale of environmental effects (assuming WGH = .75).

The hypothetical decomposition of a mean phenotypic difference, P_D, between two groups as expressed in terms of the simplest model is that the phenotypic difference between the groups is completely determined by their genetic difference and their environmental difference, or $P_D = G_D + E_D$. These variables are related quantitatively by the simple path model shown in Figure 12.8. The arrows represent the direction of causation; each arrow is labeled with the respective regression coefficients (also called path coefficients), h and e, between the variables, which, when $r_{GE} = 0$ and the variables P, G, and E are standardized, are mathematically equivalent to the respective correlation coefficients, r_{GP} and r_{EP}, and to the standard deviations of the genetic and environmental effects, σ_G and σ_E. This is the simplest model and assumes independent effects of G_D and E_D; in other words, there is no correlation between G_D and E_D. In reality, of course, there could be a causal path from G_D to E_D (with a correlation r_{GE}), but this would not alter the essential point of the present argument. We see that the phenotypic difference can be represented as a weighted sum of the genetic and the environmental effects on P_D, the weights being h and e. Since these values are equivalent to standard deviations, they cannot be summed (as previously explained). The phenotypic difference must be written as $P_D = \sqrt{h^2 P_D{}^2 + e^2 P_D{}^2}$. (Since P_D is standardized, with unit variance, we have simply $P_D = \sqrt{h^2 + e^2}$.) (See Note 32.)

A phenotypic difference between the means of two groups can be expressed in units of the standard deviation of the average within-groups environmental effect, which is $\sigma_E = \sqrt{(1 - BGH)/(1 - WGH)}$, where BGH is the between-groups heritability and WGH is the within-groups heritability. Thus the phenotypic difference between the means of the two curves in the lower half of Figure 12.7 (which represent the distribution of only environmental effects in each group) expressed in σ_E units is $\sqrt{(1 - 0)/(1 - .75)} = \sqrt{1/.25} = 2\sigma_E$. That is, the means of the two environmental-effect curves differ by two standard deviations $(2\sigma_E)$. The body of empirical evidence shows that an environmental effect on IQ this large would predictably occur only rarely in pairs of monozygotic twins reared apart (whose IQs are correlated .75) except for random errors of measurement. The difference in IQ attributable solely to nongenetic differences between random pairs of individuals in a population in which h^2 is .75 is about the same as for MZ twins reared apart. On an IQ scale with $\sigma = 15$, a difference of $2\sigma_E$ is approximately equal to 30 IQ points (i.e., 2×15). But the largest IQ difference between MZ twins reared apart reported in the literature is 1.5σ, or 23 IQ points.[33] Further, the average absolute difference in IQ (assuming a perfectly normal distribution of IQ) between all random pairs of persons in the population (who differ *both* in *g* and in E) would be 1.1284σ, or approximately 17 IQ points. (Mathematically, the mean of the absolute differences between normal deviates is $2\sigma/\sqrt{\pi} = 1.1284\sigma$.)

Now consider again the two groups in the upper half of Figure 12.7, called A and B. They differ in their mean test scores, with a phenotypic difference A $- B = +1\sigma_P$ and have a within-group environmental effect difference of $2\sigma_E$. If we hypothesize that the difference between the phenotypic means is entirely *non*genetic (i.e., environmental), then the phenotypic difference of $1\sigma_P$ must be equal to $2\sigma_E$.

By the same reasoning, we can determine the size of the environmental effect σ_E that is required to produce a phenotypic difference of $1\sigma_P$ given any values of the within-groups heritability (WGH) and the between-groups heritability (BGH). For a phenotypic difference of $1\sigma_P$, Table 12.4(A) shows the expected values (in σ_E units) of the environmental effects for various values of the within-groups heritability (WGH) and the between-groups heritability (BGH). The strong default hypothesis is defined in terms of Table 12.4(A) as BGH = WGH; the relaxed default hypothesis allows independent values of BGH and WGH.

For example, in the first column inside Table 12.4(A), the BGH = .00. This represents the hypothesis that the cause of the mean group difference in test scores is purely environmental. When WGH is also equal to .00, the environmental difference of $1\sigma_E$ between the groups accounts for all of the phenotypic difference of $1\sigma_P$ and thus accords perfectly with the environmental hypothesis that $1\sigma_P = 1\sigma_E$. Table 12.4(A) shows that when WGH = BGH = .00, the value of $\sigma_E = 1.00$.

Maintaining the same purely environmental hypothesis that the BGH = 0, but with the WGH = .10, for two groups to differ phenotypically by $1\sigma_P$ they must differ by $1.05\sigma_E$ in environmental effect, which deviates .05 from the hypothesized value of $1\sigma_E$. The critical point of this analysis is that if the BGH

Table 12.4(A)
Mean Difference in *Environmental* Effect (in σ_E Units) between Groups A and B for Different Values of WGH and BGH When the Mean Phenotypic Difference between Groups (A-B) is $1\sigma_P$.

WGH [a]	Between-Group Heritability (BGH)				
	.00	.50	.60	.70	.80
	σ_z	σ_z	σ_z	σ_z	σ_z
.00	1.00	0.71	0.63	0.55	0.45
.10	1.05	0.74	0.67	0.57	0.47
.20	1.12	0.79	0.71	0.61	0.50
.30	1.19	0.84	0.75	0.65	0.54
.40	1.77	0.91	0.82	0.71	0.57
.50	1.41	1.00	0.89	0.77	0.63
.60	1.58	1.12	1.00	0.87	0.71
.70*	1.83	1.29	1.15	1.00	0.82
.80	2.24	1.58	1.41	1.22	1.00
.90	3.16	2.24	2.00	1.73	1.41

[a]Within-group heritability.
[b]Modal value of WGH for adult IQ reported in kinship studies.
Note: All values of $\sigma^E = \sqrt{(1 - BGH)/(1 - WGH)}$.

Table 12.4(B)
Mean Difference in *Genetic* Effect (in σ_G Units) between Groups A and B for Different Values of WGH and BGH When the Mean Phenotypic Difference between Groups (A-B) is $1\sigma_P$.

WGH [a]	Between-Group Heritability (BGH)				
	.10	.50	.60	.70	.80
	σ_G	σ_G	σ_G	σ_G	σ_G
.10	1.00	2.24	2.45	2.65	2.83
.20	0.71	1.58	1.73	1.87	2.00
.30	0.57	1.29	1.41	1.53	1.63
.40	0.50	1.12	1.22	1.32	1.41
.50	0.45	1.00	1.09	1.18	1.26
.60	0.41	0.91	1.00	1.08	1.15
.70*	0.37	0.84	0.93	1.00	1.07
.80	0.36	0.79	0.87	0.93	1.00
.90	0.33	0.74	0.82	0.88	0.94

[a]Within-group heritability.
*Modal value of WGH for adult IQ reported in kinship studies.
Note: Values of σ_G (which are equal to $\sqrt{BGH/WGH}$) cannot be computed when WGH = 0, because the quotient of any value divided by zero is mathematically undefined.

= 0, values of WGH greater than 0 then require that σ_E be greater than 1.00. We can see in Table 12.4(A) that as the WGH increases, the required value of σ_E must increasingly deviate from the hypothesized value of $1\sigma_E$, thereby becoming increasingly more problematic for empirical explanation. Since the empirical value of WGH for the IQ of adults lies within the range of .60 to .80, with a mean close to .70, it is particularly instructive to examine the values of σ_E for this range in WGH. When WGH = .70 and BGH = 0, for example, the $1\sigma_P$ difference between the groups is entirely due to environmental causes and amounts to $1.83\sigma_E$. Table 12.4(A) indicates that as we hypothesize levels of BGH that approach the empirically established levels of WGH, the smaller is the size of the environmental effect required to account for the phenotypic difference of $1\sigma_P$ in group means.

Factor X. Recall that the strong form of the default hypothesis states that the average difference in test scores observed between groups A and B results from the same kinds of genetic (G) and environmental (E) influences acting to the same degree to produce individual differences within each group. The groups may differ, however, in the mean values of either G, or E, or both. Stated in terms of the demonstration in Table 12.4(A), this means that if WGH is the same for both groups, A and B, then, given any empirically obtained value of WGH, the limits of BGH are constrained, as shown. The hypothesis that BGH = 0 therefore appears improbable, given the typical range of empirical values of WGH.

To accept the preponderance of evidence that WGH > 0 and still insist that BGH = 0 regardless of the magnitude of the WGH, we must attribute the cause of the group difference to either of two sources: (1) the same kinds of environmental factors that influence the level of *g* but that do so at much greater magnitude between groups than within either group, or (2) empirically identified environmental factors that create variance *between* groups but do not do so *within* groups. The "relaxed" default hypothesis allows both of these possibilities. The dual hypothesis, on the other hand, requires either much larger environmental effects between groups than are empirically found, on average, within either group, or the existence of some additional empirically *unidentified* source of nongenetic variance that causes the difference between groups but does not contribute to individual differences *within* either group. If the two groups are hypothesized not to differ in WGH or in total phenotypic variance, this hypothesized additional source of nongenetic variance between groups must either have equal but opposite effects within each group, or it must exist only within one group but without producing any additional variance within that group. In 1973, I dubbed this hypothesized additional nongenetic effect *Factor X*.[34] When groups of blacks and whites who are matched on virtually all of the environmental variables known to be correlated with IQ *within* either racial population still show a substantial mean difference in IQ, Factor X is the favored explanation in lieu of the hypothesis that genetic factors, though constituting the largest source of variance *within* groups, are at all involved in the IQ difference *between* groups. Thus Factor X is an ad hoc hypothesis that violates Occam's razor, the well-known maxim in science which states that if a phenomenon can be explained without assuming some hypothetical entity, there is no ground for assuming it.

The default hypothesis also constrains the magnitude of the genetic difference between groups, as shown in Table 12.4(B). (The explanations that were given for interpreting Table 12.4(A) apply here as well.) For two groups, A and B, whose phenotypic means differ by $A - B = 1\sigma_P$, the strong default hypothesis (i.e., BGH = WGH) means that the groups differ on the scale of genetic effect by $BGH/WGH = 1.00\sigma_G$.

The values of σ_G in Table 12.4(B) show that the strong default hypothesis is not the same as a purely genetic hypothesis of the group difference. For example, for WGH = .70 and BGH = .70, the groups differ by $1\sigma_G$ (Table 12.4B), and also the groups differ by $1\sigma_E$ (Table 12.4A). For the relaxed default hypothesis, the environmental and genetic differences associated with each and every intersection of WGH and BGH in Tables 12.4A and 12.4B add up to $\sqrt{\sigma_G^2(WGH) + \sigma_E^2(1 - WGH)} = 1\sigma_P$.

The foregoing analysis is relevant to the often repeated "thought experiment" proposed by those who argue for the plausibility of the dual hypothesis, as in the following example from an article by Carol Tavris:[35]

> Suppose that you have a bag of tomato seeds that vary genetically; all things being equal, some seeds will produce tomatoes that are puny and tasteless, and some will produce tomatoes that are plump and delicious. You take a random bunch of seeds in your left hand and random bunch in your right. Though one seed differs genetically from another, there is no *average* difference between the seeds in your left hand and those in your right.
>
> Now you plant the left hand's seeds in Pot A. You have doctored the soil in Pot A with nitrogen and other nutrients. You feed the pot every day, sing arias to it from *La Traviata*, and make sure it gets lots of sun. You protect it from pests, and you put in a trellis, so even the weakest little tomatoes have some support. Then you plant the seeds in your right hand in Pot B, which contains sandy soil lacking nutrients. You don't feed these tomatoes, or water them; you don't give them enough sun; you let pests munch on them.
>
> When the tomatoes mature, they will vary in size *within* each pot, purely because of genetic differences. But there will also be an average difference between the tomatoes of enriched Pot A and those of depleted Pot B. This difference *between* pots is due entirely to their different soils and tomato-rearing experiences. (p. 63)

Statistically stated, the argument is that (1) WGH = 1, BGH = 0. What is the expected magnitude of the required environmental effect implied by these conditions? In terms of within-group standard deviation units, it is $\sigma_E = \sqrt{(1 - BGH)/(1 - WGH)} = \sqrt{(1 - 0)/(1 - 1)} = 1/0$. But of course the quotient of any fraction with zero in the denominator is undefined, so no inference about the magnitude of σ_E is possible at all, given these conditions. However, if we make the WGH slightly less than perfect, say, .99, the expected difference in environmental effect becomes $10\sigma_E$. This is an incredibly large, but in this case probably not unrealistic, effect given Tavris's descriptions of the contrasting environments of Pot A and Pot B.

The story of tomatoes-in-two-pots doesn't contradict the default hypothesis. Rather, it makes the very point of the default hypothesis by stating that Pots A and B each contain random samples of the same batch of seeds, so an equally massive result would have been observed if the left-hand and right-hand seeds had been planted in opposite pots. Factor X is not needed to explain the enriched and deprived tomatoes; the immense difference in the environmental conditions is quite sufficient to produce a difference in tomato size ten times greater than the average differences produced by environmental variation *within* each pot.

Extending the tomato analogy to humans, Tavris goes on to argue, "Blacks and whites do not grow up, on the average, in the same kind of pot" (p. 63). The question, then, is whether the average environmental difference between blacks and whites is sufficient to cause a $1\sigma_P$ difference in IQ if BGH = 0 and WGH is far from zero. The default hypothesis, positing values of BGH near those of the empirical values of WGH, is more plausible than the hypothesis that BGH = 0. (A third hypothesis, which can be ruled out of serious consideration on evolutionary grounds, given the observed genetic similarity between all human groups, is that the basic organization of the brain and the processes involved in mental development are qualitatively so different for blacks and whites that any phenotypic difference between the groups cannot, even in principle, be analyzed in terms of quantitative variation on the same scale of the genetic or of the environmental factors that influence individual development of mental ability within one racial group.)

The Default Hypothesis in Terms of Multiple Regression. The behavioral geneticist Eric Turkheimer[36] has proposed an approach for relating the quantitative genetic analysis of individual and of group differences. Phenotypic variance can be conceptually partitioned into its genetic and its environmental components in terms of a multiple regression equation.[37] Turkheimer's method allows us to visualize the relationship of within-group and between-group genetic effects and environmental effects in terms of a regression plane located in a three-dimensional space in which the orthogonal dimensions are phenotype (P), genotype (G), and environment (E). Both individual and group mean phenotypic values (e.g., IQ) can then be represented on the surface of this plane. This amounts to a graphic statement of the strong default hypothesis, where the phenotypic difference (P_D) between two individuals (or two group means), A and B, can be represented by the multiple regression of the phenotypic difference ($P_A - P_B = P_D$) on the genetic and environmental differences (G_D and E_D).

According to the default hypothesis, mental development is affected by the genetic mechanisms of inheritance and by environmental factors in the same way for all biologically normal individuals in either group. (Rejection of this hypothesis would mean that evolution has caused some fundamental intraspecies

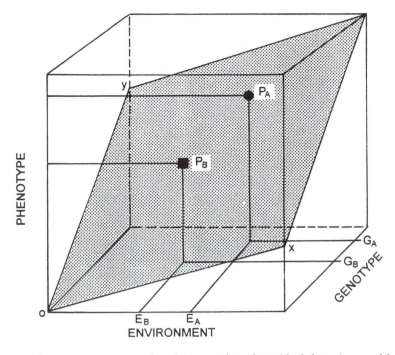

Figure 12.9. A cube representing the regression plane (shaded area) created by the multiple regression of phenotype on environment and on genotype. The slope of the regression line of phenotype on genotype (line *oy*) is h; the slope of the regression line of phenotype on environment (line *ox*) is $\sqrt{1 - h^2} = e$. A and B are two individuals (or two group means) with environmental values of E_A and E_B, genotypic values of G_A and G_B, and phenotypic values of P_A and P_B. Their phenotypic difference is given by the regression equation $P_A - P_B = h(G_A - G_B) + e(E_A - E_B)$. The positions of A and B on the regression plane are represented by the solid dot and the solid square, respectively.

differences in brain organization and mental development, a possibility which, though seemingly unlikely, has not yet been ruled out.) Thus the default hypothesis implies that a unit increase in genetic value G for individuals in group A is equal to the same unit increase in G for individuals in group B, and likewise for the environmental value E. Within these constraints posited by the default hypothesis, however, the groups may differ, on average, in the mean values of G, or E, or both. Accordingly, individuals of either group will fall at various points (depending on their own genotype and environment) on the same regression lines (i.e., for the regression of P on G and of P on E). This can be visualized graphically as a regression plane inside a square box (Figure 12.9). The G and E values for individuals (or for group means) A and B are projected onto the tilted plane; the projections are shown as a dot and a square. Their positions on the plane are then projected onto the phenotype dimension of the box.

The important point here is that the default hypothesis states that, for any value of WGH, the predicted scores of all individuals (and consequently the predicted group means) will lie on one and the same regression plane. Assuming the default hypothesis, this clearly shows the relationship between the heritability of individual differences *within* groups (WGH) and the heritability of group differences (BGH). This formulation makes the default hypothesis quantitatively explicit and therefore highly liable to empirical refutation. If there were some environmental factor(s) that is unique to one group and that contributes appreciably to the mean difference between the two groups, their means would not lie on the same plane. This would result, for example, if there were a between-groups G × E interaction. The existence of such an interaction would be inconsistent with the default hypothesis, because it would mean that the groups differ phenotypically due to some nonadditive effects of genes and environment so that, say, two individuals, one from each group, even if they had identical levels of IQ, would have had to attain that level by different developmental processes and environmental influences. The fact that significant G × E interactions with respect to IQ (or *g*) have not been found within racial groups renders such an interaction between groups an unlikely hypothesis.

It should be noted that the total nongenetic variance has been represented here as e^2. As explained in Chapter 7, the true-score nongenetic variance can be partitioned into two components: *between-families environment* (BFE is also termed *shared* environment because it is common to siblings or to any children reared together) and *within-family environment* (WFE, or *unshared* environment, that part of the total environmental effect that differs between persons reared together).

The WFE results largely from an accumulation of more or less random microenvironmental factors.[38] We know from studies of adult MZ twins reared apart and studies of genetically unrelated adults who were reared together from infancy in adoptive homes that the BFE has little effect on the phenotype of mental ability, such as IQ scores, even over a quite wide range of environments (see Chapter 7 for details). The BF environment certainly has large effects on mental development for the lowest extreme of the physical and social environment, conditions such as chronic malnutrition, diseases that affect brain development, and prolonged social isolation, particularly in infancy and early childhood. These conditions occur only rarely in First World populations. But some would argue that American inner cities *are* Third World environments, and they certainly resemble them in some ways. On a scale of environmental quality with respect to mental development, these adverse environmental conditions probably fall more than 2σ below the average environment experienced by the majority of whites and very many blacks in America. The hypothetical function relating phenotypic mental ability (e.g., IQ) on the total range of BFE

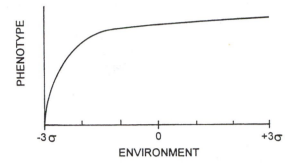

Figure 12.10. The hypothetical relationship of phenotypic values to the between-families (that is, shared) environment, represented on a normalized scale, with mean = 0, $\sigma = 1$. Note that for environments above about $-2\sigma_E$, additional increments in the environment result in small and diminishing increments in phenotypic value.

effects (termed the *reaction range* or *reaction norm* for the total environmental effect) is shown in Figure 12.10.

   Pseudo-race Groups and the Default Hypothesis. In my studies of test bias, I used what I termed pseudo-race groups to test the hypothesis that many features of test performance are simply a result of group differences in the mean and distribution of IQ per se rather than a result of any cultural differences between groups. Pseudo-race groups are made up entirely of white subjects. The *standard* group is composed of individuals selected on the basis of estimated true-scores so as to be normally distributed, with a mean and standard deviation of the IQ distribution of whites in the general population. The *pseudo-race* group is composed of white individuals from the same population as the standard group, but selected on the basis of their estimated true-scores so as to be normally distributed, but with a mean and standard deviation of the IQ distribution of blacks in the general population. The two groups, with age controlled, are intentionally matched with the white and black populations they are intended to represent only on the single variable of interest, in this case IQ (or preferably *g* factor scores). Therefore, the groups should not differ systematically on any other characteristics, except for whatever characteristics may be correlated with IQ. Estimated true-scores must be used to minimize the regression (i.e., toward the white mean of 100) effect that would otherwise result from selecting white subjects on IQ so as to form a group with a lower mean IQ than that of the population from which they were selected.

   The creation of two groups that, in this manner, are made to differ on a single trait can be viewed as another model of the strong default hypothesis. This method is especially useful in empirically examining various nonpsychometric correlates of the standard group versus pseudo-race group difference. These differences can then be compared against any such differences found between representative samples of the actual white and black populations. The critical question is, in the circumstances of daily life how closely does the behavior of the pseudo-race group resemble that of a comparable sample of actual blacks? The extent of the pseudo-race versus actual race difference in nonpsychometric or "real-life" behavior would delimit the *g* factor's power to account for the observed racial differences in many educationally, occupationally, and socially significant variables.

Notice that the standard and pseudo-race groups would perfectly simulate the conditions of the strong default hypothesis. Both genetic and environmental sources of variance exist in nearly equal degrees *within* each group, and the mean difference *between* the groups necessarily comprises comparable genetic and environmental sources of variance. If this particular set of genetic and environmental sources of IQ variance within and between the standard and pseudo-race groups simulates actual white-black differences in many forms of behavior that have some cognitive aspect but are typically attributed solely to cultural differences, it constitutes strong support for the default hypothesis. Experiments of this type could tell us a lot and should be performed.

EMPIRICAL EVIDENCE ON THE DEFAULT HYPOTHESIS

Thus far the quantitative implications of the default hypothesis have been considered only in theoretical or formal terms, which by themselves prove nothing, but are intended only to lend some precision to the statement of the hypothesis and its predicted empirical implications. It should be clear that the hypothesis cannot feasibly be tested directly in terms of applying first-order statistical analyses (e.g., the *t* test or analysis of variance applied to phenotypic measures) to determine the BGH of a trait, as is possible in the field of experimental genetics with plants or animals. In the latter field, true breeding experiments with cross-fostering in controlled environments across different subspecies and subsequent measurement of the phenotypic characteristics of the progeny of the cross-bred strains for comparison with the same phenotypes in the parent strains are possible and, in fact, common. In theory, such experiments could be performed with different human subspecies, or racial groups, and the results (after replications of the experiment to statistically reduce uncertainty) would constitute a nearly definitive test of the default hypothesis. An even more rigorous test of the hypothesis than is provided by a controlled breeding and cross-fostering experiment would involve *in vitro* fertilization to control for possible differences in the prenatal environment of the cross-fostered progeny. Such methods have been used in livestock breeding for years without any question as to the validity of the results. But, of course, for ethical reasons the methods of experimental genetics cannot be used for research in human genetics. Therefore, indirect methods, which are analytically and statistically more complex, have been developed by researchers in human genetics.

The seemingly intractable problem with regard to phenotypic group differences has been the empirical estimation of the BGH. To estimate the genetic variance *within* groups one needs to know the genetic kinship correlations based on the theoretically derived proportions of alleles common to relatives of different degrees (e.g., MZ twins = 1.00, DZ twins and full siblings, parent-child = 0.50 [or more with assortative mating], half-siblings = 0.25, first cousins = .125, etc.). These unobserved but theoretically known genetic kinship correlations are needed as parameters in the structural equations used to estimate the proportion of genetic variance (heritability) from the phenotypic correlations between relatives of different degrees of kinship. But we generally do not have phenotypical correlations between relatives that bridge different racial groups. Since few members of one racial group have a near relative (by common descent) in a different racial group, we don't have the parameters needed to estimate between-group heritability. Although interracial matings can produce half-siblings and cousins who are members of different racial groups, the offspring of interracial matings are far from ideal for estimating BGH because, at least for blacks and whites, the parents of the interracial offspring are known to be unrepresentative of these populations. Thus such a study would have doubtful generality.

An example of cross-racial kinships that could be used would be a female of group A who had two offspring by a male of group A and later had two offspring by a male of group B, resulting finally in two pairs of full-siblings who are both AA and two pairs of half-siblings who are both AB. A biometric genetic analysis of phenotypic measurements obtained on large samples of such full-siblings and half-siblings would theoretically afford a way of estimating both WGH and BGH. Again, however, unless such groups arose from a controlled breeding experiment, the resulting estimate of BGH would probably not be generalizable to the population groups of interest but would apply only to the specific groups used for this determination of BGH (and other groups obtained in the same way). There are two reasons: First, the degree of assortative mating for IQ is most likely the same, on average, for interracial and intraracial matings; that is, the A and B mates of the hypothetical female in our example would probably be phenotypically close in IQ, so at least one of them would be phenotypically (hence also probably genetically) unrepresentative of his own racial population. Therefore, the mixed offspring AB are not likely to differ genetically much, if at all, on average, from the unmixed offspring AA. Second, aside from assortative mating, it is unlikely that interracial half-siblings are derived from parents who are random or representative samples of their respective racial populations. It is known, for example, that present-day blacks and whites in interracial marriages in the United States are not typical of their respective populations in IQ-related variables, such as levels of education and occupation.[39]

How then can the default hypothesis be tested empirically? It is tested exactly as is any other scientific hypothesis; no hypothesis is regarded as scientific unless predictions derived from it are capable of risking refutation by an empirical test. Certain predictions can be made from the default hypothesis that are capable of empirical test. If the observed result differs significantly from the prediction, the

hypothesis is considered disproved, unless it can be shown that the tested prediction was an incorrect deduction from the hypothesis, or that there are artifacts
in the data or methodological flaws in their analysis that could account for the
observed result. If the observed result does in fact accord with the prediction,
the hypothesis survives, although it cannot be said to be proven. This is because
it is logically impossible to prove the null hypothesis, which states that there is
no difference between the predicted and the observed result. If there is an alternative hypothesis, it can also be tested against the same observed result.

For example, if we hypothesize that no tiger is living in the Sherwood Forest
and a hundred people searching the forest fail to find a tiger, we have not proved
the null hypothesis, because the searchers might have failed to look in the right
places. If someone actually found a tiger in the forest, however, the hypothesis
is absolutely disproved. The alternative hypothesis is that a tiger does live in
the forest; finding a tiger clearly proves the hypothesis. The failure of searchers
to find the tiger decreases the probability of its existence, and the more searching, the lower is the probability, but it can never prove the tiger's nonexistence.

Similarly, the default hypothesis predicts certain outcomes under specified
conditions. If the observed outcome does not differ significantly from the predicted outcomes, the default hypothesis is upheld but not proved. If the prediction differs significantly from the observed result, the hypothesis must be
rejected. Typically, it is modified to accord better with the existing evidence,
and then its modified predictions are empirically tested with new data. If it
survives numerous tests, it conventionally becomes a ''fact.'' In this sense, for
example, it is a ''fact'' that the earth revolves around the sun, and it is a ''fact''
that all present-day organisms have evolved from primitive forms.

Structural Equation Modeling. Probably the most rigorous methodology
presently available to test the default hypothesis is the application of structural
equation modeling to what is termed the biometric decomposition of a phenotypic mean difference into its genetic and environmental components. This methodology is an extraordinarily complex set of mathematical and statistical
procedures, an adequate explanation of which is beyond the scope of this book,
but for which detailed explanations are available.[40] It is essentially a multiple
regression technique that can be used to statistically test the differences in
''goodness-of-fit'' between alternative models, such as whether (1) a phenotypic
mean difference between groups consists of a linear combination of the same
genetic (G) and environmental (E) factors that contribute to individual differences within the groups, *or* (2) the group difference is attributable to some
additional factor (an unknown Factor X) that contributes to variance *between*
groups but not to variance *within* groups.

Biometric decomposition by this method requires quite modern and specialized computer programs (LISREL VII) and exacting conditions of the data to
which it is applied—above all, large and representative samples of the groups
whose phenotypic means are to be decomposed into their genetic and environmental components. All subjects in each group must be measured with at least

three or more different tests that are highly loaded on a common factor, such as g, and this factor must have high congruence between the two groups. Also, of course, each group must comprise at least two different degrees of kinship (e.g., MZ and DZ twins, or full-siblings and half-siblings) to permit reliable estimates of WGH for each of the tests. Further, in order to meet the assumption that WGH is the same in both groups, the estimates of WGH obtained for each of the tests should not differ significantly between the groups.

Given these stringent conditions, one can test whether the mean group difference in the general factor common to the various tests is consistent with the default model, which posits that the between-groups mean difference comprises the same genetic and environmental factors as do individual differences within each group. The goodness-of-fit of the data to the default model (i.e., group phenotypic difference = G + E) is then compared against the three alternative models, which posit *only* genetic (G) factors, or *only* environment (E), or *neither* G nor E, respectively, as the cause of the group difference. The method has been applied to estimate the genetic and environmental contributions to the observed sex difference in average blood pressure.[40]

This methodology was applied to a data set[41] that included scores on thirteen mental tests (average g loading = .67) given to samples of black and white adolescent MZ and DZ twins totaling 190 pairs. Age and a measure of socio-economic status were regressed out of the test scores. The data showed by far the best fit to the default model, which therefore could not be rejected, while the fit of the data to the alternative models, by comparison with the default model, could be rejected at high levels of confidence ($p < .005$ to $p < .001$). That is, the observed W-B group difference is probably best explained in terms of both G and E factors, while either G or E alone is inadequate, given the assumption that G and E are the same within both groups. This result, however, does not warrant as much confidence as the above p values would indicate, as these particular data are less than ideal for one of the conditions of the model. The data set shows rather large and unsystematic (though nonsignificant) differences in the WGHs of blacks and whites on the various tests. Therefore, the estimate of BGH, though similar to the overall WGH of the thirteen tests (about .60), is questionable. Even though the WGHs of the general factor do not differ significantly between the races, the difference is large enough to leave doubt as to whether it is merely due to sampling error or is in fact real but cannot be detected given the sample size. If the latter is true, then the model used in this particular method of analysis (termed the psychometric factor model) cannot rigorously be applied to these particular data.

A highly similar methodology (using a less restrictive model termed the biometric factor model) was applied to a much larger data set by behavioral geneticists David Rowe and co-workers.[42] But Rowe's large-scale preliminary studies should first be described. He began[42a,b] by studying the correlations between objective tests of scholastic achievement (which are substantially loaded on g as well as on specific achievement factors) and assessment of the quality of the child's home environment based on environmental variables that previous research had established as correlates of IQ and scholastic achievement and which, overall, are intended to indicate the amount of intellectual stimulation afforded by the child's environment outside of school. Measures of the achievement and home environment variables were obtained on large samples of biologically full-sibling pairs (N_p = 579), each tested twice (at ages 6.6 and 9.0 years). The total sample comprised three groups: white, black, and Hispanic, and represented the full range of socioeconomic levels in the United States, with intentional oversampling of blacks and Hispanics.

The data on each population group were treated separately, yielding three matrices (white, black, and Hispanic), each comprising the correlations between (1) the achievement and the environmental variables within and between age groups, (2) the full-sibling correlations on each variable at each age, and (3) the cross-sibling correlations on each variable at each age—yielding twenty-eight correlation coefficients for each of the three ethnic groups.

Now if, in addition to the environmental factors measured in this study, there were some unidentified Factor X that is unique to a certain group and is responsible for most of the difference in achievement levels between the ethnic groups, one would expect that the existence of Factor X in one (or two), but not all three, of the groups should be detectable by an observed difference between groups in the matrix of correlations among all of the variables. That is, a Factor X hypothesized to represent a unique causal process responsible for lower achievement in one groups but not in the others should cause the pattern of correlations between environment and achievement, or between siblings, or between different ages, to be distinct for that group. However, since the correlation matrices were statistically equal, there was not the slightest evidence of a Factor X operating in any group. The correlation matrices of the different ethnic groups were as similar to one another as were correlation matrices derived from randomly selected half-samples _within_ each ethnic group.

Further analyses by Rowe et al. that included other variables yielded the same results. Altogether the six data sets used in their studies included 8,582 whites, 3,392 blacks, 1,766 Hispanics, and 906 Asians.[42a] None of the analyses required a minority-unique developmental process or a cultural-environmental Factor X to explain the correlations between the achievement variables and the environmental variables in either of the minority groups. The results are consistent with the default hypothesis, as explained by Rowe et al:

> Our explanation for the similarity of developmental precesses is that (a) different racial and ethnic groups possess a common gene pool, which can create behavioral similarities, and that (b) among second-generation ethnic and racial groups in the United States, cultural differences are smaller than commonly believed because of the omnipresent force of our mass-media culture, from television to fast-food restaurants.
>
> Certainly, a burden of proof must shift to those scholars arguing a cultural difference position. They need to explain how matrices representing developmental

processes can be so similar across ethnic and racial groups if major developmental processes exert a minority-specific influence on school achievement. (p. 38)[42b]

The dual hypothesis, which attributes the within-group variance to both genetic and environmental factors but excludes genetic factors from the mean differences between groups, would, in the light of these results, have to invoke a Factor X which, on the one hand, is so subtle and ghostly as to be perfectly undetectable in the whole matrix of correlations among test scores, environmental measures, full-siblings, and ages, yet sufficiently powerful to depress the minority group scores, on average, by as much as one-half a standard deviation.

To test the hypothesis that genetic as well as environmental factors are implicated in the group differences, Rowe and Cleveland[42d] designed a study that used the kind of structural equation modeling methodology (with the biometric factor model) mentioned previously. The study used full-siblings and half-siblings to estimate the WGH for large samples of blacks and whites (total N = 1,220) on three Peabody basic achievement tests (Reading Recognition, Reading Comprehension, and general Mathematics). A previous study[42c] had found that the heritability (WGH) of these tests averaged about .50 and their average correlation with verbal IQ = .65. The achievement tests were correlated among themselves about .75., indicating that they all share a large common factor, with minor specificities for each subtest.

The default hypothesis that the difference between the black and white group means on the single general achievement factor has the same genetic and nongenetic causes that contribute to individual differences within each group could not be rejected. The data fit the default model extremely well, with a goodness-of-fit index of .98 (which, like a correlation coefficient, is scaled from zero to one). The authors concluded that the genetic and environmental sources of individual differences and of differences between racial means appear to be identical. Compared to the white siblings, the black siblings had lower means on both the genetic and the environmental components. To demonstrate the sensitivity of their methodology, the authors substituted a fake mean value for the real mean for whites on the Reading Recognition test and did the same for blacks on the Math test. The fake white mean approximately equaled the true black mean and vice versa. When the same analysis was applied to the data set with the fake means, it led to a clear-cut rejection of the default hypothesis. For the actual data set, however, the BGH did not differ significantly from the WGH. The values of the BGH were .66 to .74 for the verbal tests and .36 for the math test. On the side of caution, the authors state, "These estimates, of course, are imprecise because of sampling variation; they suggest that a part of the Black versus White mean difference is caused by racial genetic differences, but that it would take a larger study, especially one with more genetically informative half-sibling pairs, to make such estimates quantitatively precise. . . ." (p. 221).

Regression to the Population Mean. In the 1860s, Sir Francis Galton discovered a phenomenon that he first called *reversion to the mean* and later gave it the more grandiloquent title *the law of filial regression to mediocrity*. The phenomenon so described refers to the fact that, on every quantitative hereditary trait that Galton examined, from the size of peas to the size of persons, the measurement of the trait in the mature offspring of a given parent (or both parents) was, on average, closer to the population mean (for their own sex) than was that of the parent(s). An exceptionally tall father, for example, had sons who are shorter than he; and an exceptionally short father had sons who were taller than he. (The same for mothers and daughters.)

This "regression to the mean" is probably better called regression *toward* the mean, the mean being that of the subpopulation from which the parent and offspring were selected. In quantitative terms, Galton's "law" predicts that the more that variation in a trait is determined by genetic factors, the closer the degree of regression (from one parent to one child), on average, approximates one-half. This is because an offspring receives exactly one-half of its genes from each parent, and therefore the parent-offspring *genetic correlation* equals .50. The corresponding *phenotypic correlation*, of course, is subject to environmental influences, which may cause the phenotypic sibling correlation to be greater than or (more usually) less than the genetic correlation of .50. The more that the trait is influenced by nongenetic factors, the greater is the departure of the parent-offspring correlation from .50. The average of the parent-child correlations for IQ reported in thirty-two studies is +.42.[43] Traits in which variation is almost completely genetic, such as the number of fingerprint ridges, show a parent-offspring correlation very near .50. Mature height is also quite near this figure, but lower in childhood, because children attain their adult height at different rates. (Differences in both physical and mental growth curves are also largely genetic.)

Regression occurs for all degrees of kinship, its degree depending on the genetic correlation for the given kinship. Suppose we measure individuals (termed probands) selected at random from a given population and then measure their relatives (all of the same degree of kinship to the probands). Then, according to Galton's "law" and the extent to which the trait of interest is genetically determined, the expected value (i.e., best prediction) of the proband's relative (in standardized units, z) is $r_G z_P$. The expected difference between a proband and his or her relative will be equal to $z_P - z_R = z_P - r_G z_P$, where r_G is the theoretical genetic correlation between relatives of a given degree of kinship, z_P is the standardized phenotypic measurement of the proband, and z_R is the predicted or expected measurement of the proband's relative. It should be emphasized that this prediction is statistical and therefore achieves a high degree of accuracy only when averaged over a large number of pairs of relatives. The standard deviation of the errors of prediction for individual cases (known as the standard error of estimate, SE_{est}) is quite large.

For example, in the case of estimating the offspring's IQ from one parent's IQ, the $SE_{est} = \sigma_{IQ}\sqrt{1 - r_G} = 15\sqrt{1 - .50} = 10.6$ IQ points.[44]

A common misconception is that regression to the mean implies that the total variance in the population shrinks from one generation to the next, until eventually everyone in the population would be located at the mean on a given trait. In fact, the population variance does not change at all as a result of the phenomenon of regression. Regression toward the mean works in both directions. That is, offspring with phenotypes extremely above (or below) the mean have parents whose phenotypes are less extreme, but are, on average, above (or below) the population mean. Regression toward the mean is a statistical result of the imperfect correlation between relatives, whatever the causes of the imperfect correlation, of which there may be many.

Genetic theory establishes the genetic correlations between various kinships and thereby indicates how much of the regression for any given degree of kinship is attributable to genetic factors.[45] Without the genetic prediction, any particular kinship regression (or correlation) is causally not interpretable. Resemblance between relatives could be attributed to any combination of genetic and nongenetic factors.

Empirical determination of whether regression to the mean accords with the expectation of genetic theory, therefore, provides another means of testing the default hypothesis. Since regression can result from environmental as well as from genetic factors (and always does to some extent, unless the trait variation has perfect heritability [i.e., $h^2 = 1$] and the phenotype is without measurement error), the usefulness of the regression phenomenon based on only one degree of kinship to test a causal hypothesis is problematic, regardless of its purely statistical significance. However, it would be remarkable (and improbable) if environmental factors consistently simulated the degree of regression predicted by genetic theory across a number of degrees of kinship.

A theory that completely excludes any involvement of genetic factors in producing an observed group difference offers no quantitative prediction as to the amount of regression for a given kinship and is unable to explain certain phenomena that are both predictable and explainable in terms of genetic regression. For example, consider Figure 11.2 (p. 358) in the previous chapter. It shows a phenomenon that has been observed in many studies and which many people not familiar with Galton's ''law'' find wholly surprising. One would expect, on purely environmental grounds, that the mean IQ difference between black and white children should decrease at each successively higher level of the parental socioeconomic status (i.e., education, occupational level, income, cultural advantages, and the like). It could hardly be argued that environmental advantages are not greater at higher levels of SES, in both the black and the white populations. Yet, as seen in Figure 11.2, the black and white group means actually *diverge* with increasing SES, although IQ increases with SES for both blacks and whites. The specific *form* of this increasing divergence of the white and black groups is also of some theoretical interest: the black means show a significantly lower *rate* of increase in IQ as a function of SES than do the white means. These two related phenomena, black-white *divergence* and *rate* of increase in mean IQ as a function of SES, are predictable and explainable in terms of regression, and would occur even if there were no difference in IQ between the mean IQs of the black and the white parents within each level of SES. These results are expected on purely genetic grounds, although environmental factors also are most likely involved in the regression. For a given parental IQ, the offspring IQs (regardless of race) regress about halfway to their population mean. As noted previously, this is also true for height and other heritable physical traits.[46]

Probably the single most useful kinship for testing the default hypothesis is full siblings reared together, because they are plentiful, they have developed in generally more similar environments than have parents and their own children, and they have a genetic correlation of about .50. I say "about .50" because there are two genetic factors that tend slightly to alter this correlation. As they work in opposite directions, their effects tend to cancel each other. When the total genetic variance includes nonadditive genetic effects (particularly genetic dominance) it slightly decreases the genetic correlation between full siblings, while assortative mating (i.e., correlation between the parents' genotypes) slightly increases the sibling correlation. Because of nongenetic factors, the phenotypic correlation between siblings is generally below the genetic correlation. Meta-analyses[47] of virtually all of the full-sibling IQ correlations reported in the world literature yield an overall average _r_ of only slightly below the predicted +.50.

Some years ago, an official from a large school system came to me with a problem concerning the school system's attempt to find more black children who would qualify for placement in classes for the "high potential" or "academically gifted" pupils (i.e., IQ of 120 or above). Black pupils were markedly underrepresented in these classes relative to whites and Asians attending the same schools. Having noticed that a fair number of the white and Asian children in these classes had a sibling who also qualified, the school system tested the siblings of the black pupils who had already been placed in the high-potential classes. However, exceedingly few of the black siblings in regular classes were especially outstanding students or had IQ scores that qualified them for the high-potential program. The official, who was concerned about bias in the testing program, asked if I had any other idea as to a possible explanation for their finding. His results are in fact fully explainable in terms of regression toward the mean.

I later analyzed the IQ scores on all of the full-sibling pairs in grades one through six who had taken the same IQ tests (Lorge-Thorndike) normed on a national sample in all of the fourteen elementary schools of another California school district. As this study has been described more fully elsewhere,[48] I will only summarize here. There were over 900 white sibling pairs and over 500 black sibling pairs. The sibling intraclass correlations for whites and blacks were .40 and .38, respectively. The departure of these correlations from the genetically expected value of .50 indicates that nongenetic factors (i.e., environmental influences and unreliability of measurement) affect the sibling correlation similarly in both groups. In this school district, blacks and whites who were perfectly matched for a true-score[49] IQ of 120 had siblings whose average IQ was 113 for whites and 99 for blacks. In about 33 percent of the white sibling pairs both siblings had an IQ of 120 or above, as compared with only about 12 percent of black siblings.

Of more general significance, however, was the finding that Galton's "law" held true for both black and white sibling pairs over the full range of IQs (approximately IQ 50 to IQ 150) in this school district. In other words, the sibling regression lines for each group showed no significant deviation from linearity. (Including nonlinear transformations of the variables in the multiple regression equation produced no significant increment in the simple sibling correlation.) These regression findings can be regarded, not as a proof of the default hypothesis, but as wholly consistent with it. No purely environmental theory would have predicted such results. Of course, *ex post facto* and *ad hoc* explanations in strictly environmental terms are always possible if one postulates environmental influences on IQ that perfectly mimic the basic principles of genetics that apply to every quantitative physical characteristic observed in all sexually reproducing plants and animals.

A number of different mental tests besides IQ were also given to the pupils in the school district described above. They included sixteen age-normed measures of scholastic achievement in language and arithmetic skills, short-term memory, and a speeded paper-and-pencil psychomotor test that mainly reflects effort or motivation in the testing situation.[50] Sibling intraclass correlations were obtained on each of the sixteen tests. IQ, being the most *g* loaded of all the tests, had the largest sibling correlation. All sixteen of the sibling correlations, however, fell below +.50 to varying degrees; the correlations ranged from .10 to .45., averaging .30 for whites and .28 for blacks. (For comparison, the average age-adjusted sibling correlations for height and weight in this sample were .44 and .38, respectively.) Deviations of these sibling correlations from the genetic correlation of .50 are an indication that the test score variances do reflect nongenetic factors to varying degrees. Conversely, the closer the obtained sibling correlation approaches the expected genetic correlation of .50, the larger its genetic component. These data, therefore, allow two predictions, which, if borne out, would be consistent with the default hypothesis:

1. The varying magnitudes of the sibling correlations on the sixteen diverse tests in blacks and whites should be positively correlated. In fact, the correlation between the vector of sixteen black sibling correlations and the corresponding vector of sixteen white sibling correlations was $r = +.71$, $p = .002$.

2. For both blacks and whites, there should be a *positive* correlation between (a) the magnitudes of the sibling correlations on the sixteen tests and (b) the magnitudes of the standardized mean W-B differences (average difference = 1.03σ) on the sixteen tests. The results show that the correlation between the

standardized mean W-B differences on the sixteen tests and the siblings correlations is $r = +.61$, $p < .013$ for blacks, and $r = +.80$, $p < .001$ for whites.

Note that with regard to the second prediction, a purely environmental hypothesis of the mean W-B differences would predict a *negative* correlation between the magnitudes of the sibling correlations and the magnitudes of the mean
W-B differences. The results in fact showing a strong positive correlation contradict this purely nongenetic hypothesis.

CONTROLLING THE ENVIRONMENT: TRANSRACIAL ADOPTION

Theoretically, a transracial adoption study should provide a strong test of the
default hypothesis. In reality, however, a real-life adoption study can hardly
meet the ideal conditions necessary to make it definitive. Such conditions can
be perfectly met only through the cross-fostering methods used in animal behavior genetics, in which probands can be randomly assigned to foster parents.
Although adoption in infancy is probably the most comprehensive and powerful
environmental intervention possible with humans, under natural conditions the
adoption design is unavoidably problematic because the investigator cannot experimentally control the specific selective factors that affect transracial adoptions—the adopted children themselves, their biological parents, or the adopting
parents. Prenatal and perinatal conditions and the preadoption environment are
largely uncontrolled. So, too, is the willingness of parents to volunteer their
adopted children for such a study, which introduces an ambiguous selection
factor into the subject sampling of any adoption study. It is known that individuals who volunteer as subjects in studies that involve the measurement of mental
ability generally tend to be somewhat above-average in ability. For these reasons, and given the scarcity of transracial adoptions, few such studies have been
reported in the literature. Only one of these, known as the Minnesota Transracial
Adoption Study, is based on large enough samples of black and white adoptees
to permit statistical analysis. While even the Minnesota Study does not meet the
theoretically ideal conditions, it is nevertheless informative with respect to the
default hypothesis.

Initiated and conducted by Sandra Scarr and several colleagues,[51] the Minnesota Transracial Adoption Study examined the same groups of children when
they were about age 7 and again in a 10-year follow-up when they were about
age 17. The follow-up study is especially important, because it has been found
in other studies that family environmental influences on IQ decrease from early
childhood to late adolescence, while there is a corresponding increase in the
phenotypic expression of the genetic component of IQ variance. Therefore, one
would have more confidence in the follow-up data (obtained at age 17) as a test
of the default hypothesis than in the data obtained at age 7.

Four main groups were compared on IQ and scholastic performance:

1. Biological offspring of the white adoptive parents.
2. Adopted children whose biological father and mother were both white (**WW**).

3. Adopted interracial children whose biological fathers were black and whose mothers were white (**BW**).

4. Adopted children whose biological father and mother were both black (**BB**).

(A group of twelve children, consisting of Asian and Amerindian adoptees who took part in both the first study and the follow-up, were not included in the main statistical analyses.)

The adoptive parents were all upper-middle class, employed in professional and managerial occupations, with an average educational level of about sixteen years (college graduate) and an average WAIS IQ of about 120. The biological parents of the BB and BW adoptees averaged 11.5 years and 12.5 years of education, respectively. The IQs of the adoptees' biological parents were not known. Few of the adoptees ever lived with their biological parents; some lived briefly in foster homes before they were legally adopted. The average age of adoption was 32 months for the BB adoptees, 9 months for the BW adoptees, and 19 months for the WW adoptees. The adoptees came mostly from the North Central and North Eastern regions of the United States. The Stanford-Binet and the Wechsler Intelligence Scale for Children (WISC) were used in the first study (at age seven), the Wechsler Adult Intelligence Scale (WAIS) was used in the follow-up study (at age seventeen).[52]

The investigators hypothesized that the typical W-B IQ difference results from the lesser relevance of the specific information content of IQ tests to the blacks' typical cultural environment. They therefore suggest that if black children were reared in a middle or upper-middle class white environment they would perform near the white average on IQ tests and in scholastic achievement. This cultural-difference hypothesis therefore posits no genetic effect on the mean W-B IQ difference; rather, it assumes equal black and white means in genotypic g. The default hypothesis, on the other hand, posits both genetic and environmental factors as determinants of the mean W-B IQ difference. It therefore predicts that groups of black and white children reared in highly similar environments typical of the white middle-class culture would still differ in IQ to the extent expected from the heritability of IQ within either population.

The data of the Minnesota Study also allow another prediction based on the default hypothesis, namely, that the interracial children (BW) should score, on average, nearly (but not necessarily exactly) halfway between the means of the WW and BB groups. Because the alleles that enhance IQ are genetically dominant, we would expect the BW group mean to be slightly closer to the mean of the WW group than to the mean of the BB group. That is, the heterosis (outbreeding enhancement of the trait) due to dominance deviation would raise the BW group's mean slightly above the midpoint between the BB and WW groups. (This halfway point would be the expected value if the heritability of IQ reflected only the effects of additive genetic variance.) Testing this predicted heterotic effect is unfortunately debased by the fact that the IQs of the biological parents of the BB and BW groups were not known. As the BB biological parents

Table 12.5

IQ Mean and Standard Deviation of Groups in the Minnesota Transracial Adoption Study Tested at Two Ages

Group		Age 7		Age 17	
	N[a]	Mean	*SD*	Mean	*SD*
Adoptive Father	74	121.7	9.5	117.1	11.5
Adoptive Mother	84	119.1	9.7	113.6	10.5
Biological Offspring	104	116.4	13.5	109.4	13.5
Adopted White (W/W)	16	117.6	11.3	105.6	14.9
Adopted Interracial (B/W)	55	109.5	11.9	98.5	10.6
Adopted Black (B/B)	21	95.4	13.3	89.4	11.7

[a]The number of individuals tested both in 1975 and 1986.
Source: Data from Weinberg et al., 1992.

had about one year less education than the BW parents, given the correlation between IQ and education, it is likely that the mean IQ of the BB parents was somewhat lower than the mean IQ of the BW parents, and so would produce a result similar to that predicted in terms of heterosis. It is also possible, though less likely, that the later age of adoption (by twenty-one months) of the BB adoptees than of the BW adoptees would produce an effect similar to that predicted in terms of heterosis.

The results based on the subjects who were tested on both occasions are shown in Table 12.5. Because different tests based on different standardization groups were used in the first testing than were used in the follow-up testing, the overall average difference of about eight IQ points (evident for all groups) between the two test periods is of no theoretical importance for the hypothesis of interest. The only important comparisons are those between the WW, BW, and BB adopted groups *within* each age level. They show that:

• The biological offspring have about the same average IQ as has been reported for children of upper-middle-class parents. Their IQs are lower, on average, than the average IQ of their parents, consistent with the expected genetic regression toward the population mean (mainly because of genetic dominance, which is known to affect IQ—see Chapter 7, pp. 189–91). The above-average environment of these adoptive families probably counteracts the predicted genetic regression effect to some extent, expectably more at age seven than at age seventeen.

• The BB adoptees' mean IQ is close to the mean IQ of ninety for blacks in the same North Central area (from which the BB adoptees came) reared by their own parents. At age seventeen the BB group's IQ is virtually identical to the mean IQ of blacks in the North Central part of the United States. Having been reared from two years of age in a white upper-middle-class environment has apparently had little or no effect on their expected IQ, that is, the average IQ of black children reared in the average black environment. This finding specifically contradicts the expectation of the cultural-difference explanation of the W-B IQ difference, but is consistent with the default hypothesis.

• The BB group is more typical of the U.S. black population than is the BW group. The BB group's IQ at age seventeen is sixteen points below that of the white adoptees and thirteen points below the mean IQ of whites in the national standardization sample of the WAIS. Thus the BB adoptees' IQ is not very different from what would be expected if they were reared in the average environment of blacks in general (i.e., IQ eighty-five).

• The mean IQ of the interracial adoptees (BW), both at ages seven and seventeen, is nearly intermediate between the WW and BB adoptees, but falls slightly closer to the WW mean. This is consistent with, but does not prove, the predicted heterotic effect of outbreeding on IQ. The intermediate IQ at age seven is (WW + BB)/2 = (117.6 + 95.4)/2 = 106.5, or three points below the observed IQ of the BW group; at age seventeen the intermediate IQ is 97.5, or one point below the observed IQ of the BW group. Of course, mean deviations of this magnitude, given the sample sizes in this study, are not significant. Hence no conclusion can be drawn from these data regarding the predicted heterotic effect.

But all of the group IQ means do differ significantly from one another, both at age seven and at age seventeen, and the fact that the BW adoptees are so nearly intermediate between the WW and BB groups is hard to explain in purely environmental or cultural terms. But it is fully consistent with the genetic prediction. An ad hoc explanation would have to argue for the existence of some cultural effects that quantitatively simulate the prediction of the default hypothesis, which is derived by simple arithmetic from accepted genetic theory.

• Results similar to those for IQ were also found for scholastic achievement measured at age seventeen, except that the groups differed slightly less on the scholastic achievement measures than on IQ. This is probably because the level of scholastic achievement is generally more susceptible to family influences than is the IQ. The mean scores based on the average of five measures of scholastic achievement and aptitude expressed on the same scale as the IQ (with $\mu = 100$, $\sigma = 15$) were: Nonadopted biological offspring = 107.2, WW adoptees = 103.1, BW adoptees = 100.1, BB adoptees = 95.1. Again, the BW group's mean is but one point above the midpoint between the means of the WW and BB groups.

In light of what has been learned from many other adoption studies, the results of this transracial adoption study are hardly surprising. As was noted in Chapter 7 (pp. 177–79), adoption studies have shown that the between-family (or shared) environment is the smallest component of true-score IQ variance by late adolescence.

It is instructive to consider another adoption study by Scarr and Weinberg,[53] based on nearly 200 white children who, in their first year of life, were adopted into 104 white families. Although the adoptive families ranged rather widely in socioeconomic status, by the time the adoptees were adolescents there were nonsignificant and near-zero correlations between the adoptee's IQs and the characteristics of their adoptive families, such as the parents' education, IQ, occupation, and income. Scarr and Weinberg concluded that, within the range of "humane environments," variations in family socioeconomic characteristics and in child-rearing practices have little or no effect on IQ measured in adolescence. Most "humane environments," they claimed, are functionally equivalent for the child's mental development.

In the transracial adoption study, therefore, one would not expect that the large differences between the mean IQs of the WW, BW, and BB adoptees would have been mainly caused by differences in the unquestionably humane and well-above-average adoptive family environments in which these children grew up. Viewed in the context of adoption studies in which race is not a factor, the group differences observed in the transracial adoption study would be attributed to genetic factors.

There is simply no good evidence that social environmental factors have a large effect on IQ, particularly in adolescence and beyond, except in cases of extreme environmental deprivation. In the Texas Adoption Study,[54] for example, adoptees whose biological mothers had IQs of ninety-five or below were compared with adoptees whose biological mothers had IQs of 120 or above. Although these children were given up by their mothers in infancy and all were adopted into good homes, the two groups differed by 15.7 IQ points at age 7 years and by 19 IQ points at age 17. These mean differences, which are about one-half of the mean difference between the low-IQ and high-IQ biological mothers of these children, are close to what one would predict from a simple genetic model according to which the standardized regression of offspring on biological parents is .50.

In still another study, Turkheimer[55] used a quite clever adoption design in which each of the adoptee probands was compared against two _non_adopted children, one who was reared in the same social class as the adopted proband's _biological_ mother, the other who was reared in the same social class as the proband's _adoptive_ mother. (In all cases, the proband's biological mother was of lower SES than the adoptive mother.) This design would answer the question of whether a child born to a mother of lower SES background and adopted into a family of higher SES background would have an IQ that is closer to children who were born and reared in a lower SES background than to children born and reared in a higher SES background. The result: the proband adoptees' mean IQ was nearly the same as the mean IQ of the nonadopted children of mothers of lower SES background but differed significantly (by more than 0.5σ) from the mean IQ of the nonadopted children of mothers of higher SES background. In other words, the adopted probands, although reared by adoptive mothers of higher SES than that of the probands' biological mothers, turned out about the same with respect to IQ as if they had been reared by their biological mothers, who were of lower SES. Again, it appears that the family social environment has a surprisingly weak influence on IQ. This broad factor therefore would seem to carry little explanatory weight for the IQ differences between the WW, BW, and BB groups in the transracial adoption study.

There is no evidence that the effect of adoption is to lower a child's IQ from what it would have been if the child were reared by it own parents, and some evidence indicates the contrary.[56] Nor is there evidence that transracial adoption per se is disadvantageous for cognitive development. Three independent studies of Asian children (from Cambodia, Korea, Thailand, and Vietnam) adopted into white families in the United States and Belgium have found that, by school age, their IQ (and scholastic achievement), on average, considerably exceeds that of middle-class white American and Belgian children by at least ten IQ points, despite the fact that many of the Asian children had been diagnosed as suffering from malnutrition prior to adoption.[57]

The authors of the Minnesota Study suggest the difference in age of adoption of the BB and BW groups (32 months and 9 months, respectively) as a possible cause of the lower IQ of the BB group (by 12 points at age 7, 9 points at age 17). The children were in foster care prior to adoption, but there is no indication that the foster homes did not provide a humane environment. A large-scale study[58] specifically addressed to the effect of early versus late age of adoption on children's later IQ did find that infants who were adopted before one year of age had significantly higher IQs at age four years than did children adopted after one year of age, but this difference disappeared when the children were retested at school age. The adoptees were compared with nonadopted controls matched on a number of biological, maternal, prenatal, and perinatal variables as well as on SES, education, and race. The authors concluded, "The adopted children studied in this project not only did not have higher IQ than the [matched] controls, but also did not perform at the same intellectual level as the biologic children from the same high socioeconomic environment into which they were adopted. . . . the better socioeconomic environment provided by adoptive parents is favorable for an adopted child's physical growth (height and weight) and academic achievement but has no influence on the child's head measurement and intellectual capacity, both of which require a genetic influence."

In the Minnesota Transracial Adoption Study, multiple regression analyses were performed to compare the effects of *ten* environmental variables with the effects of *two* genetic variables in accounting for the IQ variance at age seventeen in the combined black and interracial groups (i.e., BB & BW). The ten environmental variables were those associated with the conditions of adoption and the adoptive family characteristics (e.g., age of placement, time in adoptive home, number of preadoptive placements, quality of preadoptive placements, adoptive mother's and father's education, IQ, occupation, and family income). The two genetic variables were the biological mother's race and education. (The biological father's education, although it was known, was not used in the regression analysis; if it were included, the results might lend slightly more weight to the genetic variance accounted for by this analysis.) The unbiased[59] multiple correlation (R) between the ten environmental variables and IQ was .28. The unbiased R between the two genetic variables and IQ was .39. This is a fairly impressive correlation, considering that mother's race was treated as a dichotomous variable with a 72%(BW mothers)/28%(BB mothers) split. (The greater the departure from the optimal 50%/50% split, the more restricted is the size of the obtained correlation. If the obtained correlation of .39 were corrected to compensate for this suboptimal split, the corrected value would be .43.) Moreover, mother's education (measured in years) is a rather weak surrogate for IQ; it is correlated about +.7 with IQ in the general population. (In the present sample, the biological mothers' years of education in the BB group had a mean of 10.9, $SD = 1.9$ years, range 6–14 years; the BW group had a mean of 12.4, $SD = 1.8$, range 7–18.)

The two critiques,[60] by Levin and by Lynn, of the authors' social-environmental interpretation of the results of their follow-up study are well worth reading, as is the authors' detailed reply, in which they state, "We think that it is exceedingly implausible that these differences are either entirely genetically based or entirely environmentally based."[60c, p. 31]

STUDIES BASED ON RACIAL ADMIXTURE

In the Minnesota Transracial Adoption Study, the interracial adoptees labeled BW (black father, white mother) had a mean IQ approximately intermediate between those of the white (WW) and the black (BB) adoptees. One might expect, therefore, that individual variation in IQ among the population of black Americans would be correlated with individual variation in the percentage of Caucasian admixture. (The mean percentage of European genes in American blacks today is approximately 25 percent, with an undetermined standard deviation for individual variation.[61a]) This prediction could be used to test the hypothesis that blacks and whites differ in the frequencies of the alleles whose phenotypic effects are positively correlated with g. The several attempts to do so, unfortunately, are riddled with technical difficulties and so are unable to reduce the uncertainty as to the nature of the mean W-B difference in IQ.

An ideal study would require that the relative proportions of European and African genes in each hybrid individual be known precisely. This, in turn, would demand genealogical records extending back to each individual's earliest ancestors of unmixed European and African origin. In addition, for the results to be generalizable to the present-day populations of interest, one would also need to know how representative of the white and black populations in each generation of interracial ancestors of the study probands (i.e., the present hybrid individuals whose level of g is measured) were. A high degree of assortative mating for g, for example, would mean that these ancestors were not representative and that cross-racial matings transmitted much the same g-related alleles from each racial line. Also, the results would be ambiguous if there were a marked systematic difference in the g levels of the black and white mates (e.g., in half of the matings the black [or hybrid] $g >$ white g and vice versa in the other half). This situation would act to cancel any racial effect in the offspring's level of g.

A large data set that met these ideal conditions would provide a strong test of the genetic hypothesis. Unfortunately, such ideal data do not exist, and are probably impossible to obtain. Investigators have therefore resorted to estimating the degree of European admixture in representative samples of American blacks by means of blood-group analyses, using those blood groups that differ most in frequency between contemporary Europeans and Africans in the regions of origin of the probands' ancestors. Each marker blood group is identified with a particular polymorphic gene. Certain antigens or immunoglobulins in the blood serum, which have different polymorphic gene loci, are also used in the same way. The gene loci for all of the known human blood loci constitute but a very small fraction of the total number of genes in the human genome. To date, only two such loci, the Fy (Duffy) blood group and the immunoglobulin Gm, have been identified that discriminate very markedly between Europeans and Africans, with near-zero frequencies in one population and relatively high frequencies in the other. A number of other blood groups and blood serum antigens also discriminate between Europeans and Africans, but with much less precision. T. E. Reed,[61b] an expert on the genetics of blood groups, has calculated that a minimum of eighteen gene loci with perfect discrimination power (i.e., 100 percent frequency in one population and 0 percent in the other) are needed to determine the proportions of European/African admixture with a 5 percent or less error rate for specific individuals. This condition is literally impossible to achieve given the small number of blood groups and serum antigens known to differ in racial frequencies. However, blood group data, particularly that of Fy and Gm, aggregated in reasonably large samples are capable of showing statistically significant mean differences in mental test scores between groups if in fact the mean difference has a genetic component.

A critical problem with this methodology is that we know next to nothing about the level of g in either the specific European or African ancestors or of the g-related selective factors that may have influenced mating patterns over the many subsequent generations of the hybrid offspring, from the time of the first African arrivals in America up to the present. Therefore, even if most of the European blood-group genes in present-day American blacks had been randomly sampled from European ancestors, the genes associated with g may not have been as randomly sampled, if systematic selective mating took place between the original ancestral groups or in the many generations of hybrid descendants.

Another problem with the estimation of racial admixture from blood-group frequencies is that most of the European genes in the American black gene pool were introduced generations ago, mostly during the period of slavery. According to genetic principles, the alleles of a particular racial origin would become increasingly disassociated from one another in each subsequent generation. The genetic result of this disassociation, which is due to the phenomena known as crossing-over and independent segregation of alleles, is that any allele that shows different frequencies in the ancestral racial groups becomes increasingly less predictive of other such alleles in each subsequent generation of the racially hybridized population. If a given blood group of European origin is not reliably correlated with other blood groups of European origin in a representative sample of hybrid individuals, we could hardly expect it to be correlated with the alleles of European origin that affect _g_. In psychometric terms, such a blood group would be said to have little or no validity for ranking hybrid individuals according to their degree of genetic admixture, and would therefore be useless in testing the hypothesis that variation in _g_ in a hybrid (black-white) population is positively correlated with variation in amount of European admixture.

This disassociation among various European genes in black Americans was demonstrated in a study[62] based on large samples of blacks and whites in Georgia and Kentucky. The average correlations among the seven blood-group alleles that differed most in racial frequencies (out of sixteen blood groups tested) were not significantly different from zero, averaging $-.015$ in the white samples (for which the theoretically expected correlation is zero) and $-.030$ in the black samples. (Although the correlations between blood groups in individuals were nil, the total frequencies of each of the various blood groups were quite consistent [$r = .88$] across the Georgia and Kentucky samples.) Gm was not included in this correlation analysis but is known to be correlated with Fy. These results, then, imply that virtually all blood groups other than Fy and Gm are practically useless for estimating the proportions of Caucasian admixture in hybrid black individuals. It is little wonder, then, that, in this study, the blood-group data from the hybrid black sample yielded no evidence of being significantly or consistently correlated with _g_ (which was measured as the composite score on nineteen tests).

A similar study,[63] but much more complex in design and analyses, by Sandra Scarr and co-workers, ranked 181 black individuals (in Philadelphia) on a continuous variable, called an "odds" index, estimated from twelve genetic markers that indicated the degree to which an individual's genetic markers resembled those of Africans without any Caucasian ancestry _versus_ the genetic markers of Europeans (without any African ancestry). This is probably an even less accurate estimate of ancestral admixture than would be a direct measure of the percentage of African admixture, which (for reasons not adequately explained by the authors) was not used in this study, although it was used successfully in another study of the genetic basis of the average white-black difference in diastolic blood pressure.[64a] The "odds" index of African ancestry showed no significant correlation with individual IQs. It also failed to discriminate significantly between the means of the top and bottom one-third of the total distribution on the "ancestral odds" index of Caucasian ancestry. In brief, the null hypothesis (i.e., no relationship between hybrid mental test score and amount of European ancestry) could not be rejected by the data of this study. The first principal component of four cognitive tests yielded a correlation of only $-.05$ with the ancestral index. Among these tests, the best measure of fluid g, Raven matrices, had the largest correlation $(-.13)$ with the estimated degree of African ancestry. (In this study, a correlation of $-.14$ would be significant at $p < .05$, one-tailed.) But even the correlation between the ancestral odds index based on the three best genetic markers and the ancestral odds index based on the remaining nine genetic markers was a nonsignificant $+.10$. A measure of skin color (which has a much greater heritability than mental test scores) correlated .27 $(p < .01)$ with the index of African ancestry. When skin color and SES were partialed out of the correlation between ancestry and test scores, all the correlations were reduced (e.g., the Raven correlation dropped from $-.13$ to $-.10$). Since both skin color and SES have genetic components that are correlated with the ancestral index and with test scores, partialing out these variables further favors the null hypothesis by removing some of the hypothesized genetic correlation between racial admixture and test scores.

It is likely that the conclusions of this study constitute what statisticians refer to as Type II error, acceptance of the null hypothesis when it is in fact false.[65] Although these data cannot reject the null hypothesis, it is questionable whether they are capable in fact of rejecting an alternative hypothesis derived from the default theory. The specific features of this data set severely diminish its power to reject the null hypothesis. In a rather complex analysis,[64b] I have argued that the limitations of this study (largely the lack of power due to the low validity of the ancestral index when used with an insufficient sample size) would make it incapable of rejecting not only the null hypothesis, but also any reasonable alternative hypothesis. This study therefore cannot reduce the heredity-environment uncertainty regarding the W-B difference in psychometric g. In another instance of Type II error, the study even upholds the null hypothesis regarding the nonexistence of correlations that are in fact well established by large-scale studies. It concludes, for example, that there is no significant correlation between lightness of skin color and SES of American blacks, despite the fact that correlations significant beyond the .01 level are reported in the literature, both for individuals' SES of origin and for attained SES.[66]

Skin Color and IQ. Earlier researchers relied on objective measures of skin color as an index of the amount of African/European admixture. In sixteen out of the eighteen studies of the IQ of American blacks in which skin color was measured, the correlations between lightness of skin color and test scores were positive (ranging from $+.12$ to $+.30$).[67]

Although these positive correlations theoretically might well reflect the proportion of Caucasian genes affecting IQ in the hybrid blacks, they are weak evidence, because skin color is confounded with social attitudes that may influence IQ or its educational and occupational correlates. It is more likely that the correlations are the result of cross-assortative mating for skin color and IQ,

Table 12.6
**Mean WISC IQ of Black Interracial Children (BW) and of White Children (WW)
of German Mothers**

Group	Boys	Girls	Difference
White (WW)	101	93	8
Interracial (BW)	97	96	1
Difference	4	-3	7

Source: Data from Eyferth (1959).

which would cause these variables to be correlated in the black population.
(There is no doubt that assortative mating for skin color has taken place in the
black population.) The same is of course true for the other visible racial characteristics that may be correlated with IQ. If, in the black population, lighter
skin color (or a generally more Caucasoid appearance) and higher IQ (or its
correlates: education, occupation, SES) are both considered desirable in a mate,
they will be subject to assortative mating and to cross-assortative mating for the
two characteristics, and the offspring would therefore tend to possess both characteristics. But any IQ-enhancing genes are as likely to have come from the
African as from the European ancestors of the hybrid descendants.

In general, skin color and the other visible physical aspects of racial differences are unpromising variables for research aimed at reducing the heredity-
environment uncertainty of the causal basis of the average W-B difference in *g*.

Black-White Hybrids in Post–World War II Germany. We saw in the
Minnesota Transracial Adoption Study that the interracial (BW) adoptees, whose
biological fathers were black and whose biological mothers were white, averaged lower in IQ than the adoptees who had two white parents (WW). (See
Table 12.5, p. 474.) This finding appears to be at odds with the study conducted
by Eyferth[68] in Germany following World War II, which found no difference
between offspring of BW and WW matings who were reared by their biological
mothers. All of the fathers (black or white) were members of the U.S. occupation
forces stationed in Germany. The mothers were unmarried German women,
mostly of low SES. There were about ninety-eight interracial (BW) children and
about eighty-three white children (WW). The mothers of the BW and WW
children were approximately matched for SES. The children averaged about 10
years of age, ranging between ages 5 and 13 years. They all were tested with
the German version of the Wechsler Intelligence Scale for Children (WISC).
The results are shown in Table 12.6. The overall WW-BW difference is only
one IQ point. As there is no basis for expecting a difference between boys and

girls (whose average IQs are equal in the WISC standardization sample), the eight-point difference between the WW boys and WW girls in this study is most likely due to sampling error. But sampling error does not only result in sample differences that are *larger* than the corresponding population difference; it can also result in sample differences that are *smaller* than the population difference, and this could be the case for the overall mean WW-BW difference.

This study, although consistent with a purely environmental hypothesis of the racial difference in test scores, is not conclusive, however, because the IQs of the probands' mothers and fathers' were unknown and the white and black fathers were not equally representative of their respective populations, since about 30 percent of blacks, as compared with about 3 percent of whites, failed the preinduction mental test and were not admitted into the armed services. Further, nothing was known about the Army rank of the black or white fathers of the illegitimate offspring; they could have been more similar in IQ than the average black or white in the occupation forces because of selective preferences on the part of the German women with whom they had sexual relations. Then, too, nearly all of the children were tested before adolescence, which is before the genotypic aspect of IQ has become fully manifested. Generally in adoption studies, the correlation of IQ and genotype increases between childhood and late adolescence, while the correlation between IQ and environment decreases markedly. (The respective correlations are the square roots of the heritability, $\sqrt{h^2}$, and of the environmentality, $\sqrt{1 - h^2} = \sqrt{e^2}$.) Finally, heterosis (the outbreeding effect; see Chapter 7, p. 196) probably enhanced the IQ level of the interracial children, thereby diminishing the IQ difference between the interracial children and the white children born to German women. A heterotic effect equivalent to about +4 IQ points was reported for European-Asian interracial offspring in Hawaii.[69]

Genetic Implications of IQ and Fertility for Black and White Women. Fertility is defined as the number of living children a woman (married or unmarried) gives birth to during her lifetime. If, in a breeding population, IQ (and therefore *g*) is consistently correlated with fertility, it will have a compounded effect on the trend of the population's mean IQ in each generation—an increasing trend if the correlation is positive, a decreasing trend if it is negative (referred to as positive or negative selection for the trait). This consequence naturally follows from the fact that mothers' and children's IQs are correlated, certainly genetically and usually environmentally.

If IQ were more negatively correlated with fertility in one population than in another (for example, the American black and white populations), over two or more generations the difference between the two populations' mean IQs would be expected to diverge increasingly in each successive generation. Since some part of the total IQ variance *within* each population is partly genetic (i.e., the heritability), the intergenerational divergence in population means would also have to be partly genetic. It could not be otherwise, unless one assumed that the mother-child correlation for IQ is entirely environmental (an assumption that has been conclusively ruled out by adoption studies). Therefore, in each successive generation, as long as there is a fairly consistent difference in the correlation between IQ and fertility for the black and white populations, some part of the increasing mean group difference in IQ is necessarily genetic. If fertility is negatively correlated with a desirable trait that has a genetic component, IQ for example, the trend is called *dysgenic*; if positively correlated, *eugenic*.

The phenomenon of regression toward the population mean (see Chapter 12, pp. 467–72) does not mitigate a dysgenic trend. Regression to the mean does not predict that a population's genotypic mean in one generation regresses toward the genotypic mean of the preceding generation. In large populations, changes in the genotypic mean of a given trait from one generation to the next can come about only through positive (or negative) *selection* for that trait, that is, by changes in the proportions of the breeding population that fall into different intervals of the total distribution of the trait in question.

It is also possible that a downward genetic trend can be phenotypically masked by a simultaneous upward trend in certain environmental factors that favorably affect IQ, such as advances in prenatal care, obstetrical practices, nutrition, decrease in childhood diseases, and education. But as the positive effect of these environmental factors approaches asymptote, the downward dysgenic trend will continue, and the phenotypic (IQ) difference between the populations will begin to increase.

Is there any evidence for such a trend in the American black and white populations? There is, at least presently and during the last half of this century, since U.S. Census data relevant to this question have been available. A detailed study[70] based on data from the U.S. Census Bureau and affiliated agencies was conducted by Daniel Vining, a demographer at the University of Pennsylvania. His analyses indicate that, if IQ is to some degree heritable (which it is), then throughout most of this century (and particularly since about 1950) there has been an overall *downward* trend in the *genotypic* IQ of *both* the white and the black populations. The trend has been more unfavorable for the black population.

But how could the evidence for a downward trend in the genotypic component of IQ be true, when other studies have shown a gradual rise in phenotypic IQ over the past few decades? (This intergenerational rise in IQ, known as the "Flynn effect," is described in Chapter 10, pp. 318–22). Since the evidence for both of these effects is solid, the only plausible explanation is that the rapid improvement in environmental conditions during this century has offset and even exceeded the dysgenic trend. However, this implies that the effect of the dysgenic trend should become increasingly evident at the phenotypic level as improvements in the environmental factors that enhance mental development approach their effective asymptote for the whole population.

Table 12.7 shows the fertility (F) of white and black women within each one-standard deviation interval of the total distribution of IQ in each population. (The average fertility estimates include women who have had children and

Table 12.7
Fertility in Each 1σ Interval of the Normal Curve and Mean IQ in Each Interval for U.S. National Probability Samples of White and Black Women Aged 25–34 in 1978

	IQ Interval					
	≤71	71–85	86–100	101–115	116–130	>130
White						
Fertility[a] (F)	1.59	1.68	1.76	1.44	1.15	0.92
Proportion (P)	.023	.136	.341	.341	.136	.023
(F × P)$_W$	.036	.228	.601	.491	.156	.021
Mean IQ	64.5	79.3	93.1	106.9	120.7	135.5
Black						
Fertility[a] (F)	2.60	2.12	1.79	1.63	1.20	0.00
Proportion (P)	.159	.341	.341	.136	.021	.001
(F × P)$_B$	.413	.723	.611	.221	.026	.000
Mean IQ	62.1	78.1	91.9	105.7	119.6	135.8
(F × P)$_B$/(F × P)$_W$	11.37	3.17	1.02	0.45	0.17	0.00

[a]From Vining (1982), Table 1, p. 247. Fertility and IQ based on probability samples (2,066 whites, 473 blacks) representing the noninstitutionalized U.S. population.

women who have not had any children by age thirty-four.) Assuming a normal distribution (which is closely approximated for IQ within the range of ±2σ), the table also shows: (a) the estimated proportion (P) of the population within each interval, (b) the product of F × P, and (c) the mean IQ of the women within each interval. The average fertility in each of the IQ intervals and the average IQs in those intervals are negatively correlated (−.86 for whites, −.96 for blacks), indicating a dysgenic trend in both populations, though stronger in the black population.

Now, as a way of understanding the importance of Table 12.7, let us suppose that the mean IQ for whites was 100 and the mean IQ for blacks was 85 in the generation preceding that of the present sample of women represented in Table 12.7. Further, suppose that in that preceding generation the level of fertility was the same within each IQ interval. Then their offspring (that is, the present generation) would have an overall mean IQ equal to the weighted mean[71] of the average IQ within each IQ interval (the weights being the proportion, P, of the population falling within each IQ interval). These means would also be 100 and eighty-five for the white and black populations, respectively.

But now suppose that in the present generation there is negative selection for IQ, with the fertility of the women in each IQ interval exactly as shown in Table 12.7. (This represents the actual condition in 1978 as best as we can determine.)

What then will be the overall mean IQ of the subsequent generation of offspring? The weights that must be used in the calculation are the products of the average fertility (F) in each interval and the proportion (P) of women in each interval (i.e., the of values F × P, shown in Table 12.7). The predicted overall weighted mean IQ, then, turns out to be 98.2 for whites and 82.6 for blacks, a drop of 1.8 IQ points and of 2.4 IQ points, respectively. The effect thus increases the W-B IQ difference from 15 IQ points in the parent generation to 15.6 IQ points in the offspring generation—an increase in the W-B difference of 0.6 IQ points in a single generation. Provided that IQ has substantial heritability within each population, this difference must be partly genetic. So if blacks have had a greater *relative* increase in environmental advantages that enhance IQ across the generations than whites have had, the decline of the genetic component of the black mean would be greater than the decline of the white genetic mean, because of environmental masking, as previously explained. We do not know just how many generations this differential dysgenic trend has been in effect, but extrapolated over three or four generations it would have worsening consequences for the comparative proportions in each population that fall above or below 100 IQ. (Of course, fertility rates could change in the positive direction, but so far there is no evidence of this.) In the offspring generation of the population samples of women shown in Table 12.7, the percentage of each population above/below IQ 100 would be: whites 43.6%/56.4%, blacks 12.4%/87.6% (assuming no increase in environmental masking between the generations). The W/B ratio *above* 100 IQ is about 43.6%/12.4% = 3.5; the B/W ratio *below* 100 IQ is .87.6%/56.4% = 1.55. These ratios or any approximations of them would have considerable consequences if, for example, an IQ of 100 is a critical cutoff score for the better-paid types of employment in an increasingly technological and information-intensive economy (see Chapter 14). Because generation time (measured as mother's age at the birth of her first child) is about two years less in blacks than in whites, the dysgenic trend would compound faster over time in the black population than in the white. Therefore, the figures given above probably underestimate any genetic component of the W-B IQ difference attributable to differential fertility.

This prediction follows from recent statistics on fertility rates. A direct test of this effect would require a comparison of the average IQ of women in one generation with the average IQ of all of their children who constitute the next generation. Such cross-generational IQ data are available from the National Longitudinal Study of Youth (NLSY).[72a] Large numbers of youths, including whites and blacks, originally selected as part of a nationally representative sample of the U.S. population, were followed to maturity. The mean IQ of the women in this group was compared with the mean IQ of their school-age children. Whereas the mean IQ difference between the white and black mothers in the study was 13.2 IQ points, the difference between the white and black children was 17.5 IQ points. That is, the overall mean W-B IQ difference in this sample had increased by about four IQ points in one generation.[72b] As there is no indication that the children had been reared in less advantaged environments than their mothers, this effect is most reasonably attributable to the negative correlation between the mothers' IQs and their fertility, which is more marked in the NLSY sample than in the Census sample represented in Table 12.7. But I have not found any bona fide data set that disconfirms either the existence of a dysgenic trend for IQ of the population as a whole or the widening disparity in the mean W-B IQ difference.

Racial Differences in Neonate Behavior. Although individual differences in infant psychomotor behavior (i.e., reactivity to sensory stimulation, muscular strength, and coordination) have very little, if any, correlation with mental ability measured from about age three years and up (and therefore are not directly relevant to individual or group differences in g), black and white infants, both in Africa and in America, differ markedly in psychomotor behavior even within the first few days and weeks after birth.[73] Black neonates are more precocious in psychomotor development, on average, than whites, who are more precocious in this respect than Asians. This is true even when the black, white, and Asian babies were born in the same hospital to mothers of similar SES background who gave birth under the same obstetrical conditions.[73a] Early precocity in motor behavior among blacks also appears to be positively related to degree of African ancestry and is negatively related to their SES. African blacks are more precocious than American blacks, and, at least in the United States, black infants of lower SES are more precocious in motor development than blacks of middle and upper-middle SES. (The same SES relationship is also observed in whites.) These behavioral differences appear so early (e.g., one or two days after delivery, when the neonates are still in hospital and have had little contact with the mothers) that purely cultural or environmental explanations seem unlikely. Substantiated in at least three dozen studies,[73b] these findings constitute strong evidence for innate behavioral differences between groups.

Relationship of Myopia to IQ and Race. In Chapter 6 (pp. 149–50) it was noted that myopia (nearsightedness) is positively correlated with IQ and that the relationship appears to be pleiotropic, that is, a gene affecting one of the traits also has some effect on the other trait. Further, there are significant racial and ethnic differences in the frequency of myopia.[74] Among the major racial groups measured, the highest rates of myopia are found in Asians (particularly Chinese and Japanese); the lowest rates among Africans; and Europeans are intermediate. Among Europeans, Jews have the highest rate of myopia, about twice that of gentiles and about on a par with that of the Asians. The same rank ordering of all these groups is found for the central tendency of scores on highly g-loaded tests, even when these groups have had comparable exposure to education. Cultural and environmental factors, except as they may have had an evolutionary impact in the distant past, cannot adequately explain the differences found among contemporary populations. Among populations of the same ethnic background, no relationship has been found between myopia and literacy. Compar-

Table 12.8
Percentages of Preinduction Whites and Blacks Diagnosed as Having Mild or Severe Myopia, and Their Sigma (σ) Equivalents in White and Black U.S. Armed Services Draftees

| | Percentage[a] | | Sigma Equivalent | | |
Group	White	Black	White	Black	B − W
Mild (Accepted)	19.3	3.4	0.87σ	1.83σ	0.96σ
Severe (Rejected)	14.7	4.6	1.05σ	1.69σ	0.64σ
All Draftees	34.0	8.0	0.41σ	1.41σ	1.00σ

[a]From Post (1982, p. 334). White $N = 1,000$; black $N = 1,000$.

isons of groups of the same ethnicity who learned to read before age twelve with those who learned after age twelve showed no difference in rates of myopia.

Table 12.8 shows the results of preinduction examinations of random samples of 1,000 black and 1,1000 white draftees for the U.S. Armed Services who were diagnosed as (a) mildly myopic and accepted for service, and (b) too severely myopic to be accepted. As myopia (measured in diopters) is approximately normally distributed in the population, the percentages of whites and blacks diagnosed as myopic can also be expressed in terms of their deviations from the population mean in standard deviation (σ) units. These average deviations are shown on the right side of Table 12.8. They indicate the approximate cutoff points (in σ units) for the diagnosis of mild and of severe myopia in the total frequency distribution of refractive error (extending from extreme hyperopia, or farsightedness [+3σ], to emmetropia, or normal vision [0σ], to extreme myopia [−3σ]). The last column in Table 12.8 shows the W-B difference in the cutoff point for the diagnosis of myopia, which is 1σ for all who had either mild or severe myopia. Unfortunately, mental test scores on these subjects were not reported, but from other studies one would expect the group diagnosed as myopic to score about 0.5σ higher than the nonmyopic. Studies in Europe and in the United States have reported differences of about seven to eight IQ points between myopes and nonmyopes.[75]

Because myopia appears to be pleiotropic with IQ, the black-white difference in myopia is consistent with the hypothesis of a genetic component in the racial IQ difference. Further studies would be needed to make it an importantly interesting hypothesis. For one thing, the pleiotropy of myopia is not yet all that firmly established. Although one study[76] provides fairly strong evidence for it, confirming studies are needed before one can make any inferences in regard to racial differences. More crucial, it is not known if myopia and IQ are also pleiotropic in the black population; there are no published studies of the correlation between IQ and myopia in blacks. Failure to find such a relationship would nullify the hypothesis.

Other testable hypotheses could also be based on various highly heritable physical traits that are correlated with g (see Chapter 6), some of which show racial differences (e.g., the ability to taste phenylthiocarbamide, color vision, visual acuity, susceptibility to perceptual illusions).[77] But it is first necessary to establish that the correlation of the physical trait with g is pleiotropic within each racial group.

As each specific gene in the human genome related to g is discovered—a search that is getting underway[78]—a determination of the genes' frequencies in different populations may make it possible to estimate the minimum percentage of the between-race variance in g that has a genetic basis. Assuming that the genetic research on quantitative trait loci already underway continues apace, it is possible that the uncertainty regarding the existence, and perhaps even the magnitude, of genetic group differences in g could probably be resolved, should we so desire, within the first decade of the next century.

ENVIRONMENTAL CAUSES OF GROUP DIFFERENCES IN g

From the standpoint of research strategy, it is sensible to ask where one can best look for the environmental variables that are the most likely to cause the nongenetic component of the black-white difference in g. The Factor X hypothesis encourages a search for nongenetic factors that are unique to the black-white difference and absent from individual differences among whites or among blacks. The default hypothesis leads us to look at the same kinds of environmental factors that contribute to g variance *within* each population as causal factors in the g difference between groups.

Among the environmental factors that have been shown to be important within either group, the between-families environmental variance markedly decreases after childhood, becoming virtually nil by late adolescence (see Chapter 7, pp. 179–81). In contrast, the within-family environmental variance remains fairly constant from early childhood to maturity, when it accounts for nearly all of the nongenetic variance and constitutes about 20 percent of the total true-score variance in psychometric g. The *macroenvironmental* variables responsible for the transient between-families variance in g would therefore seem to be an unlikely source of the observed population difference in g. A more likely source is the *microenvironment* that produces the within-family variance. The macroenvironment consists of those aspects of interpersonal behavior, values, customs, preferences, and life-style to which children are exposed at home and which clearly differ between families and ethnic groups in American society. The microenvironment consists of a great many small, often random, events that take place in the course of prenatal and postnatal life. Singly they have small effects on mental development, but in the aggregate they may have a large cumulative effect on the individual. These microenvironmental effects probably account for most of the nongenetic variance in IQ that remains after childhood.[79]

This difference in the potency and persistence of the *macro-* and *micro*environments has been consistently demonstrated in environmental enrichment and intervention programs specifically intended to provide underprivileged black children with the kinds of macroenvironmental advantages typically experienced by white middle-class children. They include use of educational toys and picture books, interaction with nurturing adults, attendance in a preschool or cognitively oriented day-care center, early adoption by well-educated white parents, and even extraordinarily intensive cognitive development programs such as the Milwaukee Project and the Abecedarian Project (Chapter 10, pp. 340–44). The effects of these programs on IQ and scholastic performance have generally been short-lived, and it is still debatable whether these improvements in the macroenvironment have actually raised the level of *g* at all. This is not surprising if we consider that the same class of environmental variables, largely associated with socioeconomic status (SES), has so little, if any, positive effect on *g* or on IQ beyond childhood within the white population. Recent research has shown that the kinds of macroenvironmental factors typically used to describe differences between white lower-middle class and white upper-middle class child-rearing environments and long thought to affect children's cognitive development actually have surprisingly little effect on IQ beyond childhood. The macroenvironmental variables associated with SES, therefore, seem unlikely sources of the black-white difference in *g*.

Hypothesizing environmental factors that are not demonstrably correlated with IQ within one or both populations is useless from the standpoint of scientific explanation. Unless an environmental variable can be shown to correlate with IQ, it has no explanatory value. Many environment-IQ correlations reported in the psychological literature, though real and significant, can be disqualified, however, because the relevant studies completely confound the environmental and the genetic causes of IQ variance. Multiple correlations between a host of environmental assessments and children's IQs ranging from below .50 to over .80 have been found for children reared by their biological parents. But nearly all the correlations found in these studies actually have a genetic basis. This is because children's IQs have 50 percent of their genetic variance in IQ in common with their biological parents, and the parents' IQs are highly correlated (usually about .70) with the very environmental variables that supposedly cause the variance in children's mental development. For children reared by adoptive parents for whom there is no genetic relationship, these same environmental assessments show little correlation with the children's IQs, and virtually zero correlation when the children have reached adolescence. The kinds of environmental variables that show little or no correlation with the IQs of the children who were adopted in infancy, therefore, are not likely to be able to explain IQ differences between subpopulations all living in the same general culture. This is borne out by the study of transracial adoptions (reviewed previously, pp. 472–78).

We can now review briefly the main classes of environmental variables that have been put forth to explain the black-white IQ difference, and evaluate each one in light of the above methodological criteria and the current empirical evidence.

Socioeconomic Status. Measures of SES are typically a composite of occupation, education, income, location of residence, membership in civic or social organizations, and certain amenities in the home (e.g., telephone, TV, phonograph, records, books, newspapers, magazines). Children's SES is that of their parents. For adults, SES is sometimes divided into "attained SES" and "SES of origin" (i.e., the SES of the parents who reared the individual). All of these variables are highly correlated with each other and they share a large general factor in common. Occupation (rank ordered on a scale from unskilled labor to professional and managerial) has the highest loading on this general SES factor.

The population correlations between SES and IQ for children fall in the range .30 to .40; for adults the correlations are .50 to .70, increasing with age as individuals approach their highest occupational level. There has probably been a higher degree of social mobility in the United States than in any other country. The attained SES of between one-third and one-half of the adult population in each generation ends up either above or below their SES of origin. IQ and the level of educational attainments associated with IQ are the best predictors of SES mobility. SES is an effect of IQ rather than a cause. If SES were the cause of IQ, the correlation between adults' IQ and their attained SES would not be markedly higher than the correlation between children's IQ and their parents' SES. Further, the IQs of adolescents adopted in infancy are not correlated with the SES of their adoptive parents. Adults' attained SES (and hence their SES as parents) itself has a large genetic component, so there is a genetic correlation between SES and IQ, and this is so within both the white and the black populations. Consequently, if black and white groups are specially selected so as to be matched or statistically equated[80] on SES, they are thereby also equated to some degree on the genetic component of IQ. Whatever IQ difference remains between the two SES-equated groups, therefore, does not represent a wholly environmental effect. (Because the contrary is so often declared by sociologists, it has been termed the *sociologist's fallacy*.)

When representative samples of the white and black populations are matched or statistically equated on SES, the mean IQ difference is reduced by about one-third. Not all of this five or six IQ points reduction in the mean W-B difference represents an environmental effect, because, as explained above, whites and blacks who are equated on SES are also more alike in the genetic part of IQ than are blacks and whites in general. In every large-scale study, when black and white children were matched within each level on the scale of the parents' SES, the children's mean W-B IQ difference *increased*, going from the lowest to the highest level of SES. A statistical corollary of this phenomenon is the general finding that SES has a somewhat lower correlation (by about .10) with children's IQ in the black than in the white population. Both of these phenomena simply reflect the greater effect of IQ regression toward the population mean for black than for white children matched on above-average SES, as previously explained in this chapter (pp. 467–72). The effect shows up not only for IQ but for all highly g-loaded tests that have been examined in this way. For example, when SAT scores were related to the family income levels of the self-selected students taking the SAT for college admission, Asians from the lowest income level scored higher than blacks from the highest, and black students scored more than one standard deviation below white students from the same income level. It is impossible to explain the overall subpopulation differences in g-loaded test performance in terms of racial group differences in the privileges (or their lack) associated with SES and income.

Additional evidence that W-B differences in cognitive abilities are not the same as SES differences is provided by the comparison of the *profile* of W-B differences with the profile of SES differences on a variety of psychometric tests that measure somewhat different cognitive abilities (in addition to g).

This is illustrated in the three panels of Figure 12.11.[81a] The W-B difference in the national standardization sample on each of the thirteen subtests of the Wechsler Intelligence Scale for Children-Revised (WISC-R) is expressed as a point-biserial correlation between age-controlled scale scores and race (quantitized as white = 1, black = 0). The upper (solid-line) profile in each panel shows the full correlations of race (i.e., W or B) with the age-scaled subtest scores. The lower (dashed-line) profile in each panel shows the partial correlations, with the Full Scale IQ partialed out. Virtually all of the g factor is removed in the partial correlations, thus showing the profile of W-B differences free of g. The partial correlations (i.e., W-B differences) fall to around zero and differ significantly from zero on only six of the thirteen subtests (indicated by asterisks). The profile points for subtests on which whites outperform blacks are positive; those on which blacks outperform whites are negative (i.e., below zero).

Whites perform significantly better than blacks on the subtests called Comprehension, Block Design, Object Assembly, and Mazes. The latter three tests are loaded on the spatial visualization factor of the WISC-R. Blacks perform significantly better than whites on Arithmetic and Digit Span. Both of these tests are loaded on the short-term memory factor of the WISC-R. (As the test of arithmetic reasoning is given orally, the subject must remember the key elements of the problem long enough to solve it.) It is noteworthy that Vocabulary is the one test that shows zero W-B difference when g is removed. Along with Information and Similarities, which even show a slight (but nonsignificant) advantage for blacks, these are the subtests most often claimed to be culturally biased against blacks. The same profile differences on the WISC-R were found in another study[81b] based on 270 whites and 270 blacks who were perfectly matched on Full Scale IQ.

Panels B and C in Figure 12.11 show the profiles of the full and the partial correlations of the WISC-R subtests with SES, separately for whites and blacks. SES was measured on a five-point scale, which yields a mean W-B difference of 0.67 in standard deviation units. Comparison of the profile for race in Panel

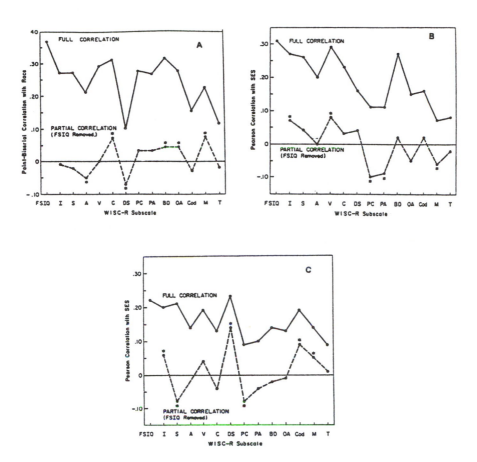

Figure 12.11. *Panel A*: Point-biserial correlation as an index of W-B difference on Full Scale IQ (FSIQ) and on each of thirteen subtests of the WISC-R. The upper profile shows the actual race × subtest correlation; the lower profile shows the correlations with FSIQ partialed out, in effect equating the groups on *g*. Partial correlations significant beyond the .05 level of confidence are indicated by asterisks. The subtests are: I = Information; S = Similarities; A = Arithmetic; V = Vocabulary; C = Comprehension; DS = Digit Span; PC = Picture Completion; PA = Picture Arrangement; BD = Block Design; OA = Object Assembly; M = Mazes; T = Tapping (Knox Cubes).

Panel B: Correlations between SES and subtest scaled scores on the WISC-R for the white sample (*N* = 1,868).

Panel C: Correlations between SES and subtest scores for the black sample (*N* = 305). Reprinted from *Personality and Individual Differences, 3*, A. R. Jensen and C. R. Reynolds, Race, social class and ability patterns on the WISC-R, 423–438, Copyright 1982, with kind permission from Elsevier Science Ltd, The Boulevard, Langford Lane, Kidlington OX5 1GB, UK.

A with the profiles for SES in Panels B and C reveals marked differences. The Pearson correlation between profiles serves as an objective measure of their degree of similarity. The profiles of the partial correlations for race and for SES are *negatively* correlated: −.45 for whites; −.63 for blacks. The SES profiles for whites and for blacks are *positively* correlated: +0.59. While the profile of race × subtest correlations and the profile of SES × subtest correlations are highly dissimilar, the black profile of SES × subtest scores and the white profile of SES × subtest scores are fairly similar. Comparable results were found in another study[82] that included racial and SES profiles based on seventy-five cognitive variables measured in a total sample of 70,000 high school students. The authors concluded, ''[C]omparable levels of socioeconomic status tend to move profiles toward somewhat greater degrees of similarity, but there are also powerful causal factors that operate differentially for race [black-white] that are not revealed in these data. Degree of [economic] privilege is an inadequate explanation of the differences'' (p. 205).

Race and SES Differences in Educational Achievement. Because the specific knowledge content of educational achievement tests is explicitly taught and learned in school, of course, scores on such tests reflect not only the individual's level of _g_ but also the amount and type of schooling, the quality of teaching, and the degree of motivation for scholastic achievement. Nevertheless, tests of educational achievement are quite _g_-loaded, especially for groups of high school age with comparable years of schooling.

It is informative, therefore, to look at the black-white difference on achievement tests for the two most basic scholastic subjects, reading/verbal skills and mathematics, when a number of SES-related factors have been controlled. Such data were obtained on over 28,000 high school students in two independent large-scale surveys, the National Longitudinal Survey of Youth (NLSY) and the National Education Longitudinal Survey (NELS). In the two studies, the actual W-B mean differences on three tests (Math, Verbal, Reading) ranged from about 0.75σ to 1.25σ. Regression analyses of the test scores obtained in each study controlled for a number of SES-related factors: family income, mother's education, father's education, age of mother at the birth of the proband, sex, number of siblings, mother single or married, mother working (or not), region of the country in which the proband lives.

When the effects of these SES factors on test scores statistically were removed by regression, the mean W-B differences in the NLSY were: for Math 0.49σ, for Verbal 0.55σ; in the NELS, for Math 0.59σ, for Reading 0.51.[83] In a multiple-regression analysis for predicting the achievement test scores from twenty-four demographic and personal background variables, no other variable among the twenty-four had a larger predictive weight (independently of all the other variables in the regression equation) than the dichotomous W/B variable. Parents' education was the next most strongly predictive variable (independently of race and all other variables), averaging only about half as much predictive weight as the W/B variable. That most of the predictive power of parental education in these analyses is genetically mediated is inferred from the studies of individuals reared by adoptive parents, whose IQs and educational attainments have a near-zero correlation with that of the adoptees. (See Chapter 7.) Thus, for measures of educational achievement, as for IQ, demographic and SES variables have been shown to account for only a small part of the W-B difference.

The Cumulative Deficit Theory. Cumulative deficit is really an empirical phenomenon that, in the 1960s, became a general theory of how environmental deprivation progressively decreased the IQ and scholastic performance of black children with increasing age relative to white age norms. The phenomenon itself is more accurately termed ''age-related decrement in IQ and achievement,'' which is neutral as regards its nature and cause. The theory of cumulative deficit, its history, and empirical literature have been reviewed elsewhere.[84a] The theory says that environmental and educational disadvantages that cause a failure to learn something at an early age cause further failure at a later age, and the resulting performance deficit, which affects IQ and scholastic achievement alike, increases with age at an accelerating rate, accumulating like compound interest. At each stage of learning, the increasing deficit of prerequisite knowledge and skills hinders learning at each later stage of learning. This theory of the cause of shortfall in IQ and achievement of blacks and other poorly achieving groups was a prominent feature of the rationale for the large-scale federal programs intended to ameliorate these conditions begun in the 1960s—interventions such as Head Start, compensatory education, and a host of experimental preschool programs for disadvantaged children.

The *raw* scores on all mental tests, including tests of scholastic achievement, show an increasing divergence among individuals as they mature, from early childhood to the late teens. In other words, both the mean and the standard deviation of raw scores increase with age. Similarly, the mean W-B difference in raw scores increases with age. This age-related increase in the mean W-B raw score difference, however, is not what is meant by the term ''cumulative deficit.'' The cumulative deficit effect can only be measured at each age in terms of the standardized scores (i.e., measures in units of the standard deviation) for each age. A significant increase of the mean W-B difference in standardized scores (i.e., in σ units) constitutes evidence for cumulative deficit, although this term does not imply the nature of its cause, which has remained purely hypothetical.

The mental test and scholastic achievement data of large-scale studies, such as those from the famous Coleman Report based on 450,000 pupils in 6,000 schools across the nation, failed to find any sign of the cumulative deficit effect for blacks in the nation as a whole. However, suggestive evidence was found for some school districts in the rural South, where the W-B difference in tests of verbal ability increased from 1.5σ to 1.7σ to 1.9σ in Grades 6, 9, and 12, respectively. These findings were only suggestive because they were entirely based on cross-sectional data (i.e., different samples tested at each grade level) rather than longitudinal data (the same sample tested at different grade levels).

Cross-sectional studies of age effects are liable to migratory and demographic changes in the composition of a local population.

Another method with fewer disadvantages even than a longitudinal study (which can suffer from nonrandom attrition of the study sample) compares the IQs of younger and older siblings attending the same schools. Cumulative deficit would be revealed by consistent IQ differences in favor of younger (Y) rather than older (O) siblings. This is measured by the signed difference between younger and older siblings (i.e., Y-O) on age-standardization test scores that constitute an equal-interval scale throughout their full range. Averaged over a large number of sibling pairs, the mean Y-O difference represents only an environmental or nongenetic effect, because there is nothing in genetic theory that relates ‘sibling differences to birth order. The expected mean *genotypic* value of the signed differences between younger and older full siblings is therefore necessarily zero. A phenotypic Y-O difference would indicate the presence of a cumulative IQ deficit with increasing age.

This method was applied to IQ data obtained from all of the full siblings from kindergarten through grade six in a total of seventeen schools in California that had about 60 percent white and 40 percent black pupils.[84a] In general, there was no evidence of a cumulative deficit effect, either for blacks or for whites, with the exception of blacks in the primary grades, who showed the effect only on the verbal part of the IQ test that required some reading skill; the effect was largely attributable to the black males' greater lag in early reading skills compared to the black females; in the early years of schooling, boys in general tend to advance less rapidly in reading than do girls. Blacks showed no cumulative deficit effect at all in nonverbal IQ, and beyond the elementary grades there was no trace of a cumulative deficit in verbal IQ.

Overall, the cumulative deficit hypothesis was not borne out in this California school district, although the mean W-B IQ difference in this school population was greater than 1σ. However, the black population in this California study was socioeconomically more advantaged and socially more integrated with the white population than is true for blacks in many other parts of the country, particular those in the rural South. It is possible that the California black pupils did not show a cumulative deficit in IQ because the vast majority of them had grown up in a reasonably good environment and the cumulative deficit phenomenon might be manifested only when the blacks' degree of environmental disadvantage falls below some critical threshold for a normal rate of mental growth.

Exactly the same methodology, based on Y-O sibling differences in IQ, was therefore applied in an entire school system of a county in rural Georgia.[84b] It perfectly exemplified a generally poor community, especially its black population, which was well below the national black average in SES. Although the school population (49 percent white and 51 percent black) had long since been racially desegregated when the test data were obtained, the blacks' level of scholastic performance was exceedingly low by national standards. The mean W-B IQ difference for the entire school population was 1.95σ (white mean 102,

SD 16.7; black mean 71, *SD* 15.1). If cumulative deficit were a genuine phenomenon and not an artifact of uncontrolled demographic variables in previous cross-sectional studies, the sibling methodology should reveal it in this rural Georgia community. One would be hard put to find a more disadvantaged black community, by all indices, anywhere in the United States. This study, therefore, provides a critical test of the cumulative deficit hypothesis.

The rural Georgia study included all of the full siblings of both racial groups from kindergarten through grade twelve. Appropriate forms of the same standardized IQ test (California Test of Mental Maturity) were used at each grade level. An examination of the test's scale properties in this population showed that it measured IQ as an interval scale throughout the full range of IQ at every age in both the black and white groups, had equally high reliability for both groups, and, despite the nearly two standard deviations IQ difference between the groups, IQ had an approximately normal distribution within each group.

No cumulative deficit effect could be detected in the white group. The Y-O sibling differences for whites showed no increase with age and they were uncorrelated with the age difference between siblings.

The result for blacks, however, was markedly different. The cumulative deficit effect was manifested at a high level of significance ($p < .001$). Blacks showed large decrements in IQ with increasing age that were almost linear from five to sixteen years of age, for both verbal and nonverbal IQ. For total IQ, the blacks had an average rate of IQ decrement of 1.42 points *per year* during their first ten or eleven years in school—in all, a total decrement of about sixteen IQ points, or about half the total W-B difference of thirty-one IQ points that existed in this population.

It would be difficult to attribute the cause of this result to anything other than the effect of an exceedingly poor environment. A genetic hypothesis of the cumulative deficit effect seems highly unlikely in view of the fact that it was not found in blacks in the California study, although the sample size was large enough to detect even a very small effect size at a high level of statistical significance. Even if the blacks in California had, on average, a larger amount of Caucasian ancestry than blacks in rural Georgia, the cumulative deficit effect should have been evident, even if to a lesser degree, in the California group if genetic factors were involved. Therefore, the cause of the cumulative deficit, at least as observed in this study, is most probably of environmental origin. But the specific nature of the environmental cause remains unknown. The fact that it did not show up in the California sample suggests that a cumulative deficit does not account for any appreciable part of the overall W-B IQ difference of about 1σ in nationally representative samples.

The overall W-B IQ difference of 1.95σ in the rural Georgia sample would be reduced to about 1σ if the decrement attributable to the cumulative effect were removed. What aspects of the environment could cause that large a decrement? It would be worthwhile to apply the sibling method used in these studies in other parts of the country, and in rural, urban or "inner city," and suburban

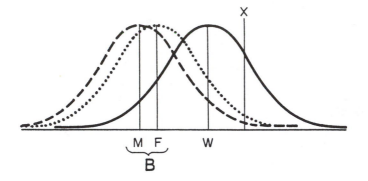

Figure 12.12. Normal curves for male (M) and female (F) blacks (B) and for whites (W) (both sexes combined) to illustrate how a relatively small average sex difference can result in markedly different proportions of males and females that fall above any given selection cutoff score, such as the vertical lines at W (the white mean) and at X.

populations of whites and blacks to determine just how widespread this cumulative deficit effect is in the black population. It is probably the most promising strategy for discovering the specific environmental factors involved in the W-B IQ difference.

The Interaction of Race × Sex × Ability. In 1970, it came to my attention that the level of scholastic achievement was generally higher for black females than for black males. A greater percentage of black females than of black males graduate from high school, enter and succeed in college, pass high-level civil service examinations, and succeed in skilled and professional occupations. A comparable sex difference is not found in the white population. To investigate whether this phenomenon could be attributed to a sex difference in IQ that favored females relative to males in the black population, I proposed the hypothesis I called the *race × sex × ability interaction.* It posits a sex difference in *g* (measured as IQ), which is expressed to some extent in all of the "real life" correlates of *g*. Because of the normal distribution of *g* for both sexes, selection on criteria that demand levels of cognitive ability that are well above the average level of ability in the population will be most apt to reveal the hypothesized sex difference in *g* and all its correlates. Success in passing high-level civil service examinations, in admission to selective colleges, and in high-level occupations, all require levels of ability well above the population average. They should therefore show a large difference in the proportions of each sex that can meet these high selection criteria, even when the average sex difference in the population as a whole is relatively small. This hypothesis is shown graphically in Figure 12.12. For example, if the cutoff score on the criterion for selection is at the white mean IQ of 100 (which is shown as 1σ above the black mean IQ of eighty-five), and if the black female-male difference (F-M) in IQ is only 0.2σ (i.e., three IQ points), the F/M ratio above the cutoff score would be about 1.4 females to 1 male. If the selection cutoff score (X) is placed 2σ above the black mean, the F/M ratio would be 1.6 females to 1 male.

This hypothesis seemed highly worthy of empirical investigation, because if the sex difference in IQ for the black population were larger than it is for the white population (in which it is presumed to be virtually zero), the sex difference could help identify specific environmental factors in the W-B IQ difference itself. It is well established that the male of every mammalian species is generally more vulnerable to all kinds of environmental stress than is the female. There are higher rates of spontaneous abortion and of stillbirths for male fetuses and also a greater susceptibility to communicable diseases and a higher rate of infant mortality. Males are also psychologically less well buffered against unfavorable environmental influences than are females. Because a higher proportion of blacks than of whites grow up in poor and stressful environmental conditions that would hinder mental development, a sex difference in IQ, disfavoring males, would be greater for blacks than for whites.

I tested this race $\times$ sex $\times$ ability interaction hypothesis on all of the test data I could find on white and black samples that provided test statistics separately for males and females within each racial group.[85a] The analyses were based on a collection of various studies which, in all, included seven highly g-loaded tests and a total of more than 20,000 subjects, all of school age and most below age thirteen. With respect to the race $\times$ sex interaction, the predicted effect was inconsistent for different tests and in different samples. The overall effect for the combined data showed a mean female-male (F-M) difference for blacks of $+0.2\sigma$ and for whites of $+0.1\sigma$. Across various tests and samples, the F-M differences for whites and for blacks correlated $+.54$ ($p < .01$), indicating that similar factors for both races accounted for the slight sex difference, but had a stronger effect for blacks. With the large sample sizes, even these small sex differences (equivalent to 3 and 1.5 IQ points for blacks and whites, respectively) are statistically significant. But they are too small to explain the quite large differences in cognitively demanding achievements between male and female blacks.[86] Apparently the sex difference in black achievement must be attributed to factors other than g per se. These may be personality or motivational factors, or sexually differential reward systems for achievement in black society, or differential discrimination by the majority culture. Moreover, because the majority of subjects were of elementary school age and because girls mature more rapidly than boys in this age range, some part of the observed sex difference in test scores might be attributable to differing rates of maturation. Add to this the fact that the test data were not systematically gathered so as to be representative of the whole black and white populations of the United States, or even of any particular region, and it is apparent that while this study allows statistical rejection of the null hypothesis, it does so without lending strong support to the race $\times$ sex interaction hypothesis.

The demise of the hypothesized race $\times$ sex interaction was probably assured

by a subsequent large-scale study[85b] that examined the national standardization
sample of 2,000 subjects on the WISC-R, the 3,371 ninth-grade students in
Project TALENT who were given an IQ test, and a sample of 152,944 pupils
in grades 5, 8, and 11 in Pennsylvania, who were given a test measuring verbal
and mathematical achievement. The subjects' SES was also obtained in all three
data sets. In all these data, the only significant ($p < .05$ with an N of 50,000)
evidence of a race $\times$ sex $\times$ ability interaction was on the verbal achievement
test for eleventh graders, and even it is of questionable significance when one
considers the total number of statistical tests used in this study. In any case, it
is a trifling effect. Moreover, SES did not enter into any significant interaction
with race and sex.

Still another large data set[85c] used the Vocabulary and Block Design subtests
of the WISC-R administered to a carefully selected national probability sample
of 7,119 noninstitutionalized children aged six to eleven years. The Vocabulary
+ Block Design composite of the WISC-R has the highest correlation with the
WISC-R Full Scale IQ of any other pair of subtests, and both Vocabulary and
Block Design are highly *g* loaded. These data also showed no effects that are
consistent with the race $\times$ sex $\times$ ability interaction hypothesis for either Vocabulary or Block Design.[87] Similarly, the massive data of the National Collaborative Perinatal Project, which measured the IQs of more than 20,000 white
and black children at ages four and seven years, yielded such a small interaction
effect as to make its statistical significance virtually irrelevant.[88]

Although the race $\times$ sex interaction hypothesis must now be discarded, it has
nevertheless raised an important question about the environmental factors that
have biological consequences for mental development as a possible cause of the
W-B difference in *g*.

NONGENETIC BIOLOGICAL FACTORS IN THE W-B DIFFERENCE

The psychological, educational, and social factors that differ between families
within racial groups have been found to have little, if any, effect on individual
differences in the level of *g* after childhood. This class of variables, largely
associated with socioeconomic differences between families, has similarly little
effect on the differing average levels of *g* between native-born, English-speaking
whites and blacks. By late adolescence, the IQs of black and white infants
adopted by middle or upper-middle SES white parents are, on average, closer
to the mean IQ of their respective populations than to that of either their adoptive
parents or their adoptive parents' biological children. Preschool programs such
as Head Start and the much more intensive and long-term educational interventions (e.g., the Milwaukee Project and the Abecedarian Project) have been shown
to have little effect on *g*.

It is reasonable, therefore, to look beyond these strictly social and educational
variables and to consider the nongenetic, or environmental, factors of a biolog-

ical nature that may have adverse effects on mental development. These include prenatal variables such as the mother's age, general health, and life-style during pregnancy (e.g., maternal nutrition, smoking, drinking, drug habits), number of previous pregnancies, spacing of pregnancies, blood-type incompatibility (e.g., kernicterus) between mother and fetus, trauma, and history of X-ray exposure. To these can be added the many obstetrical and perinatal variables, including premature birth, low birth weight, duration of labor, forceps delivery, anoxia at birth. Postnatal factors shown to have adverse effects include neonatal and child-hood diseases, head trauma, and malnutrition during the period of maximum growth of the brain (from birth to five years of age). Although each of these biological factors singly may have only a very small average effect on IQ in the population, the cumulative effect of many such adverse microenvironmental factors on any one individual can produce a decrement in g that has significant consequences for that individual's educability. Also, certain variables, though they may have a large negative effect on later IQ for some individuals, occur with such low frequency in the population as to have a negligible effect on the total variance in IQ, either within or between groups.

The largest study of the relationship between these nongenetic factors and IQ is the National Collaborative Perinatal Project conducted by the National Insti-tutes of Health.[89] The study pooled data gathered from twelve metropolitan hospitals located in different regions of the United States. Some 27,000 mothers and their children were studied over a period of several years, starting early in the mother's pregnancy, through the neonatal period, and at frequent intervals thereafter up to age four years (when all of the children were given the Stanford-Binet IQ test). Most of this sample was also tested at age seven years with the Wechsler Intelligence Scale for Children (WISC). About 45 percent of the sam-ple children were white and 55 percent were black. The white sample was slightly below the national average for whites in SES; the black sample was slightly higher in SES than the national black average. The white mothers and black mothers differed 1.02σ on a nonverbal IQ test. The mean W-B IQ dif-ference for the children was 0.86σ at age four years and 1.01σ at age seven years.

A total of 168 variables (in addition to race) were screened. They measured family characteristics, family history, maternal characteristics, prenatal period, labor and delivery, neonatal period, infancy, and childhood. The first point of interest is that eighty-two of the 168 variables showed highly significant ($p <$ .001) correlations with IQ at age four in the white or in the black sample (or in both). Among these variables, 59 (or 72 percent) were also correlated with race; and among the 33 variables that correlated .10 or more with IQ, 31 (or 94 percent) were correlated with race.

Many of these 168 variables, of course, are correlated with each other and therefore are not all independently related to IQ. However, a multiple regression analysis[90] applied to the set of sixty-five variables for which there was complete data for all the probands in the study reveals the proportion of the total variance in IQ that can be reliably accounted for by all sixty-five variables. The regression analyses were performed separately within groups, both by sex (male-female) and by race (white-black), yielding four separate analyses. The percentage of IQ variance accounted for by the sixty-five independent variables (averaged over the four sex × race groups) was 22.7 percent. This is over one-fifth of total IQ variance.

However, not all of this variance in these sixty-five variables is necessarily environmental. Some of the IQ variance is attributable to regional differences in the populations surveyed, as the total subject sample was distributed over twelve cities in different parts of the country. And some of the variance is attributable to the mother's education and socioeconomic status. (This information was not obtained for fathers.) Mother's education alone accounts for 13 percent of the children's IQ variance, but this is most likely a genetic effect, since adopted children of this age show about the same degree of relationship to their biological mothers with whom they have had no social contact. The proband's score on the Bayley Scale obtained at eight months of age also should not be counted as an environmental variable. This yields four variables in the regression analysis that should not be counted strictly as environmental factors— region, mother's education, SES, and child's own test score at eight months. With the effects of these variables removed, the remaining sixty-one environmental variables account for 3.4 percent of the variance in children's IQ, averaged over the four race × sex groups. Rather unexpectedly, the proportion of environmental variance in IQ was somewhat greater in the white sample than in the black (4.2 percent vs. 2.6 percent). The most important variable affecting the probands' IQ independently of mother's education and SES in both racial groups was mother's age, which was positively correlated with child's IQ for mothers in the age range of twelve to thirty-six years.[91]

How can we interpret these percentage figures in terms of IQ points? Assuming that the total variance in the population consisted only of the variance contributed by this large set of environmental variables, virtually all of a biological but nongenetic nature, the standard deviation of true-score IQs in the population would be 2.7 IQ points. The average absolute IQ difference between pairs of individuals picked at random from this population would be three IQ points. This is the average effect that the strictly biological environmental variables measured in the Collaborative Project has on IQ. It amounts to about one-fifth of the average mean W-B IQ difference.

Unfortunately, the authors of the Collaborative Project performed only within-group regression analyses. They did not enter race as an independent variable into the multiple regression analysis, stating explicitly that the independent effect of race was not assessed. A regression analysis in which race, as an independent variable, was entered after all of the nongenetic environmental variables could have shown the independent effect of race on IQ when the effect of the environmental variables was removed. This would have allowed testing of the strict form of the default hypothesis. It posits that the environmental variance between

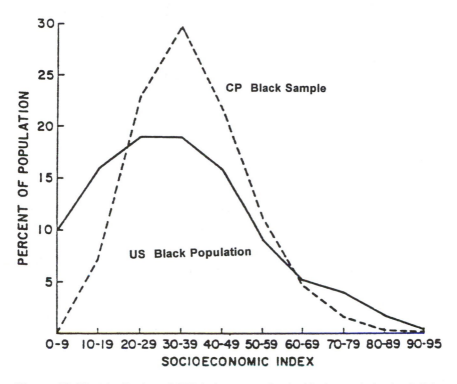

Figure 12.13. Distribution of SES index scores for the black sample in the Collaborative Project (CP) and for the U.S. black population. (From *Preschool IQ* (p. 23), by Broman et al., 1975, Hillsdale, NJ: Erlbaum. Copyright © 1975. Reprinted with permission of Erlbaum and S. H. Broman.)

groups is the same as the environmental variance within groups, in which case about three points of the fifteen points mean W-B IQ difference would be attributable to nongenetic biological environment, assuming that all of these environmental factors worked in a harmful direction for blacks.[92]

There are three reasons to suspect that this study underrepresents the effects of the nongenetic biological environment on the IQ of blacks in the general populations.

1. The black sample is somewhat above average in SES compared to the black population as a whole. What today is termed the underclass, which includes some one-fourth to one-third of the total black population, is underrepresented in the study sample; much of the U.S. black population is at or below the zero point on the scale of SES used in this study, as shown in Figure 12.13. The biological factors that adversely affect IQ almost certainly have a higher incidence in this poorest segment of the population, which was underrepresented in the Collaborative Project.

2. The selection of mothers entering the study excluded all women who had

not received care in the prenatal clinic from early in their pregnancies. All of the subjects in the study, both black and white, received prenatal care, while many underclass mothers do not receive prenatal care. The Project mothers also received comparable high-quality obstetrical and perinatal treatment, followed up with comparable neonatal and infant medical care provided by the collaborating hospitals. Pregnancies in the underclass are typically without these medical advantages.

3. Certain environmental factors that in recent years have been studied in relation to IQ, such as nutrition, breast feeding, fetal alcohol syndrome, and drug abuse, were not considered in the Collaborative Project conducted three decades ago. The causal role of these factors should be examined, as should the increasing incidence of premature delivery and low birth weight. The latter variables are in fact the strongest correlates of low IQ.

Low Birth Weight (LBW). Infant mortality can be viewed as the extreme point on a continuum of pathology and reproductive casualty. The rate of neonatal and infant mortality in a particular population, therefore, serves as an indicator of other sublethal but nevertheless damaging health conditions, which negatively affect children's mental development. While the infant mortality rate has steadily declined in the population as a whole over the last several decades, it is still about twice as great in the U.S. black population (17.6 per 1,000 live births) as in the white population (8.5 per 1,000). Other minority populations differ only slightly from whites; of the groups with lower SES than the white average (such as Hispanics, American Indians, and native Alaskans) the infant mortality rate averages about 8.6 per 1,000. Asians have by far the lowest average, about 4.3 per 1,000.[93]

LBW is defined as a birth weight under 2,500 grams (5.5 pounds). It represents a region on the risk continuum of which infant death is the end point. Therefore, the rates of LBW and of infant mortality are highly correlated across different subpopulations. Although premature birth incurs its own risks for the neonate's development, it is not the same as LBW, because a premature baby may have normal weight for its gestational age. LBW also occurs in full-term babies, who are thereby at increased risk for retarded mental development and for other developmental problems, such as behavioral adjustment, learning disabilities, and poor scholastic performance. Throughout the full range of LBW, all of these developmental risks increase as birth weight decreases. For present purposes, it is important to note that a disproportionate number of the babies born to black women are either premature or of LBW. Although black women have about 17 percent of all the babies born in the United States today, they have about 32 percent of the LBW babies.[94]

The mother's age is the strongest correlate of LBW and is probably its chief causal factor. Teenage mothers account for about one-fourth of LBW babies. Even teenage girls under age eighteen who have had proper health care during pregnancy are twice as likely to have premature or LBW babies as women in their twenties. One suggested explanation is that teenage girls are still in their growing period, which causes some of the nutrients essential for normal development to be diverted from the growing fetus to the growing mother. In addition to teenage pregnancy, other significant correlates of LBW are unmarried status, maternal anemia, substance abuse of various kinds, and low educational levels. SES per se accounts for only about 1 percent of the total variance in birth weight, and race (black/white) has a large effect on birth weight independently of SES. Most of the W-B difference in birth weight remains unaccounted for by such variables as SES, poverty status, maternal age, and education. Prenatal medical care, however, has a small effect.[95]

LBW, independently of SES, is related to low maternal IQ. Controlling for IQ reduces the B-W disparity in the percentage of LBW babies by about one-half.[96] But even college-educated black women have higher rates of LBW babies and therefore also higher rates of infant mortality than occur for white women of similar educational background (10.2 per thousand vs. 5.4 per thousand live births). When black babies and white babies, both born to college-educated parents, are statistically equated for birth weight, they have the same mortality rates in the first year of life. In the general population, however, black infants who are not of LBW have a mortality rate almost twice that of white infants.[97]

The cause of the high rate of LBW (and the consequently higher infant mortality rate) in the black population as compared with other racial or ethnic groups, including those that are less advantaged than blacks, remains a mystery. Researchers have been able to account for only about half of the disparity in terms of the combined obvious factors such as poverty, low levels of SES, education, health and prenatal care, and mother's age. The explanations run the gamut from the largely genetic to the purely environmental. Some researchers regard LBW as an inherent, evolved, genetic racial characteristic.[95,98] Others have hypothesized that black mothers may have subtle health problems that span generations, and some have suggested subtle but stressful effects of racism as a cause.[99]

Since the specific causes of LBW largely remain unidentified while the survival rate of LBW babies has been increasing over the past 20 years, researchers are now focusing on ways to mitigate its risks for developmental disabilities and to enhance the cognitive and behavioral development of LBW babies. The experimental treatment was highly similar to that provided in the Abecedarian Project described in Chapter 10 (pp. 342–44). The largest program of this kind, conducted with nearly one thousand LBW infants in eight states, showed large Stanford-Binet IQ gains (compared against a control group) for LBW children when they were tested at thirty-six months of age. The heavier LBW probands (BW between 2,001 and 2,500 grams) scored an average of 13.2 IQ points above the untreated control group (98.0 vs. 84.8); the lighter probands (<2,000 grams) scored 6.6 IQ points above the controls (91.0 vs. 84.4).[100a] Because IQ measured at thirty-six months is typically unstable, follow-up studies are crucial to determine if these promising IQ gains in the treated group would persist into the school years. The data obtained in the first follow-up, conducted when the children were five years of age, show that the apparent initial gain in IQ had not been maintained; the intervention group scored no higher than the control group.[100b] There was a further follow-up at age eight, but its results have not yet been reported.[100c]

A study of forty-six LBW black and forty-six LBW white children matched for gestational age and birth weight (all between 1,000 and 2,500 grams and averaging 1,276 grams for blacks and 1,263 grams for whites) showed that when the degree of LBW and other IQ-related background variables were controlled, the W-B IQ difference, even at three years of age, was nearly the same as that found for the general population.[101] None of the LBW children in these selected samples had any chronic illness or neurological abnormality; all were born to mothers over eighteen years of age and had parents who were married. The black mothers and white mothers were matched for educational level. (Black mothers actually had slightly more education than white mothers, although the difference was statistically insignificant, $t < 1$). When the children were tested at thirty-three to thirty-four months, the mean Stanford-Binet IQ of the black and the white groups was 90 and 104, respectively, a difference of 1.0σ. In the same study, groups of middle class black and white children of normal birth weight and gestational age, matched on maternal education, had a mean Stanford-Binet IQ of ninety-seven and 111, respectively (a 1.2σ difference).

Nutrition. A most remarkable study[102a] conducted at Cambridge University showed that the average IQ of preterm, LBW babies was strongly influenced by whether the babies received mother's milk or formula while in hospital. The probands were 300 babies who weighed under 1,850 grams at birth. While in hospital, 107 of the babies received formula, and 193 received mother's milk. The effects of breast feeding per se were ruled out (at least while the babies were in hospital), as all of the babies were fed by tube. At 7.5 to eight years of age, WISC-R IQs were obtained for all 300 children. Astonishingly, those who had received maternal milk outscored those who had been formula-fed by 10.2 IQ points (103.0 vs. 92.8). The Verbal and Performance scales showed identical effects. After a regression analysis that adjusted for confounding factors (SES, mother's age and education, birth weight, gestational age, birth rank, sex, and number of days in respirator), the difference between the two groups was still a highly significant 8.3 IQ points. Not all of the group who received mother's milk had it exclusively; some received variable proportions of mother's milk and formula. It was therefore possible to perform a critical test of whether the effect was genuinely attributable to the difference between mother's milk and formula or was attributable to some other factor. There was in fact a significant linear dose-response relationship between the amount of mother's milk the babies received and IQ at age 7.5 to eight years. Whether the milk was from the baby's own mother or from donors, it had a beneficial effect on IQ compared against the formula. The study did not attempt to determine whether mother's milk has a similarly advantageous effect for babies who are full-term and of normal birth weight.

The results, however, would seem to be highly relevant to the IQ of black children in contemporary U.S. for two reasons: (1) as was already pointed out, black infants are much more frequently of LBW than are those of other racial/ethnic groups, and (2) they are much less frequently breast fed. Surveys of the National Center for Health Statistics[102b] show that, as of 1987, 61.1 percent of non-Hispanic white babies and 25.3 percent of non-Hispanic black babies are breast fed. Black women who breast feed also end nursing sooner than do white mothers. These data suggest that some part of the average W-B IQ difference may be attributable to the combined effects of a high rate of LBW and a low frequency of breast feeding. Nationwide in the 1940s and 1950s, breast feeding declined markedly to less than 30 percent, as greater numbers of women entered the work force. But since the late 1950s there has been an overall upward trend in the percentage of babies who are breast fed, now exceeding 60 percent.

The practice of breast feeding itself is *positively* correlated with SES, maternal age and education, and, interestingly, with birth weight. The frequency of breast feeding for LBW babies (<2,500 grams) is only 38.4 percent as against 56.1 percent for babies of normal birth weight (>2,500 grams). But as regards mental development it is probably the LBW babies that stand to benefit the most from mother's milk. Human milk apparently contains factors that affect nervous system development, probably long-chain lipids, hormones, or other nutrients involved in brain growth, that are not present in formulas.

More generally, Eysenck has hypothesized that nutritional deficiencies may be major nongenetic cause of the W-B IQ difference and that research should be focused on dietary supplements to determine their effect on children's IQ.[103a] He is not referring here to the type of malnutrition resulting from low caloric intake and insufficient protein, which is endemic in parts of the Third World but rare in the United States. Rather, he is referring to more or less idiosyncratic deficiencies associated with the wide range of individual differences in the requirements for certain vitamins and minerals essential for optimal brain development and cognitive functions. These individual differences can occur even among full siblings reared together and having the same diet. The dietary deficiency in these cases is not manifested by the gross outward signs of malnutrition seen in some children of Third World countries, but can only be diagnosed by means of blood tests. Dietary deficiencies, mainly in certain minerals and trace elements, occur even in some middle-class white families that enjoy a normally wholesome diet and show no signs of malnutrition. Blood samples were taken from all of the children in such families prior to the supplementation of certain minerals to the diet and later analyzed. They revealed that only those children who showed a significant IQ gain (twice the test's standard error of measurement, or nine IQ points) after receiving the supplements for several months previously showed deficiencies of one or more of the minerals in their blood. The children for whom the dietary supplement resulted

in IQ gains were called "responders." The many children who were nonres-
ponders showed little or no blood evidence of a deficiency in the key nutrients.
Most interesting from a theoretical standpoint is that the IQ gains showed up
on tests of fluid g (Gf), which measures immediate problem-solving ability, but
failed to do so on tests of crystallized g (Gc), such as general information and
vocabulary, which measure the past learning that had taken place before dietary
supplements were begun.[103b] Eysenck believes it is more likely that a much
larger percentage of black children than of white children have a deficiency of
the nutritional elements that, when supplemented in the diet, produce the observed gain in Gf, which eventually, of course, would also be reflected in Gc
through the child's improved learning ability. This promising hypothesis, which
has not yet been researched with respect to raising black children's level of g,
is well worth studying.

Drug Abuse during Pregnancy. Many drugs can be more damaging to the
developing fetus than to an adult, and drug abuse takes a higher toll on the
mental development of newborns in the underclass than it does in the general
population. Among all drugs, prenatal exposure to alcohol is the most frequent
cause of developmental disorders, including varying degrees of mental retardation. *Fetal alcohol syndrome* (FAS), a severe form of prenatal damage caused
by the mother's alcohol intake, is estimated to affect about three per 1,000 live
births.[104a] The signs of FAS include stunted physical development and characteristic facial features, besides some degree of behavioral impairment—at
school age about half of such children are diagnosed as mentally retarded or as
learning disabled. The adverse effect of prenatal exposure to alcohol on the
infant's later mental development appears to be a continuous variable; there is
no safe threshold of maternal alcohol intake below which there is zero risk to
the fetus. Therefore the U.S. Surgeon General has recommended that women
not drink at any time during pregnancy. Just how much of the total population
variance in IQ might be attributed to prenatal alcohol is not known, but in the
underclass segment of the population its effect, combined with other microenvironmental factors that lower IQ, is apt to be considerable.

After alcohol, use of barbiturates, or sedative drugs, by pregnant women is
the most prevalent source of adverse effects on their children's IQ. Between
1950 and 1970, an estimated twenty-two million children were born in the
United States to women who were taking prescribed barbiturates. Many others,
without prescription, abused these drugs. Two major studies were conducted in
Denmark to determine the effect of phenobarbital, a commonly used barbiturate,
on the adult IQ of men whose mothers had used this drug during pregnancy.[104b]
The men's IQs were compared with the IQs of controls matched on ten background variables that are correlated with IQ, such as proband's age, family SES
when the probands were infants, parents' ages, whether the pregnancy was
"wanted" or "not wanted," etc. Further control of background variables was
achieved statistically by a multiple regression technique. In the first study, IQ
was measured by the Wechsler Adult Intelligence Scale (WAIS), an individually

administered test; the second study used the Danish Military Draft Board Intelligence Test, a forty-five-minute group test. In both studies the negative effect of prenatal phenobarbital on adult IQ, after controlling for background variables, was considerable. In the authors' words: "The individuals exposed to phenobarbital are not mentally retarded nor did they have any obvious physical abnormalities. Rather, because of their exposure more than 20 years previously, they ultimately test at approximately 0.5 *SD* or more lower on measured intelligence than otherwise would have been expected."[104b, p. 1514] Analysis of various subclasses of the total sample showed that the negative drug exposure effect was greater among those from lower SES background, those exposed in the third trimester and earlier, and the offspring of an unwanted pregnancy.

AD HOC THEORIES OF THE WHITE-BLACK IQ DIFFERENCE

The totality of environmental factors now known to affect IQ within either the white or the black population taken together cannot account for a larger amount of the total variance between groups than does the default hypothesis. The total between-populations variance accounted for by empirically demonstrable environmental factors does not exceed 20 to 30 percent. According to the default hypothesis, the remaining variance is attributable to genetic factors. But one can still eschew genetic factors and instead hypothesize a second class of nongenetic factors to explain the observed differences—factors other than those already taken into account as sources of nongenetic variance *within* groups. However, exceptionally powerful effects would have to be attributed to these hypothesized nongenetic factors if they are to explain fully the between-groups variance that the default hypothesis posits as genetic.

The explanations so far proposed to account for so large a part of the IQ variance in strictly nongenetic terms involve subtle factors that seem implausible in light of our knowledge of the nature and magnitude of the effects that affect IQ. Many researchers in the branches of behavioral science related to this issue, as opposed to journalists and commentators, are of the opinion that the W-B difference in IQ involves genetic factors. A questionnaire survey[105] conducted in 1987 solicited the anonymous opinions of 661 experts, most of them in the fields of differential psychology, psychometrics, and behavioral genetics. Here is how they responded to the question: "Which of the following best characterizes your *opinion* of the heritability of the black-white difference in IQ?"

15% said: The difference is entirely due to environmental variation.

1% said: The difference is entirely due to genetic variation.

45% said: The difference is a product of both genetic and environmental variation.

24% said: The data are insufficient to support any reasonable opinion.

14% said: They did not feel qualified to answer the question.

Those behavioral scientists who attribute the difference entirely to the environment typically hypothesize factors that are unique to the historical experience of blacks in the United States, such as a past history of slavery, minority status, caste status, white racism, social prejudice and discrimination, a lowered level of aspiration resulting from restricted opportunity, peer pressure against "acting white," and the like. The obvious difficulty with these variables is that we lack independent evidence that they have any effect on *g* or other mental ability factors, although in some cases one can easily imagine how they might adversely affect motivation for certain kinds of achievement. But as yet no mechanism has been identified that causally links them to *g* or other psychometric factors. There are several other problems with attributing causality to this class of variables:

1. Some of the variables (e.g., a past history of slavery, minority or caste status) do not explain the W-B 1σ to 1.5σ mean difference on psychometric tests in places where blacks have never been slaves in a nonblack society, or where they have never been a minority population, or where there has not been a color line.

2. These theories are made questionable by the empirical findings for other racial or ethnic groups that historically have experienced as much discrimination as have blacks, in America and other parts of the world, but do not show any deficit in mean IQ. Asians (Chinese, Japanese, East Indian) and Jews, for example, are minorities (some are physically identifiable) in the United States and in other countries, and have often experienced discrimination and even persecution, yet they perform as well or better on *g*-loaded tests and in *g*-loaded occupations than the majority population of any of the countries in which they reside. Social discrimination per se obviously does not cause lower levels of *g*. One might even conclude the opposite, considering the minority subpopulations in the United States and elsewhere that show high *g* and high *g*-related achievements, relative to the majority population.

3. The causal variable posited by these theories is unable to explain the detailed empirical findings, such as the large variability in the size of the W-B difference on various kinds of psychometric tests. As noted in Chapter 11, most of this variability is quite well explained by the modified Spearman hypothesis. It states that the size of the W-B difference on various psychometric tests is mainly related to the tests' *g* loadings, and the difference is increased if the test is also loaded on a spatial factor and it is decreased if the test is also loaded on a short-term memory factor. It is unlikely that broad social variables would produce, within the black and white populations, the ability to rank-order the various tests in a battery in terms of their loadings on *g* and the spatial and memory factors and then to distribute their effort on these tests to accord with the prediction of the modified Spearman hypothesis. (Even Ph.D. psychologists cannot do this.) Such a possibility is simply out of the question for three-year-olds, whose performance on a battery of diverse tests has been found to accord with Spearman's hypothesis (see Chapter 11, p. 385). It is hard to even imagine a social variable that could cause systematic variation in the size of the W-B difference across different tests that is unrelated to the specific informational or

cultural content of the tests, but is consistently related to the tests' g loadings (which can only be determined by performing a factor analysis).

4. Test scores have the same validity for predicting educational and occupational performance for all American-born, English-speaking subpopulations whatever their race or ethnicity. Blacks, on average, do not perform at a higher level educationally or on the job, relative to other groups, than is predicted by g-loaded tests. An additional ad hoc hypothesis is required, namely, that the social variables that depress blacks' test scores must also depress blacks' performance on a host of nonpsychometric variables to a degree predicted by the regression of the nonpsychometric variables on the psychometric variables within the white population. This seems highly improbable. In general, the social variables hypothesized to explain the lower average IQ of blacks would have to simulate consistently all of the effects predicted by the default hypothesis and Spearman's hypothesis. To date, the environmental theories of the W-B IQ difference put forward have been unable to do this. Moreover, it is difficult or impossible to perform an empirical test of their validity.

A theory that seems to have gained favor among some social anthropologists is the idea of "caste status" put forth by the anthropologist John Ogbu.[106a] He states the key point of his theory as follows: "The people who have most difficulty with IQ tests and other forms of cognitive tasks are involuntary or nonimmigrant minorities. This difficulty arises because their cultures are not merely different from that of the dominant group but may be in opposition to the latter. Therefore, the tests acquire symbolic meanings for these minorities, which cause additional but as yet unrecognized problems. It is more difficult for them to cross cognitive boundaries."[106b, p. 336]

Ogbu's answer to criticism number 2 (above) is to argue that cultural factors that depress IQ do so only in the case of *involuntary* or nonimmigrant minorities and their descendants. In the United States this applies only to blacks (who were brought to America involuntarily to be sold as slaves) and native Americans (who score, on average, intermediate between blacks and whites on tests of fluid g). This theory does not account for the relatively high test scores and achievements of East Indians in Africa, whose ancestors were brought to Africa as indentured laborers during the nineteenth century, but Ogbu could reply that the indentured Indians were not truly involuntary immigrants. American blacks, in Ogbu's theory, have the status of a caste that is determined by birth and from which there is no mobility. Lower-caste status, it is argued, depresses IQ. Ogbu cites as evidence the Harijans (untouchables) of India and the Burakumi in Japan as examples. (The Burkumi constitute a small subpopulation of Asian origin that engages in work the Japanese have traditionally considered undesirable, such as tanning leather.) Although it is true that these "lower-caste" groups generally do have lower test scores and perform less well in school than do higher-status groups in India or Japan, the body of psychometric evidence is much less than that for American blacks. We know hardly anything regarding the magnitude or psychometric nature or the degree of genetic selection for *g* in the origins of these caste-like groups in India and Japan.

Ogbu also argues that conventional IQ tests measure only those types of cognitive behavior that are culturally valued by Western middle-class societies, and IQ tests therefore inevitably discriminate against minorities within such societies. But since such tests have equal predictive validity for blacks and whites, this would have to imply that performance on the many practical criteria predicted by the tests is also lowered by involuntary but not voluntary minority status. According to Ogbu, the "Western intelligence" measured by our psychometric tests represents only a narrow set of specialized cognitive abilities and skills. These have been selected on the basis of Western values from the common species pool of capabilities for adaptation to specific environmental circumstances. It logically follows, then, that the *g* factor and the spatial factor themselves represent specialized Western cognitive skills. The question that Ogbu neither asks nor answers is why this set of Western-selected abilities has not been acquired to the same degree by a population of African descent that has been exposed to a Western society for many generations, while first-generation immigrants and refugees in America who came from the decidedly non-Western Oriental and East Indian cultures soon perform on a par with the dominant population of European descent.

A similar view of racial and ethnic IQ differences has been expressed by the economist Thomas Sowell.[107] He does not offer a formal or explanatory theory, but rather a broad analogy between American blacks and other ethnic and national groups that have settled in the United States at different times in the past. Sowell points out that many immigrant groups performed poorly on tests at one time (usually soon after their arrival in America) and had relatively low educational standing, which limited their employment to low-paying jobs. The somewhat lower test scores of recent immigrants are usually attributable to unfamiliarity with the English language, as evidenced by their relatively superior performance on nonverbal tests. Within a single generation, most immigrant groups (typically those from Europe or Asia) performed on various intellectual criteria at least on a par with the established majority population. Sowell views the American black population as a part of this same general phenomenon and expects that in due course it, too, will rise to the overall national level. Only one generation, he points out, has grown up since inception of the Civil Rights movement and the end of de jure segregation.

But Sowell's analogy between blacks and other immigrant groups seems strained when one examines the performance of comparatively recent arrivals from Asia. The W-B difference in IQ (as distinguished from educational and socioeconomic performance) has not decreased significantly since World War I, when mental tests were first used on a nationwide scale. On the other hand, the children of certain recent refugee and immigrant groups from Asia, despite their different language and culture, have scored as high as the native white population on nonverbal IQ tests and they often exceed the white average in scholastic performance.[108] Like Ogbu, Sowell does not deal with the detailed pattern of psychometric differences between blacks and whites. He attributes the lower black performance on tests involving abstract reasoning ability to poor motivation, quoting a statement by observers that black soldiers tested during World War I tended to "lapse into inattention and almost into sleep" during abstract tests.[107, p. 164] Spearman, to the contrary, concluded on the basis of factor analyzing more than 100 varied tests that "abstractness" is one of the distinguishing characteristics of the most highly g-loaded tests.[109]

Recently, a clearly and specifically formulated hypothesis, termed *stereotype threat*, has been proposed to explain at least some part of the black shortfall on cognitive tests. It should not be classed as a Factor X theory, because specific predictions can be logically derived from the hypothesis and tested empirically. Its authors have done so, with positive, though somewhat limited, results.[110]

Stereotype threat is defined as the perceived risk of confirming, as self-characteristic, a negative stereotype about one's group. The phenomenon has been demonstrated in four independent experiments. Groups of black and white undergraduates at Stanford University took mentally demanding verbal tests under preliminary instructions that were specifically intended to elicit stereotype threat. This was termed the *diagnostic condition*, since the instructions emphasized that the student's score (which they would be given) would be a true indicator of their verbal ability and of their limitations. Their test performance was statistically compared with that of a control group, for whom the preliminary instructions were specifically intended to minimize stereotype threat by making no reference to ability and telling the subjects that the results were being used only for research on difficult verbal problems. This was termed the *nondiagnostic condition*. Under both conditions, subjects were asked to do their best. The theoretically predicted outcome is that the difference in test performance between the diagnostic and the nondiagnostic conditions will be greater for blacks than for whites. With the black and white groups statistically equated for SAT scores, the hypothesis was generally borne out in the four studies, although the predicted interaction (race × condition) in two of the experiments failed to reach the conventional 5 percent level of confidence.

Standard deviations were not reported for any of the performance measures, so the effect size of the stereotype threat cannot be precisely determined. From the reported analysis of variance, however, I have estimated the effect size to be about 0.3σ, on average. Applied to IQ in the general population, this would be equivalent to about five IQ points. Clearly, the stereotype threat hypothesis should be further studied using samples of blacks and whites that are less highly selected for intellectual ability than are the students at Stanford. One wonders if stereotype threat affects the IQ scores even of preschool-age children (at age three), for whom the W-B difference is about 1σ. Do children at this age have much awareness of stereotypes?

In fact, the phenomenon of stereotype threat can be explained in terms of a more general construct, *test anxiety*, which has been studied since the early days

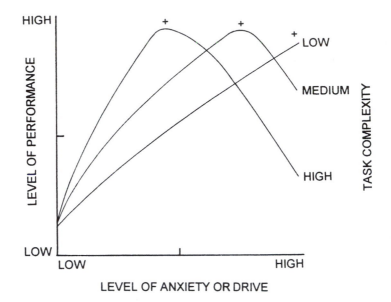

Figure 12.14. A graphic representation of the Yerkes-Dodson law, showing that the peak task performance (+) occurs at different levels of anxiety (or drive) depending on task complexity and difficulty.

of psychometrics.[111a] Test anxiety tends to lower performance levels on tests in proportion to the degree of complexity and the amount of mental effort they require of the subject. The relatively greater effect of test anxiety in the black samples, who had somewhat lower SAT scores, than the white subjects in the Stanford experiments constitutes an example of the Yerkes-Dodson law.[111b] It describes the empirically observed nonlinear relationship between three variables: (1) anxiety (or drive) level, (2) task (or test) complexity and difficulty, and (3) level of test performance. According to the Yerkes-Dodson law, the maximal test performance occurs at decreasing levels of anxiety as the perceived complexity or difficulty level of the test increases (see Figure 12.14). If, for example, two groups, A and B, have the same level of test anxiety, but group A is higher than group B in the ability measured by the test (so group B finds the test more complex and difficult than does group A), then group B would perform less well than group A. The results of the Stanford studies, therefore, can be explained in terms of the Yerkes-Dodson law, without any need to postulate a racial group difference in susceptibility to stereotype threat or even a difference in the level of test anxiety. The outcome predicted by the Yerkes-Dodson law has been empirically demonstrated in large groups of college students who were either relatively high or relatively low in measured cognitive ability; increased levels of anxiety adversely affected the intelligence test performance of low-ability students (for whom the test was frustratingly difficult) but improved the level of performance of high-ability students (who experienced less difficulty).[111c]

This more general formulation of the stereotype threat hypothesis in terms of the Yerkes-Dodson law suggests other experiments for studying the phenomenon by experimentally manipulating the level of test difficulty and by equating the tests' difficulty levels for the white and black groups by matching items for percent passing the item within each group. Groups of blacks and whites should also be matched on true-scores derived from g-loaded tests, since equating the groups statistically by means of linear covariance analysis (as was used in the Stanford studies) does not adequately take account of the nonlinear relationship between anxiety and test performance as a function of difficulty level.

Strong conclusions regarding the stereotype threat hypothesis are unwarranted at present, as the total evidence for it is based on fairly small samples of high-ability university students, with results of marginal statistical significance. Research should be extended to more representative samples of the black and white populations and using standard mental test batteries under normal testing conditions except, of course, for the preliminary instructions needed to manipulate the experimental variable (that is, the inducement of stereotype threat). Further, by conducting the same type of experiment using exclusively white (or black) subjects, divided into lower- and higher-ability groups, it might be shown that the phenomenon attributed to stereotype threat has nothing to do with race as such, but results from the interaction of ability level with test anxiety as a function of test complexity.

In contrast to these various ad hoc hypotheses intended to explain the average W-B population difference in cognitive ability, particularly g, the default hypothesis has the attributes of simplicity, internal coherence, and parsimony of explanation. Further, it does not violate Occam's razor by treating one particular racial population as a special case that is culturally far more different from any other populations. The size of the cultural difference that needs to be hypothesized by a purely environmental theory of the W-B difference is far greater than the relatively small genetic difference implied by our evolution from common human ancestors.

The default hypothesis explains differences in g *between* populations in terms of quantitative variation in the very same genetic and environmental factors that influence the neural substrate of g and cause individual variation *within* all human populations. This hypothesis is consistent with a preponderance of psychometric, behavior-genetic, and evolutionary lines of evidence. And like true scientific hypotheses generally, it continually invites empirical refutation. It should ultimately be judged on the same basis, so aptly described by the anthropologist Owen Lovejoy, for judging the Darwinian theory of human evolution:

> Evolutionary scenarios must be evaluated much in the same way that jury members must judge a prosecutor's narrative. Ultimately they must make their judgment not on the basis of any single fact or observation, but on the totality of the available

evidence. Rarely will any single item of evidence prove pivotal in determining whether a prosecutor's scenario or the defense's alternative is most likely to be correct. Many single details may actually fail to favor one scenario over another. The most probable account, instead, is the one which is the most internally consistent—the one in which all the facts mesh together most neatly with one another and with the motives in the case. Of paramount importance is the *economy of explanation*. There are always alternative explanations of any single isolated fact. The greater the number of special explanations required in a narrative, however, the less probable its accuracy. An effective scenario almost always has a compelling facility to explain a chain of facts with a minimum of such special explanations. Instead the pieces of the puzzle should fall into place.[112, p. 2]

NOTES

1. Rushton, 1989.
2. Jensen, 1994f.
3. The rate of change in the frequency of a particular allele in a population depends partly on its relative fitness, or reproductive advantage. It also depends on the amount of variation at that gene locus in the population; a rare allele, regardless of its relative fitness, spreads slowly at first and then at an accelerating rate. To take an extreme example, say that a rare allele occurs with a frequency of only 1 percent in a given population, and this allele enhances fitness by only 1 percent (i.e., those who possess the allele have 1 percent more progeny than those who do not possess it). Then, over the course of 1,000 generations, assuming the same reproductive advantage is maintained over this period, the percentage of individuals in the population who possess the allele will have risen from the original 1 percent up to 99 percent. If a change in the physical or social environment for some reason made the same allele disadvantageous in terms of fitness, its frequency in the population would gradually decrease, either to zero or to its low frequency of occurrence through spontaneous mutation of another allele at the same chromosomal locus.

4. One often hears it said that the genetic differences *within* racial groups (defined as statistically different breeding populations) is much greater than the differences *between* racial groups. This is true, however, only if one is comparing the *range* of *individual differences* on a given characteristic (or on a number of characteristics) *within* each population with the *range* of the differences that exist between the *means* of each of the separate populations on the given characteristic. In fact, if the differences *between* the means of the various populations were not larger than the mean difference between individuals *within* each population, it would be impossible to distinguish different populations statistically. Thinking statistically in terms of the analysis of variance, if we obtained a very large random sample of the world's population and computed the total variance (i.e., the total sum of squares based on individuals) of a given genetic character, we would find that about 85 percent of the total genetic variance exists *within* the several major racial populations and 15 percent exists *between* these populations. But when we then divide the sum of squares (SS) *between* populations by its degrees of freedom to obtain the mean square (MS) and we do the same for the sum of squares *within* populations, the ratio of the two mean squares, i.e., *Between MS/Within MS*, (known as the variance ratio, or *F* ratio, named for its inventor, R. A. Fisher) would be an extremely

large value and, of course, would be highly significant statistically, thus confirming the population differences as an objective reality.

5. Among the genetically conditioned physical differences in central tendency, nearly all attributable to natural selection, that exist between various contemporary breeding populations in the world are: pigmentation of skin, hair, and eyes, body size and proportions, endocranial capacity, brain size, cephalic index (100 × head-width/head-length), number of vertebrae and many other skeletal features, bone density, hair form and distribution, size and shape of genitalia and breasts, testosterone level, various facial features, interpupillary distance, visual and auditory acuity, color blindness, myopia (nearsightedness), number and shape of teeth, fissural patterns on the surfaces of teeth, age at eruption of permanent teeth, consistency of ear wax, blood groups, blood pressure, basal metabolic rate, finger and palm prints, number and distribution of sweat glands, galvanic skin resistance, body odor, body temperature, heat and cold tolerance, length of gestation period, male/female birth ratio, frequency of dizygotic twin births, degree of physical maturity at birth, physical maturation rate, rate of development of alpha (brain) waves in infancy, congenital anomalies, milk intolerance (after childhood), chronic and genetic diseases, resistance to infectious diseases (Baker, 1974; Harrison et al., 1964; Rushton, 1995). Modern medicine has recognized the importance of racial differences in many physical characteristics and in susceptibilities to various diseases, chronic disorders, birth defects, and the effective dosage for specific drugs. There are textbooks that deal entirely with the implications of racial differences for medical practice (Lin et al., 1993; Nesse & Williams, 1994; Polednak, 1989). Forensic pathologists also make extensive use of racial characteristics for identifying skeletal remains, body parts, hair, blood stains, etc.

6. Two of the most recent and important studies of genetic distances and human evolution are: (a) Cavalli-Sforza et al., 1994; (b) Nei & Roychoudhury, 1993. Although these major studies measured genetic distances by slightly different (but highly correlated) quantitative methods based on somewhat different selections of genetic polymorphisms, and they did not include all of the same subpopulations, they are in remarkably close agreement on the genetic distances between the several major clusters that form what are conventionally regarded as the world's major racial groups.

7. The genetic distances between the three largest population groupings can be represented as a triangle, with the distances between the points directly proportional to the genetic distances between the groups, as shown here. (The orientation of the triangle is irrelevant and the figure could be rotated so that any group was at the top.)

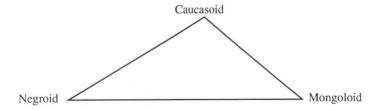

8. As it is one of the most frequently used methods of multivariate analysis in the social sciences, many behavioral scientists are familiar with varimax rotation of principal components and the eigenvalues > 1 rule for determining the number of components to be retained for rotation. Therefore, it might be instructive to demonstrate the nonhierarchical clustering of population groups by this entirely objective mathematical method.

To make the presentation of results simpler, instead of using the 42 populations studied by Cavali-Sforza et al. (1995), I have used a somewhat different collection of only 26 populations from around the world that were studied by the population geneticists Nei & Roychoudhury (1993), whose article provides the genetic distance matrix among the 26 populations samples, based on 29 polymorphic genes with 121 alleles. (They calculated genetic distances by a method different from that used by Cavalli-Sforza et al., but the two methods of computing genetic distance from allele frequencies are so highly correlated as to be virtually equivalent for most purposes.) As the index of similarity between any two populations, I used simply the reciprocal of their genetic distance. Although the reciprocals of distances do not form a Euclidian or interval scale, their scale property is such as to make for clearer clustering (since that is my purpose here), tending to minimize the variance within clusters and maximize variance between clusters. As the reciprocals of distances are not truly correlations (although they have the appearance of correlations and therefore allow a principal components analysis), a principal components analysis (with varimax rotation) of them can serve no other purpose of a principal components analysis than discovering the membership of any clusters that may exist in the data. By the eigenvalues > 1 rule, the twenty-six populations yield six components for varimax rotation. (Varimax rotation maximizes the variance of the squared loadings of each component, thereby revealing the variables that cluster together most distinctly.) Table 12.N shows the result. The population clusters are defined by their largest loadings (shown in boldface type) on one of the components. A population's proximity to the central tendency of a cluster is related to the size of its loading in that cluster. Note that some groups have major and minor loadings on different components, which represent not discrete categories, but central tendencies. The six rotated components display clusters that can be identified as follows: (1) Mongoloids, (2) Caucasoids, (3) South Asians and Pacific Islanders, (4) Negroids, (5) North and South Amerindians and Eskimos, (6) aboriginal Australians and Papuan New Guineans. The genetic groupings are clearly similar to those obtained in the larger study by Cavalli-Sforza et al. using other methods applied to other samples.

    9. Gottesman (1968) provides an account of the African origins of the African-American population. Dyer (1974) details what is known about the growth of the black population in North America since the seventeenth century, the frequency of black-white matings, and the changing proportions over time of racially mixed marriages in which the grooms were white (the latter with reference to the theoretically possible, but apparently factually negligible, genetic implications of this proportion for the degree of admixture of X-linked characters in American blacks).

    10. The two major studies are Reed (1969a) and Chakraborty et al. (1992); these articles give references to most of the scientific literature on this subject.

    11. Reed, 1969b.

    12. Thompson, 1985, p. 300.

    13. Jerison, 1973, 1982; Lynn, 1991b, 1987c.

    14. Coren (1994), a psychologist, discusses canine evolution, both natural and artificial selection, describes a variety of tests of behavioral capacities (''intelligence'') of dogs, and discusses types of canine ''intelligence.'' He also rates seventy-nine breeds on capacity for obedience training and ''working intelligence.'' Coren believes that, much as in humans, there is a general factor, as well as a number of specific factors, in dogs' mental abilities and that various breeds differ in both general and specific abilities. His book has a bibliography on the psychology and behavioral genetics of dogs.

Table 12.N
Varimax Rotated Principal Components of a Genetic Similarity Matrix among 26 Populations

Population	Varimax Rotated Components[a]					
	1	2	3	4	5	6
Pygmy	-	-	-	651	-	-
Nigerian	-	-	-	734	-	-
Bantu	-	-	-	747	-	-
San (Bushman)	-	-	-	465	-	-
Lapp	-	500	-	-	-	-
Finn	-	988	-	-	-	-
German	-	978	-	-	-	-
English	-	948	-	-	-	-
Italian	-	989	-	-	-	-
Iranian	-	635	-	-	-	-
Northern Indian	-	704	-	-	-	-
Japanese	936	-	214	-	-	-
Korean	959	-	229	-	-	-
Tibetan	855	-	-	-	-	-
Mongolian	842	-	357	-	-	-
Southern Chinese	331	-	771		-	-
Thai	-	-	814	-	-	-
Filipino	-	-	782	-	-	-
Indonesian	-	-	749	-	-	-
Polynesian	-	-	526	-	-	284
Micronesian	-	-	521	-	-	328
Australian (aborigines)	-	-	-	-	-	706
Papuan (New Guineans)	-	-	-	-	-	742
North Amerindian	-	-	-	-	804	-
South Amerindian	-	-	-	-	563	-
Eskimo	-	-	-	-	726	-

[a]Loadings ($\times$ 1000); loadings < 200 omitted; loadings > 700 in boldface type.

15. This theme has been interestingly elaborated by Lynn (1991b) and, in the same issue, is commented upon from various perspectives by several behavioral scientists, with a reply by Lynn.

16. Beals, Smith, & Dodd, 1984. This article is followed (in the same issue) by ten commentaries by experts in evolution and physical anthropology. While pointing out highly significant average differences in endocranial volume between the world's major populations, Beals et al. add a disclaimer (which nowadays is virtually pro forma doctrine for anthropologists) that "no sufficient evidence has ever been presented that population variation in brain size, head size, head shape, or cranial capacity has any connection to intelligence" (p. 324). Some physical anthropologists are perhaps less guarded. Vincent Sarich (1995), for instance, while noting the threefold increase in brain size in the course of human evolution, has argued:

[L]arge brains could not have evolved unless having large brains increased fitness through minds that could do more. . . . individuals with larger brains must have been, on average and in the long run, slightly better off than those with smaller brains. How advantaged? Dare one say it? By being smarter. What else? If variation in brain size mattered in the past, as it must have, then it almost certainly still matters. And if you are going to argue that it does not, then you are going to have to explain why it does not. . . . The evolutionary perspective demands that there be a relationship—in the form of a positive correlation—between brain size and intelligence. That proposition, I would argue, is not something that need derive from contemporary data (although . . . those data do give it strong support). It is what we would expect given our particular evolutionary history; that is, it is the evolutionary null hypothesis, and thus, something to be disproved. It seems to me that a demonstration of no correlation between brain size and cognitive performance would be about the best possible refutation of the fact of human evolution. (pp. 87–88)

17. Rushton & Ankney, 1996. The methods for estimating endocranial capacity from external head measurements (and the main references to these methods) are explained in this article, which also summarizes virtually the total world literature on the correlation between cranial capacity and IQ.

18. (a) Ho et al., 1980a, (b) 1980b, (c) 1980b, Table 5, p. 644; 1981.

19. Haug (1987) gives the regression equation for the number of cortical neurons (in billions) = 5.583 + 0.006 × brain volume in cm³. One cm³ of brain tissue weighs 1.036 grams, or only 0.036 grams more than 1 cm³ of H₂O at 4°C.

20. Lynn, 1994b; Ankney, 1992.

21. (a) Ankney, 1992. (b) Witelson et al., 1995. Haug (1987) has also found that the number of neurons for any given brain size is greater in females than in males.

22. Schoenemann, 1995.

23. (a) Broman et al., 1987; (b) Fisch, Bilek, Horrobin, & Chang, 1976; (c) Hack et al., 1991.

24. (a) Rushton & Osborne, 1995; (b) Nikolova, 1994; Bartley et al., 1997.

25. The information in this section is based on studies by Jensen & Johnson, 1994; and Jensen, 1994f. Information on the brain's growth curve from birth to maturity is given in Harrison et al., 1964, Chapter 19.

26. The statistical properties, usefulness, and theoretical and practical rationales for using group means (instead of individual measurements) as the basis for correlating variables have been fully explicated by Lubinski & Humphreys (1996).

27. Jensen (1997b) explains in greater detail the rationale for this division between the basic operating mechanisms of the brain and the aspects of brain functioning that most likely cause individual differences in speed and efficiency of information processing and largely account for _g_.

28. (a) Osborne, 1980; Scarr-Salapatek, 1971. After performing a biometrical and statistical analysis of the Scarr-Salapatek study, Eaves & Jinks (1972) concluded, "There is certainly no evidence in Scarr-Salapatek's studies that the proportion of genetic variation in either verbal or non-verbal IQ depends on race or social class" (p. 88). (b) Jensen, 1973, p. 111. (c) Loehlin et al. (1975, pp. 103–116) provide an excellent discussion of these and other studies. They conclude: "(1) Methods of estimating heritability that rely primarily on within-family variation (such as comparisons of identical and fraternal twin differences) tend not to show consistent differences in the heritability of IQ between U.S. blacks and whites in the populations so far studied. (2) Methods for estimating heritability that rely primarily on between-family variation (such as twin and sibling correlations) sometimes suggest lower IQ heritabilities for blacks, although more often they do not. When they do, it tends to be in conjunction with reduced total variance among blacks" (p. 115).

29. The formal relationship between WGH and BGH was first put forth by an animal geneticist, Jay Lush (1968), and was later introduced into the discussion of group differences in IQ by behavior geneticist John DeFries (1972). Further explanations and discussion of its implications are found in Jensen (1973, pp. 125–150) and in Loehlin et al. (1975, pp. 290–291).

30. Loehlin et al. (1975, p. 291) estimated the value of r_g from a number of randomly selected blood and protein genetic polymorphisms with known allele frequencies in the black and white populations. Entering this value of $r_g = .04$ in the equation, with realistic values for IQ of $r_p = .20$ and WGH = .75, gives BGH = .125. But of course the random sample of genetic polymorphisms on which r_g was based were neutral genes, that is, genes for which the observed small population differences in allele frequencies would largely be a result of genetic drift and would reflect little if any effects of natural selection. The abilities related to IQ, however, like the rapid increase in brain size that took place late in hominid evolution, were most probably highly selected in the course of human evolution, as described earlier in this chapter. In general, racial populations differ more in allele frequencies for adaptive characteristics that have been subject to a high degree of natural selection than they differ in allele frequencies for neutral or "housekeeping" genes. Since the specific genes that affect the development of mental ability as reflected by IQ tests are as yet unknown (with the possible exception of one or two recently, and tentatively, identified genes; see Plomon & Neiderhiser, 1992; Plomin et al., 1994, 1995; Skuder et al., 1995), a direct empirical determination of r_g for any aspect of mental ability is not possible. Large-scale research aimed at the discovery of the gene loci that affect normal variation in human mental ability, however, is well underway, and it seems only a matter of time until it will be possible to determine the allelic frequencies of these genes in different populations.

31. The baseline of the normal curve (shown in Figure 12.N) is conventionally scaled in σ units (this is also referred to as the normalized z scale). The total area under the

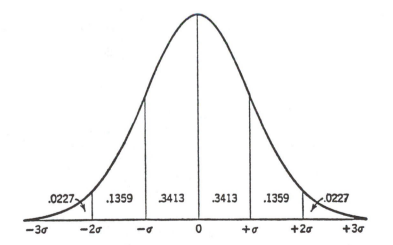

Figure 12.N. The normal curve (standardized to $\mu = 0$, $\sigma = 1$) divided into standard deviation units (σ), showing proportional areas under the curve within each σ interval. The total area under the normal curve asymptotically approaches 1.

normal curve is set at unity, or one. The mean, median, and mode of the normal curve define the zero point on this scale, which divides the total area under the normal curve into equal halves, so the probability, *p*, of $z = 0$ is ½, or .50. Positive or negative deviations from $\sigma = 0$ have lesser probabilities (i.e., $p < .50$). The *probability, p,* of a given deviation, say Xσ, from zero is defined as the proportion of the total area under the normal curve that lies beyond a cut at Xσ (i.e., the total area to the left of $-$Xσ *or* to the right of $+$Xσ). The proportional areas under the curve that fall within each of six equal intervals on the σ scale are shown; the areas only sum to .9998, because .0002 of the total area under the normal curve falls beyond $\pm 3\sigma$.

32. If the genotypic (G_D) and the environmental (E_D) differences are correlated r_{GE}, then the phenotypic difference (P_D) is $P_D = \sqrt{h^2 P_D^2 + e^2 P_D^2 + 2r_{GE} h e P_D^2}$, where h^2 is the heritability and e^2 is $1 - h^2$, the environmentality. Empirical studies have shown that the last term in the equation (called the genotype-environment covariance, or CovGE) typically accounts for relatively little of the phenotypic variance. The best meta-analysis estimate of CovGE I could obtain from IQ data on MZ and DZ twins was .07 percent of the total IQ variance, with 65 percent of the total variance due to the independent effect of genes and 28 percent due to the independent effect of environment (Jensen, 1976). In this case, $r_{GE} = .08$. As I explained in that article, the CovGE would have its maximum possible value (equal to one-half of the phenotypic variance) when $r_{GE} = 1$ and $h^2 = e^2 = 0.5$. For IQ, a number of empirically estimated values of r_{GE} center around .20 (Bouchard, 1993, pp. 74–77).

33. Newman et al., 1937. The pair of separated twins who were called Gladys and Helen in this famous study of MZ twins reared apart differed by twenty-four IQ points (or 1.5σ) on the Stanford-Binet Intelligence Scale, which was standardized to $\sigma = 16$ IQ points. (Their adult IQs were ninety-two and 116.) Not only were these twins reared in extremely different environments, but by adulthood one twin had not gone beyond the third grade, while the other had graduated from college and was a schoolteacher. Moreover, these MZ twins had extremely different health histories and also differed physically more than is typical for MZ twins (Jensen, 1972). The fact that their fingerprints differed even more than the average difference between DZ twins indicates that something affected the twins' prenatal development during the first trimester, since an individual's fingerprints do not change after that time. MZ twins typically have virtually identical fingerprints. The prenatal factor that caused the twins' fingerprints to differ may also have contributed to the difference in their mental development.

34. Jensen, 1973, pp. 137–138.

35. Tavris, 1995. This article is one of six in a pro and con (but mostly con) symposium on *The Bell Curve* by Herrnstein & Murray (1994) that appeared in *Skeptic*, Vol. 3, No. 3, pp. 58–93. (Volume 3, No. 2, contained an interview with Charles Murray. All the articles are at a level suitable for nonspecialists or undergraduate students.)

36. Turkheimer, 1990, 1991.

37. This mathematical concept is fully explained in any statistics textbook that covers regression and correlation.

38. The nature of microenvironmental effects constituting the within-family environment is fully discussed in Jensen, 1997a. Also see Turkheimer & Gottesman (1991) on a closely related topic—the canalization of certain kinds of behavior, including mental ability and the high degree of stability of individual differences throughout the course of development.

39. A few pages in books by Jensen (1973, pp. 228–229) and by Loehlin et al. (1975,

pp. 125–126) deal with black-white interracial marriage. Almost nothing is known about the actual IQs of the males and females in interracial matings, except as may be inferred approximately from their educational and occupational status. Generally, white brides average lower than their black grooms, and black brides average higher than their white grooms, which clearly suggests a trade-off between educational and occupational status, on the one hand, and the social status commonly associated with race, on the other, at least in these cases where the relationship is carried through to marriage. "Matings" as opposed to "marriages" may not be the same.

40. Dolan, 1992; Dolan et al., 1992; Dolan et al., 1994. For a technical explication, with examples, of the distinction between the psychometric (also termed the common pathway) factor model and the biometric (or independent pathway) factor model referred to in the text, see Neale & Cardon, 1992, pp. 253–259.

41. Osborne, 1980. All of the data were obtained from the appendices of this book.

42. (a) Rowe et al., 1994. (b) Rowe et al., 1995. (c) Rodgers et al., 1994. (d) Rowe & Cleveland, 1996.

43. Bouchard & McGue, 1981.

44. Psychometricians will notice that the correlation coefficient in this formula for the standard error of estimate is not squared, as it usually is in calculating the SE_{est}. The squared correlation indicates the proportion of variance in the predicted variable accounted for by its linear regression on the predictor variable. The genetic correlation between relatives already is a variance, so it need not be squared in the formula given here. A genetic correlation can be defined as the square of the correlation between genotypic and phenotypic values. For further explanation of genetic correlations, see Jensen, 1971c.

45. There should be no misunderstanding here of the fact that the genetic correlations between relatives of varying degrees of kinship, though based on genetic theory, are among the most solidly established and universally accepted parameters of quantitative, population, and behavioral genetics. The theoretical basis of this knowledge of genetic kinship correlations, which is fundamental in every genetics textbook, was originally worked out by Sir Ronald A. Fisher, in 1918, in a paper titled "The Correlation between Relatives on the Supposition of Mendelian Inheritance." It has become one of the two or three most famous and frequently cited papers in the history of genetics.

46. In terms of purely statistical prediction in a heterogeneous sample, the accuracy is improved by including in the prediction equation the mean of the particular group from which an individual was selected, along with that individual's own score. This fact represents the same phenomenon as that of Galton's "law" of regression to the mean. For example, if we use an individual's SAT score to predict his or her college freshman grade-point average in a given college, we can slightly improve, *on average*, the accuracy of the prediction by also taking account of the mean SAT score of the high school that the student attended. This may seem mysterious, but all it means is that the test (SAT) does not measure everything that is relevant to success in college (if it did, it would be a perfect predictor) and that the individual's background (e.g., characteristics of the high school attended) provides additional information about certain characteristics of that individual that are not measured by his or her own test score but which are relevant to college performance. Similarly, if in a heterogeneous population we use the parent's IQ to predict the child's IQ, we can improve the prediction by including the mean of whichever subpopulation the child's parent was selected from. Including the different mean IQs of *any* (or all) of the subpopulations (e.g., racial, regional, religious, occupational,

social class, etc.) that include the parent will, on average, improve prediction of the offspring's IQ.

47. Paul (1980), in a meta-analysis of the world literature published between 1917 and 1980 on sibling correlations from sixty-three independent samples totaling more than 27,000 sibling pairs, found an average $r = +.49$. The later compilation of kinship correlations by Bouchard & McGue (1981) based on sixty-nine independent correlations totaling over 26,000 sibling pairs produced a weighted mean correlation of $+.47$.

48. Jensen, 1973, pp. 107–119.

49. In attempting to match pairs of individuals on whatever ability or trait is measured by a test, more accurate matching is obtained by matching individuals on their estimated true-scores than on their actual obtained scores. An individual's true-score, X_T, is a statistical regression estimate of the score the individual would have obtained if the test scores had no error of measurement, that is, perfect reliability. The true-score is calculated from the individual's obtained score, X_O, the mean of the group from which the individual was selected, $\overline{X}$, and the empirically known reliability of the test or measuring instrument, r_{xx}. Thus, $X_T = r_{xx}(X_O - \overline{X}) + \overline{X}$.

50. Detailed descriptions of all of these tests are in Jensen, 1973, pp. 121–124.

51. Scarr & Weinberg, 1976; Weinberg, Scarr, & Waldman, 1992. The first paper was followed by three critiques and a rebuttal (in *American Psychologist, 32*, 1977, pp. 677–83). My own critique of the first paper is in Jensen, 1981c, in which I argued that various selection factors probably biased the sampled adoptees' IQs upward to some extent.

52. An abbreviated version of the WAIS was used, comprising only four subtests (Vocabulary, Arithmetic, Block Design, and Picture Arrangement) the combined score on which correlates .90 with the Full Scale IQ based on all of the eleven WAIS subtests.

53. Scarr & Weinberg, 1978.

54. Willerman, Loehlin, & Horn, 1990.

55. Turkheimer, 1986.

56. Capron & Duyme, 1989. Fisch, Bilek, Deinard, & Chang, 1976. The method of correlated vectors was applied to the excellent adoption data in the study by Capron and Duyme (1989, 1996) and showed that the *g* loadings of the various Wechsler subtests reflect the degree of resemblance between adoptees and the socioeconomic status (SES) of their *biological* parents (hence a genetic effect) more strongly than they reflect the SES of their *adoptive* parents (an environmental effect). The environmental effect of the adoptive environment was not significantly reflected in the adoptees' mean *g* factor scores, but the SES of the adoptees' biological parents was very significantly reflected in the adoptees' mean *g* factor scores (Jensen, 1998). It was also noted that the relative effects of the adoptees' biological background and their adoptive environmental background on the WISC-R subtests scores are significantly correlated with the magnitude of white-black differences on these subtests, consistent with the hypothesis of genetic (and/or prenatal environmental) causation of the mean W-B difference in *g*.

57. Clark & Hanisee, 1982; Frydman & Lynn, 1989; Winick, et al., 1975.

58. Fisch, Bilek, Deinard, & Chang, 1976.

59. The authors reported a multiple correlation (R) of the ten environmental variables with IQ of .41 and of the two biological variables with IQ of .40. (The two sets of variables combined give a R with IQ of .48; the unbiased R is .35.) A direct comparison of two raw multiple correlations, when each is based on a different number of independent variables, is not appropriate, because the value of R is partly a function of the

number of independent variables included in the regression equation. There is a well known standard correction for this source of bias in the R, often referred to as the "shrinkage" formula. The raw or "unshrunken" value of R applies only to the particular subject sample on which is was based; the shrunken R estimates the population value of the correlation. As the unbiased (or shrunken) R_s should have been applied in this study, I have given these values in the text. Although the same point was made by all three of the critics of the 1976 study (*American Psychologist*, 1977, *32*, 677–681), the "unshrunken" values were also used in the 1986 follow-up (Weinberg et al., 1992). Also, as pointed out by the critics of the 1976 study, the two-step hierarchical regression analysis (used in both studies) is unable to disentangle the confounded effects of the adoptive variables from the genetic variables. This is mainly because, in this data set, the race of the adoptees' mothers is so confounded with the age of adoption that these variables cannot be meaningfully assigned to distinct categories labeled "genetic" and "environmental." Thus each of these variables acts more or less as a proxy for the other in the prediction of the adoptees' IQs. The authors note, "Biological mothers' race remained the best single predictor of adopted child's IQ when other variables were controlled" (Weinberg et al., 1992, p. 132) and then suggest that their results may be due to unmeasured social variables that are correlated with the mothers' race rather than a racially genetic effect.

60. (a) Levin, 1994, (b) Lynn. 1994a. (c) Waldman et al. (1994) reply to Levin and Lynn. Their footnote 4 (p. 37) criticizing Levin's estimates of the between-groups heritability (BGH) of the mean IQ difference between blacks and whites is itself incorrect and fails to identify the actual errors in Levin's estimates of BGH. In his first estimate, for example, on the assumption that the BB adoptees (whose IQs averaged 89.4) were representative of the U.S. black population (with mean IQ = 85), Levin calculated the effect of the superior adoptive environment on IQ as $(89.4 - 85)/15 \approx 0.3\sigma$. That is, the adopted BB group presumably scored 0.3σ higher in IQ than if they had been reared in the average black environment. Levin reasoned that if 0.3σ of the average W-B IQ difference of 1σ is environmental, $1\sigma - .3\sigma = .7\sigma$ of the difference must be genetic. He then squared this genetic difference to determine the BGH, i.e., $.7^2 \approx .50$. But if the environmental proportion of the phenotypic *difference* is e, then the BGH is not $(1 - e)^2$, as Levin calculated, but $1 - e^2$, which in this case is $1 - .3^2 = 1 - .09 = .91$. For the same reason, Levin's (p. 17) three other estimates of BGH (.66, .70, .59) are similarly off the mark (being .97, .98, and .86, respectively). But even if corrected, the estimates of BGH are suspect, as they are based on certain improbable assumptions. One estimate, for example, is derived from the average IQ of the biological offspring of the white adoptive parents. Levin implicitly assumed that the difference of nine IQ points between the average IQ (109) of the white biological offspring of the adoptive parents and the white population's average IQ (100) is entirely the result of the superior home environment provided by the adoptive parents, thus neglecting any effect of the genetic correlation between parents' IQ and offsprings' IQ.

61. (a) Reed, 1971; (b) Reed, 1973.

62. Loehlin, Vandenberg & Osborne, 1973.

63. Scarr et al., 1977.

64. (a) MacLean et al., 1974. In this study, the diastolic blood pressure (DBP) of a large sample of American blacks was regressed on their percentage of Caucasian admixture (estimated from blood groups), and showed at a high level of statistical significance that the average B-W difference in DBP is negatively correlated with the blacks' per-

centage of Caucasian admixture. Given the obvious parallels between blood pressure and IQ, the methodology of the study by MacLean et al. is a model for applying exactly the same method for answering the same question for IQ (Reed, 1997). Both BP and IQ are continuous or polygenic traits, with similar reliability of measurement and similar heritability. Therefore, Reed (1997) has commented on the applicability of the methodology used by MacLean et al. for the study of racial differences in IQ. He argued that if this method had been applied in the Scarr et al. (1977) blood-group study, it would have been more apt to reveal a significant relationship between the degree of African/Causasian admixture and IQ than the "odds" method used in that study. (b) In preparing a detailed commentary (Jensen, 1981c, pp. 519–522) on the Scarr et al. study, I asked a professor of quantitative genetics at the University of California, Berkeley, to calculate the expected correlation between the "odds" index of African ancestry and mental test scores, assuming that 62.5 percent of the mean W-B difference in scores was genetic (i.e., the midpoint of the interval hypothesized in Jensen, 1973, p. 363). Given the reliability of the test scores (.90), the reliability of the blood-group index of African ancestry (.49), and the restriction of range of the ancestral index, the expected correlation is −.03. This value is not appreciably different from the reported correlation (−.05) of the ancestral odds index with the first principal component of the four most *g*-loaded tests used in the study. In her reply to my critique (in the same volume, pp. 519–522), Scarr disagrees with my conclusion that the study lacks the power to reject either the null or a reasonable alternative hypothesis, but provides no argument to disprove this conclusion. Since IQ is even more heritable than blood pressure (see Note 64a), then if the same methodology and sample size as were used in the blood pressure study by MacLean et al. (instead of the statistically weaker method used in the Scarr et al. study), a more convincing test of the genetic hypothesis should have been possible. However, there is little or no assortative mating for BP (within racial groups), while for psychometric *g* there is a higher degree of assortative mating than for any other human metric trait, either physical or mental. This factor therefore introduces a degree of uncertainty regarding the average magnitude of genetic difference in IQ between the African and white ancestry of the hybrid probands for any present-day study. Therefore, any study, however methodologically sound, would be unlikely to yield a compelling test of the critical hypothesis. Until the technical criticisms of the Scarr et al. study are adequately addressed, this study cannot be offered in good faith as direct evidence that the mean W-B IQ difference involves no genetic component.

65. Type II error also occurs in other published studies of racial differences. For example, see Jensen, 1985e.

66. Keith & Herring, 1991.

67. A review of these studies and complete references to them are provided in Jensen, 1973, pp. 219–230.

68. Eyferth, 1959, 1961; Eyferth et al., 1960. This study is described in some detail by Loehlin et al., 1975. Flynn (1980, pp. 219–261) offers a quite detailed summary and analysis of the study in support of his view that it probably constitutes the strongest of what he terms "direct" evidence against the hypothesis that the mean W-B IQ difference has a substantial genetic component.

69. Nagoshi & Johnson (1986) reported *g* factor scores averaging .26σ higher for interracial European-Asian offspring than for the offspring of same-race parents who were matched with the interracial parents in education and SES. Heterosis was greater

on the more highly g-loaded tests; the vector of heterotic effects on fifteen tests correlated $+.44$ ($p = .10$) with the vector of the tests' g loadings.

70. Vining, 1982.

71. A weighted mean is just an arithmetic mean in which different values (i.e., weights) are given to each of the N elements to be averaged. The weighted mean is calculated by (1) multiplying each element (X) by its assigned weight (w), (2) summing all the products, and (3) dividing their total by the sum of the weights. Symbolically, the simple mean is $\overline{X} = \Sigma X/N$; the weighted mean is $\overline{X}_w = \Sigma(X \times w)/\Sigma w$, where Σ means "the sum of."

72. (a) Herrnstein & Murray, 1994, pp. 355–356. (b) These authors calculated the mean W-B IQ difference for the mothers and the children in several different ways (see their Note 46, p. 737), excluding or including different age groups; the part of the mean W-B difference attributable to the dysgenic effect varied across these estimates from 1.9 to 6.1 IQ points, with a mean of 4.1 IQ points.

73. (a) D. G. Freedman (1979), who is probably the leading contemporary researcher on this topic, has reported studies of the behavior of white, Asian, black, Amerindian, African, and Australian aborigine infants at various ages from the day of birth and into early childhood; he interprets many of his findings in an evolutionary context. (b) Nearly all of the research on this subject before 1972 has been cited and summarized in Jensen, 1973, Chapter 16.

74. Post (1982) reviews most of the literature on population differences in visual defects, including myopia.

75. This literature has been reviewed by Jensen & Sinha, 1993, pp. 212–217.

76. Cohn et al., 1988.

77. Spuhler & Lindzey, 1967.

78. Skuder et al., 1995; Plomin et al., 1995.

79. The theory and empirical evidence for the microenvironmental component of IQ variance are spelled out in Jensen, 1997a.

80. Selected groups can be literally matched, person-by-person, on the measure of SES, thereby making the frequency distributions perfectly equal. Or groups can be equated statistically by regressing the variable of primary interest (say, IQ) on the measure of SES, yielding what are called SES-regressed IQ scores. Another method is to express the group difference in IQ as a point-biserial correlation and then calculate the partial correlation between race and IQ with the effect of SES removed. Values of the point-biserial correlation smaller than 0.60 have a virtually linear relationship to the size of the mean group difference. (Formulas relating these statistics are given in Jensen, 1980a, p. 121.)

81. (a) Jensen & Reynolds, 1982; (b) Reynolds & Jensen, 1983.

82. Humphreys et al., 1977.

83. Grissmer et al., 1994. This is the acclaimed RAND study of changes in student performance over the course of twenty-five years. The regression analyses referred to are fully described on pages 57–63.

84. (a) Jensen, 1974b. (b) Jensen, 1977.

85. (a) Jensen, 1971b. (b) Strauch, 1977. (c) Roberts, 1971.

86. Scholastic achievement batteries (California Achievement Test and Stanford Achievement Test), however, showed considerably larger F-M differences for blacks than

for whites. Blacks sampled in the Southeastern states showed the largest sex difference in scholastic achievement (0.24σ overall); the sex difference increased with grade level from 0.01 in grade one to 0.50σ in grade six.

87. The results of this interaction analysis of the raw score data in Roberts (1971) are as follows, where the WISC-R subscales are V = Vocabulary, BD = Block Design. The raw score means are in boldface, the standard deviations are in parentheses, and the group differences are given in σ units. Note that (1) the sex difference is greater for whites than for blacks and that (2) black males perform slightly better than black females on both Vocabulary and Block Design. Both findings are opposite to the expectation of the race × sex × ability interaction hypothesis.

	Male		Female		M-F Sex Difference
White	V: **27.5**	(10.3)	V: **25.7**	(9.8)	V: 0.18σ
	BD: **14.3**	(11.1)	BD: **13.0**	(10.4)	BD: 0.12σ
Black	V: **19.8**	(8.6)	V: **18.9**	(8.1)	V: 0.11σ
	BD: **7.1**	(6.72)	BD: **6.7**	(5.6)	BD: 0.06σ
W-B Race	V: 0.81σ		V: 0.76σ		
Difference	BD: 0.78σ		BD: 0.76σ		

88. Jensen & Johnson (1994), Table 5 (p. 318), gives the means and _SD_s of the four race × sex groups used to evaluate the interaction hypothesis at ages four and seven years.

89. This massive study is summarized by Broman et al., 1975.

90. Multiple regression analysis is a statistical procedure in which the predictor variables (usually termed _independent variables_, e.g., mother's age, baby's birth weight) are entered in the order determined by the amount of variance they account for (independently of all the other variables) in the predicted variable (termed the _dependent variable_, e.g., IQ). Beginning with whatever independent variable accounts for the most variance in the dependent variable, the second independent variable entered is the one that accounts for the next largest proportion of the variance that has not already been accounted for by the first; the third variable entered is the one that accounts for the most variance that has not been accounted for by the first and the second variable, and so on—until the proportion of variance accounted for by the next variable entered is too small to be statistically significant (at some specified level of significance, such as $p < .05$), at which point the analysis ends. The final result of this procedure is the squared multiple correlation (R^2) between the statistically selected set of independent variables and the dependent variable. R^2 is defined as the proportion of variance in the dependent variable that is accounted for by the set of independent variables.

The independent variables can also be entered _stepwise_ in some _forced_ order that the investigator may regard as most appropriate for examining a particular hypothesis. For example, in the Collaborative Perinatal Project, the independent variables were entered in three stages: (1) the prenatal variables, (2) the prenatal and neonatal variables together, and (3) the prenatal, neonatal, infancy, and childhood variables together. This permitted assessment of how much the set of variables measured at different stages of the probands' development predicted the total variance in their IQs at age four.

91. Statistics on mother's age (in years) in the study sample:

Group	N	Mean	SD	Range
White	12,210	24.74	6.04	13–47
Black	14,550	23.67	6.42	12–47

Although the mean age of mothers differs by only 1.07 years, the percentage of mothers under twenty years of age was 28.8% for blacks, 17.5% for whites.

92. Of the fifty variables that were significantly ($p < .001$) correlated with IQ in both the black and white samples, only one variable had correlations with opposite signs. The variable "Cigarettes smoked per day during pregnancy" was correlated with IQ $-.08$ for whites and $+.04$ for blacks (Broman et al., 1975, p. 280). This variable did not enter into any of the multiple regression analyses, as it made no significant independent contribution to the prediction of proband IQ. This is probably because maternal smoking habits are highly correlated with demographic, socioeconomic, and probably genetic variables that are correlated with IQ. The earlier entrance of these variables into the regression procedure left only a statistically insignificant proportion of the IQ variance to be explained by maternal smoking.

93. National Center for Health Statistics: Vital Statistics of the United States (1988). Characteristics of American Indian and Alaska native births: United States, *Monthly Vital Statistics Report, 36*, No. 3, *Supplement*, 1984.

94. *Scientific American*, April 1996, p. 25.

95. Naylor & Myrianthopoulos, 1967.

96. Herrnstein & Murray, 1994, figures on pp. 215 and 334.

97. Schoendorf et al., 1992.

98. Rushton (1995, pp. 150–152) points out consistent racial differences in LBW and mortality rates, not only for infants but throughout the life span, with Orientals showing the lowest rates, blacks the highest, and whites intermediate. He finds that this rank order holds up internationally wherever mortality rate statistics are available. Rushton sees the mortality data as part of a much broader evolutionary phenomenon that places whites intermediate between Orientals and blacks (of African origin) on some sixty physical and behavioral traits. His controversial theory explains these phenomena in terms of a sociobiological hypothesis that posits evolved differences in reproductive strategies.

99. Dr. James Collins, a researcher on LBW at Northwestern University, is quoted in the *New York Times* (June 4, 1992): "It's coming down to the fact that we are left with either it's genetic or it's some stress related to racism. At this point, there is no data to completely disprove either one." Another researcher, Dr. Paul Wise of Harvard Medical School, is quoted in the same article: "Clearly a major portion is racism. But it's difficult as a scientist to begin to determine what specific elements in racism are being expressed in infant mortality rates."

100. (a) The Infant Health and Development Program (1990). Enhancing the outcomes of low-birth-weight, premature infants: A multisite, randomized trial. *Journal of the American Medical Association, 263*, 3035–3042. (b) Brooks-Gunn et al., 1994. (c) Baumeister & Bacharach (1996) provide a comprehensive bibliography on this project and a trenchant critique of it, in which they conclude, "The bottom line is that it is unclear that there was a meaningful intervention effect at 3 years, much less at 5 years. Claims to have prevented mental retardation were decidely premature, turning out to be clearly erroneous" (p. 97).

101. Montie & Fagan, 1988.

102. (a) Lucas et al., 1992. (b) Ryan et al., 1991. Leary, 1988.

103. (a) Eysenck, 1991. (b) Eysenck, 1995; Eysenck & Schoenthaler, 1997.

104. (a) Olson (1994) provides a review and extensive bibliography on the psychological effects of fetal alcohol syndrome. (b) Reinisch et al., 1995.

105. Snyderman & Rothman, 1988, pp. 128–130, 294.

106. (a) Ogbu (1978) is the most comprehensive presentation of this view. (b) Ogbu (1994) summarizes his views on cultural determinants of intelligence differences.

107. Sowell, 1981, 1994; Chapter 6 specifically deals with race and mental ability.

108. The conspicuous success of Asian immigrants in intellectual pursuits in America is extensively documented in P. E. Vernon (1982), Flynn (1991), Caplan et al. (1992).

109. Spearman & Jones, 1950, p. 72.

110. Steele & Aronson, 1995; Steele, 1997.

111. (a) Spielberger & Sydeman (1994) provide a review and bibliography of research on test anxiety. See also Jensen, 1980a, pp. 615–616. (b) Yerkes & Dodson, 1908. (c) Spielberger, 1958.

112. Lovejoy, 1993.

Chapter 13

Sex Differences in *g*

Past studies of a sex difference in general ability have often been confounded by improper definitions and measurements of "general ability" based on simple summation of subtest scores from a variety of batteries that differ in their group factors, by the use of unrepresentative groups selected from limited segments of the normal distribution of abilities, and by the interaction of sex differences with age-group differences in subtest performance. These conditions often yield a mean sex difference in the total score, but such results, in principle, are actually arbitrary, of limited generality, and are therefore of little scientific interest. The observed differences are typically small, inconsistent in direction across different batteries, and, in above-average samples, usually favor males.

In this chapter sex differences are specifically examined in terms of their loadings on the *g* factor for a number of test batteries administered to representative population samples. When the sex differences (expressed as a point-biserial correlation between sex and scores on each of a number of subtests) were included in the correlation matrix along with the various subtests and the correlation matrix was subjected to a common factor analysis, sex had negligible and inconsequential loading on the *g* factor, averaging about .01 over five test batteries. Applying the method of correlated vectors to these data shows that the magnitude of the sex difference on various subtests is unrelated to the tests' *g* loadings. Also, the male/female variance ratio on diverse subtests (generally indicating greater male variability in scores) is unrelated to the subtests' *g* loadings. Although no evidence was found for sex differences in the mean level of *g* or in the variability of *g*, there is clear evidence of marked sex differences in certain group factors and in test specificity. Males, on average, excel on some factors; females on others. The largest and most consistent sex difference is found on a spatial-visualization factor that has its major factor loadings on tests requiring the mental rotation or manipulation of figures in an imaginary three-dimensional space. The difference is in favor of males and within each sex is related to testosterone level. But the best available evidence fails to show a sex difference in *g*.

Research on sex[1] differences in mental abilities has generated hundreds of articles in the psychological literature, with the number of studies and articles increasing at an accelerating rate in the last decade. As there now exist many general reviews of this literature,[2] I will focus here on what has proved to be the most problematic question in this field: whether, on average, males and females differ in *g*.

It is noteworthy that this question, which is technically the most difficult to answer, has been the least investigated, the least written about, and, indeed, even the least often asked.

The vast majority of studies have looked at sex differences in more specialized abilities, such as can be subsumed under the labels of certain well-established primary (first-order) or group factors in the psychometric domain. In the three-stratum hierarchy of ability factors, sex differences also appear at the second stratum.

The differences observed for specific tests and for first-order and second-order factors are now well established by countless studies. They constitute an empirical fact and the frontier of research now lies in discovering the causes of the clearly identified cognitive differences between the sexes. However, a brief examination of these first-order psychometric differences is necessary in order to understand the problem of determining whether the sexes differ in *g*.

SEX DIFFERENCES IN SPECIFIC TESTS AND IN FIRST-ORDER FACTORS

Neither Binet, in the development of his test, nor Terman, in creating the American version and the initial standardization of Binet's test (known as the Stanford-Binet), took account of sex differences. Because a sex difference in the overall test scores was of negligible size (although a minority of the individual items showed sex differences, some favoring girls and others favoring boys, and these differences at the item level largely averaged out in the composite score), it was assumed that the sexes did not differ significantly in what the test as a whole was intended to measure, namely, general intelligence. Therefore, in all subsequent revisions of the Stanford-Binet (including the latest revision, the Stanford-Binet IV) any items that showed exceptionally large and statistically significant sex differences were eliminated in order to counterbalance the sex differences for the remaining items. This counterbalancing is possible, of course, only if roughly equal numbers of sexually discriminating items favor each sex, and these discriminating items must be found throughout the range of item difficulty. Given these built-in features, obviously, the Stanford-Binet scale is hardly a suitable research instrument for studying sex differences. The negligible sex difference in Stanford-Binet IQ could be just an artifact of item selection.

A number of other standardized tests were similarly designed to minimize sex differences, the best known being the Wechsler Intelligence Scales. Because the Wechsler test consists of a dozen distinctive subscales, half of them verbal and half nonverbal (or performance), it is not easy, or perhaps not even possible, to equate the sexes on each of the subscales. These tap not only *g*, but also certain first-order factors (particularly verbal, spatial, and short-term memory). If the sexes actually differ on subtests that are aggregations of items that mainly reflect different first-order factors, the overall difference on a given subtest cannot be eliminated by item selection and still be differentiated factorially from the other subtests in the battery. This is in fact the case with the Wechsler scales. Even though the few most sexually discriminating items have been eliminated from each subtest, males and females still differ significantly on the various subtests. Females slightly but significantly exceed males on some verbal tests and on short-term memory; males exceed females on some of the performance tests, particular those calling for spatial visualization. The fact that these differences largely balance out in the overall IQ score could be a result of selection of the types of subscales used in the Wechsler, whether intentional or inadvertent. So the Wechsler IQ per se permits no conclusion about a sex difference in intelligence. Because sex differences were taken into account in the construction of the Wechsler scales, we can infer sex differences in the special abilities measured separately by each of the subtests but cannot convincingly estimate their magnitudes. For that we must turn to tests that were constructed entirely without reference to sex.

In these studies the sex difference is typically measured in terms of standard deviation units, termed the "effect size" or the *d* statistic. The value *d* is defined as the quantity male mean minus female mean divided by the average within-group standard deviation, i.e., $d = (\overline{X}_M - \overline{X}_F)/\sigma$.

Visual-Spatial Abilities. These abilities favor males and have the largest and most consistent sex differences of any psychometric abilities. The factor analysis of various kinds of tests of visual-spatial abilities reveals about ten distinct subfactors.[3] All of these analyses show a sex difference favoring males, but the largest difference is on tests that require visualizing 2-dimensional or 3-dimensional figures that have to be rotated or manipulated mentally in 3-dimensional space. For example, the testee must determine which of the following four figures on the right are the same as the figure on the left flipped over and rotated rather than merely rotated in its own plane? (*Answer*: b and c.)

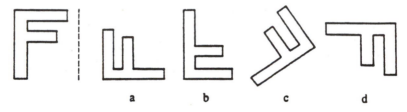

It is important to note that not every test of figural material involves the spatial ability factor. Raven's Progressive Matrices, for example, does not qualify as a spatial test. This is shown by the fact that when the Raven is factor-analyzed among a variety of tests including several tests that define a spatial factor, it does not significantly load on the spatial factor. The defining characteristic for spatial problems is that, in order to obtain the correct solution, the subject must visualize and manipulate the figural material mentally as if it were an object in three-dimensional space. Men, on average, excel women in this type of performance. Meta-analyses of the sex difference on various composites of spatial-visualization tests yield average *d* values in the range of .30 to.50 for the general population.[2c,d,i,4]

The only sex differences favoring males that are larger than this do not involve broad factors as such, but occur on tests in which spatial ability is combined with types of specific knowledge content with which males are typically more familiar (such as information about tools, auto mechanics, and electronics). Tests involving such knowledge were developed to measure vocational aptitudes for selecting individuals, usually men, for certain skilled jobs or job training. On some of these tests males exceed females by a *d* of about 1.0 ±.3. Such large sex differences occur only on tests that reflect specific achievement rather than the broad abilities that emerge at the second order in factor analyses.

Since the sex difference in spatial ability is ubiquitous throughout the human species (and is even found in other mammalian species), the consensus of expert opinion today doubts that the phenomenon is explainable purely in terms of environmental or cultural factors. The sex difference in spatial ability appears to be a *sex-limited* trait, which means that the genetic basis of individual differences in the trait is the same for both sexes, but that some other factor that differs between the sexes has the effect of limiting the expression of the trait in one sex. The best present evidence is that this additional factor involves the individual's estrogen/testosterone balance, which of course differs quite markedly in men and women.[5] Within each sex there is a nonlinear (inverted-U) relationship between an individual's position on the estrogen/testosterone continuum and the individual's level of spatial ability, with the optimal level of testosterone above the female mean and below the male mean. Generally, females with markedly above-average testosterone levels (for females) and males with below-average levels of testosterone (for males) tend to have higher levels of spatial ability, relative to the average spatial ability for their own sex. Other hypotheses based on sexual dimorphism in certain brain structures (particularly the corpus callosum) and sexual differences in the development of hemispheric dominance are also being considered, as is the evolutionary basis of these differences.[6]

Mathematical Reasoning Ability. Because mathematical or quantitative reasoning is a prominent feature of many scholastic and employment aptitude tests, including the most widely used of all such tests (the SAT), the repeated finding of a rather marked sex difference in this aptitude has given rise to a great amount of research. In recent years, this topic has even become a prominent research specialty of behavioral scientists.[7]

The sex difference favoring males does not include ability in arithmetic calculation, in which females slightly excel males, but exists for quantitative "thought problems" and especially for the more advanced and complex aspects of mathematics taught in high school and college. The sex difference in math ability in the general population is not large, with _d_ values mostly between .10 and .25 for various tests given to nationally representative samples. Much larger differences appear in subject samples that were selected from the upper-half of the distribution of math ability; the further above the general population mean, the larger the sex difference. One reason for this is the considerably greater variance of males in math ability. The variance of males' math test scores averages about 1.1 to 1.3 times greater than the variance for females. Almost twice as many males as females fall into the upper tail (>90th percentile) of the bell-curve distribution of math scores. However, males also outnumber females in the lower tail (<10th percentile) of the math score distribution. This phenomenon of greater male variance, which is most conspicuous in the extreme tails of the distribution, is generally found for most psychometric abilities. But it is more extreme in both math and spatial abilities than in any other broad ability factors. Data collected between 1970 and 1990 or so suggest that there has been a slight decrease in the sex difference in math ability in representative population samples.

Causal theories of the math sex difference are still tentative and debatable, pending further investigation. Some theorists attribute the math difference to the somewhat larger sex difference in spatial ability, in part because some types of math problems can be visualized graphically or in terms of spatial relations. But the moderate correlation of math ability with spatial ability (independent of _g_) is generally too small to account for more than a minor fraction of the sex difference in math ability. Space and math have independent determinants besides the source of variance they share in common. Biological and evolutionary psychologists have proposed theories similar to those for spatial ability, explaining the well-substantiated sex difference in math ability in terms of natural selection for the different roles performed by males and females in the course of hominid evolution and their genetically transmitted neurophysiological and hormonal mediators.[7a,b]

Verbal Abilities. The sex difference on verbal tests for young adults fluctuates around zero across various tests and studies, and seems to depend more on specific properties of each verbal test rather than reflecting any consistent difference. Girls show more rapid maturation than boys in verbal expression, but this difference begins to disappear after puberty. In general, verbal tests with the largest *g* loadings, such as tests of verbal reasoning, show differences averaging close to zero. It is possible to devise tests that use a verbal medium but that emphasize abstract reasoning more than verbal knowledge or fluency. The one type of verbal ability that most consistently favors females is *verbal fluency*. A typical-test requires the subject to produce as many common nouns beginning with a given letter within a limited time (say, thirty seconds). Scholastic-type achievement tests involving verbal content, such as reading, writing, grammar, and spelling, also consistently favor females. Tests of general information and especially science information and technical knowledge favor males.

Smaller Group Factors. Perceptual speed and short-term memory both favor females, with *d* values of $-.20$ to $-.30$. One of the larger sex differences favoring females is on a factor identified as "speed and accuracy" or "clerical checking." This factor is measured by the digit symbol or coding test of the Wechsler battery. Typical *d* values fall between $-.30$ and $-.40$. A sex difference on a test of this factor as high as $-.86$ was found for male and female twelfth-grade high school students taking the General Aptitude Test Battery's subtest Q ("clerical perception"), which makes a great demand on perceptual speed and accuracy.

THE *g* FACTOR: A NEAR-ZERO SEX DIFFERENCE

The study of a sex difference in general ability has often been confused by the use of different concepts of "general ability," and by failing to recognize that the typically greater variance of males in test scores may cause both the direction and magnitude of the mean sex differences in test scores to vary across different segments of the total distribution for the general population. The observed sex difference will therefore often vary across groups selected from different segments of the population distribution.

Many investigators have taken the sum total of the subtest scores on one or another IQ test as their operational definition of general mental ability. The total IQ is usually based on the sum of the standardized scores on the various subtests. Because there are sex differences on various types of subtests, as previously noted, the direction and magnitude of the summed sex differences will depend on the particular selection of subtests in the battery. For example, including more tests loaded on the spatial factor will favor males; including more tests loaded on verbal fluency and on clerical speed and accuracy will favor females. Thus the simple sum or mean of various subtest scores is a datum without scientific interest or generality. It cannot be considered a proper measure of general ability. If, for a particular battery, it happened to be an adequate measure of general ability, it would be so only inadvertently, as a result of averaging out sex differences that have more or less equal and opposite signs on the various subtests. This becomes more likely the greater the number of different types of subtests averaged. The essential problem is that the concept of general ability, defined as _g_, rests on the _correlations_ among test scores rather than on their simple summation. The latter, which might be referred to as "ability in general," is an arbitrary variable that fails to qualify conceptually as a scientific construct, although by happenstance it may correlate highly with general ability defined as _g_.

But even if there are many subtests in a battery, thereby tending to average out sex biases, a simple summation of sex differences over subtests is contaminated if the method of test construction included selecting test items on any criteria involving sex differences in item responses (as was done in creating the Stanford-Binet and the Wechsler intelligence scales). IQ scores on such tests can hardly be informative about the magnitude of possible sex differences in general ability, at least in principle. The study of sex differences must depend on tests in which item selection was based exclusively on the psychometric criteria used to maximize the reliability, validity, discriminability, and unidimensionality of the subtests.

Studies that are based on selected samples of males and females are highly questionable if the results are generalized to any population other than the one from which the study sample was selected. Because males' scores are more variable on most tests than are those of females, there are more males at both the upper and the lower extremes of the distribution. This is most markedly true for tests of spatial and quantitative abilities. Many of the published studies of sex differences have been based on self-selected or institutionally selected groups that score mostly in the upper half or even the upper quarter of the normal distribution of abilities, groups such as college applicants, university students, and people in highly skilled occupations, such as Air Force officers. Generally, the higher the cut-score for selection, the larger is the proportion of exceptionally high-scoring males in the group. The mean sex difference in such an above-average group would not accurately estimate the magnitude of the sex difference in the general population, but would yield a biased estimate favoring males. The opposite bias would appear if the sexes were compared in a group that scored well below the general population mean. Although greater male variance is typically found in American and north European studies, this phenomenon is not generalizable across all nations and cultures.[8] A study of sex difference in general ability intended to be generalizable to recent North American or north European populations should be based on representative samples of those populations. There are few such data sets available after excluding the national standardization samples for tests in which item selection took sex into account.

The age of the study sample must also be taken into account. Girls mature earlier than boys, which favors girls' language development and verbal facility in childhood. Also, sex differences in spatial and quantitative abilities, which are relatively nascent in childhood, are affected by the hormonal changes after puberty, although some part of the effect of testosterone on spatial ability occurs prenatally. The study of asymptotic sex differences, therefore, is focused on representative samples in adolescence and early maturity. In later maturity and old age, sex differences in health factors and in longevity interact with sex differences in cognitive abilities, limiting the generalizability of the findings. The following studies of sex differences in *g* are based largely on representative population samples of individuals in adolescence and early maturity, except for one test on children and adolescents (WISC-R, ages 5 to 16) that is included for comparison with a parallel test for young adults (WAIS, ages 23 to 34).

Factor Analyzing Sex Differences. The best method for determining the sex difference in psychometric *g* is to represent the sex difference on each of the subtests of a battery in terms of a point-biserial correlation and include these correlations with the full matrix of subtest intercorrelations for factor analysis.[9] The results of the analysis will reveal the factor loading of sex on each of the factors that emerges from the analysis, including *g*. The *g* factor loading of sex, therefore, is equivalent to the point-biserial correlation between *g* and the sex variable (quantitized as male = 1, female = 0). This method is preferable to the use of *g* factor scores (which I used in an earlier study[10] of sex differences on the WISC-R), because *g* factor scores are not a pure measure of the *g* factor of the test battery from which it was extracted. An individual's *g* factor score is calculated as a *g*-weighted mean of the individual's standardized scores on each of the subtests; it is therefore necessarily somewhat contaminated by including small bits of the other factors and test specificity measured by the various subtests. This contamination of *g* factor scores can either increase or decrease the mean sex difference, depending on the types of subtests in the battery. Therefore, it is better to factor analyze the matrix of all the subtest intercorrelations, including the correlations of sex with each of the subtests.

I have performed this analysis with five test batteries in which data were available for large and representative samples that encompass the full range of ability in the general population. The results are shown in Table 13.1. Its interpretation requires some information about the test batteries and the key variables derived from them.

For all of the test batteries, the subject samples were expressly selected to be representative of the stated age groups in the general population. For every test there were either equal or very nearly equal percentages of males and females, the largest difference (GATB) being only 1.8 percent.

The WISC-R and the WAIS are the child and adult versions of the Wechsler Intelligence Scales; the data are from the national standardization samples.[11a] The various subtests are of the same types in both batteries, but differ in the level of difficulty. Although items (within each subtest) that showed marked sex differences were eliminated in the construction of the Wechsler tests, neither the items nor the subtests were selected with any reference to factor analysis. Whatever relationship emerges between sex differences and the factor composition

Table 13.1
Relationship of Sex Differences to *g* in Five Test Batteries

Variable	Test Battery[a]					Mean	Median
	WISC-R	WAIS	GATB	ASVAB	BAS		
Number of Subtests	13	11	8	10	14		
g Loading of Sex Difference[b]	.094	.006	-.255	.180	-.001	.011	.006
d Equivalent of *g* Loading	.189	.012	-.527	.366	-.002	.008	.012
IQ Equivalent of *d*	2.83	0.18	-7.91	5.49	-0.03	0.11	0.18
Percent of Total *g* Variance Due to Sex Differences	0.19	0.00	2.27	0.54	0.00	0.60	0.19
Correlation (r_s) of Tests' *g* Loadings With Sex Differences	.364	-.036	.024	.127	.103	.116	.103
Correlation (r_s) of Tests' *g* Loadings With M/F Variance Ratios	-.261	.318	-.738	.079	-.033	-.127	-.033

[a]Wechsler Intelligence Scale for Children-Revised (WISC-R), U.S. standardization sample, ages 5 to 16 years; Wechsler Adult Intelligence Scale (WAIS), American standardization sample, ages 25 to 34 years; General Aptitude Test Battery (GATB), unselected twelfth-grade high school students; Armed Services Vocational Aptitude Battery (ASVAB), a nationally representative sample of American youths, ages 18 to 23 years; British Ability Scales (BAS), British standardization sample, ages 14 to 17 years.
[b]Positive and negative loadings indicate male superiority and female superiority, respectively.

and relative magnitudes of factor loadings of the Wechsler tests, therefore, is not an artifact of the method of test construction.

The GATB analysis was based on the normative data for twelfth-grade students in high school.[11b] Sex differences were not considered in the construction of the GATB.

The ASVAB data are based on a large probability sample of the U.S. youth population.[11c] The mean sex differences used in this analysis were based on only non-Hispanic whites. Sex differences did not enter into the construction of the ASVAB, and the various subtests show very marked sex differences, especially on subtests involving technical information to which men are generally more exposed (e.g., auto shop, mechanical reasoning, electronic information).[11d] However, the factor structure per se of the 10 ASVAB subtests combined with 17 psychomotor tests is the same for adult males and females and the *g* loadings of the 27 tests are correlated +.999 between males and females.[11f]

From a strictly psychometric standpoint, the British Ability Scales (BAS) are probably as well constructed a battery of cognitive ability tests as one can find at present. Each of the fourteen subtests was constructed by means of item selection based on item response theory, or a latent trait model (in this case the Rasch model), which, for this type of test, is the optimal psychometric procedure. Test construction is based entirely on procedures that maximize psychometric desiderata without reference to sex or other subclassifications of the normative population. The normative samples for ages fourteen to seventeen were used in the present analysis.

Most of the variables listed in Table 13.1 are self-evident: The *g* loading of the sex difference is equivalent to the point-biserial correlation of sex with the test battery's *g* factor (here represented by the first principal factor of a common factor analysis).

The *d* equivalent of the *g* loading represents the size of the mean sex difference on *g* expressed in standard deviation units.[12]

The sex difference in IQ units is simply 15*d*.

The percent of the total *g* variance due to sex differences is the squared *g* loading for sex divided by the total variance of the *g* factor (excluding sex variance) $\times$ 100.

The Spearman rank-order correlation (r_s) of the column vector of subtests' *g* loadings with the vector of the sex differences (*d*) on the subtests indicates the degree to which *g* is related to the rank order of the sex differences on the various subtests.

The method of correlated vectors was also applied to the vector of the M/F variance ratios for the various subtests, which measures the degree to which males are more variable than females. For all but one test (WAIS), greater male variability on the subtests is *negatively* correlated with the subtests' *g* loadings.

Several points are especially worth noting:

- The *g* loadings of the sex differences are all quite small; the largest difference (GATB) favors females ($-.255$). (The GATB results are somewhat discrepant from those of the other batteries because of the rather unusual psychometric sampling, with an excess of psychomotor tests designed to measure particular vocational aptitudes. This slightly compromises the *g* factor by diminishing its loadings on the more cognitive variables.[13]) The BAS, probably the best constructed of all the tests from a psychometric standpoint, shows a near-zero *g* loading ($-.001$) on sex. The mean and median *g* loadings over the five tests are near-zero and completely nonsignificant.

- The method of correlated vectors shows that in no case is there a correlation even approaching significance between subtests' *g* loadings and the mean sex differences on the various subtests.

- The method of correlated vectors shows mostly negative (but nonsignificant, except for the GATB) correlations between the M/F variance ratios on each of the subtests and the subtests' *g* loadings.

The two main conclusions supported by the analyses in Table 13.1:

- The sex difference in psychometric *g* is either totally nonexistent or is of uncertain direction and of inconsequential magnitude.

• The generally observed sex difference in variability of tests scores is attributable to factors other than _g_.

Consistent with this finding of a near-zero sex difference in _g_ is the fact that there is no consistent sex difference on Raven's Standard Progressive Matrices (SPM) test (for adults) or on the Colored Progressive Matrices (CPM) test (for children). In numerous factor analyses, the Raven tests, when compared with many others, have the highest _g_ loading and the lowest loadings on any of the group factors. The total variance of Raven scores in fact comprises virtually nothing besides _g_ and random measurement error. In a review of the entire literature (117 studies from five continents) reporting sex differences on the Raven tests, Court[14] found positive and negative mean differences in the various studies distributed about equally around zero, for both the SPM and the CPM. Court concluded that there is no consistent evidence of a sex difference in the Progressive Matrices and that the most common finding is of no significant sex difference.

Some of the recent research on sex differences in IQ has been prompted by the finding of a significant sex difference in brain size, even when body size is statistically controlled (see Chapter 6, p. 148). The fact that brain size is correlated with IQ, and particularly with _g_, would seem to make the absence of a sex difference enigmatic. In an attempt to resolve this paradox, Lynn[15] has argued that a difference of only four IQ points, favoring males, would be consistent with the prediction from the sex difference in brain size and the within-sex regression of IQ on brain size.

In a review of several tests in several population samples, he has found an overall sex difference of about four IQ points. For the reasons pointed out above, any small overall difference (even if significant) on an arbitrary collection of subtests has questionable generality across different batteries and, in principle, cannot answer the question concerning a sex difference in general ability defined as _g_. Moreover, the sex difference in brain size may be best explained in terms of the greater "packing density" of neurons in the female brain, a sexual dimorphism that allows the same number of neurons in the male and female brains despite their difference in gross size. Also, the relationship of brain size to the well-established sex difference in spatial ability (independent of _g_) has not yet been studied. But if any feature of sex differences in brain anatomy or physiology is likely to be related to cognitive abilities, spatial ability is the best bet. In any case, variation in total brain size (or in whatever causes it, such as the number of neurons, arborization of dendrites, amount of myelin, etc.) accounts for only a minor part the total variance in _g_ or in IQ. Other physiological factors unrelated to brain size, in addition to certain experiential factors, must also contribute a large part of the _g_ variance.

The theoretical importance of finding a negligible sex difference in _g_ is that it suggests that the true sex differences reside in the modular aspects of brain functioning rather than in whatever general conditions of the brain's information-processing capacity cause positive correlations among all of the modular functions on which there is normal variation and which account for the existence of *g*.

NOTES

1. Much of the recent literature on sex differences is unfortunately indexed and catalogued under the heading of *gender* differences, which is clearly inappropriate terminology for the topic of sex differences, as will be readily perceived by anyone who looks up the meaning of *gender* in an unabridged dictionary. A *sex* difference is any statistically significant difference in a characteristic between groups of individuals who posses the XY (male) and those who possess the XX (female) chromosome pairs.

2. Some key references on sex differences in mental abilities: (a) Brody, 1992, pp. 317–328; (b) Feingold, 1993, (c) Halpern, 1992; (d) Hedges & Nowell, 1995; (e) Hyde, 1981; (f) Jensen, 1980a, Chapter 13; (g) Kimura & Hampson, 1993; (h) Maccoby & Jacklin, 1974; (i) Mackintosh, 1996; (j) Stumpf, 1995.

3. Lohman's (1988) article on the nature of spatial abilities is the best treatment I have found of this topic.

4. Lubinski & Humphreys, 1990, Table 3.

5. Nyborg, 1984; Halpern, 1992, pp. 110–135; Kimura & Hampson, 1993; Feingold, 1996.

6. McKeever, 1995; Geary, 1995.

7. (a) Benbow, 1988; (b) Geary, 1996; (c) Lubinski & Humphreys, 1990. The references and peer commentaries for these key articles provide a fairly comprehensive bibliography of the modern research on sex differences in mathematical ability.

8. Feingold (1994) reviewed cross-national and cross-cultural differences in the variability of males and females on cognitive tests, concluding, "Cross-cultural comparisons . . . revealed large fluctuations in sex differences [in variability] across samples from diverse countries, suggesting that cultural factors are implicated in the results found in American samples" (p. 81).

9. The point-biserial correlation (r_{pbs}) is simply a Pearson product-moment correlation that expresses the relationship between a metric variable (e.g., test scores) and a dichotomous variable (in this case sex, quantitized as male $= 1$, female $= 0$). As the value of r_{pbs} is reduced by the amount of inequality in the sample sizes of males and females, it was corrected for this inequality where such an inequality in Ns exists. Also, as r_{pbs} is reduced by an inequality of male and female standard deviations in test scores, the r_{pbs} was adjusted accordingly. Adjustments for the inequality of Ns and SDs are accomplished simultaneously by use of the following formula for r_{pbs}:

$$r_{pbs} = d/2\sqrt{(d^2/4) + 1},$$

where d is the mean difference (males $-$ females) divided by the averaged male and female standard deviations ($\bar{\sigma}$), calculated as $\bar{\sigma} = \sqrt{\sigma_m^2 + \sigma_f^2)/2}$.

Including the sex r_{pbs} for each of the subtests in the correlation matrix to be factor analyzed had no effect on the factor structure and only a negligible effect on the subtests' *g* loadings (congruence coefficients for all batteries are .999) when the factor analyses that include r_{pbs} in the correlation matrix were compared with the analyses that excluded r_{pbs} from the matrix. Therefore, it was not necessary to perform a Dwyer (1937) extension analysis (a mathematical maneuver that would be used in this case to isolate the sex variable itself from influencing the psychometric factors while showing its loadings on the psychometric factors).

10. Jensen & Reynolds (1983, Table 3) found a sex difference (M-F) of $d = +.161$ in _g_ factor scores obtained from the national standardization sample (ages five to sixteen years) of the Wechsler Intelligence Scale for Children-Revised (WISC-R).

11. (a) The WISC-R and WAIS data (separately for males and females) were obtained from the publishers of the Wechsler tests. Factor analyses of the data separately by sex show the same factor structure for both sexes; the male × female congruence coefficients on the _g_ factor are .99+; in the present analyses the within-sex _g_ factor loadings were averaged. (b) The GATB data for high school seniors are from Tables 20-3 and 20-20 in the GATB Manual (U.S. Dept. of Labor, 1970). (c) From the Office of the Assistant Secretary of Defense, 1982, pp. 65 and 77. (d) A detailed discussion of sex differences on each of the ten ASVAB subtests and their occupational implications is provided by Bock & Moore, 1986, pp. 114–148. (e) From the Technical Handbook of the _British Ability Scales_ (Elliott, 1983, pp. 63–88 and p. 152). (f) Carretta & Ree, 1997.

12. The _g_ loading (or any point-biserial correlation, r_{pbs}, with equal N_s and equal SD_s of the dichotomous groups on the metric variable) is converted to _d_ by the formula:

$$d = \sqrt{4/[(1/r_{pbs}^2) - 1]}.$$

13. Besides containing subtests of verbal (V), numerical (N), and spatial (S) abilities, which are common to many other test batteries intended to measure general cognitive ability, the GATB also contains a number of subtests intended to measure specific vocational aptitudes that strongly involve perceptual-motor abilities, such as perceptual speed of matching figures (P), clerical speed and accuracy (Q), motor coordination (K), finger dexterity (F), and manual dexterity (M). (Females slightly exceed males to varying degrees on V, P, Q, K, and F.) The greater number of perceptual-motor subtests in the GATB causes its first principal factor (PF1) to differ considerably from that of any of the other batteries, in which strictly cognitive abilities are relatively more represented than they are in the GATB. A factor analysis of the correlation matrix including the sex difference with just the cognitive variables (i.e., V, N, S) shows a sex loading on the general factor (PF1) of $+.021$, which is negligible. The general factor of the five perceptual-motor variables (P, Q, K, F, M) shows a sex loading of $-.329$, in favor of females.

14. Court, 1983.

15. Lynn (1994b), in a review of the sex differences (M-F) on Wechsler IQ (WISC-R and WAIS) obtained in several countries, reported Full Scale IQ differences ranging from 1.0 to 5.0 IQ points, with a mean of 3.08. Lynn's review also includes other tests, which show an average M-F difference of about four IQ points. He noted that the four IQ points male advantage is "precisely the advantage that can be predicted from their larger brains" (p. 269). His prediction is based on a reported correlation of .35 between _in vivo_ brain size (measured by magnetic resonance imaging) and WAIS IQ and a reported sex difference of 0.78σ in adult brain size (based on autopsied brains), hence a predicted M-F difference in IQ of $.35 \times 0.78\sigma = 0.27\sigma \times 15 \approx 4$ IQ points.

Chapter 14

The *g* Nexus

The *g* factor derives its broad significance from the fact that it is causally related to many real-life conditions, both personal and social. These relationships form a complex correlational network, or nexus, in which *g* is a major node. The totality of real-world variables composing the *g* nexus is not yet known, but a number of educationally, socially, and economically critical elements in the nexus have already been identified and are the subject of ongoing research.

Complex statistical methods have been developed for analyzing correlational data to help determine the direction of causality among the elements of the *g* nexus. These elements include personally and socially significant variables, such as learning disabilities, level of educational attainment, illiteracy, poverty, employment and income, delinquency, crime, law abidingness, and personal integrity.

The limitations of *g* as an explanatory variable in personal achievements have also been recognized. A person's level of *g* acts only as a threshold variable that specifies the essential minimum level required for different kinds of achievement. Other, non-*g* special abilities and talents, along with certain personality factors, such as zeal, conscientiousness, and persistence of effort, are also critical determinants of educational and vocational success.

Since the psychometric basis of *g* is now well established, future *g* research will extend our knowledge in two directions. In the horizontal direction, it will identify new nodes in the *g* nexus, by studying the implications for future demographic trends, employment demands, and strategies for aiding economically developing countries. Research in the vertical direction will seek to discover the

origins of *g* in terms of evolutionary biology and the causes of individual differences in terms of the neurophysiology of the brain.

The *g* factor is not a mere statistical construct. Rather it has significant real-
world importance. The effects of *g* encompass a broader range of uniquely
human phenomena than any other psychological construct. Empirical research
on *g* extends well beyond psychometrics. The search for the causal basis of *g*
draws upon research in experimental cognitive psychology and mental chronometry, brain anatomy and physiology, quantitative and molecular genetics, and
primate evolution. Applied research has concentrated on the importance of *g* in
education, employment, economic development, health, welfare dependency,
and crime.

Researchers in the applied fields have found that variation in scores on composites of *g*-loaded tests (those measuring IQ or "general intelligence"), whatever its causal basis, provides vital information for the interpretation of many
nonpsychometric behavioral and social variables. The new field of "sociology
of intelligence" uses individual and group differences in *g* and other cognitive
variables to explain significant social outcomes.[1]

This chapter, however, will be restricted to a review of phenomena outside
the field of academic psychology in which *g* is most probably a causal agent.

CORRELATION AND CAUSATION IN THE NEXUS OF
g-RELATED VARIABLES

A *nexus* is a network of various separate but interconnected elements, or
variables. The nexus may contain as few as 3 or 4 variables to as many as 30
or 40, or more. The degree of relation between any two variables is usually
measured as a correlation coefficient (or, less often, as a covariance). In discussing the correlation of *g* (or other cognitive variables) with some variable *Y*
outside the psychometric domain (particularly social variables) we should recognize that *g* is but one of many variables that are correlated with both *g* and
Y. A correlation coefficient indicates the direction (+ or −) and the degree (0
to 1) of *relationship* between any two variables. By itself, however, a correlation
can never prove either the direction or the degree of *causation*. Causation, in
this context, means that variable X can only be said to have some degree of
causal effect on variable Y if the *experimenter-controlled* variation in X results
in significant concomitant variation in Y. This can only be determined by the
investigator's actually controlling the values taken by variable X (termed the
independent variable) while observing the effect on variation in variable Y
(termed the *dependent variable*). This paradigm is that of a true experiment.

Controlling a variable statistically (either by nonrandom selection or matching
of subjects on one or more variables, or by using formulas that partial out
[remove] the variation in one or more statistically controlled variables from the

correlation between the two variables of primary interest) is not equivalent to experimentally controlling the independent variable by direct manipulation. Neither of these purely statistical types of control can rule out with certainty the effect of some unmeasured or unknown variable besides those that were statistically controlled and which therefore could be the causal agent in the correlation of primary interest. In a true experiment, however, both the known and the unknown variables whose causal effects we wish to remove in order to determine the causal effect of the manipulated variable X (the *independent variable*) on the outcome variable Y (the *dependent variable*) are controlled by the strictly random assignment of individuals to different groups that are each given different treatments (i.e., values of X).

In differential psychology and in other social sciences, true experiments are seldom possible. When we are confronted with a number of uncontrolled but intercorrelated variables, the determination of the direction and magnitude of causality between any given pair of correlated variables is problematic. Many variables deemed important in human affairs, of course, cannot be experimentally controlled.

Given this limitation, social science research can apply several different methods for interpreting a nexus. The particular method chosen depends on both the researcher's purpose and the availability of additional information that can help interpret the correlation of interest (say, r_{XY}).

• If we know only r_{XY}, the best we can do is to note the sign and size of the correlation and its standard error (or its confidence interval). Variable X may be a pragmatically useful *predictor* of variable Y, regardless of whether there is a directly causal connection between X and Y. If one's aim is merely prediction for some practical purpose, such as selection for college admission or employment, one need not go further than establishing the reliability and validity of the correlation for the subpopulations in which predictions are to be made.

• If the correlation between X and Y is reliable and we have a theoretical interest in the causal status of the relationship, we may examine the status of r_{XY} among some nexus of other variables that are also correlated with the variable of primary interest (r_{AX}, r_{AY}, r_{BX}, r_{BY}, ...). It could be the case that variable that has no causal effect on Y at all, but is correlated with a number of other variables that together have a causal (or partially causal) effect on Y. For example, variation in X and Y could both be caused by the third variable, A. Or X could be only one among many other variables (X, A, B), each of which has a small but independent effect on Y. The causal system could consist of anything from a simple linear chain (e.g., A→B→X→Y) to a complex nexus of intercorrelated variables having multiple and interactive causal effects upon one another.

Several multivariate analytic methods[2] are available to extract particular types of information from such a nexus. Initially the nexus is represented as a matrix of the correlations among all of the variables. (Simple examples of these methods, all based on one set of actual data, are shown in Appendix C.)

• A *principal components analysis* of the correlation matrix reveals which variables form more or less distinct clusters based on their degree of relationship to each another. Variables with substantial loadings on the same mathematically extracted component have more in common (for whatever cause) than variables that have their largest loadings on different components, the components themselves being completely uncorrelated. The first principal component, which is always the largest and most general component (the component comprising the largest proportion of the total variance in the matrix) is usually the most informative. A components analysis shows which variables or subsets of variables have the most in common. But because the input data consist only of correlations, causal determination is not possible. (In scientific research, of course, causal speculation is always permissible, and indeed necessary, as a source of empirically testable hypotheses.)

• A *multiple regression analysis* reveals the degree to which any subset of the variables (called the *independent variables*) in the whole nexus predicts any given variable (called the *dependent* variable) in the nexus. The degree of prediction is measured as the multiple correlation coefficient (R), while R^2 is the proportion of the total variance in the dependent variable that is "accounted for," or "explained," by the predictor variables (also called *independent* variables). The proportion of "unexplained" variance is $1 - R^2$; its square root ($\sqrt{1 - R^2}$) is termed the coefficient of alienation. The terms "accounted for" and "explained" are perfectly synonymous in the context of any type of purely correlational analysis lacking experimental control, but they do not imply causality, nor do they imply its absence. Generally, if no additional variables can be found that, when included in the set of independent variables, significantly increase the multiple correlation (R) with the dependent variable, one can tentatively assume that some causal relationships exist between the independent variables and the dependent variable. The larger the squared multiple correlation (i.e., the proportion of the total variance accounted for) and the more numerous and diverse the sampling of variables in the nexus, the less probable it becomes that most of the causal variance lies outside the nexus of intercorrelated variables. The differing relative weight (technically termed the *standardized partial regression coefficient*) of each of the independent variables, however, does *not* indicate the relative magnitude of each independent variables' *causal* influence on the dependent variable.

The mathematical algorithm for performing a multiple regression analysis offers no leverage for discovering causality. It only ensures that the one independent variable (say, A) that has the largest *correlation* with the dependent variable is given the largest weight (i.e., the highest regression coefficient). The independent variable (B) that is assigned the next largest weight, then, is the one that has the highest correlation with the residualized dependent variable, that is, with the remaining portion of the dependent variable's total variance that was not accounted for by variable A; and the same for independent variable C, and so on, through each of the independent variables that were entered into the multiple regression equation. Variables in the nexus that contribute no increment to the predicted variance in the dependent variable that is greater than what would be expected by chance error (an example would be including an independent variable that consists only of random numbers) are termed redundant. They are redundant in the sense that all of their true-score predictive power has already been contributed by the other variables in the equation. The degree of causal influence of any one variable in the analysis cannot be determined from the regression weights (coefficients), because, for example, the one predictor variable with the largest weight may register the composite effects caused by several other predictor variables, each of whose weight, in turn, is relatively small, though they (rather than the first variable) may be the direct causes of the dependent variable. The relative weights of variables discovered in the multiple regression analysis, however, may provide clues for hypothesizing the most likely causal relationships. These relationships may be examined further by performing separate multiple regression analyses on specific subsets of variables in the whole nexus to determine which subset best predicts some highly salient variable in the nexus.

• The most appropriate type of statistical analysis for inferring causality, though it is seldom definitive (except in genetics), is the class of methods known as *structural equation models*, of which *path analysis* is most commonly applied in the behavioral sciences. (A path diagram is shown in Appendix C.) Like all the other methods described so far, these methods also begin with the matrix of correlations among the variables in a nexus. But the analytic method is intended to yield a causal explanation, or a *path model*, of the relationships between the variables in the nexus, that is, the various paths of causal influence flowing from certain variables to other variables. The *direction* and relative *strength* of each causal element are indicated by an *arrow* and its *path coefficient*, respectively. The path diagram does not actually prove the causal connection among the variables, but it may be *consistent* (or inconsistent) with the empirical data. This is determined by a statistical assessment of the "goodness of fit" between the data and the model and by comparing the measure of "goodness of fit" across alternative models to determine which model best fits the data. The model with the poorer fit is disconfirmed, while the model with the better fit is really no more than just that. It does not constitute proof (in the sense of experimental control) that the hypothesized cause-and-effect relationships depicted by the path model correctly represent the true causal relationships. But it may be the best explanation one can provide when experimental control is unfeasible or impossible.

The obvious temporal order of some of the variables in a nexus may lend plausibility, or even compelling evidence, for the causal connections shown in a path model. Path analysis was invented by the geneticist Sewall Wright, and its use is most appropriate in quantitative genetic analysis. This is because the direction of genetic influence is always inarguable; genes flow from parents to their offspring, never the reverse. A correlation of .50 between parents' height and their children's height would hardly lead anyone to suggest that the direction of the causal path was from child to parent. Or, if parents' IQ at age 12 is correlated with offsprings' IQ at age 12, one could not plausibly argue that the child's IQ caused the parent's IQ when the parent was 12 years old. But even for these seemingly unambiguous examples of parent-child correlations we still need additional information in order to determine that the direction of causality is _direct_ (that is, transmitted from parent to child) rather than indirect, whereby parents and their children alike are affected by some external variable that influences height (or IQ) in each generation. Families might differ, for example, in dietary habits that persist across generations and influence physical or mental growth. To differentiate between direct and indirect causation of the parent-child correlation, researchers in human genetics have resorted to "natural experiments," such as studying genetically unrelated children reared together and monozygotic twins reared apart. Such studies (see Chapter 7) have led to the conclusion that the correlation between parents and children, both for height and for IQ, is, for the most part, directly causal, by the transmission of the parents' genes to their offspring.

• Still another way to disentangle a nexus is to examine the correlations among _group means_ on each of the variables in the nexus. (Other statistical measures of central tendency, such as the median and the mode, may be used in the same way.) This method is used much less often in the behavioral sciences than the other methods previously mentioned, but it is commonly seen in epidemiological research.[3]

In this method, the units of analysis are groups' means. The method requires a fair number of diverse groups, each comprising a large number of individuals (e.g., every sixth-grade class in a large city, different schools, colleges, different college majors, various racial, ethnic, national, or socioeconomic groups, age groups, groups differing in education, etc.). For each group in the sample we obtain the mean on each of a number of variables. Examples are diverse psychometric tests, family background characteristics, occupational data, health records, or any other social and economic indices that describe the various groups in ways that are of interest to the investigator. The group means on these variables can then be entered into almost any type of correlational or multivariate analysis (e.g., multiple regression, principal components, factor analysis) that best suits the researcher's purpose.

The value of using group means instead of measurements on individuals as the units of correlation analysis is that correlated means have the effect of magnifying or highlighting correlations that may be hardly detectable when individuals are the units of measurement. Some variables may have considerable significance for discovering causal factors in group differences, while they are practically useless for individual prediction. A variable X that has a small correlation with Y (and therefore makes only a negligible contribution, without practical significance, to the prediction or explanation of individual performance on variable Y) when both X and Y are measured on individuals may show a very large correlation between X and Y when both variables are measured as group means. The reason is that correlating group means removes (i.e., averages out) all of the individual variability on each measure *within* each group. The pattern of correlations between those variables that best describes group characteristics, therefore, shows up very clearly, unobscured by the (typically large) amount of individual variability in the characteristics of interest. Conversely, two variables that are substantially correlated among individuals will have negligible correlations when measured as group means if the groups do not differ on both variables. The scatter diagrams for correlated means can also clearly reveal nonlinear trends in the regression of one variable on another, even when nonlinearity is totally obscured by a correlation scatter diagram based on individuals.

STUDIES OF THE *g* NEXUS

The methods described above have been used in the many studies of how *g* affects real life. These studies show that psychometric *g*, represented by IQ or other highly *g*-loaded tests, figures prominently in a large nexus of personal and social variables that most people consider important. One may wonder why individuals' scores on a single test, which has so little apparent resemblance to the practical activities of everyday life, should be correlated with so many pivotal outcomes in peoples' lives. (And the means of the same outcome variables for different subpopulations are even more highly correlated among themselves and with *g*.)

The answer, as sociologist Robert Gordon has spelled out in detail with many actual examples, is that everyday life itself acts as an intelligence test,[4] and increasingly so as technology becomes more and more a part of everyday life.

Every semantic discrimination, every decision, every choice-point, every challenge, every opportunity for performance in everyday life has some degree of *g* loading, however slight it may be. In almost every *particular* instance of individual behavior, the "signal" (*g* variance) is very small compared to the "noise" (all sources of variance other than *g*). Now these single instances of real-life behavior are perfectly analogous, statistically, to the single items of a highly heterogeneous test. Although each single item in an IQ test reflects *g* only to a very slight degree, the aggregation of a large number of similar items results in a highly reliable measure of the common factor that is reflected, however slightly, by each item. Any single item has a very small signal-to-noise ratio (typically about .05 on a scale of 0 to 1)), but the aggregation of 100 diverse items yields a total score with a signal/noise ratio of over .90. The analogy between test items and instances of everyday behavior is aptly drawn by psychologist David Lubinski:[5]

> [A]s more items are responded to (like successive opportunities in life), they begin to paint a reliable picture of the individual with respect to the attribute under analysis. When slightly correlated items are added up (much like one's track record

in life), the uniqueness associated with each individual instance does not contribute much to the final portrait because, collectively, they share nothing in common. The unique chunks of each do not coalesce. Each comprises little of the total picture. What does coalesce, however, are the slight slivers of communality running through each item (the dominant theme running through each opportunity). These bits of communality pile up. Their influences are successively augmented in a composite (in one's overall track record). The composite's variance consists mostly of the signal that the items share. What the items do not share is noise, which aggregation attenuates to a minuscule sliver within the composite. Aggregation turns the large noise/signal ratio on its head. The composite is mostly signal even though the individual items are mostly noise. (p. 197)

Of course, there are also other "signals," or stable traits, besides *g* that aggregate in the same way to have important cumulative effects on the individual's overall "track record" in life, as discussed later in this chapter. Sociologist Linda Gottfredson[6] has put it well: "The effects of intelligence—like other psychological traits—are probabilistic, not deterministic. Higher intelligence improves the *odds* of success in school and work. It is an advantage, not a guarantee. Many other things matter" (p. 116).

Some sociologists regard individual and group differences in the level of *g* as wholly a result of inequalities in schooling and in social and economic privilege. In this view, *g* is merely an epiphenomenon in the nexus of all the socially valued variables with which *g* is so ubiquitously correlated. However, there are compelling reasons for believing that *g* is a central and generative causal force in the nexus. As pointed out, while multivariate statistical methodologies, by their inherent nature, cannot prove causality but at best can only increase its plausibility, there are empirical facts which, if taken into consideration, make it extremely probable that *g* itself is a causal force in the greater social nexus.

First, there is the high heritability of *g*, which simply means that the single largest source of individual differences in *g* is attributable to genetic factors. We therefore know that various social, economic, or environmental variables are not a main cause or explanation of most of the observed variance in *g*. Moreover, the part of the nongenetic variance in IQ that is commonly attributed to between-families differences in socioeconomic status (SES) constitutes only a very small proportion of the total environmental variance, most of which results from *within*-family environmental effects. In fact, large IQ differences exist among individuals when SES is taken account of, but SES factors are not related to individuals' IQs after genetic variability is accounted for. Attempts to discredit the evidence for the heritability of *g*, or to belittle its magnitude, are motivated by the wish to explain all of the variance it has in common with many real-life variables entirely in terms of socioeconomic variables, thereby denying the causal role of *g* (and along with it, genetics) in human affairs.

The most effective method for controlling what sociologists refer to as family background and socioeconomic variables (e.g., parents' education, occupation, income, and other variables that are correlated with *g*) is the use of *within*-

family correlations. About one-half of the total population variance in adult IQ exists among full siblings who have shared the same family background from birth to maturity. Yet the IQs of full siblings (measured when they are children or adolescents) are positively correlated (+.30 to .+40) with measures of their educational, occupational, and economic status as adults. That is, IQ predicts these and many other kinds of individual outcomes independently of differences in family and social background, which, independently of IQ, typically have lesser predictive power than does IQ.[7]

It is obvious to parents as well as to teachers in all levels and types of education that providing equal opportunities to learn does not result in equal rates of learning or in the level of performance after a given amount of instruction and practice. This is true for every kind of learning, though certain types of learning are much more (or much less) *g* loaded than other types. This is true regardless of social class, race, or family background. Yet highly *g*-loaded tests can predict learning outcomes under equal opportunity for learning far in advance of the actual learning experience. Additional measures of group factors, special abilities, or talents, of course, can usually improve the prediction (or explanation) of success for certain types of learning—music, art, mechanics, athletics, manual skills, and athletics, to name a few. Individual differences in certain ability factors, especially *g*, are measurable or identifiable long before the initiation of many of the learning opportunities whose outcomes are correlated with the measures of *g* that were obtained much earlier. To infer that the causal path goes in the direction from *g* to the learning outcome is certainly more plausible than the reverse.

Causal interpretation of the pathways in a nexus should be informed by the results of experimental and quasi-experimental studies of the direct effects of social, cultural, and educational variables on *g*. When massive and long-term interventions, such as the Milwaukee Project, the Abecedarian Project, the Minnesota Transracial Adoption Study, and adoption studies in general (see index), produce only slight or transitory effects on *g*-loaded performance, imputing large causal effects to variables that empirically have proven to be exceedingly weak is implausible and improbable. A classic example is the so-called "Pygmalion effect," or "teacher expectancy"—the claim that children's IQs can be raised or lowered by such a subtle condition as the classroom teacher's being told (even falsely) that certain children have either a low or a high potential for mental growth. A meta-analysis of eighteen studies of the purported effect of this kind of teacher expectancy on children's IQ lends no support for its reality.[8] The overall average effect size for seventeen studies (excluding the methodologically defective original Pygmalion study) is $+.025\sigma$, that is, less than one-half of an IQ point.

Low Levels of *g*. Applied psychologists working in personnel selection have established that low IQ is more reliably predictive of vocational outcomes than is high IQ. This is because *g* is only one of the many psychological factors and personal characteristics that affect how one responds to the various challenges of life and thereby influences the opinions of other people—parents, teachers, classmates, employers, and co-workers—with whom one interacts. Ability creates opportunity to a large extent. A person with a high IQ but lacking other desirable traits can fare worse in life than many people with a low IQ who have these other qualities. A low IQ, however, provided it is a valid assessment of the individual's standing on *g*, invariably restricts an individual's educational and occupational options, the more so, the further their IQ falls below 100 (the average level). This is true regardless of the person's standing on other traits, which, when favorable, to some extent mitigate the disadvantaging effects of low *g*.

Contrary to much popular wisdom, the IQ score per se does not act as a self-fulfilling prophecy. IQ predicts and is related to certain life outcomes not because the person's IQ happens to have been measured, or because anyone happens to know the person's IQ as such. If mental tests had never been invented, parents, teachers, and employers would still be able to make successful predictions about individuals. The IQ is simply a rough index of *g*, which reflects underlying individual differences in the efficiency of certain brain processes that are manifested as one of the important factors in human affairs.

A critical threshold in the distribution of *g* lies near the tenth percentile, that is, the level of general ability below which 10 percent of U.S. adults fall, with 90 percent being above that level. The tenth percentile corresponds to an IQ of eighty-one in the nationally representative standardization sample of the Wechsler Adult Intelligence Scale. Considering the standards of today's education-demanding, knowledge-intensive society, the American Association on Mental Retardation has classified IQs between seventy and eighty-five as "borderline retarded." Most persons in this IQ range exhibit about a fifth- or sixth-grade level of educational achievement, even after twelve years of school attendance.

The U.S. Congress recognized this critical threshold when it mandated that the minimum mental ability requirement for induction into any branch of the armed services be set at the tenth percentile on the Armed Forces Qualification Test (a highly *g*-loaded scale), even in time of war. This mandate was based on the practical experience gained in training recruits for the various jobs required in the armed services. The problem is not just that individuals below the tenth percentile lack the specific knowledge and skills needed in the armed services, but rather it is a problem in trainability. All new recruits, regardless of IQ, have to undergo training for the specific jobs they will perform in the military. But when recruits scoring below the tenth percentile have been admitted on an experimental basis, it has generally been impossible, given the time that can pragmatically be devoted to training, to bring them up to a useful standard of performance on even the least complex jobs available in the military. Nor is this a literacy problem per se (although the vast majority of illiterates are found in this group). Rather, it is essentially a comprehension problem; trainees below the tenth percentile typically cannot understand verbal instructions any better when they hear them clearly read aloud than when they are required to read the instructions by themselves.

In a largely urbanized industrial and technological society, with its ever-increasing information-intensive demands, life for those with IQs below eighty becomes a series of frustrating trials. Using a telephone directory, getting through a voice-mail system, reading bus or train schedules, banking, keeping financial records, filling out forms and dealing with the bureaucracy, using a VCR, cooking food in a microwave, following directions on prescriptions or over-the-counter drugs, passing drivers' tests, knowing where, when, and how to shop economically, and countless other routine demands of daily life in modern society are all cognitive challenges for individuals with low IQ, and are often beyond their capability.

Specific training for any one of these demands can only do so much. Earl Hunt, a leading researcher in cognitive psychology, provides the following example[9a] from the U.S. Army's experience in training Category IV personnel for specialized jobs. (Category IV recruits are those whose scores on the Armed Forces Qualification Test fall between the tenth and thirtieth percentiles [equivalent to IQs of about 81 to 92]): "[T]he Category IV soldier did quite well so long as it was clear exactly what was to be done. For instance, these soldiers were able to perform engine maintenance operations that involved long sequences of operations, providing that there were no choices at each step. On the other hand, the same soldiers were unable to carry out relatively simple repairs in situations where they had to decide what had to be done" (p. 10). The two types of tasks described by Hunt clearly differ in their *g* demand. The first represents a well-learned and routinized skill, the second involves thinking and problem solving. It is the latter type that, so far, has been least responsive to training in the below-eighty IQ range, probably because the very process of learning the kinds of algorithms, schemata, and strategies that constitute the teachable aspect of thinking and problem-solving skills are themselves too *g*-demanding to be mastered by persons of low IQ. Productive thinking and problem solving depend upon having a store of relevant information that can be readily accessed from long-term memory. However, the amount and level of complexity of the information that can be acquired through training and experience are highly correlated with *g*. And therein lies the problem.

In a recent book,[9b] Hunt examined the problem of supply and demand for cognitive ability and the higher levels of specialized skills needed for employment in the coming decades. Making a legitimate distinction between *g* and acquired skills, he proposes using methods based on cognitive theory to improve the required work-related thinking and problem-solving skills for persons at almost every level of general ability. The methods are not intended as a prescription for equalizing people in general ability or, for that matter, even in specific skills, but for increasing the level of various needed skills in the whole population, especially those in the lower half of the IQ distribution, in order to increase the supply of workers who can better fulfill demands that will be made on our future work force. Whether Hunt is overly optimistic about the efficacy of these methods for the lower IQ segment of the population remains to be seen. So far, most advances in technology (for example, the use of personal computers) have accentuated the effects of individual differences in _g_, dividing the population into those who can and those who cannot become proficient in using the new technology. Those who cannot are then further disadvantaged.

Lloyd Humphreys[10a] coined the term _inadequate learning syndrome_ (ILS) to describe deficits in basic intellectual skills and information. He believes ILS is a social epidemic "as serious in its way as the AIDS epidemic." ILS is primarily a result of an insufficient level of _g_ and is seen in the presence of _adequate_ educational opportunity. This is what makes ILS so visible. The adverse consequence of ILS in the nation's work force is not a result of any marked change in the total population distribution of _g_. It is a product of the increasing demand for formal educational credentials in today's job market. As such credentials and diplomas have become spread over a greatly increased range of individual differences in actual educational achievements and qualifications, many employers have found today's high school diploma, or even a college degree, of little value in the absence of additional information about a job applicant's ability. Employers increasingly come to rely on specific screening tests to assess actual levels of relevant achievement. And what these tests too often reveal is ILS.

For the most part, ILS only comes to public attention because of its disproportionate frequency among identifiable subpopulations whose distribution of _g_ is considerably below the overall national average. Humphreys is much less optimistic than Hunt, not only because ILS is so strongly _g_ related, but because it is so often enmeshed in the whole nexus of other _g_-related variables that are inimical to the development of employable skills. Humphreys notes "the prevalence of ILS among parents and other relatives, neighborhood adults, and peers" and how it is "embedded in a complex of problems that include teen pregnancy, illegitimacy, female-headed families, welfare, drugs, prostitution, and violent crime" (p. 259).

People with IQs below eighty commonly run into difficulties unless assisted in the management of their affairs by relatives or social agencies. The problem is accentuated socially and politically by the visibility of marked disparities between the proportions of different subpopulations that fall below this critical threshold. The social importance of these proportional below-threshold differences is that they are also reflected in statistical differences in many "real life" variables that constitute the _g_ nexus—education, employment, income, poverty, crime, and other social pathologies.

The major social problems involving _g_ arise from the dual conditions of _critical threshold_ and _critical mass_. Largely because of economic selection, people in the lower segment of the normal distribution of _g_ gradually become segregated from the rest of the community, not only in regard to where they live but also in how they live. People of a given ability level tend to be less conspicuous among a community of similar individuals and operate more comfortably within it. People's environments, or their perceptions of them, differ in complexity and cognitive demands. One might even characterize different environments in terms of their *g* loadings. As the selection process accelerates, the percentage of low-ability persons residing in the same locality approaches what might be called a *critical mass*, in which a majority of the inhabitants of the neighborhood segregated by low *g* falls below the critical threshold. The more able and ambitious residents leave the area; its economic viability dwindles; and those left behind come to constitute what is now referred to as the *underclass*.[10b] This is the blight of the so-called "inner city" of many metropolitan areas. The "culture of poverty" spontaneously engendered by these conditions hinders upward mobility, most unfortunately even for those youths who possess an average or above-average level of *g* and would predictably succeed in a decent environment. This is indeed the gloomy side of the *g* nexus.

The problems of inner-city schools are *g* related and epitomize what Humphreys has referred to as the inadequate learning syndrome, or ILS. Observing educators' attempts to improve learning in inner-city schools, Maeroff[11] noted: "[T]here is a tendency to revel in delusions of improvement. Order may be restored, but oppression reigns. Test scores may rise, but concepts remain ungrasped. Facts may be memorized, but students cannot apply them in solving problems. Dropouts may be kept in school, but the diplomas they receive are not backed by skills and knowledge" (p. 638).

Persons of subthreshold *g* who are not members of the underclass constitute a relatively small percentage of the general population that is gainfully employed and lives in wholesome neighborhoods. Although low IQ persons who are reared in the favorable environment of fully capable parents and relatives experience the usual cognitive disadvantages of subthreshold *g* in scholastic performance and level of employment, their disadvantage in dealing with novelty and complexity is generally "buffered" by their relatives and caring neighbors, who can mediate for them when necessary in their encounters with the more *g*-demanding problems of daily life. When the cognitively disadvantaged are sparsely dispersed among responsible relatives and neighbors of average and higher IQ, they escape the multiplier effect of their disadvantage that results when many low-IQ persons are segregated together in a neighborhood. In a neighborhood that has reached "critical mass," on the other hand, cognitive disadvantage is the majority condition for parents and children and their extended families and neighbors, who can provide little if any mediation or "buffering" when needed.[12] There are families, and even whole apartment blocks, that require almost daily intervention by social workers to help in the management of what most people would consider routine contingencies in the affairs of daily life.

EDUCATION AND FUNCTIONAL LITERACY

After *g* itself, education is the most important variable in the nexus. This is because the effects of general education and of specialized intellectual skills (whether acquired in school or elsewhere) are the main mediators for the *indirect effects* of *g* as manifested in present-day society. Performance in life (outside the testing room) reflects in large part the interaction of *g* and education. The effects of education and *g* are not additive, but multiplicative. (That is, their joint effect can be represented as the product of *g* × education.) When educational opportunity is equalized, *g* becomes the major predictor of performance. (Only when *g* is held constant does education become the major predictor.) For persons in the same educational setting and at every level from first grade to graduate school, highly *g*-loaded tests predict more of the variance in educational performance than any other single variable or set of variables *independent* of *g*, including all of the usual SES or family background variables that are so commonly regarded as the major determinants of educational achievement. (As selection for and by education, from elementary school through college, progressively reduces the variance in *g*, special talents and certain noncognitive traits come to play an increasingly important role in successful performance.) It is important to note that, independent of *g*, the variables of race or ethnicity per se contribute virtually nothing to the prediction of educational achievement.

It is instructive in this regard to look at multiple regression analyses based on four data sets from large independent samples that were given various tests at different stages of schooling.

• Psychometric data from the National Longitudinal Study of Youth (NLSY) provide test scores that measure two core aspects of scholastic achievement (mathematics and verbal/reading skills) obtained on large regional samples of youths fifteen to eighteen years of age. The National Education Longitudinal Survey (NELS) provides achievement scores in mathematics and reading skills obtained from large regional samples of eighth-graders (aged twelve to fourteen years). The NLSY and NELS data sets both include the same measures of family background, along with the region of the country, as independent (predictor) variables. The family background variables include family income, father's and mother's education, age of mother at child's birth, number of siblings, mother's marital status, mother's employment status, and ethnicity (black, Hispanic, and non-Hispanic white).[13] If we use all of the background variables, *except* race/ethnicity, as independent variables in a multiple regression to predict scholastic achievement in math and reading, the multiple correlation, R, in each study is:

	NLSY	NELS
Math	.39	.39
Reading	.47	.37

All of the correlations are highly significant ($p < .001$). It is apparent that the background variables are substantial predictors of achievement. Among all of the independent variables, by far the largest share of the predictive weight is carried by the parents' level of education. We know from other studies that the level of education is also related ($r \approx .60$) to the mid-parent IQ, which is correlated ($r \approx .50$) with the offspring's IQ. IQ is highly predictive $r \approx .75$ of the child's overall level of scholastic achievement from grades one through twelve. Most, though not quite all, of the power of parental education as a predictor of their offspring's achievement, therefore, is mediated both by the parents' level of *g* and by the substantial (narrow) heritability of *g*.

When race/ethnicity is included among the predictor variables in the multiple regression, the *R*s are:

	NLSY	NELS
Math	.53	.53
Reading	.60	.48

Comparing these values of *R* with those in the preceding table, it is apparent that the addition of race/ethnicity to the prediction equation increases *R* substantially.

From the difference[14] between these two tables, we can determine the predictive value of the race/ethnicity variable independent of all of the other background variables, that is, when the total effect of all of the other measured background variables has been statistically removed. Thus the *R* for the independent effect of race/ethnicity on scholastic achievement in this analysis is:

	NLSY	NELS
Math	.37	.35
Reading	.38	.31

These are also substantial predictive values, which appear to contradict the earlier statement that race/ethnicity contributes nothing to the prediction of scholastic achievement. That statement is true, however, when we take individual differences in level of *g* into account in addition to background variables. This tells us that the effect of the variable labeled race/ethnicity on educational achievement is largely mediated by other variables and especially by *g*.

• Consider the following study[15] of nearly 6,000 pupils (2,237 white, 2,025 Hispanic [Mexican-American], and 1,694 black) in grades one through eight in one California school district in which the test scores of the three groups closely matched the normative distribution of scores for these populations on two nationally standardized tests. Multiple regression analyses were performed separately within each school grade. Race or ethnicity was included as a binary variable in three separate analyses—white/black, white/Hispanic, and black/Hispanic.

The *predictor variables* were age, sex, a SES index that summarized 25 family and home background variables in 4 separate scores, a battery of 7 highly diverse cognitive ability tests chosen to not measure scholastic subject matter (1 verbal IQ test and 5 nonverbal tests whose composite score is highly *g* loaded), and a personality inventory for assessing introversion-extraversion and neuroticism (anxiety) in children (not used below fourth grade).

The *predicted variables* were each of the nine subtests of the Stanford

Achievement Test battery, which assess basic elements of scholastic achievement such as various aspects of reading, spelling, language, and arithmetic. Scores on each subtest were regressed separately on the set of predictor variables (described above).

The results of these analyses were highly similar for all nine achievement variables. The predictive validity of the independent (predictor) variables increased monotonically with grade level, the overall average value of R increasing from .37 at grade 1 to .76 at grade 8, averaging .70 across grades 1 to 8. This set of independent variables thus predicts educational achievement to a high degree.

Now look at the simple correlation of race or ethnicity with achievement (averaged over all subtests and grades): For white/black, $r = .38$; for white/ Hispanic, $r = .31$, and for Hispanic/black, $r = .12$. These correlations are modest but significant (all with $p < .01$). But when we partial out (remove) the effects of the set of predictor variables (absent race/ethnicity) from these correlations, the corresponding values of the partial correlations drop to .05, $-.08$, and .08, each of which is nonsignificant (average $p > .30$). That is, race/ethnicity made no significant contribution to the prediction of achievement independent of the effects of the measures of individual differences in the cognitive abilities and family background variables that constitute the core of the whole *g* nexus. No uniquely racial or ethnic characteristics of the students or racial biases imposed by the schools need be invoked to explain the observed racial/ethnic differences in educational achievements.

• In data obtained from 339 college students, the *g* factor proved to be the central element in the path analysis[16] of a nexus of nine intercorrelated variables that included *college aptitude* (SAT-Verbal, SAT-Math, ACT college aptitude test), *academic performance* in high school and college (high school grade average, college grade average in math and in English, and *family variables* (income, parent's age, family size).

Five different path models were fitted to the data. The path model that best explained the nexus, that is, the model that provided the most parsimonious or "best fit" to the data, is shown in Figure 14.1. Both *g* and academic performance (AP) are called *latent traits* in this model, as they are not observed variables; that is, they are not measured directly, but are derived as factors from the observed data. (Latent traits are conventionally shown in path analyses as circles, observed variables as squares.) Note that there are no direct paths connecting any of the three family variables (or their common factor) to the common factor of academic performance or to any of its three elements. Including another path that directly connects the family variables (or from their common factor) to academic performance (**AP**) does not improve the model's fit in the least. In the best-fitting model (Figure 14.1), *g* is shown with a path coefficient of .672 going to **AP**; thus *g* accounts for $(.672)^2$, or 45.2 percent of the variance in AP. The circles containing **E** represent measurement error and unmeasured sources of true-score variance in the observed variables. The square of the path coeffi-

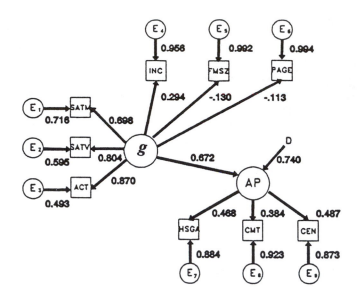

Figure 14.1. Path analysis of a nexus consisting of 3 college aptitude measures: SAT-M (math), SAT-V (verbal), ACT (American College Test); 3 family variables: INC (family income), FMSZ (family size), PAGE (parent age); and 3 measures of academic performance: HSGA (high school grade average), CMT (college math grades), CEN (college grades in English. *g* and **AP** (academic performance) are derived general factors, or the *latent* variables in the path model. **E** and **D** are "error" or unexplained sources of variance in the respective variables. Arrows indicate the hypothesized paths between the latent variables (in circles) and the observed variables (in squares). (Brodnick, R. J. & Ree, M. J., A structural model of academic performance, socioeconomic status, and Spearman's *g*. *Educational and Psychological Measurement, 55,* pp. 583–594, copyright © 1995 by R. J. Brodrick and M. J. Ree. Reprinted by permission of Sage Publications, Inc.)

cient coming from any **E** is the proportion of variance in the given variable that remains *unexplained* by the latent variables in the model. Similarly, D^2 is the unexplained variance in the latent trait labeled **AP.** [*Note*: $(.672)^2 + (.740)^2 = 1.00.$]

Functional Literacy. The general level of literacy in America, partly as a result of comparisons with that of other industrialized nations, has become a major concern to educators and an issue of acute public awareness.[17] The skill known as reading comprehension is certainly a major element in the *g* nexus. Reading comprehension is a complex information-processing skill, the acquisition of which, like other complex processing skills, reflects individual differences in *g*.

Although literacy and illiteracy are often treated as "either-or categories," there is actually a perfect continuum of individual differences in the ability to comprehend the meaning of printed text and to express one's thoughts in writing. Illiteracy once meant the complete lack of reading or writing skills. Since this lowest-level definition now applies to only about 1 percent of American adults and therefore conveys little information, illiteracy has come to be defined as the inability to read and write well enough to function adequately in modern society. More specifically, the U.S. Public Health Service, in 1971, adopted the definition of *functional literacy* as being the average level of reading comprehension attained by school children at the *beginning of fourth grade* (at about age nine). The *mean* on an objective test of reading comprehension given to a representative sample of children just entering the fourth grade was used as the cut-score for classifying persons as either functionally literate or functionally illiterate. This test was given to a national probability sample, ages twelve to seventeen.[18] The estimated relative frequency (and its standard error) of functional illiteracy among seventeen-year-old Americans in 1971 was 4.4 ± 0.73 percent (white, 2.8 ± 0.65; black, 14.8 ± 4.32). In the years from 1971 to 1984, however, surveys by the National Assessment of Educational Progress (NAEP) have shown significant gains in the level of reading proficiency, especially for racial/ethnic minority groups (see Figure 14.2). The reading tests are all scored on a common scale representing different levels of the complexity and difficulty of the reading material. Key scores on the reading scale are characterized as follows:

Score Reading Level

150—*Rudimentary* (typical 2nd-grade readers)

200—*Basic* (4th-grade reading matter)

250—*Intermediate* (8th-grade reading matter)

300—*Adept* (high school college preparatory material)

350—*Advanced* (4-year college reading level)

The cause of the increase in scores for each age group (9, 13, and 17 years) between 1971 and 1984 is uncertain, but is probably related to the schools' increased focus on the improvement of reading instruction and the increased attention given to raising the achievement levels of minority students. Other contributing factors are possibly secular changes in birthrates in different socioeconomic levels of the population and the conditions hypothesized as causes of the "Flynn effect" (see Chapter 10, pp. 318–32).

From first grade through high school, reading proficiency (defined as reading comprehension), becomes increasingly *g* loaded. Skill in word reading per se normally becomes automatized in the early grades. Unusual difficulty in acquiring automatized word reading, or *decoding*, if it persists into the fourth grade, becomes relatively unrelated to *g*. It is then typically taken as evidence of a specific learning disability, or *dyslexia*, which occurs in about 5 to 15 percent of the school population, the precise frequency depending on the diagnostic criteria used. Beyond fourth grade, however, the correlation of reading

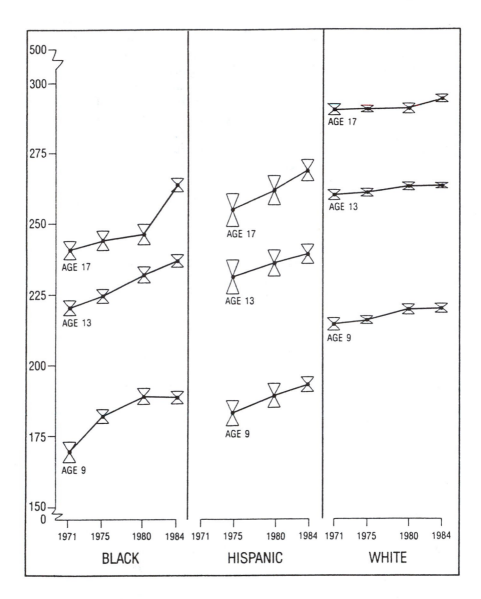

Figure 14.2. Trends in average reading proficiency as a function of race/ethnicity, age, and the year of testing (1971–1984), in a national probability sample of the U.S. population. The ''hourglass'' figures indicate the estimated population mean level of reading proficiency and the 95 percent percent confidence interval around the mean (i.e., the level of certainty that the mean reading proficiency in the given population falls within the interval between the top and bottom of the ''hourglass''). See text for explanation of the scale of reading proficiency. (*Source*: National Assessment of Educational Progress, 1985, p. 32.)

comprehension with IQ and its *g* loading in factor analyses of reading tests along with various other kinds of cognitive tests is almost as high as the reliability of the tests themselves. Also, mean racial/ethnic group differences in reading comprehension are highly comparable to the corresponding mean differences in verbal and nonverbal IQ for native-born, English-speaking groups. The sex difference in reading—females are higher at every age—is one instance where the group differences in reading proficiency and in *g* are slightly at variance. Most of the sex difference occurs at the lower levels of reading proficiency; for example, among persons seventeen years of age, more than twice as many males as females are functionally illiterate (6.5 percent vs. 2.3 percent).[18] The sex difference is negligible in the functionally literate segment of the population.

Because reading is a learned skill, of course, it improves with training and practice, and reading comprehension increases with growth in vocabulary and with the increasing fund of information stored in long-term memory. But as reading is a complex information-processing skill, all these aspects of reading also reflect individual differences in the efficiency of information processing, which includes speed of intake of information, working memory capacity, and the accessibility of information from long-term memory.[19] It is these basic processing components in reading that are less easily influenced by training and practice. In the absence of a specific reading disability (such as dyslexia or aphasia), *reading* comprehension and *listening* comprehension are highly correlated. It is comprehension itself that is by far the more complex aspect of the skill involved in reading. Reading comprehension is correlated nearly as much with nonverbal as with verbal IQ. Even performance on a task as simple as reaction time (RT) measured with the Hick paradigm, which does not use alphanumeric symbols at all (see Chapter 8, pp. 211–14), shows correlations with scores on a reading comprehension test comparable to those for the highly *g*-loaded Raven's matrices (a nonverbal test of reasoning). Intraindividual trial-to-trial variability in RT, which has the highest *g* loading of any measure derived from the RT procedure, showed a correlation of $-.71$ with reading comprehension in a group of ninth graders, while total RT correlated $-.54$ with reading comprehension.[20]

EMPLOYMENT AND INCOME

Adam Smith's dictum that a nation's wealth depends on the developed abilities of its people is the basis of the public concern in this technological era that we have a well-educated work force. In the information age, a nation's most important resource in the modern world is not its material natural wealth but its human capital, that is, the overall level of its population's developed abilities that are in demand in a free market. The economic value of *g*, therefore, is a function of the particular knowledge and skills in which it is most highly loaded, and in which proficiency depends upon education, training, and experience. Developed ability, in other words, is a product of *g* × education—education that inculcates the knowledge and skills that are productively relevant to the culture and the times. But, as already noted, there is a strong causal dependence between the level of _g_ and the level of educational attainments, a dependence that only increases as educational opportunity is extended throughout a nation's entire population. Most economists recognize causal connections between economic factors and developed abilities, but they generally underestimate them, because the measure of developed ability most often used in economic analyses is the number of years of schooling.[21] This is at best a crude index of actual educational attainment and poorly reflects its _g_ component, as the correlation between years of schooling and _g_ is about .6 as compared with about .8 for the correlation between measures of scholastic achievement and _g_. (The average of school or college grades is also only moderately correlated with psychometric assessments of actual attainments.) Specialized tests of the types of knowledge and skills that are most relevant to certain occupations may have more predictive validity for personnel selection, but they, too, have a large _g_ component when all the applicants have had equivalent training for the specialized job.

R. B. Cattell's[22] formulation of the supply/demand relationship between the _supply_ of developed abilities and the economic _demand_ for these abilities in a particular culture at any given time can be depicted as two bell-like curves, one curve representing the _supply distribution_ of developed ability in the population, the other curve representing the _demand distribution_ at a given time. When the two distribution curves completely overlap or coincide, supply and demand are in perfect equilibrium, which is presumably the ideal condition. When the two curves are markedly offset, however, there is a scarcity of supply at the higher end of the ability spectrum and an excess supply at the lower end, as shown in Figure 14.3. (This is intended as a theoretical model and does not represent actual data or measurements.) The model predicts that changes in the unemployment rate due to fluctuations in the economy mostly affect the lower segment of the ability spectrum. The supply distribution is shown as quite skewed to the right, because it represents the distribution of developed ability, which is a form of achievement. (Because achievement is a product of a number of more basic, normally distributed traits, it always has a skewed distribution when measured on an absolute scale.) Note that in any complex industrialized society the demand distribution spans a very wide range on the ability scale, although the actual population frequencies (supply) at each point on the scale may depart markedly from the frequency of demand. The cognitive requirements for various occupations, of course, fall in different segments of the ability scale.

The _economic value_ per se (and hence the monetary reward) for persons at any given point on the ability scale is a positive function of the ratio of demand (D) frequency to supply (S) frequency (i.e., demand/supply). For example, at -1σ below the mean (zero) in Figure 14.3, the demand/supply ratio (D_1/S_1) is .3; at $+1\sigma$ above the mean, the demand/supply ratio (D_2/S_2) is 2.4.[23] At the mean (M) of the ability scale, the demand is only slightly less than the supply (a D_M/S_M ratio of .8 in Figure 14.3). Developed ability in most of the population

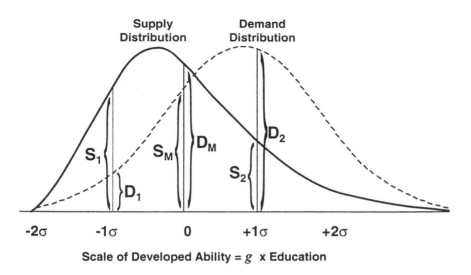

Figure 14.3. Theoretical frequency distribution of the *supply* (S) of developed abilities in a population and the distribution of the economic *demand* (D) for those abilities in a given culture at a given time, represented on a *z* scale ($\mu = 0$, $\sigma = 1$) of developed ability, which is conceived as a product of *g* and education (or training) and experience. (Adapted from Cattell, 1983, p. 163.)

is mainly a product of $g \times$ education (or training), but this ability continuum may be conceived as also including special artistic and athletic talents and personality traits that potentiate developed ability, such as conscientiousness, drive, persistence, emotional stability, and stress tolerance.

The regions of the IQ scale from which various occupations are typically recruited have been determined empirically using large data sets that sample virtually the entire employed population of adults. An analysis based on the Wonderlic Personnel Test (WPT), for which the normative data comprise many thousands of persons employed in every level of the occupational status, was summarized, along with other descriptive indices of ability, in a figure devised by Gottfredson,[24] as shown in Figure 14.4.

Various subpopulations have more or less bell-shaped frequency distributions with different means and different standard deviations on the scale of developed ability. In recent years, the relevance of these statistical differences to problems of unemployment, unequal representation of various subpopulations at different levels of the job status hierarchy, and related disparities in personal income have been widely discussed in newspaper and magazine articles. These inequalities are most conspicuous at the higher levels of the scale of developed ability, particularly in science, engineering, and computer technology—fields in which the supply generally lags far behind the demand. In fact, large numbers of workers are imported from Asia and Europe to fill the employment opportuni-

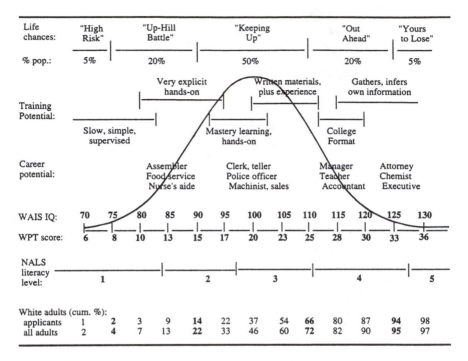

Figure 14.4. Overall life chances associated with different ranges in the normal distribution of IQ in the general population. The sources of data on which this figure is based are referenced by Gottfredson (1997, Figure 3, p. 117). (Used with permission of Ablex.)

ties. At the same time, there is extreme underrepresentation of U.S. blacks and (to a lesser degree) Hispanics in science and engineering. This disparity is of such major concern that the American Association for the Advancement of Science devoted a large part of one issue of its official journal, *Science*,[25] to an examination of the topic. Despite an increase in population between 1979 and 1988, the total number of blacks earning Ph.D. degrees in science and engineering declined by 20 percent over that period. Although blacks make up 11 percent of the working-age population, they constitute only 1 percent of all doctoral degrees in all of the natural sciences and engineering. The range of developed ability (as assessed by the SAT) that includes all those high school students who go on to college and major in science or engineering comprises nearly 8 percent of white students, 1.2 percent of Hispanic students, and .3 percent of black students.[26] There is no evidence that these disparities are due to racial or ethnic bias or discrimination in the selection of students who major in science and engineering. The National Science Foundation commissioned a large-scale investigation of this question, and found that although a larger proportion of blacks than of whites were interested in majoring in science when

Table 14.1
Theoretically Predicted versus Actual Percentages of Blacks and Whites Employed in Various Occupations That Differ in Mean IQ

Occupation	B%/W% in Recruiting Range	B%/W% in Occupation 1970	1980
Physician	0.05	0.23	0.30
Engineer	0.05	0.12	0.25
Secondary teacher	0.10	0.59	0.59
Real estate sales	0.10	0.18	0.23
Fireman	0.49	0.27	0.65
Policeman	0.49	0.69	0.87
Electrician	0.49	0.33	0.50
Truck driver	0.72	1.59	1.48
Meat cutter	0.72	0.98	0.98

Source: Adapted from Gottfredson, 1986, pp. 400–401.

they entered college, only 34 percent of blacks as compared with 60 percent of whites ended up majoring in any science field. On the basis of measured aptitudes related to a science major, the study concluded that "equal developed ability among students interested in science predicts equal persistence, regardless of ethnic or racial affiliation."[27]

This question can be broadened to include examination of a wide spectrum of occupations for which there are different percentages of blacks and whites (and other subpopulations). Sociologist Linda Gottfredson[28] began with the observation that various occupations "recruit" their members from different segments of the normal distribution of IQ in the general population (see Figure 14.3). Then, from employment and test data gathered in 1970 and in 1980, she determined empirically the percentage of the white population and of the black population that fall in the "recruiting range" of IQ for each of nine occupations that vary widely in central tendency on the nationally normed IQ scale. The black/white ratio (i.e., B%/W%) within each IQ recruiting range was then compared with the ratio of blacks to whites (B%/W%) actually employed in each occupation, in 1970 and 1980. These ratios are shown in Table 14.1. Obviously, many other personal characteristics besides IQ, in addition to circumstances and opportunities, determine a person's occupation. However, this does not contradict the essential point conveyed by Table 14.1, which is that if recruitment standards were the same for blacks and whites with respect to the *g* demands in each occupation (as indicated by its IQ recruitment range) the B%/W% ratio in the recruitment range for a given occupation should be equal to the B%/W% ratio actually employed in that occupation. If there were racial discrimination against blacks, we should expect the recruitment ratio to be larger than the employment ratio. But in fact the opposite is true for many of the more *g*-demanding occupations, in which blacks are quite considerably overrepresented, especially in the 1980 data. For some of these occupations (and probably many others) it appears that blacks were recruited from a somewhat lower IQ range than whites. This is consistent with independent data showing that mean IQs are lower for blacks than for whites in the same occupational category. Gottfredson[28] concluded: "*If* black-white differences in *g* remain large and *if* jobs remain *g* loaded, then black-white parity in employment may be possible only by lower intelligence recruitment standards for blacks. Unless blacks possess compensatory non-*g* traits in greater measure than do whites for any particular job, then lower intelligence standards for blacks than for whites will also result in lower mean performance levels for blacks than for whites in those jobs" (p. 402).

Income. In the *g* nexus, earned income is closely related to education and occupational status. But even when education, occupation, and socioeconomic background are held constant, income is correlated with IQ. The correlation of income with IQ, which averages about .40, increases with age and stabilizes when people are middle-aged and have reached their highest career potential. Also, the IQ-income correlation itself increases at higher levels of education; the lower the level of education, the weaker is the relation of income to IQ. This is because the variation in IQ decreases going from low-status to high-status occupations; the lower bound of the IQ range in different occupations rises markedly in the upper half of the occupational scale, while the upper bound of the IQ range increases relatively little. Typical path analyses best fit a causal model leading from IQ independently to each of the three variables in the nexus (education, occupation, income), with paths also causally connecting the these variables (education → occupation → income). The causal direction of IQ has been established in studies in which the IQ was measured in childhood and parental SES is statistically controlled. Individuals' IQ, even when measured in childhood, is a considerably larger independent source of variance in educational attainment and occupational status than is parental SES.[29] Intergenerational mobility in SES is largely determined by IQ; for example, a son whose IQ is higher (or lower) than his father's IQ, on average, moves up (or down) the scale of occupational status and income, and siblings with quite different IQ, though reared together, often differ in occupational status and earned income as adults. In fact, full siblings who were reared together differ, on average, almost as much in occupational status as persons picked at random in the population.

Economists Brown and Reynolds[30] have formulated a mathematical model of the relationship between IQ and income. It states: $Y_{ij} = a_j + b_j(IQ_i - t_j) + e_{ij}$, where Y_{ij} is the income for the *i*th individual in the *j*th occupation; t_j is the threshold IQ for occupation *j*; b_j is a slope parameter > 0; IQ_i is the *i*th individual's IQ; and e_{ij} is a random effect (uncorrelated with IQ) with an expected value of 0 and a constant σ. The model theoretically makes a number of predictions that accord with empirical findings:

1. Mean IQ in higher occupations exceeds mean IQ in lower occupations.
2. Variation in IQ is greater in lower occupations.
3. Mean earnings are greater in higher occupations.
4. Implied by items 1 and 2: There is a negative correlation between mean IQ and IQ variance across occupations.
5. Variation in earning is greater in higher occupations.
6. In two subpopulations, A and B, where the mean IQ of A is less than the mean IQ of B and the groups have the same IQ variance, then, if the population ratio of A to B is R, the relative frequency of A will increasingly fall further below R at each higher level of the occupational hierarchy.
7. Assuming that all individuals with the same IQ earn equal incomes (on average), the average earnings of A will be less than those of B within all occupations.
8. If the mean IQ of subpopulation A is less than the mean IQ of subpopulation B, then within occupations A will have a smaller range and variance in both IQ and income.
9. Within a given occupation, the correlation between earned income and IQ will be lower for subpopulation A than for subpopulation B, and the slope of the regression of earnings on IQ will be lower for A than for B.

Brown and Reynolds show empirically how the model fits the above predictions and also helps to explain the occupational patterns of certain minority groups (Chinese Americans, Jews, and blacks) that have historically been victims of discrimination but, on average, attain different levels in the occupational hierarchy. As the IQ-based model of income differences predicts slightly less than half of the black-white earnings gap, however, there are obviously other factors that must account for the remaining income difference, such as disadvantages in non-*g* characteristics that are related to job performance, and perhaps racial discrimination in hiring and promotion.

The fact that the average black-white difference in *g* cannot explain entirely the black-white differences in various educational, occupational, economic, and social variables is clearly shown by the differences that remain after the black and white groups are statistically equated for IQ. This has been done with a national probability sample from the National Longitudinal Study of Youth[31] (see Table 14.2).

CRIME, DELINQUENCY, AND MORALITY IN THE *g* NEXUS

Chapter 9 (pp. 297–98) discussed the relationship between antisocial behavior and the predictive validity of *g*. However, it is only within the context of the whole *g* nexus that the causal role of *g* in these societal variables can be properly understood. This is especially so since some criminologists, sociologists, and psychologists have argued that individual and group differences in mental

Table 14.2
Percentages of Blacks and Whites (Statistically Matched for IQ) in Various Educational and Social Conditions

	Percentage	
Condition[1]	Blacks	Whites
High school graduation (103)	91	89
College graduation (114)	68	50
High-Level Occupation (117)	26	10
Living in poverty (100)	14	6
Unemployed for 1 month or more (100)	15	11
Married by age 30 (100)	58	79
Unwed mother with children (100)	51	10
Has ever been on welfare (100)	30	12
Mothers in poverty receiving welfare (100)	74	56
Having a low birth-weight baby <5.5 lbs (100)	6	3
Average annual wage (100)	$25,001	$25,546

[1]The number in parentheses is the IQ on which blacks and whites were statistically equated within
    each category.
Source: Herrnstein & Murray, 1994, Chapter 14.

abilities are important causal effects in delinquency and crime.[32] The argument that some part of the conspicuous racial differences in crime rates is related to the statistical differences between races in the measures of cognitive ability that are empirically correlated with antisocial behavior[33] is based on four established facts:

• There is a negative correlation ($-.3$ to $-.5$ in various studies, slightly more so for verbal than for nonverbal tests) between IQ and measures of delinquency and criminality, such as police and court records and self-reports of criminal activity. Delinquents and adult criminals typically average ten to twelve IQ points below law-abiding persons living in similar circumstances. Juvenile delinquents who become adult criminals have lower IQs than delinquents who do not become criminals. Recidivists have lower IQs than one-time offenders. In home environments or in neighborhoods that are conducive to delinquent or criminal behavior, an above-average IQ acts as a protective factor against the influences toward antisocial behavior.

• The above-mentioned correlation between crime and IQ is clearly nonlinear. That is, the rate of serious crimes against persons, such as robbery, assault, rape, and homicide, is very low and nearly constant across IQ levels above IQ 100, but below IQ 100 the rate rises steeply, and then declines rapidly below IQ 70. The peak crime rate occurs in the IQ range from 75 to 90, with the highest rate for violent crime in the IQ range from 80 to 90. The vast majority of both petty

crimes and violent crimes are committed by the segment of the population ranging from IQ 60 to 100. (So-called white-collar criminals and leaders of organized
crime generally have IQs above 100.) These findings apply to both males and
females, although the rate for most types of antisocial behavior is much lower
for females, especially violent crime.

Low IQ is obviously not the only, or even the main, causal factor in crime,
since the vast majority of people with IQs in the sixty to 100 range never become
delinquents or criminals. However, in addition to all other causes of criminal
behavior, whatever these may be, low IQ is clearly a statistical risk factor. But
no single factor has been identified as either a necessary or a sufficient cause
of antisocial behavior.

• IQ is a more important statistical predictor of delinquency and crime than
is socioeconomic status (SES) independent of IQ (when SES is controlled, the
inverse correlation between IQ and delinquency or crime is hardly diminished).
The correlation exists largely _within_-families. That is, delinquents average about
ten IQ points lower than their nondelinquent siblings reared by the same par-
ent(s) in the same social-class environment. So for individuals with IQs below
100, having a lower IQ than one's siblings or classmates increases the risk for
antisocial behavior.

• The above observations apply to the population in general and to different
racial and ethnic groups. Group differences in crime rates are attributed, at least
in part, to the proportion of each group with IQs in the range of maximum risk
for antisocial behavior. Groups with a mean IQ above 100, therefore, show lower
crime rates than groups with a mean IQ below 100. For example, the Asian
(Chinese and Japanese) population of the United States, which has an average
IQ of about 105 and only about 15 percent falling below IQ 90 (the region of
highest crime rates), has a crime rate lower than that of the white population
(which has a mean IQ of 100, with 25 percent falling below IQ 90). Jews,
another group with a mean IQ well above 100, also have a relatively low crime
rate.[34] The black population, with a mean IQ of 85 and approximately 60
percent falling below IQ 90, has higher rates of delinquency and criminality
than any other racial or ethnic group in the United States.[35] On the basis of such
statistics, sociologist Robert Gordon has coined the term _IQ-commensurability_
for his discovery that nearly all of the _mean_ black-white differences in delinquency and crime rates can be accounted for in terms of the mean black-white
difference in IQ.[36] Within any given segment of the IQ distribution, the black
and white crime rates are approximately the same, so much so as to leave little,
if any, variance needing to be explained by any other variables. In statistical
terms, Gordon's analysis means that one and the same regression line for the
regression of mean crime rates on mean IQ levels would fit the data on the IQ
× crime rate × race interaction.

Why should there be a negative correlation between _g_ (or IQ) and delinquent
or criminal behavior? Three explanations have been proposed. They are not
mutually exclusive and all three probably play a part.

One hypothesis is that low IQ causes difficulty in school and in failure to receive the rewards of scholastic success, which, in turn, lowers both self-esteem and the respect of one's peers; the resulting frustration leads to the individual's failure to internalize the rules by which approval is normally gained, instead resorting to aggressive and delinquent acts. Membership in a gang of youths who also have rejected the usual sources of self-esteem provides a means of gaining peer approval and self-esteem through antisocial behavior. The rewards that cognitive deficiencies make it difficult or impossible for these individuals to obtain by conventional and legitimate means are obtained in illegitimate and socially disapproved ways.

Another hypothesis posits a more direct causal relationship between low IQ and most forms of criminal behavior. It claims that low IQ individuals have a short *time horizon*; that is, they are more present-oriented and more lacking in *foresight* than most people. Persons with low IQ fail to adequately and realistically *imagine* the future consequences of their actions. Their immediate behavior is therefore less thoughtful and more impulsive. And they are also less apt to be guided by the *recall* of past experience because long-range foresight, imagination, and recall of past experience are all *g*-loaded cognitive functions.

A third hypothesis emphasizes the individual's level of moral reasoning. Research in child development has shown that moral reasoning, like most other forms of reasoning, develops as a function of mental age. A certain level of mental maturity is necessary for the kind of reasoning that underlies moral and ethical behavior. Hence there is a correlation between IQ and moral reasoning. In specific moral-dilemma situations, for example, high IQ children are able to give reasons for moral behavior that are on a level of sophistication comparable to that of less exceptional youths four or five years older than themselves.[37] In fact, understanding moral principles forms a series of steps going all the way from the simple rule of "don't do what you were told is wrong, otherwise you might be caught and punished" to a deep appreciation of Kant's Categorical Imperative. At least an average level of reasoning ability (*g*) is probably needed to apply this most universal principle of morality in every specific situation. Persons who are unable to understand the Kantian ethic or who do not comprehend what is wrong with their transgressions, or their seriousness, within the broad social context, are more prone to offensive or immoral behavior. In his research on the personal correlates of *g*, Raymond Cattell concluded, "There is a moderate tendency . . . for the person gifted with higher general ability, to acquire a more integrated character, somewhat more emotional stability, and a more conscientious outlook. He tends to become 'morally intelligent' as well as 'abstractly intelligent.' "[38]

THE LIMITATIONS OF *g*

As this book is about the *g* factor, more has been said about *g* than about any other aspects of human variation. This fact, however, should not leave readers with the impression that g is the all-important, or even the most important, variable in life. To be sure, it is one of the psychobiological variables having many important personal and societal correlates. But its expression in any person's life and in the character of a society depends on other factors, equally important, that are independent of g per se. Indeed, it is the *interaction* between g and these other factors that accounts for much, probably most, of the enormous variance in the visible aspects of what most people regard as worldly success. Success in life, of course, is not at all unidimensional. It has many dimensions, forms, and facets, and g plays an important part in only some of them.

The distinctness of g from many other valued personal characteristics was clearly recognized within ten years after Spearman discovered it. In 1915, one of Spearman's doctoral students, E. Webb, published a factor analysis of a matrix of correlations including a number of highly g-loaded tests and a number of ratings of character, or personality.[39a] The particular personality traits chosen for study and obtained from ratings by students' teachers and associates were actually selected because they were expected to be related to g, and hence to show significant loadings on the g factor. This expectation, however, was completely contradicted by Webb's analysis, which yielded two wholly distinct factors—g and a general "character" factor, which Webb labeled w and characterized as "will" and "persistence of motives." The types of items most highly loaded on the w factor were described as: perseverance, as opposed to willful changeability; perseverance in the face of obstacles; kindness on principle; trustworthiness; and conscientiousness. It seemed puzzling that this cluster of traits would emerge independent of g. Teachers' and other people's subjective impressions of any given person's level of intelligence create a "halo effect" which biases the observers' ratings of that person's personality traits. Despite this bias of the personality ratings by halo effects, Webb's factor analysis, because it included objective tests of g, gave a clean-cut separation of the two domains. What Webb's study and subsequent studies seemed to indicate was that g, even as fallibly measured by psychometric tests, is an entirely cognitive variable.

Later studies of the relationship between personality factors and g have fully substantiated this conclusion.[39b] The most thorough and systematic research I have found in this vein is that by Philip Ackerman and his associates.[40] They have correlated the so-called "Big Five" personality factors (Neuroticism, Extraversion, Openness, Agreeableness, Conscientiousness), which account for most of the variance measured by many different personality inventories, with measures of fluid and crystallized ability, or Gf and Gc. (Recall from Chapter 5 [pp. 122–25] that when a large number of diverse tests are factor analyzed, the second-order factor Gf and the third-order g are virtually identical.)

The Goff and Ackerman study[40] found that the correlations between thirteen personality scales and Gf (or g) were nonsignificant ($p > .05$) and close to zero (r ranging from $-.167$ to $+.131$, with the average $r = -.034$, the average absolute $|r| = .071$). Crystallized abilities, or the Gc factor, showed three significant ($p < .05$) but small correlations (r ranging from $-.138$ to $+.238$ with the average $r = +.087$, $|r| = .109$). The pattern of the thirteen Gf correlations is quite different from that of the thirteen Gc correlations, as these two column vectors of correlations are correlated with each other $-.263$.

The difference between Gf and Gc in relation to personality variables, however, is consistent with a key hypothesis advanced by Ackerman, which holds that "when considering the development and expression of intellect in adulthood, no theory can be comprehensive if it does not portray how personality, interests, and ability interact to determine the level of knowledge that individuals develop throughout the adult lifespan."[41] Ackerman makes an important distinction between the individual's level of *maximal performance* on highly g-loaded tests and that individual's level of *typical performance* in everyday life, or what Ackerman labels as *Typical Intellectual Engagement* (or *TIE*). Most people perform at near their maximum level while taking a cognitive test. However, even among persons who show exactly the same level of g, there is great variation in TIE, which is assessed with a fifty-nine-item self-report questionnaire. The TIE inventory assesses the degree to which the individual typically engages in g-demanding activities, vocationally and especially avocationally, and has what would ordinarily be regarded as intellectual interests (reading, learning, thinking, a wide range of interests, particularly in literature, science, and mentally challenging activities, such as chess, being absorbed by the subjects of one's interests and delving into them in depth).

TIE is much more a personality factor than an ability factor. It does not correlate at all with Gf (or a third-order factor g), but has significant but small correlations ($r = +.3$ to $+.4$) with verbal IQ and Gc. (Tests for IQ and Gc involve specific knowledge content and hence reflect intellectual achievement as well as the information-processing capacity that is measured more purely by Gf.) For a given level of g, a higher level of TIE in adulthood leads to somewhat higher levels of real-world intellectual achievement. But TIE itself clearly belongs in the personality domain, as shown by its correlations of about $+.60$ with two of the "Big Five" personality factors ("Openness" and "Conscientiousness"), as well as with another personality factor, "self-directed activity," which reflects energy level, absorption, and lack of distractibility. Ackerman and Heggestad summarize as follows, "[A]bilities, interests, and personality develop in tandem, such that ability level and personality disposition determine the probability of success in a particular task domain, and interests determine the motivation for attempting the task. Thus, subsequent to successful attempts at task performance, interest in the task domain may increase. Conversely, unsuccessful attempts at task performance may result in a decrement in interest for that domain."[42]

This is all reminiscent of R. B. Cattell's *investment theory*,[43] which is essentially a theory of the experientially acquired components of mental abilities, particularly crystallized abilities (Gc) and other non-g second-order factors. Different types and levels of achievement result from the different ways that persons "invest" their *g* resources. These, in turn, are largely determined by interests and personality factors, which themselves have both genetic and environmental variance components.

An individual's investment of *g* is never spread equally or randomly over every type of knowledge or skills offered by the environment. Rather, it is highly selective, depending on interests and personality and chance events. These non-cognitive factors are themselves hardly, if at all, correlated with *g*, yet they are strong determinants of achievement, provided the individual's level of *g* exceeds the threshold required for initially acquiring the basic knowledge or skills in a particular field of achievement. A particular interest tends to focus one's *g* resources. But I would hypothesize that there is also what might be termed the "spread of *g*" effect in knowledge acquisition (analogous to E. L. Thorndike's "spread of effect"), which would account for the fact that high-*g* persons show a lot of *incidental* learning; that is, they soak up bits of information from the environment even on subjects in which they have little or no interest. (Hence the high *g* loading of tests of "general information," which sample a wide variety of factual information.) More of their experience of the world "sticks" in their incidental knowledge repertoire, even though much of this experience is adventitious and never really aroused the person's interest or focus of attention.

What are the chief personality traits which, interacting with *g*, relate to individual differences in achievement and vocational success? The most universal personality trait in this respect is *conscientiousness*, that is, being responsible, dependable, caring, organized, and persistent. It applies to every kind of job success from professional and managerial to semiskilled work. It is commonly thought that persons who are high in conscientiousness are not apt to be successful in the creative arts. But this is a false perception based on observation of the often highly egocentric, unconventional, nonconformist, or eccentric lifestyle of certain famous composers, artists, and writers. The one thing that the biographies of such individuals consistently show, however, is that, without exception, they have been exceedingly conscientious in the work for which they are famous. While their personal lives may often seem chaotic, their work habits and their work products are not.

Besides a reasonably high level of *g*, those who are successful in the realm of intellectual achievement also have high levels on two highly correlated personality factors, TIE (typical intellectual engagement) and "openness to experience."

The sine qua non of truly exceptional achievement, or greatness, in *any* field is an extraordinary level of ambition and zeal in one's endeavors. It is the opposite of a lackadaisical attitude toward one's work. Zeal is probably what makes possible the enormous amount of diligent practice in one's pursuit without which a world-class level of performance is simply not possible. The extraordinary level of virtuoso skill seen in great musicians, Olympic athletes, world-class mathematicians, chess champions, and top-level surgeons, for example, owes at least as much to their many years of disciplined study and practice as to their inborn talent. Their talent, in fact, might actually consist in large part of their unusual drive and capacity for assiduous persistence in developing their specialized skills over many years.[44a] Ten years seems to be about the minimum amount of "practice time" needed for attaining a high level of expertise in one's vocation, even for famous geniuses.[44b]

Ambition seems to consist of a high level of goal-directed drive, persisting in the face of difficulties and obstacles. It is possessed to an extraordinary degree by the world's greatest achievers. The personal sources of the immense ambition that overrides all obstacles are scarcely understood and, as yet, have not been very much studied by psychologists. Dean Simonton, the leading contemporary researcher on the origins of high-level achievement, has remarked that the source of the exceptional level of drive and ambition evinced by the most illustrious achievers in history is still one of the great mysteries of psychology.[45] Psychologists often speak of "achievement motivation," but this simply names the phenomenon without explaining it. The topic is crying out for scientific research.

Other personality traits are less universal in their importance, although they are important for success in vocations in which effective interpersonal relations are especially important. Among the major personality factors that enhance the predictability of success in these types of work are *extraversion* (or sociability), *agreeableness*, being *decisive* and *action-oriented, stress tolerance, emotional stability*, and the trait known as *locus of control*, that is, the belief that one has control over what happens in life through one's own actions and efforts and is not a helpless victim of circumstances.

The term "emotional intelligence" has gained momentary popularity,[46] but it is something of a misnomer, as it is not a cognitive variable at all. It actually comprises several relatively uncorrelated personality traits, mainly management of feelings (low neuroticism), motivation, zeal, and persistence of optimism and effort in the face of obstacles and setbacks, empathy for others and the ability to read their unspoken feelings, self-awareness, and social skills. To note that these traits are independent of *g* and factor-analytically fall within the personality domain rather than the cognitive domain does not at all lessen their importance in life, and no one would argue that positive values on any of these facets of personality are not desirable and advantageous personal qualities.

What has been termed "social intelligence" is better termed *social competence*, or the tendency to act wisely in human relations. It is not a unitary dimension of personality, but is analyzable into a number of distinct factors (seven, in the most comprehensive study[47]), each of which is correlated with a number of well-known personality factors. The dimensions of social competence, however, surprisingly lie outside the domain of cognitive abilities and therefore are distinct from *g*. They show remarkably low correlations with psychometric abilities, both verbal and quantitative. In summarizing the results of their impressive studies of social competence, Schneider, Ackerman, and Kanfer[47] have noted that "it is time to lay to rest any residual notions that social competence is a monolithic entity, or that it is just general intelligence [*g*] applied to social situations'' (p. 479). Because most people live and work in a world in which much depends on interpersonal relations, the traits that constitute social competence are unquestionably of major personal and societal importance.

Robert Sternberg's view of *practical intelligence* as being something distinct from general intelligence, or *g*, is best understood, I believe, in terms of Cattell's investment theory. Practical intelligence refers to various kinds of knowledge and skills (''practical know-how'') that lie outside the sphere of abilities associated with scholastic or academic aptitude and achievement.[48] Rather, it consists of abilities required by problems and tasks faced in the everyday world. Hence practical intelligence consists of various types of achievement, in which individuals differ as a result of their unique experiences and the specialized investment of their *g* resources. Measures of practical intelligence are of such a nature that, if they were included in a factor analysis along with many diverse cognitive tests, most of their variance would consist of specificity, and the rest would be absorbed into the other well-established factors, and mostly into *g*.

Practical intelligence is not really a unitary factor, because it consists of skills or ''know-how'' or ''tricks of the trade'' specific to particular fields. The several tests of practical intelligence that I have seen are designed to tap specific items of knowledge relevant to these different fields and appear to have very little variance in common, other than *g*. As yet there has been no systematic factor analytic study of the relationship between practical intelligence and the established cognitive factors. Any specific and highly practiced skill in a particular occupation would be expected on theoretical grounds to have little communality with many other abilities and little correlation with *g*. The fact that many such narrow types of knowledge and skills have been found, and that they are scarcely correlated with each other or with already established cognitive factors, is to be expected. But there is no evidence that the various examples of practical intelligence intercorrelate highly enough to form a single group factor *independent* of *g*.[49]

Creativity and *genius* are unrelated to *g* except that a person's level of *g* acts as a threshold variable below which socially significant forms of creativity are highly improbable. This *g* threshold is probably at least one standard deviation above the mean level of *g* in the general population. Besides the traits that Galton thought necessary for ''eminence'' (viz., high ability, zeal, and persistence), *genius* implies outstanding creativity as well. Though such exceptional creativity is conspicuously lacking in the vast majority of people who have a high IQ, it is probably impossible to find any creative geniuses with low IQs. In other words, high ability is a necessary but not sufficient condition for the emergence of socially significant creativity. Genius itself should not be confused with merely high IQ, which is what we generally mean by the term ''gifted'' (which also applies to special talents, such as music and art).[50] True creativity involves more than just high ability. It is still uncertain what this is, but the most interesting theory that I have seen spelled out in detail is Eysenck's. He hypothesizes that the essential personality factor in creative genius is what he terms *trait psychoticism*, which has a genetic basis and is explainable in part in terms of brain chemistry and physiology. Explication of Eysenck's rather complex theory is beyond the scope of this chapter, but those with an interest in the subject will find Eysenck's comprehensive and fascinating book[51] well worth reading.

THE FUTURE OF g

Since its discovery by Spearman in 1904, the g factor has become firmly established as a major psychological construct. Further psychometric and factor analytic research is unlikely either to disconfirm the construct validity or predictive validity of g, or to add anything essentially new to our understanding.

How then will research on g proceed in the future? I see two directions, which I refer to as the *horizontal* and the *vertical*.

The *horizontal* direction refers to the further exploration and broadening of our knowledge of the g nexus, that is, the interactions of g with the many variables of importance in the modern world. Those nodes of the g nexus that have been well studied were reviewed earlier in this chapter, but investigations of other nodes are still at a rudimentary stage. For example, it seems likely that g could play a much more prominent role in economic theory than has yet been fully recognized. The population distribution of g would also seem an important factor in development strategies for countries that have only limited resources for public education as well as in allocating international aid.[52] Greater consideration could be given to the relevance of g to domestic policies on poverty, welfare, job training, and public education.[53] The demographic study of the population distribution of g resulting from differential trends in the birth and mortality rates within different segments of the normal curve has recently received renewed interest.[54]

The *vertical* direction refers to researching the factors that cause individual differences in g, particularly in terms of evolutionary biology, genetics, and brain anatomy, chemistry, and physiology. Unlike any of the primary, or first-order, psychometric factors revealed by factor analysis, g cannot be described in terms of the knowledge content of mental test items, or in terms of skills, or even in terms of theoretical cognitive processes. It is not fundamentally a psychological or behavioral variable, but a biological one. We know that g reflects certain properties of the human brain because of its correlations with individual differences in a number of brain variables, such as size, metabolic rate, nerve conduction velocity, and the latency and amplitude of evoked electrical potentials.

Although correlated with g, these physiological variables have not yet provided an integrated explanatory theory. The empirically established phenomena in this field greatly exceed our theoretical understanding. The known properties of neural processes, brain organization, and localization of functions all serve to narrow the possible hypotheses to those most likely to prove fruitful for integrating all of the disparate facts revealed by research on individual differences in information processing.

However, it is important to distinguish between the explanation of *intelligence* and the explanation of *g*. The explanation of intelligence calls for the description of the operating principles of the nervous system that make the functions of intelligence possible in all normal members of the same species. Individual differences in the efficiency, capacity, and power of the nervous system with respect to its information-processing functions are most strongly reflected by the *g* factor. But the explanation of *g* per se is an essentially different task from that of explaining intelligence, in that it calls for the discovery specifically of those features of the nervous system that are associated with individual differences in the *effectiveness* of the organism's neural information processes, particularly those feature(s) of the nervous system that cause positive covariance (or correlation) among virtually all cognitive abilities, which is what *g* is all about.[55] A theory that integrates these empirical discoveries would explain the biological basis of psychometric *g*.

As a possible heuristic for research on the neurophysiological basis of *g*, therefore, I propose consideration of the following working hypothesis: Individual differences in behavioral capacities do not result from intraspecies differences in the brain's structural operating mechanisms per se, but result entirely from other aspects of cerebral physiology that modify the sensitivity, efficiency, and effectiveness of the basic information processes that mediate the individual's responses to certain aspects of the environment. Thus research on the neurophysiology of mental ability has two aspects, the first dealing with the brain structures and neural processes that make possible intelligent behavior, the second dealing with the physical conditions that produce individual differences in intelligent behavior. The first aspect will probably be more difficult to resolve than the second, but investigation of the second need not depend upon a prior resolution of the first. Investigation can be directed at discovering the relationship between *g* and the neural conditions that affect a number of different elementary cognitive processes or behavioral capacities which, though served by different brain modules, are nevertheless correlated for individuals.

The highest priority in *g* research, therefore, is to discover how certain anatomical structures and physiological processes of the brain cause individual differences in *g*. Advanced technology of brain research has brought *g* research to the threshold presaged by Spearman himself over seventy years ago, that the final understanding of *g* "must needs come from the most profound and detailed direct study of the human brain in its purely physical and chemical aspects."[56]

NOTES

1. A special issue of the journal *Intelligence* (1997, 24, 1–320), edited by Linda Gottfredson, is largely devoted to theoretical, methodological, and empirical articles on the sociology of intelligence.

2. The methods briefly described here are more fully explicated in verbal and math-

ematical terms in books by Loehlin (1992) and Li (1975), which are suitable for those with the equivalent of at least a two-semester college course in statistical methods.

3. This methodology, the interpretation of which presents certain pitfalls to the statistically unsophisticated, is well explicated and empirically illustrated in articles by Lubinski & Humphreys (1996, 1997); also see Humphreys (1994). Lynn (1988) has analyzed correlations among IQ and many educational, social, and economic variables measured as the mean IQ of each of the regions of Britain, or France, or the districts of New York, or the boroughs of London. From his study of the nexus of IQ and many socioeconomic variables in each of these populations, Lynn states, "It should be apparent that social class as such can have no causal effects, and its correlations with educational attainment, infant mortality, and so on arise only because social class is itself a correlate and effect of a variety of psychological variables of which intelligence is at present the best understood and quantified" (p. 960).

4. Gordon, 1997.

5. Lubinski, 1996.

6. Gottfredson, 1997.

7. Partialing out a measure of parental socioeconomic status or other family background variables from the proband sample's correlation between IQ and some outcome variable (e.g., education, occupation, income, etc.) and then interpreting the partial correlation to mean that IQ accounts for very little, if any, of the outcome variance is known as the "sociologist's fallacy." It is a fallacy because the measured "family background" includes the direct and indirect effects of the parents' own level of *g*, which causally accounts for at least 50 percent of the variance in their offspring's IQ. Therefore, partialing out (or otherwise statistically controlling) "family background" spuriously robs the IQ of much of its predictive and causal-explanatory power.

8. Snow, 1995.

9. (a) Hunt, 1992; (b) Hunt, 1995.

10. (a) Humphreys, 1988. (b) Mincy et al. (1990) consider various technical definitions and characteristics of the underclass, including the conditions of selection I have referred to as producing a "critical mass" for social pathology concentrated in certain neighborhoods.

11. Maeroff, 1988.

12. Herrnstein & Murray (1994), in their Chapter 16, clearly and accurately spell out the relationship between low cognitive ability and many variables in the *g* nexus, including poverty, employment and unemployment, crime, welfare dependency, illegitimacy, low-birth-weight babies, deprived home environments, and developmental problems. Using data from the National Longitudinal Study of Youth (NLSY), they present simple graphs which show the relationship of each of these variables to IQ. Kaus (1992) provides statistics and describes in considerable detail many of the characteristics of the underclass culture as it exists at present in the large metropolitan areas of the United States.

13. Statistical summaries and multiple regression analyses of these NLSY and NELS data are reported in Grissmer et al., 1994.

14. These values of R are obtained from the difference between the two matrices above. The difference between two values of R, say, R_a and R_b, expressed on the same scale, is equal to $\sqrt{R_a^2 - R_b^2}$. (R is always without sign, as it is the square root of the variance accounted for, and any variance greater than zero is necessarily a positive value.) R (instead of R^2) was used in this example, because it represents degree of correlation

on the same scale as the simple _r_, in terms of which correlation and predictive validity are usually expressed.

15. Jensen, 1974c.

16. Brodnick & Ree, 1995. This study is instructive in showing how path analysis can be used to compare statistically the "goodness-of-fit" of the observed correlations for various alternative models of the hypothesized causal relationships among the variables in a complex nexus. Besides the observed variables, the path models in this study all involve three latent (unobserved) variables implicit in the data, namely, _g_, scholastic aptitude, and SES.

17. National Commission on Education, 1983; Thorndike, 1973.

18. Vogt, 1973.

19. Daneman (1984) provides an excellent exposition of the psychology of reading as information processing and its dependence upon the capacity and efficiency of working memory. Thorndike (1973–74) argues, on the basis of psychometric data, that reading comprehension is a form of reasoning and therefore reflects individual differences in the same fundamental source of individual differences, namely _g_, as do tests of IQ, whether they are verbal or nonverbal.

20. Carlson & Jensen, 1982.

21. Lerner (1983) provides an excellent essay on the relation of test scores (as opposed to merely amount of schooling) as a measure of what she refers to in economic terms as "human capital."

22. Cattell, 1971, pp. 477–483; 1983, pp. 161–164.

23. In examining many pages of "help wanted" advertisements in the newspapers of large cities and tabulating the types of job being advertised according to the mean IQ levels of employees in these jobs (as given in by the U.S. Employment Service), I find that virtually all of the listed openings are for jobs that call for above-average levels of developed ability.

24. Gottfredson, 1997. All of the data sources for the elements in Gottfredson's graph are described in her article.

25. _Science_, 1993, _262_, 1089–1134. (November 12 issue.)

26. Pool, 1990, p. 435.

27. Holden, 1995.

28. Gottfredson, 1986. (Also see Gottfredson & Sharf, 1988.) These articles appear in two special issues of the _Journal of Vocational Behavior_ (edited by Gottfredson and by Gottfredson & Sharf) that deal extensively with "The _g_ Factor in Employment" (1986) and "Fairness in Employment Testing" (1988), respectively.

29. Duncan, et al., 1972. The key literature on this topic is reviewed by Jencks (1979).

30. Brown & Reynolds, 1975.

31. Herrnstein & Murray, 1994, Chapter 14.

32. Wilson & Herrnstein (1985, Chapter 6) review most of the key references on this topic. Levin (1997, Chapter 9), a philosopher, treats the comprehension of moral principles in greater depth than any other source on this topic.

33. Gordon, 1975, 1980, 1987a, 1997.

34. Gottfredson & Hirschi (1990, pp. 149–150) report Asian and Jewish crime rates in the United States. Most of the studies of Jewish IQ are referenced in MacDonald (1994, pp. 188–199). The evidence leaves little question that the mean IQ of Jews is above the mean of the general U.S. population, though by how much is considerably less certain; MacDonald claims about seventeen IQ points, the difference being larger

on verbal than on nonverbal tests. But I have not found a proper meta-analysis of the available data that would permit a strong conclusion on this point.

35. Based on 1990 FBI statistics for the United States, the arrest rate for violent crimes is about six times higher for blacks than for whites (Reiss & Roth, 1993, pp. 71–72). Black and white crime rates and victimization rates are reported for various types of crime in Jaynes & Williams, 1989, Chapter 9. The black-white rate differences are largest for serious personal crimes such as robbery, assault, rape, and homicide; they are the smallest for impersonal crimes such as tax fraud, embezzlement, counterfeiting, and the like (also, Wilson & Herrnstein, 1985).

36. Gordon, 1980; Gordon (1997), besides showing evidence for *IQ-commensurability* with respect to racial differences in delinquency and crime, extended this analytic paradigm to other variables, including opinions and social attitudes, in which there are also marked racial differences.

37. Sanders et al., 1995.

38. Cattell, 1950, pp. 98–99.

39. (a) Webb, 1915. Also reported in considerable detail by Spearman, 1927, pp. 345–348. Eysenck (1953, see "*w*" in the index) described most of the subsequent research related to the *w* factor and also its distinctness from the *g* factor (pp. 42–46). (b) P. E. Vernon (1971), in factor analyses including tests of cognitive abilities and of scholastic subject-matter knowledge, found two major factors, *g* and educational achievement, the latter interpreted by Vernon as a product of *g*, interest, and industriousness.

40. Goff & Ackerman, 1992; Ackerman & Heggestand, 1997.

41. Ackerman, 1996, p. 237.

42. Ackerman & Heggestad, 1997, p. 239.

43. Cattell, 1971, Chapter 6.

44. (a) Ericsson & Charness, 1994; Ericsson & Lehmann, 1996; (b) Gardner, 1993.

45. Simonton (1994) has written a fascinating book on the psychology of world-class levels of achievement, which he labels "greatness."

46. Goleman, 1995.

47. Schneider, Ackerman, & Kanfer, 1996.

48. Sternberg & Wagner, 1986. (Jensen [1988b] provides a critical review of this book.) For an updated review of the literature on practical intelligence, see Wagner, 1994.

49. Willis & Schaie (1986), in their chapter in the book *Practical Intelligence* edited by Sternberg & Wagner (1986), report a study showing that measures of proficiency in a great many practical skills of everyday life are substantially correlated with psychometric *g*.

50. Jensen, 1996b.

51. Eysenck, 1995b.

52. Klitgaard (1985) deals with the issues involved in selecting those potentially ablest members of developing countries who can be most instrumental in the economic advancement of their society.

53. Herrnstein & Murray (1994) in their signal book *The Bell Curve* broach the topic of the public policy implications of *g* more fully than any other work to date, and their effort has elicited extraordinarily vehement pro and con reactions in the media and in academe. One should hope that the door will remain wide open for further research on the critically important issues raised by their work. A recent but more narrowly focused book, *Intelligence Policy* (Browne-Miller, 1995), deals mainly with the implicit assump-

tions about intelligence as they influence college admission policies; Gordon (1996) provides an insightful review of this book.

54. Lynn (1996) provides an extensive review of the genetic theory and the empirical data on historical changes in intelligence and conscientiousness in Western and non-Western societies, which, he argues, have been on a dysgenic trend in the twentieth century.

55. Jensen (1997b) further elaborates this theme.

56. Spearman, 1927, p. 403.

Appendix A

Spearman's "Law of Diminishing Returns"

Spearman (1927, pp. 217–21) compared the disattenuated correlation matrices (based on 12 diverse cognitive tests) of 78 "normal" children and 22 "defective" children. He found that the mean r of the matrix for the normal children was $+.466$; for the retarded children the mean r was $+.782$. Deary and Pagliari (1991) performed principal components analyses of Spearman's correlation matrix for the normal children and the correlation matrix for the defective children. The average loadings on the first principal component (PC1) of each matrix were $+.725$ and $+.899$, respectively. Yet the PC1 was clearly the same factor in both the normal and retarded groups, as indicated by a congruence coefficient of $+.988$. Spearman also noted in other data sets that tests' intercorrelations (and average g loadings) were larger for younger children than for older children. These findings suggested that the higher the level of g, the less is the amount of g variance in any particular mental test.

Spearman rather grandiosely likened this phenomenon to the "law of diminishing returns," as it applies in physics and in economics. That is, the higher a person's level of g, the less important it becomes in the variety of abilities the person possesses. High-g persons have more diversified abilities, with more of the total variance in their abilities existing in non-g factors (i.e., the various group factors and specificity). Others have explained this phenomenon in terms of what has become known as the *differentiation* theory, that higher g level (and the increase in mental abilities from childhood to early maturity) is accompanied by an increasing differentiation of general ability and the development of special abilities independent of g. (In the elderly, the reverse occurs for novel tests and tasks; there is dedifferentiation of abilities variance and a consequent increase in various tests' g loadings.) One might say that in the course of mental development g (or fluid ability, Gf) becomes increasingly invested in specialized skills, in which proficiency becomes partly automatized through practice. The automatized aspects of the special skills lose their g loading, and the non-g part of the skills variance forms first-order group factors and specificity. In this way, g is somewhat like money—the poor can only afford to spend their money on little besides the few necessities and have nothing left over to invest in other things, while the rich can afford to spend their money on a great variety of things and have many diversified investments. Like money, g isn't very important if one has enough of it.

In recent times, the British factor analyst A. E. Maxwell (1972b) rediscovered Spearman's "law of diminishing returns" by comparing the correlation matrices of the subtests of the Wechsler Preschool and Primary School Intelligence (WPPSI) test given to children who were good and poor readers, as assessed independently by tests of reading ability. (Reading ability, particularly reading comprehension, as contrasted with "word reading," is itself highly g loaded.) Good readers showed lower correlations (hence lower g loadings) among the WPPSI subtests than did poor readers. This would seem to substantiate Spearman's "law."

The first really systematic and methodologically convincing study of this phenomenon was conducted by Detterman and Daniel (1989). They demonstrated the effect both with a variety of computer-administered cognitive tasks and with the subtests of Wechsler Adult Intelligence Scale-Revised (WAIS-R) and the Wechsler Intelligence Scale for Children-Revised (WISC-R). The latter demonstration, based on very large subject samples on the Wechsler tests, was particularly impressive. The entire subject sample (on the WISC-R and on the WAIS-R) was divided into five levels of IQ (<78, 78–92, 83–107, 108–122, >122), with the IQ equivalent based on only one subtest. In the first analysis the Vocabulary subtest was the basis of classification; in the second analysis, Information. Within each of the five ability levels, the average intercorrelation among all the Wechsler subtests (except Vocabulary or Information) was obtained. These average intercorrelations among subtests decreased monotonically from about $+.7$ for the IQ < 78 group to about $+.35$ for the IQ > 122 group.

The result was interpreted in terms of Detterman's (1987) systems theory of mental retardation. This theory posits that mental ability involves a number of distinct systems or processes, and that some processes are more "central" than others, in the sense that their functioning is crucial to a wider range of cognitive operations. A deficiency in a highly central process will therefore handicap a great many mental functions and result in low scores on every type of test. Variation in less central functions will affect only certain narrow abilities (group factors and specificity) but not most abilities. Persons with low IQs have less efficient central processes, hence overall low performance on most kinds of cognitive tasks. Persons with higher IQs have more efficient central processes but may vary considerably in the less central, narrower processes. Consequently, there should be higher correlations (and more g variance) among various tests in a low-IQ group and lower correlations (less g variance) in a high-IQ group. A corollary of this theory is that the "profile" or pattern of subtest scores should be flatter (i.e., lower standard deviation among the individual's subtest scores) for low-IQ persons than for high-IQ persons. Detterman and Daniel applied corrections in each IQ group for restriction of range, so that the observed differences in average correlations could not be attributed to differences in the variance of test scores within each group. This is a problematic and less than ideal practice, because the correction of correlations for restriction of range assumes that the "true" correlation between the variables in question is the same throughout the full range of the latent trait (i.e., g), which is the very assumption that is contradicted by Spearman's "law of diminishing returns." The only really adequate means for dealing with the restriction-of-range problem is to select the high- and low-g groups so that they have the same *SD* on the selection test. The demonstrations of Spearman's "law" in other studies (e.g., Lynn, 1992; Lynn & Cooper, 1993, 1994) that did not take test reliabilities or restriction of range into account, therefore, provide only weak evidence. Differences in average correlations between the higher- and lower-IQ groups in these studies could simply be an artifact of the smaller variance of IQ in the higher groups. In fact, the test variances in the lower-IQ groups in these studies are larger, but whether the test intercorrelations would still be significantly larger in the lower- than in the higher-IQ group if the groups were equated for variance remains unknown. As these two phenomena (i.e., different test variances and different test intercorrelations in high and low IQ groups) are conceptually distinct effects, they should not be confounded in studies of Spearman's "law of diminishing returns."

A large-scale and methodologically sophisticated test of Spearman's "law" was carried out (Deary et al., 1996) both on high- and low-ability groups (mean difference = 1σ) and for younger and older groups (mean ages ~ 170 vs. 201 months) within each ability level. The test score distributions of the four comparison groups were equated for variance but, of course, not for mean ability level. (This article also provides a comprehensive review of the history of the theory and research on Spearman's "law" and the differentiation hypothesis.) The g factor (first principal component) of the subtests of the Differential Aptitude Test (DAT) was extracted for each group. As predicted by Spearman's "law," g accounted for more of the total variance in the low-ability groups at both age levels, especially when the high- and low-ability groups were selected on the basis of the most highly g-loaded tests. Selection of high- and low-ability groups on the basis of tests with relatively small g loadings resulted in very little difference between the groups in the proportions of total variance accounted for by the g extracted from the Differential Aptitude Test (DAT) battery. (*Note*: Selection of subjects for the high- and low-ability groups was never based on a test contained in the DAT battery from which the g was extracted to examine Spearman's "law.") There was little difference in the total g variance for either high- or low-ability groups as a function of age. This could be because the age groups differed by only about two and a half years. Other studies (reviewed by Deary et al., 1997) have shown the differentiation effect in groups differing more widely in age.

Heritability as a Function of IQ Level. Because Detterman found higher test intercorrelations (hence larger g loadings) for low- than for high-IQ groups, he went on to ask whether tests also have higher heritability (h^2) in low- than in high-IQ groups. A genetic analysis based on MZ and DZ twins seemed to show that something akin to Spearman's "law" applied to h^2 as well as to g loadings (Detterman, Thompson & Plomin, 1990). On the other hand, another study conducted in Norway, using very large samples of MZ and DZ twins (Ns of 862 and 1,325, respectively), found not the slightest evidence that h^2 differs across ability levels (Sundet et al., 1994). However, Bailey and Revelle (1991), using a simpler but arguably better methodology than that used by Detterman et al. (1990), applied to a number of very large twin samples (twenty-one samples comprising about 3,000 twin pairs) found an opposite result: an increase in h^2 at higher levels of IQ. Bailey and Revelle concluded, "[T]he bulk of the available evidence suggests that the specific finding of Detterman *et al.* does not reflect a general phenomenon" (p. 403). Bailey and Revelle tried but were unable to come up with any promising hypothesis for the increase in h^2 at higher levels of IQ. So we have three large and apparently methodologically sound studies that have shown entirely different results—positive, negative, and zero. The reality of the phenomenon as it applies to the heritability of IQ, therefore, remains in question.

I have found (Jensen, 1997a), in some fine-grained twin analyses, that favorable and unfavorable nongenetic influences on mental development are not symmetrically distributed, and that lower IQs have a larger component of nongenetic variance due to largely biological environmental prenatal and early childhood influences (e.g., poor nutrition, disease, head trauma, mother-fetus incompatibility in blood antigens, prematurity, and low birth weight). This finding would seem to favor the hypothesis that h^2 decreases at lower levels of IQ.

Appendix B

Method of Correlated Vectors

The method of correlated vectors is one way of testing whether the g factor extracted from a battery of diverse tests is related to some variable, X, which is external to the battery of tests. If the degree to which each of the various tests is loaded on g significantly predicts the relative magnitudes of the various tests' correlations with the external variable X, it is concluded that variable X is related to g (independently of whether or not it is related to other factors or test specificity). The significance level is determined from the rank-order correlation between the elements in the column vector of the various tests' g loadings and the elements in the column vector of the tests' correlations with variable X.

As the size of a test's factor loading (in this case its g loading) and the size of the test's correlation with an external variable (X) are both affected by the test's reliability, and as various tests may differ in reliability, it is necessary to rule out the possibility that the correlation between the vector of the tests' g loadings and the vector of the tests' correlations with X is not attributable to the tests' differing reliability coefficients. This is accomplished by correcting the g loadings and the correlations for attenuation, or by obtaining the correlation of the column vector of the tests' reliability coefficients with both the vector of g loadings and the vector of correlations, and using the three correlations between the three vectors to calculate the partial correlation between the g vector and the X vector (with the vector of reliability coefficients partialed out). If the partial correlation is large enough to be statistically significant, the tests' varying reliability coefficients are not responsible for the correlation between the g and X vectors. (Note: The degrees of freedom for testing the significance of the correlation [or the partial correlation] is based, not on the number of subjects in the study, but on the number of tests [i.e., number of elements in the vector of g loadings]).

An actual example of the use of correlated vectors is shown in connection with the information in Table B.1, from a study (Schafer, 1985) on the relation

Table B.1

Example of the Method of Correlated Vectors Based on the Evoked Potential Habituation Index (EPHI) and the *g* Factor Loadings of the Wechsler Adult Intelligence Scale (WAIS)

WAIS Subtest	*g* Factor Loadings				Subtest X EPHI Correlation			
	Uncorrected		Corrected		Uncorrected		Corrected	
	g	Rank	*g'*	Rank'	*r*	Rank	*r'*	Rank'
Information	.71	10	.74	10	.41	8	.43	7
Comprehension	.49	5	.55	5	.39	7	.44	8
Arithmetic	.57	7	.64	7.5	.32	5	.37	4
Similarities	.59	9	.64	7.5	.50	11	.53	10
Digit Span	.32	2	.38	2	.03	1	.04	1
Vocabulary	.77	11	.80	11	.45	10	.46	9
Digit Symbol	.26	1	.27	1	.17	2	.18	2
Picture Completion	.46	3.5	.50	3	.21	3	.23	3
Block Design	.50	6	.54	4	.38	6	.41	6
Picture Arrangement	.58	8	.71	9	.44	9	.54	11
Object Assembly	.46	3.5	.57	6	.31	4	.38	5
Column Vectors	A	B	C	D	E	F	G	H

of the *g* factor (of the Wechsler Adult Intelligence Scale) to the habituation of the evoked potential, a measure of the brain's electrical activity in response to an external stimulus (an auditory "click" in this study).

What was referred to above as variable *X* is the evoked potential habituation index in this example. The subjects were fifty-two normal young adults with IQs ranging from ninety-eight to 142. The habituation index was correlated +.59 with Full Scale IQ; corrected for restriction of range of IQ in this sample, the correlation was +.73. The method of correlated vectors, illustrated in Table B.1 shows that it is principally the *g* factor that is related to the brain-evoked potential. When *g* was statistically removed from the WAIS, in fact, the remaining non-*g* variance showed virtually zero correlation with the evoked potential habituation index.

EXPLANATION OF THE COLUMN VECTORS

A. The *g* loadings (first principal factor) of the eleven WAIS subtests (without correction for attenuation).

B. The rank order of the uncorrected *g* loadings, ranked from the smallest (rank = 1) to the largest (rank = 11).

C. The *g* loadings after correction for attenuation (i.e., each subtest's *g* loading is divided by the square root of the subtest's reliability coefficient).

D. The rank order of the corrected (disattenuated) *g* loadings.

E. The Pearson correlation (*r*) of each WAIS subtest and the evoked potential habituation index (EPHI). (The EPHI is the difference between the average amplitude of the evoked potential obtained in the first block of twenty-five trials and the second block of twenty-five trials.)

F. The rank order of the correlations in Column **E**.

G. The Pearson correlations (Column **E**) corrected for attenuation of the subtest score (i.e., dividing each correlation in Column **E** by the square root of the subtest's reliability coefficient).

H. The rank order of the corrected (disattenuated) correlations in Column **G**.

CORRELATED VECTORS

The Pearson correlation (r_{AE}) between the column vector **A** (the subtests' uncorrected g loadings) and the column vector **E** (the subtests' correlations with the EPHI) is $r_{AE} = +.81$. The correlation between the column vectors **B** and **F** is the corresponding Spearman rank-order correlation (r_s), which here is $+.91$. With $n = 11$ variables in each of the correlated vectors, the rank-order correlation is significant at $p < .01$, which means that a correlation this large has less than 1 percent probability of occurring by mere chance if the true correlation in the population were 0; therefore, the obtained correlation is regarded as significant. This scatter diagram for this correlation is plotted in Figure 6.2 in Chapter 6 (p. 156).

The Pearson correlation (r_{CG}) between the column vector **C** (corrected g loadings) and column vector **G** (correlated correlations of subtests with the EPHI) is $r_{CG} = +.80$. The corresponding rank-order correlation $r_{DH} = +.77, p < .01$.

A test of whether the correlation between vectors **A** and **E** is a result of the vector of the subtests' differing reliability coefficients attenuating both the g loadings (in vector **A**) and the correlations (in vector **E**) is to calculate the partial correlation between vectors **A** and **E**, with the vector of subtest reliability coefficients (Vr_{xx}) partialed out. The partial correlation, in effect, holds constant the subtests' reliability coefficients, removing whatever effect they might have on the correlation between vectors **A** and **E**. (Statistics textbooks give the formula for calculating the partial correlation.) In the present example, the partial correlation between vectors **A** and **E**, removing the effect of Vr_{xx}, is $+.79$, or hardly different from the original correlation of $+.81$, which therefore clearly cannot be attributed to the differing reliability coefficients of the various subtests. (The original correlation is technically termed a *zero-order* correlation. If one variable is partialed out, the resulting coefficient is termed a first-order partial correlation. With two variables partialed out, it is a second-order partial correlation, and so on.)

Appendix C

Multivariate Analyses of a Nexus

The following multivariate analyses of a small nexus of five interrelated variables are intended only as a didactic example of different ways of looking at a nexus. They merely illustrate what the results of these analyses look like when applied to a real (but small) nexus. The example is not intended to make any particular argument. Detailed computational algorithms for the various types of analysis can be found in textbooks on multivariate statistical methods. The correlation matrix and computational procedure for the path analysis were taken from Li (1975, pp. 324–328).

The five variables in the nexus, listed in temporal order, are: *father's education* (FED), *father's occupation* (FOC), his *child's IQ* in childhood (CIQ), the *child's education* as total years of schooling (CED), and the *child's adult IQ* (CAIQ).

A. The correlations among these five variables, based on a large sample of white males, aged twenty-five to sixty-four, are shown in Table C.1.

B. A principal components PC analysis yields two meaningful components, labeled I and II (see Table C.2). The remaining three PCs have been dropped based on the criterion that their eigenvalues (or latent roots) are less than one.

C. Also shown are the multiple correlations (Rs) of each variable with every other variable in the matrix. They indicate the degree to which any given variable in the nexus can be predicted by all of the other variables in the nexus. The proportion of variance that any given variable has in common with all of the other variables is indicated by R^2. The fact that all of the loadings on PC I (i.e., the general factor in this matrix) are all fairly large indicates that this is a quite close-knit nexus; the main division among the variables is clear from the opposite signs for the father and child variables in PC II. The multiple R and the R^2 for Father's Education are the smallest in the whole set, showing that it is the least well predicted by all of the other variables. The Child's Education

Table C.1

Variable	FED	FOC	CIQ	CED	CAIQ
Father's Education	1	.509	.300	.382	.305
Father's Occupation		1	.300	.420	.314
Child's IQ			1	.550	.830
Child's Education				1	.630
Child's Adult IQ					1

(From Li, 1975.)

Table C.2

Variable	PC I	PC II	R	R²
Father's Education	.616	-.600	.547	.299
Father's Occupation	.633	-.589	.566	.320
Child's IQ	.827	.410	.832	.692
Child's Education	.808	.072	.680	.463
Child's Adult IQ	.856	.404	.856	.732
Eigenvalue	2.85	1.04		
Percent Variance	57	21		

is much better predicted because of the presence of Child IQ in the nexus. Subsets of the variables entered into multiple correlations help to highlight the more important relationships, but are not necessarily causal. The temporal order of the variables, however, may suggest the direction of causality; the Child's IQ, for example, is unlikely to be a cause of his Father's Education or Occupation.

   D. Table C.3 shows values of the multiple correlation R obtained from different sets of independent variables for predicting different dependent variables. The amount by which a given multiple R is increased by the addition of a another variable to the regression equation can be determined by subtracting the first R^2 from the second R^2 and taking the square root of the difference to express it on the scale of R. For example, the contribution of Child's IQ to the prediction of Child's Education, independent of the Father's Education + Occupation, is $R = \sqrt{[(.623)^2 - (.463)^2]} = .417$.

Table C.3

Independent Variables	Dependent Variable	R
Father's Education + " Occupation	Child's IQ	.345
Father's Education + " Occupation	Child's Adult IQ	.356
Father's Education + " Occupation	Child's Education	.463
Father's Education + " Occupation + Child's IQ	Child's Education	.623
Father's Education + " Occupation + Child's Education	Child's Adult IQ	.634
All 4 other variables	Child's Adult IQ	.732

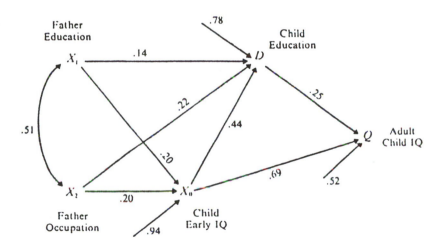

Figure C.1. From Li, 1975. Used with permission of Boxwood Press.

E. A path analysis based on the correlation matrix in Table C.1 is shown in Figure C.1. It is taken from Li (1975, p. 325), which fully explains the method of deriving the path coefficients (arrows) from the correlation matrix. The path analysis is a model of the causal relationships between the variables. A path coefficient (which reflects the causal effect of one variable on another) is indicated by an arrow. A simple correlation (which imputes no causality) is indicated by a curved line with arrow tips at each end. Note that the locations of the variables are shown according to their temporal or chronological order, going from left to right. The arrows that appear to come out of nowhere are causal paths originating from variables that were not included in the nexus. The variable (or variables) that might account for them are open to speculation. Note that the child's early IQ is largely determined (path coefficient = .94) by causes that lie outside this set of only five variables. (Also note that the main determinants [.78] of the child's education are not included among the variables in this nexus. But among the variables within the nexus, the child's IQ is the main cause of the child's education.) However, some of the causal factors in this path may be investigated by some larger nexus, such as one that includes children adopted at birth and then reared by adoptive parents whose IQ, education, and occupation are included in the analysis, along with the IQ, education, and occupation of the biological parents of the adopted children. (This sort of study has been done, giving the results that were summarized in Chapter 7.) There are important caveats in the interpretation of causality from any path analysis. Path analysis is best considered as but one investigative tool among many others, which must essentially be worked in combination with one another to discover the causal relationships among the variables of interest.

References

Ackerman, P. L. (1996). A theory of adult intellectual development: Process, personality, interests, and knowledge. *Intelligence, 22,* 227–257.

Ackerman, P. L. & Heggestad, E. D. (1997). Intelligence, personality, and interests: Evidence for overlapping traits. *Psychological Bulletin, 121,* 218–245.

Adams, M. S. & Neel, J. V. (1967). Children of incest. *Pediatrics, 40,* 55–62.

Afzal, M. (1988). Consequences of consanguinity on cognitive behavior. *Behavior Genetics, 18,* 583–594.

Afzal, M. & Sinha, S. P. (1984). Consanguinity effect on intelligence quotient of Bihari Muslim children. In G. K. Manna & U. Sinha (Eds.), *Perspectives in Cytology and Genetics, 4,* 114–117.

Agrawal, N., Sinha, S. N. & Jensen, A. R. (1984). Effects of inbreeding on Raven Matrices. *Behavior Genetics, 14,* 579–585.

Ahern, S. & Beatty, J. (1979). Pupillary responses during information processing vary with Scholastic Aptitude Test scores. *Science, 205,* 1289–1292.

Alderton, D. L. & Larson, G. E. (1994). Cross-task consistency in strategy use and the relationship with intelligence. *Intelligence, 18,* 47–76.

Alliger, G. M. (1988). Do zero correlations really exist among measures of different intellectual abilities? *Educational and Psychological Measurement, 48,* 275–280.

Anderson, B. (1993). Evidence from the rat for a general factor that underlies cognitive performance and that relates to brain size: Intelligence? *Neuroscience Letters, 153,* 98–102.

Anderson, B. (1994). Speed of neuron conduction is not the basis of the IQ-RT correlation: Results from a simple neural model. *Intelligence, 19,* 317–324.

Andreasen, N. C., Flaum, M., Swayze II, V., O'Leary, D. S., Alliger, R., Cohen, G., Ehrhardt, J. & Youh, W. T. C. (1993). Intelligence and brain structure in normal individuals. *American Journal of Psychiatry, 150,* 130–134.

Angoff, W. H. (1984). *Scales, norms, and equivalent scores.* Princeton, NJ: Educational Testing Service. (Reprint of chapter in R. L. Thorndike [Ed.], *Educational measurement* [2nd ed.]). Washington, DC: American Council on Education, 1971.

Ankney, C. D. (1992). Sex differences in relative brain size: The mismeasure of woman, too? *Intelligence, 16,* 329–336.

Austin, G. R. & Garber, H. (Eds.) (1982). *The rise and fall of national test scores.* New York: Academic Press.

Badaruddoza & Afzal, M. (1993). Inbreeding depression and intelligence quotient among North Indian children. *Behavior Genetics, 23,* 343–347.

Bailey, J. M. & Revelle, W. (1991). Increased heritability for lower IQ levels? *Behavior Genetics, 21,* 397–404.

Baker, J. R. (1974) *Race.* New York: Oxford University Press.

Baker, L. A., Vernon, P. A. & Ho, H-Z. (1991). The genetic correlation between intelligence and speed of information processing. *Behavior Genetics, 21,* 351–367.

Barrett, P. T., Daum, I. & Eysenck, H. J. (1990). Sensory nerve conduction and intelligence: A methodological study. *Journal of Psychophysiology, 4,* 1–13.

Barrett, P. T. & Eysenck, H. J. (1994). The relationship between evoked potential component amplitude, latency, contour length, variability, zero-crossings, and psychometric intelligence. *Personality and Individual Differences, 16,* 3–32.

Bartley, A. J., Jones, W. D. & Weinberger, D. R. (1997). Genetic variability of human brain size and cortical gyral patterns. *Brain, 120,* 257–269.

Bashi, J. (1977). Effects of inbreeding on cognitive performance. *Nature, 266,* 440–442.

Baumeister, A. A. & Bacharach, V. R. (1996). A critical analysis of the Infant Health and Development Program. *Intelligence, 23,* 79–104.

Bayroff, A. G. (1963). *Successive AFQT forms—Comparisons and evaluations.* Technical Research Note 132. Washington, DC: U.S. Army Personnel Research Office.

Beals, K. L., Smith, C. & Dodd, S. M. (1984). Brain size, cranial morphology, climate, and time machines. *Current Anthropology, 25,* 301–318. (Comments and Reply by Beals et al., pp. 318–330.)

Beer, J., Markely, R. P. & Camp, C. J. (1989). Age and living conditions as related to perceptions of ambiguous figures. *Psychological Reports, 64,* 1027–1033.

Bellugi, U., Wang, P. P. & Jernigan, T. L. (1994). Williams syndrome: An unusual neurophysiological profile. In S. H. Broman & J. Grafman (Eds.), *Atypical cognitive deficits in developmental disorders: Implications for brain function* (pp. 23–56). Hillsdale, NJ: Erlbaum.

Benbow, C. P. (1988). Sex differences in mathematical reasoning ability in intellectually talented preadolescents: The nature, effects, and possible causes. *Behavioral and Brain Sciences, 11,* 169–183; Peer Commentary, pp. 183–232.

Benbow, C. P. (1992). Academic achievement in mathematics and science of students between ages 13 and 23: Are there differences among students in the top one percent of mathematical ability? *Journal of Educational Psychology, 84,* 51–61.

Bender, B. G., Linden, M. G. & Robinson, A. (1994). Neurocognitive and psychosocial phenotypes associated with Turner syndrome. In S. H. Broman & J. Grafman (Eds.), *Atypical cognitive deficits in developmental disorders: Implications for brain function* (pp. 197–216). Hillsdale, NJ: Erlbaum.

Benton, D. (1995). Do low cholesterol levels slow mental processing? *Psychosomatic Medicine, 57,* 50–53.

Benton, D. (1996). Dietary fat and cognitive functioning. In M. Hillbrand & R. T. Spitz (Eds.) *Lipids, health and behavior* (pp. 227–243). Washington, DC: American Psychological Association.

Blake, J. (1966). Ideal family size among white Americans: A quarter of a century's evidence. *Demography, 3*, No. 1.

Blinkhorn, S. F. (1995). Burt and the early history of factor analysis. In N. J. Mackintosh (Ed.), *Cyril Burt: Fraud or framed?* (pp. 13–44). Oxford: Oxford University Press.

Block, J. B. (1968). Hereditary components in the performance of twins on the WAIS. In S. G. Vandenberg (Ed.), *Progress in human behavior genetics* (pp. 221–228). Baltimore, MD: The Johns Hopkins University Press.

Blomquist, K. B. & Danner, F. (1987). Effects of physical conditioning on information-processing efficiency. *Perceptual and Motor Skills, 65*, 175–186.

Bock, R. D. & Kolakowski, D. (1973). Further evidence of sex-linked major gene influence on human spatial visualizing ability. *American Journal of Human Genetics, 25*, 1–14.

Bock, R. D. & Moore, E. G. J. (1986). *Advantage and disadvantage: A profile of American youth.* Hillsdale, NJ: Erlbaum.

Böök, J. A. (1957). Genetical investigation in a North Swedish population: The offspring of first-cousin marriages. *Annals of Human Genetics, 21*, 191–221.

Boring, E. G. (1950). *A history of experimental psychology* (2nd ed.). New York: Appleton-Century-Crofts.

Bouchard, T. J., Jr. (1987). The hereditarian research program: Triumphs and tribulations. In S. Modgil & C. Modgil (Eds.), *Arthur Jensen: Consensus and controversy* (pp. 55–70). New York: Falmer.

Bouchard, T. J., Jr. (1993). The genetic architecture of human intelligence. In P. A. Vernon (Ed.), *Biological approaches to the study of human intelligence* (pp. 33–85). Norwood, NJ: Ablex.

Bouchard, T. J., Jr., Lykken, D. T., McGue, M., Segal, N. L. & Tellegen, A. (1990). Sources of human psychological difference: The Minnesota study of twins reared apart. *Science, 250*, 223–228.

Bouchard, T. J., Jr., Lykken, D. T., Tellegen, A. & McGue, M. (1996). Genes, drives, environment, and experience: EPD theory—revised. In C. P. Benbow & D. Lubinski (Eds.), *Intellectual talent: Psychometric and social issues* (pp. 5–43). Baltimore: Johns Hopkins University Press.

Bouchard, T. J., Jr. & McGue, M. (1981). Familial studies of intelligence: A review. *Science, 212*, 1055–1059.

Bouchard, T. J., Jr. & Segal, N. L. (1985). Environment and IQ. In B. B. Wolman (Ed.), *Handbook of intelligence: Theories, measurements, and applications* (pp. 391–464). New York: Wiley.

Brand, C. (1987a). The importance of general intelligence. In S. Modgil & C. Modgil (Eds.), *Arthur Jensen: Consensus and controversy* (pp. 251–265). New York: Falmer.

Brand, C. (1987b). Interchange: Brand replies to Pellegrino. In S. Modgil & C. Modgil (Eds.), *Arthur Jensen: Consensus and controversy* (pp. 278–283). New York: Falmer.

Brand, C. (1987c). Bryter still and bryter? *Nature, 328*, 110.

Brand, C. R. & Deary, I. J. (1982). Intelligence and "inspection time." In H. J. Eysenck (Ed.), *A model for intelligence* (pp. 133–148). New York: Springer-Verlag.

Brand, C. R., Freshwater, S. & Dockrell, W. B. (1989). Has there been a "massive" rise in IQ levels in the West? Evidence from Scottish children. *Irish Journal of Psychology, 10,* 388–394.

Brodnick, R. J. & Ree, M. J. (1995). A structural model of academic performance, socioeconomic status, and Spearman's *g. Educational and Psychological Measurement, 55,* 583–594.

Brody, N. (1992). *Intelligence* (2nd ed.). San Diego, CA: Academic Press.

Broman, S. H., Nichols, P. L. & Kennedy, W. A. (1975). *Preschool IQ: Prenatal and early developmental correlates.* Hillsdale, NJ: Erlbaum.

Broman, S. H., Nichols, P. L., Shaughnessy, P. & Kennedy, W. (1987). *Retardation in young children.* Hillsdale, NJ: Erlbaum.

Brooks-Gunn, J., McCarton, C. M., Casey, P. H., McCormick, M. C., Bauer, C. R., Bernbaum, J. C., Tyson, J., Swanson, M., Bennett, F. C., Scott, D. T., Tonascia, J., & Meinhert, C. L. (1994). Early intervention in low birthweight premature infants. *Journal of the American Medical Association, 272,* 1257–1262.

Brown, A. L. & Campione, J. C. (1982). Modifying intelligence or modifying cognitive skills: More than a semantic quibble? In D. K. Detterman & R. J. Sternberg (Eds.), *How and how much can intelligence be increased,* pp. 215–230. Norwood, NJ: Ablex.

Brown, W. W. & Reynolds, M. O. (1975). A model of IQ, occupation, and earnings. *American Economic Review, 65,* 1002–1006.

Browne-Miller, A. (1995). *Intelligence policy: Its impact on college admissions and other social policies.* New York: Plenum Press.

Burt, C. (1909). Experimental tests of general intelligence. *British Journal of Psychology, 3,* 94–177.

Burt, C. (1911). Experimental tests of higher mental processes and their relation to general intelligence. *Journal of Experimental Pedagogy, 1,* 93–112.

Burt, C. (1941). *The factors of the mind.* New York: Macmillan.

Burt, C. (1949a). The two-factor theory. *British Journal of Psychology, Statistical Section, 2,* 151–178.

Burt, C. (1949b). The structure of the mind: A review of the results of factor analysis. *British Journal of Educational Psychology, 19,* 100–111, 176–199.

Burt, C. (1955). The evidence for the concept of intelligence. *British Journal of Educational Psychology, 25,* 159–177.

Burt, C. (1962). Francis Galton and his contributions to psychology. *British Journal of Statistical Psychology, 15,* 1–49.

Burt, C. (1966). The genetic determination of differences in intelligence: A study of monozygotic twins reared together and apart. *British Journal of Psychology, 57,* 137–153.

Burt, C. (1972). General ability and special aptitudes. In R. M. Dreger (Ed.), *Multivariate personality research: Contributions to the understanding of personality, in honor of Raymond B. Cattell* (pp. 411–450). Baton Rouge, LA: Claitor's Publishing Division.

Callaway, E. (1979). Individual psychological differences and evoked potential variability. *Progress in Clinical Psychophysiology, 6,* 243–257.

Camilli, G. & Shepard, L. A. (1994). *Methods for identifying biased test items.* Thousand Oaks, CA: Sage.

Campbell, F. A. & Ramey, C. T. (1990). The relationship between Piagetian cognitive development, mental test performance, and academic achievement in high-risk students with and without early educational experience. *Intelligence, 14*, 293–308.

Campbell, F. A. & Ramey, C. T. (1994). Effects of early intervention on intellectual and academic achievement: A follow-up study of children from low-income families. *Child Development, 65*, 684–698.

Campbell, F. A. & Ramey, C. T. (1995). Cognitive and school outcomes for high-risk African-American students at middle-adolescence: Positive effects of early intervention. *American Educational Research Journal, 32*, 743–772.

Caplan, N., Choy, M. H. & Whitmore, J. K. (11992). Indochinese refugee families and academic achievement. *Scientific American, 266*, 18–24.

Capron, C. & Duyme, M. (1989). Assessment of effects of socioeconomic status on IQ in a full cross-fostering design. *Nature, 340*, 552–553.

Capron, C. & Duyme, M. (1996). Effect of socioeconomic status of biological and adoptive parents on WISC-R subtest scores of their French adopted children. *Intelligence, 22*, 259–275.

Cardon, L. R., Fulker, D. W. & DeFries, J. C. (1992). Multivariate analysis of specific cognitive abilities in the Colorado Adoption Project at age 7. *Intelligence, 16*, 383–400.

Carlson, J. S. & Jensen, C. M. (1982). Reaction time, movement time, and intelligence: A replication and extension. *Intelligence, 6*, 265–274.

Carretta, T. R. (1997). Group differences on U.S. Air Force selection tests. *International Journal of Selection and Assessment, 5*, 115–127.

Carretta, T. R. & Ree, M. J. (1995a). Near identity of cognitive structures in sex and ethnic groups. *Personality and Individual Differences, 19*, 149–155.

Carretta, T. R. & Ree, M. J. (1995b). Air Force Officer Qualifying Test validity for predicting pilot training performance. *Journal of Business and Psychology, 9*, 379–388.

Carretta, T. R. & Ree, M. J. (1997). Negligible sex differences in the relation of cognitive and psychometor abilities. *Personality and Individual Differences, 22*, 165–172.

Carroll, J. B. (1976). Psychometric tests as cognitive tasks: A new ''Structure of Intellect.'' In L. B. Resnick (Ed.), *The nature of intelligence* (pp. 27–56). New York: Wiley.

Carroll, J. B. (1991a). Cognitive psychology's psychometric lawgiver. *Contemporary Psychology, 36*, 557–559.

Carroll, J. B. (1991b). No demonstration that *g* is not unitary, but there's more to the story: Comment on Kranzler & Jensen. *Intelligence 15*, 423–436.

Carroll, J. B. (1991c). Still no demonstration that *g* is not unitary: Further comment on Kranzler and Jensen. *Intelligence, 15*, 449–453.

Carroll, J. B. (1993a). *Human cognitive abilities: A survey of factor-analytic studies.* Cambridge, UK: Cambridge University Press.

Carroll, J. B. (1993b). The unitary *g* problem once more: On Kranzler and Jensen. *Intelligence, 17*, 15–16.

Carter, C. O. (1967). Risk to offspring of incest. *Lancet, 1*, 436.

Cattell, R. B. (1950). *Personality.* New York: McGraw-Hill.

Cattell, R. B. (1971). *Abilities: Their structure, growth, and action.* Boston: Houghton Mifflin.

Cattell, R. B. (1978). *The scientific use of factor analysis in behavioral and life sciences.* New York: Plenum Press.

Cattell, R. B. (1983). Some changes in social life in a community with a falling intelligence quotient. In R. B. Cattell (Ed.), *Intelligence and national achievement*, pp. 156–176. Washington, DC: Cliveden Press.

Cavalli-Sforza, L. L., Menozzi, P. & Piazza, A. (1994). *The history and geography of human genes*. Princeton, NJ: Princeton University Press.

Cavanagh, J. P. (1972). Relation between the immediate memory span and the memory search rate. *Psychological Review, 79*, 525–530.

Ceci, S. J. (1991). How much does schooling influence intellectual development and its cognitive components? A reassessment of the evidence. *Developmental Psychology, 27*, 703–722.

Ceci, S. J. (1992). Schooling and intelligence. *Psychological Science Agenda, 5*, 7–9.

Cerella, J. (1985). Information processing rates in the elderly. *Psychological Bulletin, 98*, 67–83.

Chaiken, S. R. (1994). The inspection time not studied: Processing speed ability unrelated to psychometric intelligence. *Intelligence, 19*, 295–316.

Chaiken, S. R. & Young, R. K. (1993). Inspection time and intelligence: Attempts to eliminate the apparent movement strategy. *American Journal of Psychology, 106*, 191–210.

Chakraborty, R., Kamboh, M. I., Nwankwo, M. & Ferrell, R. E. (1992). Caucasian genes in American blacks: New data. *American Journal of Human Genetics, 50*, 145–155.

Christal, R. E. (1991). *Comparative validities of ASVAB and LAMP tests for logic gates learning* (AL-TP-1991–0031). Brooks, AFB, TX: Manpower and Personnel Division, Air Force Human Resources Laboratory.

Clark, E. A. & Hanisee, J. (1982). Intellectual and adaptive performance of Asian children in adoptive American settings. *Developmental Psychology, 18*, 595–599.

Clarke, A. M. & Clarke, A. D. B. (1976). *Early experience: Myth and evidence*. New York: Free Press.

Cohen, T., Block, N., Flum, Y, Dadar, M. & Goldschmidt, E. (1963). School attainments in an immigrant village. In D. Goldschmidt (Ed.), *The genetics of migrant and isolate populations*. Baltimore: Williams & Wilkins.

Cohn, S. J., Carlson, J. S. & Jensen, A. R. (1985). Speed of information processing in academically gifted youths. *Personality and Individual Differences, 6*, 621–629.

Cohn, S. J., Cohn, C. M. G. & Jensen, A. R. (1988). Myopia and intelligence: A pleiotropic relationship? *Human Genetics, 80*, 53–58.

Cole, N. S. & Moss, P. A. (1989). Bias in test use. In R. L. Linn (Ed.), *Educational measurement* (3rd ed., pp. 201–219). New York: Macmillan.

Comrey, A. L. & Lee, H. B. (1992). *A first course in factor analysis* (2nd ed.). Hillsdale, NJ: Erlbaum.

Conry, R. & Plant, W. T. (1965). WAIS and group test predictions of an academic success criterion: High school and college. *Educational and Psychological Measurement, 25*, 493–500.

Coren, S. (1994). *The intelligence of dogs: Canine consciousness and capabilities*. New York: Free Press.

Court, J. H. (1983). Sex differences in performance on Raven's Progressive Matrices: A review. *Alberta Journal of Educational Research, 29*, 54–74.

Coward, W. M. & Sackett, P. R. (1990). Linearity of ability-performance relationships: A reconfirmation. *Journal of Applied Psychology, 75*, 297–300.

Crinella, F. M. & Yu, J. (1995). Brain mechanisms in problem solving and intelligence: A replication and extension. *Intelligence, 21*, 225–246.

Cronbach, L. J. (1971). Test validation. In R. L. Thorndike (Ed.), *Educational measurement* (2nd ed., pp. 443–507). Washington, DC: American Council on Education.

Currie, J. & Thomas, D. (1995). Does Head Start make a difference? *American Economic Review, 85*, 341–364.

Daneman, M. (1984). Why some people are better readers than others: A process and storage account. In R. J. Sternberg (Ed.), *Advances in the psychology of human intelligence*, Vol. 2 (pp. 367–384). Hillsdale, NJ: Erlbaum.

Daniels, D., Plomin, R., McClearn, G. & Johnson, R. C. (1982). Fitness behaviors and anthropometric characters for offspring of first-cousin matings. *Behavior Genetics, 12*, 527–534.

Davis, K. (1947). Final note on a case of extreme isolation. *American Journal of Sociology, 52*, 432–457.

Dawis, R. V. (1994). Occupations. In R. J. Sternberg (Ed.), *Encyclopedia of human intelligence*, Vol. 2 (pp. 781–785). New York: Macmillan.

Deary, I. J. (1994a). Sensory discrimination and intelligence: Postmortem or resurrection? *American Journal of Psychology, 107*, 95–115.

Deary, I. J. (1994b). Intelligence and auditory discrimination: Separating processing speed and fidelity of stimulus representation. *Intelligence, 18*, 189–213.

Deary, I. J. & Caryl, P. G. (1993). Intelligence, EEG, and evoked potentials. In P. A. Vernon (Ed.), *Biological approaches to the study of human intelligence* (pp. 259–315). Norwood, NJ: Ablex.

Deary, I. J., Egan, V., Gibson, G. J., Austin, E., Brand, C. R. & Kellaghan, T. (1996). Intelligence and the differentiation hypothesis. *Intelligence, 23*, 105–132.

Deary, I. J. & Pagliari, C. (1991). The strength of *g* at different levels of ability: Have Detterman and Daniel resdiscovered Spearman's "Law of Diminishing Returns"? *Intelligence, 15*, 247–250.

Deary, I. J. & Stough, C. (1996). Intelligence and inspection time: Achievements, prospects, and problems. *American Psychologist, 51*, 599–608.

DeFries, J. C. (1972). Quantitative aspects of genetics and environment in the determination of behavior. In L. Ehrman, G. S. Omenn & E. Caspari (Eds.), *Genetics, environment, and behavior* (pp. 5–16). New York: Academic Press.

Dempster, F. N. & Brainerd, C. J. (Eds.) (1994). *New perspectives on interference and inhibition in cognition.* San Diego, CA: Academic Press.

Derr, R. L. (1989). Insights on the nature of intelligence from ordinary discourse. *Intelligence, 13*, 113–118.

Detterman, D. K. (1987). Theoretical notions of intelligence and mental retardation. *American Journal of Mental Deficiency. 92*, 2–11.

Detterman, D. K. (Ed.) (1992). *Current topics in human intelligence*, Vol. 2, *Is mind modular or unitary?* Norwood, NJ: Ablex.

Detterman, D. K. & Daniel M. H. (1989). Correlations of mental tests with each other and with cognitive variables are highest for low IQ groups. *Intelligence, 13*, 349–359.

Detterman, D. K. & Sternberg, R. J. (Eds.) (1982). *How and how much can intelligence be increased?* Norwood, NJ: Ablex.

Detterman, D. K., Thompson, L. A. & Plomin, R. (1990). Differences in heritability across groups differing in ability. *Behavior Genetics, 20*, 369–384.

Diascro, M. N. & Brody, N. (1994). Odd-Man-Out and intelligence. *Intelligence, 19*, 79–92.

Dolan, C. V. (1992). *Biometric decomposition of phenotypic means in human samples.* Amsterdam: University of Amsterdam.

Dolan, C. V., Molenaar,, P. C. M. & Boomsma, D. I. (1992). Decomposition of multivariate phenotypic means in multigroup genetic covariance structure analysis. *Behavior Genetics, 22*, 319–335.

Dolan, C. V., Molenaar, P. C. M. & Boomsma, D. I. (1994). Simultaneous genetic analysis of means and covariance structure: Pearson-Lawley selection rules. *Behavior Genetics, 24*, 17–24.

Draycott, S. G. & Kline, P. (1994). Further investigation into the nature of the BIP: A factor analysis of the BIP with primary abilities. *Personality and Individual Differences, 17*, 201–209.

Drews, C. D., Yeargin-Allsopp, M., Decouflé, P. & Murphy, C. C. (1995). Variation in the influence of selected sociodemographic risk factors for mental retardation. *American Journal of Public Health, 85*, 329–334.

Duncan, O. D., Featherman, D. L. & Duncan, B. (1972). *Socioeconomic background and achievement.* New York: Seminar Press.

Dwyer, P. S. (1937). The determination of the factor loadings of a given test from the known factor loadings of other tests. *Psychometrika, 2*, 173–178.

Dyer, K. F. (1976). Patterns of gene flow between Negroes and whites in the US. *Journal of Biosocial Science, 8*, 309–333.

Earles, J. A. & Ree, M. J. (1992). The predictive validity of the ASVAB for training grades. *Educational and Psychological Measurement, 52*, 721–725.

Eaves, L. J. & Jinks, J. L. (1972). Insignificance of evidence for differences in heritability of IQ between races and social classes. *Nature, 240*, 84–88.

Egan, V., Chiswick, A., Santosh, C., Naidu, K., Rimmington. J. E. & Best, J. J. K. (1994). Size isn't everything: A study of brain volume, intelligence and auditory evoked potentials. *Personality and Individual Differences, 17*, 357–367.

Elliott, C. D. (1983). *British Ability Scales, Manual 2, Technical handbook.* Windsor, Berks., England: NFER-Nelson.

Ericsson, K. A. (1988). Analysis of memory performance in terms of memory skills. In R. J. Sternberg (Ed.), *Advances in the psychology of human intelligence*, Vol. 4 (pp. 137–179). Hillsdale, NJ: Erlbaum.

Ericsson, K. A. & Charness, N. (1994). Expert performance: Its structure and acquisition. *American Psychologist, 49*, 725–747.

Ericsson, K. A. & Lehman, A. C. (1996). Expert and exceptional performance: Evidence of maximal adaptation to task constraints. *Annual Review of Psychology, 47*, 273–305.

Eyferth, K. (1959). Eine Untersuchung der Neger-Mischlingskinder in Westdeutschland. *Vita Humana, 2*, 102–114.

Eyferth, K. (1961). Leistungen verschiedener Gruppen von Besatzungskindern in Hamburg-Wechsler Intelligenztest für Kinder (HAWIK). *Archiv für die gesamte Psychologie, 113*, 222–241.

Eyferth, K., Brandt, U. & Hawel, W. *Farbige Kinder in Deutschland.* München: Juventa Verlag.

Eysenck, H. J. (1953). *The structure of human personality.* New York: Wiley.

Eysenck, H. J. (1967). Intelligence assessment: A theoretical and experimental approach. *British Journal of Educational Psychology, 37*, 81–98.

Eysenck, H. J. (1984a). Behavioral genetics. In R. J. Corsini (Ed.), *Encyclopedia of psychology*, Vol. 1 (pp. 121–124). New York: Wiley.

Eysenck, H. J. (1984b). The effect of race on human abilities and mental test scores. In C. R. Reynolds & R. T. Brown (Eds.), *Perspectives on bias in mental testing* (pp. 249–291). New York: Plenum Press.

Eysenck, H. J. (1987a). Thomson's "bonds" or Spearman's "energy": Sixty years on. *Mankind Quarterly, 27*, 259–274.

Eysenck, H. J. (1987b). Speed of information processing, reaction time, and the theory of intelligence. In P. A. Vernon (Ed.), *Speed of information-processing and intelligence* (pp. 21–67). Norwood, NJ: Ablex.

Eysenck, H. J. (1991). Race and intelligence: An alternative hypothesis. *Mankind Quarterly, 32*, 123–125.

Eysenck, H. J. (1993). The biological basis of intelligence. In P. A. Vernon (Ed.), *Biological approaches to the study of human intelligence* (pp. 1–32). Norwood, NJ: Ablex.

Eysenck, H. J. (1995a). Can we study intelligence using the experimental method? *Intelligence, 20*, 217–228.

Eysenck, H. J. (1995b). *Genius: The natural history of creativity*. Cambridge: Cambridge University Press.

Eysenck, H. J. & Barrett, P. (1985). Psychophysiology and the measurement of intelligence. In C. R. Reynolds & P. C. Willson (Eds.), *Methodological and statistical advances in the study of individual differences* (pp. 1–49). New York: Plenum Press.

Eysenck, H. J. & Eysenck, S. B. G. (Eds.) (1991). Improvement of IQ and behavior as a function of dietary supplementation: A symposium. *Personality and Individual Differences, 12* (Special Issue).

Eysenck, H. J. & Schoenthaler, S. J. (1997). Raising IQ level by vitamin and mineral supplementation. In R. J. Sternberg & E. Grigorenko (Eds.) *Intelligence, heredity and environment* (pp. 363–392). New York: Cambridge University Press.

Fairbank, B. A., Jr., Tirre, W. C. & Anderson, N. S. (1991). Measures of 30 cognitive tasks: Analysis of reliabilities, intercorrelation, and correlations with aptitude battery scores. In P. L. Dann, S. H. Irving & J. M. Collis (Eds.), *Advances in computer-based human assessment* (pp. 51–101). Dordrecht, Amsterdam: Kluwer.

Falconer, D. S. (1981). *Introduction to quantitative genetics*. New York: Longman.

Fan, X., Willson, V. L. & Reynolds, C. R. (1995). Assessing the similarity of the factor structure of the K-ABC for African-American and white children. *Journal of Psychoeducational Assessment, 13*, 120–131.

Fancher, R. E. (1983a). Alphonse de Candolle, Francis Galton, and the early history of the nature-nurture controversy. *Journal of the History of the Behavioral Sciences, 14*, 341–352.

Fancher, R. E. (1983b). Francis Galton's African ethnography and its role in the development of his psychology. *British Journal for the History of Science, 16*, 67–79.

Fancher, R. E. (1983c). Biographical origins of Francis Galton's psychology. *Isis, 74*, 227–233.

Fancher, R. E. (1984). The examined life: Competitive examinations in the thought of Francis Galton. *History of Psychology Newsletter, 16*, 13–20.

Fancher, R. E. (1985a). *The intelligence men: Makers of the IQ controversy.* New York: W. W. Norton.

Fancher, R. E. (1985b). Spearman's original computation of *g*: A model for Burt? *British Journal of Psychology, 76*, 341–352.

Faulstich, M. E., McAnulty, D., Carrey, M. P. & Gresham, F. M. (1987). Topography of human intelligence across race: Factorial comparison of black-white WAIS-R profiles for criminal offenders. *International Journal of Neuroscience, 35*, 181–187.

Feingold, A. (1993). Cognitive gender differences: A developmental perspective. *Sex Roles, 2*, 91–112.

Feingold, A. (1994). Gender differences in variability in intellectual abilities: A cross-cultural perspective. *Sex Roles, 30*, 81–92.

Feingold, A. (1996). Cognitive gender differences: Where are they, and why are they there? *Learning and Individual Differences, 8*, 25–32.

Ferguson, G. A. (1956). On transfer and the abilities of man. *Canadian Journal of Psychology, 10*, 121–131.

Fisch, R. O., Bilek, M. K., Deinard, A. S. & Chang, P-N. (1976). Growth, behavioral, and psychologic measurements of adopted children: The influences of genetic and socioeconomic factors in a prospective study. *Behavioral Pediatrics, 89*, 494–500.

Fisch, R. O., Bilek, M., Horrobin, J. M. & Chang, P-N. (1976). Children with superior intelligence at 7 years of age. *Archives of American Journal of Diseases of Children, 130*, 481–487.

Fisher, R. A. (1970). *Statistical methods for research workers* (14th ed.). New York: Hafner Press.

Fleishman, E. A. & Hempel, W. C., Jr. (1955). The relation between abilities and improvement with practice in a visual discrimination task. *Journal of Experimental Psychology, 49*, 301–312.

Flynn, J. R. (1980). *Race, IQ and Jensen.* London: Routledge & Kegan Paul.

Flynn, J. R. (1984). The mean IQ of Americans: Massive gains 1932 to 1978. *Psychological Bulletin, 95*, 29–51.

Flynn, J. R. (1987a). Massive gains in 14 nations: What IQ tests really measure. *Psychological Bulletin, 101*, 171–191.

Flynn, J. R. (1987b). Race and IQ: Jensen's case refuted. In S. Modgil & C. Modgil (Eds.), *Arthur Jensen: Consensus and controversy* (pp. 221–232). New York: Falmer.

Flynn, J. R. (1987c). The ontology of intelligence. In J. Forge (Ed.), *Measurement, realism and objectivity* (pp. 1–40). New York: D. Reidel.

Flynn, J. R. (1990). Massive IQ gains on the Scottish WISC: Evidence against Brand et al.'s hypothesis. *Irish Journal of Psychology, 11*, 41–51.

Flynn, J. R. (1991). *Asian Americans: Achievement beyond IQ.* Hillsdale, NJ: Erlbaum.

Flynn, J. R. (1993). Skodak and Skeels: The inflated mother-child gap. *Intelligence, 17*, 557–561.

Flynn, J. R. (1994). IQ gains over time. In R. J. Sternberg (Ed.), *Encyclopedia of human intelligence* (pp. 617–623). New York: Macmillan.

Flynn, J. R. (1996). What environmental factors affect intelligence: The relevance of IQ gains over time. In D. K. Detterman (Ed.), *Current topics in human intelligence*, Vol. 5, *The environment* (pp. 17–29). Norwood, NJ: Ablex.

Fodor, J. A. (1983). *The modularity of mind.* Cambridge: MIT Press.

Forrest, D. W. (1974). *Francis Galton: The life and work of a Victorian genius.* New York: Taplinger.

Frearson, W. M. & Eysenck, H. J. (1986). Intelligence, reaction time (RT) and a new "odd-man-out" RT paradigm. *Personality and Individual Differences, 7,* 808–817.

Freedman, D. G. (1979). *Human sociobiology.* New York: Free Press.

Freedman, D. H. (1994). A romance blossoms between gray matter and silicon. *Science, 265,* 889–890.

Fry, P. S.(Ed.) (1984). *Changing conceptions of intelligence and intellectual functioning: Current theory and research.* Amsterdam, The Netherlands: Elsevier Science.

Frydman, M. & Lynn, R., (1989). The intelligence of Korean children adopted in Belgium. *Personality and Individual Differences, 10,* 1323–1326.

Galton, F. (1908). *Memories of my life.* New York: AMS Press (1974).

Garber, H. L. (1988). *The Milwaukee Project: Preventing mental retardation in children at risk.* Washington, DC: American Association on Mental Retardation.

Gardner, H. (1983). *Frames of mind.* New York: Basic Books.

Gardner, H. (1993). *Creating minds.* New York: Basic Books.

Gazzaniga, M. S. (1989). Organization of the human brain. *Science, 245,* 947–952.

Geary, D. C. (1995). Sexual selection and sex differences in spatial cognition. *Learning and Individual Differences, 7,* 289–301.

Geary, D. C. (1996). Sexual selection and sex differences in mathematical abilities. *Behavioral and Brain Sciences, 19,* 229–247; Peer Commentary, pp. 247–284.

Gedye, C. A. (1981). *Longitudinal study (grades 1 through 10) of school achievement, self-confidence, and selected parental characteristics.* Doctoral dissertation, University of California, Berkeley.

Gettinger, M. (1984). Individual differences in time needed for learning: A review of literature. *Educational Psychologist, 19,* 15–29.

Ghiselli, E. E. (1966). *The validity of occupational aptitude tests.* New York: Wiley.

Gibbons, A. (1993). The risks of inbreeding. *Science, 259,* 1252.

Gill, C. E., Jardine, R. & Marin, N. G. (1985). Further evidence for genetic influences on educational achievement. *British Journal of Educational Psychology, 55,* 240–250.

Glover, J. A. & Ronning, R. R. (Eds.) (1987). *Historical foundations of educational psychology.* New York: Plenum Press.

Glutting, J. J. & McDermott, P. A. (1990). Principles and problems in learning potential. In C. R. Reynolds & Kamphaus, R. W. (Eds.), *Handbook of psychological and educational assessment of children:: Intelligence and achievement* (pp. 296–347). New York: Guilford Press.

Goff, M. & Ackerman, P. L. (1992). Personality-intelligence relations: Assessment of typical intellectual engagement. *Journal of Educational Psychology, 84,* 537–552.

Goldman-Rakic, P. S. (1994). Specification of higher cortical functions. In S. H. Broman & J. Grafman (Eds.), *Atypical cognitive deficits in developmental disorders: Implications for brain function* (pp. 3–17). Hillsdale, NJ: Erlbaum.

Goleman, D. (1995). *Emotional intelligence.* New York: Bantam.

Gordon, R. A. (1975). Crime and cognition: An evolutionary perspective. Paper presented at the Second International Symposium on Criminology, São Paulo, Brazil.

Gordon, R. A. (1980). Research on IQ, race, and delinquency: Taboo or not taboo? In E. Sagarin (Ed.), *Taboos in criminology* (pp. 37–66). Beverly Hills, CA: Sage.

Gordon, R. A. (1987a). SES versus IQ in the race-IQ-delinquency model. *International Journal of Sociology and Social Policy, 7*, 30–96.

Gordon, R. A. (1987b). Jensen's contributions concerning test bias: A contextual view. In S. Modgil & C. Modgil (Eds.), *Arthur Jensen: Consensus and controversy* (pp. 77–154). New York: Falmer.

Gordon, R. A. (1996). How intelligent is our intelligence policy? (Review of "Intelligence policy" by A. Browne-Miller). *Contemporary Psychology, 41*, 573–576.

Gordon, R. A. (1997). Everyday life as an intelligence test: Effects of intelligence and intelligence context. *Intelligence, 24*, 203–320.

Gorsuch, R. L. (1983). *Factor analysis* (2nd ed.). Hillsdale, NJ: Erlbaum.

Gottesman, I. I. (1968). Biogenetics of race and class. In M. Deutsch, I. Katz & A. R. Jensen (Eds.), *Social class, race, and psychological development* (pp. 11–51). New York: Holt, Rinehart & Winston.

Gottfredson, L. S. (1985). Education as a valid but fallible signal of worker quality: Reorienting an old debate about the functional basis of the occupational hierarchy. In A. C. Kerckhoff (Ed.), *Research in sociology of education and socialization*, Vol. 5 (pp. 123–169). Greenwich, CT: JAI Press.

Gottfredson, L. S. (Ed.) (1986). "The g factor in employment," Special issue of the *Journal of Vocational Behavior, 29*, 293–450.

Gottfredson, L. S. (1997). Why g matters: The complexity of everyday life. *Intelligence, 24*, 79–132.

Gottfredson, L. S. & Sharf, J. C. (Eds.) (1988). "Fairness in employment testing," Special issue of the *Journal of Vocational Behavior, 33*, 225–477.

Gottfredson, M. R. and Hirschi, T. (1990). *A general theory of crime.* Stanford, CA: Stanford University Press.

Graziano, W. G., Varca, P. E. & Levy, J. C. (1982). Race of examiner effects and the validity of intelligence tests. *Review of Educational Research, 52*, 469–497.

Grissmer, D. W., Kirby, S. N., Berencs, M. & Williamson, S. (1994). *Student achievement and the changing American family.* Santa Monica, CA: RAND.

Guilford, J. P. (1964). Zero correlations among tests of intellectual abilities. *Psychological Bulletin, 61*, 401–404.

Guilford, J. P. (1967). *The nature of human intelligence.* New York: McGraw-Hill.

Guilford, J. P. (1985). The Structure-of-Intellect model. In B. B. Wolman (Ed.), *Handbook of intelligence: Theories, measurements, and applications* (pp. 225–266). New York: Wiley.

Gustafsson, J-E. (1988). Hierarchical models of individual differences in cognitive abilities. In R. J. Sternberg (Ed.), *Advances in the psychology of human intelligence*, Vol. 4 (pp. 35–71). Hillsdale, NJ: Erlbaum.

Gustafsson, J-E. (1992). The "Spearman hypothesis" is false. *Multivariate Behavioral Research, 27*, 265–267.

Guttman, L. & Levy, S. (1991). Two structural laws for intelligence tests. *Intelligence, 15*, 79–103.

Hack, M., Beslau, N., Weissman, B, Aram, D., Klein, N. & Borawski, E. (1991). Effect of very low birth weight and subnormal head size on cognitive abilities at school age. *New England Journal of Medicine, 325,* 231–237.

Haier, R. J. (1993). Cerebral glucose metabolism and intelligence. In P. A. Vernon (Ed.), *Biological approaches to the study of human intelligence* (pp. 317–373). Norwood, NJ: Ablex.

Haier, R. J., Siegel, B., Tang, C., Abel, L. & Buchsbaum, M. S. (1992). Intelligence and changes in regional cerebral glucose metabolic rate following learning. *Intelligence, 16,* 415–426.

Haier, R. J., Robinson, D. L., Braden, W. & Williams, D. (1983). Electrical potentials of the cerebral cortex and psychometric intelligence. *Personality and Individual Differences, 4,* 591–599.

Hall, V. C. & Kleinke, D. (1971). The relationship between social class and cognitive abilities: A test of Jensen's cognitive levels hypotheses. Paper presented at the annual meeting of the Society for Research in Child Development, Minneapolis, April 1971.

Halpern, D. F. (1992). *Sex differences in cognitive abilities* (2nd ed.). Hillsdale, NJ: Erlbaum.

Hambleton, R. K. (1989). Principle and selected applications of item response theory. In R. L. Linn (Ed.), *Educational measurement* (3rd ed., pp. 147–200). New York: Macmillan.

Hamilton, J. A. (1935). The association between brain size and maze ability in the white rat. Unpublished doctoral dissertation, University of California, Berkeley.

Harman, H. H. (1976). *Modern factor analysis* (3rd ed.). Chicago: University of Chicago Press.

Harrison, G. A., Weiner, J. S., Tanner, J. M. & Barnicot, N. A. (1964). *Human biology: An introduction to human evolution, variation and growth.* London: Oxford University Press.

Haug, H. (1987). Brain sizes, surfaces, and neuronal sizes of the cortex cerebri: A stereological investigation of man and his variability and a comparison with some species of mammals (primates, whales, marsupials, insectivores, and one elephant). *American Journal of Anatomy, 180,* 126–142.

Hawk, J. A. (1970). Linearity of criterion-GATB aptitude relationships. *Measurement and Evaluation in Guidance, 2,* 249–256.

Heath, A. C., Berg, K., Eaves, L. J., Solaas, M. H., Corey, L. A., Sundet, J., Magnus, P. & Nance, W. E. (1985). Educational policy and the heritability of educational attainment. *Nature, 314,* 734–736.

Hedges, L. V. & Nowell, A. (1995). Sex differences in mental test scores, variability, and number of high-scoring individuals. *Science, 269,* 41–45.

Hemmelgarn, T. E. & Kehle, T. J. (1984). The relationship between reaction time and intelligence in children. *School Psychology International, 5,* 77–84.

Herrnstein, R. J. & Murray, C. (1994). *The bell curve: Intelligence and class structure in American life.* New York: Free Press.

Hick, W. E. (1952). On the rate of gain of information. *Quarterly Journal of Experimental Psychology, 4,* 11–26.

Hirschi, T. & Hindelang, M. J. (1977). Intelligence and delinquency: A revisionist view. *American Sociological Review, 47,* 571–587.

Ho, H-Z., Baker, L. A. & Decher, S. N. (1988). Covariation between intelligence and speed of cognitive processing: Genetic and environmental influences. *Behavior Genetics, 18*, 247–261.

Ho, K-c., Roessmann, U., Hause, L. & Monroe, G. (1981). Newborn brain weight in relation to maturity, sex, and race. *Annals of Neurology, 10*, 243–246.

Ho, K-c., Roessmann, U., Straumfjord, J. V. & Monroe, G. (1980a). Analysis of brain weight: I. Adult brain weight in relation to sex, race, and age. *Archives of Pathology and Laboratory Medicine, 104*, 636–639.

Ho, K-c., Roessmann, U., Stramfjord, J. V. & Monroe, G. (1980b). Analysis of brain weight: II. Adult brain weight in relation to body height, weight, and surface area. *Archives of Pathology and Laboratory Medicine, 104*, 640–645.

Holden, C. (1995). No hostile climate found for minorities. *Science, 269*, 1047.

Holland, P. W. & Wainer, H. (Eds.) (1988). *Differential item functioning*. Hillsdale, NJ: Erlbaum.

Holt, G. L. & Matson, J. L. (1974). Necker cube reversals as a function of age and IQ. *Bulletin of the Psychonomic Society, 4*, 519–521.

Horn, J. (1985). Remodeling old models of intelligence. In B. B. Wolman (Ed.), *Handbook of intelligence: Theories, measurements and applications* (pp. 267–300). New York: Wiley.

Horn, J. (1986). Intellectual ability concepts. In R. J. Sternberg (Ed.), *Advances in the psychology of human intelligence*, Vol. 3 (pp. 35–77). Hillsdale, NJ: Erlbaum.

Horn, J. (1989). Models of intelligence. In R. L. Linn (Ed.), *Intelligence: Measurement, theory, and public policy* (pp. 29–73). Urbana: University of Illinois Press.

Hotelling, H. (1933). Analysis of a complex of statistical variables into principal components. *Journal of Educational Psychology, 24*, 498–520.

Humphreys, L. G. (1971). Theory of intelligence. In R. Cancro (Ed.) *Intelligence: Genetic and environmental influences* (pp. 31–42). New York: Grune & Stratton.

Humphreys, L. G. (1976). A factor model for research on intelligence and problem solving. In L. B. Resnick (Ed.), *The nature of intelligence* (pp. 329–339). Hillsdale, NJ: Erlbaum.

Humphreys, L. G. (1984). General intelligence. In C. R. Reynolds & R. T. Brown (Eds.) *Perspectives on bias in mental testing* (pp. 221–247). New York: Plenum Press.

Humphreys, L. G. (1985a). Race differences and the Spearman hypothesis. *Intelligence, 9*, 275–283.

Humphreys, L. G. (1985b). Attenuated hypothesis or attenuated test of hypothesis? *Intelligence 9*, 291–295.

Humphreys, L. G. (1988). Trends in levels of academic achievement of blacks and other minorities. *Intelligence, 12*, 231–260.

Humphreys, L. G. (1989). Intelligence: Three kinds of instability and their consequences for policy. In R. L. Linn (Ed.), *Intelligence: Measurement, theory, and public policy* (pp. 193–216). Urbana: University of Illinois Press.

Humphreys, L. G. (1994). Intelligence from the standpoint of a (pragmatic) behaviorist. *Psychological Inquiry, 5*, 179–192.

Humphreys, L. G., Fleishman, A. I. & Pang-Chieh-Lin. (1977). Causes of racial and socioeconomic differences in cognitive tests. *Journal of Research in Personality, 11*, 191–208.

Hunt, E. (1992). Why is it hard to improve mental competence? A cognitive science perspective. *Advances in Cognition and Educational Practice*, Vol. 1A (pp. 3–24). Greenwich, CT: JAI Press.

Hunt, E. (1995). *Will we be smart enough? A cognitive analysis of the coming workforce.* New York: Russell Sage Foundation.

Hunt, E., Frost, N. & Lunneborg, C. J. (1973). Individual differences in cognition: A new approach to intelligence. In G. H. Bower (Ed.), *Psychology of learning and motivation*, Vol. 7 (pp. 87–122). New York: Academic Press.

Hunt, E., Lunneborg, C. & Lewis, J. (1975). What does it mean to be high verbal? *Cognitive Psychology, 7*, 194–227.

Hunter, J. E. (1989). *The Wonderlic Personnel Test as a predictor of training success and job performance.* Northfield, IL: E. F. Wonderlic Personnel Test.

Hunter, J. E. & Hunter, R. F. (1984). Validity and utility of alternative predictors of job performance. *Psychological Bulletin, 96*, 72–98.

Hunter, J. E. & Schmidt, F. L. (1990). *Methods of meta-analysis: Correcting error and bias in research findings.* Newbury Park, CA: Sage Publications.

Hunter, J. E., Schmidt, F. L. & Judiesch, M. K. (1990). Individual differences in output as a function of job complexity. *Journal of Applied Psychology, 75*, 28–46.

Hyde, J. S. (1981). How large are cognitive gender differences? A meta-analysis using ω^2 and *d. American Psychologist, 36*, 892–901.

Inbaraj, S. G. & Rao, P.S.S.S. (1978). Mental development among children in relation to parental consanguinity. Preliminary communication presented at the Vth Annual Conference of the Indian Society of Human Genetics, Bombay, Dec.

Irvine, S. H. & Berry, J. W. (Eds.) (1988). *Human abilities in cultural context.* Cambridge: Cambridge University Press.

James, W. (1894/1950). *The principles of psychology.* New York: Dover.

Jaynes, G. D. & Williams, R. M., Jr. (Eds.) (1989). *A common destiny: Blacks and American society.* Washington, DC: National Academy Press.

Jenkinson, J. C. (1983). Is speed of information processing related to fluid or to crystallized intelligence? *Intelligence, 7*, 91–106.

Jenks, C. (1979). *Who gets ahead? The determinants of economic success in America.* New York: Basic Books.

Jensen, A. R. (1967). Estimation of the limits of heritability of traits by comparison of monozygotic and dizygotic twins. *Proceedings of the National Academy of Sciences, 58*, 149–156.

Jensen, A. R. (1971a). Individual differences in visual and auditory memory. *Journal of Educational Psychology, 62*, 123–131.

Jensen, A. R. (1971b). The race $\times$ sex $\times$ ability interaction. In R. Cancro (Ed.), *Intelligence: Genetic and environmental influences*, (pp. 107–161). New York: Grune & Stratton.

Jensen, A. R. (1971c). A note on why genetic correlations are not squared. *Psychological Bulletin, 75*, 223–224.

Jensen, A. R. (1972). The causes of twin differences in IQ: A reply to Gage. *Phi Delta Kappan, 53*, 420–421.

Jensen, A. R. (1973). *Educability and group differences.* London: Methuen.

Jensen, A. R. (1974a). Kinship correlations reported by Sir Cyril Burt. *Behavior Genetics, 4*, 1–28.

Jensen, A. R. (1974b). Cumulative deficit: A testable hypothesis? *Developmental Psychology, 10*, 996–1019.

Jensen, A. R. (1974c). Ethnicity and scholastic achievement. *Psychological Reports, 34*, 659–668.

Jensen, A. R. (1976). The problem of genotype-environment correlation in the estimation of heritability from monozygotic and dizygotic twins. *Acta Geneticae et Gammellogiae, 25,* 86–99.

Jensen, A. R. (1977). Cumulative deficit in IQ of blacks in the rural south. *Developmental Psychology, 13,* 184–191.

Jensen, A. R. (1978). Genetic and behavioral effects of nonrandom mating. In R. T. Osborne, C. E. Noble & N. Weyl (Eds.), *Human variation: The biopsychology of age, race, and sex* (pp. 51–105). New York: Academic Press.

Jensen, A. R. (1980a). *Bias in mental testing.* New York: Free Press.

Jensen, A. R. (1980b). Uses of sibling data in educational and psychological research. *American Educational Research Journal, 17,* 153–170.

Jensen, A. R. (1981a). *Straight talk about mental tests.* New York: Free Press.

Jensen, A. R. (1981b). Précis of *Bias in mental testing. Behavioral and Brain Sciences, 3,* 325–333.

Jensen, A. R. (1981c). Obstacles, problems, and pitfalls in differential psychology. In S. Scarr, *Race, social class, and individual differences in I.Q.* (pp. 483–514). Hillsdale, NJ: Erlbaum.

Jensen, A. R. (1982a). Reaction time and psychometric g. In H. J. Eysenck (Ed.), *A model for intelligence* (pp. 93–132). New York: Springer.

Jensen, A. R. (1982b). The chronometry of intelligence. In R. J. Sternberg (Ed.), *Advances in the psychology of human intelligence,* Vol. 1 (pp. 255–310). Hillsdale, NJ: Erlbaum.

Jensen, A. R. (1983). Effects of inbreeding on mental-ability factors. *Personality and Individual Differences, 4,* 71–87.

Jensen, A. R. (1984a). Test validity: g versus the specificity doctrine. *Journal of Social and Biological Structures, 7,* 93–118.

Jensen, A. R. (1984b). Test bias: Concepts and criticisms. In C. R. Reynolds & R. T. Brown (Eds.), *Perspectives on bias in mental testing* (pp. 507–586). New York: Plenum Press.

Jensen, A. R. (1984c). The black-white difference on the K-ABC: Implications for future tests. *Journal of Special Education, 18,* 377–408.

Jensen, A. R. (1985a). The nature of the black-white difference on various psychometric tests: Spearman's hypothesis. *Behavioral and Brain Sciences, 8,* 193–219.

Jensen, A. R. (1985b). The black-white difference in g: A phenomenon in search of a theory. *Behavioral and Brain Sciences, 8,* 246–263.

Jensen, A. R. (1985c). Methodological and statistical techniques for the chronometric study of mental abilities. In C. R. Reynolds & V. L. Willson (Eds.), *Methodological and statistical advances in the study of individual differences* (pp. 51–116). New York: Plenum Press.

Jensen, A. R. (1985d). Humphreys's attenuated test of Spearman's hypothesis. *Intelligence, 9,* 285–289.

Jensen, A. R. (1985e). Race differences and Type II errors: A comment on Borkowski and Krause. *Intelligence, 9,* 33–39.

Jensen, A. R. (1987a). Individual differences in mental ability. In J. A. Glover & R. R. Ronning (Eds.), *Historical foundations of educational psychology* (pp. 61–88). New York: Plenum Press.

Jensen, A. R. (1987b). Psychometric g as a focus of concerted research effort. *Intelligence, 11,* 193–198.

Jensen, A. R. (1987c). Process differences and individual differences in some cognitive tasks. *Intelligence, 11*, 107–136.

Jensen, A. R. (1987d). Individual differences in the Hick paradigm. In P. A. Vernon (Ed.), *Speed of information-processing and intelligence* (pp. 101–175). Norwood, NJ: Ablex.

Jensen, A. R. (1987e). The *g* beyond factor analysis. In R. R. Ronning, J. A. Glover, J. C. Conoley & J. C. Witt (Eds.), *The influence of cognitive psychology on testing* (pp. 87–142). Hillsdale, NJ: Erlbaum.

Jensen, A. R. (1987f). Process differences and individual differences in some cognitive tasks. *Intelligence, 11*, 107–136.

Jensen, A. R. (1987g). Further evidence for Spearman's hypothesis concerning the black-white differences on psychometric tests. *Behavioral and Brain Sciences, 10*, 512–519.

Jensen, A. R. (1988a). Speed of information processing and population differences. In S. H. Irvine & J. W. Berry (Eds.), *Human abilities in cultural context* (pp. 105–145). Cambridge: Cambridge University Press.

Jensen, A. R. (1988b). A review of *Practical Intelligence* by R. J. Sternberg and R. Wagner. *Personality and Individual Differences, 9*, 199–200.

Jensen, A. R. (1989a). The relationship between learning and intelligence. *Learning and Individual Differences, 1*, 37–62.

Jensen, A. R. (1989b). Raising IQ without increasing *g*? A review of *The Milwaukee Project: Preventing mental retardation in children at risk* by H. L. Garber. *Developmental Review, 9*, 234–258.

Jensen, A. R. (1991a). Speed of cognitive processes: A chronometric anchor for psychometric tests of *g*. *Psychological Test Bulletin, 4*, 59–70.

Jensen, A. R. (1991b). Spearman's *g* and the problem of educational equality. *Oxford Review of Education, 17*, 169–187.

Jensen, A. R. (1992a). Commentary: Vehicles of *g*. *Psychological Science, 3*, 275–278.

Jensen, A. R. (1992b). Scientific fraud or false accusations? The case of Cyril Burt. In D. J. Miller & M. Hersen (Eds.), *Research fraud in the behavioral and biomedical sciences* (pp. 97–124). New York: Wiley.

Jensen, A. R. (1992c). Understanding *g* in terms of information processing. *Educational Psychology Review, 4*, 271–308.

Jensen, A. R. (1992d). The importance of intraindividual variability in reaction time. *Personality and Individual Differences, 13*, 869–882.

Jensen, A. R. (1992e). The relation between information processing time and right/wrong responses. *American Journal on Mental Retardation, 97*, 290–292.

Jensen, A. R. (1992f). Spearman's hypothesis: Methodology and evidence. *Multivariate Behavioral Research, 27*, 225–234.

Jensen, A. R. (1992g). More on psychometric *g* and "Spearman's hypothesis." *Multivariate Behavioral Research, 27*, 257–260.

Jensen, A. R. (1993a). Psychometric *g* and achievement. In B. R. Gifford (Ed.), *Policy perspectives on educational testing* (pp. 117–227). Boston: Kluwer Academic Publishers.

Jensen, A. R. (1993b). Why is reaction time correlated with psychometric *g*? *Current Directions in Psychological Science, 2*, 53–56.

Jensen, A. R. (1993c). Spearman's *g*: Links between psychometrics and biology. *Annals of the New York Academy of Sciences, 702*, 103–131.

Jensen, A. R. (1993d). Spearman's hypothesis tested with chronometric information-processing tasks. *Intelligence, 17,* 47–77.

Jensen, A. R. (1993e). Test validity: g versus "tacit knowledge." *Current Direction in Psychological Science, 2,* 9–10.

Jensen, A. R. (1994a). Sir Francis Galton. In R. J. Sternberg (Ed.), *Encyclopedia of intelligence* (pp. 457–463). New York: Macmillan.

Jensen, A. R. (1994b). Charles Edward Spearman. In R. J. Sternberg (Ed.), *Encyclopedia of intelligence* (pp. 1007–1014). New York: Macmillan.

Jensen, A. R. (1994c). Phlogiston, animal magnetism, and intelligence. In D. K. Detterman (Ed.), *Current topics in human intelligence,* Vol. 4, *Theories of intelligence* (pp. 257–284). Norwood, NJ: Ablex.

Jensen, A. R. (1994d). Humphreys's "behavioral repertoire" an epiphenomenon of g. *Psychological Inquiry, 5,* 208–210.

Jensen, A. R. (1994e). Reaction time. In R. J. Corsini (Ed.), *Encyclopedia of psychology,* Vol. 3, 2nd ed., (pp. 282–285). New York: Wiley.

Jensen, A. R. (1994f). Psychometric g related to differences in head size. *Personality and Individual Differences, 17,* 597–606.

Jensen, A. R. (1996a). Secular trends in IQ: Additional hypotheses. In D. K. Detterman (Ed.), *Current topics in human intelligence,* Vol. 5, *The environment* (pp. 147–150). Norwood, NJ: Ablex.

Jensen, A. R. (1996b). Giftedness and genius: Crucial differences. In C. P. Benbow & D. Lubinski (Eds.), *Intellectual talent: Psychometric and social issues* (pp. 393–411). Baltimore: The Johns Hopkins University Press.

Jensen, A. R. (1997a). The puzzle of nongenetic variance. In R. J. Sternberg & E. L. Grigorenko (Eds.) *Heredity, intelligence, and environment* (pp. 42–88). Cambridge: Cambridge University Press.

Jensen, A. R. (1997b). The neurophysiology of g. In C. Cooper & V. Varma (Eds.), *Processes in individual differences* (pp. 108–125). London: Routledge.

Jensen, A. R. (1998). Adoption data and two g-related hypotheses. *Intelligence, 25,* 1–6.

Jensen, A. R., Cohn, S. J. & Cohn, C. M. G. (1989). Speed of information processing in academically gifted youths and their siblings. *Personality and Individual Differences, 10,* 29–34.

Jensen, A. R. & Faulstich, M. E. (1988). Differences between prisoners and the general population in psychometric g. *Personality and Individual Differences, 9,* 925–928.

Jensen, A. R. & Figueroa, R. A. (1975). Forward and backward digit span interaction with race and IQ: Predictions from Jensen's theory. *Journal of Educational Psychology, 67,* 882–893.

Jensen, A. R. & Johnson, F. W. (1994). Race and sex differences in head size and IQ. *Intelligence, 18,* 309–333.

Jensen, A. R., Larson, G. E. & Paul, S. M. (1988). Psychometric g and mental processing speed on a semantic verification test. *Personality and Individual Differences, 9,* 243–255.

Jensen, A. R. & McGurk, F. C. J. (1987). Black-white bias in "cultural" and "noncultural" test items. *Personality and Individual Differences, 8,* 295–301.

Jensen, A. R. & Osborne, R. T. (1979). Forward and backward digit span interaction with race and IQ: A longitudinal developmental comparison. *Indian Journal of Psychology, 54*, 75–87.

Jensen, A. R. & Reed, T. E. (1990). Simple reaction time as a suppressor variable in the chronometric study of intelligence. *Intelligence, 14*, 375–388.

Jensen, A. R. & Reynolds, C. R. (1982). Race, social class and ability patterns on the WISC-R. *Personality and Individual Differences, 3*, 423–438.

Jensen, A. R. & Reynolds, C. R. (1983). Sex differences on the WISC-R. *Personality and Individual Differences, 4*, 223–226.

Jensen, A. R., Saccuzzo, D. P. & Larson, G. E. (1988). Equating the Standard and Advanced forms of the Raven Progressive Matrices. *Educational and Psychological Measurement, 48*, 1091–1095.

Jensen, A. R., Schafer, E. W. & Crinella, F. M. (1981). Reaction time, evoked brain potentials, and psychometric g in the severely retarded. *Intelligence, 5*, 179–197.

Jensen, A. R. & Sinha, S. N. (1993). Physical correlates of human intelligence. In P. A. Vernon (Ed.), *Biological approaches to the study of human intelligence* (pp. 139–242). Norwood, NJ: Ablex.

Jensen, A. R. & Weng, L-J. (1994). What is a good g? *Intelligence, 18*, 231–258.

Jensen, A. R. & Whang, P. A. (1993). Reaction time and intelligence: A comparison of Chinese-American and Anglo-American children. *Journal of Biosocial Science, 25*, 397–410.

Jensen, A. R. & Whang, P. A. (1994). Speed of accessing arithmetic facts in long-term memory: A comparison of Chinese-American and Anglo-American children. *Contemporary Educational Psychology, 19*, 1–12.

Jerison, H. J. (1973). *Evolution of brain and intelligence*. New York: Academic Press.

Jerison, H. J. (1982). The evolution of biological intelligence. In R. J. Sternberg (Ed.), *Handbook of human intelligence* (pp. 723–791). Cambridge: Cambridge University Press.

Johnson, F. W. (1991). Biological factors and psychometric intelligence: A review. *Genetic, Social, and General Psychology Monographs, 117*, 313–357.

Johnson, R. C., McClearn, G. E., Yuen, S., Nagoshi, C. T., Ahern, F. M. & Cole, R. E. (1985). Galton's data a century later. *American Psychologist, 40*, 875–982.

Jonçich, G. (1968). *The sane positivist: A biography of Edward L. Thorndike*. Middletown, CT: Wesleyan University Press.

Jones, L. V. (1981). Achievement test scores in mathematics and science. *Science, 213*, 412–416.

Jöreskog, K. G. & Sörbom, D. (1989). *LISREL 7: A guide to the program and applications* (2nd ed.) Chicago: SPSS Inc.

Judson, H. J. (1979). *The eighth day of creation*. New York: Simon & Schuster.

Kail, R. (1991). Development of processing speed in childhood and adolescence. In H. W. Reese (Ed.), *Advances in child development and behavior*, Vol. 23 (pp. 151–185). New York: Academic Press.

Kail, R. (1992). General slowing of information processing by persons with mental retardation. *American Journal on Mental Retardation, 97*, 333–341.

Kail, R. (1994). Processing time, articulation time, and memory span. *Journal of Experimental Child Psychology, 57*, 281–291.

Kaiser, H. F. (1968). A measure of the average intercorrelation. *Educational and Psychological Measurement, 28*, 245–247.

Kaiser, H. F. (1987). An interesting probability problem, with an example and an experiment. *Psychological Reports, 60*, 509–510.

Kaiser, H. F. & Caffrey, J. (1965). Alpha factor analysis. *Psychometrika, 30*, 1–14.

Kaus, M. (1992). *The end of equality*. New York: Basic Books.

Keith, V. M. & Herring, C. (1991). Skin tone and stratification in the black community. *American Journal of Sociology, 97*, 760–778.

Kendall, M. G. & Stuart, A. (1973). *The advanced theory of statistics*, Vol. 3. London: Griffin.

Keynes, M. (Ed.) (1993). *Sir Francis Galton, FRS: The legacy of his ideas*. London: Macmillan.

Kimura, D. & Hampson, E. (1993). Neural and hormonal mechanisms mediating sex differences in cognition. In P. A. Vernon (Ed.) *Biological approaches to the study of human intelligence* (pp. 375–397). Norwood, NJ: Ablex.

Kline, P. (1991). Sternberg's components: Non-contingent concepts. *Personality and Individual Differences, 12*, 873–876.

Kline, P., Draycott, S. G. & McAndrew, V. M. (1994). Reconstructing intelligence: a factor analytic study of the BIP. *Personality and Individual Differences, 16*, 529–536.

Klitgaard, R. (1985). *Choosing elites: Selecting "The best and the brightest" at top universities and elsewhere*. New York: Basic Books.

Kranzler, J. H. (1992). A test of Larson and Alderton's (1990) worst performance rule of reaction time variability. *Personality and Individual Differences, 13*, 255–261.

Kranzler, J. H. & Jensen, A. R. (1989). Inspection time and intelligence: A meta-analysis. *Intelligence, 13*, 329–347.

Kranzler, J. H. & Jensen, A. R. (1991a). The nature of psychometric *g*: Unitary process or a number of independent processes? *Intelligence, 15*, 397–422.

Kranzler, J. H. & Jensen, A. R. (1991b). Unitary *g*: Unquestioned postulate or empirical fact? *Intelligence, 15*, 437–448.

Kranzler, J. H. & Jensen, A. R. (1993). Psychometric *g* is still not unitary after eliminating supposed "impurities": Further comment on Carroll. *Intelligence, 17*, 11–14.

Kranzler, J. H., Whang, P. A. & Jensen, A. R. (1994). Task complexity and the speed and efficiency of elemental information processing: Another look at the nature of intellectual giftedness. *Contemporary Educational Psychology, 19*, 447–459.

Kutas, M., McCarthy, G. & Donchin, E. (1977). Augmenting mental chronometry: The P300 as a measure of stimulus evaluation time. *Science, 197*, 792–795.

Kyllonen, P. C. (1993). Aptitude testing inspired by information processing: A test of the four-sources model. *Journal of General Psychology, 120*, 375–405.

Kyllonen, P. C. (1994). CAM: A theoretical framework for cognitive abilities measurement. In D. K. Detterman (Ed.), *Current topics in human intelligence*, Vol. 4, *Theories of intelligence* (pp. 307–359). Norwood, NJ: Ablex.

Kyllonen, P. C. & Christal, R. E. (1990). Reasoning ability is (little more than) working memory capacity?! *Intelligence, 14*, 389–433.

Larson, G. E. & Alderston, D. L. (1990). Reaction time variability and intelligence: A "worst performance" analysis of individual differences. *Intelligence, 14*, 309–325.

Larson, G. E., Haier, R. J., LaCasse, L. & Hazen, K. (1995). Evaluation of a "mental effort'' hypothesis for correlations between cortical metabolism and intelligence. *Intelligence, 21*, 267–278.

Larson, G. E. & Lattin, K. E. (1989). Discriminant validity and information processing: the case of "verbal correlates." *Personality and Individual Differences, 10*, 1185–1188.

Larson, G. E., Merritt, C. R. & Williams, S. E. (1988). Information processing and intelligence: Some implications of task complexity. *Intelligence, 12*, 131–147.

Larson, G. E., Succuzzo, D. P. & Brown, J. (1994). Motivation: Cause or confound in information processing/intelligence correlations? *Acta Psychologica, 85*, 25–37.

Leary, W. E. (1988). Why fewer blacks choose to breast-feed than do whites. *New York Times*, April 7, 1988, (p. B6).

Lehmann, J. E. (1937). The effects of changes in pH on the action of mammalian nerve fibers. *American Journal of Physiology, 118*, 600–612.

Lehrl, S. & Fischer, B. (1988). The basic parameters of human information processing: Their role in the determination of intelligence. *Personality and Individual Differences, 9*, 883–896.

Lehrl, S. & Fischer, B. (1990). A basic information psychological parameter (BIP) for the reconstructions of concepts of intelligence. *European Journal of Personality, 4*, 259–286.

Lerner, B. (1983). Test scores as measures of human capital and forecasting tools. In R. B. Cattell (Ed.), *Intelligence and national achievement* (pp. 70–99). Washington, DC: Cliveden Press.

Levin, M. (1994). Comment on the Minnesota Transracial Adoption Study. *Intelligence, 19*, 13–20.

Levin, M. (1997). *Why race matters*. Westport, CT: Praeger.

Levine, G., Preddy, D. & Thorndike, R. L. (1987). Speed of information processing and level of cognitive ability. *Personality and Individual Differences, 8*, 599–607.

Li, C. C. (1975). *Path analysis—A primer*. Pacific Grove, CA: Boxwood Press.

Libet, B. (1985). Unconscious cerebral initiative and the role of conscious will in voluntary action. *Behavioral and Brain Sciences, 8*, 529–566.

Libet, B. (1987). Consciousness: Conscious, subjective experience. In G. Adelman (Ed.), *Encyclopedia of neuroscience*, Vol. 1 (pp. 272–275). Boston: Birkhäuser.

Libet, B., Pearly, D. K., Moreledge, D. E., Gleason, C. A., Hosobuchi, Y. & Barbara, N. M. (1991). Control of the transition from sensory detection to sensory awareness in man by the duration of a thalamic stimulus: The cerebral "time-on" factor. *Brain, 114*, 1731–1757.

Lin, K-M., Poland, R. E., & Nakasaki, G. (Eds.). (1993). *Psychopharmacology and psychobiology of ethnicity*. Washington, DC: American Psychiatric Press.

Lipsey, M. W. & Wilson, D. B. (1993). The efficacy of psychological, educational, and behavioral treatment: Confirmation from meta-analysis. *American Psychologist, 48*, 1181–1209.

Locurto, C. (1990). The malleability of IQ as judged from adoption studies. *Intelligence, 14*, 275–292.

Loehlin, J. C. (1984). Nature/nurture controversy. In R.J. Corsini (Ed.), *Encyclopedia of psychology*, Vol. 2 (pp. 418–420). New York: Wiley.

Loehlin, J. C. (1989). Partitioning environmental and genetic contributions to behavioral development. *American Psychologist, 44*, 1285–1292.

Loehlin, J. C. (1992). *Latent variables models: An introduction to factor, path, and structural analysis* (2nd ed.). Hillsdale, NJ: Erlbaum.

Loehlin, J. C., Lindzey, G. & Spuhler, J. N. (1975). *Race differences in intelligence.* New York: W. H. Freeman.

Loehlin, J. C., Vandenberg, S. G. & Osborne, R. T. (1973). Blood group genes and Negro-White ability differences. *Behavior Genetics, 3*, 263–270.

Loevinger, J. (1951). Intelligence. In H. Helson (Ed.), *Theoretical foundations of psychology* (pp. 557–601). New York: Van Nostrand.

Lohman, D. F. (1988). Spatial abilities as traits, processes, and knowledge. In R. J. Sternberg (Ed.), *Advances in the psychology of human intelligence*, Vol. 4 (pp. 181–248). Hillsdale, NJ: Erlbaum.

Lovejoy, C. O. (1993). Modeling human origins: Are we sexy because we are smart, or smart because we're sexy? In D. T. Rasmussen (Ed.), *The origin and evolution of humans and humanness* (pp. 1–28). Sudbury, MA: Jones & Bartlett.

Lovie, A. D. & Lovie, P. (1993). Charles Spearman, Cyril Burt, and the origins of factor analysis. *Journal of the History of the Behavioral Sciences, 29*, 308–321.

Lovie, P. & Lovie, A. D. (1995). The cold equations: Spearman and Wilson on factor indeterminacy. *British Journal of Mathematical and Statistical Psychology, 48*, 237–253.

Lubinski, D. (1996). Applied individual differences research and its quantitative methods. *Psychology, Public Policy, and Law, 2*, 187–203.

Lubinski, D. & Dawis, R. V. (1992). Aptitudes, skills, and proficiencies. In M. D. Dunnette & L. M. Hough (Eds.) *Handbook of industrial/organizational psychology*, Vol. 3 (2nd ed., pp. 1–59). Palo Alto, CA: Consulting Psychology Press.

Lubinski, D. & Humphreys, L. G. (1990). A broadly based analysis of mathematical giftedness. *Intelligence, 14*, 327–355.

Lubinski, D. & Humphreys, L. G. (1992). Some bodily and medical correlates of mathematical giftedness and commensurate levels of socioeconomic status. *Intelligence, 16*, 99–115.

Lubinski, D. & Humphreys, L. G. (1996). Seeing the forest from the trees: When predicting the behavior or status of groups, correlate means. *Psychology, Public Policy, and Law, 2*, 363–376.

Lubinski, D. & Humphreys, L. G. (1997). Needed: Incorporating general intelligence into epidemiology and the social sciences. *Intelligence, 24*, 159–201.

Lucas, A., Morley, R., Cole, T. J., Lister, G. & Leeson-Payne, C. (1992). Breast milk and subsequent intelligence quotient in children born preterm. *Lancet, 339*, 261–264.

Luce, R. D. (1986). *Response times: Their role in inferring elementary mental organization.* New York: Oxford University Press.

Luo, D., Petrill, S. A. & Thompson, L. A. (1994). An exploration of genetic g: Hierarchical factor analysis of cognitive data from the Western Reserve Twin Project. *Intelligence, 18*, 335–347.

Lush, J. L. (1968). Genetic unknowns and animal breeding a century after Mendel. *Transactions of the Kansas Academy of Sciences, 71*, 309–314.

Lutzenberger, W., Burbaumer, N., Flor, H., Rockstroh, B. & Elbert, T. (1992). Dimensional analysis of the human EEG and intelligence. *Neuroscience Letters, 143*, 10–14.

Lynam, D., Moffitt, T. & Stouthamer-Loeber, M. (1993). Explaining the relation between

IQ and delinquency: Class, race, test motivation. school failure, or self-control? *Journal of Abnormal Psychology, 102*, 187–196.

Lynn, R. (1987a). Nutrition and intelligence. In P. A. Vernon (Ed.), *Biological approaches to the study of human intelligence* (pp. 243–258). Norwood, NJ: Ablex.

Lynn, R. (1987b). Japan: Land of the rising IQ: A reply to Flynn. *Bulletin of the British Psychological Society, 40*, 464–468.

Lynn, R. (1987c). The intelligence of Mongoloids: A psychometric, evolutionary, and neurological theory. *Personality and Individual Differences, 8*, 813–844.

Lynn, R. (1988). Multivariate analyses of the sociology of intelligence. In J. Nesselroade & R. B. Cattell (Eds.), *Handbook of multivariate experimental psychology* (pp. 939–960). New York: Plenum Press.

Lynn, R. (1989). Positive correlations between height, head size and IQ: A nutrition theory of the secular increases in intelligence. *British Journal of Educational Psychology, 59*, 372–377.

Lynn, R. (1990a). Differential rates of secular increase of five major primary abilities. *Social Biology, 38*, 137–141.

Lynn, R. (1990b). The role of nutrition in secular increases in intelligence. *Personality and Individual Differences, 11*, 273–285.

Lynn, R. (1991a). Race differences in intelligence: A global perspective. *Mankind Quarterly, 31*, 254–296.

Lynn, R. (1991b). The evolution of racial differences in intelligence. *Mankind Quarterly, 32*, 99–121.

Lynn, R. (1992). Does Spearman's g decline at high IQ levels? Some evidence from Scotland. *Journal of Genetic Psychology, 153*, 229–230.

Lynn, R. (1994a). Some reinterpretations of the Minnesota Transracial Adoption Study. *Intelligence, 19*, 21–28.

Lynn, R. (1994b). Sex differences in intelligence and brain size: A paradox resolved. *Personality and Individual Differences, 17*, 257–271.

Lynn, R. (1996). *Dysgenics: Genetic deterioration in modern populations.* Westport, CT: Praeger.

Lynn, R. & Cooper, C. (1993). A secular decline in Spearman's g in France. *Learning and Individual Differences, 5*, 43–48.

Lynn, R. & Cooper, C. (1994). A secular decline in the strength of Spearman's g in Japan. *Current Psychology, 13*, 3–9.

Lynn, R. & Hampson, S. (1986). The rise of national intelligence: Evidence from Britain, Japan and the U.S.A. *Personality and Individual Differences, 7*, 23–32.

Lynn, R., Hampson, S. L. & Mullineux, J. C. (1987). A long-term increase in the fluid intelligence of English children. *Nature, 328*, 797.

Lynn, R. & Holmshaw, M. (1990). Black-white differences in reaction times and intelligence. *Social Behavior and Personality, 18*, 299–308.

Lynn, R. & Owen, K. (1994). Spearman's hypothesis and test score differences between whites, Indians, and blacks in South Africa. *Journal of General Psychology, 12*, 27–36.

Lynn, R. & Pagliari, C. (1994). The intelligence of American children is still rising. *Journal of Biosocial Science, 26*, 65–67.

Lynn, R,, Wilson, R. G. & Gault, A. (1989). Simple musical tests as measures of Spearman's g. *Personality and Individual Differences, 10*, 25–28.

Maccoby, E. E. & Jacklin, C. N. (1974). *The psychology of sex differences.* Stanford, CA: Stanford University Press.

MacDonald, K. (1994). *A people that shall dwell alone.* Westport, CT: Praeger.

Mackintosh, N. J. (Ed.) (1995). *Cyril Burt: Fraud or framed?* Oxford: Oxford University Press.

Mackintosh, N. J. (1996). Sex differences and IQ. *Journal of Biosocial Science, 28,* 559–572.

Mackintosh, N. J. & Mascie-Taylor, C. G. N. (1985). The IQ question. Annex D to *Education for all.* (Chairman, Lord Swann) Report of the Committee of Inquiry into the Education of Children from Ethnic Minority Groups. London: Her Majesty's Stationery Office.

MacLean, C. J., Adams, M. S., Leyshon, W. C., Workman, P. L., Reed, T. E., Gershowitz, H. & Weitkamp, L. R. (1974). Genetic studies on hybrid populations. III. Blood pressure in an American black community. *American Journal of Human Genetics, 26,* 614–626.

Maeroff, G. E. (1988). Withered hopes, stillborn dreams: The dismal panorama of urban school. *Phi Delta Kappan, 69,* 633–638.

Manning, W. H. & Jackson, R. (1984). College entrance examinations: Objective selection or gatekeeping for the economically privileged. In C. R. Reynolds & R. T. Brown (Eds.), *Perspectives on bias in mental testing.* New York: Plenum Press.

Marshalek, B., Lohman, D. F. & Snow, R. E. (1983). The complexity continuum in the radex and hierarchical models of intelligence. *Intelligence, 7,* 107–127.

Martin, N. G. (1975). The inheritance of scholastic abilities in a sample of twins, II. Genetical analysis of examination results. *Annals of Human Genetics, 39,* 219–229.

Mascie-Taylor, C. G. N. (1989). Spouse similarity for IQ and personality and convergence. *Behavior Genetics, 19,* 223–227.

Matarazzo, J. D. (1972). *Wechsler's measurement and appraisal of adult intelligence* (5th ed.). Baltimore: Williams & Wilkins.

Maxwell, A. E. (1972a). Factor analysis: Thomson's sampling theory recalled. *British Journal of Mathematical and Statistical Psychology, 25,* 1–21.

Maxwell, A. E. (1972b). The WPPSI: A marked discrepancy in the correlations of the subtests for good and poor readers. *British Journal of Mathematical and Statistical Psychology, 25,* 283–291.

Maxwell, A. E., Fenwisk, P. B., Fenton, G. W. & Dollimore, J. (1974). Reading ability and brain function: A simple statistical model. *Psychological Medicine, 4,* 274–280.

McGarry-Roberts, P. A., Stelmack, R. M. & Campbell, K. B. (1992). Intelligence, reaction time, and event-related potentials. *Intelligence, 16,* 289–313.

McGue, M. & Bouchard, T. J., Jr. (1989). Genetic and environmental determinants of information processing and special mental abilities: A twin analysis. In R. J. Sternberg (Ed.), *Advances in the psychology of human intelligence* (pp. 7–45). Hillsdale, NJ: Erlbaum.

McGue, M., Bouchard, T. J., Jr., Iacono, W. G. & Lykken, D. T. (1993). Behavioral genetics of cognitive ability: A life-span perspective. In R. Plomin & G. E. McClearn (Eds.), *Nature, nurture, and psychology* (pp. 59–76). Washington, DC: American Psychological Association.

McGue, M., Bouchard, T. J., Jr., Lykken, D. T. & Feuer, D. (1984). Information processing abilities in twins reared apart. *Intelligence, 8,* 239–258.

McHenry, J. J., Hough, L. M., Toquam, J. L., Hanson, M. L., & Ashworth, S. (1990). Project A validity results: The relationship between predictor and criterion domains. *Personnel Psychology, 43,* 335–354.

McKeever, W. F. (1995). Hormone and hemisphericity hypotheses regarding cognitive sex differences: Possible future explanatory power, but current empirical chaos. *Learning and Individual Differences, 7,* 323–340.

Meeker, M. (1966). Immediate memory and its correlates with school achievement. Unpublished Ed.D. thesis, University of Southern California.

Messick, S. (1989). Validity. In R. L. Linn (Ed.), *Educational measurement* (3rd ed., pp. 13–103). New York: Macmillan.

Messick, S. (1992). Multiple intelligences or multilevel intelligence? Selective emphasis on distinctive properties of hierarchy: On Gardner's *Frames of Mind* and Sternberg's *Beyond IQ* in the context of theory and research on the structure of human abilities. *Psychological Inquiry, 3,* 365–384.

Miller, E. M. (1994). Intelligence and brain myelination: A hypothesis. *Personality and Individual Differences, 17,* 803–832.

Mincy, R. B., Sawhill, I. V. & Wolf, D. A. (1990). The underclass: Definition and measurement. *Science, 248,* 450–453.

Modgil, S. & Modgil, C. (Eds.) (1987). *Arthur Jensen: Consensus and controversy.* New York: Falmer.

Moffitt, T. E., Caspi, A., Harkness, A. R. & Silva, P. A. (1993). The natural history of change in intellectual performance: Who changes? How much? Is it meaningful? *Journal of Child Psychology and Psychiatry, 14,* 455–506.

Moffitt, T. E., Caspi, A., Silva, P. A. & Stouthamer-Loeber, M. (1995). Individual differences in personality and intelligence are linked to crime: Cross-context evidence from nations, neighborhoods, genders, races, and age-cohorts. In J. Hagan (Ed.), *Current perspectives on aging and the life cycle,* Vol. 4, *Delinquency and disrepute in the life course: Contextual and dynamic analyses* (pp. 1–34). Greenwich, CT: JAI Press.

Moffitt, T. E., Gabrielli, W. F., Mednick, S. A. & Schulsinger, F. (1981). Socioeconomic status, IQ, and delinquency. *Journal of Abnormal Psychology, 90,* 152–156.

Montie, J. E. & Fagan, J. F. (1988). Racial differences in IQ: Item analysis of the Stanford-Binet at 3 years. *Intelligence, 12,* 315–332.

Morris, R. D. & Hopkins, W. D. (1995) Amount of information as a determinant of simple reaction time in chimpanzees (*Pan troglodytes*). Unpublished report. Yerkes Regional Primate Center, Emory University, Atlanta, GA.

Mulaik, S. A. (1972). *The foundations of factor analysis.* New York: McGraw-Hill.

Murray, C. & Herrnstein, R. J. (1992). What's really behind the SAT-score decline? *Public Interest,* no. 106 (Winter), 32–56.

Naglieri, J. A. & Jensen, A. R. (1987). Comparison of black-white differences on the WISC-R and the K-ABC: Spearman's hypothesis. *Intelligence, 11,* 21–43.

Nagoshi, C. T. & Johnson, R. C. (1986). The ubiquity of *g. Personality and Individual Differences, 7,* 201–208.

Nagoshi, C. T. & Johnson, R. C. (1987). Between- versus within-family factor analyses of cognitive abilities. *Intelligence, 11,* 305–316.

Nagoshi, C. T., Johnson, R. C. & Honbo, K. A. M. (1993). Family background, cognitive abilities, and personality as predictors of educational and occupational attainment across two generations. *Journal of Biosocial Science, 25,* 259–276.

National Assessment of Educational Progress (1985). *The reading report card.* Princeton, NJ: Educational Testing Service.

National Commission on Excellence in Education (1983). *A nation at risk: The imperative for educational reform.* Washington, DC: U.S. Government Printing Office.

Naylor, A. F. & Myrianthopoulos, N.C. (1967). The relation of ethnic and selected socioeconomic factors to human birth-weight. *Annals of Human Genetics, 31,* 71–83.

Neale, M. C. & Cardon, L. R. (1992). *Methodology for genetic studies of twins and families.* Boston: Kluwer.

Neel, J. V., Schull, W. J., Yamamoto, M., Uchida, S., Yanase, T. & Fujiki, N. (1970). The effect of parental consanguinity and inbreeding in Hiado, Japan: II. Physical development, tapping rate, blood pressure, intelligence quotient, and school performance. *American Journal of Human Genetics, 22,* 263–286.

Nei, M. & Roychoudhury, A. K. (1993). Evolutionary relationships of human populations on a global scale. *Molecular Biology and Evolution, 10,* 927–943.

Nesse, R. M. & Williams, G. C. (1994). *Why we get sick: The new science of Darwinian medicine.* New York: Random House.

Nettelbeck, T. (1985). Inspection time and mild mental retardation. In N. R. Ellis & N. W. Bray (Eds.), *International review of research on mental retardation,* Vol. 13 (pp. 109–141). New York: Academic Press.

Nettelbeck, T. (1987). Inspection time and intelligence. In P. A. Vernon (Ed.), *Speed of information-processing and intelligence* (pp. 295–346). Norwood, NJ: Ablex.

Nettlebeck, T. & Rabbitt, P. M. A. (1992). Aging, cognitive performance, and mental speed. *Intelligence, 16,* 189–205.

Neubauer, A. C. & Freudenthaler, H. H. (1994). Reaction time in a sentence-picture verification test and intelligence: Individual strategies and effects of extended practice. *Intelligence, 19,* 193–218.

Newman, H. H., Freeman, F. N. & Holzinger, K. J. (1937). *Twins: A study of heredity and environment.* Chicago: University of Chicago Press.

Nichols, P. L. (1984). Familial mental retardation. *Behavior Genetics, 14,* 161–170.

Nichols, R. C. (1987a). Interchange: Nichols replies to Flynn. In S. Modgil & C. Modgil (Eds.), *Arthur Jensen: Consensus and controversy* (pp. 233–234). New York: Falmer.

Nichols, R. C. (1987b). Racial differences in intelligence. In S. Modgil & C. Modgil (Eds.), *Arthur Jensen: Consensus and controversy* (pp. 213–220). New York: Falmer.

Nikolova, M. (1994). Genetic and environmental influences on morphological characteristics. *Mankind Quarterly, 35,* 27–38.

Nyborg, H. (1984). Performance and intelligence in hormonally different groups. In G. J. DeVries et al. (Eds.), *Progress in brain research,* Vol. 61 (pp. 491–508). Amsterdam: Elsevier.

Office of the Assistant Secretary of Defense (Manpower, Research Affairs, and Logistics). (1982). *Profile of American youth: 1980 nationwide administration of the Armed Services Vocational Aptitude Battery.* Washington, DC: Department of Defense.

Ogbu, J. U. (1978). *Minority education and caste: The American system in cross-cultural perspective.* New York: Academic Press.

Ogbu, J. U. (1994). Culture and intelligence. In R. J. Sternberg (Ed.), *Encyclopedia of human intelligence*, Vol. 2 (pp. 328–338). New York: Macmillan.

Olea, M. M. & Ree, J. M. (1994). Predicting pilot and navigator criteria: Not much more than *g*. *Journal of Applied Psychology, 79*, 845–851.

Olson, H. C. (1994). Fetal alcohol syndrome. In R. J. Sternberg (Ed.), *Encyclopedia of human intelligence*, Vol. 1 (pp. 439–443). New York: Macmillan.

Osborne, R. T. (1980). *Twins, black and white*. Athens, GA: Foundation for Human Understanding.

Osborne, R. T. & McGurk, F. C. J. (1982). *The testing of Negro intelligence*, Vol. 2. Athens, GA: Foundation for Human Understanding.

O'Toole, B. J. (1990). Intelligence and behavior and motor vehicle accident mortality. *Accident Analysis and Prevention, 22*, 211–221.

O'Toole, B. J. & Stankov, L. (1992). Ultimate validity of psychological tests. *Personality and Individual Differences, 13*, 699–716.

Owen, K. (1989). *Test and item bias: The suitability of the Junior Aptitude Test as a common test battery for white, Indian, and black pupils in Standard 7* (Report P-96, Institute for Psychological and Edumetric Research). Pretoria, South Africa: Human Sciences Research Council.

Owen, K. (1992). The suitability of Raven Standard Progressive Matrices for various groups in South Africa. *Personality and Individual Differences, 13*, 149–159.

Page, E. B. & Jarjoura, D. (1979). Seeking the cause of correlations among mental abilities: Large twin analyses in a national testing program. Special Invited Issue on "Intelligence," *Journal of Research and Development in Education* (pp. 208–210). Baltimore: Johns Hopkins University Press.

Paul, S. M. (1980). Sibling resemblance in mental ability: A review. *Behavior Genetics, 10*, 277–290.

Pearson, K. (1901). On lines and planes of closest fit to systems of points in space. *Philosophical Magazine, 2*, 559–572.

Pedersen, N. L., Plomin, R. & McClearn, G. E. (1994). Is there G beyond *g*? (Is there genetic influence on specific cognitive abilities independent of genetic influence on general cognitive ability?) *Intelligence, 18*, 133–143.

Pedersen, N. L., Plomin, R., Nesselroade, J. R. & McClearn, G. E. (1992). A quantitative genetic analysis of cognitive abilities during the second half of the life span. *Psychological Science, 3*, 346–352.

Peoples, C. E., Fagan, J. F, III & Drotar, D. (1995). The influence of race on 3-year-old children's performance on the Stanford-Binet: Fourth edition. *Intelligence, 21*, 69–82.

Plomin, R. (1987). Genetics of intelligence. In S. Modgil & C. Modgil (Eds.), *Arthur Jensen: Consensus and controversy* (pp. 41–53). New York: Falmer.

Plomin, R. (1988). The nature and nurture of cognitive abilities. In R. J. Sternberg (Ed.), *Advances in the psychology of human intelligence*, Vol. 4 (pp. 1–33). Hillsdale, NJ: Erlbaum.

Plomin, R. (1990). *Nature and nurture: An introduction to human behavioral genetics*. Pacific Grove, CA: Brooks/Cole.

Plomin, R. (1994). *Genetics and experience*. Thousand Oaks, CA: Sage.

Plomin, R. & Bergeman, C. S. (1991). The nature of nurture: Genetic influences on "environmental" measures. *Behavioral and Brain Sciences, 14*, 373–387.

Plomin, R. & Daniels, D. ((1987). Why are children in the same family so different from one another? *Behavioral and Brain Sciences, 10,* 1–16.

Plomin, R., DeFries, J. C. & Loehlin, J. C. (1977). Genotype-environment interaction and correlation in the analysis of human behavior. *Psychological Bulletin, 84,* 309–322.

Plomin, R., Defries, J. C. & McClearn, G. E. (1990). *Behavioral genetics: A primer* (2nd ed.). New York: W. H. Freeman.

Plomin, R. & McClearn, G. E. (Eds.) (1993). *Nature nurture and psychology.* Washington, DC: American Psychological Association.

Plomin, R., McClearn, G. E., Smith, D. L., Skuder, P., Vignetti, S., Chorney, M. J., Chorney, K., Kasarda, S., Thompson,, L. A., Detterman, D. K., Petrill, S. A., Daniels, J., Owen, M. J. & McGuffin, P. (1995). Allelic associations between 100 DNA markers and high versus low IQ. *Intelligence, 21,* 31–48.

Plomin, R., McClearn, G. E., Smith, D. L., Vignetti, S., Chorney, M. J., Corney, K., Venditti, C. P., Kasarda, S., Thompson, L. A., Detterman, D. K., Daniels, J., Owen, M. & McGuffin, P. (1994). DNA markers associated with high versus low IQ: The IQ Quantitative Trait Loci (QTL) Project. *Behavior Genetics, 24,* 107–118.

Plomin, R. & Neiderhiser, J. M. (1992). Quantitative genetics, molecular genetics, and intelligence. *Intelligence, 15,* 369–387.

Plomin, R., Pedersen, N. L., Lichtenstein, P. & McClearn, G. E. (1994). Variability and stability in cognitive abilities are largely genetic later in life. *Behavior Genetics, 24,* 207–215.

Plomin, R. & Rende, R. (1991). Human behavioral genetics. *Annual Review of Psychology, 42,* 161–190.

Polednak, A. P. (1989). *Racial and ethnic differences in disease.* Oxford: Oxford University Press.

Polich, J. & Kok, A. (1995). Cognitive and biological determinants of P300: An integrative review. *Biological Psychology, 41,* 103–146.

Pool, R. (1990). Who will do science in the 1990s? *Science, 248,* 433–435.

Poortinga, Y. H. (1971). Cross-cultural comparison of maximum performance tests: Some methodological aspects and some experiments with simple auditory and visual stimuli. *Psychologica Africana* (Monograph Supplement No. 6).

Posner, M. I. (1978). *Chronometric explorations of mind.* Hillsdale, NJ: Erlbaum.

Posner, M. I., Petersen, S. E., Fox, P. T. & Raichle, M. E. (1988). Localization of cognitive operations in the human brain. *Science, 240,* 1627–1631.

Post, R. H. (1982). Population differences in visual acuity: A review, with speculative notes on selection relaxation. *Social Biology, 29,* 319–343.

Pressey, S. L. & Teter, G. F. (1919). Minor studies from the psychological laboratory of Indiana University: I. A comparison of colored and white children by means of a group scale of intelligence. *Journal of Applied Psychology, 3,* 277–282.

Rae, C., Scott, R. B., Thompson, C. H., Kemp, G. J., Dumughn, I., Styles, P., Tracey, I. & Radda, G. K. (1996). Is pH a biochemical marker of IQ? *Proceedings of the Royal Society* (London), *263,* 1061–1064.

Ramey, C. T. (1992). High-risk children and IQ: Altering intergenerational patterns. *Intelligence, 16,* 239–256.

Ramey, C. T. (1993). A rejoinder to Spitz's critique of the Abecedarian experiment. *Intelligence, 17,* 25–30.

Ramey, C. T. (1994). Abecedarian Project. In R. J. Sternberg (Ed.), *Encyclopedia of human intelligence*, Vol. 1 (pp. 1–3). New York: Macmillan.

Raz, N., Torres, I. J., Spencer, W. D., Millman, D., Baertschi, J. C. & Sarpel, G. (1993). Neuroanatomical correlates of age-sensitive and age-invariant cognitive abilities: An *in vivo* MRI investigation. *Intelligence, 17*, 407–422.

Raz, N., Willerman, L., Ingmundson, P. & Hanlomnf, M. (1993). Aptitude-related differences in auditory recognition masking. *Intelligence, 7*, 71–90.

Ree, M. J. & Carretta, T. R. (1994). The correlation of general cognitive ability and psychomotor tracking tests. *International Journal of Selection and Assessment, 2*, 209–216.

Ree, M. J. & Earles, J. A. (1991a). The stability of convergent estimates of *g*. *Intelligence, 15*, 271–278.

Ree, M. J. & Earles, J. A. (1991b). Predicting training success: Not much more than *g*. *Personnel Psychology, 44*, 321–332,

Ree, M. J. & Earles, J. A. (1992a). Intelligence is the best predictor of job performance. *Current Directions in Psychological Science, 1*, 86–89.

Ree, M. J. & Earles, J. A. (1992b). *Subtest and composite validity of ASVAB Forms 11, 12, and 13 for technical training courses* (AL-R 1991–0107). Brooks Air Force Base, TX: Air Force Human Resources Laboratory, Manpower and Personnel Division.

Ree, M. J. & Earles, J. A. (1993). *g* is to psychology what carbon is to chemistry: A reply to Sternberg and Wagner, McClelland, and Calfee. *Current Directions in Psychological Science, 2*, 11–12.

Ree, M. J. & Earles, J. A. (1994). The ubiquitous predictiveness of *g*. In M. G. Rumsey, C. B. Walker & J. H. Harris (Eds.), *Personnel selection and classification* (pp. 127–135). Hillsdale, NJ: Erlbaum.

Ree, M. J., Earles, J. A. & Teachout, M. S. (1994). Predicting job performance: Not much more than *g*. *Journal of Applied Psychology, 79*, 518–524.

Reed, T. E. (1969a). Caucasian genes in American Negroes. *Science, 165*, 762–768.

Reed, T. E. (1969b). Letters. *Science, 165*, 1353.

Reed, T. E. (1971). The population variance of the proportion of genetic admixture in human intergroup hybrids. *Proceedings of the National Academy of Science U.S.A. 68*, 3168–3169.

Reed, T. E. (1973). Number of gene loci required for accurate estimation of ancestral population proportions in individual human hybrids. *Nature, 244*, 575–576.

Reed, T. E. (1984). Mechanism for heritability of intelligence. *Nature, 311*, 417.

Reed, T. E. (1988a). Narrow-sense heritability estimates for nerve conduction velocity and residual latency in mice. *Behavior Genetics, 18*, 595–603.

Reed, T. E. (1988b). A neurophysiological basis for the heritability of intelligence. In H. J. Jerison & I. Jerison (Eds.), *Intelligence and evolutionary biology*. Berlin: Springer.

Reed, T. E. (1997). ''The genetic hypothesis'': It could have been better tested. *American Psychologist, 52*, 77–78.

Reed, T. E. & Jensen, A. R. (1991). Arm nerve conduction velocity (NCV), brain NCV, reaction time, and intelligence. *Intelligence, 15*, 33–47.

Reed, T. E. & Jensen, A. R. (1992). Conduction velocity in a brain nerve pathway of normal adults correlates with intelligence level. *Intelligence, 16*, 259–272.

Reed, T. E. & Jensen, A. R. (1993). Choice reaction time and visual pathway nerve conduction velocity both correlate with intelligence but appear not to correlate with each other: Implications for information processing. *Intelligence, 17,* 191–203.

Reinisch, J. M., Sanders, S. A., Mortensen, E. L. & Rubin, D. B. (1995). In utero exposure to phenobarbital and intelligence deficits in adult men. *Journal of the American Medical Association, 274,* 1518–1525.

Reiss, A. J., Jr. & Roth, J. A. (Eds.) *Understanding and preventing violence.* Washington, DC: National Academy Press.

Reiss, A. L., Abrams, M. T., Singer, H. S., Ross, J. L., & Denckla, M. B. (1996). Brain development, gender and IQ in children: A volumetric imaging study. *Brain, 119,* 1763–1774.

Reynolds, C. R. (1980). Differential construct validity of intelligence as popularly measured: Correlations of age with raw scores on the WISC-R for blacks, whites, males, and females. *Intelligence, 4,* 371–379.

Reynolds, C. R. & Brown, R. T. (Eds.) (1984). *Perspectives on bias in mental testing.* New York: Plenum Press.

Reynolds, C. R. & Jensen, A. R. (1983). WISC-R subscale patterns of abilities of blacks and whites matched on Full Scale IQ. *Journal of Educational Psychology, 75,* 207–214.

Ricciuti, H. N. (1994). Nutrition. In R. J. Sternberg (Ed.), *Encyclopedia of human intelligence,* Vol. 2 (pp. 775–779). New York: Macmillan.

Rijsdijk, F. V., Boomsma, D. L. & Vernon, P. A. (1995). Genetic analysis of peripheral nerve conduction velocity in twins. *Behavior Genetics, 25,* 341–348.

Roberts, J. (1971). Intellectual development of children: By demographic and socioeconomic factors. *Vital and health statistics,* Series 11, No. 10 (DHEW Publication No. (HSM) 72–1012.) Rockville, MD: National Center for Health Statistics, Department of Health, Education, and Welfare.

Roberts, R. D., Beh, H. C. & Stankov, L. (1988). Hick's law, competing-task performance, and intelligence. *Intelligence, 12,* 111–130.

Rodgers, J. L., Rowe, D. C. & May, K. (1994). DF analysis of NLSY IQ/Achievement data: Nonshared environmental influences. *Intelligence, 19,* 157–177.

Rowe, D. C. (1994). *The limits of family influence: Genes, experience, and behavior.* New York: Guilford Press.

Rowe, D. C. & Cleveland, H. H. (1996). Academic achievement in Blacks and Whites: Are the developmental processes similar? *Intelligence, 23,* 205–228.

Rowe, D. C., Vazsonyi, A. T. & Flannery, D. J. (1994). No more than skin deep: Ethnic and racial similarity in developmental process. *Psychological Review, 101,* 396–413.

Rowe, D. C., Vazsonyi, A. T. & Flannery, D. J. (1995). Ethnic and racial similarity in developmental process: A study of academic achievement. *Psychological Science, 6,* 33–38.

Rushton, J. P. (1989). Japanese inbreeding depression scores: Predictors of cognitive differences between blacks and whites. *Intelligence, 13,* 43–51.

Rushton, J. P. (1995). *Race, evolution, and behavior.* New Brunswick, NJ: Transaction Books.

Rushton, J. P. & Ankney, C. D. (1996). Brain size and cognitive ability: Correlations with age, sex, social class, and race. *Psychonomic Bulletin and Review, 3,* 21–36.

Rushton, J. P. & Endler, N. S. (1977). Person by situation interactions in academic achievement. *Journal of Personality, 45,* 297–309.

Rushton, J. P. & Osborne, R. T. (1995). Genetic and environmental contributions to cranial capacity in black and white adolescents. *Intelligence, 20,* 1–13.

Ryan, A. S. Pratt, W. F., Wysong, J. L., Lewandowski, G., McNally, J. W. & Krieger, F. W. (1991). A comparison of breast-feeding data from the National Surveys of Family Growth and the Ross Laboratories mothers' surveys. *American Journal of Public Health, 81,* 1049–1052.

Salthouse, T. A. (1985). *A theory of cognitive aging.* Amsterdam: North-Holland.

Sanders, C. E., Lubinski, D. & Benbow, C. P. (1995). Does the Defining Issues Test measure psychological phenomena distinct from verbal ability? An examination of Lykken's query. *Journal of Personality and Social Psychology, 69,* 498–504.

Sarich, V. M. (1995). In defense of *The Bell Curve*: The reality of race and the importance of human differences. *Skeptic, 3,* 84–93.

Scarr-Salapatek, S. (1971). Race, social class, and IQ. *Science, 174,* 1285–1295.

Scarr, S. (1989). Protecting general intelligence: Constructs and consequences for interventions. In R. L. Linn (Ed.), *Intelligence: Measurement, theory, and public policy* (pp. 74–118). Chicago: University of Illinois Press.

Scarr, S. (1996). How people make their own environments: Implications for parents and policy makers. *Psychology, Public Policy, and Law, 2,* 204–228.

Scarr, S. (1997). Behavior-genetic and socialization theories of intelligence: Truce and reconciliation. In R. J. Sternberg & E. Grigorenko (Eds.), *Intelligence, heredity, and environment* (pp. 3–41). Cambridge: Cambridge University Press.

Scarr, S., Caparulo, B. K., Ferdman, B. M., Tower, R. B. & Caplan, J. (1983). Developmental status and school achievements of minority and non-minority children from birth to 18 years in a British Midlands town. *British Journal of Developmental Psychology, 1,* 31–48.

Scarr, S. & Carter-Saltzman, L. (1982). Genetics and intelligence. In R. J. Sternberg (Ed.), *Handbook of human intelligence* (pp. 792–896). Cambridge: Cambridge University Press.

Scarr, S. & McCartney, K. (1983). How people make their own environments: A theory of genotype → environment effects. *Child Development, 54,* 424–435.

Scarr, S., Pakstis, A. J., Katz, S. H. & Barker, W. B. (1977). Absence of a relationship between degree of white ancestry and intellectual skills within a black population. *Human Genetics, 39,* 69–86.

Scarr, S. & Weinberg, R. A. (1976). IQ test performance of black children adopted by white families. *American Psychologist, 31,* 726–739.

Scarr, S. & Weinberg, R. A. (1978). The influence of "family background" on intellectual attainment. *American Sociological Review, 43,* 674–692.

Schafer, E. W. P. (1982). Neural adaptability: A biological determinant of behavioral intelligence. *International Journal of Neuroscience, 17,* 183–191.

Schafer, E. W. P. (1985). Neural adaptability: A biological determinant of *g* factor intelligence. *Behavioral and Brain Sciences, 8,* 240–241.

Schafer, E. W. P., Amochaev, A. & Russell, M. J. (1982). Brain response timing correlates with information mediated variations in reaction time. *Psychophysiology, 19,* 345.

Schafer, E. W. P. & Marcus, M. M. (1973). Self-stimulation alters human sensory brain responses. *Science, 181,* 175–177.

Schaie, K. W. (1994). The course of adult intellectual development. *American Psychologist, 49*, 304–313.

Schmid, J. & Leiman, J. M. (1957). The development of hierarchical factor solutions. *Psychometrika, 22*, 53–61.

Schmidt, F. L. (1992). What do data really mean? Research findings, meta-analysis, and cumulative knowledge in psychology. *American Psychologist, 47*, 1173–1181.

Schmidt, F. L. & Hunter, J. E. (1981). Employment testing: Old theories and new research findings. *American Psychologist, 36*, 1128–1137.

Schmidt, F. L., Hunter, J. E. & Outerbridge, A. N. (1986). Impact of job experience and ability on job knowledge, work sample performance, and supervisory ratings of job performance. *Journal of Applied Psychology, 71*, 432–439.

Schmidt, F. L., Hunter, J. E., Outbridge, A. N. & Goff, S. (1988). Joint relation of experience and ability with job performance: Test of three hypotheses. *Journal of Applied Psychology, 73*, 46–57.

Schmidt, F. L., Law, K., Hunter, J. E., Rothstein, H. R., Pearlman, K. & McDaniel, M. (1993). Refinements in validity generalization methods: Implications for the situational specificity hypothesis. *Journal of Applied Psychology, 78*, 3–12.

Schmidt, F. L., Ones, D. S. & Hunter (1992). Personnel selection. *Annual Review of Psychology, 43*, 627–670.

Schneider, R. J., Ackerman, P. L. & Kanfer, R. (1996). To ''act wisely in human relations'': Exploring the dimensions of social competence. *Personality and Individual Differences, 21*, 469–482.

Schoendorf, K. C., Hogue, C. J. R., Kleinman, J. C. & Rowley, D. (1992). Mortality among infants of black as compared with white college-educated parents. *New England Journal of Medicine, 326*, 1522–1526.

Schoenemann, P. T. (1995). Brain size scaling and body composition in mammals: Implications for sex difference in brain size in *Homo sapiens*. Paper presented at the annual meeting of the American Association of Physical Anthropologists. (Department of Anthropology, University of California, Berkeley).

Schoenemann, P. T. (1997). The evolution of the human brain and its relationship to behavior. Unpublished doctoral dissertation. Berkeley: University of California.

Schoenthaler, S. J., Amos, S. P., Eysenck, H. J., Peritz, E. & Yudkin, J. (1991). Controlled trial of vitamin-mineral supplementation: Effects on intelligence and performance. *Personality and Individual Differences, 12*, 351–362.

Schull, W. J. & Neel, J. V. (1965). *The effects of inbreeding on Japanese children*. New York: Harper & Row.

Seemanova, E. (1971). A study of children of incestuous matings. *Human Heredity, 21*, 108–128.

Segal, N. L. (1985). Monozygotic and dizygotic twins: A comparative analysis of mental ability profiles. *Child Development, 56*, 1051–1058.

Segal, N. L. (1997). Same-age unrelated siblings: A unique test of within-family environmental influences on IQ similarity. *Journal of Educational Psychology, 89*, 381–390.

Shuey, A. M. (1966). *The testing of Negro intelligence* (2nd ed.). New York: Social Science Press.

Silverstein, A. B. (1973). Factor structure of the Wechsler Intelligence Scale for Children for three ethnic groups. *Journal of Educational Psychology, 65*, 408–410.

Silverstein, A. (1982). Factor structure of the Wechsler Adult Intelligence Scale. *Journal of Consulting and Clinical Psychology, 50*, 661–664.

Simonton, D. K. (1994). *Greatness: Who makes history and why*. New York: Guilford Press.

Skodak, M. & Skeels, H. M. (1949). A final follow-up study of one hundred adopted children. *Journal of Genetic Psychology, 75*, 85–125.

Skuder, P., Plomin, R., McClearn, G. E., Smither, D. L., Vignetti, S., Chorney, M. J., Chorney, K., Kasarda, S., Thompson, L. A., Detterman, D. K., Petrill, S. A., Daniels, J., Owen, M. J. & McGuffin, P. (1995). A polymorphism in mitochondrial DNA associated with IQ? *Intelligence, 21*, 1–11.

Slatis, H. M. & Hoenne, R. E. (1961). The effect of consanguinity on the distribution of continuously variable characteristics. *American Journal of Human Genetics, 13*, 28–31.

Smith, G. A. & McPhee, K. A. (1987). Performance on a coincidence timing task correlates with intelligence. *Intelligence, 11*, 161–167.

Smith, G. A. & Stanley, G. (1987). Comparing subtest profiles of *g* loadings and correlations with RT measures. *Intelligence, 11*, 291–298.

Snow, R. E. (1995). Pygmalion and intelligence? *Current Directions in Psychological Science, 4*, 169–171.

Snow, R. E., Kyllonen, P. C. & Marshalek, B. (1984). The topography of ability and learning correlations. In R. J. Sternberg (Ed.), *Advances in the psychology of human intelligence*, Vol. 2 (pp. 47–103). Hillsdale, NJ: Erlbaum.

Snow, R. E. & Yalow, E. (1982). Education and intelligence. In R. J. Sternberg (Ed.), *Handbook of human intelligence* (pp. 493–585). Cambridge: Cambridge University Press.

Snyderman, M. & Rothman, S. (1988). *The IQ controversy: The media and public policy*. New Brunswick, NJ: Transaction Books.

Sowell, T. (1981). Assumptions versus history in ethnic education. *Teachers College Record, 83*, 37–71.

Sowell, T. (1994). *Race and culture: A world view*. New York: Basic Books.

Spearman, C. (1904). General intelligence, objectively determined and measured. *American Journal of Psychology, 15*, 201–293.

Spearman, C. (1923). *The nature of "intelligence" and the principles of cognition*. London: Macmillan.

Spearman, C. (1927). *The abilities of man: Their nature and measurement*. New York: Macmillan.

Spearman, C. (1930). Autobiography. In C. Murchison (Ed.), *A history of psychology in autobiography*, Vol. 1 (pp. 299–333). Worcester, MA: Clark University Press. (Reprinted 1961 by Russell & Russell, New York).

Spearman, C. & Jones, L. W. (1950). *Human ability: A continuation of* The abilities of man. London: Macmillan.

Spielberger, C. D. (1958). On the relationship between anxiety and intelligence. *Journal of Consulting Psychology, 22*, 220–224.

Spielberger, C. D. & Sydeman, S. J. (1994). Anxiety. In R. J. Sternberg (Ed.), *Encyclopedia of human intelligence* (pp. 102–105). New York: Macmillan.

Spitz, H. H. (1986). *The raising of intelligence: A selected history of attempts to raise retarded intelligence*. Hillsdale, NJ: Erlbaum.

Spitz, H. H. (1988). Wechsler subtest patterns of mentally retarded groups: Relationship to g and to estimates of heritability. *Intelligence, 12,* 279–297.

Spitz, H. H. (1992). Does the Carolina Abecedarian early intervention project prevent sociocultural mental retardation? *Intelligence, 16,* 225–237.

Spitz, H. H. (1993a). When prophecy fails: On Ramey's response to Spitz's critique of the Abecedarian Project. *Intelligence, 17,* 17–23.

Spitz, H. H. (1993b). Spitz's reply to Ramey's response to Spitz's first reply to Ramey's first response to Spitz's critique of the Abecedarian Project. *Intelligence, 17,* 31–35.

Spuhler, J. N. & Lindzey, G. (1967). Racial differences in behavior. In J. Hirsch (Ed.), *Behavior genetic analysis* (pp. 366–414) New York: McGraw-Hill.

Staats, A. W. & Burns, G. L. (1981). Intelligence and child development: What intelligence is and how it is learned and functions. *Genetic Psychology Monographs, 104,* 237–301.

Steele, C. M. (1997). A threat in the air: How stereotypes shape intellectual identity and performance. *American Psychologist, 52,* 613–629.

Steele, C. M. & Aronson, J. (1995). Stereotype threat and the intellectual test performance of African Americans. *Journal of Personality and Social Psychology, 69,* 797–811.

Sternberg, R. J. (1977). *Intelligence, information processing, and analogical reasoning: The componential analysis of human abilities.* Hillsdale, NJ: Erlbaum.

Sternberg, R. J. (1980). Sketch of a componential subtheory of human intelligence. *Behavioral and Brain Sciences, 3,* 573–614.

Sternberg, R. J. (1984a). A contextualist view of the nature of intelligence. *International Journal of Psychology, 19,* 307–334.

Sternberg, R. J. (1984b). Toward a triarchic theory of human intelligence. *Behavioral and Brain Sciences, 7,* 269–315.

Sternberg, R. J. (1985). *Beyond IQ: A triarchic theory of human intelligence.* New York: Cambridge University Press.

Sternberg, R. J. (1987). "Gee, there's more than g!" A critique of Arthur Jensen's views on intelligence. In S. Modgil & C. Modgil (Eds.), *Arthur Jensen: Consensus and controversy.* New York: Falmer.

Sternberg, R. J. (1988). *The triarchic mind: A new theory of intelligence.* New York: Viking Press.

Sternberg, R. J., Conway, B. E., Ketron, J. L. & Bernstein, M. (1981). People's conceptions of intelligence. *Journal of Personality and Social Psychology, 41,* 37–55.

Sternberg, R. J. & Detterman, D. K. (1986). *What is intelligence? Contemporary viewpoints on its nature and definition.* Norwood, NJ: Ablex.

Sternberg, R. J. & Gardner, M. K. (1982). A componential interpretation of the general factor in human intelligence. In H. J. Eysenck (Ed.), *A model for intelligence* (pp. 231–254). New York: Springer-Verlag.

Sternberg, R. J. & Wagner, R. (1986). *Practical intelligence: Nature and origins of competence in the everyday world.* Cambridge: Cambridge University Press.

Sternberg, R. J., Wagner, R. K., Williams, W. M. & Horvath, J. A. (1995). Testing common sense. *American Psychologist, 50,* 912–926.

Sternberg, S. (1966). High-speed scanning in human memory. *Science, 153,* 652–654.

Sternberg, S. (1969). Memory-scanning: Mental processes revealed by reaction-time experiments. *American Scientist, 57,* 421–457.

Sticht, T. G., Hooke, L. R. & Caylor, J. S. (1981). *Literacy, oracy, and vocational aptitude as predictors of attrition and promotion in the Armed Services.* Alexandria, VA: Human Resources Research Organization.

Stoddard, G. D. (1943). *The meaning of intelligence.* New York: Macmillan.

Strauch, A. B. (1977). More on the sex × race interaction on cognitive measures. *Journal of Educational Psychology, 69*, 152–157.

Stumpf, H. (1995). Gender differences in performance on tests of cognitive abilities: Experimental design issues and empirical results. *Learning and Individual Differences, 7*, 275–287.

Sundet, J. M., Eilertsen, D. E., Tambs, K. & Magnus, P. (1994). No differential heritability of intelligence test scores across ability levels in Norway. *Behavior Genetics, 24*, 337–339.

Sundet, J. M., Tambs, K., Magnus, P. & Berg, K. (1988). On the question of secular trends in the heritability of intelligence scores: A study of Norwegian twins. *Intelligence, 12*, 47–59.

Tambs, K., Sundet, J. M. & Magnus, P. (1984). Heritability analysis of the WAIS subtests. *Intelligence, 8*, 283–293.

Tan, Ü. (1996). Correlations between nonverbal intelligence and peripheral nerve conduction velocity in right-handed subjects: Sex-related differences. *International Journal of Psychophysiology, 22*, 123–128.

Tavris, C. (1995). A place in the sun. *Skeptic, 3*, 62–63.

Teasdale, T. W. & Owen, D. R. (1984). Heredity and familial environment in intelligence and educational level—A sibling study. *Nature, 309*, 620–622.

Teasdale, T. W. & Owen, D. R. (1987). National secular trends in intelligence and education: A twenty-year cross-sectional study. *Nature, 325*, 119–121.

Teasdale, T. W. & Owen, D. R. (1989). Continuing secular increases in intelligence and a stable prevalence of high intelligence levels. *Intelligence, 13*, 255–262.

Terman, L. M. (1917). The intelligence quotient of Francis Galton in childhood. *American Journal of Psychology, 28*, 209–215.

Thompson, L. A., Detterman, D. K. & Plomin, R. (1991). Associations between cognitive abilities and scholastic achievement: Genetic overlap but environmental differences. *Psychological Science, 2*, 158–165.

Thompson, R. F. (1985). *The brain: A neuroscience primer* (2nd ed.). New York: W. H. Freeman.

Thomson, G. (1947). Charles Spearman 1863–1945. *Obituary Notices of Fellows of the Royal Society, 5*, 373–385.

Thomson, G. (1951). *The factorial analysis of human ability* (5th ed.). London: University of London Press.

Thorndike, E. L. (1917). Reading as reasoning: A study of mistakes in paragraph reading. *Journal of Educational Psychology, 8*, 323–332.

Thorndike, E. L. (1927). *The measurement of intelligence.* New York: Teachers College.

Thorndike, R. L. (1935). Organization of behavior in the albino rat. *Genetic Psychology Monographs, 17*, 1–70.

Thorndike, R. L. (1973). *Reading comprehension education in fifteen countries.* International Studies in Evaluation III. Stockholm: Almquist & Wiksell.

Thorndike, R. L. (1973–74). Reading as reasoning. *Reading Research Quarterly, 9*, 135–147.

Thorndike, R. L. (1984). *Intelligence as information processing: The mind and the computer.* Bloomington, IN: Center on Evaluation, Development, and Research.

Thorndike, R. L. (1985). The central role of general ability in prediction. *Multivariate Behavioral Research, 20,* 241–254.

Thorndike, R. L. (1987). Stability of factor loadings. *Personality and Individual Differences, 8,* 585–586.

Thorndike, R. L. (1994). g (Editorial). *Intelligence, 19,* 145–155.

Thorndike, R. L., Hagen, E. P. & Sattler, J. M. (1986). *Technical manual for the Stanford-Binet Intelligence Scale: Fourth edition.* Chicago: Riverside.

Thorndike, R. M. & Lohman, D. F. (1990). *A century of ability testing.* Chicago: Riverside.

Thurstone, L. L. (1931). Multiple factor analysis. *Psychological Review, 38,* 406–427.

Thurstone, L. L. (1947). *Multiple factor analysis.* Chicago: University of Chicago Press.

Toomepuu, J. (1986, November). Education and military manpower requirements. Paper presented at the annual meeting of the Council of Chief State School Officers, Louisville, KY.

Tuddenham, R. D. (1948). Soldier intelligence in World Wars I and II. *American Psychologist, 3,* 54–56.

Turkheimer, E. (1986). Cognitive development of adopted and fostered children. Unpublished doctoral dissertation, University of Texas, Austin.

Turkheimer, E. (1990). On the alleged independence of variance components and group differences. *European Bulletin of Cognitive Psychology, 20,* 686–690.

Turkheimer, E. (1991). Individual and group differences in adoption studies of IQ. *Psychological Bulletin, 110,* 392–405.

Turkheimer, E. & Gottesman, I. I. (1991). Individual differences and the canalization of human behavior. *Developmental Psychology, 27,* 18–22.

U.S. Department of Labor (1970). *Manual for the USES General Aptitude Test Battery* (4th ed.). Washington, DC: Government Printing Office.

Vandenberg, S. G. & Vogler, G. P. (1985). Genetic determinants of intelligence. In B. B. Wolman (Ed.), *Handbook of intelligence: Theories, measurements, and applications* (pp. 3–57). New York: Wiley.

Vernon, P. A. (1981a). Reaction time and intelligence in the mentally retarded. *Intelligence, 5,* 345–355.

Vernon, P. A. (1981b). Level I and Level II: A review. *Educational Psychologist, 16,* 45–64.

Vernon, P. A. (1983). Speed of information processing and general intelligence. *Intelligence, 7,* 53–70.

Vernon, P. A. (Ed.) (1987a). *Speed of information-processing and intelligence.* Norwood, NJ: Ablex.

Vernon, P. A. (1987b). Level I and Level II revisited. In S. Modgil & C. Modgil (Eds.) *Arthur Jensen: Consensus and controversy* (pp. 17–24). New York: Falmer.

Vernon, P. A. (1987c). New developments in reaction time research. In P. Vernon (Ed.), *Speed of information processing and intelligence* (pp. 1–20). Norwood, NJ: Ablex.

Vernon, P. A. (1988). Intelligence and speed of information processing. *Human Intelligence Newsletter, 9,* 8–9.

Vernon, P. A. (1989a). The heritability of measures of speed of information-processing. *Personality and Individual Differences, 10,* 573–576.

Vernon, P. A. (1989b). The generality of *g. Personality and Individual Differences, 10*, 803–804.

Vernon, P. A. (1990). The use of biological measures to estimate behavioral intelligence. *Educational Psychologist, 25*, 293–304.

Vernon, P. A. (1992). Intelligence, reaction times, and peripheral nerve conduction velocity. *Intelligence, 16*, 273–288.

Vernon, P. A. (1993a). Intelligence and neural efficiency. In D. K. Detterman (Ed.), *Current topics in human intelligence*, Vol. 3 (pp. 171–187). Norwood, NJ: Ablex.

Vernon, P. A. (Ed.) (1993b). *Biological approaches to the study of human intelligence*. Norwood, NJ: Ablex.

Vernon, P. A. & Jensen, A. R. (1984). Individual and group differences in intelligence and speed of information processing. *Personality and Individual Differences, 5*, 411–423. (Corrigendum to Fig. 1: *PAID, 6*, 291.)

Vernon, P. A. & Kantor, L. (1986). Reaction time correlations with intelligence test scores obtained under either timed or untimed conditions. *Intelligence, 10*, 315–330.

Vernon, P. A. & Mori, M. (1990). Physiological approaches to the assessment of intelligence. In C. R. Reynolds & R. Kamphaus (Eds.), *Handbook of psychological and educational assessment of children: Intelligence and achievement* (pp. 389–402). New York: Guilford Press.

Vernon, P. A., Nador, S. & Kantor, L. (1985). Reaction times and speed-of-processing: Their relationship to timed and untimed measures of intelligence. *Intelligence, 9*, 357–374.

Vernon, P. E. (1971). *The structure of human abilities* (3rd ed.). New York: Wiley.

Vernon, P. E. (1982). *The abilities and achievements of Orientals in North America*. New York: Academic Press.

Vincent, K. R. (1991). Black/white IQ differences: Does age make the difference? *Journal of Clinical Psychology, 47*, 266–270.

Vining, D. R., Jr. (1982). On the possibility of the reemergence of a dysgenic trend with respect to intelligence in American fertility differentials. *Intelligence, 6*, 241–264.

Vogt, D. K. (1973). *Literacy among youth 12–17 years*. DHEW Pub. No. (HRA) 74–1613, National Center for Health Statistics. Washington, DC: U.S. Government Printing Office.

Wagner, R. (1994). Practical intelligence. In R. J. Sternberg (Ed.), *Encyclopedia of human intelligence*, Vol. 2 (pp. 821–828). New York: Macmillan.

Waldman, I. D., Weinberg, R. A. & Scarr, S. (1994). Racial-group differences in IQ in the Minnesota Transracial Adoption Study: A reply to Levin and Lynn. *Intelligence, 19*, 29–44.

Walker, H. M. & Lev, J. ((1953). *Statistical inference*. New York: Holt.

Walters, L. C., Miller, M. R. & Ree, M. J. (1993). Structured interviews for pilot selection: No incremental validity. *International Journal of Aviation Psychology, 31*, 25–38.

Webb, E. (1915). Character and intelligence. *British Journal of Psychology, Monograph Supplement III*.

Weinberg, R. A., Scarr, S. & Waldman, I. D. (1992). The Minnesota Transracial Adoption Study: A follow-up of IQ test performance in adolescence. *Intelligence, 16*, 117–135.

West, A. M., Mackintosh, N. J. & Mascie-Taylor, C. G. N. (1992). Cognitive and educational attainment in different ethnic groups. *Journal of Biosocial Science, 24*, 539–554.

Wherry, R. J. (1959). Hierarchical factor solutions without rotation. *Psychometrika, 24*, 45–51.

Wickett, J. C. & Vernon, P. A. (1994). Peripheral nerve conduction velocity, reaction time, and intelligence: An attempt to replicate Vernon and Mori (1992). *Intelligence, 18*, 127–131.

Wickett, J. C., Vernon, P. A. & Lee, D. H. (1994). *In vivo* brain size, head perimeter, and intelligence in a sample of healthy adult females. *Personality and Individual Differences, 16*, 831–838.

Wickett, J. C., Vernon, P. A. & Lee, D. H. (1996). General intelligence and brain volume in a sample of healthy adult male siblings. *International Journal of Psychology, 31*, 238–239. (Abstract).

Wigdor, A. K. & Garner, W. R. (Eds.) (1982). *Ability testing: Uses, consequences, and controversies*, Part I. *Report of the Committee*, Part 2: *Documentation section*. Washington, DC: National Academy Press.

Wilks, S. S. (1938). Weighting systems for linear functions of correlated variables when there is no dependent variable. *Psychometrika, 3*, 34–40.

Willerman, L. & Bailey, J. M. (1987). A note on Thomson's sampling theory for correlations among mental tests. *Personality and Individual Differences, 8*, 943–944.

Willerman, L., Loehlin, J. C. & Horn, J. M. (1990). A 10-year follow-up of adoptees whose biological mothers had differed greatly in IQ. (Abstract). Behavior Genetics Association, 20th Annual Meeting, p. 62.

Willerman, L., Rutledge, J. N. & Bigler, E. D. (1991). *In vivo* brain size and intelligence. *Intelligence, 15*, 223–228.

Willis, S. L. & Schaie, K. W. (1986). Practical intelligence in later adulthood. In R. J. Sternberg & R. K. Wagner (Eds.), *Practical intelligence: Nature and origins of competence in the everyday world* (pp. 236–268). Cambridge: Cambridge University Press.

Wilson, E. B. (1928). Review of C. Spearman's *The abilities of man. Science, 67*, 244–248.

Wilson, J. Q. & Herrnstein, R. J. (1985). *Crime and human nature*. New York: Simon & Schuster.

Wilson, R. S. (1983). The Louisville Twin Study: Developmental synchronies in behavior. *Child Development, 54*, 298–316.

Winick, M., Meyer, K. K. & Harris, R. C. (1975). Malnutrition and environmental enrichment by early adoption. *Science, 190*, 1173–1175.

Wittelson, S. F., Glezer, I. I. & Kigar, D. L. (1995). Women have greater density of neurons in posterior temporal cortex. *Journal of Neuroscience, 15*, 3418–3428.

Yerkes, R. M. & Dodson, J. D. (1908). The relation of strength of stimulus to rapidity of habit formation. *Journal of Comparative Neurology and Psychology, 18*, 458–482.

Zindi, F. (1994). Differences in psychometric performance. *The Psychologist, 7*, 549–552.

Name Index

Subject Index

About the Author

ARTHUR R. JENSEN is Professor Emeritus of Educational Psychology, Graduate School of Education, University of California, Berkeley. During the 40 years of his tenure at Berkeley, he has been a prolific researcher in the psychology of human learning, individual differences in cognitive abilities, psychometrics, behavioral differences in cognitive abilities, psychometrics, behavioral genetics, and mental chronometry. His work, published in six earlier books and some 400 articles in scientific and professional journals, has placed him among the most frequently cited figures in contemporary psychology.